ACC Basketball
AN ILLUSTRATED HISTORY

BY RON MORRIS
With Contributions from John Feinstein, Barry Jacobs and Dick Herbert.

ACC Ba

AN ILLUSTRA

sketball

TED HISTORY

ACC Basketball
AN ILLUSTRATED HISTORY

Publisher ■ Art Chansky
Editor/Designer ■ Lee Pace
Executive Editor ■ Tony Britt
Editorial Assistants ■ Ed Price, Alfred Hamilton, Jim Wilson
Research Assistants ■ Adam Zinn, Ron Smith

Printing ■ PBM Graphics, Research Triangle Park, N.C.
Typesetting and Composition ■ Azalea Typography, Durham, N.C.
Color Separations ■ Hi-Ke Color, Greensboro, N.C.

Published By

Four Corners Press
P.O. Box 793
Chapel Hill, NC 27514

A Proud Part Of The Village Companies

Copyright © 1988 by Ron Morris

All rights reserved. No part of this publication may be reproduced in any form without the prior written permission of the publisher.

Library of Congress—Cataloging in Publication Data

Morris, Ron, 1954-
 ACC basketball.

 Includes index.
  1. Basketball—Tournaments—United States—History.
 2. Atlantic Coast Conference—History. 3. Basketball
 —United States—Records. 4. College sports—United
 States—History. I. Feinstein, John. II. Jacobs,
 Barry. III. Herbert, Dick. IV. Title.
 GV885.49.A84M66 1988   796.32'372   88-80981
 ISBN 0-9609548-9-9

Printed in the United States.

To anyone who has given a damn
about a basketball game at
Clemson, Duke, Georgia Tech, Maryland,
North Carolina, North Carolina State,
South Carolina, Virginia or Wake Forest.

TABLE OF

THE '50s
Pages 17-72

Spotlight:

Case Of The Hoosier Hotshot
Indiana to Raleigh pipeline spurred ACC's growth.
Pages 65-72

One-On-One:

Bill Yarborough Clemson □ 59	**Ronnie Shavlik** N.C. State □ 56
Joe Belmont Duke □ 28	**Grady Wallace** South Carolina □ 38
Bud Millikan Maryland □ 52	**Buzz Wilkinson** Virginia □ 62
Lennie Rosenbluth North Carolina □ 26	**Dickie Hemric** Wake Forest □ 40

THE '60s
Pages 73-144

Spotlight:

Era Of The Executive Coach
Duke's Bubas elevated profession to new heights.
Pages 129-137

EXTRA:

The Recruiting Of Tom McMillen
Pages 138-144

One-On-One:

The Mahaffeys Clemson □ 90	**Press Maravich** N.C. State □ 110
Art Heyman Duke □ 84	**Frank McGuire** South Carolina □ 122
Billy Jones Maryland □ 98	**Bill Gibson** Virginia □ 94
Larry Miller North Carolina □ 104	**Bones McKinney** Wake Forest □ 116

CONTENTS

THE '70s
Pages 145-208

Spotlight:

The Remarkable King David

Pack's "eighth wonder of the world" dazzled the ACC.

Pages 201-208

One-On-One:

Tree Rollins
Clemson □ 184

Gene Banks
Duke □ 194

John Lucas
Maryland □ 196

Phil Ford
North Carolina □ 182

Tom Burleson
N.C. State □ 158

John Roche
South Carolina □ 162

Wally Walker
Virginia □ 180

Charlie Davis
Wake Forest □ 157

THE '80s
Pages 209-275

Spotlight:

Born To Lead And Compete

Dean Smith's Tar Heels set lofty ACC standards.

Pages 265-273

One-On-One:

Horace Grant
Clemson □ 239

Mike Krzyzewski
Duke □ 260

Bobby Cremins
Georgia Tech □ 244

Len Bias
Maryland □ 250

Michael Jordan
North Carolina □ 220

Jim Valvano
N.C. State □ 236

Ralph Sampson
Virginia □ 226

Tyrone Bogues
Wake Forest □ 252

REFERENCE 277-313

INDEX, PHOTO CREDITS 314-320

Letter From The Publisher
The ACC's family photo album.

Art Heyman not only personifies the history of ACC basketball, but he also best represents the task of publishing a book on what we've come to know as "the best college basketball league in the nation."

Heyman was the subject of an intense recruiting battle in 1959 and committed to UNC before changing his mind amidst a near fistfight between his stepfather and Tar Heel Coach Frank McGuire.

Heyman went on to land All-America honors and lead Duke to national prominence as one of the conference's most colorful, controversial and talented players. Nothing with him was ever routine, and after he completed a brief pro career, he all but disappeared.

Finding him, and the more than 70 other ex-players and coaches interviewed within these pages, is a memorable part of putting together *ACC Basketball: An Illustrated History*.

Heyman turned up in New Jersey last year. Ron Morris, the intrepid author, found him at the Colonia Country Club in Colonia, N.J. And Heyman, who with a Duke coed once checked into a motel under the name of Mr. and Mrs. Oscar Robertson, was up to his old tricks.

When Morris flew to New Jersey to spend two days with Heyman, the irrepressible "Pest," as he became known during his time at Duke, made a reservation for his guest at a local "hotel." When Morris checked in, the desk clerk asked him how many *hours* he would need the room for. "Uh. . . 24, or at least 12," said Morris, who like Heyman refused to sign his own name to the register book. He left and found his own hotel.

Practical jokes aside, Heyman was typical of most ACC "graduates" by gleefully recounting his days in the league. His story, one of 36 individual profiles on former players or coaches, can be found on Pages 84-85.

Heyman wasn't the hardest subject to find. That distinction goes to Don Gallagher, the erstwhile point-shaver who attended N.C. State in the late 1950s and early '60s. Uncovering Gallagher and his exclusive story was a case of "blind, dumb luck," according to Morris.

Any history of the ACC must include the scandals that rocked State, UNC, South Carolina and, by association, every other school. How and why it happened were pre-eminent questions in Morris' research.

Poring over Durham and Wake County, N.C., court records wasn't enough. He had to find someone who was there and hear his side of it. Some of the players involved couldn't be found, one had died and others wouldn't talk about the past. One player's mother cried when reminded what her son had done.

With his sources dwindling by the day, Morris starting calling directory assistance in the old hometowns of the players he couldn't find, compiling a list of people with the same last names. Finally, in Binghamton, N.Y., he talked to a Daniel Gallagher (no relation), who helped Morris locate the brother of Don Gallagher in another part of the country.

Gallagher's brother gave Morris the number he needed. Cordial but reluctant to talk about the point-shaving scandals over the phone, Gallagher agreed to meet with Morris and tell how he got hooked.

The fascinating account of the ACC's darkest days begins on Page 74, as an introduction to the 1960s. Ironically, it is a warm, gripping story about an impressionable kid led astray. Like Gallagher and other point-shavers who went on to live respectable, prosperous lives, the ACC recovered to send seven teams to the Final Four in the '60s.

The last two decades have been distinctly different from those early, turbulent days when the fledgling ACC scratched and clawed for its place among older, more established leagues. The late Commissioner Bob James, who succeeded Jim Weaver, implemented the corporate image and set the stage for unprecedented prosperity the conference enjoys today under Gene Corrigan's leadership.

That great variance of personalities and styles, both on and off the court, over the last 35 years has made this such a wonderful tale to tell. We knew it would be interesting when we started in January of '87, but we never imagined it would be as poignant or this much fun.

Morris criss-crossed the ACC states in search of old stories, photographs and, yes, vintage ACC game jerseys. Upon returning from each trip, Morris magically made our offices smaller. By the

The editorial team (L-R): Britt, Morris, Chansky and Pace.

end of his odyssey, we were stepping over and around the carefully arranged files mushrooming from his desk.

Meanwhile, as Morris was busy squinting at the microfilm machine, transcribing tapes and setting world keypunch records at his computer, the editors were putting *ACC Basketball: An Illustrated History* into book form: 320 pages, more than 350 photos and 250,000 words, including the name of every player to ever wear an ACC uniform.

Besides presiding over an editing and proofreading staff, designer Lee Pace laid out the pages and photos, carefully mixing in the right school colors where he could. Executive editor Tony Britt coordinated a promotional plan in which regular releases were mailed to the media and brochures were sent to ACC fans and boosters.

At the same time, freelance contributors Dick Herbert, Barry Jacobs and John Feinstein were carving out their pieces of ACC history.

Herbert, now retired to fishing and golf daily, profiles old coaches and friends Everett Case and Vic Bubas with the reverence and respect they deserve. Jacobs recaptures David Thompson's magical ACC days after chasing the now-reclusive DT, futilely, from Seattle to his parents' home outside of Shelby, N.C. And Feinstein does with Dean Smith exactly what he did to Bob Knight in *A Season On The Brink*—he tells it like it is. Of course, Smith's story is one the whole family can read!

That's good because, after all, ACC basketball has been part of your family, and ours, for a long time. We sincerely hope you enjoy *ACC Basketball: An Illustrated History* as much as we have.

Art Chansky

**Art Chansky
Publisher**

game /ˈgām/ *n* [ME] **1 a** (1): a physical or mental competition conducted for fun or amuse-

ment according to rules with the participants in direct opposition to each other.

fan / ˈfan / n [ME] *(prob. short for fanatic)*
1: an enthusiastic devotee (as of a sport or

a performing art) usually as a spectator, often prone to extreme behavior.

hys·te·ria / his-'ter-ē-a / *n* [NL] **1:** a psycho-neurosis marked by emotional excitability and

disturbances of the psychic, sensory, vasomotor, and visceral functions. **2: ACC Basketball.**

On the preceding six pages:

■ First-round games from the 1988 ACC Tournament included: (top left) Sam Ivy of Wake Forest slamming home two points against UNC and Clemson's Elden Campbell lofting a jumper against N.C. State; Georgia Tech's Tom Hammonds (bottom left) driving by Maryland's Derrick Lewis; and Duke's Quin Snyder (top right) defending against Virginia's John Crotty. The intensity of the championship game, won 65-61 by Duke, is mirrored on the faces of Blue Devil Robert Brickey and Tar Heels Pete Chilcutt and Rick Fox.

■ N.C. State's Reynolds Coliseum builds to a crescendo during a 1956 Dixie Classic confrontation between the Wolfpack of Coach Everett Case and Iowa, won by State 84-70.

■ Duke fans erupt during a second half run against archrival UNC in 1988. The Blue Devils broke a three-game losing streak with a 96-81 win before advancing to the Final Four.

THE '50s

THE '50s

The Die Is Cast

When North Carolina's high-rolling Tar Heels took an improbable fourth win over Wake Forest in 1957, the ACC hauled in a jackpot.

As was their custom, Lennie Rosenbluth, Joe Quigg and Ken Rosemond piled into the light blue Ford station wagon driven by Joel Fleishman, the team manager. Rosenbluth was an All-America center for North Carolina's basketball team, Quigg a starting forward and Rosemond a reserve guard. The common denominator was that all three players smoked cigarettes.

As long as Fleishman stayed in the rear of a three-car caravan, Coach Frank McGuire, who rode shotgun in the lead car, would know nothing of the players' smoking habits. Always looking for an edge, Quigg served as campus representative for the Philip Morris Company. He'd get Marlboros by the case load to distribute throughout the Chapel Hill campus. More often than not, the smokes ended up in the pockets of Rosenbluth and Rosemond.

The travel arrangement usually worked well, although once on a trip to the University of South Carolina, Fleishman took a wrong turn and the three players arrived in Columbia at tipoff.

It could have been worse. They had heard of the time Wake Forest star Lefty Davis was caught smoking. Davis would wait until Coach Murray Greason dozed off in the back seat, then light up in front. On one trip, Davis flipped a spent cigarette out the front window and the wind pushed it in the back window. The butt not only set the ball bag on fire but also ignited the temper of a startled Greason.

So it was on the damp, chilly Friday afternoon of March 8, 1957, Rosenbluth and company were on their way from Chapel Hill to Raleigh, chain-smoking down Highway 54. "Killed the nerves," Rosenbluth said.

Davis wasn't with Wake Forest anymore, but Jackie Murdock, Ernie Wiggins and the rest of the Deacons

A stunned Bones McKinney afterward: "This was the saddest moment of my entire basketball career."

ACC BASKETBALL / THE '50s

climbed into Greason's car at about the same time for the short trip to Raleigh from the old Wake Forest campus.

Little did either group know it was about to participate in a game that would help change the face of ACC basketball. The Tar Heels, unbeaten and ranked No. 1 in the country, were playing Wake Forest, unranked with a 19-8 record, in the semifinals of the ACC Tournament at Reynolds Coliseum.

UNC would eventually capture the NCAA Championship with back-to-back, triple-overtime victories over Michigan State and Kansas in the Final Four. But neither of those was more dramatic, nor more important, than the Tar Heels' improbable fourth win over Wake Forest that season.

If UNC had not survived that game, the ACC would have waited another 17 years for its first national championship; ACC fans would have waited another decade for television coverage of regular-season games; and critics would have claimed once again that the league was cutting its throat by playing a postseason tournament.

As it turned out, the ACC could rightfully call itself the best basketball conference in the country.

•

Frank McGuire was greeted at the players' entrance to Reynolds Coliseum by John Baker, a bailiff for the Wake County Courthouse when he wasn't guarding the back door of the Coliseum. Baker welcomed all to Reynolds Coliseum, but McGuire was one of his favorites. McGuire took pride in talking to bellhops as well as businessmen, security guards as well as state senators. It was all part of his charm.

Beyond being gracious, McGuire was superstitious. He would wear the same silk suit, purchased on his Christmas trip to New York City, all three days of the Tournament, assuming the Tar Heels had a three-day run.

Unlike the other teams, UNC commuted daily to the Tournament, remaining in Chapel Hill Friday to attend class. Because Rosenbluth was such a movie buff, McGuire sent Assistant Coach Buck Freeman to the Varsity Theater on Franklin Street to make sure he wasn't skipping class. Freeman once found Rosenbluth in the theater and got so engrossed in the movie he forgot to run his star player off to class.

McGuire's teams enjoyed a pregame meal precisely four hours before tipoff. For home games, or for those in nearby cities such as Raleigh, the team usually ate at The Pines, where the prime rib and steak drew customers from around the state. For most of the players, the pregame meal was steak, baked potato, dry toast and hot tea.

"Give the fellas whatever they want," McGuire invariably told the waitress. All the fellas, that was, except for Rosie, as Rosenbluth was known to his teammates. He preferred to not eat at all, saving his appetite for a pastrami sandwich at The Goody Shop in Chapel Hill after the game. If Rosenbluth ate anything before a game, it was shrimp cocktail. Legend has it, and McGuire confirms, that Rosenbluth sat down to 11 shrimp cocktails before one game.

"If that's what he wants . . ." McGuire said.

Once the team arrived at Reynolds, the players were allowed to watch the first half of the other ACC Tournament semifinal between South Carolina and Maryland. Rosenbluth, again, bucked the norm. He preferred to watch every second of any game he could. On this occasion, he wanted to see if South Carolina forward Grady Wallace, the nation's leading scorer that season, would break the ACC Tournament record of 45 points scored by Rosenbluth in the first round. Following that performance, Clemson Coach Press Maravich passed a rabbit's foot on to Rosie. "I've tried everything, but nothing seems to work against him," Maravich said.

Clemson's Press Maravich waved a white flag and presented Rosenbluth a rabbit's foot.

When the team was assembled and dressed in the UNC locker room, Freeman listed player matchups on the chalkboard. Only then was McGuire prepared for some final words to his team. It was pretty much an unspoken truth that Freeman, McGuire's coach at St. John's, managed the team's strategy. McGuire, meanwhile, was the club's firebrand. On this occasion, McGuire used the Tar Heels' 77-56 loss to Wake Forest in the '56 ACC Tournament as motivational fodder.

"Wake Forest is a big opponent of mine," McGuire said in the spacious dressing room beneath the din of the Coliseum. "I have not forgotten how those boys celebrated last year in this building, how they humiliated us. We've had such a great, great year. Don't let them spoil the year for you.

"They'll do anything, anything to try and win. We've never had an easy game against Wake, those sons-a-bitches. I've never had an easy game against Wake Forest. It's a big thing for them to beat us. They play like they're possessed."

He reminded his team of the game against Wake Forest in Chapel Hill the previous season. Fans came out of the stands while the two teams squared off in fisticuffs.

McGuire then clenched his fist and glared into the eyes of his players.

"I want to beat the hell out of them," he said, shaking his fist.

Next door, Greason and Assistant Coach Bones McKinney engaged in their own pregame strategy session. There was an unspoken truth about that coaching tandem as well. Greason, by then in his 23rd and final season as head coach at Wake Forest, had pretty much turned his duties over to McKinney. A Baptist preacher on the side, McKinney knew a little about motivation. But on this day, he figured his team needed no pep talk.

What Wake Forest needed, Bones figured, was a little luck and an excellent game plan. He took care of the luck by wearing red socks, which had become tradition at Wake Forest. The student government at the tiny Baptist school had taken to selling red socks to fans at all home games.

As for the game plan, McKinney checked his players out of the Plantation Inn north of Raleigh early that morning. He took them to the town of Wake Forest for a special practice session at Gore Gymnasium. Nearly all of them had played in Gore before the Z. Smith Reynolds Foundation moved the school 100 miles west to Winston-Salem in 1956. To the players, Gore was still home.

To McKinney, Gore was a place to work on a game plan in private. Earlier in the season, when the two teams played in Winston-Salem, McKinney suspected the Tar Heels had a spy at one of his practices. McKinney had planned to spring a full-court press on UNC because he didn't particularly respect the ball-handling skills of Tar Heel guards Tommy Kearns and Bob Cunningham. McKinney claimed that the janitor in the Winston-Salem Coliseum was a "Carolina man" and tipped off McGuire. How else would McGuire have known to play 5-foot-8 guard Rosemond, an excellent dribbler, in place of 6-9 center Quigg?

McGuire termed such charges "preposterous" and claimed that Quigg had a virus. McGuire's squad came from one point down in the final minute to win, 72-69. The Tar Heels had also come from behind to defeat Wake Forest 63-55 and win the Dixie Classic championship back in December. When they met in Chapel Hill, UNC again staved off Wake Forest for a 69-64 victory.

McGuire said "the bounce of the ball" made the difference in at least two of the three games. McGuire actually would not have minded a loss in one of those games. He knew how difficult it was to defeat an ACC team four times in one season. N.C. State had pulled off the hat trick—plus one—against Wake Forest in 1956, and it would be done twice more in league history—Duke over Wake Forest in '58 and Duke over N.C. State in '79.

Odds aside, Wake Forest gave UNC fits whenever they played. No doubt that was because of McKinney's coaching. Even McGuire admitted McKinney's days as a player and coach in the National Basketball Association pushed him to the forefront of the ACC coaching ranks.

For games against UNC, McKinney concocted a "fruit salad" defense, which was a variation of the 1-3-1 zone with emphasis on denying the ball to Rosenbluth. McKinney had actually designed the defense the previous season and showed it to Vic Bubas, then an assistant at N.C. State, to use against North Carolina. Rosenbluth got his points as usual, but at least N.C. State won.

Shutting down Rosenbluth was virtually impossible. At 6-5 he was as good a shooter as any in the league. He ranked eighth in the ACC in shooting as a sophomore, third as a junior and second in 1957 on a variety of shots, ranging from a hook at 5 feet to a soft jumper from 20 feet. His shooting touch would have been uncanny for a guard. For a center, it was unheard of.

Quigg and Pete Brennan helped free Rosenbluth for shots. Quigg was excellent around the basket and had a nose for the ball. Brennan's forte was a corner jump shot, which would account for 16 points against Wake Forest. The inside trio presented a dilemma for opponents—spend too much time worrying about Rosenbluth and the others hurt you.

Rosenbluth was everybody's All-America because he could also rebound. Teammates called him "The Goose" for the one-handed way he snatched the ball out of the air. At age 25 after taking three extra years to get out of high school, he was older and wiser than most ACC players. He was experienced at every level, having played against the Boston Celtics at a summer camp in upstate New York.

So as Wake Forest walked through its defensive assignments on the Gore Gymnasium floor, how to defend Rosenbluth was the focus of attention. Wiggins, a guard, practiced playing in front of Rosenbluth. Jim Gilley, the center, practiced playing behind him. When UNC passed the ball to either corner, Rosenbluth followed it to the low post. Wiggins was quick enough to run between Rosenbluth and the ball. Gilley also planned to jump in front of Rosenbluth while one of Wake's forwards, either Jack Williams or Olin Broadway, planned to move behind the UNC star.

"They'll do anything, anything to try and win. We've never had an easy game against Wake. ... It's a big thing for them to beat us. They play like they're possessed."
☐ **UNC Coach Frank McGuire**

"We have to trap him at all times," McKinney said. "The big thing is, deny him the ball and block out."

McKinney repeated the same instructions to his team minutes before leaving the Reynolds Coliseum locker room that night.

Down a long hallway, which ran the width of the Coliseum basement, officials John Nucatola and Jim Mills readied for the game in a dressing room infamous for not having a door. Coaches often dropped by before and after games to visit with officials. On one occasion, however, McKinney took exception to a call and charged into their quarters in rage. After that, a security guard was stationed outside the doorway.

Nucatola was considered the top official in the East, and perhaps the best in the nation. He was from New York City and known as Madison Square Garden's best man in stripes. So respected was Nucatola, he later was among the few officials inducted into the Basketball Hall of Fame. Mills was a long-time ACC ref whose only limitation was that he could not call games involving N.C. State. Mills played for the Wolfpack in 1940 and 1941 along with his identical twin, Joe, who was also an ACC official.

Despite being from Apex, on the outskirts of Raleigh, Mills was required by the league to stay in a downtown Raleigh hotel throughout the Tournament. College basketball had just survived a massive point-shaving scandal in the Northeast, and there was talk that gamblers were working officials as well as players to fix games. Nucatola and Mills were under tight security, although Mills did manage to slip away Friday afternoon to tend to his garden in Apex.

Nucatola and Mills ascended the long, steep steps from the basement to the main floor of the rectangular arena, shaped like a shoe box. To reach the court, the officials came from beneath the stands of one end zone and through a tunnel of seated fans. The two teams followed up the same stairs, then entered the court from opposite sides of the end zone.

McKinney and McGuire had already led their teams onto the court. McKinney looked like he had already spent a hard day at the office. His bow tie was loose at the neck and his shirttail slipped from the back of his trousers. McGuire was all New

ACC BASKETBALL / THE '50s

York City, unlike anything North Carolina had previously seen. His suit was perfectly tailored, his white shirt starched and crisp against his chest with his necktie pulled tight. As he adjusted the red scarf in his jacket pocket and flashed his diamond cuff links, every head turned to notice the coach lauded by one magazine as "one of America's best-dressed men."

Every one of Reynolds' 12,400 seats was filled, many fans arriving in time to see the end of South Carolina's 74-64 victory over Maryland. Wallace, Rosenbluth was told just before UNC's tipoff, scored 31. Rosie's record was safe.

Before tossing the ball toward the overhanging scoreboard to start play, Nucatola looked to the radio booth where Ray Reeve sat high above the court. Reeve's play-by-play coverage crossed the state, and the officials always made sure the voice of ACC basketball was ready.

"The Tar Heels and Demon Deacons are coming out onto the court now," Reeve said in his creaking shrill. "North Carolina is wearing home white uniforms with blue numerals outlined in black piping. Wake Forest is in gold uniforms with black numerals outlined in white piping.

"And we are ready to go. Rosenbluth will jump in the tapoff against Gilley."

The jump ball at the beginning of each half marked the only time Rosenbluth matched up man-for-man against an opponent. Because of Rosenbluth's deficiencies on defense, UNC was forced to play a 2-3 zone at all times.

North Carolina controlled the tip and most of the early action. A 10-point outburst with Rosenbluth and Kearns scoring four apiece gave the Tar Heels a 22-11 lead. Wake Forest, stunned by the quick UNC start, called a timeout with 8:32 left in the half.

"Look, you didn't lose it in two minutes and you're not going to get it back in two minutes," McKinney told the Wake players. "Let's cut the lead down and get within five points of them by the end of the half."

On the other bench, McGuire was calm as ever.

"Keep working the offense," McGuire said. "They've got to give us something, just keep working it. Get the ball to Rosie."

McGuire was long an advocate of the star system in coaching. His teams at St. John's, UNC and later at South Carolina always had one big scorer and four contributors. When he first assembled the '57 team, McGuire figured Rosenbluth to be the star and the scorer.

Kearns, a prolific scorer in high school and potential star in his own right, had difficulty accepting McGuire's system initially. During one practice session, McGuire tossed two balls on the court for a scrimmage. When Kearns threw one ball out, McGuire tossed it back into play.

"One's for Tommy," McGuire said, "and one's for the rest of the team. Tommy, if you want to hog the ball, take one for yourself."

Kearns enlisted the support of teammates on the issue, and it wasn't long into preseason practice that the Tar Heels were rife with dissension. Most of the players formed a tight-knit group off the court. But Rosenbluth, the only one with a steady girlfriend, went his own way. While the rest of the players gathered at student hangouts on campus, Rosenbluth was off with Pat Oliver, a coed from Mt. Airy, N.C., who became his wife three months after the season.

Most of McGuire's boys went along with the coach's rules. Haircuts were mandatory the day of a game and a player could not practice unless he was clean-shaven. Rosenbluth often tried to bend the rules. He missed a few practices during the season when Freeman deemed his facial growth too thick.

Finally, McGuire met with Rosenbluth and pleaded with him to solve the team's problems. A squad meeting was called, without the coaching staff.

"I thought we'd go undefeated and win the national championship," Rosenbluth told the team. "I know we can do it. But there is one thing that could stop us—dissension."

Anybody who had a beef got it off his chest. Nothing was held back. The air was cleared and weekly meetings were scheduled for the remainder of the season. The players emerged from the skull session in the Woollen Gym locker room with a new purpose. Winning was always paramount, but now Kearns and the rest realized for the Tar Heels to be ACC champions, the ball needed to be in Rosie's hands. McGuire told the team often during the season, "Feed the animal."

Deacons Jim Gilley (12) and Jack Williams vie for rebound at left, while UNC's Tommy Kearns (40) drives on Jackie Murdock.

ACC BASKETBALL / THE '50s

In exchange, Rosenbluth abided by team rules. Now, he was truly the team's captain.

So when McGuire urged the Tar Heels to feed the animal, they knew it was for their own good. Denying Rosenbluth the ball could mean a loss, and a loss in the ACC Tournament meant the end of the season. Only one team represented the ACC in the NCAA Tournament.

McGuire never had to mention the importance of rebounding to his team. Along with the 6-5 Rosenbluth, there was 6-9 Quigg and 6-6 Brennan. No front line in the country had that much overall height, and each averaged at least eight rebounds a game. Against Wake Forest, Quigg would get 14.

Then there was Cunningham, who was 6-4 but played guard. He was the tallest at his position in the country and took advantage of his height to get nearly seven rebounds a game. Cunningham needed to rebound because a high school hand injury severely hampered his shooting. He could clutch a ball, as he did against Wake Forest with 13 rebounds, but he could not shoot it well.

Wake bench ignites during rally late in "guinea pig" half.

There weren't many rebounds to be had in the first half. The Demon Deacons gradually sliced away at the lead with some remarkable outside shooting. UNC was most aware of Wake guard Ernie Wiggins, a streak shooter. Against N.C. State the previous season, Wiggins made 12 straight two-handed set shots. After that game, a writer asked McKinney, "Have you ever seen Wiggins shoot better than that?" Bones shrugged and said, "Many times . . . in practice."

UNC didn't know Wiggins had lost confidence in his shot. Greason had criticized Wiggins during the season for shooting from too far out. Wiggins, a quiet and sensitive youngster, got gun-shy. Although he would make only three of 10 attempts against UNC, Wiggins still drew the Tar Heels' attention.

While UNC tended to Wiggins, Murdock and Jack Williams were flipping in jump shots from all over the court. Murdock was often the target of insults from the UNC bench. The Tar Heels called him "squirrel." When the teams met for the Dixie Classic championship earlier in the season, the UNC bench jockeys were particularly harsh on Murdock, who finally walked in front of the Tar Heels and spit at their toes.

Although UNC played zone defense, Kearns paid close attention to Murdock. Brennan checked Williams, a deadly outside shooter who at only 6-3 could also power inside.

By halftime, Wake Forest had done just as McKinney asked, cutting an 11-point deficit to 33-29 on the outside shooting of Murdock and Williams.

The Coliseum crowd buzzed over Wake's comeback. Many in the crowd were N.C. State fans accustomed to seeing their team in the Tournament semifinals and championship. State had won all three ACC championships and six of the last seven Southern Conference titles before the ACC was formed. But in 1957, the Wolfpack lost to Wake Forest in the first round.

Giving up the crown was bad enough. But losing to Wake Forest made matters worse because the Demon Deacons had knocked off State to win the final Southern Conference championship in 1953 and Wake was led by Murdock, who grew up only a short distance from Reynolds.

If Wake Forest was disliked by the State faithful, North Carolina was despised. The Tar Heels were trying to end State's dominance of the early ACC after hiring a Yankee who, ironically, had been discovered in Reynolds Coliseum.

McGuire brought his St. John's team to Raleigh for the NCAA East Regional in 1952, beating Case and his Wolfpack by 11 points. Chuck Erickson, North Carolina's athletic director, watched from the stands and figured McGuire knew better than anyone how to beat Case. A few months later, Erickson convinced McGuire to move South.

McGuire beat Case the next time they met in January of 1953. But it wasn't until '57 that McGuire really gained the upper hand. By then, his "underground railroad" had transported an entire team of Yankees to Chapel Hill. Twice the Tar Heels defeated State during '57 on their way to an undefeated regular season. The first-round Tournament win over Clemson gave them a 25-0 record.

That depressed some State fans and may have contributed to a near riot outside Reynolds following the opening round of the Tournament. A demonstration was touched off when dormitory parking areas were blocked by Coliseum visitors, many presumably from Winston-Salem and Chapel Hill. A reported 26 suspected rioters were hauled downtown after police used six tear gas bombs to disperse the crowd. Twenty-five car tires were reportedly slashed, one automobile was overturned, two police car windshields were shattered and three patrolmen suffered minor injuries.

In the middle of it all, ACC Commissioner Jim Weaver was hung in effigy. Weaver was instrumental in forming the ACC, whose original seven members broke from the old Southern Conference in June of 1953. Virginia then joined the ACC six months later, also believing the Southern Conference was too big with 17 members. "It was so big," Clemson Football Coach Frank Howard once said, "I felt like a member of the Rotary Club and the Ku Klux Klan."

Weaver also helped the NCAA investigate N.C. State's recruiting practices in luring Louisiana schoolboy Jackie Moreland to the Raleigh campus in August of 1956. The NCAA, as well as the ACC, found those practices illegal and the NCAA handed State a four-year probation in all sports. It was by far the stiffest penalty in the short history of the NCAA.

Some State fans may have considered selling their tickets to the semifinal games or, in protest, staying home to watch the all-new Everett Case Show on their black-and-white TVs.

But basketball ran too deeply in their blood, regardless of who was playing, so they sat in Reynolds and turned their attention to the game at hand. If only they could hear what McGuire was telling his fellas, and McKinney his boys, downstairs at halftime.

"That was the guinea pig half," McGuire told his team. "It doesn't mean anything. We just played it because it was 20 minutes that needed to be played. You have to win the game in the second half."

Rosie and the fellas had heard McGuire's halftime talk so many times they could practically recite it. Even when the Tar Heels had a big lead, which they often did that season, McGuire talked of how the first half was meaningless. Once, when UNC had a huge lead over Virginia at halftime, the players hid their faces in towels to keep from laughing at the coach.

23

ACC BASKETBALL / THE '50s

This time, though, they listened intently.

"You've got to play like men out there," McGuire said. "If you commit a foul, make it a good foul. No baby fouls. No three-point plays. Wake Forest is going to come at us. They're a bunch of demons. Don't ever forget what they did to us last year, right here in this building. I've never forgotten that, and you shouldn't either."

McGuire made one tactical move. He had Kearns and Cunningham exchange places at the top of UNC's zone defense so Cunningham played in front of Murdock. Cunningham had long arms that made it difficult for Murdock to shoot.

McKinney had few changes for Wake Forest. He was concerned that UNC had a 29-8 rebounding advantage in the first half, but he also realized the "fruit salad" defense put his team in awkward rebounding position. In an effort to deny Rosenbluth the ball, Wake gave up some rebounds. Against UNC, opponents had to give up something.

"Look, we have accomplished everything we set out to do," McKinney told his players, who sat and sucked on sliced oranges. "Forget all about that 10 straight points they scored and how far we were behind. We have accomplished what we wanted to do. We got ourselves back in the ball game. We made a great comeback. All we have to do is play the same way the rest of the game, the same way we did the last 10 minutes of the half."

McGuire and McKinney had prepared their respective teams for one of the most incredible finishes in league history.

Wake Forest held its own on the boards in the second half but gave up some outside shots to Rosenbluth, who would finish with 23 points. In an attempt to stop Rosenbluth, Williams got into foul trouble. Cunningham shut down Murdock, who wouldn't score a second-half field goal, so Wake turned to Gilley for scoring. Gilley had an excellent saddle—or pivot—move inside and could draw fouls with his hook shot.

The game remained close throughout the second half, and, with 2:17 remaining, UNC still led, 58-53. A Tar Heel victory and trip to the championship game seemed inevitable. Not only did UNC hold the lead, but it also forced Wake Forest out of its "fruit salad" defense and into man-to-man.

Then the tide turned. In quick succession over the next 82 seconds, Williams hit a shot from the side; Kearns missed the front end of a 1-and-1; Broadway sank a shot from the corner; and Cunningham charged into Gilley. Suddenly, it was 58-57 and Gilley was going to the line for a 1-and-1 and a chance for Wake Forest to take its first lead. Less than a minute remained.

On the Wake bench, McKinney grabbed a dipper and scooped a mouthful of water from the bucket he kept under his chair. He thought about calling time to set his defense, but decided against it.

"Go back to the 'fruit salad,'" McKinney yelled to Murdock, who passed the defensive change along to Wiggins. Word got around to Broadway and to Wendell Carr, who had replaced Williams when he fouled out with 24 points late in the game. But word never got to Gilley because McKinney had a rule that no player talked to the free throw shooter. It had something to do with breaking his concentration.

Gilley, white as cotton when he toed the line, swished both free throws and Wake Forest led 59-58. Fifty-five seconds remained.

Under these circumstances, McGuire usually called time out and set a final play. But the Tar Heels knew the ball needed to go to Rosie and the quicker they worked it upcourt, the less time Wake Forest would have to set its defense.

Kearns quickly moved the ball up the floor and passed to Cunningham on the wing. Rosenbluth broke from the baseline across the key. For one of the few times in the game, Cunningham had little trouble throwing a direct pass into Rosie.

Gilley thought the Deacons were still playing man-to-man and stayed with Quigg on the baseline. Carr noticed the mistake and quickly charged out to defend Rosenbluth.

Poor Wendell Carr. If ever there was a victim of circumstance, he was it.

Carr had wanted to attend N.C. State after a stint in the Army. But on the way to a tryout in Raleigh, Carr got off the train in Wake Forest and loved the town's hospitality. It was the milk shake he bought at Holding Drug Store, thick enough to eat with a spoon, that sold Carr on Wake Forest.

Just as Wake was not a bad choice of schools, it was not a bad decision to charge up the lane and challenge Rosenbluth. Carr could have been the game's hero.

Rosie turned and dribbled toward the middle. He planted his left foot just inside the foul line and lofted a hook shot toward the basket. On his release, Rosie collided with Carr. The ball swished through the hoop, and the crowd roared so loud it drowned out the sound of a whistle. Gilley and Broadway turned to Mills, the official nearest the play, under the basket.

The crowd quieted as Mills walked to the scorer's table. He had to make one of three calls: a charging foul on Rosenbluth, disallowing the basket and giving the ball to Wake; a foul on Carr before the shot, disallowing the basket and sending Rosenbluth to the free throw line; or a blocking foul on Carr, counting the basket and awarding Rosenbluth one shot.

He made the last call.

"At the time, I didn't think I missed the call," Mills recalls. "But I've heard so much about it since, I wonder now. Maybe I missed it because Bones has always wanted me to look at the film."

McKinney said: "I'll always contend Rosenbluth drove into Carr. The film clearly showed it. There's no question about it."

Rosenbluth said: "It was a very, very close play. It would have been a shame if we lost the whole year on a charging foul. That would have been a shame. But the way we won games, we probably would have intercepted a pass and won the game, anyway."

Chuck Taylor, the basketball expert and shoe manufacturer, was at courtside and said, "I would have called it a double foul."

A film of the play, watched frame by frame, shows that Mills made the proper call. Carr reached across and hit Rosenbluth before the two collided.

As his Catholic teammates made the sign of the cross, Rosenbluth made the free throw and UNC had a 61-59 lead with 46 seconds left. Wake Forest had time for a game-tying shot, but a 20-footer by Wiggins bounded off the rim and dropped to the floor. After a wild scramble for the ball, Cunningham came up with it and dribbled to midcourt as time expired.

UNC had survived another scare, a game it could not afford to lose in the Tournament McGuire would come to call "Russian Roulette."

Dick Herbert, writing for *The News and Observer* of Raleigh the following day, said: "If the Tar Heels are calling their shots with such a narrow margin allowed for error, they should change their procedure or else carry the responsibility of weakening thousands of hearts. Their followers can't stand many more like that one."

ACC BASKETBALL / THE '50s

At courtside sat Castleman D. Chesley, an independent TV producer who had experimented in 1956 with regional telecasts of college football. Chesley had an idea that basketball on television might have a future.

When the Tar Heels coasted past South Carolina to win the ACC Tournament, then beat Yale, Canisius and Syracuse to reach the Final Four, Chesley decided to test his idea. As the Tar Heels went three overtimes to defeat Michigan State, and three more extra periods to down Kansas and Wilt Chamberlain for the national championship, thousands of North Carolinians watched back home.

The ACC had officially entered the television era.

McGuire told a TV announcer that, after beating Michigan State and Kansas, Wake Forest was still the toughest team UNC had played all season. That boast, along with the national championship and live television coverage for the first time, gave the ACC unprecedented exposure and credibility.

When the Tar Heels returned from Kansas City, hundreds of fans stampeded the runway at Raleigh-Durham Airport to get a glimpse of the national champs. The Tar Heels were the darlings of an entire state after their charmed 32-0 season.

Lost in history, though, is just how close UNC came to not surviving against Wake Forest in the ACC semifinals.

McKinney hid his face in his hands as he walked off the Reynolds Coliseum floor that night. In the Wake Forest locker room, the players sat with their heads bowed. Tears streamed from their eyes as Lefty Davis, the player who once set the ball bag on fire, walked in.

"Can't you see these fellows are eating their hearts out?" Davis said to the smattering of newsmen who hovered around. "Why don't you get out and leave them alone? The real story, as you surely must know, is the way the referees choked up."

Bill Gibson, Wake Forest's athletic director, asked all visitors to leave the room, and McKinney hugged every player. The coach and the team cried together in privacy.

"That place was like a tomb. Of all my days in the pros, all my playing and all my coaching days, this was the saddest moment of my entire basketball career," McKinney said 30 years later. "The whole damn place was broken up. I've never seen anything like it in my life. There wasn't one dry eye in the place, mine included.

"To be honest, I've always thought God had a hand in that game. I don't think He cares a whole lot about ACC basketball, but I think He had something to do with that one."

Billy Carmichael, comptroller for the UNC system and McKinney's friend, tried to console the coach.

"Bones," he said, "I know you feel bad, but I thought it was funny as hell that you Baptists and Catholics were out there fighting like hell and a Jew stepped in and settled the whole thing."

Rosenbluth, the only Jewish player on the team, led the wild celebration in the UNC locker room. He even put on a new shirt after wearing the same button-down the previous three days as a good luck charm. Mostly, he looked forward to that pastrami sandwich at The Goody Shop.

Rosie then piled into the station wagon with Fleishman, Quigg and Rosemond and smoked Marlboros all the way back to Chapel Hill. In his hands he also carried the future of ACC basketball.

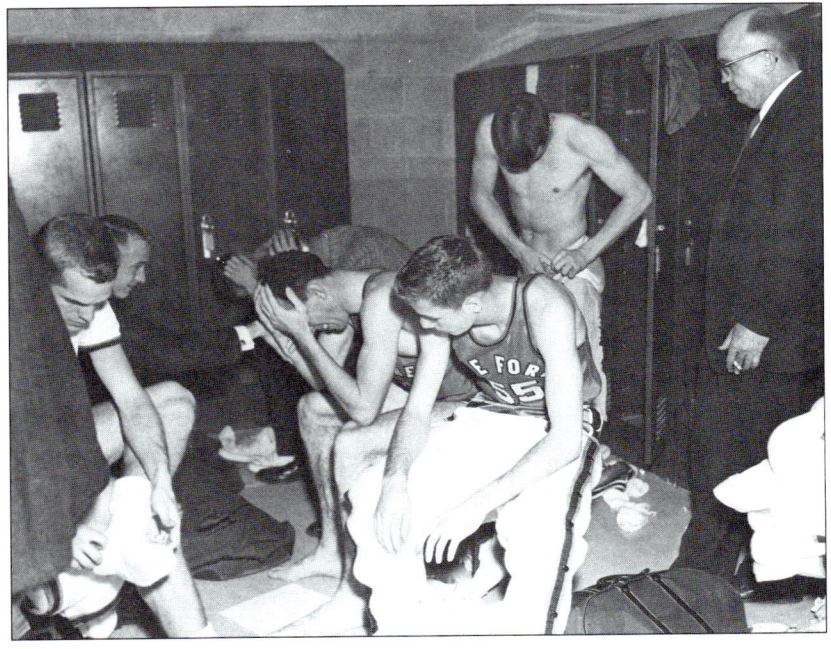

Semifinal postmortem: Smiles and sweat for McGuire and Heels, tears in a tomb for Deacs.

25

ACC BASKETBALL / **THE '50s**

Tar Heel championship drive came up Rosie.

Lennie Rosenbluth is remembered by North Carolina fans as captain of the Tar Heels' NCAA championship team in 1957, when he was National Player of the Year. What UNC and ACC fans probably do not remember is that Rosenbluth very nearly was not a Tar Heel.

As a junior in high school, Rosenbluth was courted by the Boston Celtics before the National Basketball Association prohibited the signing of prep players. Two years later, he was set to attend N.C. State before Wolfpack Coach Everett Case decided the 6-foot-5 youngster was not prepared for college ball.

The '50s

North Carolina

At the time, high schools in the Bronx were crowded with veterans who were back from the service. The vets, stronger and more mature when they returned, dominated the New York athletic scene. The younger, less-developed kids such as Rosenbluth were often victims of a numbers game.

As a result, Rosenbluth was cut from his high school basketball team his sophomore and junior years. He took a minimum number of courses to remain a junior, and he finally made the team in his third try. Then came a strike of New York's coaches that left the city without high school athletics for two years.

The strike sent Rosenbluth scurrying for a place to play. He found it in neighborhood parks and at the 92nd Street YMCA, where Hy Gotkin coached the team. Rosenbluth was the only white player on the squad, whose star player, Sihugo Green, went on to Duquesne and the NBA. The team once won 65 straight, and Rosenbluth landed a spot on a summer league roster in the Catskill Mountains, where the area's best pro, college and high school players annually polished their games.

Rosenbluth's playing time for the Laurel Country Club team in the Catskills was limited at first. Then a teammate was killed and two others were injured in an automobile accident and Rosenbluth stepped into the starting lineup.

By summer's end, Rosenbluth was scoring more than 20 points a game and catching the eyes of not only college recruiters but pro scouts. Red Auerbach, then coach of the Boston Celtics, extended an official invitation to attend his club's rookie camp. Rosenbluth spent two weeks in September of 1951 working out with the Celtics. Among the players in camp were Bob Cousy, Bill Sharman and a former all-league center named Bones McKinney.

Auerbach was impressed enough to offer Rosenbluth a pro contract even though he had little prep playing experience and had not graduated from high school. When the NBA saw Rosenbluth's name on a list of prospective players, it ruled that high school players could not be signed.

"For a kid to play with the Boston Celtics?" Rosenbluth says. "Yes, I probably would have signed."

Rosenbluth's fascination with the game began at age 14

Little-known lore: "Boston" or "N.C. State" might well have adorned chest of Rosenbluth, UNC's '57 captain.

when his father, a former minor league baseball player, took Lennie to an NYU-Bowling Green game at Madison Square Garden. Rosenbluth would have attended NYU, City College of New York or Long Island University, but the point-shaving scandals of the early '50s sent most of the city's top talent South.

Hy Gotkin's brother, Davey, was playing at N.C. State, and they both told Rosenbluth to take the same route. But before signing Rosenbluth to a scholarship, State's Case wanted a firsthand look. The tryout was in the spring of 1952, and Rosenbluth was admittedly out of shape.

"Scholarships are hard to come by and I can't use your son," Case told Rosenbluth's father.

Harry Gotkin, Hy's cousin and a talent scout in New York, knew of Rosenbluth and asked St. John's Coach Frank McGuire to take a look. McGuire was impressed but was certain he would not be at St. John's by the time Rosenbluth enrolled in school. McGuire suggested that Rosenbluth attend Virginia's Staunton Military Academy for one season, then join him at either Alabama or North Carolina, two schools McGuire was considering moving to.

"No matter where you go, I'll go with you," Rosenbluth told McGuire.

"Knowing McGuire and his teams at St. John's," Rosenbluth says, "I knew it wasn't going to be long before he started bringing in (good) ballplayers."

In addition to wanting the extra year to improve his basketball game, Rosenbluth needed a foreign language class and several mathematics courses to qualify for college. He met those needs at Staunton and followed McGuire to UNC in 1953.

For Rosenbluth's first freshman game at UNC, the Tar Heels found themselves locked out of Woollen Gym.

"When they finally got the door open, there might have been four kids in the stands, either friends of players or just managers," Rosenbluth says.

By the end of that season, the stands in Woollen were packed for freshman games. Some UNC followers watched Rosenbluth perform, then left during the varsity contest. Rosenbluth's biggest explosion as a frosh came when he scored 51 points against Chowan Junior College.

Rosie was hardly a one-dimensional player. During his sophomore season, 1955, he twice had 25 rebounds in a game. He averaged 11.7 rebounds that year to go with the 25.5 points he scored per game. He also caused a great deal of friction among teammates.

"There was dissension because there were a lot of seniors on that ballclub, and I was a sophomore doing everything," Rosenbluth says of the team that finished with a 10-11 record.

An 84-80 victory at N.C. State helped ease the tension, and the enthusiasm carried over to Rosenbluth's junior year, when the Tar Heels were 18-5 and ranked as high as fifth nationally.

Then came the magical season of 1957.

"When McGuire made me captain of the team my senior year, I got everyone together and we had weekly meetings," Rosenbluth says. "If anybody had any gripes it would come out in the open. No one would hold anything back. That's one thing I made sure we didn't have my senior year, dissension on the team."

Rosenbluth was the star, and the others had to accept his status for the team to be successful. He proved it on the court from the start. In the '57 season opener against Furman, Rosenbluth scored a Woollen Gym and school-record 47 points.

When a game was on the line, the ball went to Rosie. Only five times during the 1957 season did Rosenbluth not lead the Tar Heels in scoring. His game-winning, three-point play against Wake Forest in the ACC Tournament semifinals kept alive Carolina's undefeated march to the national championship. The previous night, Rosenbluth scored a Tournament-record 45 points.

Prior to Rosenbluth, State's Ronnie Shavlik was the only ACC center who could rebound *and* shoot from outside. Even more than Shavlik, Rosenbluth was both strong and quick afoot.

McGuire once said of Rosenbluth: "This kid is versatile, more so than any other player I have ever coached and for that reason I'd have to call him the greatest player I've ever had. He does a fine job at everything he tries on a basketball court.

"More than that, Lennie gives you that big performance when the chips are down. Every time he goes on a basketball court you know the quality of the performance you're going to get. This boy is an All-American if I ever saw one, and I've seen plenty."

The highlight of Rosenbluth's career was, of course, the 1957 NCAA Championship. As national Player of the Year, Rosenbluth's No. 10 jersey was later retired by the school. His 26.9 scoring average remains the best in UNC history and second in league annals. Three times he was first-team All-ACC, unanimous selections in 1956 and '57.

Once called a "Jewish Joe DiMaggio" by McGuire, Rosenbluth was the lone Jewish member of an otherwise all-Catholic team and coaching staff in 1957. He was the only starter who didn't make the sign of the cross before going to the foul line.

During one close game, McGuire urged Rosie to say a Hail Mary and make an important free throw. Rosenbluth told McGuire he didn't know how to say a Hail Mary.

"We'll say a Hail Mary," said teammate Pete Brennan. "You make the shot."

Rosenbluth's pro career was limited to 53 games for Philadelphia in 1958 and another 29 in 1959. He was too short to be an NBA center, too frail to be a power forward and not agile enough to play small forward. Rosie was also short on defensive skills, having played mostly zone at UNC.

Rosenbluth had visions of forming a professional league among former college players in North Carolina. His team of UNC all-stars traveled the state for two seasons. When that didn't last, he took up coaching at Wilson (N.C.) High School and eventually migrated to Miami, where he coached for 18 seasons at the high school and junior high school levels. His teams were 378-126 and won a state championship at Coral Gables High.

Rosenbluth has since retired from coaching. At 54, he still teaches American history at Coral Gables and plans to give that up in a few years. He and his wife, Helen, plan to return to where he is best remembered for leading UNC to the ACC's first national championship.

"The greatest thing is just being remembered," Rosenbluth says. "It's nice to know that in my lifetime, and long after I'm gone, my name and jersey will still be hanging around."

ACC BASKETBALL / THE '50s

Frank McGuire returned often to his native New York City during a nine-year span as basketball coach at North Carolina. While in the City to recruit some of its best basketball talent, McGuire would invariably tell of a revival going on in the Carolinas.

"When I first went to Carolina," McGuire would say, "we went over to play Wake Forest. They called it Baptist Hollow—and I was baptized, brother. That crowd sang the Wake Forest (fight) song and the light bulbs broke. But when they started singing *Dixie*—oh, brother."

McGuire was speaking to a group of basketball fans accustomed to seeing the finest the college game had to offer during the '40s and '50s. The best basketball in the country was played at old Madison Square Garden with the likes of LIU, NYU and CCNY knocking heads throughout the season.

McGuire was beginning to see the same kind of rivalries develop in the South, and he was in New York to tell the tales. He told of the time at UNC's Woollen Gym when members of the Tar Heel football team sat behind the Wake Forest bench for the purpose of harassing the Demon Deacons. Wake Forest got the last laugh, though. On UNC's next trip to Wake Forest's Gore Gym, members of the Deacon football team dressed in full gear, shoulder pads and all, and situated themselves behind the Tar Heel bench. The Wake football team even went through pregame layup drills, in full gear.

Basketball, McGuire told whomever would listen, had replaced football as the top spectator sport in North Carolina. With Maryland, Virginia, South Carolina and Clemson in the Atlantic Coast Conference fold, the basketball craze was spreading throughout the South.

Most ACC followers believe Indianan Everett Case brought basketball fever to the Carolinas when he moved to N.C. State in 1946 and promptly won six straight Southern Conference championships. In part, that is true. But it was probably McGuire who fanned the fire by creating a heated rivalry between himself and Case as well as UNC and N.C. State. Once those rivalries were established, there was a snowball effect. Others were quickly fostered and nourished over the years.

If Case was indeed the father of ACC basketball, then McGuire was certainly the godfather.

Only a few months after Virginia became the eighth school to split from the bloated, 17-member Southern Conference in December of 1953 and form the ACC, McGuire began to draw the battle lines with Case.

Case's Wolfpack dominated the Tar Heels from 1947 through 1952, winning 15 straight games. UNC could stand no more and hired McGuire to challenge the Case dynasty.

In his first meeting against Case, McGuire coached the Tar Heels to a 70-69 victory. But UNC paid dearly for that victory as the Wolfpack whipped the Tar Heels by 21 and 32 points in their next two meetings. Then, following State's 84-77 victory at UNC on Jan. 19, 1954, McGuire decided he had had enough.

"He (Case) ruined the game by using the (full-court) press," McGuire charged. "It was ridiculous. He could beat us 25 points without doing it and he comes over here and tries to lick us by 40. If that's the way he wants to play, I'll fight him right back when we get the boys to compete with him."

Case, usually the gentleman who would turn his cheek to such charges, dropped his guard and responded to this one.

Philly-to-Duke torch sparkled for savvy Belmont.

When Joe Belmont relaxes in his suburban Denver home with his wife of 27 years and two teen-age children, he can reflect with satisfaction on a career in basketball as a player, official and coach.

His fondest memory is from the 1954 Dixie Classic. Belmont was a guard for the Blue Devils, and a picture in the den of his home shows him clipping the net after Duke defeated Navy to win its only Dixie Classic Championship. The net from Reynolds Coliseum still hangs near the picture.

"That was the highlight," Belmont says. "That was it."

The '50s

Duke

Belmont played on Duke's first three entries in the ACC, teams that posted splendid records of 22-6, 20-8 and 19-7. The 1954 club was ranked eighth nationally at midseason and finished first in the ACC's regular-season race. The 1955 team represented the league in the NCAA Tournament, only to lose in the first round. The Blue Devils were ranked in the Top 20 during Belmont's senior season.

Bernie Janicki and Rudy D'Emilio played on those teams. So did Ronnie Mayer and Junior Morgan. All were stars, and all were among the ACC's top players.

But above all, there was Belmont. He stood only 5-foot-11, but sportswriter Jack Horner of the *Durham Morning Herald* described him as a "white Marcus Haynes as a dribbler." Although his career field-goal percentage was under .400, Belmont could shoot if necessary. He was primarily a ball handler and a passer, one who carried the torch of Philadelphia guards who attended Duke. Bill Fleming came first, then Dave Scarborough, then D'Emilio. Finally, Belmont.

"He was a typical Philadelphia guard, smart and heady," says former Maryland Coach Bud Millikan.

Beyond his abilities as a player, there was a bit of ham in Belmont. His antics on the court, which ranged from looking falsely fatigued at times to boyish exuberance, reminded ACC fans of former Duke All-America Dick Groat. Belmont, in fact, played much of his career with a toothpick in his mouth.

"He was a cutie out there," says longtime ACC official Lou Bello. "He'd beat you somehow. He'd tug at your shirt, push you on a layup. He knew how to get away with things, but boy could he play."

Grady Wallace, the great scorer at South Carolina for two seasons, said Belmont would try to sucker an opponent into believing he was exhausted.

"When he walked out to warm up, he looked like he

ACC BASKETBALL / THE '50s

Belmont would "beat you somehow" with scoring, ball handling and smarts.

First-team All-ACC honors were awarded to Belmont following his senior season, and he was drafted under territorial rights by the Warriors in the fifth round.

"To this day I don't know why I didn't go to the Warriors' camp," says Belmont. "You always think about what could have happened, but you had to play 10 to 15 years to get any money in the NBA then."

The going salary rate for a middle-round pick in 1956 was between $8,000 and $10,000. While confident of his basketball skills, Belmont was equally proud that he was the first in his family to graduate from college. His parents did not make it through high school.

So when it came to making a decision, Belmont opted for the security of a regular job with AAU basketball on the side. The Denver-Chicago Truckers of the National Industrial Basketball League gave him a job making $400 a month to go with a $1,200 basketball bonus. A friend got him interested in officiating, and he was wearing stripes for the ABA during its initial season, 1967, for $75 a game. His connections led to a front-office job with the Denver Rockets and eventually the head-coaching job when John McLendon was fired early in the 1970 season.

"I was the only guy in the organization who had ever worn a jock, other than the players," says Belmont, who lost his first game as a professional coach and then saw his team reel off 16 straight wins.

With Spencer Haywood as their star, the Rockets were 42-14. Without Haywood, the Rockets were 3-10 to start the 1971 season, and Belmont was fired in favor of Stan Albeck. Belmont returned to officiating for a brief period in the NBA before arthritis in his legs and hips forced him to retire. He now manages a Ferrari dealership in Denver.

"If it wasn't for basketball, I probably would never have left Philly," Belmont says.

was about ready to drop any second," Wallace recalls. "He'd let his pants sag. I always wondered what kept his pants up. It seemed to me like he was whipped all the time. But he didn't know when to quit."

Belmont learned the tricks of his trade on the streets of Philadelphia. He and Guy Rodgers formed a backcourt at Northeast Public High School. Summer pickup games would include the likes of Wilt Chamberlain, Tom Gola, Wayne Hightower and Ernie Beck. The dream of every Philadelphia kid was to some day play for the Warriors. Chamberlain did. So did Gola. And Hightower. Beck, too. When Belmont headed off to Duke, he intended to return to Philadelphia as a Warrior.

Belmont had the credentials. With 1,338 points, he left Duke as its third leading all-time scorer behind Dick Groat and Mayer. He was also outstanding on defense, once holding West Virginia star Hot Rod Hundley to seven points.

ACC BASKETBALL / **THE '50s**

If Everett Case was indeed the father of ACC basketball...

"Since when did he get to the place where he could coach my ballclub? I'll do anything I please as long as it's within the rules."

☐ **Everett Case**

"Why that's the most childish thing I've ever heard of," Case said. "Since when did he get to the place where he could coach my ballclub? I'll do anything I please as long as it's within the rules. Didn't he press us over here last year?"

McGuire was known as a fighter. Once, while playing for St. John's, he threatened to take on the entire Providence team in a fistfight. He took his aggressiveness into coaching, where his teams were known for a bruising style of play, a characteristic that carried his St. John's squad to the national championship game in 1952, only to lose to Kansas.

Some might interpret McGuire's remarks about Case's style of play in January of '54 as mere heat-of-the-battle comments. But those who knew McGuire knew better. He was sending a message to Case and to N.C. State that the war had begun. The first battle of words had been waged in the ACC, and the rest of the league schools could join in if they pleased. Duke, Wake Forest and Maryland would all take their shots at Case and the Wolfpack in the '50s.

Wake Forest stepped to the fore in '54. The Deacons took State to overtime in the inaugural ACC Tournament before dropping the championship game by two points.

That first Tournament was a far cry from what ACC fans know today. A book of tickets for the entire Tournament cost $10, yet not a single game was sold out at State's Reynolds Coliseum in Raleigh.

The 10,000 or so fans who attended each game saw plenty of exciting action. Wake Forest was taken to overtime in wins over South Carolina and Maryland, then again in the championship game against State. Wake was the talk of the Tournament because of Dickie Hemric, a 6-foot-6, 227-pound junior center from Jonesville, N.C., who was ACC Player of the Year in 1954 and 1955.

Hemric was the most dominant player in a league that featured only three other starters as tall as 6-7. Hemric's 24.3 scoring average was second in the ACC to the 30.4 of Virginia's Buzz Wilkinson. Hemric led the league in rebounds with 15.1 a game, and his .504 shooting percentage was second to the .505 of Maryland's Gene Shue. Hemric was an aggressive player with a soft shooting touch. In 1954, the player was rare who could rebound as well as shoot.

The rules of the day helped Hemric and other players his size. The foul lane was only 6 feet wide, compared to the current 12 feet, allowing Hemric position within easy reach of the basket without being called for a 3-second lane violation. Each team also was allowed to claim one of the inside foul lane positions during a free throw attempt, meaning players such as Hemric could easily tap in missed free throws as field goals. For the 1954 season, the NCAA also adopted an unusual bonus free throw, whereby a player was awarded a second shot if he missed the first. Teams were known to intentionally miss second free throws to the side of the basket in which their teammate was standing.

While interest in basketball was increasing in North Carolina, it was not nearly as hot an item throughout the rest of the ACC. The Associated Press report of Maryland's 81-41 victory over Clemson on Dec. 3, 1954 did not even mention that it was the first official game between two league teams.

Maryland's interest was in football—the Terrapins had just won a national championship. In fact, the ACC was formed more with football in mind than basketball. A round-robin

ACC BASKETBALL / THE '50s

... then Frank McGuire was certainly the godfather.

"I am declaring open war against Everett Case. And some day, perhaps in a year or two, the shoe will be on the other foot."

☐ **Frank McGuire**

schedule was possible in an eight-team football league, and with national football powers at Maryland and Duke, the ACC was able to secure an automatic berth for its league champion in the annual Orange Bowl. Not all of the 17 Southern Conference schools could possibly keep up with Duke and Maryland, so the better football schools were most interested in forming the new league.

For the first few years of the league's operation, basketball played second fiddle. But interest in basketball was slowly developing.

"There's no doubt," said Duke Coach Hal Bradley, "that this area is a hotbed of college basketball and in another few years we will rank with any such area in the nation. Basketball in the high schools of our state is improving steadily and this, too, will hasten the growth and popularity of the sport in North Carolina."

Perhaps nothing hastened that growth more than the McGuire-Case feud.

Following that January game in which the Wolfpack used a full-court press to defeat the Tar Heels by seven, McGuire said: "I don't mind losing, but when a team takes advantage of your weak spot, especially when it can win by other means, well, that's not cricket in my book.

"I'll never forget this night. The tide will turn some day. You can quote me as saying I am declaring open war against Everett Case. And some day, perhaps in a year or two, the shoe will be on the other foot.

"I thought he was my friend, but I know better now. I just can't wait until the day comes when I can meet him on equal terms. I'll get even with that rascal."

The two coaches refused to shake hands following N.C. State's 57-48 victory over UNC in Raleigh a month later. McGuire said it was up to the winning coach to offer a handshake. Case claimed the losing coach should be first to offer congratulations. McGuire did not cotton to the way State played keep-away for the final six minutes of the game. Neither did some of the Reynolds Coliseum fans who threw orange peelings and even a liquor bottle onto the floor.

"He'd always say, 'Don't shake hands on the court. Let the people think we're mad at each other,'" said McGuire in an attempt to brush aside the differences between the two.

The Case-McGuire feud reached the point where Billy Carmichael Jr., the longtime comptroller at UNC, got the two together for lunch to pass a peace pipe. McGuire and Case attempted to bury the hatchet further during a pre-Tournament function, but the hard feelings between the coaches and their teams carried into the 1954 ACC Tournament first round. A shoving match near the end of the game resulted in a technical foul against State guard Dave Gotkin, who threw the basketball at UNC forward Gerry McCabe.

State escaped with that win and eventually qualified for the NCAA Tournament for the fourth time in five seasons. At the time, the NCAA invited only the ACC champion to its tournament. The ACC also adopted a rule that no team could participate in the National Invitational Tournament. The NIT ban was a carryover rule from the Southern Conference and it stood until 1967.

The Wolfpack represented the ACC well with a victory over George Washington before losing to All-America Tom Gola and La Salle in the East Regional semifinals, 88-81.

31

ACC BASKETBALL / THE '50s

N.C. State remained the ACC's kingpin through the 1955 and 1956 seasons, but the Wolfpack had to pay dearly for violations of NCAA rules. State was banned from participation in the 1955 NCAA Tournament for paying the travel expenses of prospects to Raleigh for tryouts in 1953. The key figure in those recruiting violations was believed to be Ronnie Shavlik, an All-America whom the Wolfpack successfully wooed out of Denver.

Another four-year NCAA probation in the '50s and a point-shaving scandal in the '60s tainted what was otherwise a polished program at State under Case.

The formula by which Case established a winner was no secret. He used his connections from coaching high school basketball in Indiana to secure players out of the Midwest and Northeast. Once he got signed players on campus, Case taught a fast-break game foreign to ACC fans as well as a relentless full-court defensive pressure—the kind that so aggravated McGuire.

There was another key to Case's success at State: scheduling. In 1949, he helped N.C. State realize a dream with the completion of a grand new playing facility. It took 10 years, three governors, four General Assemblies, four Budget Commissions, two Budget Directors and $3 million to build Reynolds Coliseum.

Reynolds' initial design was the same as that of Indoor Stadium on the Duke University campus and was to be constructed for a mere $300,000. Since the rectangular arena would also serve as an ROTC Armory, the Federal Government authorized a $100,000 grant through the Work Progress Authority (WPA). The Council of State, on Governor J. Melville Broughton's recommendation, allocated $100,000 to the project. The late William Neal Reynolds of Winston-Salem furnished the remaining $100,000.

At the N.C. State commencement in June, 1941, Governor Broughton announced that the $300,000 coliseum would be built. The Secretary of War certified the project as one of importance to national defense and the WPA grant was approved. But the project was stalled during World War II.

The steel girders stood as a skeleton frame of the coliseum during the war. Once the war ended, the project was continued and expanded. By then, N.C. State officials decided that a 9,000-seat facility was not big enough, so they extended both end zones to increase the capacity. The additional seats account for its unusual shoebox shape.

With 12,400 seats, Reynolds was the largest arena in the ACC when completed for the 1950 season. Case first convinced Southern Conference officials, then the ACC, that the league Tournament should be played there. He also fostered the idea of playing a Christmas tournament in Reynolds with the four North Carolina schools in the ACC playing four of the nation's top teams in a three-day event. The Dixie Classic, as the tournament was named, began in 1950.

By playing the ACC Tournament and the Dixie Classic in Reynolds, Case and the Wolfpack rarely had to pack a suitcase to play. From 1954 through 1960, a period which covered the birth of the ACC and the death of the Dixie Classic, the Wolfpack never played more than 10 games in one season outside Reynolds. During that stretch, State posted an impressive 108-22 (.831 winning percentage) record at home. Not nearly as impressive was the 36-29 (.554) record away from Reynolds. In 1956, the Wolfpack played only five of its 28 games on the opposing team's court.

When Case's teams enjoyed only mild success (6-6 and only a 1950 trip to the Final Four) in the NCAA Tournament, he came under some criticism for slanted scheduling.

Duke Coach Hal Bradley got in a parting shot when he said: "I'm not criticizing State, I just wish we didn't have to do it (play in Reynolds) so many times. It's tougher to win away from home, and even tougher when you are going into the other team's gym."

Even opposing players spoke out on the subject. "State is 100 percent and two men better when they play at home," said Wake Forest's Dave Budd. "There ought to be a law against the home-court advantage they have. Every team has an advantage at home, but let's face it, it is beyond reasonable limits in Raleigh."

After dropping an 82-60 decision to State for the Dixie Classic championship in 1955, UNC's McGuire said: "Each time I go to New York I rave and rave about State. Then when they go north they never live up to expectations."

When the Wolfpack lost a four-overtime thriller to lightly regarded Canisius in the 1956 NCAA Tournament in New York, veteran Madison Square Garden publicist Lester Scott said: "Case-coached teams always play poorly here for some reason. I don't know if it's because they play so many games at home and aren't used to those crowds on the road or what."

McGuire got in his usual jab at Case when in December of 1956 he said: "Good teams win on the road. Fair ones do not. Basketball is a game where the home court has its advantages. A good team, in order to stay on top, has to win on the road."

McGuire was never one to avoid pointing a finger at Case and N.C. State. During the 1954 season, he said that the use of music at Reynolds Colisum was a tremendous advantage to the Wolfpack. In addition to being the first school to use a pep band at home games, State employed an organist at Reynolds. McGuire claimed that when the organist let out with *Dixie* it meant at least 10 points for the Wolfpack.

By 1955, every coach in the ACC was acutely aware of the advantages in playing before a home crowd.

Clemson rarely fielded good teams during the '50s, but every ACC team knew it was in for a battle when the game was played at Clemson's Fike Field House. The tiny gymnasium seated just 3,500 and was almost always filled to capacity. Randy Mahaffey, who played his entire career in the '60s at Fike, figured there wasn't much else to do in Clemson during the winter, so basketball games became social events.

"I absolutely cannot imagine anyplace, anywhere an athlete could be more pumped up than coming out in playing in that old field house," Mahaffey said. "It was just an incredible feeling to come out on that floor with that damn pep band playing *Tiger Rag*, thousands of people just clapping and raising hell. You got so much adrenaline running in you, you just couldn't contain yourself."

Fan involvement was part of the game at Fike, which was known mostly as the Tiger Den, but was also called the Snake Pit, the Sweat Box or the Cow Palace. Opposing players were greeted in pregame introductions with chants of "Tiger meat, Tiger meat, Tiger meat." So loud was Fike, Duke Coach Vic Bubas often huddled his team at midcourt during timeouts.

The tiny gymnasium, which was also used for dances and boxing matches, once provided primal scream therapy sessions for the cadets when Clemson was both an agriculture and all-male military school.

ACC BASKETBALL / THE '50s

"Students were still all dressed up in military uniforms," said Grady Wallace, who played at Fike for South Carolina in 1956 and 1957. "You'd get up there to shoot a free throw and everyone was whipping around. After a while, it looked like they were sitting still and the goal was moving."

Fike was not very well lighted. Once, Bubas threatened to have his players warm up with miner's helmets. Following Duke's final trip to Fike in 1968, Bubas stooped and left a goodbye kiss for the Tiger emblem at midcourt.

For the first season of ACC play, Maryland played at tiny Ritchie Coliseum where, according to Terp John Sandbower, "you always ended up in a lap here and there." Capacity at Ritchie was 4,200.

The Terps moved into the 12,000-seat Student Activities Building in 1955. The building, later renamed Cole Field House, was the third largest arena on the East Coast to New York's Madison Square Garden and N.C. State's Reynolds Coliseum. In 1957, Wake Forest players complained that the bright lights caused a glare, so they smeared grease under their eyes.

Bones McKinney, Wake's head coach from 1958 through 1965, recalled how difficult it was to win games at Maryland. "They wanted to make us feel right at home," McKinney said, "so they put a brass band right behind our bench. Now the gym was practically empty because this game was played during the holidays, but the band winds up right behind my back.

"Every time I called a timeout to give instructions to my fellows, the music would start — loud and clear. No soft numbers, mind you, just brassy ones. That trombone player was leaning right over my shoulder all afternoon. The music was pretty, but my boys never heard a word I said."

Woollen Gym in Chapel Hill was built under the same premise as the other arenas in the ACC, during an era when basketball was more of an intramural sport. Capacity was only 6,000. By 1959, the Woollen Gym roof leaked so badly that five buckets were on the court to catch rain drops. Children were stationed on the sidelines to rush out during games and wipe water.

South Carolina played in 3,200-seat Carolina Field House, which was affectionately known to all as The Pit because the court was surrounded by a 2-foot concrete wall.

"I used to say they emptied the damn swimming pool and we played in it," said Bud Millikan, who took his Maryland teams to Carolina Field House from 1951 through 1967. Referee Lou Bello said he always feared that a fire would force evacuation and the players and officials would be trapped on the court inside those walls.

Virginia never posted a winning record against ACC opponents in 11 seasons at its old Memorial Gymnasium, but that didn't mean it was an easy place for opponents to play. When nationally ranked Duke played at Virginia in 1963, Cavalier fans pelted Bubas with paper cups every time he stood to instruct his team.

"I was trying to calm my players in all the noise and din of the game—and it was a new twist when Art Heyman came over and put his arms around me," Bubas said. "He said in a soft voice: 'Take it easy, coach. Take it easy. Everything will work out okay.' "

Memorial Gymnasium, which seated 5,000, featured an old track that circled the upper deck. Virginia fans were known on occasion to reach down and shake the basket supports when an opposing player was shooting a free throw.

Most unique of all the gymnasiums was probably Wake Forest's Gore. It measured only 90 feet in length instead of the NCAA regulation 94.

"You'd run down the floor in that old gym and they'd put their legs up right from the first row of the stands and they'd trip you," says Joe Belmont, who played for Duke. "They'd kill you over there. It was a disaster going over to that place. You had to be careful where you were running. You had to run your fast-break lanes closer to the center of the court."

Wake Forest games against State, North Carolina or Duke drew more than capacity crowds of 2,200. Children were known to climb trees and sneak through the bathroom windows upstairs to the gymnasium, where they would sit in the rafters.

Only at N.C. State did ACC teams experience playing inside what would be considered a big-time arena.

"It was the Taj Mahal of the country," said Wake Forest's Dickie Hemric. "When I tried out there my senior year in high school, I looked at that big edifice and couldn't believe it."

Case made the mammoth facility even more special by adding unique touches such as the pep band and the now-famous applause meter, which measured the noise level of the crowd. Everything was meant by Case to entertain the fans as well as provide more of a home-court edge.

Though State enjoyed the home-court advantage in 1955, the Wolfpack probably would have finished first in the regular season and won the ACC Tournament no matter where it was played. Some observers, including Case on occasion, thought the 1955 squad was his best at State. The Wolfpack lost only four games, including a 91-78 decision at Villanova when John Maglio and Nick Pond were slowed by illnesses, and 6-foot-10 senior center Cliff Dwyer was nursing an injured elbow.

To defeat N.C. State in 1955 was cause for celebration.

When Maryland, which played a style of basketball known to ACC fans as "possession ball," defeated the Wolfpack 68-64 at Maryland, Terp fans carried players Bob Kessler and Bob O'Brien off the floor. Then when UNC downed N.C. State 84-80 in Reynolds Coliseum, McGuire and his Tar Heels clipped the nets in an obvious gesture of one-upmanship on Case, who brought the net-cutting tradition to N.C. State from Indiana.

Prior to the UNC-State game, Case said McGuire's slowdown tactics that season were "not basketball and not good for the game." McGuire's team ran the court freely in this victory, one he called "the sweetest since I have been at North Carolina." State's other loss came at home to Villanova, 107-96, despite a magnificent 49-point, 35-rebound performance

Juco Giant

Walt Hambrick had a sterling record as a junior college coach, leading Pikeville (Ky.) JC to a 63-9 record during the '54 and '55 seasons. South Carolina Coach Frank Johnson noticed, recruiting five players off the '54 team and two more in '55. For good measure, he brought Hambrick along as an assistant coach.

33

ACC SCRAPBOOK

Some vintage scenes from old ACC gyms (clockwise from top left): An experimental rule in 1955 allowed both teams to line a player up under the basket on free throws. Here UNC's Lennie Rosenbluth shoots while N.C. State's Cliff Dwyer (87) and Carolina's Bob Young (20) await the rebound. ■ Thousands of fans attired in their Sunday-go-to-meeting best watch as a Duke player dives over press row at Reynolds Coliseum in Raleigh. ■ Player introductions in the late '50s and early '60s meant the house lights went down and the spotlights went up. ■ Eager Tiger fans await tip-off in Clemson's Fike Field House, known around the league under assorted monikers: Tiger Den, Sweat Box and Snake Pit. ■ TV gave the ACC much of its identity. Here a WUNC-TV camera catches the action of a Duke-Carolina game in '58.

ACC BASKETBALL / THE '50s

Molodet, Maglio State's Magic "M Twins"
N.C. State's backcourt combo of Vic Molodet (73, shooting) and John Maglio were the lightning-quick guards that ran and pressed their way to ACC Tournament titles in '55 and '56. "I match my guards against any in the country," Coach Everett Case said of his "M Twins."

from All-America Ronnie Shavlik.

State featured a double-post offense in '55 with the 6-10 Dwyer low and the 6-9 Shavlik high. A tandem with such height was considered extraordinary at the time. Each averaged in double figures in points and rebounds. Vic Molodet and Maglio were the lightning-quick guards and 6-5 Phil DiNardo averaged just under 10 points and 10 rebounds a game at forward. This State team was deep in talent with Ronnie Scheffel, Pond and Cliff Hafer off the bench.

A most unusual incident occurred late in the season when ACC official Phil Fox received a threatening letter from La Salle Coach Ken Loeffler. In the letter, Loeffler was critical of several calls Fox made the previous season when State lost 88-78 to La Salle at Reynolds. Loeffler wrote that La Salle would film the game against State this season with the purpose of watching Fox's calls. Fox turned the letter over to the FBI and Loeffler later apologized for the incident. (Loeffler was later the coach at Texas A&M when that school was put on probation, along with State, for illegal recruiting tactics of Louisiana schoolboy Jackie Moreland.)

That probation came later. In 1955, State served a one-year sentence from the NCAA for violations in 1953 when it illegally paid travel expenses and held tryouts for recruits. The probation prevented the Wolfpack from representing the ACC in the NCAA Tournament.

Duke, which placed second to N.C. State in the regular season and lost the ACC Tournament title game 87-77 to the Wolfpack, represented the ACC in postseason play. Duke's first-ever NCAA Tournament appearance was short-lived as the Blue Devils fell behind Villanova by 16 points in the East Regional and lost 74-73. "I'm afraid our boys were too awestruck over appearing in Madison Square Garden," said Duke Coach Bradley.

N.C. State, perhaps in defiance of the ACC's policy that prohibited league teams from participating in the NIT, opted to play in the 25-team national AAU Tournament in Denver. Playing in his hometown, Shavlik scored 20 points in each game as State defeated Wuthnow Furniture of Hope, Kan., then lost to the San Francisco Olympic Club.

Neither game counted in State's final record, and following the season, the ACC voted to not allow league schools to participate in the AAU Tournament.

ACC BASKETBALL / THE '50s

'56

N.C. State was the favorite to retain the ACC crown for the '56 season, with Ronnie Shavlik, Vic Molodet, John Maglio, Cliff Hafer, Phil DiNardo, Bob Seitz, Nick Pond and Lou Dickman returning. The Wolfpack won 24 of 28 games, and for the second straight season there was talk that this was Case's best team.

Case admitted: "My present team is the fastest I have ever had at State. I match my guards (Maglio and Molodet, who were known to State fans as the 'M Twins') against any in the country. Ronnie Shavlik has hit his stride and there aren't any better ones around when he is right."

Following the season, Shavlik was the first-round pick of the New York Knicks in the NBA draft. Molodet was the first-round pick of the Boston Celtics. Maglio, Seitz and Hafer would be selected in the NBA draft a year later.

Early in the season, State defeated fifth-ranked Brigham Young 95-81, then rolled through a Dixie Classic field that included two other unbeaten and Top 10 teams. By the time State had run its two-year win streak to 23 games by whipping its first 11 opponents, the Wolfpack was ranked No. 2 behind San Francisco with center Bill Russell. The streak was snapped when 11th-ranked Duke handed the Wolfpack a 68-58 defeat on Jan. 7 in Durham. State played the game without Molodet, who picked up a viral infection during a holiday hunting trip. The Wolfpack's only other losses during the regular season were at North Carolina 73-69 and to Maryland 71-62.

Heading into the ACC Tournament, State looked like a lock to win its third straight championship and ninth conference title (counting the Southern Conference) in 10 years. But the Wolfpack had lost Hafer in mid-February when the school ruled he violated its honor code. Then, in the regular-season finale, Shavlik broke his wrist and was not expected to play again in '56. Surprisingly, Shavlik played 10 minutes as the Wolfpack survived a scare from Clemson in its first-round victory, 88-84. The powerful Wolfpack defeated Duke 91-79 in the Tournament semifinals and Wake Forest 76-64 in the championship with Shavlik at half-speed.

The strain of beating North Carolina in the semifinals, then challenging State on its home court in the championship, probably caught up with Wake Forest. "Tournaments are just like airplanes," Deacon Coach Murray Greason said. "One drop and you're a goner."

When asked if he tired of winning championships, Case said: "No, it's just like eating. You don't get tired of eating, do you?"

Shavlik, playing with a cast on his wrist, scored eight points and had 16 rebounds against Duke. "In my book," Case said, "I can't recall a greater demonstration of courage than was displayed by his boy tonight."

Shavlik scored another eight points and had 17 rebounds against Wake Forest. "He gives the entire team confidence. When we shoot, we know we've got a rebounder," Maglio said of Shavlik.

With a week to prepare for the NCAA Tournament, it appeared Shavlik would have enough time to return to top form. Shavlik became a celebrity because of his courage to play with a broken wrist. Prior to the NCAA Tournament, he made an appearance on the Perry Como Show. Shavlik and classmates Molodet, DiNardo and Dickman—a group tagged the "Fabulous Freshmen of '53"—were ready to win a tournament they had set their sights on four years earlier.

State's first-round opponent was Canisius, which had a 17-6 record and had won 15 of its last 16 games. The site of the game was Madison Square Garden, which had long been a house of horrors for the Wolfpack. "I don't think the Garden will bother us this time," Molodet said. "We're going all the way."

State fell behind early against Canisius, but rallied to tie the game 65-all at the end of regulation. It was tied at 69 following the first overtime and at 71 following two overtimes. Neither team scored in the next 5-minute period, and the game went to a fourth overtime. The Garden crowd was up and down. It booed the stall tactics of both clubs and cheered the prospect of such a tense and lengthy game.

The Wolfpack led 78-77 when Maglio was fouled with 14 seconds remaining in the fourth OT. But Maglio, a 73 percent free throw shooter for the season, failed to seal the victory when he missed the free throw. Canisius rushed down the court and scored on a basket by Frank Corcoran, a little-used substitute who averaged less than a point a game during the regular season. Corcoran's name did not appear in the official Tournament program, and the winner was his only basket of the game.

Shavlik was fabulous in his final game. He scored 25 points

Case congratulates Shavlik, bandage and all, after '56 Tournament triumph.

37

USC a country boy's sweet dream of heaven.

Grady Wallace arrived in Columbia, S.C., with a suitcase half full of clothes, a $10 bill in his pocket and a dream to wear a University of South Carolina basketball jersey.

Walt Hambrick, an assistant coach for the Gamecocks who came with Wallace from Pikeville (Ky.) Junior College, once said all the 6-foot-4 Wallace needed to be happy was a pound of grapes and a Western movie.

"They told me I got $15-a-month laundry allowance, and my mother sent me a little money. They fed me three times a day," Wallace says. "The next thing I knew, every time I go the post office there are passes for me to the theater. I was just shelling them out to everybody. We all went to the movie. He (Hambrick) was right, it didn't take much to make me happy. Life was great. Never had to spend money going to the movies. Never had a car so I didn't have to worry about gasoline or anything.

"It was just a country boy's dream of heaven."

The '50s
South Carolina

Two years later, Wallace pocketed a national scoring title. With a 31.2 average in 1957, Wallace edged Mississippi's Joe Gibbon, later a major-league baseball pitcher, Seattle's Elgin Baylor and Kansas' Wilt Chamberlain. He remains the only player in ACC history to do so.

"It was an accomplishment, really, but you wonder why and how it happened, the why of it more than the how," Wallace says. "The only thing I ever wanted to do was get out there and play."

Wallace first learned to play on the dirt court behind Bunk Crum's house in Mare Creek, which is tucked deep in the mountains of eastern Kentucky and where living off the land has long meant topping a peak and stripping it for coal. Wallace's father was a coal miner, as was the head of every other family in the community of about 15 households. If their children escaped the mine shafts, more than likely it was to join the service or head for the automobile factories in "Deee-troit," Wallace says.

Wallace was lucky just to be alive. Typhoid fever struck when he was 8. He missed an entire year of school, and at one point during the illness a doctor ordered the nurse to "draw the curtain" and call a priest.

But Wallace survived, and his good health led to an affection for athletics, which he saw early as a way out of the mines. "I was always held to a very sincere promise that my mother got out of me," Wallace says. "That promise was never to go into a coal mine."

Football was appealing to Wallace, but few of the high schools in the Mare Creek area had teams since there wasn't enough level ground to clear out a 100-yard field. So he turned to basketball, a Kentucky craze.

After Adolph Rupp guided the University of Kentucky to national championships in 1948, 1949 and 1951, the crudest of basketball goals went up in backyards from Louisville to Lebanon Junction. Mare Creek was no exception.

Wallace's first goal was really no goal at all. He and Bunk Crum got a piece of guide wire, like that used to hold telephone poles in place, made a circle out of it and pinned it to the top of a barn.

"We'd play until our hands got numb. We played day after day, 12 months out of the year," he said. "I played in snowstorms where you couldn't see the goal from 15 feet away."

When the two weren't playing basketball, they joined the rest of the community and listened to University of Kentucky games by radio. For better reception, townsfolk drove their cars atop the nearest mountain and listened to the raspy voice of Claude Sullivan.

Wallace couldn't imitate the playing styles of Kentucky stars Alex Groza, Ralph Beard, Cliff Hagan and Frank Ramsey because he never saw them play in person or on television. Instead, his idols were the prep stars in the area, most notably Frankie Gene Crum (no relation to Bunk) of Betsy Layne High School, where Wallace went, and Paul Maye from nearby Mayetown High School. Games between the Betsy Layne Bobcats and the rival Van Leer Mule Banks were just as important as any Kentucky-Indiana matchup.

Wallace noticed that Frankie Gene Crum always took one dribble to his right and leaned into his defender while shooting his jump shot. Paul Maye, on the other hand, took the same dribble to his right, leaned *back* and released his jumper.

"I always thought if I could do that, exactly like they did, it would work for me too," Wallace says. "I would go out from daylight until dark and practice those shots. As fast as I could go get the ball, I'd go back and shoot it again. One time like Frankie Gene. Another time like the Maye boy."

Wallace's patience paid off. By his sophomore year at Betsy Layne High, he was in the same starting lineup with his all-time idol, Frankie Gene Crum. When the Bobcats were eliminated in the District Tournament that season, Frankie Gene removed his jersey No. 42 for the last time.

"I want you to wear that thing," Frankie Gene said as he tossed the jersey to Wallace.

Six years later, Wallace would win the national scoring title at South Carolina, primarily because he perfected the Crum lean-in shot and the Maye fall-away. He still wore jersey No. 42, which South Carolina retired.

South Carolina almost didn't get the services of Wallace. Rupp showed some interest, but Wallace was so scared of going to school in a big city like Lexington that he ducked out of a possible recruiting session with The Baron. Instead, Wallace headed off to Eastern Kentucky before a severe case of homesickness led him back to Mare Creek after one semester.

Next, he enrolled at Pikeville Junior College, partly because his longtime friend Benny Fannin and defensive star Bobby McCoy were both there. "I don't know what bulldog tenacity means, but I think that's what he demonstrated," Wallace says of McCoy.

Pikeville Coach Walt Hambrick arranged a tuition

waiver for Wallace as well as free tokens for the 15-mile daily bus ride south on Highway 23 from Mare Creek to Pikeville. Wallace didn't need the tokens.

"Basketball was a pretty popular item at that time and everybody had a little interest in it, so I guess they probably knew me," Wallace says. "I'd just stand out there beside the road. I didn't even have to stick a thumb out. They'd stop and I'd hop in the car and I'd always beat the bus to school.

"I used to get there so early I could stop off at the smokehouse and shoot a couple of games of pool before I went and headed off to school."

Fannin, Woody Preston, Sam Smith, Russ Porter and Sol Richardson all played with Wallace on the 1954 Pikeville team, then all five went to South Carolina. His last year at Pikeville, Wallace averaged 32.4 points a game to lead all junior college players. When South Carolina Coach Frank Johnson hired Hambrick as an assistant coach, Wallace and McCoy went along as part of the package.

In 1956, the Gamecocks managed only nine wins in 23 games, but Wallace helped carry them to a 17-12 record in 1957. Although they won only five of 14 conference games during the regular season, the Gamecocks took unbeaten North Carolina to overtime before losing and were a threat to win the ACC Tournament.

"Sure, he has a weakness," said The Citadel Coach Norm Sloan after watching Wallace score 43 points in one game. "I noticed that he doesn't dribble too well with his left foot."

By ACC Tournament time, Wallace was racing neck-and-neck with Gibbon, Chamberlain and Baylor for the national scoring leadership. Wallace assured himself of the crown by scoring 41 points against Duke, 31 against Maryland and 28 more against North Carolina in the championship game.

"I felt like if I was 1-on-1 and I had the ball, I don't think there were too many people who were going to stop me from taking a fairly good percentage shot," Wallace says. "They might stop me from making it, but not from taking it."

Wallace took only a few more shots after college. He chose AAU basketball over the NBA, played two seasons, then returned to Columbia to work in his current capacity as Commissioner of Parole and Community Corrections for the state of South Carolina. He coached on a volunteer basis for nine years at Cardinal Newman High School in Columbia and helped win two state championships, including one with future major league baseball player Gorman Thomas as a star center.

Wallace says his name is still recognized on occasion around Columbia. But rarely is he recognized as the only ACC player to lead the nation in scoring.

"Just because you went out there and played a game, and maybe had a pretty good night, that didn't make you an author of wisdom," Wallace says. "Hell, you just went out there and had a pretty good night, maybe took advantage of somebody else's deficiency. It didn't make you any smarter or any wiser. It just meant you had a pretty good night." ∎

From Kentucky dirt court to ACC hardwood, Gamecock Wallace was naturally hot-handed.

ACC BASKETBALL / THE '50s

and had 17 rebounds. "I would hate to see Shavlik with two arms," said Canisius Coach Joe Curran. Said Shavlik, "I just don't know what happens to us in New York." Said Molodet: "I hate to end like this. I had a feeling we were going all the way."

Said Case: "It is the greatest disappointment I've suffered in my 36 years in basketball. If I hadn't recognized the players on the floor I wouldn't have believed this was the same State team. The boys were so high. They wanted to do the right thing so badly that they did everything wrong."

The '56 season signaled the end of State's grip on the ACC championship. While winning along the way, Case had established himself as one of the outstanding coaches in college basketball. He also set the standard for the rest of the league. McGuire at UNC, Bradley at Duke, Greason at Wake Forest and Millikan at Maryland watched how Case operated and followed his lead. They all recognized how Case gathered excellent talent to the west Raleigh campus, and they all went about securing the same kind of talent.

The ACC had entered the age of recruiting.

It was no coincidence that the two leading scorers during the '56 season were recruited from outside the region— Lennie Rosenbluth (26.7 average) to North Carolina and Grady Wallace (23.9 average) to South Carolina.

Rosenbluth's recruitment was part of what was to be known as McGuire's "Underground Railroad" from New York City to Chapel Hill. Rosenbluth was one of seven New Yorkers on UNC's national championship team of 1957, known affectionally as the "Flatbush Tar Heels." Two of the other six team members were from New Jersey.

As McGuire said in *Sports Illustrated* that season: "New York is my personal territory. Duke can scout in Philadelphia and North Carolina State can have the whole country. But if anybody wants to move into New York, they need a passport from me . . . All the people in New York are my friends. No one gets paid for helping, but everybody looks out for me. The whole police department looks for players for me. So do the high school coaches, so do the brothers at the Catholic schools. Even the waterfront looks out for me."

As in the recruiting of Rosenbluth, a 6-foot-5 forward out of the Bronx, McGuire usually enlisted the help of Harry Gotkin, his New York buddy.

Gotkin also worked for McGuire to land the likes of Danny Lotz, Tommy Kearns, Bob Cunningham, Joe Quigg and Pete Brennan, a group that formed the nucleus of UNC's '57 championship team.

Before long, McGuire and North Carolina basketball were known to all in New York.

What wasn't known to the prospects and their parents was the South. But Gotkin worked to break those stereotypes. "No, they don't kill Catholics down there," Gotkin said, according to Dan Klores in his book *Roundball Culture*. "No, they don't have a Newman Club, but they will. Yes, Frank will make sure they won't lose their religion."

They didn't lose their religion in North Carolina, they only gained another: ACC basketball. It was a fascination with a game that was spreading fast, from the tip of the league's geographic lines in Maryland to the bottom in South Carolina.

Basketball fans in Columbia were excited about a 6-4 forward from Mare Creek, Ky., named Grady Wallace. "Both are great shooters," South Carolina Coach Frank Johnson said in comparing Wallace to Rosenbluth, "but my boy is superior on defense." Even so, Wallace was best on offense where he led

No bones about it: Hemric a Demon in hardwood jungle.

The '50s

Wake Forest

Dickie Hemric doesn't have to search for reasons why he was All-America at Wake Forest.

"There was a will to achieve in the lifestyle I had lived prior to that," Hemric says. "It was not the law of the jungle, but we were taught to establish goals and go after them. For me, the goals were to succeed and be a contributor to anything I participated in."

Hemric more than reached his goals.

After four seasons at Wake Forest, Hemric left for the Boston Celtics of the NBA as the NCAA's all-time leading scorer. His 2,587 points were more than the previous NCAA high set by Furman's Frank Selvy. Hemric's total still ranks 15th in NCAA history. His 1,802 career rebounds rank fifth all-time.

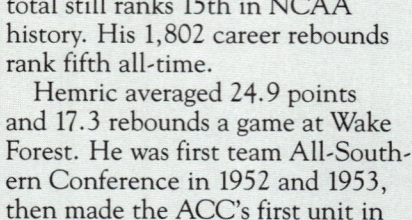

Hemric averaged 24.9 points and 17.3 rebounds a game at Wake Forest. He was first team All-Southern Conference in 1952 and 1953, then made the ACC's first unit in 1954 and 1955, both times being named the league's Player of the Year. He remains the ACC's all-time leading scorer and rebounder.

All that from a youngster who arrived on the Wake Forest campus in the fall of 1951 with an idea of devoting as much time to football as basketball. Hemric had the body for both sports. He stood 6-foot-6 and weighed a healthy 230 pounds.

Hemric's bulk helped him hold his own, especially as a freshman. He was strong enough to plant himself near the basket, which was easier to do in those days of the 6-foot foul lane. He was also adept at drawing fouls and is still the all-time NCAA leader in free throws attempted (1,359).

Not until his sophomore year, which coincided with the arrival of Bones McKinney as an assistant coach, did Hemric begin to polish his game. Hour after hour, day after day, McKinney drilled Hemric in the fundamentals of playing the center position.

"Dickie learned more in a month than any man I ever saw," McKinney says. "I don't know of any man who ever progressed as quickly as he did. When he came he did not have a hook and could not shoot a foul shot."

McKinney, fresh off a six-year career as a center in the NBA, taught Hemric how to make a hook shot with either hand as well as how to pivot off either foot before moving to the basket. The grueling practice sessions often centered around McKinney keeping possession of the ball in 1-on-1 games against Hemric, who was even-

40

tually feared as much by opponents as a shot blocker as a scorer.

The long hours of work in practice made Hemric dominant in ACC games. That he once scored 41 points against Clemson was not so unusual. But Hemric also had 36 rebounds, which remains the ACC single-game record.

Against Duke during the 1954 season, Hemric limped to a 44-point performance on what later proved to be a broken ankle. He often played his best against the best, outscoring Kentucky's Cliff Hagan 28-18, La Salle's Tom Gola 23-20 and Duquesne's Jim Tucker 23-15.

"That guy is going to score about 30 or more points against you, regardless, so why bother to concentrate on him?" said UNC Coach Frank McGuire following one game. "We just try to stop the other guys on the team."

That was often difficult, as Wake Forest's offense centered around Hemric. The first pass was usually to the pivot, and the offense evolved from there. It worked well enough for Hemric and Wake Forest to stop N.C. State's six-year hold on the Southern Conference crown with a championship in the 1953 tournament.

That title was particularly gratifying to Hemric. Two years earlier, Wolfpack Coach Everett Case called Hemric to Raleigh for a tryout against the N.C. State varsity. Hemric was impressive, but not enough to be offered a scholarship by Case.

Hemric had already committed himself to Wake Forest, primarily because he had caddied for several Demon Deacon fans at the golf course in his hometown of Jonesville, N.C. The smaller size of the school and the charm of the old Wake Forest campus also appealed to Hemric, who was near the top of his Jonesville High School class.

As the ninth of 10 children of a carpenter in the Jonesville community of 2,000 near Winston-Salem, Hemric had little time for athletics. His newspaper routes helped the family spring for the one pair of overalls each of the Hemric children had for school and the one suit each had for church. When the knees of the pants wore through from shooting marbles, the overalls became cutoff shorts for summer work in the tobacco fields.

Hemric's attention eventually turned to football and basketball, and he became a star for the Jonesville High School Blue Jays. Unlike his five older brothers, all of whom entered the military service following high school, Hemric used athletics as a vehicle to attend college and eventually to play on the world champion Boston Celtics of 1957.

Hemric retired from professional basketball after two seasons, and for the past 30 years has worked in marketing management for Goodyear in North Canton, Ohio.

When Hemric left Wake Forest, his old coach paid him the supreme compliment. Said McKinney, "Dick is the best basketball player North Carolina has ever produced." ∎

Grueling 1-on-1 sessions with McKinney made Hemric double trouble, first at scoring goals, then at blocking them.

ACC BASKETBALL / THE '50s

the ACC in scoring in 1957, capping his senior season by winning the national scoring title over Kansas center Wilt Chamberlain.

Wallace, still the only ACC player ever to lead the nation in scoring, also led the nation's junior college players with a 32.4 average at Pikeville (Ky.) JC during his sophomore season. It was purely by coincidence, Johnson said, that Pikeville Coach Wally Hambrick was hired as a South Carolina assistant coach a few months prior to Wallace showing up on the Columbia campus. Hambrick had done Johnson, a longtime friend, a favor by sending four Pikeville players to South Carolina the previous season. By the time Wallace arrived, half of the Gamecocks' roster was from the state of Kentucky.

That's the way recruiting of players was done in the '50s. Friends sent ballplayers to their coaching friends. ACC coaches generally had a region of the country they worked: McGuire, New York; Case, Indiana and New Jersey; Bradley, Philadelphia; Millikan, western Pennsylvania.

There were exceptions, like when Case went to Colorado to find Shavlik. Another was a gifted high school ballplayer from Minden, La., who drew the attention of nearly every college coach across the country. Case wanted the services of Jackie Moreland as much as anyone, and he got him.

Moreland was the most highly recruited player by ACC schools in the '50s, just as Art Heyman, Dick DeVenzio and Larry Miller were in the '60s, Tom McMillen, Moses Malone, David Thompson, Gene Banks and Ralph Sampson in the '70s, and Michael Jordan, Danny Ferry and J.R. Reid in the '80s. But none caused more of a storm than Moreland.

In his first appearance in a Wolfpack uniform, the 6-7 center scored 30 points as his freshman team dropped an 88-87 decision to the State varsity. Moreland did not play the game's final 10 minutes, presumably because Case did not want to see the freshmen defeat the varsity.

That was the only game in which Moreland would play for the Wolfpack. He was illegally recruited to State, according to the NCAA, and the school's entire athletic program was placed on probation for four years. It was one of the stiffest NCAA penalties until SMU's football program was dissolved in 1987. The penalty was harsh, the NCAA said, because State had been on probation once before (1955). In response to the ruling, ACC Commissioner Jim Weaver said that Moreland was ineligible to play at State.

Before enrolling at State, Moreland had also signed letters-of-intent to attend Texas A&M, Kentucky and Centenary College. Texas A&M was also placed on probation by the NCAA for its recruiting of Moreland.

The NCAA found that N.C. State was guilty of the following violations in recruiting Moreland:
- Moreland was promised $200 a year for clothing.
- He was also promised an annual gift of $1,000.
- His girlfriend, Betty Clara Rhea of Minden, La., was promised an expense-paid trip to Raleigh to meet Moreland at Thanksgiving.
- Rhea was promised a seven-year college medical education.
- Moreland was given $80 for transportation to enroll at N.C. State.
- He was also promised a five-year scholarship at N.C. State.

The NCAA ruled that State was ineligible to participate in any NCAA championships and postseason events. As a result, when the Wolfpack won the ACC football championship in 1956, it was unable to play in the Orange Bowl. Instead, Duke represented the league in the 1957 New Year's Day bowl which, at the time, had a tie-in with the ACC champion. The NCAA also ruled that State could not participate in any NCAA televised event for four years, be represented on any NCAA committee or vote on any questions before the NCAA.

"We have enough concrete evidence to convince a board of 18 men from all parts of the country," said Walter Byers, executive director of the NCAA. "In other words, our decisions aren't based on hearsay."

The ACC conducted an investigation and agreed with the NCAA's findings. In addition to ruling Moreland ineligible to play at State, the ACC also denied contact with prospective athletes by all Wolfpack basketball staff members for one year and fined State $5,000. The ACC ruled that the fine would be waived should Moreland remain a student at State on athletic scholarship.

The basketball program pleaded innocent to all counts and drew the support of State Chancellor Carey H. Bostian. The school conducted its own investigation, and its Athletic Council gave a vote of confidence to the athletic staff. Bostian eventually asked all principal witnesses in the case, as well as representatives from the ACC and the NCAA, to appear at an open hearing in Louisiana. He eventually dropped the idea when witnesses were not willing to appear, and the ACC ultimately reduced its fine against State to $2,500.

Although the second probation was another black mark on his program, Case remained clean in the eyes of Wolfpack and ACC followers. He said he knew nothing of the illegal doings, presumably by the assistant coaches who remained on his staff, and cooperated with the NCAA and ACC throughout their investigations.

"If you're going to convict schools on charges like these, I

Moreland (L) was all smiles in this freshman pose with Bill Haig.

ACC BASKETBALL / THE '50s

can tell you that there wouldn't be very many left to play basketball, or anything," Case said. "They are getting mighty thin, splitting hairs, grasping at technicalities." Case admitted guilt on one charge, that Dwight L. Laughlin, a resident of Bossier City, La., offered Moreland $80 to cover transportation costs to Raleigh. Case denied all other charges, including one that Assistant Coach Vic Bubas had offered Moreland a five-year scholarship.

Upon learning of the probation placed upon State by the NCAA and the ACC, Moreland left Raleigh and landed at Louisiana Tech, where he played for two seasons. He later played five years of professional basketball with the Detroit Pistons of the NBA and another three with the New Orleans Buccaneers of the ABA. He died of cancer in 1971 at age 33.

Beyond the Case-McGuire feud of the early '50s, the extensive and perhaps excessive recruiting of Moreland stood as another indication that the ACC was beginning to take its basketball seriously.

The rest of the nation was beginning to take note, as well. *Sports Illustrated* explained just how McGuire landed such a healthy lot of players in Chapel Hill via New York City. The story, titled "Basketball's Underground Railroad," told of a little-known group of talent scouts who worked on behalf of McGuire and UNC. The article tabbed Gotkin, a New York garment manufacturer, as UNC's chief scout. Howard Garfinkel was named as the chief scout in New York for Case and State.

"I scout for N.C. State," Garfinkel said in the story, "but I don't get paid for it. Far as I know, Gotkin's the only scout who gets paid. I don't know why the hell anyone pays him."

The story said Mike Tynberg, an alumnus of UNC, also helped the school in the area of scouting. "I'm on the North Carolina payroll," Tynberg said. "So is Uncle Harry (Gotkin). We're listed as assistant coaches."

McGuire, of course, denied the charges, saying only that Gotkin and Tynberg were friends who helped in recruiting. Whatever the process, McGuire began the 1957 season with a lineup that probably would feel more at home on 42nd Street than Franklin Street in Chapel Hill. The season-opening lineup of Rosenbluth, Quigg, Kearns, Brennan and Bill Hathaway was entirely from the New York area.

'57

Frank McGuire had some reservations about his fifth UNC team. Harvey Salz, a sharp-shooting, 6-foot-1 sophomore, dropped out of school, thinning the ranks. McGuire was also aware that 6-2 senior guard Tony Radovich was only eligible for the first semester. Later in the season, the 6-11 Bill Hathaway and 6-0 sophomore reserve Stan Groll were declared academically ineligible. To get his roster to 10 players, 6-6 center Bob Young, who was also ineligible at one point because of poor grades, was added to the team.

"Frankly," McGuire said, "I'd set 18 victories in the 24-game regular season as my goal. I thought if we did that it would be a good year."

McGuire, perhaps knowing he was blessed with a gifted lot of players, scheduled a particularly demanding slate of games. In an attempt to make his team road-tough, only eight games were scheduled for tiny Woollen Gym on the UNC campus.

In an early season game against New York University at Madison Square Garden, the Violets elected to triple-team Lennie Rosenbluth, and he managed only nine points. But Bob Cunningham, Joe Quigg, Pete Brennan and Tommy Kearns picked up the scoring and the Tar Heels won, 64-59. In another game, at William & Mary, Rosenbluth was limited to only one field goal. Again, the Tar Heels passed around the scoring load and won, 71-61.

"Everybody has one thing in mind—stop Lennie," McGuire said. "Every team we play tries to defense him. But we keep right on winning."

As the Tar Heels kept winning, the pressure kept mounting. At one point McGuire said: "I don't know how we keep winning. Every opponent is playing harder against us and our kids are feeling the pressure building up from our winning streak. I think we'd be a better ballclub if we got knocked off in a couple of games. There's no such thing as an undefeated season in basketball."

"Rattled? These boys are too young to get rattled. They haven't got enough sense to get rattled. Nothing bothers them, they just play ball, they don't worry."
☐ **UNC Coach Frank McGuire**

McGuire underestimated his troops, who were outfitted for the first time in knee-high, blue-and-white stockings. By mid-January, Kansas and center Wilt "The Stilt" Chamberlain had lost to Iowa State, and UNC was the nation's top-ranked team.

"It's a coach's dream," McGuire said. "The boys can do everything. They can adapt themselves against any defense. They're big, they can run and they're all good outside shooters. Most of all, however, they play as a unit. It's easily the best-coordinated team I ever coached. I can't say too much about them."

The season came to be known as "McGuire's Miracle," and the Tar Heels created a few along the way to preserve their perfect record. The biggest scare of the regular season came at Maryland in early February before a crowd of 14,000, the largest ever to see an ACC game and 2,000 over capacity.

According to newspaper accounts of the game, UNC trailed 53-49 with two minutes to play in regulation. In retelling the story over the years, the deficit has increased proportionally as the time remaining has decreased. A 1982 *Sports Illustrated* story said the deficit was four points with 40 seconds remaining. The same year, a Raleigh *News and Observer* story quoted UNC players as saying the Maryland lead was somewhere between three and six points with perhaps just a few seconds left. McGuire was quoted as saying UNC was down four points with 18 seconds left.

Whatever the particulars, McGuire was preparing his team for the worst when he called the timeout.

"It looks rough, boys," McGuire said. "It looks like we can't catch 'em . . . I want you to do this: Make sure you don't make any mistakes and if we have to lose, I want you to go down like a true champion. If we lose, we lose just like we win. Be a good loser as well as a good winner and the people will think just as much of you."

43

ACC BASKETBALL / THE '50s

Baskets by Cunningham and Kearns, sandwiched around a free throw miss by Maryland, tied the game at 53 and forced overtime. At the end of regulation and at the conclusion of the first overtime, Maryland missed last-second shots to win the game. Finally, Kearns' basket gave UNC a 63-61 lead and eventually a 65-61 victory in the second overtime.

"Rattled?" McGuire said. "These boys are too young to get rattled. They haven't got enough sense to get rattled. Nothing bothers them. They just play ball, they don't worry. They're just kids, and they're all going to get better."

Looking back, Kearns says the victory over Maryland meant more than simply extending a winning streak.

"That game was the turning point of the season for us," he says. "It gave us the lift we needed in those close ones which followed. When things looked bad after that, we'd just remind ourselves that we had done it at Maryland and we could do it again. When we pulled that one out, it seemed to give us more confidence."

One week later, UNC lost an eight-point lead in the final 1:50 against Duke at Woollen Gym. Only a bad-luck play by Duke's Bobby Joe Harris saved the Tar Heels. Harris had made two key interceptions that led to baskets and tied the game with 21 seconds left. But following the tying basket, Harris looked at the scoreboard and it read: UNC 73, Duke 71. Before the numbers could be changed to indicate a tie, Harris intentionally fouled Kearns with 16 seconds remaining.

Kearns sank two free throws, and UNC remained unbeaten —barely—in 18 games.

"I wouldn't have fouled him if I had known the score was tied," Harris said. "The scorekeeper was slow putting our points on the board. He cost us the game. They didn't beat us. That scorekeeper caused it. They are no better than we are. We will get 'em when we play again in Durham March 1."

UNC won the rematch handily. Following the 86-72 UNC victory, McGuire told his team: "This is the happiest night of my life. I didn't think you could do it (24-0 in the regular season), but you fooled me."

Perhaps because it rarely overpowered opponents and because it had a knack for escaping with last-second victories, UNC had many skeptics.

"They've got a fine ballclub," said State's Case. "But I believe somebody'll knock 'em off before the end of the season."

Added Bradley of Duke: "Carolina has a fine team and I'm glad to see it ranked No. 1 in the nation. It looks good for our conference. But I don't think they have a great team. They are experiencing too many scares."

No team scared UNC more than Wake Forest. The Demon Deacons lost to the Tar Heels four times in 1957, by margins of eight, three, five and two points. The last defeat was the most crushing for Wake Forest because it came in the semifinals of the ACC Tournament.

After the Tar Heels coasted past Grady Wallace and South Carolina 95-75 for the ACC Tournament championship, Rosenbluth talked of UNC's inevitable meeting with Kansas and Wilt Chamberlain.

"How's he going to defense us?" Rosenbluth said. "We're No. 1. They gotta play us. If they pull inside on me or Pete (Brennan), we go outside. They box me and Joe (Quigg) has the corner open. They have to worry about us as much as we have to worry about them. He's just one man. And he doesn't score as many points as Wallace . . . This is a team that honestly feels it can lick the world."

Wins over Yale, Canisius and Syracuse in the first three rounds of the NCAA Tournament backed Rosenbluth's claim

Title Team '57
Lennie Rosenbluth (opposite) drives past Wilt Chamberlain during the Tar Heels' 54-53 NCAA title win over Kansas. Coach Frank McGuire (above) enjoyed a victory ride after the game, while UNC fans feted Joe Quigg upon his arrival at RDU Airport.

ACC BASKETBALL / **THE '50s**

and thrust UNC into the Final Four in Kansas City. But Michigan State, with Johnny Green as its star, had other ideas. The Spartans also wanted a crack at Kansas for the national title and took UNC to three overtimes before losing, 74-70.

Michigan State's Jack Quiggle made a shot at the end of regulation, but officials ruled that it came after time had expired and the game went to overtime tied at 58. At the end of the first extra period, Brennan grabbed a missed free throw by Green, drove the length of the court and sank a 15-footer to tie the game at 64 with four seconds left. The teams matched baskets in the second overtime before Rosenbluth, Kearns and Young scored in the final period for the victory.

"No, I never felt like we would lose," McGuire said. "I have had too many close scares this year to give up on these kids. I knew they had guts. Everyone should know that by now. It's hard to beat a team with guts."

So Kansas found out in the championship. The Jayhawks had a partisan crowd of 10,500 in Kansas City behind them, as well as the nation's tallest and best college player in Chamberlain. He scored 32 points as Kansas romped past defending national champion San Francisco 80-56 in the semifinals.

What Kansas did not have was the determination of Rosenbluth, Quigg, Kearns, Cunningham, Brennan and Young.

Through 40 minutes of regulation and three overtimes against Kansas, UNC again fought for its life. And once again, the Tar Heels survived not only to win a national championship but also complete a perfect 32-0 season. Quigg's two free throws with six seconds remaining were the winners in a 54-53 decision.

UNC gained a psychological edge at the center jump when McGuire had Kearns, the shortest player on the team at 5-11, jump against the 7-2 Chamberlain. McGuire picked up the strategy from Assistant Coach Buck Freeman, who used it against Duquesne when McGuire played for him at St. John's 20 years earlier.

"Wilt looked 10 feet tall towering over Tommy, but they made such a ridiculous picture together that Chamberlain must have felt no bigger than his thumb," McGuire said. "At least, that's the state of mind we wanted to get him into. North Carolina had to stop Chamberlain to win, and anything we could do to harass him would help. We wanted him thinking, 'Is this coach crazy? What other tricks does he have up his sleeve?' What I wanted was for Chamberlain to get a good shock."

The strategy worked. Chamberlain did not make his first field goal until UNC had jumped to a 9-2 lead. That seven-point edge held until halftime, thanks to some sound strategy and perfect execution. UNC played carefully and deliberately on each ball possession. Kansas employed a box-and-1 defense with Maurice King guarding Rosenbluth all over the court.

Just as UNC had difficulty shutting down Chamberlain, who finished with 23 points, Kansas could not stop Rosenbluth, who had 20. Kansas' box-and-1 tactics left corner shots for Quigg and Brennan, who scored 10 and 11 points, respectively. Kearns operated on the perimeter, where he scored 11 points. By halftime, UNC had made 64.7 percent of its field goal attempts.

On defense, the Tar Heels put a human fence around Chamberlain and took their chances on the outside shooting of the other Kansas players. The Jayhawks could not take advantage of the situation and made only 27.3 percent of their shots in the first half. More importantly, UNC planned to keep Chamberlain away from any stray shots. That's where the Tar Heels were most successful; they outrebounded the Jayhawks 42-28.

"The better team won," said Kansas Coach Dick Harp, who 30 years later would become an assistant coach at North Carolina. "The rebounds played an important part in the outcome."

UNC was hurt in the second half by foul trouble. Quigg picked up his fourth foul just after halftime. At the same time, Rosenbluth and Kearns each had three as they attempted to contain Chamberlain. By the midway point of the second half, Kansas had forged a 40-37 lead and decided to give UNC a dose of its own medicine. In what McGuire later termed "bonehead" strategy, Harp ordered his team to play keepaway. For five minutes, McGuire went along with the strategy as his players rested and stayed away from further foul trouble.

Rosenbluth fouled out with 1:45 remaining in regulation, but UNC held on and it ended in a 46-all deadlock. Each team scored one basket in the first overtime as Chamberlain batted away a shot by Kearns as time expired.

Neither team scored in the second overtime, except for an alleged punch to the stomach of McGuire during a scuffle. Chamberlain and Brennan had to be pulled apart as they wrestled for a loose ball. Harp rushed onto the court because he "wanted to try to prevent a fight." Kansas players said McGuire called them an ugly name, and McGuire said that Harp told him to "shut up." McGuire also said a "big guy" on the Kansas bench belted him in the stomach. McGuire later said the punch was thrown by Kansas Assistant Coach Jack Eskridge. Courtside observers said what McGuire described as a "punch" was more like a shove.

After the coaches shook hands and order was restored, UNC managed a 52-48 lead. But Kansas charged back to take a 53-52 lead on a free throw by Gene Elstun with 25 seconds remaining.

In the game's final 10 seconds, Quigg drove toward the basket in the direction of Chamberlain, who moved out to challenge Quigg's shot. Before Quigg could release his shot, he was fouled by King with six seconds remaining. Normally the opposing team calls time out in this situation to make the free throw shooter think about the situation. In this case, McGuire bucked the odds and called a timeout to set his team's defense.

"I was really feeling good," Quigg told the Raleigh *News and Observer* in 1982. "I knew I could do it. I just had a great feeling that I would make the shots. I told coach I would make them and he said, always confident, 'After Joe makes the shots, we'll go to a zone.' "

Before Quigg went back out, Freeman told him to follow through and end up on his toes. Quigg, a 72 percent free throw shooter for the season, made both for a 54-53 UNC lead.

Kansas immediately called time out, which under the rules of the day gave the Jayhawks the ball at halfcourt. The ball went to King on the inbounds pass, but his attempt to get the ball in the hands of Chamberlain was foiled by Quigg. Knowing Kansas wanted Chamberlain to take the final shot, Quigg had dropped back on defense and deflected the pass. Then Kearns got control of the ball with two seconds remaining and tossed it high into the air. The horn sounded to end the game before the ball came down.

"It's uncanny how we could have kept our undefeated season going," McGuire said. "We were lucky, awfully lucky, all season long in the close games. But our boys always kept their poise and came through in the clutch. I guess that's the mark of champions."

Upon their return to North Carolina the following day, the champions were greeted by a wild mob of fans at RDU airport.

ACC BASKETBALL / THE '50s

UNC fans told McGuire "Thanks" with a new car.

It was a reception like the state of North Carolina, and the ACC, had never seen before. Fans poured onto the airport runway and delayed the team plane's landing for several minutes. When they departed the plane, many of the players were carried to the terminal.

To show their support for McGuire and what he had done for the UNC program, fans later presented him with a sparkling new, blue and white, air-conditioned Cadillac. "Gosh, I've seen Cadillacs being given away on TV programs, but I never thought it would happen to a basketball coach," said McGuire, who was also awarded a five-year contract with an annual salary of $11,500.

About the only loss UNC suffered was Pete Brennan's car. His old Buick had been abandoned in front of the Monogram Club on campus since the beginning of the season. The longer UNC's winning streak stretched, the more Brennan believed it would be bad luck to move the car, which by then had been painted Carolina blue. At one point, N.C. State students painted the car red. But when the Tar Heels defeated the Wolfpack, students put another coat of blue paint on the body. Figuring UNC had used all its luck in winning the NCAA title, Brennan put the car up for sale when he returned from Kansas City.

'58

As it turned out, North Carolina's NCAA championship in 1957 was the ACC's only trip to the Final Four in the '50s.

When Maryland dropped out in the second round of the NCAA Tournament in 1958 and UNC went down in the opening round a year later, followers of the league began to wonder why their teams rarely did well in postseason play.

ACC teams had a 9-5 record in the NCAA Tournament during the '50s, but five of those wins were by UNC in 1957, and another two were in regional consolation games. Otherwise, the ACC was a dismal 2-5. For a league that boasted of being one of the best in the country, those numbers were hard to swallow.

Throughout the '50s, some league coaches howled about the ACC Tournament. They believed the Tournament placed too much unnecessary pressure on the players and the strain of a three-day event to pick the NCAA Tournament representative was simply too great. By the time the ACC champion reached the NCAA playoffs, they figured, it was drained physically as well as emotionally.

The ACC Tournament was a carryover from the old Southern Conference Tournament. With member schools in 15 different states, the Southern Conference could not possibly establish a home-and-home series between each school during the regular season. So the league teams would meet in Atlanta every March and play morning, noon and night for several days to decide the conference champion. In 1922, North Carolina emerged from a huge field of 25 teams to win the five-day event. By 1933, a new Southern Conference was formed with 15 members, and a tournament was still played.

That first Southern Conference Tournament, played in Raleigh's Memorial Auditorium, netted the league $250. The first ACC Tournament, played in 1954 at Reynolds Coliseum in Raleigh, netted the league treasury almost $40,000. By comparison, Duke's appearance in the Orange Bowl football game that year netted the league about half that amount.

While the ACC Tournament was not necessary since the eight members could play on a home-and-home basis during the regular season by 1954, it fast became apparent that the three-day extravaganza was a boon to the league's coffer.

Maryland Coach Bud Millikan still took exception to the Tournament, calling it the "$60,000 farce" as it continued to make money. Millikan suggested the team that finished first in the regular season represent the league in the NCAA Tournament, and that the ACC Tournament be held during the Christmas holidays, like the Big Eight Conference did each season.

In a poll of ACC coaches conducted by *The Charlotte News* in 1957, seven of the eight opposed having the ACC Tournament determine a league champion. The only coach in favor of the system was Case of N.C. State. "It's always been this way and nobody is going to change it," Case said. "The money from the Tournament is too important. Why make so much noise over nothing?"

UNC Coach Frank McGuire, whose team came within an official's call of being eliminated from the ACC Tournament in the 1957 semifinals, was naturally opposed to its existence.

"The way it is now, these regular-season games mean nothing," McGuire said. "We're just providing entertainment for the students. Why should anyone play 14 league games that will be junked at the season's end?"

Wake Coach Murray Greason proposed a rather unique alternative. "If a team finished first in the regular season and was then beaten in the Tournament, that team would play the Tournament champ (in a one-game playoff) for the title," he suggested.

Another reason the coaches opposed the ACC Tournament was scheduling. Beginning in 1956, the NCAA allowed a team to play only 26 regular-season games. Included in that count were the three possible games in the ACC Tournament. The NCAA considered the ACC Tournament part of the regular season because all eight teams qualified. At one point, the ACC considered a seven-team Tournament with the last-place finisher during the regular season not participating and a bye going to the team finishing first. That never passed.

The coaches also didn't like extending the season by a week. Since only the ACC and the Southern Conference played such tournaments, the champion often was not well-rested for NCAA play. While other league champions had at least one week to rest and prepare for the NCAAs, the ACC and Southern Conference champion often had only two days between games.

Since the ACC was not thought to be a particularly strong basketball league until the late '50s, the NCAA made its champion play a preliminary-round game in the national tournament. Not until 1963 did the ACC champion receive a first-round bye. As a result, during the '50s, the ACC cham-

47

pionship was decided on a Saturday night and the preliminary round of the NCAA Tournament was held the following Tuesday. The ACC champ often had to play in New York on Tuesday night, then advance to the East Regional elsewhere on Thursday or Friday.

For UNC to reach the Final Four in 1957, the Tar Heels had to defeat Clemson, Wake Forest and South Carolina on Thursday, Friday and Saturday in Raleigh, then down Yale in New York on Tuesday and finally Canisius and Syracuse on Friday and Saturday in Philadelphia—six tournament games in nine days.

The coaches believed the ACC Tournament hindered scheduling, was unfair to the team that finished first in the regular season, and put too much pressure on the Tournament champion. So why did the ACC continue to stage the Tournament, which was even criticized by coaches from other leagues? Money was certainly a contributing factor. But the interest the Tournament created each season could not be discounted.

Among the coaches, only Case saw the benefits of helping the league's treasury as well as sustaining interest for every league team throughout the regular season.

ACC Commissioner Jim Weaver had good reason to believe such an event could only help a newly formed league get its feet on the ground. From the outset, the Tournament was a moneymaker, but not nearly the financial bonanza it became in the '70s and '80s.

In fact, the ACC Tournament was not a sellout for all three rounds until 1965. For the first 11 Tournaments, tickets could be purchased at the door on the day of most games. In 1961, when North Carolina did not participate in the Tournament because of NCAA probation and N.C. State was eliminated by South Carolina in the first round, the average attendance for the six Tournament games was only 9,525 in 12,400-seat Reynolds Coliseum. By comparison, the 1976 event that was held in Landover, Md., drew an average crowd of 19,600 for six games.

As long as 10,000 or more fans attended each game and the conference continued to put money in its pocket, the coaches had to concede that the Tournament was a permanent fixture for the league.

As it turned out, the uniqueness of the ACC Tournament played a big part in gaining recognition nationally for the league.

"The Tournament helped make the league what it is today," says UNC's Dean Smith, who has been an assistant or head coach in all four ACC decades.

Although the ACC coaches of the '50s eventually admitted that the Tournament was worthwhile, they could not go along with playing the annual event on N.C. State's home court in Raleigh. As early as 1957, league coaches began to speak out.

"Let's go to Maryland, Chapel Hill, Wake Forest, Duke or somewhere," said UNC Coach McGuire. "You can't beat State here. Going up against State in the Coliseum is a big handicap, believe me."

Opposing coaches had a good beef when pointing to the home-court advantage enjoyed by the Wolfpack. Granted, State was perennially one of the nation's top teams. Still, the Wolfpack enjoyed unusual success in the ACC Tournament during the 13 seasons it was held in Raleigh. State had a 20-8 record during that period, won the championship five times and lost in the title game on one other occasion.

Of the seven coaches who were opposed to playing on State's home court, the most vehement objectors were those from Clemson, South Carolina, Virginia and Maryland. Only once

Deacons' Two-Sport Standout
Wake Forest's Lefty Davis was among the ACC's top 10 scorers from 1954-56, and he was a standout on the pitcher's mound, too, helping the Deacons win the 1955 NCAA baseball championship. Davis was killed in a car accident in 1986.

a season did those four teams get a chance to play in Raleigh while UNC, Duke and Wake Forest became familiar with Reynolds by playing three additional games there in the Dixie Classic until 1960.

The Tournament was initially based in Raleigh because of Reynolds' seating capacity. By the end of the '50s, however, there were new, spacious arenas in Charlotte (11,666 seats), Greensboro (8,766 at the time) and College Park (12,000 permanent seats with capacity to handle 14,500). Millikan, whose team defeated then-No. 1 ranked North Carolina in mid-January of 1958 before a crowd of 15,100 in College Park, was particularly adamant about shifting the Tournament site.

However, as long as the ACC made money and everyone remained reasonably happy, the Tournament had little chance of moving. For that reason, Millikan took particular pleasure

48

ACC BASKETBALL / THE '50s

in Maryland being the first non-Big Four team to win the league championship.

Millikan's Terrapins defeated Virginia (70-66), Duke (71-65 in overtime) and North Carolina (86-74) to win the title in '58. Perhaps as a carryover from having to take sixth-ranked Duke to overtime as well as defending champion and 13th-rated UNC to the wire in the championship game, the Terps lost to fifth-ranked Temple in the second round of the NCAA Tournament. Center Al Bunge, who averaged 10 points a game and led Maryland with nine rebounds a game, was sick with an intestinal disorder and scored only five points in the Terps' 71-67 NCAA loss to the Owls.

The early NCAA Tournament defeat did not take away from an outstanding season for Maryland. The Terps' 22-7 record included an 86-63 victory over Boston College in the first round of the NCAA East Regional and a 59-55 consolation win over Manhattan. By season's end, Maryland was the nation's sixth-ranked team.

Lending credence to Maryland's arrival as a threat to the ACC's top teams, UNC Coach McGuire engaged in a tit-for-tat with Millikan prior to the two teams' midseason meeting at Maryland. McGuire complained that Maryland now played in a 14,500-seat arena yet only gave UNC 25 tickets for the game. "That's ridiculous," McGuire said.

Millikan responded: "Where does that guy get that stuff? That's all the tickets we ever exchange with out-of-town teams —25. That's what we get when we go to Chapel Hill." Maryland officials eventually gave UNC another 25 tickets, but the Terps got the final say on the court.

Maryland, a team which had defeated nationally ranked Kentucky earlier in the season, routed the Tar Heels 74-61 in the biggest victory in the school's history to that point.

"You could say that this wasn't Carolina's night," Millikan said, "but that is only half of the story. The truth of the matter is that it was Maryland's night in a big way."

McGuire said: "Don't compare this Maryland team with past Maryland squads. It's strictly a metropolitan team. They play the Eastern style of run and shoot. No more of that Oklahoma control stuff. Defensively, it's still Oklahoma. They play a compact man-to-man and jam up the middle. It's almost impossible to drive the middle against Maryland."

Maryland's faster style was the result of the newfound size and quickness along the Terps' front line, where 6-foot-6 sophomore forward Charles McNeil and 6-9 sophomore center Bunge were the stars. "For the first time since I have been at Maryland, we have some good big men," Millikan said.

Maryland appeared on its way to a first-place finish during the regular season. But a late-season road swing took its toll on the Terps.

"A coach is a fool to travel Tobacco Road," Richmond Coach Malcolm Pitt once said. Maryland learned that hard lesson in losses at Duke, UNC and N.C. State during a one-week period, leaving the Terps with a fourth-place finish in the conference.

"Those didn't count," Millikan said of the three losses. "I told my boys after each one of those games not to feel bad, they didn't mean a thing. I think losing those games helped us win the Tournament."

Maryland was also helped by a couple of key injuries that hurt UNC. One week prior to the season opener, the defending national champions lost Joe Quigg with a broken leg.

"I honestly think we lost our chance to repeat as national champions when he went to the hospital," McGuire said. Two weeks later, UNC lost key reserve Danny Lotz, a 6-7 junior center, for eight games with an injury.

"If you think Sputnik has been flying high, we have too," McGuire said. "But Sputnik is going to come down and so are we. And it will be a good thing for us."

The Tar Heels came down to earth not long after extending their two-year winning streak to 37 games, losing 75-64 in the Kentucky Invitational to a West Virginia team that would replace UNC as the nation's top-ranked team. UNC remained ranked with an 11-1 record in the early season, but it faltered down the stretch and finished with a 19-7 record that included the 86-74 loss to Maryland in the ACC Tournament championship.

By winning the ACC title, Maryland became the first outsider to join North Carolina's Big Four schools as champion of what was fast becoming the nation's top basketball conference.

Maryland and coach Bud Millikan (front row, right) were the first non-Big Four champions in the ACC Tournament.

ACC SCRAPBOOK

Coaches didn't like the "Russian Roulette" pressure, but from the beginning the ACC Tournament proved unique: Kids cheered their heroes and flocked around them for autographs—State's Cliff Dwyer is approached while trailing Coach Everett Case (right)—while their folks picnicked and partied outside Reynolds Coliseum before tipoff (top right). ■ The Tournament was held on State's home court for 13 years (opposite), and although a money-maker, it didn't sell out for all three rounds until 1965. ■ Note signs of the times as UNC's Lennie Rosenbluth (above) lofts a jumper in '56 first round: A referee in sneakers, a battery of Western Union operators and nine white players making little effort to jockey in case of a rebound.

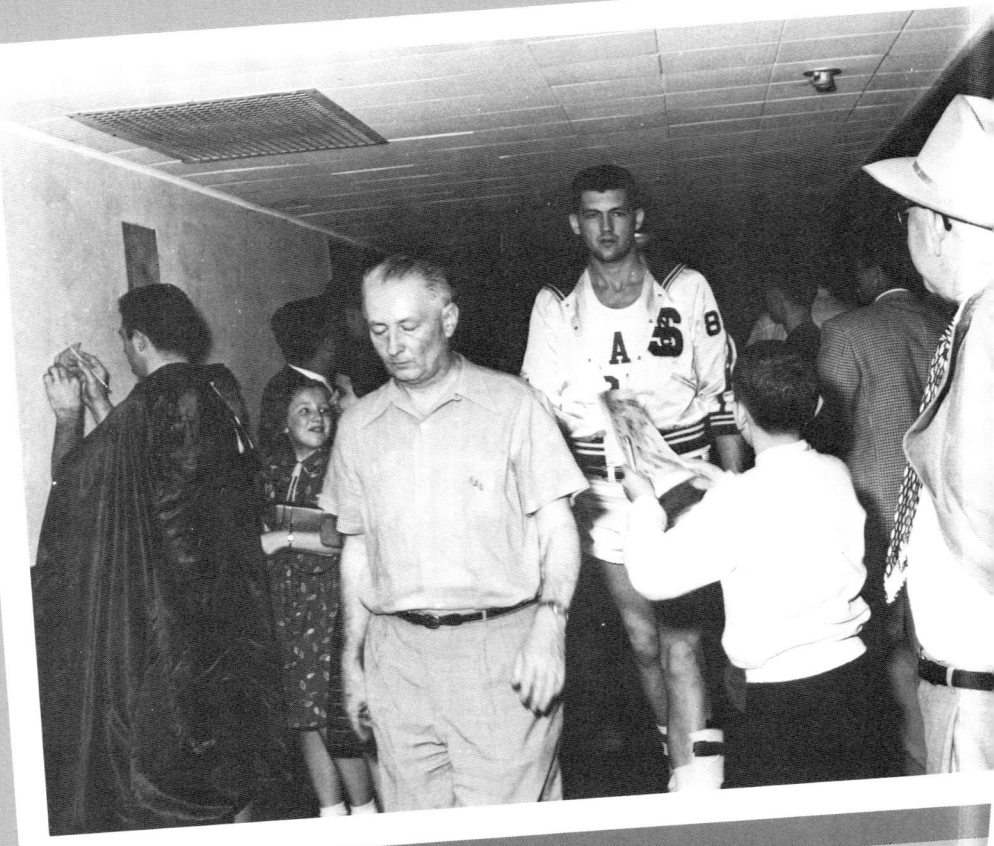

Coca-Cola

Second Annual
ATLANTIC COAST CONFERENCE
BASKETBALL TOURNAMENT

'59

With more teams fighting for the championship, unruly behavior followed.

Why were there so many instances of fighting in the '50s? Perhaps not enough attention was given by school administrators to fan behavior and player conduct. Perhaps players were growing faster than the game and it was difficult to deal with bigger bodies taking up more space on the court. Or perhaps tempers were being tested in the cramped facilities.

For whatever reason, violence erupted among the Big Four schools almost as soon as the ACC was formed. Much of it had to do with the festering rivalry between Case and McGuire.

In the State-UNC game of Jan. 19, 1954, officials Lou Bello and Dallas Shirley attempted to control play by calling 74 personal fouls. By game's end, McGuire had been charged with three technical fouls and spectators had thrown paper, fruit and combs onto the Woollen Gym floor.

When State and UNC met in the ACC Tournament in March of 1954, the game ended in a brief scuffle. The Wolfpack elected to freeze the ball in the final minutes of a close contest, and fans pelted the court with trash. With eight seconds remaining, Gerry McCabe of UNC tackled State's Dave Gotkin, who wheeled and threw the ball in McCabe's face. Gotkin was called for a technical foul that nearly cost the Wolfpack the first-round game. UNC made the technical free throw to cut State's deficit to the final 52-51 margin.

The incidents of fan violence were not restricted to Big Four schools. University of Virginia President Colgate W. Darden approached the student body during the early '50s with an ultimatum. "Either you act like gentlemen and treat our visitors as guests should be treated, or we will cancel the remainder of our basketball schedule," he said.

The bigger the game, the more likelihood there would be a fight. N.C. State's Dick Tyler and George Washington's Ed Catino were ejected for fighting during the fourth quarter (the NCAA played four, 10-minute quarters until switching to two, 20-minute halves for the 1954-55 season) of an NCAA East Regional game in 1954.

The ACC was quickly earning a reputation as a fighters' league. After losing a game to Wake Forest in 1955, Seton Hall Coach Honey Russell said the Demon Deacons were the "dirtiest team we've played all year."

In 1955, the State-Duke game in Durham was held up for 10 minutes in the second half when Duke center Marty Doherty was injured in a scramble under the basket. Doherty was carried off the floor on a stretcher with a cut ear, a gash on his forehead and an ankle sprain. "At least three women reportedly fainted in the balcony at the sight of blood gushing out of Doherty's head wound," according to the *Durham Morning Herald* report. ACC Commissioner Jim Weaver reviewed films of the incident and reprimanded State's Cliff Dwyer for swinging elbows.

Later that season, Maryland and Wake Forest got into the act. With a two-point lead and possession of the ball in the final seconds, Wake Forest attempted to run out the clock. But Wake's Jackie Murdock was hugged by Maryland's John Sandbower. Murdock took exception to the intentional foul and swung a wild blow that just missed hitting Sandbower. Fans streamed onto the Gore Gymnasium court at Wake Forest and one struck Sandbower from behind.

In Chapel Hill the following night, Feb. 22, students from UNC and State had an issue to settle after the Wolfpack's 79-75 victory over the Tar Heels, a win that clinched first

Millikan taught Terrapins to win, slowly but surely.

The '50s — Maryland

A fresh-faced Bud Millikan strolled into Ritchie Coliseum on the University of Maryland campus, eager to begin his first day of practice as the school's new head basketball coach. After entering through the rear entrance of the antiquated arena, Millikan circled a portable boxing ring to reach the gymnasium floor.

Boxing was big at Maryland in 1950, so big that bouts were often the headliner with a basketball game as the preliminary in an athletic double-header. That boxing was *the* winter sport at Maryland was only one reason for Millikan's apprehension about his new position.

At age 29, Millikan was only two years older than his starting center. Scholarships were limited, little money was budgeted for recruiting, assistant coaches served only on a volunteer basis, travel was by bus and accommodations for away games were usually cots in the opposing team's gym.

Apprehension aside, Millikan liked the challenge.

He walked swiftly to midcourt and blew his whistle to signal the start of practice. Nothing happened. Basketballs continued to bounce off the rim at one end of Ritchie as jump ropes popped the floor at the other. Millikan blew his whistle again, and again.

The team finally huddled around the new coach. "Everybody who last touched a basketball, go get it," Millikan said. "If you're going to play the type of basketball we'll have to play to win at Maryland, you've got to have some discipline. Putting the basketballs in the cardboard box before practice is just the start of it."

The finished product for Millikan was a precision game of basketball, almost identical to that played by Henry Iba-coached teams at Oklahoma A&M. On defense, Millikan's teams played tight man-to-man at all times. On offense, Maryland played "possession ball," which meant walking the ball up court at a turtle's pace while other ACC teams were "blowing and going," in Millikan's words.

A disciplined team to Millikan was a winning team. His first one quickly learned the system, posted a winning record and reached the Southern Conference Tournament semifinals, both firsts in over a decade at Maryland. By 1958, Millikan's Terps had a championship in the powerful ACC.

Jim Tatum, Maryland's athletic director as well as football coach, envisioned that kind of success for the basketball program when he made two important tele-

52

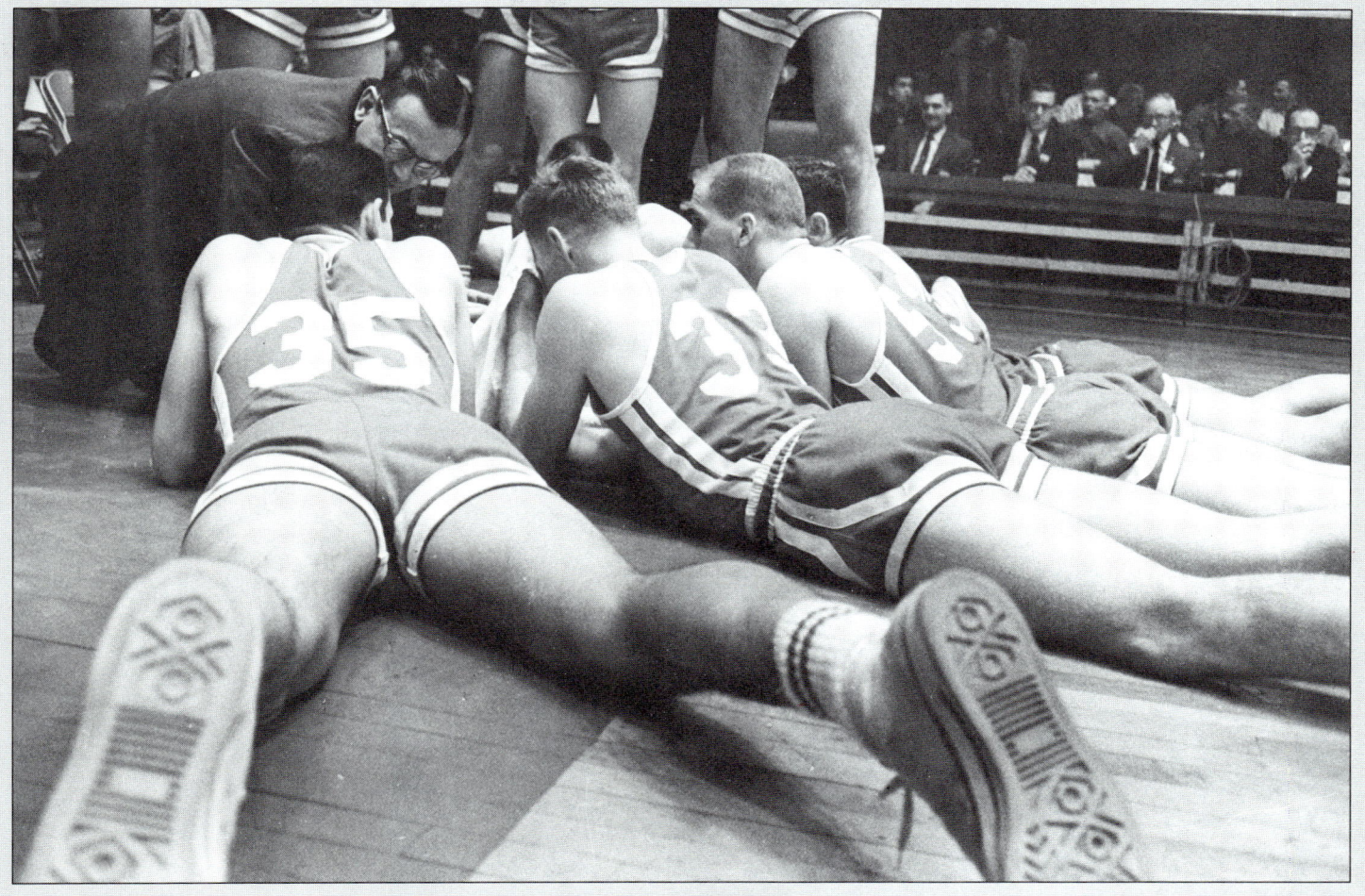

The Millikan earmuff: Ground level strategy sessions turned volume down on crowd's din.

phone calls in 1950. The first was to Kentucky Coach Adolph Rupp, but the line was busy. The second went to Iba, who recommended Millikan.

Millikan had played guard on a Maryville (Ohio) High School team in the mid-'30s that won 53 straight games, including one by a 35-0 score. He played pickup games at Northwest Missouri State Teachers College, where Iba coached, and served as mascot and batboy for Iba's baseball team. When it came to choosing a college, Millikan was going where Iba coached, and by then that was Oklahoma A&M.

Millikan played on four winning teams at A&M, one placing third in the NIT, and he earned All-America honors as a senior. Then he served as an assistant under Iba when A&M won national championships in 1945 and 1946.

After apprenticeships at Maryville High and Newton (Iowa) High, Millikan figured what was good for Oklahoma A&M was good for Maryland. Millikan had helped Iba invent the stack formation for inbounds plays, the same set used by nearly every college team today. Millikan's teams, like Iba's, laid flat-out on their stomachs on the court during timeouts to combat crowd noise. The Terps often chewed gum as a form of relaxation. More than anything, they drove opponents crazy with their slow style of play.

"Holy hell, if you've got to walk to get it up there, you better walk," says Millikan, now retired in Atlanta, and at age 66 a Jonathan Winters look-alike. "If you can fly, we'll fly. But when you get there, you've got to have the ball. What's wrong with that?"

Not a thing, apparently. Maryland won 23 games in 1954, 22 and the ACC Tournament in 1958. After losing in the second round of the '58 NCAA Tournament, the Terps were ranked No. 6 nationally. Unfortunately for Millikan, success did not mean more funding for the basketball program. Without a full-time assistant coach, recruiting became more difficult.

Millikan's program eventually slipped. Possession ball was successful, but it was generally unappealing not only to Washington-area professional sports fans, but also to high school recruits. In Millikan's first nine seasons, Maryland was 146-82. In his final eight, the Terps were 97-100. By 1963, Millikan had been hanged in effigy by Maryland students. By the end of 1965, he had stepped into retirement.

When he left, Millikan was the only coach outside the Big Four to win an ACC Tournament. He was perhaps the lone coach in ACC history who graduated every player he had who completed his eligibility.

For that and more, Maryland athletic officials were always grateful that Adolph Rupp's telephone line was busy back in 1950. ∎

Deacon Olin Broadway (44) steps between Dave Budd (far left) and Cincinnati's Oscar Robertson (12) in '58 Dixie Classic.

place in the regular season. State students cut down the net at one goal and tossed it into the UNC student section. Before the State students could clip the net at the other end of the floor, shoving and pushing among the students from both schools ended in a wild, fist-swinging melee.

During a 1956 game between Wake Forest and Duke in Durham, students showered the court with apple cores and coins. Duke's Ronnie Mayer was struck on the arm by a flying apple core, another hit referee Cart Howerton and Wake Forest's Jim Gilley slipped on a core and pulled a leg muscle. Wake Forest Assistant Coach Bones McKinney said he objected to the throwing of apple cores, but didn't mind the tossing of coins. "I picked up enough change to buy me a carton of Cokes," McKinney said.

The fighting and fan violence was a point of deep concern for the ACC when UNC met Wake Forest on Feb. 15, 1956, in Chapel Hill. As the clock was running out in UNC's 77-73 victory, the Tar Heels' Joe Quigg and Wake's Gilley tripped over each other near midcourt. Before the two could get on their feet, fans swarmed the floor and fights broke out. Bob Cunningham of UNC and Wake Forest reserve Bill Tucker were two among the mob who squared off and fought.

"I didn't know who was fighting who—and I don't believe anybody else knew either," said UNC's McGuire. "All I know is that I got hit in the head a couple of times and got a kick on my leg a few times. I couldn't stop the fight." McGuire later went into the Wake Forest locker room and apologized for the incident.

Uniformed police restored order in the second such incident during a UNC-Wake Forest athletic event in two years. A free-swinging fight broke out two years earlier at the conclusion of a football game between the two schools in Chapel Hill.

"Our series with North Carolina has become bitter in all sports," McKinney said.

Commissioner Weaver reviewed films of the game and suspended Cunningham and Tucker. Weaver said that although he did "not minimize nor condone the behavior of each player involved, it is my judgment that the preponderance of guilt lies with those players, Cunningham and Tucker, who first committed an unsportsmanlike act of disqualifying nature, thereby inciting their teammates to retaliatory measure."

Cunningham appealed the decision but lost his case, and

both players were suspended for the remainder of the regular season and ACC Tournament (four games for Cunningham, five for Tucker). Additionally, Weaver fined each of the schools $500 and reprimanded both schools because of "unsportsmanlike conduct."

Neither team was particularly hurt by the loss of the players, who each averaged fewer than three points a game. When the teams met in the '56 ACC Tournament semifinals, the game was played without incident.

Weaver's suspension of Cunningham and Tucker apparently had an effect on the league. Only one minor skirmish occurred during the 1957 season. Dick Hoffman of South Carolina and Olin Broadway of Wake Forest exchanged punches in a battle for a loose ball during a game in Columbia, and both players were ejected from the game.

Early in 1958, as State left the court following a 58-57 overtime victory in UNC's Woollen Gym, the Wolfpack's Bob MacGillivray engaged in a fistfight with a Tar Heel football player in attendance. Perhaps proving that basketball was the rougher sport in the ACC, MacGillivray reportedly got the best of the UNC football player.

By mid-season of 1958, McGuire decided to take the issue of fan behavior into his own hands. During introduction of lineups during the State-UNC game in Raleigh, Tar Heel starter Pete Brennan was booed by Wolfpack fans. Incensed by Brennan's reception, McGuire did not allow his remaining starters to run to center court during the introductions. A spotlight, used in almost every ACC arena for introductions, spanned Reynolds Coliseum in search of the UNC players who stood by McGuire in front of the bench.

"Listen, I'm not letting those kids get another boo from 12,000 fans," McGuire said. "All the time Lennie Rosenbluth was with us we had to put up with that loud booing by 12,000 fans. Our players represent the University of North Carolina. That's no disgrace. And I am not going to let them be exposed to bad treatment by the fans. We went to Kentucky and we didn't hear a single boo. At Chicago the other night, before 17,000 fans, we were treated royally. That's the way it should be."

Once the game began, McGuire went to the scorer's table and asked that an announcement be made that fans refrain from booing, particularly when UNC had a player at the free throw line. That failing, McGuire had official Phil Fox ask the fans to refrain from booing. The threat of a technical foul against the home team brought an end to the booing.

Several weeks earlier McGuire had pleaded with UNC fans in Woollen Gym to show Duke better sportsmanship. Once the fans quieted, UNC lost a lead and the game to the Blue Devils.

"Sure, that could have cost us the ball game," McGuire said. "I have received letters from people telling me that. It's time for student fans to act like grownups. Winning a game isn't so important after all when you have to get barbaric to do it. Legislation? There isn't any use in trying to set up rules to govern the thing. Students are intelligent enough to understand the principle of sportsmanship. You don't need rules.

"When I first came to Chapel Hill, the football players would line up behind the visiting team's bench and razz the visiting coach and players. I immediately stopped those things and have done my best to maintain order at our ball games. I'm sorry to say I have found no such order at any other place in the conference."

Following UNC's loss to Duke in the 1958 regular-season

State's Russ Marvel brandishes his fist at Clemson's Tommy Mahaffey during turn-of-the-decade heated moment.

finale at Durham, McGuire held his team on the court until it was cleared of Duke fans. The fans carried Duke Coach Vic Bubas off the floor in celebration of a first-place finish in the regular season, while McGuire requested a police escort.

"I told my players to come back to the bench and let the crowd get off the floor," McGuire said. "My appeals for sportsmanship have backfired. I've carried this thing long enough. Maybe restraining barriers for the crowd would help. It's not fair to the ballplayers. But I've done all I can possibly do."

McGuire's actions at Duke did not sit well with Duke Football Coach Bill Murray, who was in charge of stadium operation for the UNC game.

"It was an uncalled-for demonstration," Murray said. "No athletic team will have trouble walking off this court. The Carolina team could have gone off the court without trouble. When the time comes that we have to have police protection to escort a team off our court, well, we should quit playing.

"In all my coaching experience, I have never seen a more obvious exhibition. It was the most revolting act by a college coach I've ever witnessed. The very idea of McGuire requiring police protection to go to his dressing room is absurd. He has created a monster in his publicity-seeking statements suppos-

ACC BASKETBALL / **THE '50s**

Shavlik a giant in games of hoops and life.

The '50s

N.C. State

Perhaps the proudest witness of N.C. State's national championship victory over Houston in 1983 was Ronnie Shavlik. Stricken with cancer, Shavlik made the trip to Albuquerque to watch his beloved Wolfpack for the final time. He died less than three months later at age 49.

"It seemed like it might have been for Ronnie," said Charlie Bryant, once an assistant coach at N.C. State and now the executive director of the Wolfpack Club, State's booster organization.

Not even a championship could begin to repay Shavlik for the contributions he made to N.C. State University as a two-time All-America center and to the city of Raleigh as a civic leader.

Shavlik was a giant of a man, in every respect. He stood 6-foot-9 on the basketball floor and even taller in the community.

During his undergraduate days at State, Shavlik did volunteer work with children at the Governor Morehead School for the Blind. He served as a Big Brother to an 8-year-old and provided counseling and leadership to children in the Raleigh Recreation Department.

After a brief professional basketball career, Shavlik returned to Raleigh where his business, Carolina Maintenance Company, Inc., grew into a $250 million janitorial service. He helped found the National Association of Building Service Contractors and the Shavlik Summer Basketball League for Wake County high school players, financing the 20-team league by himself for the first three years. He was active in the Boys Club of America, the Raleigh Chamber of Commerce, worked in several organizations to aid the handicapped, and was a one-time president of N.C. State's Student Aid Foundation.

"I have often said I would like my two boys to grow up to be just like Ronnie Shavlik," Bryant told *The News and Observer* of Raleigh.

"Basketball and business are correlated," Shavlik once told *The Raleigh Times*. "You have to discipline yourself, work at it and never accept failure."

Prior to Shavlik's arrival on the ACC scene, fast-break basketball was limited. Few teams pushed the ball up the court because centers and forwards were generally too slow and bulky.

Then came Shavlik, who not only ran like a smaller forward but was as coordinated as a guard. Working in the pivot, Shavlik was once likened to a T-formation quarterback in football because of his abilities to fake and pass. Perhaps his best skill was as an offensive rebounder. He might have been the first in the ACC to make the tap shot a lethal weapon.

"I worked hard on the timing of getting the ball back through the net," Shavlik said years ago. "Nobody suggested it to me. It was the easy way to score and it came natural to me."

Shavlik's skills first drew national notice when he led East High School in Denver to consecutive Colorado state championships, then took his summer team to the semifinals of the National AAU Tournament. Among the college coaches who visited Shavlik in Denver was N.C. State's Everett Case. Shavlik, in turn, visited Case on the State campus.

Shavlik bagged championship nets and lots of business in Raleigh.

So intent was Case on corralling Shavlik, he bent the rules and held an illegal tryout for him that resulted in an NCAA probation for the Wolfpack during the 1955 season. Shavlik was the first player from the West to play in the ACC. Previously, players migrated primarily from the Chicago area, Philadelphia or New York.

"I think the fact that he came here from Denver, in and of itself, made people sit up and look at him," says former State teammate Nick Pond, who hailed from New Jersey. "Where we grew up, we were bar rats, beer drinkers. We all grew up that way. Shavlik was never one of those type of guys."

Shavlik further removed himself from the team's social circle when he was married before his senior season. The wedding reception was held at Coach Case's house, one of several favors Case apparently granted Shavlik. Pond says he and his teammates also suspected that under-the-table payments of between $100 and $200 a month were made to Shavlik.

"Some of us average players kind of resented the fact that the big, big Wolfpack supporters always looked out for the big stars, but didn't much look out for us little guys," Pond says. "It was kind of a foregone conclusion that the big stars are there to be taken care of. But we all respected Ronnie. He was our leader. He was the guy. We looked to him."

With Shavlik as its center, State had records of 26-7 in 1954, 28-4 in '55 and 24-4 in '56. Against ACC competition during that period, State was a remarkable 40-9. The Wolfpack won the ACC Tournament all three seasons with Shavlik averaging 18.5 points and 16.8 rebounds for his career. His 55 points against William & Mary during the '55 season stood as an ACC record for 15 seasons and has been topped only twice (South Carolina's John Roche scored 56 points in 1971 and State's David Thompson scored 57 in 1974). In 1955 against Villanova, Shavlik also had a school-record 35 rebounds, a mark that still stands.

Shavlik was first-team All-ACC his junior and senior years and received votes for Player of the Year all three seasons, sweeping the honor as a senior in 1956. He won back-to-back MVP awards for leading the Wolfpack to Dixie Classic championships in 1954 and 1955.

Shavlik, who constantly tugged at the bottom of his shorts during games, was as gracious as he was great. He once had a violent collision with a bespectacled opponent and then helped search the floor for pieces of the shattered specs.

Unfortunately for Shavlik and the Wolfpack, his illustrious playing career ended on a sad note. N.C. State was ranked second to Bill Russell-led San Francisco in the national polls when the Wolfpack defeated Wake Forest for the 1956 ACC Tournament championship. But Shavlik broke his wrist during the game and was believed lost for the NCAAs.

Shavlik returned to play with a cast on his wrist, but was slowed as State lost a four-overtime decision to lightly regarded Canisius at Madison Square Garden. It was the final time that Shavlik wore State jersey No. 84, which the school later retired.

In 1976, Shavlik recalled the pain of the last college game: "That was the most sickening thing. I can still feel it. I couldn't believe we lost. We were mentally prepared to play San Francisco in the finals."

While in school, Shavlik was also preparing for the remainder of his life. During his summer visits to Denver, he noticed the dog track there used part-time help for maintenance. He formed a company, washed windows and swept the track with the idea of starting a similar business in Raleigh.

> "Basketball and business are correlated. You have to discipline yourself, work at it and never accept failure."
> — **Ronnie Shavlik**

In time, his Raleigh-based company served some 40 states. He also formed sister companies, Trash Disposal, Inc., and Southeastern Sales Co. But Shavlik still had to give pro basketball a shot.

He was the fourth player selected in the 1956 NBA draft, going to the New York Knicks. Shavlik received a $5,000 signing bonus from the Knicks and an annual salary of $14,000. He later claimed the pro game was too much of a business and played only seven games for the Knicks in 1957 and one in 1958.

"He was probably not aggressive enough," says Joe Belmont, a former Duke standout and good friend. "This is going to sound crazy, but if he would have grown up on the East Coast where he would have understood the game better and played 365 days a year, Shavlik would probably have been in the Hall of Fame.

"Ronnie could play. He could handle the ball, hook, go outside and shoot the jumper. But he just happened to go to New York and the Knicks were hurting for bangers. It was a survival test, and I don't think Ronnie was prepared to go in and have a fistfight every night."

Shavlik migrated to the Baltimore Bullets of the Eastern League, where he played for several seasons. He commuted from Raleigh to Baltimore for games while his wife, Beverly, stayed behind to run the maintenance business.

"There comes a day when you can't eat that basketball," Shavlik said when he left pro ball to concentrate on his business as well as charity work. So successful was Shavlik in both areas, he received the NCAA's 1980 Silver Anniversary Award given annually to five former athletes who distinguish themselves in business careers and community service.

Perhaps the highest compliment of Shavlik was paid by his coach, Everett Case.

"I have never had a better player or a better boy in my 36 years in basketball," Case said in 1956. "Shavlik is one of the truly great players of our time, and he's my candidate for all sportsmanship awards." ∎

ACC BASKETBALL / THE '50s

Duke's Decade Steady Under Bradley
Duke Coach Hal Bradley (center, top) led the Blue Devils to consistent finishes in the top half of the ACC standings, taking first in 1954 and '58, but he could never win the league tournament. Bradley left for the University of Texas in '59. Some light moments were provided by personalities like Larry Bateman (L) and Bobby Joe Harris (R). When Vic Bubas took over as coach and opened 1959-60 preseason practice, he asked each Blue Devil to grab a basketball and go to the spot he would shoot from during a game. Bateman took a ball and sat on the bench. Harris had a steady girlfriend in Winston-Salem, and the love birds would exchange two to three letters a day. "One day I got five letters from my girlfriend," Harris said.

edly made to stop such things as this. I once admired him, now I blame him."

McGuire, not one to remain silent, responded.

"I wish Murray had come to me with those remarks," he said. "I'd tell him he has enough to worry about in (UNC football coach) Jim Tatum to keep him occupied. I'd tell him he'll never beat Carolina in football as long as Tatum's around."

Murray, in an effort to get in the last word, said, "I'm wondering what Tatum's whipping me has got to do with McGuire's campaign to handle basketball crowds."

Finally, McGuire claimed that Murray made an "unwarranted attack" on him by taking his remarks to the media instead of speaking to McGuire personally.

Matters grew worse in the ACC during the 1959 season. The seed was planted during the Dixie Classic when powerful Cincinnati, with All-America guard Oscar Robertson, played Wake Forest in the opening round. Robertson and Wake Forest forward Dave Budd engaged in a shoving match.

"Robertson tripped me as we started up court a few minutes before the scuffle," Budd was quoted in a *Durham Morning Herald* account. "I guess both our tempers were building up to a hot point. Then under the basket, we got tangled up in a scramble for a rebound and that was it. We fell to the floor and I was on top. I could have hit him, but I didn't. I happened to think about his race, and I knew if I hit him it would cause a lot of trouble. If it had been any other player, no one would have thought too much about it. But because of his race, I guess it will look bad for this section (of the country). It's a shame because he is a great player."

Of the incident, Robertson said: "We went up for a rebound and I came down on his back. It wasn't anybody's fault. It was just one of those things."

Following the game, Robertson and Budd refused to shake hands.

"I don't shake hands during or after a game," Robertson said.

ACC BASKETBALL / THE '50s

Yarborough lone diamond in Clemson rough.

As the newest and youngest member of the 1951 Chicopee Mills basketball team in Walhalla, S.C., Bill Yarborough dreamed of some day playing college basketball.

Yarborough was anxious for his first minute of competition as he and his five teammates drove some 30 miles to Central for Chicopee's season opener. Unfortunately for both teams, there were no fans in the tiny gymnasium. Unfortunately for Yarborough, the officials also failed to show.

"Time came to start," Yarborough recalls, "and our coach had to officiate. So I had to keep score. I didn't get to play a single second."

Yarborough would not be held out of a game again until he had become the only player in ACC history to earn five letters in basketball. For good measure, Yarborough stuck around an extra semester at Clemson to earn a letter in golf, a game he played for the first time in college.

Yarborough first played on the 1952-53 Clemson basketball squad when freshmen were eligible. He earned a second letter for his play during the first semester of his sophomore season, 1953-54, but dropped out of school for the second semester. Yarborough then resumed play at Clemson during his junior year (1954-55) and played during what normally would have been his senior season (1955-56).

Prior to the 1956-57 season, North Carolina Coach Frank McGuire requested an extra year of eligibility for Tar Heel Jerry Vayda, who, like Yarborough, had sat out one semester for academic reasons. When the vote came before the ACC athletic directors, Frank Howard of Clemson suggested that Vayda be granted the extra year of eligibility only if the same grace year were given to Yarborough.

Perhaps figuring that the return of a star player could make hapless Clemson more competitive within the league, the athletic directors bought Howard's idea and Yarborough returned for a fifth season.

Yarborough's return actually didn't help the Tigers' cause much. Their record was 7-17, which fell right in line with the other marks during his career: 8-10, 5-18, 2-21 and 9-17.

Those marks accurately reflect basketball's place on the Clemson athletic department pecking order during the early days of the ACC. Howard, who doubled as Clemson's athletic director and football coach, once said of crew that he would not fund a sport in which people "sat on their butts and moved backwards." Basketball, as an intercollegiate sport, rated only slightly above crew in Howard's view. Howard wasn't much interested in a sport that was not revenue producing, and basketball at Clemson did not make enough money "to pay the gymnasium's light bill," according to Yarborough.

Banks McFadden was one of Howard's chief assistants in football and filled his spare time during the winter coaching basketball. Many of the basketball players were actually football players who merely wanted to stay in shape year round.

Yarborough was an exception. After leading Walhalla to 33 straight wins and the South Carolina Class C high school championship in 1952, he was recruited by Wake Forest and Clemson. He selected Clemson only because Wake Forest Coach Murray Greason thought that the 6-foot Yarborough was too small to play forward.

Yarborough played guard at Clemson and developed into the Tigers' top reserve as a freshman. He was a starter the remaining four years and eventually earned second-team All-ACC honors in 1955 and 1956. His two-hand set shot from outside the key was deadly, and he eventually copied the running one-hand shot of his hero, N.C. State's Sammy Ranzino. Yarborough's 46-point effort against South Carolina in 1955 remains the modern-day scoring record at Clemson and was never topped in Clemson's old Fike Field House.

"That game was actually one of my biggest disappointments," says Yarborough, who now teaches and coaches golf at West-Oak High School in Pendleton, S.C. "We didn't win, and that really taught me a lesson about one player not being good enough to beat an entire team."

Yarborough learned to lose at Clemson. In his five seasons, the Tigers were 31-83, including a woeful 4-47 mark against ACC competition. Clemson lost its first 26 games in the ACC before defeating Virginia for its lone league win in 1956.

"I thought we'd never win that first one," Yarborough recalls. "It was a tough go at Clemson in those days, but it was an educational experience."

The '50s

Clemson

Yarborough shot basketballs for five letters and golf balls for one more.

THE DIXIE CLASSIC

Holiday Cheer in Big Four Country.

Everett Case loved tournament basketball. He marveled as a high school coach in Indiana at how an entire state got caught up in the madness of a postseason tournament. When he got to N.C. State, Case saw the same potential for allegiance to a college Christmas tournament.

Case's idea was to attract four of the nation's top-caliber teams to Raleigh each December and see how they fared against North Carolina's Big Four schools. Four games were to be played each day for three successive days between Christmas and New Year's Day. From the outset, the Dixie Classic was special. Book tickets, costing $5 and $3, provided perfect Christmas gifts.

The first Dixie Classic was played in December of 1949, only four weeks after the doors were opened to 12,400-seat Reynolds Coliseum. The first afternoon session drew 10,500, and rarely did attendance dip below 10,000, even when non-ACC teams were playing afternoon games.

"I never saw anything like it in the heydays of Madison Square Garden," UNC Coach Frank McGuire said of the Classic atmosphere in *On Tobacco Road*. "It was there in the air for four or five days ahead, and I can certainly say we gave the people of North Carolina wonderful entertainment for a week. They forgot all their worries and the front-page troubles."

State won the first four Dixie Classics when the Big Four teams were still members of the Southern Conference. Duke then inaugurated the ACC's influence in 1953, advancing past the first round for the first time and going on to win with victories over 12th-ranked Oregon State (71-61), Wake Forest (83-66) and previously unbeaten Navy (98-83).

State won one of the most exciting Classic finals in '54 when it edged Minnesota. Trailing by one, the Wolfpack called time out with 17 seconds to play, presumably to plan one last shot by star Ronnie Shavlik. Instead, guard John Maglio drove into the lane and made a hook shot with eight seconds remaining to give the Wolfpack an 85-84 victory.

State also won the '55 Classic, but UNC broke the Wolfpack's stronghold the following season en route to the national championship, beating Wake Forest 63-55 in the final. UNC also won in '57, beating State 39-30 in a controversial slow-down game.

The Classic played in December of 1958 was unquestionably the greatest of them all. It featured a field of four nationally ranked teams. Cincinnati was top-ranked, unbeaten in five games and featured the nation's leading scorer, Oscar Robertson, and his 38-point average. UNC was 5-0 and ranked third, State was 6-1 and ranked sixth, and Michigan State was unbeaten in four games and ranked ninth.

Robertson and Cincinnati survived the first round with a 94-70 victory over Wake Forest, but not before the All-America guard was involved in a brief scuffle with Demon Deacon forward Dave Budd. After watching the game, State's Case said, "I don't think it's possible for us to win against Cincinnati."

The Wolfpack paid no attention to that. John Richter stole the spotlight from Robertson as State slowed the tempo and defeated Cincinnati 69-60. Richter finished

60

with 26 points and 15 rebounds. Robertson had 29 and eight. In the championship, Richter and Lou Pucillo led State to a 70-61 victory over Michigan State and All-America Johnny Green.

Little respect was given Wake Forest at the start of the 1959 Dixie Classic. The Demon Deacons had won only six and 10 games in their first two seasons under Coach Bones McKinney. But Wake Forest, behind the play of sophomore guard Billy Packer, turned back Holy Cross (80-71), Dayton (61-50) and UNC (53-50) to win its lone Classic championship. Packer was in tears when he was named the tournament MVP.

In the postgame celebration, McKinney put his arms around former Coach Murray Greason and kissed his bald head. They danced arm in arm at midcourt.

Their joy turned to tragedy on New Year's Day, however, when Greason was killed in an automobile accident while on a hunting trip.

The Tar Heels came back in the 1960 Dixie Classic to sweep past Maryland (81-57), Villanova (87-67) and Duke to win the title. Doug Moe was the hero for UNC as he put the clamps on Duke scoring ace Art Heyman and earned MVP honors with a 16-point, 17-rebound performance in the 76-71 championship game victory. Moe held Heyman to four points over the game's final 29 minutes.

The Classic was discontinued the following year in the wake of the point-shaving scandals, and although much talk circulated later in the decade about reviving it, the Classic had enjoyed its last hurrah.

"It's like the State Fair, it's part of the people," McKinney said in 1962. "In 1964, I plan to run for governor on a platform favoring the elimination of the sales tax on food and the restoration of the Dixie Classic. I don't see how I can lose."

State polishes off Cincinnati (top) in '58, while MVP Billy Packer (R) and Coach Bones McKinney celebrate Wake Forest's '59 title.

"I shake hands before the game."

Budd was again the center of controversy when perhaps the wildest free-for-all in league history occurred during UNC's 75-66 victory over Wake Forest on Feb. 12, 1959, in Winston-Salem. With 30 seconds remaining in the game, Memorial Coliseum turned into a madhouse.

UNC forward Lee Shaffer came down with a rebound and was harassed by Wake Forest guard Charlie Forte. When Shaffer threw an elbow at Forte, Budd joined the fracas. Shaffer, Forte and Budd all tumbled to the floor in a free-swinging fight. Players from both sides joined in the melee and fans swarmed onto the court. Winston-Salem police officers attempted to restore order as fights broke out all over the court.

Wake Forest Coach McKinney was decked during the fight, UNC's McGuire was hit atop the head and UNC forward Doug Moe wore a black eye from a fist thrown by a Wake Forest fan. The fights continued as the Wake Forest pep band first played the national anthem, then *Dixie* in an attempt to settle the crowd. UNC reserve guard Lou Brown was seen throwing punches. Even mild-mannered Wake Forest forward Winston Wiggins got involved. Wiggins' wife, who had been seated behind the Deacon bench, walked to the edge of the court and yelled, "Winston, you get out of there right this minute." (Her request went unnoticed.)

Once order was restored, McKinney and McGuire sent their starting five players to the locker room and completed the final seconds with reserves.

Wake Forest Athletic Director Bill Gibson said, "This is a terrible thing and something we will have to stop if we hope to continue our rivalry with Carolina."

Commissioner Weaver again reviewed films of the fight and placed the two squads on strict probation. He warned that any unsportsmanlike conduct in the future would endanger the players' eligibility. Weaver also ruled that a 1960 game between the two teams could not be played in Winston-Salem. He also recommended that the game scheduled for Chapel Hill in 1960 be moved to a neutral site. Finally, Weaver censured McGuire and McKinney and said that Budd would lose his eligibility if involved in another unsportsmanlike act. Shaffer, Forte, Wiggins, Brown and Wake's Dickie Odom were all reprimanded with probation.

Weaver's decision was not well received.

UNC Chancellor William B. Aycock first ordered McGuire to remain mum on the issue. Then Aycock said UNC did not believe Shaffer should be reprimanded.

Forrest W. Clonts, faculty chairman of athletics at Wake Forest, said the school would appeal Weaver's decision on three counts. Wake officials wanted to keep the 1960 game against UNC in Winston-Salem. If a game was to be played in Chapel Hill, Wake Forest wanted its student tickets honored at the gate. Finally, Wake protested the reprimand of Budd.

Keeping McGuire mum was impossible. While the UNC coach did not say anything for print, he instead sent a letter to members of the university's Educational Foundation. In the letter, McGuire wrote, "I emphatically do not agree with his (Weaver's) judgment, and I truly believe he is prejudiced, having been the athletic director at Wake Forest for a number of years."

Wake Forest's Dave Budd

Cavaliers abuzz with Wilkinson's scoring artistry.

The '50s
Virginia

Coach Frank McGuire was determined to take the buzz out of Virginia's high-powered offense when his Tar Heels met the Cavaliers early in the 1954 season. McGuire assigned one of his players specifically to stick like glue on Virginia guard Buzz Wilkinson.

"Every time we would take possession of the ball, there was a guy standing behind me so that when I turned to go down the floor, I would run over him," says Wilkinson, who quickly picked up four fouls in the game's first six minutes. "I guess that was one way to stop me."

Wilkinson scored only nine points that night, the only time in a three-year career he was held under double figures. But McGuire was soon to learn that keeping Wilkinson down for long was next to impossible. Twenty-three days later, Wilkinson scored 45 points against the Tar Heels in Charlottesville.

Such feats were not unusual for Wilkinson, who scored 30 or more points in a game on 35 occasions from 1953 to 1955. Ten times he topped 40. The 6-foot-2 guard twice averaged more than 30 points in a season, and his 28.6 career average remains the best in ACC history.

"I've laughingly told others that I was a poor little man's Ralph Sampson," says Wilkinson, who was nicknamed by his grandmother after a comic strip character who buzzed around a lot. "Ralph was there (at Virginia) in the days of television and was the most visible athlete in the country his senior year. I did it without TV. Nobody knew of me."

Wilkinson was actually the subject of a *Sports Illustrated* story late in the 1955 season. And he was certainly known well enough around the ACC. No one dribbled the ball between his legs and behind his back like Wilkinson, at least not in the ACC. He was extremely quick, having once been timed in the 100-yard dash at 9.9 seconds, and an excellent passer. Virginia Coach Bus Male called Wilkinson a "real artist who is a generation ahead of his time."

More than an artist, Wilkinson was a shooter. "Oh, what a shooter," said Maryland Coach Bud Millikan. "Heck of a shooter."

At times, Wilkinson was called a gunner. His reputation of shooting from anywhere on the court at any time was fostered from an opening-round game in the 1954 ACC Tournament. Given the green light by Male, Wilkinson attempted 44 shots. He made 13, which was pretty good shooting considering the rest of his team-

62

ACC BASKETBALL / THE '50s

Coach Bus Male and guard Bill Miller (5) had plenty to smile about with Wilkinson (14) pouring in 32.1 points a game in '55.

mates combined made only six of 47 shots.

"That was the only game I really felt I overshot," Wilkinson says. "Bus kept saying to me, 'They're going to remember that you shot so many times.' My feeling was that we were behind and we were trying to catch up."

Wilkinson got a chance to redeem himself for that performance a year later in the 1955 ACC Tournament. He scored 30 and 32 points in an overtime win over Maryland and an overtime loss to Duke, respectively.

Wilkinson's shot at the end of regulation against Duke was blocked and prevented Virginia from advancing to the NCAA Tournament. The winner of the Duke-Virginia semifinal game qualified for the NCAAs because N.C. State was on probation for one year.

That was the final game in an illustrious college career for Wilkinson. More than anything, he brought attention to a sport that had previously been ignored on the Virginia campus.

"When I went to school there, you could go to a game at 8 o'clock and sit at midcourt with probably a hundred other people," Wilkinson says. "By the time I left, if you wanted to go to a game and you didn't have a season ticket, you had to get there at 6 o'clock just to get in."

Wilkinson, the son of a doctor in Pineville, W.Va., attended Virginia because he wanted to be a lawyer. The only other school he even considered was Kentucky, but Wilkinson says Adolph Rupp did not seem much interested in academics when he visited the legendary coach.

More than a passion, basketball was a means for Wilkinson to obtain a college scholarship and free education. He never took his preparation lightly. When his mother sent him off to piano lessons as a youngster, Wilkinson often ended up on the basketball court instead. It was a game he dreamed of playing professionally.

A car accident following Wilkinson's senior season at Virginia left him with several broken ribs and hindered his chances of playing for the Boston Celtics, who drafted him. It didn't help matters that Boston had a backcourt of Bob Cousy and Bill Sharman.

Wilkinson eventually graduated from Virginia Law School, then began a banking career in Bluefield, W.Va., where he still lives. Richard Wilkinson is president of First National Bank of Bluefield and has been honored numerous times in that city and in the state for his community service work.

"The greatest carry-over from basketball to management is working with people," Wilkinson says. "You learn in a team sport to be a team player. You can work for somebody or work with somebody. It's a difference in attitude. When the door is closed and we're in a meeting, most of the people in the bank still call me Buzz."

ACC BASKETBALL / THE '50s

All appeals by both schools were denied by the ACC.

While the league closed out the '50s on an ugly note with unruly fan behavior and player fights, it had another interesting season on the court in 1959. N.C. State and UNC were clearly the top teams in the league, at one point ranked first and third in the nation, respectively. Both held No. 1 national rankings at one time and both reached the final of the ACC Tournament.

UNC and State were among four Top 10 teams in the Dixie Classic field. The Wolfpack defeated second-ranked Cincinnati 69-60 and ninth-ranked Michigan State 70-61 to win the title for the seventh time in 10 years.

The big game of the season was played on Jan. 14 in Raleigh when third-ranked UNC pulled out a 72-68 overtime victory over the top-ranked Wolfpack. Shaffer's driving layup with 25 seconds left gave the Tar Heels the lead for keeps in overtime.

"This is the one we wanted," McGuire said. "I'd rather win this one than win the Dixie Classic." McGuire let his players celebrate in front of the crowd of 12,400 by calling a timeout with a two-point lead and one second to go.

The teams met again on Feb. 18 in Chapel Hill with UNC ranked No. 1 this time and State ranked No. 5. The Tar Heels held off a late rally and won again, 74-67. The win kept UNC unbeaten in the ACC at the time, but the Tar Heels would lose to Maryland and Virginia to finish in a first-place tie with State, which lost only twice to UNC.

A third meeting came between the two clubs in the ACC Tournament championship. But the Wolfpack was serving the third of four seasons of probation by the NCAA, so UNC automatically qualified for the NCAA Tournament by reaching the ACC title game.

With more incentive to win, N.C. State got 23 points from senior guard Lou Pucillo in an 80-56 rout of UNC for the championship.

"This is the greatest thrill of my college career," Pucillo said, "and my last."

Early in the game, McGuire pulled most of his starters, as he explained later, to rest them for NCAA Tournament play. State rolled to a lopsided lead, and one insulted fan went to the Reynolds Coliseum basement and cut off the lights in protest. An eight-minute delay ensued.

When it became clear that the Wolfpack was going to win the title with a 65-52 lead and 4:29 remaining, McGuire removed his starters for good and the rout was on. ACC followers were irate at McGuire for not taking the championship game more seriously.

"You always want to win the game you're playing," McGuire said. "That's basketball. We put the second string in there to rest our regulars. It's an old trick. Howard Cann used to do it 20 years ago at NYU. You put the second team in and tell them not to take shots. Just hold the ball and move it. All this time, your regulars are resting. Don't forget, the game was lost when the regulars were in there. Not when the subs were in there. The game was lost with about eight minutes to go."

State relished its fourth championship of the decade by calling a timeout with four seconds to play.

"That was some of the boys' doing," Case said. "I had nothing to do with it. In fact, I wish they hadn't done it. But you know how boys are. On second thought, Carolina called time out on us once with one second showing on the clock."

The extra rest for the Tar Heels didn't help much. They fell in the opening round of the NCAA Tournament 76-63 to a Navy team that was given little chance against a team that many thought was better than McGuire's national champions of '57. The loss to Navy was UNC's fourth in its final seven games after winning 17 of its first 18.

"I believe we reached our peak too soon," said UNC guard Harvey Salz.

The NCAA Tournament disaster was typical for the ACC in the '50s as only the '57 Tar Heels reached the Final Four during the decade. UNC became the third team in the league's six-year history to bow out in the first round of the NCAAs.

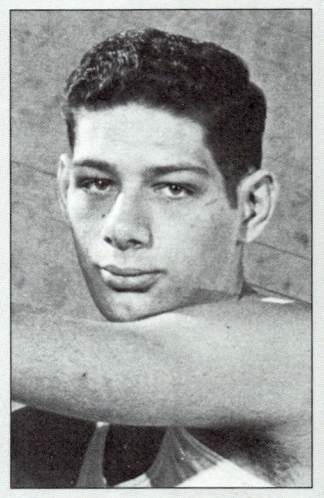

Tragedy Under State Goal

These four played center for Everett Case during the '50s, and each has met with tragic circumstances. The recruiting of Cliff Dwyer (top left), a native Kentuckian, helped fuel the war between Case and Kentucky Coach Adolph Rupp; he died of a heart attack in 1975. John Richter (top right) was a straight-A major in nuclear engineering; he committed suicide in 1985. Bob Seitz (bottom left) suffered from a gland problem that forced him to grow out of control; he died of the disease in 1967 at age 33. And Ronnie Shavlik (bottom right) was ACC Player of the Year in '56; he died of cancer in 1983, shortly after watching State win the national title.

ACC Basketball / **THE '50s**

SPOTLIGHT

Everett Case:

"It was easy to play for him because he was a winner and demanded a lot. He didn't want to be second best."

By DICK HERBERT

ACC BASKETBALL / THE '50s

Midnight was approaching as the chartered bus pulled to a stop on the shoulder of Highway 70 a few miles west of Raleigh on March 25, 1974. Snow covered the adjacent cemetery. The jubilant passengers on the bus stopped celebrating for a moment of silence and a salute to the legend who was buried facing the highway so he could forever "wave to the team when it goes to Durham to play Duke."

The bus was returning from Greensboro, where a few hours earlier North Carolina State had defeated Marquette for the NCAA Championship. Buried on the side of the hill is Everett Norris Case, who in 1946 launched the program that brought State into national basketball prominence. He also had brought to Raleigh as a member of his first team Norman Sloan, coach of the 1974 champions.

"Every game was a championship game, every meal was a banquet while we were here," Sloan said of the Case years. "He was a little dynamo. He just crackled with energy. There was nothing routine or average about anything he undertook."

Sloan represented one of many effective players, policies, and practices that made Case a legend in his time and the father of the basketball hysteria in the ACC area today. The great interest in his teams brought the completion of the 12,400-seat Reynolds Coliseum, and soon Raleigh was hailed as the "Basketball Capital of the World."

No man in the long history of basketball devoted more time, contributed more to its successful promotion, and better knew how to prepare for big games and tournaments than Case, who began coaching at the age of 18 and continued until failing health forced him to retire 47 years later. He is a member of the Indiana and North Carolina Sports Halls of Fame, as well as the Basketball Hall of Fame.

His teams created excitement with a fast-break offense and pressing defense, forced rivals to upgrade their programs, and brought championship trophies to Raleigh with amazing regularity. All of this, though, was mixed with some adversity, such as NCAA probation, players involved in point-shaving and, finally, the onslaught of a terminal illness. Still, the "Old Gray Fox" maintained his perky, cheerful outlook on basketball and life.

•

During the World War II years, N.C. State officials decided when the war was over a strong effort would be made to strengthen the school's basketball program because the Wolfpack could not maintain success in football. In the last prewar season (1942) the Wolfpack had a young, promising team under the late Bob Warren, who elected to go into business after his wartime service. Chuck Taylor, who gave basketball clinics all over the country on behalf of Converse, was asked by State officials for advice on the selection of a coach.

Taylor said Case, a prominent high school coach in Indiana who was then coaching in the Navy, was "the best available man in the country." Dr. H.A. Fisher, faculty chairman of athletics, and J.L. Von Glahn, business manager, met Case in Atlanta and offered him the job at N.C. State.

Case was told he would have an adequate number of full scholarships, worth far more than the approximately $2,000 a year Warren had to glean from concession profits at the Southern Conference Tournament. In a few days Case accepted the offer without having seen the State campus.

Before coming to Raleigh, Case had won Indiana state high school championships at Frankfort in 1925 and 1929. After the 1929 title, the state high school association suspended Frankfort for a year for using undue influence in getting Herman Yeager and Bernard Lowe to move to Frankfort from Jennings County. Case was not implicated in the charge.

In 1931, Case moved to Anderson High, also in Indiana, where he met young Butter Anderson, who had just graduated. Controversy soon followed Case to Anderson, where the boosters had arranged for Joe Hallman of Akron, Ohio, to move to Anderson. The high school association ruled Hallman ineligible for not passing the required school work and suspended Anderson High for a year, from February, 1933 to January, 1934.

Case left Anderson to become an assistant to Sam Barry at the University of Southern California, where he had sent Butter Anderson to play. Case spent two years on the West Coast and earned a Masters degree in English. (His thesis was on free-throw shooting.) Case returned to Frankfort in 1935 and won the state championship in his first season. He also showed his abilities as a businessman, opening a successful drive-in restaurant called the Campus Castle, which he patterned after California drive-ins he had seen.

When Anderson graduated from Southern Cal in 1938, Case made him an assistant in Frankfort. Another state championship, his fourth, followed in 1939, but when World War II erupted both Case and Anderson entered the Navy V-5 program. Case, after a 726-75 high school record, became a successful Navy coach at Depauw University in 1944 (29-3) and for the Ottumwa Iowa Seahawks in 1945 (27-2).

Then came the offer from N.C. State, and a decision had to be made on whether to remain in the Navy, where he had the rank of commander, return to Frankfort or try college coaching in Raleigh.

When Anderson was discharged from the Navy, he again joined his friend in the new venture in North Carolina. They had shared a house in Frankfort and "he was like a father to me," recalled Butter.

Along with Anderson, Case brought to State a talented group of players he had seen in Indiana high schools and service basketball, or who had been recommended highly by his many coaching friends. Leo Katkaveck returned to State from the service and was captain of Case's first two teams. The other players were Dick Dickey, Pete Negley, Eddie Bartels, Warren Cartier, Jack McComas, Charles Stine, Bob Hahn, Norman Sloan and Harold Snow.

Few teams in any sport made such a strong, quick impact as did Case's first at State. The 1947 club, tabbed by many as the "Hoosier Hotshots," won 26 games and lost only five. Because other North Carolina teams did not schedule games prior to Christmas, Case took his first Wolfpack team on a six-game tour of the Midwest. State won all six games, including a 16-point decision over Bob Cousy-led Holy Cross, which went on to win the NCAA Championship.

The Wolfpack immediately attracted a strong following. The Carolina game, scheduled for old Frank Thompson Gym, was canceled by the fire marshal after students had knocked down the doors and created bedlam.

Interest now was so great that the Southern Conference Tournament, held in Raleigh's Memorial Auditorium since 1933, had to be switched to Duke and its 9,000-seat facility. The Wolfpack won that tournament and the next five South-

This portrait of the "Old Gray Fox," painted posthumously in the early '70s, hangs today in the lobby of Reynolds Coliseum.

ern Conference crowns. In his first 13 years, Case's teams won 10 conference championships (six Southern and four ACC) and seven of 10 Dixie Classics.

In his 18 full seasons and two games in the 19th, Case won 377 and lost only 135. Fifty-two of the defeats came in his last five seasons, when NCAA probation and the point-shaving scandal took their toll.

The long, successful tenure almost never happened. After his second season, Case was ready to accept a job as head coach of a proposed professional team in Louisville, Ky. The promoters there thought it was all set. The deal was to include Anderson, who was in Louisville the night of the supposed signing. But Case called promoters and said he was going to stay at State.

There were two reasons for the change of mind. First, Case had been informed that State would be permitted to establish a school for Industrial and Rural Recreation that he had proposed to make it easier to recruit and keep players in school. Second, he had attended a banquet that evening for the new White Memorial Presbyterian Church and had been so moved by the adulation and attention from youngsters and their parents he felt he should stay in Raleigh.

In the great years at State, Case was blessed by having outstanding assistants. Three who served long, hard terms

ACC BASKETBALL / THE '50s

under him—Anderson, Vic Bubas and Lee Terrill—all say working for Case was very difficult but rewarding in many ways. Each finally had to break away from the position because of family and financial obligations. Case never married and did not fully understand the obligations of parents to children.

Bubas, one of many Indiana natives Case lured to Raleigh, was in Case's second recruiting class and was a standout guard. He was made freshman coach after graduation and then succeeded Anderson as top assistant.

"It was easy to play for him because he was a winner and demanded a lot," Bubas says. "He didn't want to be second best. He liked the fast break and so did I. He had a sense of humor along with his demanding style. He did not believe in long practices all year long. He would vary them according to need, and he did not overwork his players. He would use multiple offenses and defenses and not be stereotyped. Players usually are happier when they win, and we won a lot!"

Bubas, who eventually won a lot (213-67 record) in 10 seasons as Duke's coach and is now commissioner of the Sun Belt Conference, was a Case assistant for eight years.

"The first six years were hell," Bubas says. "I was always away from home (recruiting) and in bringing me around as a coach, he was relentless. But there was a method in his madness—he didn't want me to be second best either. He drove me hard, criticized me hard, pushed me, pulled me, shoved me, encouraged me, led me—he did it all, and at all hours of the day and night.

"Then came a big change. In my last two years he must have felt that I had arrived because he left me alone. Almost anything I wanted to do in coaching, recruiting, administering and advising, was almost gospel to him. It was scary that he gave me that much leverage. It was like being the head coach without the monkey being on your back because if we lost, he had the burden. But we didn't lose much. After those eight years, I knew I was ready and so did he."

Terrill says being an assistant was hard because of the long hours that made normal home life impossible. He had just about decided to go into another field when the point-shaving scandals involved four State players he had recruited. He left coaching, joined Eastman Kodak and became head of that huge company's textile, chemical and plastic operations.

Lou Pucillo, an All-America guard, had a brief fling with the pros before going into coaching. Then, he says, he "had the pleasure" of working with Case for three years.

"He was one of the brightest, most organized and competitive individuals I have ever known," says Pucillo, now a businessman in Raleigh. "He won too much; he had a fear of losing. He once made the statement that his biggest problem at State was that during the prime of his career he won too much. He believed the last few years of his coaching would have been easier had he not won so many games and

The house that Case built: Everett Case is shown in February 1948, standing in front of an unfinished Reynolds Coliseum. Case enjoyed many glorious moments in the building, winning seven Dixie Classics and four ACC Tournament titles there.

championships.

"The saddest part of his career was his early death at 65. He told me he was thinking of becoming a counselor for children with problems. He believed he could continue to contribute to Raleigh by helping youngsters.

"He was a great man. Every time I drive on Highway 70 and pass his cemetery, I blow the horn and say, 'Thanks, Coach.' "

Willis Casey, the former athletic director at State, was assistant AD during the Case regime and knew the coach well during those 19 years.

"He was well read and one of the most intelligent coaches I ever knew," Casey says. "He was an astute businessman. He was a likeable individual. He never lost his cool. He had a great sense of public relations. He enjoyed the media and knew the power it could assert in the promotion of his program. He was a great promoter."

Case created the highly successful Dixie Classic, which became the premier sports event in the South Atlantic from its inception in 1949 to its death because of the point-shaving scandals in 1960. He adopted the current pre-game introductions now used everywhere. The Tipoff Club, which hosted visiting teams as part of its functions, was another Case idea. He spent his life trying to make his program and the game of basketball better.

Case was one of the first coaches known to have filmed games, doing so during his high school coaching days in Indiana. His Frankfort High School team's stall tactics over the entire court in a 1927 game led to the adoption of the 10-second midcourt line. At N.C. State, Case had a telephone placed adjacent to his seat on the bench with a direct line to an assistant coach who provided strategies from the press box upstairs at Reynolds Coliseum.

Tournaments were the grandest form of promotion to Case, and he was at his best coaching in them. In Indiana, where all high schools in the state competed in the same tourney, Case won four titles, a record that stood until 1986.

Anderson remembers that about a month before the playoffs, Case called the players and their parents together for a meeting. The players signed a pledge to eat the proper food, be in bed early, always have their ankles taped and wear hats during the Indiana winter so they would not catch colds.

"He would go back to fundamentals," Bubas says. "If a playoff game were in the afternoon, we practiced at the same time. If it were at night, we practiced at night. He did everything as close to game conditions as possible. He would use

---

"He was one of the brightest, most organized and competitive individuals I have ever known. He won too much; he had a fear of losing."

☐ **Lou Pucillo**

---

different combinations of players so that in case of foul trouble the team was used to the combination on the court. He stressed not turning the ball over and worked on backboard play, the fast break and pressing defenses."

Bubas points out that two or three weeks before the tournament Case would discard about one-third of his offense and about one-third of his defense. "We would review fundamentals and simplify and execute," Bubas says. "He reduced practice time drastically, dropping from two hours to an hour, and sometimes practicing not at all."

In the final practice before a tournament Case often threw his sixth man—and sometimes the whole squad—off the court for playing poorly. This usually brought an intense performance in the opener.

Generally there were not many training rules for the other weeks of the season. Case believed that because of squad depth the players knew they had to be in shape or they wouldn't play. During a slump in February, 1958, however, Case got word that some of the players had been drinking.

"He called Vic and me in and ranted and raved about a half hour," Terrill says. "He said we were to let the players know this had to stop and any player caught would be kicked out of school. As we were leaving, he said, 'Wait. You better not go into the Players Retreat (lounge) or any other bar because you might find (John) Richter.' He knew John loved his beer and he was our star center and only big man and would be a tremendous loss."

Case was also a master at scheduling. He spent many hours figuring when and where it would be best to play certain teams and when to schedule name non-conference opponents. He spent the summer with a master sheet. He knew when an opponent had a tough game before the one with State. He would schedule strong teams after State had a week off.

"He liked to play an easy schedule in December leading up to the Dixie Classic," Terrill recalls. "He was willing to travel and play hard teams in January and early February but then build up again with many home games from the middle of February on so that he'd be on a roll going into the Tournament."

Case, unlike many other coaches, never complained about finishing first for the regular season and then having to win the ACC Tournament to go to the NCAA playoffs. He knew how much the Tournament meant to the growth of basketball at State and in the area. It was only appropriate that the most valuable player award, beginning with the 1965 ACC Tournament, was named in honor of Case.

In the early years of the ACC Tournament, conference officials wanted to have the top-ranked team play in the second game of the Friday night semifinals as a better drawing card. Case complained bitterly about this, saying the top-seeded team should have the early game because it deserved to get several more hours of rest. "It was worth six points in the title game the next day," said Case, who eventually won his point when it no longer was necessary to promote Tournament ticket sales.

•

Some credit Case with introducing the fast break and pressing defenses to the ACC area. All had been used before, but not to the extent that the Wolfpack employed them. Their first real display came during State's 1947 Southern Conference Tournament championship game against UNC. The Wolfpack trailed 22-7 early when Case ordered his team into a full-court press, and it rallied to a 50-48 victory.

Bubas still ranks Case as the finest teacher of the fast break. "I have not seen anyone as good," Bubas says. "He explained as he taught, and it was a sight to behold. The emphasis was on the wing men crossing with stops and pivots and never throwing the ball away. If you ran the break the way he wanted, it was almost impossible to throw the ball away."

Case always kept up with developments in basketball around the country and was quick to adopt anything that worked. For a number of years the Wolfpack used a zone defense that rival coaches had a difficult time figuring out.

"We got a head start on the use of the matchup zone," Bubas says. "We had watched some teams up North—mostly Villanova—and copied it. By being the only one in the area with it gave us an advantage for several years."

Practice gimmicks were used that usually, but not always, brought success.

"We were to play the Rhode Island State team that moved the ball up the court much faster than anyone," Terrill recalls of the 1949 Dixie Classic. "So we added a sixth man to our second team when we scrimmaged, and we had two basketballs. It was ridiculous, but when we played the game under regular conditions, the Rhode Island fast break was easy to defend and we won (81-64)."

Another time, the second team center was placed on a chair in front of the basket in the practices before playing South Carolina, which had 7-foot Jim Slaughter at center. "After having shots batted away in practice, our players hardly noticed Slaughter in the game and we won by 30 points," Bubas says of State's 83-53 win over South Carolina in the 1951 Southern Conference Tournament.

The thoroughness with which Case prepared for games was amazing. He knew the floor at old Madison Square Garden, put down in 1933 and never replaced, was 4 feet short of the regulation 94 feet. Since the center line was only 41 feet from the backboard instead of the customary 43, Case moved the backboards at Reynolds Coliseum to that distance for practice before games at the old Garden. His wing men crisscrossed on the fast break at a certain point on the court and

ACC BASKETBALL / THE '50s

In this early '60s Christmas card, Case bemoans the loss of the Dixie Classic, an annual holiday bonanza he conceived in 1949 pitting State, Carolina, Duke and Wake Forest against four top national teams. The tournament was discontinued in 1961 amid reforms following point-shaving scandals.

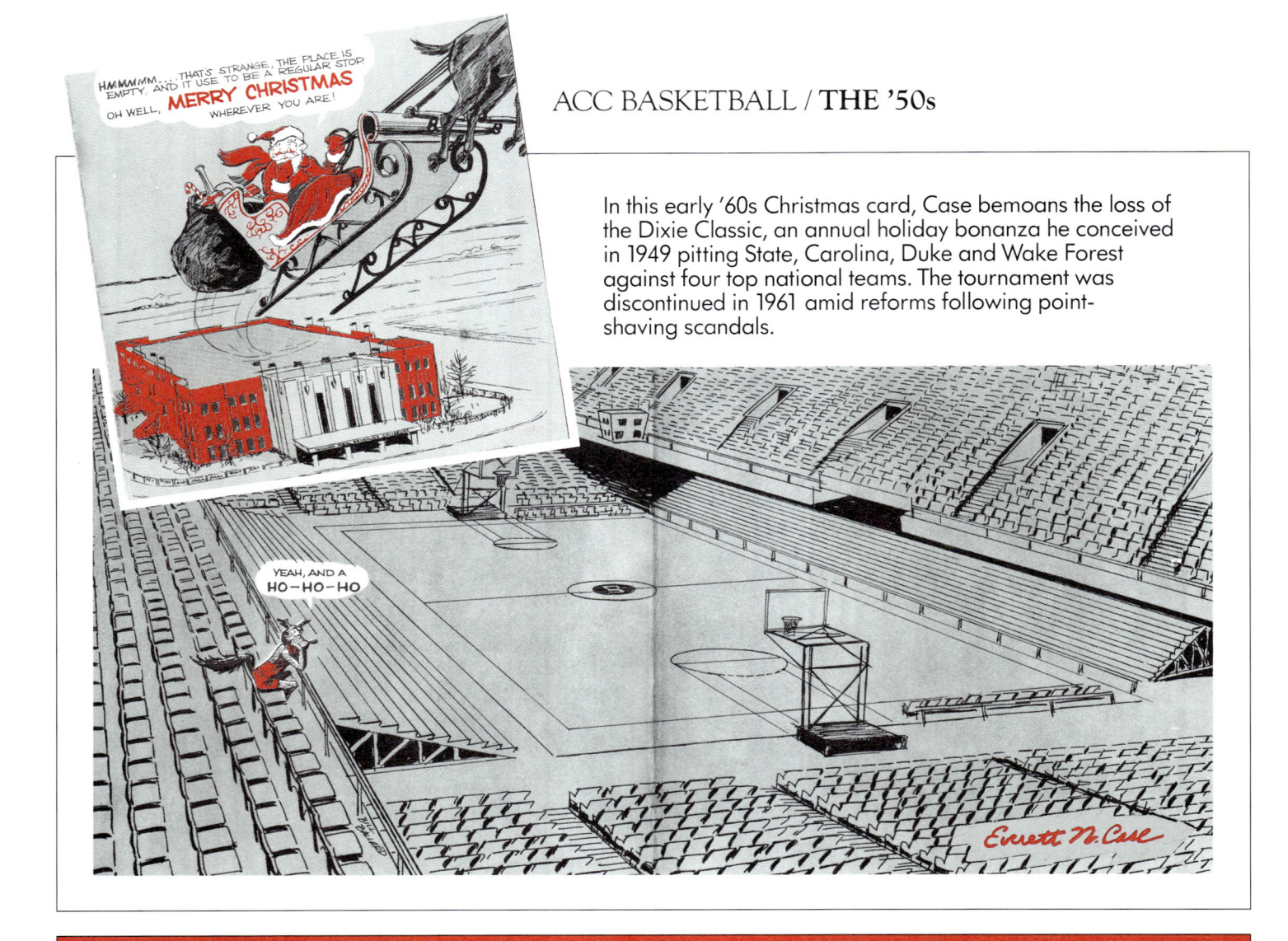

the shorter distance changed the break.

Regardless of Case's knowledge of the Madison Square Garden court, his teams often seemed to have trouble playing there. Case's most crushing defeat came in the first round of the 1956 NCAA Tournament at the Garden. The second-ranked Wolfpack, perhaps Case's best team, lost a four-overtime decision to lightly regarded Canisius.

Case's planning also included close study of game officials. The coaches watched film to see what they called and what they let go. Statistics were kept on their calls.

Recalls Terrill: "We had learned that Phil Fox, who called many of our games, was tough on the play in the pivot early in the game. So we usually played a zone defense at the start to keep our big men out of foul trouble. In intersectional games, the other teams often found their big men in foul trouble in the early minutes and that made it a lot easier for us."

To increase the home-court advantage, Case had a sound meter installed at Reynolds. Bulbs mounted on a board and suspended from the ceiling would light up from the bottom as the crowd grew louder. State fans tried to make the lights go on all the way to the top of the sound meter, which was really controlled by a man and a switch at courtside.

Like other coaches, Case might show displeasure with the officiating early in the game to help arouse the crowd. Overall, he was not rough on officials, leaving that task to Anderson when necessary. As selector of officials for the prestigious Dixie Classic, Case sought the best in the country and few officials wanted to risk his ire.

Lou Bello, the colorful official who worked many State games, says he has a recurring dream about meeting Case in heaven. "You owe me two," Case greets Bello, who officiated a controversial loss State suffered in South Carolina's old gym.

"South Carolina scored to go ahead by a point," Bello remembers. "State signalled for time, and I called time. My back was to the clock, so I checked with the timer and he said the game was over. State claimed time had been called with two seconds to play. I asked the timer again, and he said the game was over before time was called. Every time I saw Everett after that he'd say, 'You owe me two.'"

Generally, Case was gracious in defeat and almost never had an alibi for a loss. He often complimented the opposing team and its coach. On rare occasion was there an unfavorable remark. Some believe there was a feud between Case and UNC's Frank McGuire. But the two coaches respected each other and often played up the rivalry for promotional reasons.

McGuire, at the time of Case's death said: "Everett and I were very close. You can't replace him in our conference. Nobody ever dreamed it, but Everett and I were close friends until the nights we played and then were mad at each other.

"The conference lost a great deal of color and appeal when he became sick. He was a big leaguer—there is no other way to describe the man. I loved to compete against him and you didn't mind losing to him because he was a big leaguer."

If Case had a legitimate feud, it was with the late Adolph Rupp, the legendary coach at Kentucky. Rupp resented the

ACC BASKETBALL / THE '50s

attention Case got for bringing big-time basketball to the South, and he was probably justified since his program was established at Kentucky long before Case arrived at State.

Neither would agree to play the other away from home, so they never met during the regular season. Their only meeting came in Case's first season when the Wildcats won, 60-42, in the NIT in New York. While they never met again on the court, the two coaches often bumped heads in the recruiting of the nation's best high school players.

Case's successful recruiting for most of his years at State did not have any special gimmicks. He relied on the word from hundreds of high school coaches, many of whom had attended his popular high school clinics in Indiana. In the early years, tryouts were permitted and several dozen standout prospects were brought to Raleigh.

Once Case and Anderson were in the home of recruit Lou Dickman, who was trying to decide which of many schools to attend. Mrs. Dickman got down on her knees to pray. Case quickly followed and nudged Butter to do the same.

Mrs. Dickman finally looked up and said, "Well, the Lord has spoken."

Case asked, "What did He say?"

She answered, "The boy is going to State College."

Everett said, "AAAmen!"

Case didn't miss often, but two mistakes came back to haunt him. He did not offer a scholarship to Dickie Hemric, who became an all-time great at Wake Forest and helped the Deacons stop State's string of six conference championships in 1953. Lennie Rosenbluth was also rejected and became the scoring leader on the 1957 North Carolina team that went 32-0 and won the NCAA Championship. Rosenbluth went through a tryout for Case during the spring of 1952, and his lack of defensive skills, plus the fact that Rosenbluth was out of shape, turned Case off. McGuire hid Rosenbluth's defensive deficiencies inside a zone at Carolina.

Case landed a couple of others at a high cost. State was given a one-year probation by the NCAA for the recruiting of Ronnie Shavlik in 1953, and a four-year sentence in all sports for the recruiting of Jackie Moreland in 1956. State was charged with conducting illegal tryouts for Shavlik. State assistant coaches and school boosters were charged with inducing Moreland with illegal offers. In each case, Case claimed innocence.

Terrill recounts an amusing story about a large and capable player with marginal scholastic ability who Case recruited out of Chicago. Case decided to bring him to Raleigh and use tutors to get him through school. The player arrived and, within a few days, grew homesick.

"Several days later," Terrill recalls, "He came in the office and appeared to be quite happy. We asked what the big change was. He explained that he didn't like the strange music on the radio in his room. He wanted the Chicago Beat he was used to and had called his mother and asked her to send down his Chicago radio so that he could enjoy the Chicago Beat. We realized then that he would never play for NCSU. He left school one day after plugging in his Chicago radio and getting the same music that had depressed him before."

Under Case, State recruited players who lived some distance from Raleigh. Indiana, of course, was the prime recruiting area and where he found All-Americas Sammy Ranzino and Dick Dickey. Only Bob Speight among Case's All-Americas was from North Carolina. He was a Raleigh native. Otherwise, Case found All-Americas from Pennsyl-

Case was a public relations whiz and jockeyed carefully for favorable coverage in the media.

vania, Richter and Pucillo; from Illinois, Vic Molodet; and even from Denver, where he landed one of his greatest prizes, Shavlik. Soon, rival schools spread their recruiting areas.

"He sold his ideas to his players, he sold his basketball team to the public via imaginative ideas and good public relations," Bubas says. "He sold N.C. State on having a good basketball program, and he sold me on the advantages of coming to North Carolina (from Indiana) with a new building going up, the Coliseum, and a good basketball program, and a fine educational institution. He sold a lot of players from far away to come to N.C. State."

Perhaps because of his salesmanship, Case was secure financially, listing over a quarter of a million dollars in assets at the time of his death in 1965.

In Indiana, he made money on clinics, the sale of schedules and All-America certificates, and his drive-in restaurant. At State, he seldom spent much money. He drove his car—a Cadillac, given by boosters—back and forth to the campus, which was only a few blocks away. His thriftiness was famous among his friends.

Lou Pucillo tells of the time he received his first paycheck as an assistant coach: "I asked Coach out to have dinner with me. At the restaurant one of the big boosters came over to our table and insisted he wanted to pay the check. I told him no, but Coach gave me a nudge under the table and whispered, 'Let him do it and then you can take me out again.'"

Harry E. Stewart, executive director of the Wolfpack Club for most of the Case years, remembers the time in New York when he got out of a cab and Everett tipped the driver a dime. The cabbie looked at the coin in his open palm and then moved his hand toward Case. He said, "I think you might need this more than I do." Everett reached out, plucked the coin and said, "You know, I believe I do."

Stewart tells of another time when Frank Gallagher, a strong booster, and Case were in New York recruiting and traveling by subway. Each trip, Gallagher paid for it. Finally he got fed up and dropped only his fare. The conductor saw there was one fare short and announced that until it was paid the train would not move. Case finally had to come forward when Gallagher told him he no longer was paying.

ACC BASKETBALL / THE '50s

Case was 46 when he arrived in Raleigh. Mrs. Laura Stevens, whose two sons had played for Everett in Indiana and who talked basketball with him hours on end, was brought along as a housekeeper. She was grandmotherly and enjoyed having a nice home to look after for the coach. She was known affectionately by everyone as "Mamar."

Away from basketball, Case's only hobby was tastefully decorating his home. He was of medium size with sharp features and hair that was turning gray. Thus the nickname of the "Old Gray Fox." Some later thought it more appropriate to call him the "Old Silver Fox." He had a cheerful demeanor and a good sense of humor. He liked to talk basketball with anyone at anytime.

His friends thought he drank too much for his health, but it never interfered with his basketball. In his early years at State, visiting coaches would join him after the games for skull sessions that lasted until early morning. Many members of the press had the same relationship.

It wasn't long after Case arrived in Raleigh that he began taking a nap after lunch. Nothing could keep him from it.

"He would ask to be on the morning program when he was speaking at clinics," Bubas says. "He scheduled our trips so that he could nap."

Frank Weedon, sports information director at State during Everett's last six years, recalls a time in Greenville, S.C., when the Wolfpack was to play Furman.

"He always was most helpful to the media," says Weedon, now the senior associate director of athletics at State, "and I was surprised when a Greenville writer called me and told me he couldn't reach Coach and that he was not registered at the hotel. I knew he was in the hotel and finally found out he had registered under the name of Mr. Simmons, for the well-known mattress that he must have been on at the time."

The nap kept the coach perky, and he predicted he would live to be 100. But in 1962 his health began to fail. He was found to have multiple myeloma, cancer of the bone marrow.

At the time his illness was disclosed, Case was going through the most trying period of his coaching career. Four of his players had been involved in the point-shaving scandals of 1960-61. For many years, at the beginning of the season, Case had a representative of the FBI or SBI talk to his squad about gambling. But prior to the 1961 season, Case had overlooked this precaution. In an early season game in Reynolds against Georgia Tech, it was obvious to Case that something was wrong and he called in the SBI the next day. That warning, however, did not stop the point-shaving.

Although he liked to gamble, he never bet on team sports. Once, not long after the scandals of the '50s, he asked a sportswriter about how the point spread worked. The exposure of the State players was a severe blow to his program as well as to him personally. Terrill, his top assistant, was so upset he left coaching.

Case's illness got so bad that after the second game of the 1964-65 season he had to give up coaching. He turned the team over to Press Maravich, the former Clemson coach who had been brought in as an assistant for the 1963 season with the understanding he probably would be Case's successor.

Dr. Newton G. Pritchett, Case's physician in Raleigh, said: "He had this disease some three-plus years before he died. He knew that we had no specific cure for it. His attitude toward this was that he lived each day for itself without really looking down the road too far."

Case intended to do some traveling in retirement, but on his first trip to Las Vegas he fell and fractured a hip. After that, he stayed close to Raleigh. He was at Reynolds Coliseum to see State win the ACC Tournament in 1965 and presented the first Everett Case Award to MVP Larry Worsley. The Wolfpack players had Case clip the championship nets.

"I've never been happier," Case said. "The last taste is always the best."

Shortly before his death on April 30, 1965, Case revised his will and left $69,525 of his estate to most of those who played for him and the Wolfpack. One sister, Blanche Jones, was the only surviving relative. She was left $198,000.

The funeral was attended by hundreds of friends and associates. The eight members of Case's last recruiting class served as pallbearers. Honorary pallbearers were former players, fellow coaches, officials of N.C. State University and the ACC, and his friends in the media.

On the next-to-last row of the sanctuary sat three elderly ladies who had never met Case. "We came just because we love basketball," one of them said, "and because of what Coach Case meant to the game."

When the ceremony moved to the grave on the hill facing Highway 70, a pelting rain fell. As the group huddled against the rain and the final words were said, an era of ACC basketball ended.

ACC

Champs again: Case gets joy ride from '55 ACC Tournament champs (L-R) Phil DiNardo, Ronnie Shavlik, Cliff Hafer, Bob Seitz, Bucky Waters, Tom Hopper and Nick Pond.

THE '60s

THE '60s

ACC's Close Shave

The decade opens with the league in a fix as gambling and bribery scandals taint three schools.

A midnight knock at Don Gallagher's front door was unusual, but this time Gallagher knew exactly who was there.

It was Joe Greene, who wore an exasperated look on his face. His eyes were puffed. Beads of sweat glistened on his balding head as he waited outside of Gallagher's Clark Avenue apartment in Raleigh.

Gallagher opened the door and invited his visitor in.

The two walked through the living room of the two-bedroom flat, stopping long enough to acknowledge Gallagher's wife, Betty. She was unaware of her husband's involvement with Greene, and Gallagher wanted to keep it that way.

"What went wrong?" Greene asked Gallagher as they stood in the kitchen.

"Look," Gallagher said, "it's important to me to remain a starter on the ballclub or else I wouldn't be any help to you guys. I had to do a few things right. I had to play well enough to stay in the game."

Gallagher stammered while explaining how his North Carolina State team had posted a 63-53 ACC victory over Duke several hours earlier at nearby Reynolds Coliseum. The more he talked, the more Gallagher realized he was in a compromising position. He would normally have celebrated the Wolfpack's win. But on this February night of 1960, the beer Gallagher shared with his wife after the game was more a tranquilizer than a toast.

Gallagher was deeply involved in a point-shaving scheme gone sour. He was paid $1,000 by Greene to make sure N.C. State lost to Duke by at least 12 points. It didn't help matters that Gallagher contributed 10 points to the Wolfpack's victory, thereby making Greene and his gambling buddies big-money losers.

"Duke just didn't play a good game," said Gal-

Don Gallagher was an ideal target for gamblers: He came from a poor background, was married with one child and scraped to make ends meet. He was handsomely rewarded for helping to alter the outcome of four N.C. State games in 1960. "I had choices to make and I made the wrong choices then," he says today. "... I hope that people can forgive."

ACC BASKETBALL / THE '60s

lagher, who at 6-foot-4 had finally earned a starting spot for State in his senior season. "Our ballplayers seemed to be clicking tonight. We could do no wrong and Duke could do no right. I'm sorry, but it was just one of those games."

"How do you explain the points you scored?" asked Greene, who at age 34 knew how to put some heat on a 24-year-old college student.

"It was the momentum of the game," Gallagher said. "I'm not sure one guy can control a game. Oscar Robertson might be able to do that, but I'm no Oscar Robertson."

Greene seemed willing to accept the explanation, but he wasn't finished with Gallagher.

"Listen," Greene said. "There are some people outside that want to talk to you . . . be careful. Someone has a gun in that car."

Gallagher swallowed hard. Three months of participation in an underhanded plot to make fast cash had finally caught up with him. His life was on the line.

After slowly descending the 12 steps in front of his apartment, Gallagher carefully kept Greene between himself and the 1960 Buick sedan parked across the street. As they approached the car, a dark-haired man with a receding hairline got out of the back seat.

"This is Dave," Greene said, introducing Gallagher to Dave Goldberg, who was in his early 40s. Goldberg lived in St. Louis but worked wherever there was a college basketball player willing to change the outcome of a game.

Goldberg had been to North Carolina several times during the 1959-60 season. Through Greene, Goldberg employed Gallagher to "work" N.C. State games.

Goldberg and Gallagher walked two blocks east on Clark Avenue until they reached Oberlin Road, across from Cameron Village Shopping Center.

"I had an awful lot of money involved in that game tonight," Goldberg said. "We lost a few thousand dollars."

Gallagher was scared. He looked over Goldberg's clothing, worried there was a gun under his overcoat.

"I'm sorry, really sorry," Gallagher said. "There was nothing I could do to change it. We were just clicking and Duke was not. I did the best I could. Did you see me draw up on a couple of those layups? I started going in for a layup that one time and just threw up any old kind of shot. The damn thing went in. That happened to me twice.

"I'm sorry, but things just didn't turn out the way they were supposed to turn out."

Goldberg told Gallagher to return the $1,000 cash he was paid by Greene. Gallagher handed Goldberg fifty $20 bills. Twenty dollars bought a lot of 15-cent loaves of bread in 1960. The thousand dollars would have covered half the cost of a new Buick Special.

"What can we do about the next game?" Goldberg asked.

Gallagher suggested he enlist the help of another N.C. State player, Stan Niewierowski, Gallagher's sidekick forward for the Wolfpack. Goldberg listened and agreed.

By season's end, Gallagher would shave points in four games, including one in which Niewierowski assisted. The following season, 1960-61, Niewierowski, along with teammates Anton Muehlbauer and Terry Litchfield, shaved points in five more games.

Four players were involved in point-shaving at South Carolina from 1957 through 1961. Three players were contacted at North Carolina and one, Lou Brown, conspired to fix numerous games at schools in the Northeast.

When it was reported in 1960 that a college football game in Florida was fixed, suspicions of bribes arose across campuses with big-time athletics. Everett Case, N.C. State's coach, sensed some wrongdoing in the Wolfpack's loss to Georgia Tech in 1961 and called for a North Carolina SBI agent to address the team about gambling.

By the time a nationwide investigation by the New York District Attorney's office and by Wake County Solicitor Lester Chalmers was completed in 1962, more than 50 players from 25 schools across the country were accused of fixing 54 games between 1956 and 1961. Close to $45,000 in bribe money was paid to players, and gamblers made millions.

Gallagher swallowed hard. Three months of participation in an underhanded plot to make fast cash had finally caught up with him. His life was on the line.

Four N.C. State players and Brown of North Carolina were charged with bribery and granted immunity in Wake County Superior Court for testifying against the conspirators. The five were later indicted, convicted and given suspended sentences for fixing games in Durham County. Bribers from New York to North Carolina were convicted and given prison terms.

In an effort to bring basketball back into "educational perspective," officials of the consolidated University of North Carolina system de-emphasized the sport. Included in the cutback was cancellation of the Dixie Classic, a 12-year-old Christmas tournament played annually before sold-out crowds at Reynolds Coliseum. The Classic was instrumental in creating widespread interest in ACC basketball.

A point-shaving scandal in the early 1950s left basketball fans in the Northeast stunned. This one in the '60s had the same effect on ACC fans.

"You look these kids in the eye and you say, 'Why, why . . . ?' You look them in the eyes and you know it isn't so," Frank McGuire, then the coach at North Carolina, told *The Charlotte Observer*. "These aren't boys you pass on the street. These are your own. Your family.'"

•

The hundred-mile bus ride from Raleigh to Winston-Salem on Dec. 5, 1959, seemed to take an eternity to Don Gallagher. Earlier in the day, Gallagher had seen a $100 bill for the first time in his life. Five of them, in fact. That was half his pay to make sure N.C. State lost to Wake Forest by at least 12 points. The other half would be paid if Wake Forest "beat the spread."

Gallagher hid the $500 in a footlocker at his apartment. On the way to Winston-Salem, he considered telling Case what he had done. He changed his mind several times during the bus ride, finally deciding that a confession would end his playing career.

Before each basketball season, members of the Wolfpack were required to read a scrapbook of clippings from the point-shaving scandals of the '50s. Each player had to sign a statement saying he would not involve himself with gamblers. Gallagher signed Case's proclamation all four years at State.

He considered other options as he slipped the red No. 43 State jersey over his head in the locker room at the Winston-

76

Salem Coliseum. He could back out of the bribe and be held accountable by the gamblers. Or he could feign an injury or illness and not play in the game. After all, Wake Forest, with senior Dave Budd and super sophs Len Chappell and Billy Packer, was heavily favored to win.

Gallagher mulled those options in his mind as he listened to Case's pregame talk.

"Wake Forest is a very disciplined team," Case said of Coach Bones McKinney's team. "Any time you play against Bones, you better have your ducks lined up. They're going to give us 40 minutes of tough, tenacious, no-turnover basketball. We have to protect the ball and play tight defense."

Gallagher listened and realized he was playing two games. He wore the uniform of N.C. State, but he was essentially going out to play for Wake Forest.

As he went through pregame layup drills, Gallagher searched the crowd for Greene, who was there to make sure Gallagher earned his pay. Gallagher was a prime target for the bribers, who carefully researched the background of potential point-shavers. He met all the qualifications—from a poor background, married with a baby, scraping to make ends meet. He was vulnerable.

Gallagher grew up on the east side of Binghamton, N.Y., the youngest of eight children. His father went from job to job while his mother raised the five girls and three boys. Each of the kids had a daily chore. Don Gallagher learned to stoke a fire that burned through the night. Occasionally, that fire warmed water borrowed from neighbors after the Gallaghers had their main turned off for not paying the bill.

Gallagher recognized from an early age that athletics could provide a way out of Binghamton and the near-poverty.

The streets of Binghamton served as the ballparks, stadiums and gymnasiums. Stickball, football and basketball were the games. Gallagher actually happened into basketball. He was a track star at school, thanks to his high-jumping abilities. He figured if he could jump, he could probably rebound, so as a junior he tried out for the Binghamton North High School junior varsity. He finished the season as a starter on the varsity.

To improve his shooting, Gallagher built a basketball goal in his family driveway with a rim 4 inches less than regulation diameter. Gallagher's shooting touch and his jumping ability made him a college prospect.

He took the advice of college scouts and attended Fishburne Military School in Waynesboro, Va., before migrating to N.C. State on a basketball scholarship.

As a sophomore for the Wolfpack, Gallagher averaged 5.3 points and nearly six rebounds a game in a reserve role. His playing time was sliced in half during his junior season because of an injury, but he was primed for stardom as a senior.

Greene had kept an eye on Gallagher's situation as a sophomore and junior, but waited until he won a starting position for the Wolfpack. It was important for a "bought" player to get quality playing time and thereby have more opportunities to alter the game's score.

When Gallagher accepted his first payoff from Greene, he was also told exactly how to fix a game. Most of Gallagher's work was done on defense, where it was more difficult for a coach to detect wrongdoing. Instead of playing tight against an opponent, Gallagher occasionally sloughed off and gave up open shots. On rebounds, Gallagher often failed to box his opponent out and allowed other uncontested baskets.

There were more obvious ways, but they were saved only for drastic situations. Gallagher could miss a shot intentionally, or make an errant pass, or step out of bounds on purpose. Eventually, he perfected the art of shooting at the back of the rim on free throws to intentionally miss.

In his first "fixed" game against Wake Forest, Gallagher helped the Demon Deacons to an early 11-point lead. But State pulled within 41-35 by halftime and, in the stands, Greene was concerned. So were Goldberg and Steve Lekometros, another of the fixers who was also from St. Louis. As they smoked cigarettes in the Coliseum corridor, Lekometros suggested one of them talk with Gallagher when State returned to the court for the second half. Greene and Goldberg nixed the idea.

When the Demon Deacons won 73-59, Gallagher was safe. He scored six points for State but, more importantly, allowed Budd to have an outstanding game. Budd, a bruising 6-6, 210-pound forward who averaged 11 points and 10 rebounds that season, had 17 points and 19 rebounds against Gallagher.

From Winston-Salem on Saturday, the Wolfpack traveled by bus to Columbia, S.C., for a Tuesday night game against South Carolina. Late that afternoon, Gallagher met Greene in front of the Hotel Carolina, where the State team was housed for the evening. Greene paid Gallagher the remaining $500 for his work in the Wolfpack's loss to Wake Forest.

Greene also told Gallagher to play his very best against South Carolina.

"There might be a little extra cash in it for you," Greene said. That confused Gallagher, but he assumed he wasn't needed to fix the game. According to later court testimony, South Carolina players Larry Dial and Robert Frantz were paid $500 each by Greene to lose by more than three points.

The deal backfired when South Carolina's Ronnie Johnson made a shot with two seconds left and the Gamecocks defeated the Wolfpack 71-70. Dial and Frantz returned the money to Greene, and Gallagher got nothing. Later court testimony in Wake County also revealed that Dial, Frantz and South Carolina teammates Richard Hoffman and Mike Callahan were involved in the point-shaving of six games over three seasons. The state of South Carolina never brought a point-shaving case to court and none of those players were charged.

Back home in Raleigh following State's game against South Carolina, Gallagher discovered a problem. He could not spend what he had earned for fear someone might ask how he got it. So he continued to hide the $100 bills in his apartment. One day, he drove his Ford an hour and a half south on U.S. 401 to Lumberton, where he had the 100s broken into 20s. For future games, Gallagher asked Greene to pay in $20 bills.

Next on N.C. State's schedule was a double-header against Kansas State and Kansas at Reynolds Coliseum, with North Carolina and the Wolfpack alternating opponents on consecutive nights. Greene decided it was best to see how the four teams played on Friday, then pick which games to fix Saturday.

Having returned from Atlanta, where he arranged the fixing of a Georgia Tech game, Greene tried numerous times Saturday afternoon to contact Gallagher at his apartment in Raleigh. When Greene failed, he left a message with Gallagher's wife, Betty.

"Tell him the game is a pick 'em," Greene told Betty by telephone. "Get the message to him at the Coliseum that it's a pick 'em."

By "pick 'em," Greene meant the game was a toss-up. Gallagher was to do his best to make sure N.C. State lost to Kansas. Gallagher's wife relayed the message to Richard Pons, a student at N.C. State and a friend of the Gallaghers. But Pons could not reach Gallagher prior to the game.

As it turned out, Kansas won easily, 80-58, and Greene's bets on the game were good. Gallagher was not paid because he did not participate in the fix. At this point, Gallagher began to realize more people than Greene were involved in the point-shaving scheme.

Goldberg and Lekometros were paying Greene to enlist Gallagher's help. So when the N.C. State-Kansas game worked without Gallagher's aid, Greene kept his cut, plus that intended for Gallagher.

Next, N.C. State took a 2-5 record into the opening round of the 11th annual Dixie Classic. Times were tough for the Wolfpack and Everett Case. Gallagher was part of a class four years earlier that included Harold Atkins, Willett Bennett, Walter Bortko, Ken Clark, Dan Englehardt, Harold Estis and Jackie Moreland. Only Gallagher, Englehardt and Clark remained as seniors. State landed the much-ballyhooed Moreland but paid a heavy price. The Wolfpack was placed on probation for one year by the NCAA for recruiting violations and eventually lost Moreland to Louisiana Tech.

The Moreland incident, plus the other player defections, left Case on the verge of suffering his first losing season as a head coach. He knew it, and the players knew it. Yet the Dixie Classic always provided a struggling team with a second chance. That's what N.C. State looked for when it met powerful Dayton in the first round.

Case decided it was time for a change and ordered the Wolfpack to play slowdown basketball. Prior to the game, Greene met Gallagher and promised him $1,000 if the Wolfpack won by fewer than four points—or lost.

With State and Dayton playing slowdown, there was very little room for error on either side. That put Gallagher in a very awkward position, leaving him almost powerless. He could not make a poor pass for fear of being noticed. Although Gallagher made no attempt to change the game's outcome, State lost to Dayton, 36-32, and Gallagher got his grand. Greene slipped the cash inside a comic book and handed it to Gallagher in the men's restroom at Reynolds Coliseum following the game.

By this point, Gallagher had $2,000 and was worried about keeping that much cash hidden in his apartment. He finally made a $1,500 deposit in the Raleigh Savings & Loan Bank in Cameron Village, all the while praying the teller wouldn't question where a college student had gotten all that money.

Aside from the lump he carried in his stomach, things were going well for Gallagher. He was making easy money and really believed he was in some kind of wonderland. He finally had spending cash for his wife and son. He stocked the family's refrigerator with food and purchased a new black-and-white television console.

He even had enough spare change to socialize with his teammates.

State basketball players hung out at The Profile, a bar and grill next door to the bowling alley on Hillsborough Street in Raleigh. If not at The Profile, they congregated down the street at Red's Grill or just around the corner from the Bell Tower at Players Retreat on Oberlin Road. They drank beer, played bridge, hobnobbed with state legislators and argued about whether the best high school basketball was played in Indiana or New York, where most of the players came from.

Nick Pond said when his playing days ended at State in 1957 he owed more than $1,000 at bars, restaurants and clothing stores along Hillsborough Street.

"If it wasn't for those people," Pond said, "we wouldn't have gotten through school."

Life was fun for State basketball players. Dave Gotkin owned an old 24-foot-long hearse station wagon, and Pond bought a 1939 blue Packard hearse for $50. All 22 players jumped into the funeral limos for beach weekends.

Everett Case knew the score. He just asked that his players stay out of trouble. No fights. No drunken binges.

"Old Joe Hayes is watching my boys," Case often told his players.

A player was once known to ask, "What does Joe Hayes look like, Coach?"

Case responded, "Well, he stands about 6-foot-9, weighs about 290 pounds, and he's black."

Hayes was, of course, a myth created by Case.

There was nothing false about Case's rapport with his players. When they and their wives or girlfriends were out on the town, Case sometimes telephoned the bowling alley, trying to track them down on Hillsborough Street. He occasionally invited them to his house for the evening.

Case lived by himself near Cameron Village. His home on the hill at 611 Daniels Street was a meeting place for basketball cronies. Case always sat in his special easy chair in the den, adjacent to the wet bar. A first-time visitor quickly learned where Case kept the Imperial whiskey and how to mix it with water for the coach's drink. It was okay for the players to drink alcohol with Case. Once, when senior George Stepanovich gave up scotch and popcorn for Lent, he carried three six-packs of beer to Case's house instead.

His players were tremendously loyal. Gallagher learned of that loyalty during his recruiting visit to State and turned down Adolph Rupp and Kentucky to play for Case.

The Rev. Harkness Howard, a Baptist minister from Wyomissing, Pa., first spotted Gallagher playing basketball in an industrial league near Binghamton. Howard, known affectionately throughout the Northeast as "Heaven and Hell," recruited behind the scenes for Rupp. Howard often sent good prospects off to a military school before passing them on to "the Baron of the Bluegrass."

Gallagher made the first step of Howard's planned journey. But when he got to Fishburne Military Academy, Gallagher was also recruited by N.C. State. Gallagher had heard about the tight rein Rupp kept on his players, and was easily swayed by the gentlemanly manners of Case and his assistant coaches, Butter Anderson, Vic Bubas and Lee Terrill. On his recruiting visit to Raleigh in 1957, Gallagher watched a game at massive Reynolds Coliseum in awe.

"They don't have anything like this in Binghamton, I can tell you that," Gallagher told Case.

A full athletic scholarship at State included room, board, tuition and $15 a month for laundry expenses. If a player needed extra spending money, Case arranged for him to work as an usher at the Ice Capades in Reynolds or sell programs at State home football games.

Gallagher joined Delta Sigma Phi fraternity as a freshman, and on one weekend gave up his room to one of the visiting girls from Averett College in Danville, Va. N.C. State admitted only 100 female students each year in the late '50s, so for weekend dances girls were imported from neighboring colleges.

Gallagher met Betty Gray that weekend. Within a year, they jumped in Gallagher's banged-up '54 Ford, drove to Dillon, S.C., and were married by a justice of the peace. By his

ACC BASKETBALL / THE '60s

senior season, Gallagher was the father of one son, Craig. Although Betty worked as a waitress at a cafeteria in Cameron Village, the Gallaghers found it difficult to make ends meet.

Instead of attending summer school and working out at Reynolds Coliseum with the rest of his teammates, Gallagher played basketball and waited tables for Klein's Hillside Hotel in Liberty, N.Y. Many of the hotels in the Catskill Mountains, known to New Yorkers as the Jewish Alps or the Borscht Belt, employed good high school and college players from New York City. They bussed tables by day and played basketball by night. The games were entertainment for hotel guests twice a week, just like the comedians, ventriloquists and big bands on other nights.

When patrons of the restaurant heard Gallagher's last name, they often asked his hometown.

"Binghamton," Gallagher said.

"Ah, Birmingham," they said. "We figured someone named Gallagher was a Southerner."

One who took a particular liking to Gallagher in the Catskills was Tom Scott, a 30-year-old high school teacher and basketball coach in Memphis, Tenn., who served as an athletic director for Klein's Hillside Hotel during the summer. Gallagher and Scott were among the few Gentiles at Klein's and became close friends. Gallagher liked hearing Scott talk about playing for the Washington Generals, the team that lost night after night to the Harlem Globetrotters.

One evening, Scott called Gallagher to the sideline of the basketball court and introduced him to Joe Greene.

That meeting was in August of 1959. Two months later, Greene telephoned Gallagher at his apartment in Raleigh.

"Just passing through town on the way to Cuba," Greene said. "You ought to come down with me sometime. There's nothing like a Cuban woman. Better than their cigars."

Gallagher thought the conversation was unusual. He knew Greene only through a formal meeting. Why the telephone call?

On his return trip from Cuba one week later, Greene called Gallagher again.

"I think you might be interested in a way to make some extra cash," Greene said. "Let's get together and talk about it."

Greene drove to Gallagher's apartment and explained how point-shaving worked. Greene preferred to call it "arranging games." His pitch to Gallagher was softsell.

Warrants were issued in May, 1961, for Stan Niewierowski, Anton Muehlbauer and Terry Litchfield (top to bottom).

"You don't have to dump games," Greene told Gallagher. "All you have to do is be involved in changing the point spread. Instead of winning the game by 10 points, just make sure you only win by four points."

Sucked in by the chance to make easy money, Gallagher said he was interested. After "arranging" the Wake Forest game in December for Greene, Gallagher was hooked.

"They needed to find a guy who had a character weakness and flaw, and at the time that was me," Gallagher said years later. "Once they get started on something like that, there are options available. But I didn't think there were any. You get in deep, then deeper and deeper."

By January of 1960, N.C. State was struggling with a 3-8 record and faced the bulk of a difficult ACC schedule. Next up was a game at Duke. Gallagher was told by Greene that Duke was favored by 14 points, and he agreed to help Duke win by more than that.

Duke led 35-34 with 4:27 remaining when Gallagher went to work. His errant passes, two missed field-goal attempts and a couple of untimely fouls helped Duke score the last 12 points of the game. Still, the Blue Devils' 13-point victory was not enough for Gallagher to collect. Following the game, he met Greene at the Seaboard Railroad Station in Durham and returned $1,000 in cash.

"That's the first time I feared for my life," Gallagher said years later. "I thought I was going to get killed that night. It was very dark and dingy, a very lousy meeting place. I thought somebody was out to waste me. It would have been a perfect place to get killed. I was beginning to get frightened, really frightened, about the elements on the bad side."

Gallagher decided to back off the point-shaving for a few games. He was also concerned that teammates suspected him. Gallagher reversed his role in consecutive victories over Eastern Kentucky, Clemson and Virginia. He was sensational, getting 15 points and seven rebounds against Eastern Kentucky, 25 and eight against Clemson and 19 and 10 against Virginia.

One month following State's loss at Duke, the two teams played again in Raleigh. Greene paid Gallagher $1,000 to make sure the Wolfpack lost by at least 12 points. When State won by 10 points, Gallagher knew he was in trouble.

That's when Greene, Goldberg and Lekometros visited Gallagher's apartment and Gallagher agreed to enlist Niewierowski's help for the next game against Maryland.

The day before the game, Gallagher approached Niewierowski about point-shaving. Niewierowski needed very little convincing. A happy-go-lucky member of the team, he was the first to organize a party and usually had a girl by his side. He charmed people with his engaging smile and boyish looks. He also was known by teammates to have bet on college football and basketball games.

"Throw a feather in the air and he'd bet whether it would hit the floor or not," Bob DiStefano said when he heard of Niewierowski's involvement in the scandal.

Niewierowski was an exceptional athlete. A shortstop and third baseman for his high school team in New York, he was courted by pro baseball scouts. He was also good at handball, golf, ice skating, swimming, bowling and boxing. On the basketball court, Niewierowski had a jump shot that earned him the nickname "The Blond Bombshell."

With Niewierowski's help, Gallagher made sure N.C. State did not defeat Maryland by more than three points. It was close, but the Wolfpack escaped with a 48-46 victory. Niewierowski and Gallagher were happy on all counts. State won, and each received $1,000 cash.

Three days later, Greene approached Gallagher and Niewierowski about fixing State's home game against North Carolina. The three went for a short ride in Greene's rented Ford. The players refused to cooperate with Greene because they both wanted to beat their archrivals, who were favored. Greene upped the ante from $1,000 to $1,250, but the players still refused.

State lost to UNC by four points. After earning $3,000 for three fixed games, Gallagher was through with point-shaving. The Wolfpack closed out the regular season with a lopsided victory over La Salle, then defeated Maryland in the first round of the ACC Tournament before losing to Wake Forest in the semifinals.

Following the season, Gallagher was named winner of the Alumni Trophy, given annually to N.C. State's outstanding senior athlete. He averaged nearly 10 points a game in basketball, then high jumped and ran the 400 meters for the track team. Gallagher graduated with honors from State in August of 1960. He also was cited for being in the best platoon in the school's ROTC program.

"He just seemed to epitomize the choirboy kind of existence," says Bucky Waters, who played with Gallagher and later was an assistant coach at State. "He was the kind of guy that everybody respected. He and (former North Carolina) Governor (Jim) Hunt were in school at the same time. Those were two guys you would say, if one was to be governor some day, it would be Gallagher."

Gallagher had other ideas. He joined the Army, figuring that would keep him away from any possible investigation. But the guilt of having shaved points lived with Gallagher.

Seven months into his Army duty, Gallagher learned that basketball betting was under investigation in North Carolina. He knew it was a matter of time before his name was linked. On May 13, 1961, warrants were issued in Wake County Superior Court for the arrests of Muehlbauer, Litchfield and Niewierowski for point-shaving during the 1960-61 season. On September 12, 1961, Gallagher was named by a Wake County Grand Jury for being implicated during the 1959-60 season. True bills of indictment were issued against six New York men accused of fixing games.

New York District Attorney Frank Hogan had broken the case. His office arrested Aaron "The Bagman" Wagman, Joseph Hacken, Jack Molinas and Greene. Wagman was a 29-year-old souvenir-stand operator outside Yankee Stadium who lived around the corner in The Bronx from Molinas, an attorney. Wagman and Hacken were believed to be members of a national crime syndicate. Molinas was a 30-year-old former Columbia University basketball player. All were eventually convicted in New York and served time in prison. Thirteen years later, in 1975, Molinas was shot to death outside his luxurious Hollywood Hills, Calif., home.

"Things began to happen. Mistakes, poor ball handling. I began to think we were getting bad calls from the officials. It was the first game I sensed anything wrong."
☐ **State Coach Everett Case**

Gallagher, Niewierowski, Muehlbauer and Litchfield of N.C. State, and Lou Brown of UNC were granted immunity in New York state for their testimony in North Carolina.

In New York, Brown admitted helping to arrange fixes of seven games not involving UNC, earning $4,500, and making more money by betting on the fixed games. He also testified that teammate Doug Moe accepted $75 from Wagman, spent the money and never reported the incidents with Wagman. Moe was not charged with fixing a game but was suspended from school, along with Brown, by UNC Chancellor William B. Aycock.

Also suspended for not reporting a bribe attempt was UNC teammate Ray Stanley. According to Brown's testimony, Stanley refused to accept $1,000 and did not participate in point-shaving.

Brown entered a guilty plea of bribery charges in Durham County and was given an 18-to-24-month suspended sentence on five years good behavior and payment of court costs. Before testifying in New York and North Carolina, Brown sold his story to *Look* magazine.

In Wake County, Greene, Wagman, Goldberg, Lekometros, Paul Walker, Lou Barshak, Michael Siegal and Jerry Vogel faced charges of bribery and conspiracy. All but Goldberg and Lekometros entered guilty pleas and were convicted. Wagman's case was turned over to New York state officials. Barshak and Siegal, only 23 and 22 years old at the time of the trial, were given three-year, suspended sentences with supervised probation. Walker was sentenced to 18 months in prison and Vogel was given a one-year sentence.

The trial of Goldberg and Lekometros, who were both handed two five-year sentences and served 22 months each in a North Carolina prison, began on Nov. 20, 1962 in Wake County Superior Court.

The testimony was astounding.

In addition to the revelations by Gallagher, who was subpoenaed from his Army assignment in West Germany to testify, Greene told how he and Wagman received $2,200 to $2,300 each from Goldberg and/or Lekometros for their part in arranging a game to be fixed. Greene said that since his conviction in New York City, he had attempted suicide by slashing his wrists in a jail cell.

Niewierowski said he earned $3,250 for shaving points in two

ACC BASKETBALL / **THE '60s**

Good times before the storm: Gallagher (42, top right) and Niewierowski (44) celebrate '58 Dixie Classic championship. Gallagher fell prey to gamblers a year later and then enlisted Niewierowski's help.

games, one against Maryland in 1960 with Gallagher and one against Duke in 1961. He turned down two other offers totaling $2,250, both times to fix games against UNC.

Muehlbauer accepted $50 to alter the score of N.C. State's game against George Washington in 1961 and $1,250 for fixing a game against Duke the same season. He accepted $1,000 to change the outcome of the Wolfpack's game against Georgia Tech in '61, but said he returned the cash after the fix failed.

Muehlbauer was an all-star performer at Lincoln High School in New York City who was known for his play on defense. Once, when he heard of a battle among Muehlbauer, Jon Speaks and Ken Rohloff for the two guard spots at N.C. State, Wake Forest star Billy Packer said, "I hope Muehlbauer loses because he was the toughest man to guard me . . . I don't care if I never have to face him again."

Muehlbauer's poor defensive play in the Georgia Tech game led Case to suspect something was wrong. Later, Case showed films of the game to other State players to watch Muehlbauer's lackadaisical play on defense.

"Things began to happen," Case told the court on a day he said was the saddest of his illustrious coaching career. "Mistakes, poor ball handling. I began to think we were getting bad calls from the officials. It was the first game I sensed anything wrong."

81

ACC BASKETBALL / THE '60s

Litchfield was the most tragic story of all. He accepted $50 to shave points against George Washington and another $1,000 for the Georgia Tech game. "I never shaved any points in any game," Litchfield told *The News & Observer* of Raleigh prior to his testimony. He said he returned the money for the Georgia Tech game.

Pronounced blind when he was 6, Litchfield overcame severe nearsightedness to play college basketball. He transferred to N.C. State from the University of Richmond.

"I used to watch Terry in his high school games," said his father, Alfred, who once was executive director of the Kentucky YMCA. "He wore those big thick glasses and when they were knocked off he'd have to stand right where he was. He couldn't even see well enough to pick them up off the court. But he made it in spite of . . . "

Litchfield was not an exceptional player for the Wolfpack. But he made a memorable, desperation, last-second corner shot to give State a 61-59 win over third-ranked Duke in February of 1961.

After leaving State, Litchfield returned home to Louisville. He later was a successful salesman for Mrs. Smith's Frozen Foods out of Philadelphia. He died of a heart attack in California in 1974, and one week later his wife committed suicide by shooting herself. The Litchfields were survived by a handicapped daughter.

"He enjoyed life very much," Alfred Litchfield said. "He was a man of his word. That was an ordeal I had to go through, but somehow or another you get the strength to deal with those things and you rely on your Christianity to pull you through."

Other players involved in the point-shaving scandal gained the strength to recover, just as the ACC pulled its bootstraps up and went on to have its most successful decade of basketball with seven teams reaching the NCAA Final Four in the '60s.

One of the players involved in the scandal earned a Ph.D. and became a noted professor in Madison, Wisc. Another earned undergraduate and graduate degrees from St. John's University and went on to be a successful businessman in New York. Another became a mailman in Sheepshead Bay, N.Y.

Gallagher retired from the Army in 1981 after serving tours of duty in the Dominican Republic, West Germany and Vietnam twice. While in the service, he earned a masters degree in public administration from the University of Georgia. He and Betty, who died of cancer in 1986, had three sons and a daughter. The family lives on the West Coast.

Gallagher had vowed to never return to N.C. State, but he went back to Binghamton on occasion and never felt comfortable doing so.

"I had choices to make and I made the wrong choices then," Gallagher says today. "But I have made a lot of right choices since that time. I hope that people can forgive. I hope that people are big enough to understand that people make mistakes and can overcome those mistakes.

"You don't ever receive a day in jail, but the repercussions are very vivid in your mind. You are scorned by your neighbors, your friends, your past friends, people who defended you for many, many years. To be scorned by your friends at your high school and in your hometown is worse than a sentence in jail, I can assure you that . . .

"Your inability to return to the campus in any kind of admirable way and be able to identify yourself to people and ask around, to join the alumni association, those kind of things hurt.

"You lose your identity for a long period of your life."

Public feuding between coaches during the '50s usually involved Frank McGuire of North Carolina and Everett Case of N.C. State. But by the first week of February in 1960, other league coaches were joining in.

Wake Forest's Bones McKinney exchanged remarks with Maryland's Bud Millikan following the Demon Deacons' 65-64 victory over the Terps in Winston-Salem.

The incident stemmed from a letter Millikan wrote to Commissioner Jim Weaver, asking that Deacon star Dave Budd remain on probation for fighting during the 1959 season. McKinney read the letter to his team before the Maryland game, and Millikan believed the letter should have been kept between the coaches.

Much as the earlier feuds between McGuire and Case were a sign the Tar Heels were ready to challenge for a championship in the ACC, the McKinney-Millikan conflict signaled that Wake Forest had emerged once again as a solid contender.

Wake Forest's resurgence in 1960 made the ACC Tournament a wide-open affair. UNC and Wake had tied for first place in the regular season, Maryland was three games behind and Duke managed a .500 record. For the first time, no ACC team was ranked among the nation's Top 20 as the Tournament approached. When N.C. State upset third-seeded Maryland in the first round, a Big Four field remained for the semifinals.

Wake Forest defeated State 71-66 in a semifinal game that saw Budd and State's Anton Muehlbauer ejected for fighting with 18 seconds remaining. The other semifinal game was expected to be a blowout since UNC defeated Duke by margins of 22, 27 and 25 points during the regular season.

In what is generally regarded as the biggest upset in Tournament history, Duke registered a stunning 71-69 victory. Behind a 30-point effort by center Carroll Youngkin, the Blue Devils held on to win in the final seconds after leading throughout.

"It was like Christmas in March," said Duke Coach Vic Bubas.

"I'll bet they'd trade all three of those (during the regular season) for this one," Youngkin said.

"To this minute, I can't understand how they beat us," UNC center Lee Shaffer said years later.

As Wake Forest and Duke prepared to meet for the ACC championship and the right to represent the league in the NCAA Tournament, questions arose about Budd's eligibility. The morning of the game, Commissioner Weaver conferred with Footsie Knight, the ACC's supervisor of officials, as well as game officials Red Mihalik and Lou Eisenstein. Weaver wanted more information about Budd's fight with Muehlbauer in the semifinals at State's Reynolds Coliseum.

Weaver declared Budd ineligible for the championship game, and at Wake Forest's request the executive committee was asked to review Weaver's decision. The committee overruled the commissioner.

"They reinstated him at 5 o'clock (for the 8 o'clock championship game)," McKinney said. "We would have beaten the hell out of Duke without Budd, so the last thing I said to Dave in front of the ballclub was that the fans were going to boo the hell out him, but stand there with your damn head up.

"When they called his name, they threw that spotlight on him and (the fans) started to boo. Then they started to applaud, then they gave him a standing ovation. We were 20 points better than Duke, but that made pussycats out of us. Pussycats."

Budd was a tiger as he scored 10 points to go with his 15 rebounds. But that was not enough as Duke pulled out a 63-59 victory after dropping 17 and 19-point decisions to the Demon Deacons during the regular season.

"I'm deeply grateful to Coach (Everett) Case," Bubas said after guiding Duke to its first league championship since winning the 1946 Southern Conference Tournament. "No words can explain what he's done to make this minute possible. He's put so many pages in my book that I can never call it my own."

Throughout the Tournament, Bubas used his "Birmingham Five" lineup of Youngkin, Howard Hurt, Jack Mullen, John Frye and Doug Kistler. That unit earned its nickname when it won the Birmingham Classic in December, then upset highly touted Utah in the Dixie Classic.

The Blue Devils continued to play well in the NCAA Tournament with victories over Princeton 84-60 and St. Joseph's 58-56. They came within one game of reaching the NCAA semifinals, losing 74-59 to 12th-ranked New York University, which got 22 points from star forward Satch Sanders.

"I'm real proud of our kids. They gave us all they had, and we came a long way," Bubas said. "I'm very happy with my first year as a head coach."

Bubas and Duke had only scratched the surface. He had built a solid foundation for a program that would dominate the ACC in the mid-'60s. His work at Duke helped make the '60s the most glorious of times for ACC basketball. By the end of the decade, the ACC had sent seven teams to the Final Four. Wake Forest went in 1962, then Duke in 1963, 1964 and 1966. Finally, UNC made the trip in 1967, 1968 and 1969.

Duke's Doug Kistler slams home two of his game-high 22 points during the Blue Devils' 63-59 ACC final win over Wake Forest in 1960.

'61

The decade proved to be dandy for the league, but not before the ACC survived more fighting among players and poor behavior by fans—carry-overs from the late '50s—and a point-shaving scandal.

Players from N.C. State and UNC admitted altering final scores of games during the 1959, 1960 and 1961 seasons for money from organizers of the point-shaving scheme. The indicted players who admitted guilt were granted immunity in Wake County, N.C., for testimony against the bribers. The players were later prosecuted in Durham County.

The Board of Trustees of the Consolidated University, with recommendations from North Carolina Governor Terry Sanford and UNC President William C. Friday, judged point-shaving the result of big-time athletics. The Board canceled the annual Dixie Classic, limited schedules at UNC and N.C. State to 14 league games and two non-conference games and allowed both schools to sign only two scholarship players per year from outside the ACC region. That restriction lasted two years.

The ACC would recover from the scandals, but most Big Four fans could not get over losing the Dixie Classic, a festival of basketball held each December in Raleigh. Well into the '70s, fans and writers occasionally talked about bringing back the famed eight-team tournament.

UNC won the final Dixie Classic in December of 1960, sweeping past Maryland 81-57, Villanova 87-67 and Duke. Doug Moe was the hero for putting the clamps on Duke scoring ace Art Heyman, as Moe earned MVP honors with 16 points and 17 rebounds in the 76-71 championship game victory. Moe held Heyman, who averaged 25.2 points a game that season, to four points over the final 29 minutes.

Moe teamed with guard York Larese as the famous one-two punch that led UNC to a Top 10 ranking in the 1961 season and prompted Tar Heel Coach Frank McGuire to say, "I wouldn't take any other two college players for Dougie and Yorkie." Moe was a rugged inside player who averaged 20.4 points and 14 rebounds and was considered the league's best defensive player. Larese was a whiz with the basketball and an exceptional outside shooter who averaged 23.1 points a game.

Primarily due to Moe and Larese, Clemson Coach Press

Heyman king in Blue Devil checker game.

Art Heyman's ill-balanced gait has always been as recognizable as his happy-go-lucky grin. Heyman, 45 years old and the owner of a Long Island restaurant, remains today as knock-kneed and pigeon-toed as during his playing days at Duke. His strut is exaggerated in its bounce, and he tilts forward in deference to a severe back injury that cut short his pro basketball career.

"The first time I saw him," says Vic Bubas, Heyman's coach at Duke, "I wasn't so much concerned over his basketball ability as whether or not he was going to fall down."

Bubas speaks of Heyman's walk, but he could very well be talking of Heyman's checkered college career. On the Duke Indoor Stadium basketball floor, there was no one better. Heyman was a three-time All-America selection and national Player of the Year in 1963. Some would argue that Heyman was the best player ever to wear a Duke uniform, and he was certainly one of the best in ACC history.

Off the court, Heyman was an enigma. He worked diligently to earn a history degree in four years, was the first among team members to volunteer for visits to Durham-area hospitals and rarely turned his back on an autograph seeker. Heyman once went so far as to strip off his sweat suit and present it to an awestruck young fan.

The other side of Heyman was not nice. He was involved in numerous fights—on court, off court and in court. When Heyman was inducted into the Duke Sports Hall of Fame in 1978, he joked that for his career the school had to keep a Durham attorney on retainer.

Heyman was a much-ballyhooed athlete out of Rockville Centre (N.Y.) High School on Long Island. He was a goalie on an unbeaten soccer team and got looks from major league scouts until he was kicked off the baseball team for fighting with the coach. In basketball, he averaged 30 points and 25 rebounds a game as a senior and broke the Long Island career scoring record of Jim Brown, who would make a name for himself in pro football.

Heyman says that when a University of Cincinnati coach placed $10,000 cash on his bed, he was ready to sign. But his parents vetoed that idea, so he turned to Coach Frank McGuire and UNC. McGuire was more than happy to have Heyman aboard and announced the signing of his services in early May of 1959. During Heyman's official recruiting visit to Chapel Hill, however, Heyman's stepfather engaged in a shouting match with McGuire. Heyman says he had to step between the two.

When Bubas was named Duke's new coach on May 6, his first order of business was to go after Heyman.

"I was the first break for Bubas. I started all that down there," says Heyman, who was once described by a writer as wearing his modesty like a loud sports jacket.

From the outset, Heyman was a very special basketball player. At a rugged 6-foot-5 and 205 pounds, he specialized in hanging around the basket much like he did around his high school gymnasium on Saturday afternoons. Despite his awkward appearance, Heyman was quick on his feet. More than that, he was strong and quite capable of mixing it up with bigger players inside the foul lane. He was best at taking the ball on the wing and driving, no holds barred, to the basket.

"If there are two points on the other side of a brick wall, he'd go through it to get 'em," Princeton Coach Butch van Breda Kolff would later say of Heyman.

Word spread quickly that Heyman was a sight to see, and attendance at Duke freshman games increased dramatically during the 1960 season. He averaged 30 points a game and was mentioned by area writers as being for Duke what Lennie Rosenbluth was for UNC in the mid '50s.

As a sophomore, Heyman began as a reserve in Duke's lineup. The Blue Devils returned five starters from a team that won the ACC Tournament the previous season. But Heyman quickly showed he belonged in the starting five. He scored Duke's initial six points in his first varsity game and finished with 23.

"He's just like a king in a checker game," Bubas said. "I can move him anywhere and he gets the job done."

Sixteen games into the season, Duke had lost only once and Heyman was averaging close to 30 points a game. The lone loss was in the Dixie Classic championship when UNC's Doug Moe held Heyman to five points over the final 35 minutes. Heyman clipped a picture of Moe out of the newspaper, pinned it to his bulletin board and vowed to get revenge. In a return match, Heyman scored 36 points.

With nine seconds remaining in the rematch, Heyman grabbed UNC's Larry Brown on a breakaway layup. Brown wheeled and swung the ball at Heyman. Films showed that Brown and several UNC players first jumped on Heyman, and a wild free-for-all followed with 10 Durham policemen needed to restore order. Heyman was suspended from Duke's three remaining ACC games, while Brown and Donnie Walsh were not allowed to play in UNC's final four league games.

At halftime of the same game, a UNC male cheerleader patted Heyman on the back as he was headed to the locker room. Heyman swung at the cheerleader. A Durham attorney and UNC alumnus, Blackwell M. Brogden, saw the incident and swore out a warrant charging Heyman with assault. When the cheerleader refused to testify, the attorney had him subpoenaed. The case was eventually dismissed as a crowd of 300 jammed a Durham courtroom to watch.

Heyman says he was also arrested and jailed that school year in Myrtle Beach, S.C., for transporting an underage female across the state line. He had registered at a beach hotel under the names of Mr. and Mrs. Oscar Robertson. Heyman says Bubas pulled some political strings to get him out of jail and have the charges dropped.

"I wasn't a Boy Scout," Heyman says, "But I never drank, never smoked and always took care of myself. I went down

Heyman's drive and determination sparked Duke past St. Joe's in '63 East Regional and into Final Four.

there as a kid and came out as a man. You had to be a man to survive all the crap I went through there."

By the start of his junior season, Heyman had been labeled "The Pest" by his teammates. The nickname was appropriate on two counts. Heyman says he was the chief prankster on the team, once taking over the wheel of a Duke bus and driving it through campus. He was even more of a nuisance to opponents. He scored 39 points in one game against South Carolina, 38 in another against Maryland and 36 against Penn State.

Prior to the 1962 season, Heyman was convicted of assaulting a Duke student and fined $25 and costs of court. Three years later, the assaulted student filed an $85,000 civil suit against Heyman, claiming he sustained a severe eye injury and possible loss of eyesight. The suit was dismissed.

"A weaker person would have left," Heyman says. "I was so oblivious to the notoriety. I lived in my own little world. I did what I wanted to do. I was basically oblivious to people around me."

Heyman took out his frustrations on the basketball floor, where his goal was to take Duke to a national championship. With Heyman as the ACC's Player of the Year in 1963, Duke went unbeaten against the league during the regular season and won the ACC Tournament.

Heyman's final trip around the league was memorable. was given a rousing standing ovation by Clemson fans following a 30-point performance. Apparently upset by foul language directed his way during the game, Heyman flashed an obscene gesture to the crowd and said, "I nearly started a riot."

For his finale at Duke Indoor Stadium, Heyman was given free rein by Bubas to score as he wished. Heyman closed out his home career, where Duke was 30-1 during his stay, in spectacular fashion. He scored 40 points and had 24 rebounds in Duke's 106-93 victory over UNC.

A 20-game winning streak carried Heyman and Duke to the semifinals of the NCAA Tournament, where the Blue Devils lost to Loyola of Chicago despite his 29 points and 12 rebounds.

The performance capped a college career that was most remarkable for its consistency. Heyman averaged 25.2, 25.3 and 24.9 points per game to go with rebound averages of 10.9, 11.2 and 10.8 in his three seasons. He and N.C. State's David Thompson remain the only players to be three-time, unanimous All-ACC choices, and he was the ACC's Athlete of the Year in 1963.

"I put on some shows there," Heyman says. "Look at the films."

The New York Knicks saw enough to make Heyman the first pick in the 1963 NBA draft, ahead of West Virginia's Rod Thorn and Bowling Green's Nate Thurmond. For one season, Heyman was the toast of New York. But in his second, and last, with the Knicks, Heyman sulked on the bench and faced numerous fines from management for "conduct detrimental to the club." He later played briefly with the Cincinnati Royals and Philadelphia 76ers, then jumped to the ABA where he played with New Jersey, Pittsburgh, Minnesota and Miami before retiring in 1970.

"I could have been something special," Heyman says of his pro career. "That's reality. I should have been 100 percent better . . . Maybe I wasn't mature and didn't grow up. I just wasn't ready . . . it's really sad, but I have no one to blame but myself. It was all my fault. Sometimes I didn't listen."

Heyman regrets only one thing about his college career. He says his jersey, No. 25, should be retired by Duke. Bubas agrees.

"I'm still hopeful that something will be done to right that wrong," Bubas says.

Heyman says: "I don't understand those people. Who gave that school more publicity, good or bad, than me? Hey, everybody doesn't go to church. Everybody doesn't cross their Ts and dot their Is. It takes a lot of different people. To have a Bloody Mary, you need salt and pepper."

Maravich said of the Tar Heels, "I think they're every bit as good as they were in 1957 when they went all the way."

Earlier in the season, following UNC's 70-65 loss to Kentucky in Greensboro, legendary Wildcat Coach Adolph Rupp said: "This is the biggest team I've sent one of my teams against in all of my 30 years of coaching. I think it (UNC) is going to be a great club. It can go all the way like it did in 1957. It's a well-coached, smart, good-shooting squad."

UNC went as far as it could go in 1961. The Tar Heels finished first in the regular season, 12-2 in the league and 19-4 overall. One of those wins was over Notre Dame at the Charlotte Coliseum in a game that featured a most unusual ending. Notre Dame led 71-68 when Larese was fouled while attempting a shot with 1:32 remaining.

Notre Dame Coach Bill Crosby questioned the foul call and said to official Joe Mills, "You're sure going to take care of your boys down here, aren't you?" Mills promptly called a technical foul on Crosby, and Larese made all three free throws to tie the game. UNC got possession of the ball, ran the clock down for a final shot and won when Jim Hudock tipped in a missed shot by Moe.

UNC was not so fortunate later in the season when it dropped an 81-77 decision at Duke in perhaps the ugliest night of fighting in conference history.

The fisticuffs started in the freshman game played prior to the varsity game and won by Duke, 79-52. The UNC frosh finished the game with just three players on the court. The Tar Heels lost one man for tackling a Duke player on a layup, another when he threw a punch at a Blue Devil and five others to personal foul disqualifications. UNC actually outscored Duke 1-0 in the final 11 seconds when the Tar Heels had only three players.

Those incidents were mild compared to the varsity game. Early in the first half, Moe and Heyman almost came to blows. Later, McGuire walked the length of the floor to criticize Duke's assistant trainer, Jim Cunningham, for chatting with UNC player Dieter Krause. At halftime, while leaving the court, Heyman slapped a UNC male cheerleader on the back of the head after the cheerleader touched him. (Heyman was later charged with simple assualt, but the case was thrown out of a Durham court.)

Nine seconds remained in the game when Heyman and UNC's Larry Brown engaged in a fistfight that erupted into a free-for-all. Both benches emptied, and some fans spilled onto the floor. Moe, who had fouled out of the game earlier, was in the middle of the court throwing punches.

The fight occurred directly in front of the UNC bench. At one point, as many as eight UNC players piled on top of Heyman. One official, Jim Mills, attempted to break up the fight but his partner, Charlie Eckman, watched from behind the basket support.

It took 10 Durham policeman several minutes to restore order and resume play. Finally, with three seconds remaining and Duke leading by four points, McGuire went to the scorer's table to dispute how much time was left on the clock. When Duke's Bubas joined the discussion, he and McGuire exchanged harsh words. Duke won the game, but the fight captured most of the headlines.

Commissioner Weaver reviewed films of the fight and suspended Heyman, Brown and UNC's Donnie Walsh for all remaining ACC games. The suspension most hurt Duke, which lost two of its last three conference games without Heyman. The losses cost Duke, 10-4 in the conference, a first-place finish in the regular season. UNC won both of its remaining league games without Brown and Walsh and finished first at 12-2. Wake wound up second at 11-3.

Despite its first-place finish, UNC did not participate in the NCAA Tournament. On Jan. 10, the NCAA placed the school basketball program on one year's probation for violating recruiting rules.

The NCAA Council charged that in at least 15 instances UNC entertained prospective players, their parents and sometimes their high school coaches away from the campus at Chapel Hill. The Council said that some players' parents went to Raleigh annually for the Dixie Classic, and the university paid for their lodging and part of their food.

The Council ruled that McGuire and a talent scout in New York, Harry Gotkin, had picked up entertainment bills and had failed to account in detail for the expenditures.

Wolfpack's Marathon Man

"Larry Lakins has been around so long he voted for FDR," Wake Forest Coach Bones McKinney quipped in 1964. He wasn't far off, as the N.C. State forward endured a career that spanned nearly a decade. Lakins entered State as a freshman in 1957. Halfway through the '58-59 season, he entered the Army and served 18 months in Korea. He returned to State but was summoned back into the service during an international crisis situation. He returned for the '62-63 season but was declared academically ineligible halfway into the following year. Finally, Lakins returned to the Pack for the '65 season and finished second in the league in field goal percentage at 53.4.

Art Heyman (left center) is restrained as melee rages with UNC's Larry Brown, Don Walsh and a cast of thousands.

The Council also ruled that Billy Galantai of Brooklyn, N.Y., was ineligible for one year at UNC. Galantai, a highly recruited 6-foot-6 player, had already been declared ineligible for freshman ball at UNC because he filed a false statement regarding his eligibility. Galantai eventually played the 1963 and 1964 seasons but was never a standout.

"The University of North Carolina and its basketball program have been penalized by the NCAA for errors in judgment rather than for a deliberate violation of rules," said university Chancellor William B. Aycock.

In late January, UNC notified the ACC it would not participate in the 1961 ACC Tournament. The decision was made by the school's Faculty Committee. In a telegram to Commissioner Weaver, the Committee said, "Such withdrawal would preclude the possibility of an ineligible team eliminating one or more eligible teams."

The most eligible team was Wake Forest, which now pointed to N.C. State since UNC was on probation. At one point during the 1961 season, Wake Coach McKinney presented to N.C. State athletic officials a symbol of supremacy in the Deacons' rivalry with the Wolfpack. UNC and Duke had a victory bell in football, just as Michigan and Minnesota had the Little Brown Jug. So McKinney came up with a chair painted Wake gold and black on top and State red and white on the bottom.

The idea came about after McKinney objected to a call during the 1960 Dixie Classic and broke a chair. State officials billed McKinney $14.33 for damages. In lieu of payment, McKinney had the chair repaired and painted in the colors of the two schools. State's Case liked the idea, but the ritual lasted only until Case retired during the 1965 season.

McKinney predicted in February that his Demon Deacons would win the 1961 ACC Tournament. Wake Forest had an outstanding team with 6-8 junior center Len Chappell, 5-11 junior guard Billy Packer, 6-6 junior forward Bill Hull and 5-10 senior guard Alley Hart as its stars.

How they got together at Wake Forest is a story in itself. Packer's father, Tony, the basketball coach at Lehigh University, wrote to Duke's Ace Parker about the chances of his son landing a baseball scholarship to Duke. Having no baseball scholarships, Parker checked with Duke Basketball Coach Hal Bradley, who was holding one basketball scholarship open for a prized recruit. Packer then elected to go to Wake Forest, and the prized recruit turned out to be Chappell, who also opted for Wake Forest instead of Duke.

Hull, originally a football player at Wake Forest, was asked

ACC BASKETBALL / THE '60s

by McKinney to join the basketball team during preseason when center Bob Woollard and forward Jerry Steele went down with injuries. "Not a bad pickup," McKinney said of Hull after he scored 17 points and had 12 rebounds in a 68-67 victory over State. "I told Hull after the game that I loved only my wife and children better than him. He was absolutely amazing. Before the game I told him to play like a basketball player, not a football player. And he did, too."

Hart was a walk-on who earned a partial scholarship by his junior season and a full ride by his senior year. He earned McKinney's respect in his junior season during a victory over UNC in a televised game at Chapel Hill.

"Playing on television sometimes upsets a kid," McKinney said. "But Hart acted like a veteran. One time he was on the foul line preparing to shoot when his chewing gum slipped out. Casually he bent down, picked up the gum and, although it had dirt on it, he put it back in his mouth. Then he sank the free throw. I said to myself, 'He's my boy.'"

Packer and Hart averaged 17.2 and 13.7 points, respectively. Hull averaged 9.5 points and 9.9 rebounds a game. Chappell led the league in scoring (26.6) and rebounding (14.0) for the first of two straight seasons. His play led one North Carolina newspaper to proclaim, "Baptist Certain They Have Finest Chappell In Country."

The Deacons missed a chance for a three-way tie when Duke could not defeat UNC in the regular-season finale. Wake Forest, which finished second behind UNC and received a first-round bye, took out its wrath on Maryland 98-76 in the semifinals and on Duke 96-81 in the championship.

"I knew after our pregame pep talk that they were hungry," McKinney said. "Listen, they charged out of the dressing room so fast that they knocked over the water cooler and broke it. I never saw a more determined bunch than they were before the game. You don't knock down and tear up water jugs as big as that one every day, my friend."

Wake then buried St. John's in the opening round of the NCAA Tournament, 97-74, in New York's Madison Square Garden. In the East Regional semifinals at Charlotte, Wake turned back St. Bonaventure 72-67.

Wake missed a trip to the Final Four when St. Joseph's put six players in double figures in a 96-86 victory for the East Regional championship. "Their hearts were in it," McKinney said of his players, "but their bodies couldn't quite match their hearts."

ACC fans soon learned that the outcomes of many games over the previous three seasons had been fixed. Point shaving was rampant throughout the country, including games involving N.C. State and South Carolina. Before the point-shaving case was closed, 12 ACC players were believed to be involved, either through unreported contacts with bribers or actual point shaving.

UNC player Lou Brown was granted immunity in New York and North Carolina for his testimony against bribers. He admitted accepting bribes to arrange games outside of the ACC to be fixed. State players Don Gallagher, Anton Muehlbauer, Terry Litchfield and Stan Niewierowski admitted accepting bribes to fix games they played in during the 1960 and 1961 seasons.

Deacon Coach Bones McKinney delighted in talking about ACC scoring leader Len Chappell (51) and the '61 ACC champs.

ACC BASKETBALL / THE '60s

'62

The point-shaving scandals left the ACC in a quandary as the 1962 season approached, especially at UNC and N.C. State. Both had schedules trimmed and recruiting limited by the Consolidated University. UNC also played under NCAA probation for recruiting violations.

A cloud of skepticism loomed not only over those two programs but over all of college basketball. Was the game on the up and up? Would fans turn their backs on a sport that had been wracked by scandals the previous three seasons?

Duke Coach Vic Bubas predicted, "College basketball will come back this season—bigger and better than ever before."

The game was back, all right, but the league carried on without the Dixie Classic and without Frank McGuire.

The point-shaving incidents only sealed McGuire's exit after a long-standing feud with the UNC administration. McGuire never believed he was rewarded properly for taking the Tar Heels to the national championship in 1957. Several incidents made McGuire's final seasons uncomfortable.

On the night the Tar Heels defeated Kansas for the national title in Kansas City, McGuire wanted a first-class party thrown for his champions. The school obliged—to a point. When the party became too extravagant, McGuire reluctantly paid for a few special items out of his pocket.

Following the '57 season, McGuire signed a five-year contract. The $11,600 annual salary was adequate, but certainly not what he thought a national championship coach should be paid. Although he received a new car from boosters, McGuire was denied a weekly press conference like that held for UNC Football Coach Jim Tatum. For road games, McGuire wanted to carry along some of his friends at the school's expense, but UNC refused.

More than anything, McGuire wanted a better playing facility than tiny Woollen Gym. He claimed it was just too small for a big-time college program, and when he resigned in August of 1961 to coach Wilt Chamberlain and the Philadelphia Warriors of the NBA, the roof still leaked in the old gym. With the Warriors, McGuire was to be paid $22,500 a year, plus $2,500 for travel expenses so he could continue living in Chapel Hill.

The same day McGuire announced his resignation, assistant Dean Smith was elevated to head coach. With the promotion, Smith received a raise from $8,000 to $9,500 but operated without a contract.

"I hope to carry on Coach McGuire's program, although I realize I have some big shoes to fill," Smith said.

Smith's coaching debut was a success as the Tar Heels rolled past Virginia 80-46 at Woollen Gym. Smith was so nervous he forgot to set aside a game ball and had to send a manager after one just before tipoff. Smith also forgot about his team's tired signal, the traditional raised fist that would become a trademark of his program. When Larry Brown signaled to the bench, Smith ignored his guard's request to take a breather and shouted words of encouragement, thrusting a fist back at Brown.

By UNC's fourth game of the season, Smith had settled into his job and began showing opposing coaches he was an exceptional coach. Following Notre Dame's 99-80 loss to UNC at the Charlotte Coliseum on Jan. 6, 1962, Fighting Irish Coach Johnny Jordan said: "Frank (McGuire) was all right, but this Dean Smith is a heck of a fine basketball coach, believe me. He's one of the best."

Fans were not as quick to jump on the Smith and UNC bandwagon that season. A crowd of only 3,016 turned out at the Greensboro Coliseum in December to see the Tar Heels play Indiana.

Wake Forest and Duke were the focus of ACC fans' attention, with Wake ranked fifth in the preseason and Duke eighth. Without a Dixie Classic, the Deacons and Blue Devils seized the opportunity to play a "non-league" game in Greensboro on Dec. 30.

A sellout crowd showed up to watch a matchup of Wake Forest's Len Chappell and Duke's Art Heyman. Chappell scored 37 points and Heyman had 33 in Duke's 75-73 victory. The crowd was also enthralled by the flashy new uniforms worn by the Blue Devils, the first college team to have players' names on the backs of their jerseys. At the time, the Chicago White Sox in baseball and the Los Angeles Lakers in basketball were the only pro teams to do it.

"I do believe that uniforms bearing the names of the players will be a big help to the fans," Duke's Bubas said.

Another interesting sidelight to the season occurred during a January game when Florida State visited Clemson. In an effort to curb coaches' poor sideline behavior, Clemson's Press Maravich and Florida State's Bud Kennedy agreed to sit together at midcourt through the entire game. Maravich had the most control of his team from afar as the Tigers prevailed, 75-69.

Maravich probably should have tried the same coaching tactics within the ACC. His Tigers finished below .500 (4-10) for a ninth straight season. Meanwhile, N.C. State surprised the rest of the league by winning 10 ACC games. But the race for first place really came down to powers Wake Forest and Duke.

The Deacons won the regular season with losses to Duke and Maryland. They returned starters Len Chappell and Billy Packer, as well as center Bob Woollard and guard Dave Wiedeman, from the 1961 squad that won 19 games. Sophomore forward Frank Christie moved up from the freshman team, and forward Bill Hull and guard Tommy McCoy gave the Deacons excellent depth.

Wake Forest, due in part to a rigorous schedule, struggled early in the season and was 7-7 at one point. "What's wrong with Wake Forest?" fans asked around the league.

The question started popping up along Tobacco Road following an early season meeting in Winston-Salem between No. 3-ranked Wake Forest and No. 1 Ohio State. For the first time, Wake Forest students camped overnight to get tickets.

One Moment of Glory

Neil Brayton's career at Maryland was steady but unspectacular; the 6-4 guard averaged 9.4 points from 1964-66. He found the limelight one time, however, hitting a 20-foot jumper with 17 seconds left to give the Terps a 69-68 win over Houston and Elvin Hayes in the 1965 Sugar Bowl Tournament.

89

ACC BASKETBALL / THE '60s

Mahaffeys dealt Clemson four of a kind.

Working as a ball boy at local tennis tournaments was more practical than profitable in La Grange, Ga., during the early 1950s. Eight-year-old Tommy Mahaffey's remuneration for a week's work was a worn basketball.

"They were fixing to discard it," Tommy says. "I took that sucker home. Finally, the next Christmas, we talked our dad into giving us a basketball goal. He put it up on the garage, and we got another three or four years out of that basketball."

The '60s
Clemson

The story goes that H.T. Mahaffey's 1955 investment of $35 for a basketball goal ultimately paid for four college educations. Tommy, Donnie, Randy and Richie Mahaffey all learned the game in the family driveway. Then all played it skillfully at Clemson University.

By the time Richie left the program following the 1970 season, the Mahaffeys had played 251 games for Clemson over 11 straight seasons. A Mahaffey led Clemson in rebounding all but one of those years. All totaled, the Mahaffeys scored 3,556 points and had 2,728 rebounds. Collectively, they averaged 11.4 points and 9.1 rebounds a game. Randy and Richie still rank among the top 20 scorers in Clemson history, and the four brothers are bunched among the top seven rebounders in school history.

"We're a peas-in-a-pod bunch," says Randy as he sits today in the offices of Ply-Mart, a building supply business owned and operated by the four brothers in Atlanta. They turned a $15,000 investment two decades ago into a $35 million operation today.

Sit with Randy for any length of time and he's bound to point out a much-treasured, small-framed picture displayed prominently behind his desk. In the picture, H.T. and his four young boys are posed, shovels in hand, on the land where the Mahaffeys would one day build a new home in La Grange.

"Our father ingrained the old American work ethic in us," Randy says. "On Saturdays, when the other kids were maybe going to the movies, or playing or watching TV, we were out there clearing that land, pulling honeysuckle vines, putting a garden in. We hated it. But both of our parents demonstrated hard work to us."

H.T. Mahaffey was superintendent of the Elm City Textile Mill in La Grange. He taught his boys the values of hard work, as well as the pleasures of athletics. H.T. played baseball at Clemson during the 1930s, and he liked the idea of his boys doing the same. The Mahaffeys would travel the 70 miles northeast to Atlanta to see Clemson play Georgia Tech in football, and on a special occasion, the family would make the longer drive north for a Clemson home football game.

Football was mostly a spectator sport for the Mahaffeys. All other sports, particularly basketball since their mother was a shooting star at Asheville Women's College, were to be played and enjoyed. H.T. was 6 foot 5 and his wife 5-10, and each of the Mahaffeys grew to be at least 6-7. Donnie was tallest at 6-8.

"We got our height from our dad," Randy says. "Mother was particularly concerned about our diet. It was incredible what we ate and what we did not eat." Daily breakfast at the Mahaffey household included a bowl of cereal, a couple of eggs, bacon, sausage, ham, grits, toast, juice, milk and sliced oranges. An even healthier lunch included five or six vegetables, and supper was another feast.

The Mahaffeys were not only raising young men but building a work force as well. By the time the Mahaffeys had constructed their new home in La Grange, there was spare time to spend at the Calloway Community Center several hundred yards through the woods from their front doorsteps. Tommy was the first to pass through the Community Center and on to La Grange High School.

When Tommy scored 42 points in one high school game, Clemson Coach Press Maravich telephoned the Mahaffey home the next morning. Then Maravich sent an assistant coach to watch Tommy play in the Georgia state AAA Tournament. The coach liked what he saw and offered him a basketball scholarship. So, too, did the University of Georgia, which also guaranteed a full ride for Donnie when he graduated high school.

"We didn't want anything to do with a package deal," Tommy says. "But the real reason I went to Clemson was because of the ACC. North Carolina had won the national championship the year before (1957). I wanted to play against the best, and at Clemson I felt I would have an opportunity to play right off the bat."

Tommy was a rugged player at 6-7, 220 pounds. He liked to bang his body against the bigger players inside, then go outside and take jump shots. He led the Clemson freshmen to an undefeated season in 1959, then moved into the starting varsity lineup as a sophomore. Little did anyone know that when Tommy scored 11 points in the season opener against Erskine, a Mahaffey would be in the Clemson starting lineup for the next 11 years.

Tommy's senior season of 1962 found sophomore Donnie in the starting lineup. The Tigers won at Virginia and at Maryland to close out the regular season. In the first round of the ACC Tournament, they stunned N.C. State and celebrated by hoisting Maravich to their shoulders to clip down the nets. Then Clemson defeated Duke in the semifinals.

"Damn, we'll never see that again," Tommy said, elbowing his younger brother in the ribs and pointing to Clemson Athletic Director and Football Coach Frank Howard celebrating in the stands at Reynolds Coliseum, where the Tournament was played until 1967.

"First time I ever saw him get excited over a basketball game," Tommy said.

Clemson lost the championship game to Wake Forest. So it was up to Donnie to carry the Mahaffey torch in search of a championship for another two years. Donnie was as strong

ACC BASKETBALL / THE '60s

For 11 consecutive seasons from 1960 to 1970, the name Mahaffey graced the Clemson roster (L-R): Tommy, Donnie, Richie and Randy. The "peas-in-a-pod" clan lit the scoreboards for 3,556 points and had 2,728 rebounds.

under the boards as Tommy, but he liked to work more with his back to the basket. Donnie had a hook shot and turnaround jump shot.

Donnie was even more heralded than Tommy out of La Grange High School. He was the Georgia Player of the Year his senior season when La Grange lost only one game, the state championship, for the second straight year.

Donnie played in only six losing games at La Grange, and he expected to play on winners at Clemson as well. But it wasn't until Clemson defeated Maryland in the first round of the 1964 ACC Tournament, in Donnie's senior year, that the Tigers clinched their first winning season since 1952. A loss to Wake Forest in the Tournament semifinals left Clemson with a 13-12 record. But the winning record was a major breakthrough for the program and something to be proud of for Donnie.

At 6-7 and 200 pounds, Randy was the model power forward. He could shoot, rebound and run. Kentucky had wanted his services, as did most of the other Southeastern Conference schools, but his sights were set on Clemson.

Randy was left-handed and modeled his game after Billy Cunningham, North Carolina's "Kangaroo Kid." And who should Mahaffey match up against in his first college game but Cunningham? When Randy held his own by scoring 15 points to go with 11 rebounds, it marked the start of an illustrious career for yet another Mahaffey.

Before Randy left Clemson, he had earned second-team All-ACC honors in 1965 and first-team honors in 1967. The Tigers had winning records, overall and within the ACC, during Randy's junior and senior seasons. He and brother Richie were part of perhaps the grandest moment in Clemson basketball history late in the 1967 season, when the Tigers swept North Carolina's Big Four schools in an eight-day period.

Off the court, Randy served as junior class president at Clemson. He graduated in pre-medicine with a 3.5 grade point average. Along the way, he also helped recruit Richie for Clemson.

Duke was playing at Clemson during Randy's sophomore year. The game was particularly important to Randy because he was matched against 6-10 Hack Tison. On one play early in the game, Randy perfectly timed his jump and blocked a shot by Tison that brought the Clemson fans to their feet as old Fike Field House shook with noise.

At that moment, Richie was listening to the crowd roar on the radio back in La Grange and was certain he wanted to play college basketball in Fike. In addition to being an outstanding basketball player in La Grange, Richie was also a state high jump champion.

He played parts of four seasons at Clemson after being granted an extra year of eligibility following an injury in 1969. Although Richie averaged 14 points and nine rebounds a game, Clemson enjoyed only one winning season during his stay — 17-8 in 1967.

"Richie is the last of the Mahaffeys, and I will certainly hate to see the string run out," Clemson Coach Bobby Roberts said in 1967. "Perhaps if I stay at Clemson long enough, we can start recruiting their children."

Randy played four seasons in the American Basketball Association with Kentucky, New York and the Carolina Cougars. When he retired from pro basketball, Randy settled in with his brothers outside Atlanta. He and Tommy married sisters. At one point, the four brothers all lived in renovated houses in the same neighborhood, attended the same church and had three children each.

Richie finally broke the pattern with a fourth child. Donnie, who founded the family business, has since branched into other ventures. The brothers also formed the nucleus of a Decatur First Methodist Church basketball team that dominated the Atlanta recreation circuit.

Finally, after an 11-year period in which Tommy, Randy, Donnie and Richie starred for Clemson at different times, they got to play together.

ACC BASKETBALL / THE '60s

Tigers howl following 67-46 win over State in '62 ACC Tourney, Clemson's first postseason triumph since 1939.

A standing-room only crowd of 8,200 packed Memorial Coliseum, only to see Wake Forest embarrassed by Ohio State 84-62.

"I still think we've got the better team," McKinney said after the game in which Jerry Lucas scored 23 points and had 20 rebounds for the Buckeyes. John Havlicek added 18 points for Ohio State, and a reserve guard named Bobby Knight had seven.

The game became the rallying cry for the Demon Deacons. More than anything, they wanted another shot at Ohio State. To get that chance, Wake Forest would have to meet the Buckeyes sometime during the NCAA Tournament.

Not to be denied, Wake Forest ran off six straight conference wins to close the regular season, then rolled past Virginia, 81-58, and South Carolina, 88-75, to reach the final of the ACC Tournament for a third straight year.

Clemson was Wake Forest's opponent in the championship game. The Tigers stunned State in the opening round, winning 67-46 for Clemson's first Tournament victory since 1939 when the Tigers won the Southern Conference Tournament.

"Man, it's been a long dry spell," said Clemson's Maravich. "It was time for us to break the jinx. We even moved to a new hotel this year just for luck. The law of averages was with us, just like shooting craps. You can't roll box cars and snake eyes all the time. Once in a while you will come up with 7 or an 11."

State's Case said, "We looked like Meredith College girls playing."

Clemson then upset Duke in the semifinals 77-72 behind a 34-point effort by Jim Brennan.

"We were gutty beyond human endurance," Maravich said.

The clock struck midnight for Cinderella Clemson in the final as Wake Forest built a 20-point lead and coasted to a 77-66 victory and the championship in Raleigh.

"I don't think the Boston Celtics could beat State, Duke and Wake Forest on three successive days," Maravich said.

Of Wake Forest's recovery from early season struggles, McKinney said: "It's much harder to get up off the floor and become a champion than it is to stand up and be a champ. It's easier to be a nice guy when you're rich, a lot different than when you're scrapping for something to eat."

ACC fans thought maybe the Deacons were on another championship roll, like UNC in 1957, when Wake Forest won its first two NCAA Tournament games in overtime. The Deacons defeated Yale 92-82 despite the fact that Chappell fouled out with two seconds left in regulation.

"Before the start of the five-minute extra period, I told my

ACC BASKETBALL / THE '60s

boys that we had rode Chappell's back this far, now let's do something for him," McKinney said. Before Chappell departed, he scored 25 points to break the ACC career scoring mark of 2,045, previously held by UNC's Lennie Rosenbluth.

Wake Forest trailed St. Joseph's by six points with 1:02 remaining in regulation in the second-round game. But the Deacons rallied, and a 30-foot jump shot by Packer with four seconds remaining forced overtime. It was no contest in overtime as Wake Forest outscored the Hawks 22-11 for a 96-85 victory.

The Deacons then dealt Villanova a fatal one-two punch in the East Regional final. Chappell scored 22 points and had 21 rebounds, while Woollard scored 19 and had 18 rebounds in the Deacons' 79-69 victory.

"We've come a long way since the last time we played Ohio State," McKinney said upon learning that Wake Forest would meet the Buckeyes in the Final Four in Louisville, Ky., "and I just hope we can keep going."

But Ohio State was again too much for Wake Forest, killing the Deacons' shot at the national championship, 84-68. In an attempt to stop Lucas, who scored 19 points, Wake Forest allowed Havlicek to shoot. Hondo scored 25 points.

"I thought Ohio State played as great a game as any college team I ever saw," McKinney said. "Any doubt in my mind that they were not great was certainly dispelled by their magnificent performance."

The next night, Ohio State lost to Cincinnati 71-59 in the championship game. Wake Forest rebounded to defeat UCLA for third place as Chappell scored 26 points and Packer added 22 in an 82-80 victory. The loss was the last for UCLA in the NCAA Tournament until N.C. State defeated the Bruins in the 1974 semifinals at Greensboro.

Wake Forest's run to the Final Four concluded an important season for the ACC. On the heels of the scandals, the league rebounded to have a year in which there were few, if any, on-court or off-court incidents. Respect and dignity had returned to the game and to the league.

'63

Duke and Wake Forest were again considered contenders for the national championship in 1963, while youthful Coach Dean Smith had quickly rebuilt UNC into a solid team.

The rest of the league had fallen on hard times, particularly N.C. State. Everett Case, perhaps never able to overcome the sting of the point-shaving scandals, could not get his program turned around.

Case's health also continued to fail, and the Wolfpack reached new lows. It lost twice to Virginia for the first time in history and set another precedent by dropping home games to Duke, UNC and Wake Forest in the same season.

One of the few celebrations in a 10-11 season for the Wolfpack came in a season-opening victory at Clemson. The State players carried Assistant Coach Press Maravich off the court following the game. Maravich had been wooed to State from Clemson following the 1962 season, presumably to take over when Case retired.

The UNC players also carried Smith off the floor following a December game in Lexington, Ky. The Tar Heels had just stunned ninth-rated Kentucky 68-66, dealing Wildcat Coach Adolph Rupp only his 15th home-court loss in 21 seasons.

"This is equal to the spirit and thrill we had at Kansas City in 1957 when we won the national crown," said UNC Assistant Coach Ken Rosemond, a member of the '57 team. The victory vaulted the Tar Heels into the Top 20 for the first time in Smith's tenure.

The next day, second-ranked Duke was upset 72-69 by a Davidson team coached by former Blue Devil player Lefty Driesell. The win was particularly sweet for Driesell, who had interviewed for the Duke coaching job when Hal Bradley departed following the 1959 season. Driesell lost out to Bubas.

Leading the Davidson win with 27 points was Fred Hetzel, who nearly attended Duke. The Blue Devils withdrew their scholarship offer to Hetzel when Bill Bradley of Crystal River,

Duke's Space Man
Jay Buckley, a Duke forward from 1962-64, listed an IQ of around 160 and spent one summer at Columbia University on a special grant from NASA. Coach Vic Bubas once told him, "Jay, one of these days I'll be reading about you being the first man on the moon." Buckley responded: "No coach, you'll be there first— looking for ballplayers." Two more Buckleys have played in the ACC: Brother Bruce was a UNC forward from 1974-77, and son Clay joined the Blue Devil program in '88.

ACC BASKETBALL / **THE '50s**

Mo., signed a letter of intent to Duke in the summer of 1961.

"When he (Bradley) told us he was going to Duke, it was such a profound happening, we closed the offices, got some pizzas and in the middle of the afternoon had more beer than we should have," recalled Bucky Waters, then an assistant to Bubas. "We were happy. We had our napkins out diagramming plays with Bradley here, (Art) Heyman here, (Jeff) Mullins here, (Hack) Tison here, (Buzzy) Harrison here."

On the first day of classes at Duke, Sept. 8, 1961, Bubas received a message to telephone Warren Bradley, Bill's father, in Missouri.

"Vic returned the call to Warren Bradley," Waters said. "Mr. Bradley said: 'Coach Bubas, I remained in the background throughout the recruiting process and allowed Bill to basically go through and make his decision. He made his decision. But Bill is not coming to Duke. He's in Princeton. I sent him there. It is my wish that he go to an Ivy League school and I am happy that he is at Princeton. I regret deeply that this process has injured your program, but that's the way the cookie crumbles.'"

The younger Bradley sent Bubas a seven-page letter thanking him for the courtesies shown during recruiting. The letter was little consolation to Bubas; Bradley went on to make All-America at Princeton and become one of the best forwards in college basketball history. He was later an outstanding professional player and now is a U.S. Senator.

Three days following the loss to Davidson, Duke was stunned again. This time the Blue Devils fell to Miami (Fla.), 71-69. Miami got 26 points from 7-1 center Mike McCoy and a sterling defensive performance from forward Rick Barry, who limited Heyman to 11 points.

Then came the showdown between Heyman and Bradley at Duke's Indoor Stadium. Both players were brilliant with Heyman scoring 27 and grabbing eight rebounds and Bradley getting 24 and seven. Duke also had Jeff Mullins, who scored 28 and had six rebounds in the Blue Devils' 85-74 victory.

Bubas said of Bradley: "I experience a sharp pain in my stomach when I think about it now. And when I see Bradley play, I almost become ill."

The win over Princeton was the first of 20 straight for Duke, a string that led to an unbeaten record within the league during the regular season, an ACC Tournament championship and an NCAA Tournament East Regional title. Previously, the 1957 UNC Tar Heels had gone unbeaten in the league and won the ACC Tournament; only the N.C. State teams of 1973 and 1974 have completed the sweep since.

The journey to the NCAA semifinals was fairly smooth for the Blue Devils. UNC and Wake Forest, the two other ACC teams to post better than .500 overall records in 1963, provided the only stiff competition within the league.

The road was rougher for Heyman, then a senior. In an early season victory over Wake Forest in Greensboro, Heyman was punched in the nose by Deacon Frank Christie during a scuffle.

"Please tell them I didn't start this one," Heyman pleaded with reporters following the game. "Honest, I was just trying to play basketball. I wasn't trying to fight. I'll take a lie detector test if they want me to."

Heyman overcame the physical shots of opposing players and the verbal assaults of fans to have a splendid season. He averaged nearly 25 points and 11 rebounds a game and was a near-unanimous choice as the league's top player. He received 88 of the 93 votes cast for Player of the Year, with UNC's Billy Cunningham getting the other five. No vote was as lop-

Hooter's heroes give Cavaliers victory song.

The '60s

Virginia

Not long after Bill Gibson suffered a heart attack in July of 1974, doctors suggested that he give up coaching at the University of South Florida.

"I suggest he had that level of confidence that said, 'I can do it,'" says Chip Conner, an assistant under Gibson for eight seasons at Virginia and South Florida. "My guess is that he said, 'Others can't do it, but I can and I will. It won't get me.'"

Gibson coached the inaugural team at South Florida to a 15-10 record in 1975. But a second heart attack got Gibson in July of that year, and he died at age 47.

"I just think he had an incomparable self-confidence and self-determination," Conner says. "He really thought no matter the obstacle, no matter the lack of resources . . . by God, he was good enough to do it and he was going to do it, no matter what."

The biggest challenge in Gibson's coaching career, and perhaps in his life, was an attempt in the late '60s to build a respectable basketball program at the University of Virginia. By all accounts, Gibson succeeded despite having to overcome every imaginable obstacle.

Gibson came to Virginia after a successful coaching stint at Mansfield (Pa.) State College, where his teams were 102-37 in seven seasons. So convinced was Gibson of his coaching abilities, he fully believed that Virginia could compete with the ACC powers despite several major disadvantages. For one, Virginia was not awarding a full allotment of scholarships when Gibson arrived in the fall of 1963. While other ACC schools had two full-time assistant coaches, one of whom was usually assigned to recruiting, Virginia had only one. The ACC had a college board score entrance requirement of 800 for athletes, but Virginia set its standards even higher.

For five seasons, Gibson's teams struggled along with records of 8-16, 7-18, 7-15, 9-17 and 9-16. A string of 14 consecutive losing seasons lent credence to the thinking that Virginia could never produce a winner. Undaunted, Gibson stood firm that respectability could be attained.

"I think he was very frustrated by the fact that it was far more difficult than he might have imagined," Conner says. "He didn't have very good players and there was not a real commitment to the program in terms of dollars or scholarships . . . but I think, honestly, in his first four or five years those things didn't matter to him. He continued to believe he had done it before and he would do it again. He didn't necessarily have to have those things."

ACC BASKETBALL / THE '60s

Gibson stood firm in his quest to end a 14-season UVa losing streak.

What could have been the most damaging of circumstances ultimately proved to be what turned the tide for Gibson and Virginia. During the week prior to the 1969 ACC Tournament in Charlotte, N.C., the Virginia players revolted against Gibson and demanded his ouster as coach.

The players listed their grievances against Gibson and presented them to Virginia Athletic Director Steve Sebo. *The Cavalier Daily,* Virginia's student newspaper, ran a four-part series under the headline: "Gibson Must Go." Gibson and several players were called before an Athletic Council board that eventually gave full support to the coach.

Prior to the start of the 1970 season, a close-knit group of sophomore basketball players wrote a letter to the student newspaper saying they were fully committed to Gibson.

"That was a difficult period for those guys," Conner says of Frank DeWitt, Scott McCandlish, Chip Miller and Tim Rash. "They had been freshmen who looked up to their varsity peers. The fact that those players spoke in support of him created a bond that was an absolute joy from that time until he died."

The experience of the player revolt had an immediate impact on Gibson. Realizing he was held accountable for Virginia's lack of success, Gibson sought more of a commitment to the program. Previously, he had helped raise money to build a new gym, University Hall. He sought a second full-time assistant coach and a full allotment of scholarships. Then Gibson figured it was time to sell the program.

The man who was affectionately known to all as "Hoot" formed a basketball support club in Charlottesville. He started wearing orange ties, then orange pants and finally an orange jacket that would become his trademark. In recruiting, Gibson went all out. Even though he lost Tom McMillen to Maryland, his efforts were a sign that Virginia was serious about securing top-notch players.

The initial sign that times were changing at Virginia was the Cavaliers' 95-93 victory over North Carolina in the first round of the 1970 ACC Tournament. A year later, Virginia was 11-2 at one point and ranked 15th in the nation. Chants of "Boot the Hoot" were replaced at U-Hall by the pep band playing "Hooter's Heroes," a rendition of the theme song from the TV show *Hogan's Heroes.*

Attendance at home games went from 4,000 in previous seasons to 7,500 per game in 1971. The enthusiasm carried over to the following year when Virginia won 18 of its first 19 games and was ranked sixth nationally. With Barry Parkhill joining the senior class of DeWitt, McCandlish, Miller and Rash, the Cavaliers enjoyed a 21-7 season and trip to the NIT.

"Once success arrived, he enjoyed it because he had gone through all that frustration," Conner says. "But I don't think he was surprised by it. He just thought he should have maintained it."

When Virginia dropped to 11-16 in 1974, Gibson decided to attack another project at South Florida. He was on his way to making that program respectable when he died.

Among those who attended Gibson's funeral in Tampa were DeWitt, McCandlish, Miller and Rash, the four very special members of Virginia's basketball class of 1972. ∎

Duke's Heyman gets VIP ride after helping beat Wake for '63 ACC title. Note one interested observer (second from right, sitting at press table): South Carolina Assistant Coach Dwane Morrison, later to become the head coach at Georgia Tech.

sided until David Thompson won the 1974 award.

Heyman saved his best performance at Duke for last. In a spectacular closing chapter, Heyman had a career high of 40 points and added 24 rebounds in his final game at Duke Indoor Stadium, a 106-93 win over UNC.

"Heyman is one of the greatest I have ever seen," said UNC's Smith. "We had two of the best defensive men in the conference on him, Larry Brown and Yogi Poteet. But he kept making baskets."

Heyman was removed from the game with 22 seconds remaining and received a three-minute standing ovation from the crowd.

"This was the first time I recall in coaching that I've given a player free rein," Bubas said. "I just wanted to let Art go. It was a gamble, but it turned out all right. I told him before the game that I hoped he'd have a good one, and he did.

"Everyone talks about how great Dick Groat was. Groat was a great basketball player. I guarded him and he's a good friend of mine. But Heyman is bigger and stronger. He's got to be the best player who ever put on a Duke uniform."

Oddly, Heyman's jersey No. 25 was not retired by Duke. Gary Melchionni (1971-73), Mark Crow (1974-77) and Greg Wendt (1982-83) have since worn the number for the Blue Devils.

While Heyman was the focus of Duke's attack on offense, he was certainly not the Blue Devils' only weapon. They were a smooth-working, fast-breaking, intelligent team with excellent shooters throughout the lineup. Of the five starters, Harrison, Fred Schmidt and Jay Buckley were Dean's List students. The Blue Devils were the first team in ACC history to shoot better than 50 percent from the floor. They made 51.1 percent of their field goal attempts, including a league-leading 60 percent by Buckley.

Duke got outstanding play from guards Harrison, Schmidt and Denny Ferguson as well as from centers Buckley and Tison. Buckley averaged 11.2 points and 9.9 rebounds a game. Mullins and Heyman gave Duke the best forward combination in the country.

"I think that's the most overall talent I've seen on one ballclub in our league," said State's Case. "Carolina in 1957 didn't have a lot of depth. Duke's got a lot of 'em (talented players) and they can vary their lineup . . . just take 'em in and out and it doesn't make much difference."

The Blue Devils' power was most noticeable in the ACC Tournament, where they swept past Virginia 89-70, State 82-65 and Wake Forest 68-57. Wake led Duke by four at halftime of the championship game and held a slight edge early in the second half.

At one point, Heyman called a timeout and told his teammates, "Give me the ball and get out of my way." He finished with 24 points and 11 rebounds.

Heyman's take-charge style helped Duke defeat 18 ACC opponents by an average of 17.5 points. Only four times did the Blue Devils win a league game by less than 10 points.

"We have confidence, have a right to have it, and I believe we can win it, the national crown," Bubas said following the ACC Tournament.

Duke advanced to the Final Four by beating NYU 81-76 and St. Joseph's 73-59 in the East Regional at College Park, Md., despite rare back-to-back poor performances by Heyman. He made only three of 14 field goal attempts against St. Joseph's and only six of 21 against NYU. But Mullins picked up the slack by scoring 49 points in the two games to earn regional tournament MVP honors.

Duke faced a Loyola of Chicago team in the NCAA semifinals that was noted for its scoring balance as well as for having four black starters. Adding to Blue Devil problems, Heyman denied rumors that he had been married during the

ACC BASKETBALL / THE '60s

season. Also, Buckley had a sore right shoulder.

Not much went Duke's way as it dropped a 94-75 decision to Loyola, which won the NCAA Championship the following night by dethroning Cincinnati.

The Blue Devils made only one field goal in the first 10 minutes of the game, trailed by 17 points early and were down 13 at halftime. Duke twice pulled within three points in the second half with possession of the ball but could get no closer.

"When you reach this level of competition, you have to play 40 minutes of good basketball," Bubas said. "We played only 30."

The loss was particularly difficult for Heyman, who refused to talk to reporters. His last chance at winning a national championship was gone, and Heyman looked for someone to blame.

"That was the worst officiating the world has ever seen," Heyman shouted in the Duke locker room.

Heyman, who scored 29 points and had 12 rebounds against Loyola, came back to score 22 in an 85-63 consolation victory over Oregon State. Thus Heyman would become only one of four players in NCAA Tournament history to be named MVP despite not playing in the championship game.

'64

Although Art Heyman would be missed by Duke, Coach Vic Bubas seemed to have an endless supply of talent. To replace Heyman for the 1964 season, Bubas went to a tall lineup of 6-foot-10 postmen Jay Buckley and Hack Tison. He also had Jeff Mullins on the front line and newcomer Jack Marin. In the backcourt, Denny Ferguson and Buzzy Harrison returned with sophomore Steve Vacendak available for relief.

The Blue Devils were ranked preseason No. 4 in the country behind Loyola, Cincinnati and NYU. Interest in Duke basketball was at an all-time high. More than 3,000 season tickets were sold to watch the Blue Devils in Duke Indoor Stadium. For the first time, Duke had near sellouts for every home game.

That was a breakthrough for Duke and Bubas, who had started a major ticket-selling campaign when he took over before the 1960 season. Previously, only N.C. State among the schools in the ACC with large arenas had consistent sellouts. The Wolfpack sold out nearly every game from 1951 through 1953 and again during the 1955 and 1956 seasons. But by 1964, N.C. State's home attendance had fallen to an average of 5,713 a game in 12,400-seat Reynolds Coliseum.

Maryland occasionally played before sellout crowds, usually when a nationally ranked opponent was in College Park. When Cole Field House was opened during the 1956 season, there was rarely a need for Maryland officials to install portable seats on the lower part of the arena.

North Carolina was still playing home games at cramped Woollen Gymnasium, although the Tar Heels were moving more and more games to Charlotte and Greensboro. From 1962 through 1965, UNC played no more than eight home games in one season. But even the games at Charlotte and Greensboro did not always sell out.

South Carolina and Clemson tried to keep up with the demands of their fans and played annually in the North-South Double-headers in Charlotte. The two South Carolina schools were willing to sacrifice a home-court advantage every other season against UNC and N.C. State to draw more spectators in Charlotte.

Hello to Coach No. 5
The NCAA doesn't keep records on such matters, but Wake Forest's Paul Long (12) probably holds the record for having played under the most head coaches. He entered Virginia Tech for the 1962-63 season and played under Guy Strong, who was replaced the following year by Bill Matthews. Long transferred to Wake Forest and sat out during Bones McKinney's last season, then played under Jackie Murdock as a junior in '66 and Jack McCloskey (above) as a senior.

With little success in basketball, Virginia rarely played before a sellout crowd at tiny Memorial Gym. And Wake Forest, despite its success in the early '60s, could not consistently sell out Memorial Coliseum in Winston-Salem.

Winning seemed to be the magic formula for drawing fans at Duke. According to the *Converse Basketball Yearbook*, Duke played before more fans (274,103) than any team in the country during the 1963 season. With continued success in 1964, Duke was assured of drawing another big following.

Among the early season wins for Duke were two over Ohio State and West Virginia for the championship of the West Virginia Centennial in Morgantown, W.Va., and a hard-fought, 82-75 decision over fourth-ranked Davidson.

Following the loss to Duke, Davidson Coach Lefty Driesell said Bubas was "yellow" for not scheduling a return game in Charlotte for the 1965 season. Davidson had lost to Duke three times in Durham but had defeated the Blue Devils in the teams' only meeting in Charlotte. Driesell later apologized

ACC BASKETBALL / THE '60s

for his remarks but stood by his challenge to play Duke in Charlotte.

Those games were only part of a rigorous non-conference schedule resulting in three early season losses. The Blue Devils dropped an overtime decision at Vanderbilt, then were beaten at No. 1-ranked Michigan (83-67) and, later, by Kentucky (81-79) in New Orleans when the Wildcats were No. 1.

Against league competition, Duke looked like it could go unbeaten for a second straight season. The Blue Devils were hardly challenged in winning their first 10 conference games to give them 28 straight victories against ACC opponents. Among those wins was an 84-64 decision over North Carolina that led UNC's Smith to say, "Duke reminds me of that old high school yell, 'Buckley's our man, if he can't do it, Marin can; if Marin can't do it, Kitching can . . .'"

Buckley was not only a consistent player who averaged 13.8 points and nine rebounds a game, but he was also a brilliant student. The summer prior to his senior season, Buckley worked with NASA under a special grant.

"Jay, one of these days I'll be reading about you being the first man on the moon," Bubas once told Buckley.

"No coach," Buckley said, "you'll be there first—looking for ballplayers."

Bubas went to Lexington, Ky., to find Mullins, who chose Duke because he wanted to escape the shadow of Kentucky basketball. Mullins led the Blue Devils in scoring with a 24-point average and, despite being only 6-4, was just behind Buckley with 8.9 rebounds a game. He also had a couple of unique aspects to his game, including an off-balance bank shot. By the end of his career, Mullins also had Duke students counting to 13 as he dribbled the basketball that many times before each free throw attempt.

The third member of Duke's front line, Tison, was a credit to hard work and determination. As a sophomore, Tison averaged only 4.7 points and 4.4 rebounds a game. As a junior in 1964, his numbers jumped to 11.8 points and 7.6 rebounds. His scoring average remained the same and his rebounds improved by one as a senior.

Marin was most valuable as a sixth man because of his ability to play inside as well as outside. He was a 6-6 guard at a Farrell, Pa., high school because he was the only player on the team who could shoot. Marin also had good genes. His father played in the first Orange Bowl game for Duquesne, his older brother played basketball at Penn State and his younger brother played at Louisville.

Harrison, named Frank Late Harrison at birth, was perhaps the best outside shooter on the team. His backcourt mate, Ferguson, was the team's floor leader. Then there was Vacendak, of whom Bubas said, "The way that boy plays his heart out, sometimes it doesn't make any difference whether he's scoring or not."

Excellent depth gave Bubas many options. Mostly, he liked the Blue Devils to play pressure defense. They quickly earned the nickname of "Bubas' Bandits." Where they had relied on Heyman for scoring the previous season, this Duke team went to one of seven players for points.

For the second straight season, State Coach Everett Case said the Blue Devils were the best team in ACC history.

"That national championship team of North Carolina's in 1957 didn't have the bench like this Duke team," Case said. "No, none of my good teams here at State did either."

Only once during the season did Duke falter against an ACC opponent. Surprisingly, the Blue Devils' 28-game win streak came to an end against Wake Forest. The Demon Dea-

Jones first black to join ACC warfare.

The '60s
Maryland

By the time Billy Jones played his first varsity game for the Maryland Terrapins in December of 1965, Jackie Robinson had been retired nine years from a 10-year career in major league baseball. The Civil Rights Act had been in effect for 11 years. Three months later, Texas Western would win the NCAA basketball championship with an all-black starting lineup.

Yet when Jones took the court for Maryland's game at Penn State University, he was going where no other black had been. He was the first black to play basketball in the Atlantic Coast Conference.

Unlike Robinson, Jones was never considered a pioneer. It could have been because Jones was not the instant star for Maryland that Robinson was for the Brooklyn Dodgers. It could also have been that blacks had played against ACC teams since the early '50s. For whatever reason, Jones' arrival as the first black in the ACC went almost unnoticed, save for the standing ovation he received during introductions at the 1966 ACC Tournament.

There were no racial slurs directed at Jones. No heckling by fans. Quite simply, Jones says, there were no incidents.

"The ACC, I can honestly say, was so fired up about its basketball, the people didn't have time to deal with it," Jones says. "As long as you had a road uniform on, they weren't particularly fond of you. But they didn't care what color your skin was."

It comes as a surprise to Jones that any kind of hullabaloo is made today about his place in ACC history. In six years as an assistant coach at four different colleges and another 12 years as head coach at the University of Maryland-Baltimore County, there was hardly a reference made to Jones breaking the league's color line.

Perhaps the nostalgia craze, or the arrival of Maryland's Bob Wade as the first black coach in the ACC, prompted more recognition for Jones.

"It's not that I downplay it," Jones says. "I understand the significance of it, I guess. But at the same time, while it was happening to me there were more important things than being a so-called first. It really wasn't a matter of me being first at anything. I just thought I had a right to play and couldn't find a reason why I couldn't play or shouldn't play."

Maryland Coach Bud Millikan had the same line of thinking when he recruited Jones out of Towson, Md., and Pete Johnson (also black) out of Seat Pleasant, Md.,

98

in the fall of 1964. Millikan had tried other black players as walk-ons for the Maryland freshman team, but none were prepared for varsity action. Jones and Johnson were recruited for the express purpose of helping Maryland win basketball games.

Jones and Johnson liked Maryland because the College Park campus was not far from home. Both had played in Maryland's Cole Field House during the state high school basketball championships. Both liked the idea of playing in a league with some of the nation's best players. But neither Jones nor Johnson had any idea there had not been a black varsity player at Maryland or in the ACC before them. That fact didn't seem to bother Millikan either.

"I guess I was color blind," Millikan says.

"That was never discussed," Jones says. "We never thought about it, talked about it or discussed it. I just wanted to play at College Park. That was it. It was that simple. It didn't dawn on me at that point. I was kind of naive, and I guess in some ways I'm glad I was."

Jones, a 6-foot-1 swingman, became the first ACC black quite by accident. Prior to the 1966 season, Millikan decided it was best to red-shirt Johnson. Jones, meanwhile, had earned a spot on the varsity squad as a backup forward. It was not a position Jones was accustomed to playing, but he was more than willing to accept the switch from guard.

Millikan took a liking to Jones because he was particularly aggressive on defense. But the position change, coupled with Jones' relative inexperience, resulted in his playing sparingly in 16 games as a sophomore. He averaged 2.8 points per game.

"Going from playing freshman ball to that level and seeing guys like Henry Finkel, Elvin Hayes and Don Chaney, it's like a different world," Jones says. "It takes you a while to step in and challenge at that level. No matter how good you think you are, that's a different world. I learned a lot watching those other guys."

Jones returned to the backcourt during his junior season and averaged 11.6 points per game. He was a co-captain his senior season and averaged 10.2 points. Although Maryland's record was 33-41 during Jones' three seasons, there were a few highlights. The Terps defeated Hayes and Houston in 1966. They also downed Davidson, coached by Lefty Driesell, and Army, coached by Bobby Knight, on consecutive nights to win the Charlotte Invitational championship in 1967.

"I have no regrets," says the 41-year-old Jones, who went on to work for Southwestern Bell Publications in Baltimore. "I really appreciated playing in the ACC. It was a great experience. It was something in my life that really gave me a lot of direction. The fact that the competition was so keen I think really helped me as a person.

"I did what I wanted to do. I wanted a chance to play, to see the country and get an education. I did all that." ∎

Jones averaged in double figures during his junior and senior seasons and made little fanfare over his breaking the color barrier: "As long as you had a road uniform on, (fans) weren't particularly fond of you. But they didn't care what color your skin was."

Jeff Mullins was a three-time All-ACC selection and helped Duke advance to the Final Four in '63 and '64.

cons entered the mid-February game with a 10-9 record but managed a 72-71 victory before 8,320 fans at Winston-Salem's Memorial Coliseum.

Junior Richard Herring of Winston-Salem, the lone substitute by Wake Forest, made the key basket for a one-point lead late in the game. Following the victory, the Deacons carried Coach Bones McKinney off the floor.

While Duke's 13-1 record during the ACC regular season was a worthy accomplishment, it should be noted that the league was down as a whole. Wake Forest finished second with a 9-5 conference record, 16-11 overall. Clemson was the only other league team to finish better than .500, and the Tigers were only 13-12.

Thus, it was easy to see why Duke breezed to the ACC Tournament championship. The Blue Devils defeated N.C. State 75-44 in the first round, UNC 65-49 in the semifinals and Wake Forest 80-59 for the championship.

The competition was stiffer for the first round of the NCAA East Regional in Raleigh, but Mullins had the best game of his career and the Blue Devils defeated Villanova 87-73. Mullins made 19 of 28 shots from the floor, scored 43 points and had 12 rebounds.

Duke then got a break when Connecticut stunned heavily favored Princeton 52-50 in the other first-round game in Raleigh. Connecticut was coached by former Duke Assistant Fred Shabel, but the Huskies were hardly a match for the powerful Blue Devils. Duke led 62-27 at halftime and coasted to a 101-54 victory.

In the postgame celebration, the Blue Devils sang Wilbert Harrison's *Kansas City*. That's where Duke was headed to meet Michigan in the Final Four.

Getting to Kansas City proved more difficult for Duke off the court. The 85-seat charter airplane skidded off the rain-slick runway upon landing at Municipal Airport. Although no one was injured, the shaky landing threw a scare into the team.

"We hope to repay Michigan this week," Bubas said upon arriving in Kansas City. He did not want the Blue Devils to forget the 83-67 loss to the Wolverines earlier in the season.

With all five starters scoring in double figures, Duke overcame a 31-point performance by All-America Cazzie Russell to defeat Michigan 91-80. Buckley had 25 points and 14 rebounds, while Mullins added 21 points. Ferguson ran the club brilliantly, scored 12 points and had only one turnover.

"I can't remember a game when all of us played any better than we did tonight," Mullins said.

Duke's opponent in the championship game was UCLA, which did not have a starter taller than 6-5. The Bruins' battle cry all season was "Tall Ain't All." That proved true as UCLA completed a 30-0 season with a 98-83 pasting of Duke for the national championship.

Duke held a 30-29 lead seven minutes into the game, but the Bruins' full-court zone press took its toll as they ran off 16 straight points. Twice Duke called time out during the spree, but the Blue Devils could not recover from the blitz.

"We just lost our poise against their pressure defense and went to pieces," Bubas said.

Unheralded Kenny Washington scored 26 points and had 12 rebounds to lead UCLA, which not only forced Duke into numerous turnovers but also outrebounded the taller Blue Devils 43-35.

"It was like fighting gnats," Buckley said. "They are so little and quick. They came crawling under my arms to take the ball. You can feel a big guy behind you and you can block him out, but not UCLA."

ACC BASKETBALL / THE '60s

'65

During Duke's waltz to the 1964 East Regional championship, rumors out of South Carolina had Frank McGuire returning as a coach in the ACC. McGuire, who had coached the Philadelphia Warriors of the NBA for two seasons and had been out of basketball for one year, was named South Carolina's head coach in February of 1964.

Just as North Carolina had hired McGuire to compete with Everett Case and N.C. State in the early '50s, South Carolina hired McGuire to make the Gamecocks competitive in the ACC. Thus South Carolina joined Virginia and Clemson among the non-Big Four schools taking a greater interest in basketball.

Virginia, a perennial doormat in the ACC, had hired youthful and energetic Bill Gibson prior to the 1964 season. Gibson set out to make Virginia respectable within the league. Although it was a long and difficult struggle, Gibson accomplished that before departing Virginia in 1974. His teams had winning seasons in 1971, 1972 and 1973, including a 21-7 record in 1972.

Press Maravich took Clemson to the championship game of the ACC Tournament in 1962, marking the first time the Tigers had advanced past the first round. When Maravich became an assistant coach at N.C. State, the school turned to Bobby Roberts for the 1963 season. In less than five years, Roberts moved Clemson out of the basement to the middle of the ACC pack.

McGuire's task of building a winning program at South Carolina was much more difficult than what he faced at UNC in the '50s. The Gamecocks had no basketball tradition. South Carolina's winning seasons in 1957 and 1962 were basically a reflection of weak non-conference schedules. The Gamecocks were not competitive within the league, where they were 47-118 prior to McGuire's arrival.

It took McGuire much longer to bring respectability to South Carolina than it did at UNC. His Gamecocks were 6-17 during the 1965 season, then went 11-13, 16-7, 15-7, 21-7, 25-3 and 23-6 before South Carolina withdrew from the ACC following the 1971 season.

The other coaching change during the 1965 season was a surprise to all. Just two games into the season, on Dec. 7, 1964, Case announced his retirement as N.C. State's head coach. Maravich, Case's assistant since the previous season, was named the Wolfpack's new coach.

"I would like to have finished," Case said of the 1965 season, which was expected to be his last, "but it was not the proper thing to do."

Case said he had suffered severe headaches and extreme fatigue during preseason practice. Following State's season-opening win over Furman, Case recalled, "I thought I never would get home, get my clothes off and get into bed." Then, following a loss to Wake Forest in Winston-Salem, Case said it was time to retire.

"I had to get a chair and sit down," Case said of his final game on the sideline.

Case had gone to State in July of 1946 after four years in the Navy, where he coached service teams to a 56-5 record. Prior to that, Case's Indiana high school teams were 726-75 in

A Passel of Hassells

Four members of the Hassell family of Beaufort, N.C., wore an ACC uniform: Cousins Pud (middle left) and Ray (middle right) played at UNC, Pud during the '64 and '65 seasons and Ray from '64-66; cousin Butch (R) played under Bones McKinney at Wake Forest from '62-64; and John (L), Ray's younger brother, played freshman ball at State in 1964. All four played at Beaufort High and were members of teams that won 91 straight games from 1958 through '62. That streak is still a North Carolina high school record.

101

ACC BASKETBALL / THE '60s

23 years that included four state championships. State was 377-134 in 18 seasons under Case, giving him a career coaching record of 1,159-214, an incredible .844 winning percentage. His Wolfpack won 10 league titles, six in the Southern Conference and four in the ACC. He was ACC Coach of the Year three times.

"Everybody who loves and admires Coach Case will be sorry that he cannot finish his last season in harness," said N.C. State Chancellor John T. Caldwell. "We can all be grateful, though, that we have such able hands to carry on with full momentum."

That momentum was far more than anyone expected. Under Maravich, State reeled off 11 straight wins, including six against ACC opponents. The Wolfpack's fast start under Maravich was the result of a rebuilding program started under Case the previous season.

Thanks to the botched recruiting of prep star Jackie Moreland, the resulting NCAA probation and the point-shaving scandals of the early '60s, Case's program was in shambles by the start of the 1964 season. He had only two returning players, so Case went with a lineup of one senior, one junior and three sophomores.

By the 1965 season, those young players had experience, and with sophomore guard Eddie Biedenbach running the show, the Wolfpack was fast developing poise. State's 6-1 start in the league made the hunt for first place one of the most competitive in ACC history.

Duke, of course, was still on top after consecutive trips to the Final Four. UNC's Smith had his team in contention with star forward Billy Cunningham. So, too, was Maryland as Coach Bud Millikan relied on the one-two punch of forwards Jay McMillen and Gary Ward.

Duke had a couple of new wrinkles under Coach Vic Bubas for the 1965 season. After failing to solve UCLA's full-court zone press in the 1964 NCAA championship game, the Blue Devils employed the same defensive tactics in 1965. For the most part, the strategy worked for Duke, which wore warmup jackets that had "ACC Champs '64" stitched across the back.

Duke's lone loss outside the league was an early season rematch of the 1964 NCAA semifinal against Michigan. Michigan won this time, in Duke Indoor Stadium, 86-79, but the loss seemed to spark the Blue Devils to 17 wins in their next 18 games.

UNC certainly did its part in an attempt to knock Duke from the top spot the Blue Devils had held the previous two seasons. The Tar Heels won both regular-season meetings against the Blue Devils as Smith snapped a seven-game losing streak in head-to-head competition with Bubas.

Despite the two victories over Duke, 1965 was perhaps the strangest of all seasons for Smith. Following a 107-85 loss at Wake Forest, the UNC team returned to Woollen Gym only to find a dummy of Smith hanging in effigy. Cunningham was among the players who jumped from the bus and ripped the dummy from a tree.

Exactly one week later, following the Tar Heels' 65-62 loss at home against N.C. State, Smith was again hanged in effigy. This time, a burning took place among 100 or so students near Saunders Hall. The dummy burned while one of the students played taps.

The Tar Heels split their next two games before reeling off seven straight victories to end the regular season.

Cunningham was very much responsible for UNC's late surge. He finished as the league's leading scorer (25.4 average) and rebounder (14.3). In one early season game against Tulane, Cunningham scored a Woollen Gym record 48 points and had 25 rebounds. In another game against Vanderbilt, Cunningham with 30 points and Bob Lewis with 31 became the first ACC teammates to score 30 in the same game.

UNC's final game of the regular season was also the last played at Woollen, home court of the Tar Heels since 1939. Cunningham closed out his college career and shut the Woollen doors with a 25-point, 16-rebound performance in UNC's 71-66 victory over Duke.

Despite the loss, Duke finished first in the regular season with an 11-3 record. UNC, N.C. State and Maryland all tied for second at 10-4. That set up a most interesting ACC Tournament, which was a sellout for the first time in Raleigh's Reynolds Coliseum.

UNC was stunned by Wake Forest 92-76 in the opening round of the Tournament, and Duke survived a scare to defeat South Carolina, 62-60. Maryland and N.C. State easily

Larry Worsley scored 30 points in leading State over Duke in the '65 Tournament final, then was all smiles upon accepting the inaugural Everett Case Award from its namesake.

Karolina's Kangaroo Kid

Billy Cunningham earned the nickname "Kangaroo Kid" from his extraordinary leaping ability during his days at UNC from 1963-65. "I don't know whether it will be John Glenn or Cunningham who will make the first trip to the moon," said Wake Forest Coach Bones McKinney. "Cunningham is already in striking distance." Cunningham chose No. 32 upon his arrival in Chapel Hill because it was the number worn by Bob Cunningham (no relation) during UNC's '57 championship season.

---

advanced to the semifinals. Then, when Duke and N.C. State coasted into the final, the Wolfpack was primed to win the championship dedicated to Case.

"We all would like to win it for him," N.C. State center Larry Lakins said of Case, who was sick and unable to attend the Wolfpack's semifinal victory but promised to be on hand for the championship.

The emotion of winning one for Case, as well as the play of junior forward Larry Worsley, proved too much for Duke. Worsley made 14 of 19 shots, had eight rebounds and scored 30 points as State defeated Duke 91-85 for the championship. Worsley, who came off the bench when starter Billy Moffitt got into foul trouble, was named the winner of the first Everett Case Award as the Tournament's Most Valuable Player.

Following the game, State players first hoisted Maravich on their shoulders so he could clip the nets. Then they lifted Case and he clipped a set of nets in a tradition he brought south from Indiana in 1946.

There was no net-clipping for the Wolfpack in the NCAA East Regional the following week in College Park, Md. Princeton, which got 27 points and 14 rebounds from Bill Bradley, defeated State 66-48 in the first round as the Wolfpack made only 17 of 66 field goal attempts. State then rebounded to defeat St. Joseph's 103-81 in the third-place game.

"I told them they had forgotten they were champions of the Atlantic Coast Conference and to go out and play like the true champions they are," Maravich said of his team, which finished 21-5 in his first season.

Miller time at UNC meant Captain Clutch.

The ball was loose at midcourt as the final seconds ticked off the overhanging scoreboard clock at Memorial Coliseum in Winston-Salem. North Carolina and Wake Forest were deadlocked at 74, and overtime seemed imminent.

UNC's Dick Grubar had knocked the ball away from Wake Forest guard Jerry Montgomery. Tar Heel forward Larry Miller raced downcourt, swept the ball off the floor and drove straight to the basket for the winning goal as time expired.

The '60s

North Carolina

"I didn't even watch it go in," said Miller, who continued to sprint off the court, through a tunnel of fans and toward the locker room. Jack Williams, the sports information director at UNC, extended a hand to congratulate Miller but was plowed over by the Tar Heel star.

"I just darted straight for that door," Miller says. "When it wasn't open, I broke it down."

Most in the partisan Wake Forest crowd of 8,200 were left stunned by the dramatic ending. Again, Miller had displayed remarkable ability to make the biggest plays when they counted the most. Long before he left UNC, Miller became known to Tar Heel fans as "Captain Clutch."

"In the clutch, the guy was incredible," Duke Coach Vic Bubas said.

"He was a lot like Joe Namath," UNC Coach Dean Smith said. "When he made up his mind to do something, he would do it and do it well."

"I've seen a lot of college teams that couldn't beat Larry Miller and four girls," said Oregon State Coach Paul Valenti after Miller earned MVP honors in the 1967 Far West Classic.

Three days after his brilliant play against Wake Forest, Miller made a driving layup with six seconds remaining to give UNC a three-point victory over Duke. Following his performance in an early season win over Kentucky, Wildcat Coach Adolph Rupp made a personal visit to Miller in the UNC locker room. Later that season—Miller's junior year—he scored 29 points in the second half on 11-of-15 shooting as UNC rallied to defeat Wake Forest in the ACC Tournament semifinals. The next night, in the championship, Miller scored 32 points on 13-of-14 shooting and had 11 rebounds as the Tar Heels defeated Duke.

As a sophomore, Miller had scored 22 points and grabbed 16 rebounds against William & Mary in the first game played at Carmichael Auditorium. Later, he arrived as a star player by scoring 12 of UNC's final 14 points as the Tar Heels went from a 68-64 lead with two minutes remaining to an 82-72 victory at Ohio State.

Never was Miller better, however, than when the fourth-ranked Tar Heels defeated third-ranked and unbeaten St. Bonaventure in the semifinals of the 1968 NCAA East Regional. He scored 27 points and had 16 rebounds in the UNC victory over Bob Lanier and the Bonnies.

"I always enjoyed having the ball at the end of games because I could pass, I could handle the ball and I had the ability to drive . . . ," Miller said. "I really thought I should have the ball at the end.

"I remember we lost a game in the (Pennsylvania) state high school final when I brought the ball down the floor and passed off to one of my teammates who had a layup. It went through his hands when I could have taken it in to the basket . . . It was kind of a lesson I learned and it stuck with me."

"I've seen a lot of college teams that couldn't beat Larry Miller and four girls."
☐ **Oregon State Coach Paul Valenti**

Miller learned quite a few other lessons while growing up in Catasauqua, a town of 5,000 on the outskirts of Allentown that had as many saloons as churches. Growing up in the rough-and-tumble neighborhood, Miller had a choice between playing basketball or flirting with reform school. He learned the game could keep him out of trouble, and instead of stealing hubcaps, Miller stole the hearts of basketball fans in the area.

He worked out daily on an isometrics rack built by his father. He wore ankle weights in practice as well as a weighted vest that his father made out of a hunting jacket. He was strong enough to play for the Allentown Jets of the old Eastern Basketball League when he was in the eighth grade. The team featured Ed Burton, who played for the Harlem Globetrotters, and Boo Ellis, who played for the Minneapolis Lakers. By the time Miller was a senior in high school, his vertical jump allowed him to put both elbows over the rim.

Miller averaged more than 30 points and 30 rebounds a game during his senior year. In one game, he outscored the opponent 65-59. In one loss, Miller scored 48 of his team's 54 points. He was strong and quick at 6-foot-3 and 210 pounds.

He was courted by coaches from across the country, but finally selected UNC over Duke and Michigan State. When Miller's signing with UNC was announced, Chapel Hill restaurant owner Tom West served T-bone steaks for 98 cents in celebration.

Miller felt so badly about disappointing Bubas that he could not face the Duke coach in person. Miller kept his last letter from Bubas sealed until he left UNC and, four years later, opened it to find that Bubas wished him well in his college career.

That career was splendid from start to finish. Some 14 busloads of fans from Catasauqua attended Miller's first freshman game and were not disappointed as he scored 39

Miller lofts jumper against Davidson and Coach Lefty Driesell in '68 East Regional final.

points. Those same fans sold $4,000 worth of advertising the following year to have UNC games broadcast on radio back home.

The "Big Cat From Catasauqua" finished as the second leading scorer and third leading rebounder in UNC history and in the top 11 in scoring and rebounding each of his three seasons in the ACC. He averaged 21.8 points and 9.2 rebounds over his career, was named ACC Player of the Year in 1967 and 1968 and was the league's Athlete of the Year in '68. The consensus All-America team that season included Miller, UCLA's Lew Alcindor, Houston's Elvin Hayes, LSU's Pete Maravich and Louisville's Wes Unseld.

Miller had the tough luck of leading the Tar Heels during the same era that Alcindor and UCLA dominated college basketball. UNC was 70-21 during Miller's career, finished fourth in the NCAA Tournament in 1967 and lost the 1968 national title game to Alcindor and the Bruins.

"That's always been a regret of mine, that we couldn't win it," Miller has said. "We were good enough to win it. Sure, we had letdowns, but when we got up for games, I don't think anybody could beat us except UCLA . . . I don't think anybody could have beaten that team."

Miller's trademarks at UNC were a picture-perfect, left-handed jump shot, a medallion that flew recklessly around his neck and a handsome face and floppy hairstyle that made him a candidate for an acting career.

Miller got as far as an appearance on *The Dating Game* television show. His pro basketball career lasted seven seasons with five teams in the ABA, where he scored a league-record 67 points in one game for the Carolina Cougars in 1972.

He retired from basketball in 1976 and went full-steam into a successful career selling commercial real estate in Virginia and later North Carolina. Like that long-ago layup against Wake Forest, Miller never looked back. ■

ACC SCRAPBOOK

Four men claim the distinction of having played basketball at an ACC school and later been a head coach in the league, and only one has done both at the same school. Bucky Waters (below left), lettered at N.C. State from 1956-58 and coached Duke from 1970-73, compiling a 63-45 record. Bobby Cremins (below right) lettered at South Carolina from 1968-1970, and through the 1988 season had a 133-80 record through seven years at Georgia Tech. Charles G. "Lefty" Driesell (near right) lettered at Duke in 1953 and '54 and compiled a 348-159 record in 17 years at Maryland from 1970-86. Jackie Murdock (far right) lettered at Wake Forest from 1955-57 and coached the Deacons to an 8-18 season in 1966.

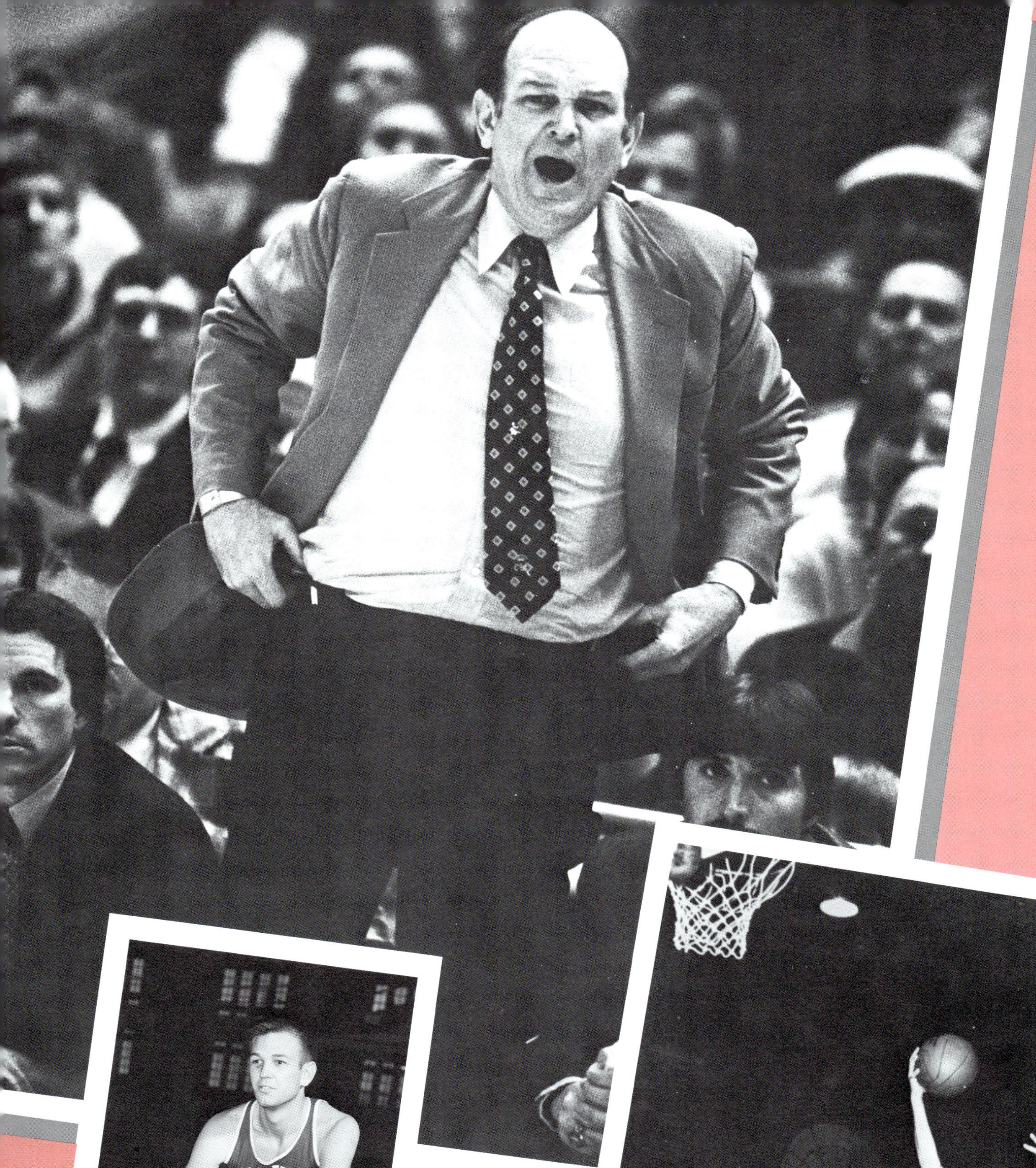

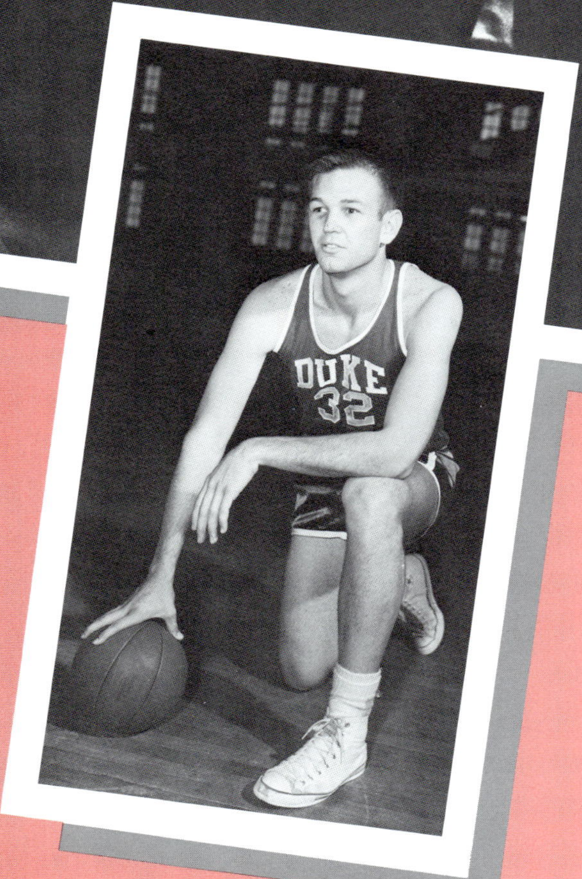
DUKE
32

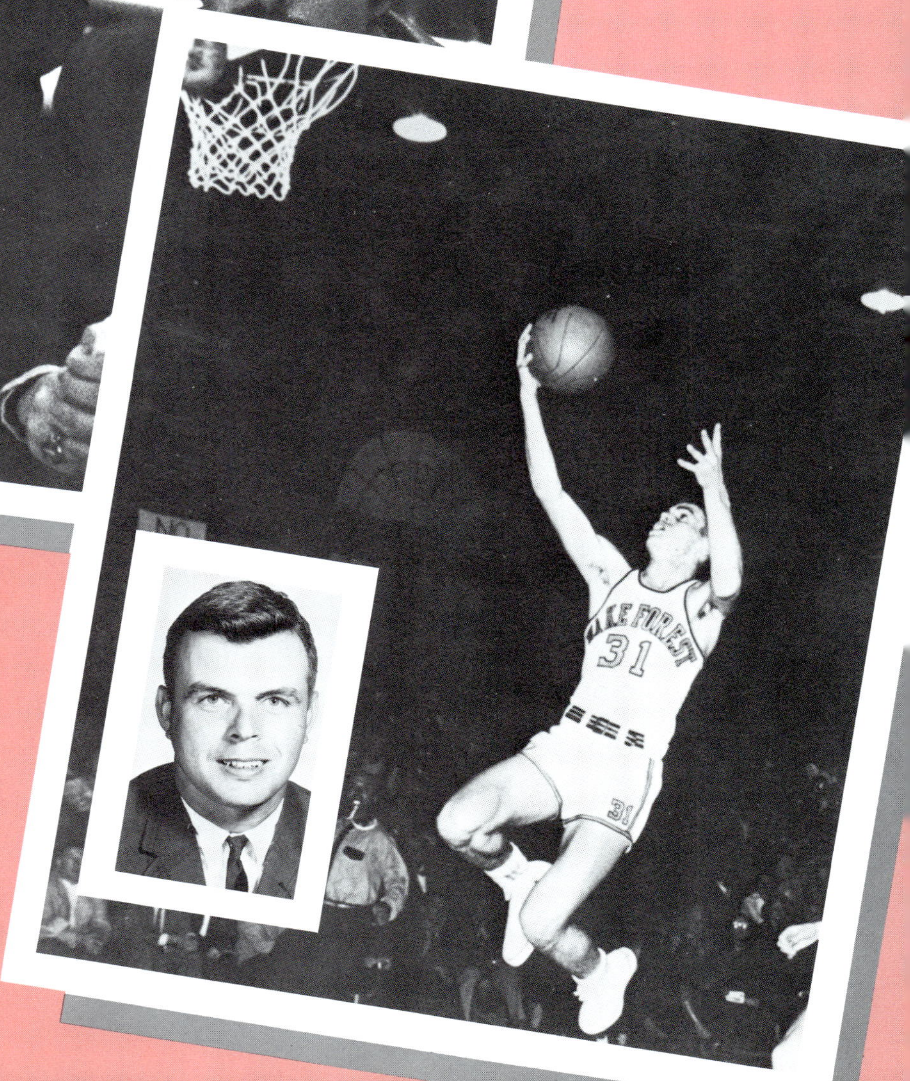
31

ACC BASKETBALL / THE '60s

'66

ACC teams were accustomed to playing against black players by the mid-1960s. Aside from a brief altercation between Wake Forest forward Dave Budd and Cincinnati All-America guard Oscar Robertson in the 1958 Dixie Classic, blacks had played without incident against ACC teams.

Oddly enough, though, the first black did not play in the ACC until 12 years after the Civil Rights Act of 1954.

Billy Jones, a 6-foot-1 guard from Towson, Md., broke the ACC's color barrier at Maryland. He did so with little fanfare, perhaps because such a breakthrough was so long in coming. After all, Jackie Robinson had broken baseball's color line nearly two decades earlier.

There had been some earlier attempts, however feeble, by ACC schools to recruit black basketball players.

Almost by accident, North Carolina nearly recruited a black in the first season of ACC basketball, 1953-54. Don Byrd, a center for the Fort Belvoir (Va.) team, mistakenly received a form recruiting letter from UNC Coach Frank McGuire.

"Birdie," said former Duke All-America Dick Groat, who coached the Fort Belvoir team that year, "is good enough to make the starting five on any college team in the United States."

McGuire had written Byrd to say that the coach would be interested in meeting the player when Ft. Belvoir played a benefit game against Duke in February of 1954. McGuire was unaware that Byrd did not have a high school diploma or that he was black.

ACC coaches and fans were certainly aware that blacks were worthy of athletic scholarships. Jesse Arnelle of Penn State received a standing ovation for his play in the 1949 Dixie Classic at Reynolds Coliseum. The great Robertson, as well as Johnny Green of Michigan State, opened the eyes of ACC coaches and players with their play in the 1958 Dixie Classic.

"Great Scott," N.C. State Coach Case said of Robertson. "I know a lot of Southern coaches who would like to pull a Branch Rickey with that boy."

The rest of the country had already recognized that blacks were making significant contributions on the basketball floor. The consensus All-America team of 1958 included Guy Rodgers of Temple, Robertson of Cincinnati, Wilt Chamberlain of Kansas, Elgin Baylor of Seattle and Bob Boozer of Kansas State, all black players.

UNC Coach Dean Smith might have made the ACC's first legitimate attempt to recruit a black. In 1962, Smith's first season in Chapel Hill, he recruited Lou Hudson of Greensboro. Hudson, instead, attended Minnesota and went on to a long and prosperous career in the NBA.

N.C. State was the first ACC school to allow a black to compete in intercollegiate athletics when Irwin Holmes of Durham earned a varsity tennis letter in 1960. His breakthrough did not go without incident, as Clemson switched its home match with State to Raleigh rather than have Holmes play at Clemson.

Two years later, Daryl Hill became the first black football player in the ACC at Maryland. By then, Maryland basketball Coach Bud Millikan had made it known he would recruit black players. "We've had some out now and then for freshman teams," Millikan said, adding they "apparently just weren't good enough to make the team."

Sonny Jackson, a baseball and basketball star at nearby

Tigers' Mr. Everything
Choppy Patterson played guard for Clemson during basketball season from 1960-62. The rest of the time he played baseball, majored in pre-med and even served as student body president. Patterson once scored 60 points and had 28 rebounds for Piedmont (S.C.) High. His 19-point scoring average in '61 fell to 8.8 in '63 after he fractured his pelvis in an auto accident.

Montgomery Blair High School in Silver Springs, Md., was one of the first blacks to be recruited by Maryland. But Jackson chose instead to play professional baseball with the Houston Colt .45s and was an infielder for 12 seasons in the major leagues.

Millikan next wanted John Austin of DeMatha High School in Hyattsville, Md., to be the first black, but Austin also declined the offer. Chris Richmond, a transfer from Citrus (Fla.) Junior College, was ready to break the barrier for the 1965 season, but he was cut from the team before playing in a varsity game.

Then came Jones and Julius "Pete" Johnson. Jones was a product of Towson (Md.) High School who also made a recruiting visit to Michigan. Johnson hailed from Fairmont Heights High School near the Maryland campus. He also considered attending Syracuse, where he could have teamed in the backcourt with Dave Bing.

Johnson was held out of the 1965-66 season to improve his

ACC BASKETBALL / THE '60s

academic standing. Thus, Jones became the league's first black player.

"It so happened that Billy Jones was a very fine young man," Millikan recalled years later. "There was never any problem that I was aware of, or have been aware of. Really, I had forgotten, or hadn't realized, that he was the first black to play in the ACC. Our housing situation, our food situation, there was just no problem. So I didn't think anything about it."

In his first varsity season, Jones averaged 2.8 points while playing in 16 of Maryland's 25 games during 1965-66. His scoring average increased to 11.6 as a junior, then was 10.2 as a senior.

Once Jones broke the barrier, other ACC schools quickly followed. In 1967, C.B. Claiborne of Danville, Va., was the first black to play at Duke. A year later, Charlie Scott and Norwood Todmann of New York were the first black scholarship players at North Carolina and Wake Forest, respectively. Al Heartley of Clayton, N.C., broke the color barrier at N.C. State in 1969, then Craig Mobley of Chester, S.C., and Casey Manning of Dillon, S.C., did so for Clemson and South Carolina, respectively, in 1971. Virginia was the last league team to play a black when Al Drummond of Waverly, N.Y., made the team for the 1972 season.

Only Scott among the first group of blacks established himself as an outstanding player over three years. He was a first-team All-ACC performer and an All-America in 1969 and 1970. Scott finished second to South Carolina guard John Roche, who was white, in the 1969 and 1970 voting for ACC Player of the Year. Scott was a loser by 17 votes (56 to 39) in '69 and by four votes (51 to 47) in 1970. Both times, Scott claimed he lost the vote because of his race.

Cries of racism in the ACC lost some validity the following year when Wake Forest guard Charlie Davis, a black, was named ACC Player of the Year by a vote of 86 to 30 over Roche. Counting Davis, blacks were then named Player of the Year 14 of the next 17 ACC seasons.

Not long after the league's integration, every team's roster included blacks. By 1977, all of the first-team All-ACC players were black. In 1981 and again in 1983, blacks captured nine of the 10 all-league spots. By 1984, nearly 50 percent of the league's players were black, and in 1986 Maryland had the first all-black team. Maryland's Bob Wade became the league's first black coach for the 1987 season.

Those figures provide a stark contrast to the 1966 season when Jones was the league's lone black. Duke again fielded a magnificent team under Bubas and advanced to the Final Four for the third time in four years. But the Blue Devils were the lone all-white team in the Final Four.

Seniors Jack Marin and Steve Vacendak teamed with juniors Bob Verga and Bob Riedy, all of whom welcomed 6-foot-7 sophomore center Mike Lewis from Missoula, Mont., to the starting lineup. Rival coaches claimed that Lewis had been wrestling broncos all summer in Montana to prepare for the rough-and-tough life of rebounding in the ACC. Lewis jumped right into the fire and led the league in rebounding with 11 a game. He also averaged 13.9 points.

"The other day," Bubas said early in the season, "Chuck Daly, our assistant coach, was telling the little fellows on the club to shine Lewis' shoes and to serve him coffee—because he's the guy who's going to get the ball for you."

Although this Duke team was not as deep as the previous three Blue Devil squads, its starting five was as sound as any in the country. Duke finished first in the ACC's regular season race for the fourth straight season and captured the ACC Tournament championship for the third time in four years. Over that period, the Blue Devils posted a 99-17 record, including a sparkling 61-7 ACC mark.

One of those seven losses came early and proved to be one of two monumental upsets of the season. The Blue Devils dropped a 73-71 decision to a South Carolina team that would win only four conference games and finish the season 11-13.

After Frank Standard's field goal with 15 seconds to play clinched the biggest victory in South Carolina's basketball history, students poured onto the court and cut down the nets.

"Now I can go fishing," said South Carolina Coach Frank McGuire.

Speculation of the day was that Duke was looking past the lowly Gamecocks to a two-game showdown with two-time, defending national champion and No. 1-ranked UCLA. The first game was scheduled for Duke Indoor Stadium on Dec. 10, 1965, with the scene shifting to the Charlotte Coliseum the following night.

"By Christmas I'll either be drowning myself or throwing one huge party," Duke's Bubas said.

The party must have been pretty big because sixth-ranked Duke handed UCLA an 82-66 defeat in Durham, then downed the Bruins 94-75 in Charlotte. Ten days later, the Blue Devils turned back third-ranked Michigan 100-93 in overtime in the Wolverines' back yard of Detroit.

In the first meeting against UCLA, Duke beat the Bruins where the Devils had lost to them in the NCAA championship two years earlier—on the backboards. Duke held a 58-34 rebounding advantage with Lewis getting 21.

"Yes, we were after Lewis," UCLA Coach John Wooden said of his recruiting efforts. "We called him up several times, but every time we did, (then Duke assistant coach) Bucky Waters answered the telephone."

(As a footnote to that first game, Pete Maravich of Southwood [Va.] College scored 27 points, but his team dropped a 106-77 decision to the Duke freshman team in a preliminary game.)

Following Duke's victory, Bubas addressed his team.

"I told them I knew how happy they were and they knew how happy I was," he said. "Then I asked them if they were men enough to forget it and dedicate themselves to one more great game."

And would a neutral site in Charlotte help the Bruins' cause?

"Neutral court?" Wooden said. "Well, that's sort of like our football team playing Notre Dame in Rome."

UCLA held its own on the boards during the second game, but the Bruins could not handle the outstanding shooting of Marin and Verga. Marin scored 23 points on 10-of-15 shooting, and Verga scored 22 on 10-of-14 shooting.

In addition to excellent rebounding and shooting, Duke was superb handling the Bruins' full-court pressure. In 75 possessions over the two games, Duke had the ball stolen by UCLA in the backcourt only six times. At one point, with Vacendak doing most of the ball handling, Duke went 32 straight possessions without a turnover. To beat UCLA's press, Duke's starters had practiced bringing the ball up the court against six reserves.

"Duke never lost its poise," said Wooden, whose club would lose more games that season (eight) than it would in the next seven combined (five).

The Blue Devils kept their poise through a 13-game streak in which they beat opponents by an average of 16 points and solidified their No. 1 national ranking. One of those victories came over Michigan after Duke trailed by 14 points early in the second half.

For nearly two months, Duke stood atop the college basketball world. Then the Blue Devils tumbled after blowing a 19-point lead in a 94-90 loss at West Virginia. The Mountaineers were coached by former Duke and Bubas assistant Bucky Waters, who was carried off the court on his players' shoulders.

Two weeks later, Duke was stunned again, 99-98—this time by a Wake Forest team that finished last in the league and won only eight of 26 games. It was easily the biggest victory in the one-year term of Demon Deacons' Coach Jackie Murdock, whose club rallied from 15 points down and trailed 90-87 with 13 seconds remaining in regulation. But Bob Leonard made the first of two free throws, and teammate Paul Crinkley followed the missed second shot to force overtime.

Wake Forest won in overtime when Marin and Lewis fouled out for Duke. The Blue Devils would not lose again until the Final Four.

While the focus of the ACC's regular season was on Duke, there were other noteworthy incidents in 1966. North Carolina moved into Carmichael Auditorium and defeated William & Mary 82-68 in the first game at the 8,800-seat arena.

In the third game played at Carmichael, junior forward Bob Lewis scored a school-record 49 points in UNC's 115-80 win over Florida State. The point total was the third highest in ACC history, as Lewis made 18 of 25 field goal attempts and 13 of 16 free throws before leaving the game with 2:01 remaining.

Twenty-two years later, UNC would close the Carmichael doors to men's college basketball after winning 169 of 189 games in the building that came to be known as "Blue Heaven."

Winston-Salem's Memorial Coliseum was closed down on the night of Dec. 11. Two transformers in the main lobby caught fire during the first half of Wake Forest's game against N.C. State, and more than 7,000 spectators were evacuated so firemen could put out the blaze.

State was leading 23-13 with 10:02 remaining in the half when the lights went out. The game was resumed at that point on Feb. 23 in Winston-Salem, and the Wolfpack posted a 101-75 victory.

The off-the-court news centered around South Carolina and Coach Frank McGuire. The Gamecocks, as well as Clemson, were fined $2,500 by the ACC for having too many athletes on scholarship. Because both schools were five scholarships over the 140 limit for all sports, they were allowed to have only 135 scholarship athletes for the 1966-67 academic year.

McGuire exchanged heated words with Duke's Bubas during the Blue Devils' 41-38 victory in Durham on Feb. 14.

"I was talking to Curly White (one of the officials) and he (Bubas) came over and interfered," McGuire said. "I told him to mind his own business."

As McGuire left the court following the game, he was twice pelted by apples, hit once in the leg and once in the neck. Why apples? Duke had long sold fruit at its concession stands.

Duke survived the game against South Carolina without Bob Verga, who was serving the second of a two-game suspension for a curfew violation. Riedy had also been suspended for Duke's previous game against Virginia.

Both players were back and Duke was at full strength by ACC Tournament time. Excitement for the postseason event was at an all-time high. This was the first year in which each school sold its full allotment of tickets to the Tournament, and there was no public sale.

Duke rolled past Wake Forest 103-73 in the first round and

ACC Pressed in two colors by Maravich.

The '60s

N.C. State

Press Maravich wanted to go to his grave with a basketball by his side.

"He was all consumed with basketball," says Tommy Mahaffey, who played for Maravich at Clemson. "That game was everything to him, and to his family. He just lived basketball."

Growing up in Pittsburgh, Maravich played basketball in the streets, shooting a tin can stuffed with paper and wrapped in black tape into a goal made of an apple basket. In 17 seasons of coaching at Clemson, N.C. State, Louisiana State and Appalachian State, Maravich's trademark was his towel-chewing on the bench. Upon his retirement from coaching, he often carried a piece of chalk in his coat pocket, just in case an offense or defense needed further explanation.

Maravich played at Davis & Elkins College in West Virginia, then professionally with the Detroit Eagles, Youngstown Bears and Pittsburgh Ironmen of the National Basketball League, which later became the NBA. He started coaching at the high school level and later was a pro scout. If there was a way, Maravich certainly had the will to serve as a counselor at any summer basketball camp in the country. Clinics were his specialty.

Maravich gave the rest of the ACC a clinic during the 1965 season at N.C. State. Two games into the season, Everett Case turned the coaching reins over to Maravich, who many thought to be the legendary coach's hand-picked successor. The N.C. State program had slipped some in Case's final years, partly because of the point-shaving scandals earlier in the decade and partly because of Case's failing health.

When Maravich took control, he made only a few subtle changes. He used a few Xs to implement more of a fast-break offense, then a few Os to show his team the finer points of a pressing defense. The results were astounding. The Wolfpack won its first 11 games under Maravich's tutelage. By season's end, N.C. State had a 21-5 record and its first ACC Tournament title since 1959.

The Wolfpack, wrote Bill Ballenger of *The Charlotte News*, was "the motliest gang of backyard athletes" ever to win the ACC. "(Maravich) had a guard who was offered only one scholarship (Larry Worsley), a pot-bellied, bald Korean War veteran (Larry Lakins) at center, an Ivy League transfer (Pete Coker) with lungs so under-sized he could play only 10 minutes at a time between

ACC BASKETBALL / THE '60s

Maravich took his intensity out on his towels—orange ones for six years at Clemson and red ones for four more at State.

rests and a thieving guard named 'Wild Horse' (Eddie Biedenbach) who couldn't shoot."

Maravich was best able to display his immense coaching skills at N.C. State, where he had enough talent to compete equally with other ACC schools. His second Wolfpack team had an 18-9 record before he left for LSU as part of a package with son Pete. Prior to his arrival at N.C. State, Maravich coached six seasons at Clemson, where he had overmatched personnel.

"No speed, no height, no bench, no stamina," Maravich said in describing his 1961 Clemson team. Maravich's problems stemmed from poor recruiting at a school that seemed to have little interest in basketball.

"I believe I'd give my right arm for a big man," he once said. "No, I'll change that. I'd give both of them."

Maravich gave neither, but he did throw all his eggs into one season's recruiting basket in 1962. He started an all-sophomore lineup in the ACC Tournament and marched Clemson to the championship game, where the Tigers lost to Wake Forest. Clemson had not previously won an ACC Tournament game and had not won a post-season game in 23 years.

That and the ACC title team at N.C. State were Maravich's crowning moments in coaching, although his 1970 LSU team was 22-10 and advanced to the semifinals of the NIT. His overall coaching record was 183-259.

"I don't believe if you lose that you are a loser," Maravich said during a 1983 interview. "If I did, I would have had a bunch of losers at Clemson. And I didn't. Every one of them graduated and is successful. They've all got nice jobs and they're all married. There are no divorces in their families. No hangups. I'm proud of that."

Maravich was also proud of his unusual first name, his keen sense of humor and, above all, for being the dad of Hall of Famer Pete.

His Yugoslavian parents christened him Peter at birth, but Maravich changed it to Press when he began delivering the Pittsburgh Press newspaper as a youngster. "Peter was a fistfight name," Maravich explained.

When Maravich was hung in effigy by Clemson fans during the 1960 season, he said, "I'm glad to see somebody around here is that interested in basketball." The following day, Maravich found a calendar from a mortuary in his mailbox and responded, "At least someone thinks I'll make it through the year."

Adding to Maravich's charm was a voice that, according to Ballenger, sounded like "a 45 (rpm record) on 78 when he really got worked up." For the longest time, Maravich was in a class with Johnny Unitas and Pete Rose as the only sports figures still wearing a crew cut.

Once, about 3 a.m. following an ACC Tournament game in Raleigh, Maravich had an urge for a cup of coffee. He gathered with friends in the hotel lobby, noticed it was raining outside and summoned a cab. Minutes later, Maravich dashed through the rain to enter the cab, slammed the door and told the driver to take him to the all-night diner—directly across the street.

Maravich kept that sense of humor through some difficult days of coaching at LSU and Appalachian State and a fatal illness. He had cancer in his later years and died in April of 1987.

"He always said he wanted to be buried with a basketball by his side," Pete said just two weeks before he himself died of a heart attack in January of 1988. "But, by the time he died, basketball was no longer the focus of his life. We had turned our lives over to Christ. He didn't need to be buried with a basketball by his side because God had really touched his heart, just as He has touched mine." ■

ACC BASKETBALL / THE '60s

was a heavy favorite to turn back UNC in the semifinals. But Tar Heel Coach Smith had other ideas about how to handle the Blue Devils.

UNC opened the game in a delay offense and continued to play that way throughout, sometimes keeping possession of the ball for as long as four minutes. By halftime, UNC had attempted only five field goals and trailed 7-5. Finally, with four seconds remaining in the game, Duke's Mike Lewis sank the second of two free throws to give the Blue Devils a 21-20 victory.

"I didn't want a good game, I wanted to win it," Smith said. "We thought we could win with this kind of game. It has won for us against other teams."

The Tar Heels, using only five players the entire game, actually held a 17-12 lead with 10:03 remaining. But Duke rallied to tie the game at 20, then Verga fouled UNC's Johnny Yokley with 1:40 to play. Yokley missed the free throw and Duke rebounded.

The Blue Devils held the ball until 16 seconds remained and called time out to set a final play. Verga was unable to shoot on the final play, so he passed the ball to Lewis, who was fouled under the basket by Bob Bennett.

Lewis missed his first free throw attempt, saying the basket appeared to be about the size of a dime. He made the second attempt for a 21-20 lead, and UNC could not get off a shot in the game's final four seconds.

"We won under the toughest of conditions, but it is a tribute to our courage and poise," Bubas said. "It's in the books for a coach to choose his style of play. If he wants to slow it down, that's his business. If we had lost, I told myself, I would have said the very same thing I'm telling you fellas right now. You can't be a cry baby."

The Duke-UNC stall game made the Blue Devils' 71-66 championship victory over N.C. State somewhat anti-climactic. All five Duke starters scored in double figures, while Riedy, Marin and Lewis each had at least 13 rebounds.

"That was balance and it was the kind of balance that we had to have tonight," said Bubas, whose club played in the championship for the sixth time in his seven years at Duke and won its fourth title.

Preparing for the NCAA Tournament was nothing new to Bubas and his Blue Devils, who survived an opening-round scare in Raleigh from an excellent St. Joseph's team coached by Jack Ramsay, 76-74. The second-round East Regional game was not as difficult for Duke, which registered a 91-81 victory over Syracuse. Once again, Duke placed all five starters in double figures. The Blue Devils employed an unusual 3-2 zone defense, with the 6-6 Marin playing at the top of the key. His presence prevented Syracuse from shooting open jump shots and throwing easy passes inside.

Syracuse All-America guard Dave Bing, who was held to 10 points, said: "Duke is the best team I've seen. I think they can go all the way. No team has stood up to us like they did."

In 1964, Duke had to deal with a near plane crash as it arrived in Kansas City for the Final Four. This time, the Blue Devils had no trouble as their plane landed safely in College Park, Md. Instead, there was a problem with Verga, who was slowed by the flu. He was hospitalized with a throat infection the entire week prior to Duke's semifinal meeting against Kentucky, which practiced without senior forward Larry Conley, also hospitalized with the flu.

Verga was not near full strength and scored only four points

A flu-ridden Bob Verga drives against Kentucky in 83-79 loss in 1966 Final Four semifinals.

Blue Devil assets in '66 were Steve Vacendak (taking a tumble above) and Jack Marin (lofting a hook at right).

(14 below his average) on 2-of-7 shooting in Kentucky's 83-79 victory. Conley was slightly better with 10 points.

"I don't want a man to go out of this room and write that I said we could have beaten Kentucky with a well Bobby Verga," Bubas said. "I don't know what the score would have been, but I know Bobby is a better ball player than he showed and we are a stronger club when he is well. We are better—a whole lot better—when he is healthy."

Marin and Lewis picked up some of the scoring slack for Duke with 29 and 21 points, respectively. But that was not enough to counter Kentucky's balance. Louie Dampier had 23 points and Pat Riley 19 for the Wildcats.

The Blue Devils rebounded, as did Verga with 15 points, to defeat Utah 79-77 for third place before Texas Western (now Texas-El Paso) stunned Kentucky to win the national championship.

"Naturally, we were keenly disappointed that we could not win the national championship," Bubas said, "but third place in a country as large as ours isn't bad."

ACC BASKETBALL / THE '60s

'67

It would be another 12 years before Duke returned to the Final Four. The Blue Devils slipped to 18-9 in 1967 and did not finish first in the ACC's regular season for the first time in five years, finishing second with a 9-3 league record.

North Carolina lost only two league games to claim first place in the regular season. The Tar Heels' rise to the top represented a changing of the guard in the ACC, one that would have the rest of the league shooting at UNC for most of the next 21 years.

There was another significant change in 1967. After five years in which there were few fights and little fan violence, the league erupted in a flurry of off-the-court incidents.

The fireworks were set off when the ACC ruled that 6-foot-9, 230-pound sophomore center Mike Grosso was ineligible to play basketball at South Carolina. Grosso had scored 789 on his college board scores, thus falling below the 800 necessary to receive an athletic scholarship under ACC guidelines. The 800 rule had been adopted by the ACC Faculty Chairmen in May of 1966, one year after Grosso enrolled at South Carolina.

Instead of accepting one of 40 scholarship offers from other schools where he would have been eligible, Grosso elected to attend South Carolina and pay his own way. Duke University, and Athletic Director Eddie Cameron, suspected that Grosso was getting financial assistance from South Carolina and asked for an investigation of the situation by the ACC.

Grosso was an exceptional talent. He led his high school team to the New Jersey state championship. In a first-round tournament game, Grosso scored 43 points and had 45 rebounds. His senior season of high school, Grosso averaged 30 points and 31 rebounds a game. As a non-scholarship player, Grosso averaged 22.7 points for South Carolina's freshman team. In one freshman game against Duke, Grosso scored 29 points and had 41 rebounds.

Grosso never completed his freshman season of play, however. He suffered an arm cut while opening a window and needed 50 stitches.

As for Grosso's investigation, the ACC found that South Carolina had not conducted illegal tryouts as charged. There was no proof that South Carolina illegally arranged testing for Grosso to reach 800 on his board scores. But the ACC claimed that Grosso's middle-class parents could not afford to pay Grosso's way to South Carolina.

"I'm in a rat race, but the rats are winning," South Carolina Coach Frank McGuire said of the investigation.

Grosso said his uncle, the owner of Grosso's Bar & Grill in New Jersey, paid his expenses at South Carolina. After ACC officials visited the Grosso family in New Jersey, they found evidence to suggest Grosso was being helped from other sources.

On Oct. 29, 1966, Grosso was declared ineligible by the ACC Executive Committee. Dr. Ralph E. Fadum of N.C. State, a member of the Committee, read the league's official statement: "Any student athlete enrolled or incoming at the University of South Carolina whose eligibility is questioned (by the Commission) will be withheld from competition unless and until it is established to the satisfaction of the Commission that there has been no violation in each individual case."

In essence, it appeared the ACC was saying an athlete could be assumed guilty until proven innocent.

McGuire steamed over the decision.

He said the decision was directed at him "and is being taken out on this boy." He said the conference was lined up against South Carolina and charged Duke with starting the action. McGuire also hinted at possible court action.

McGuire's comments drew a reprimand from the University of South Carolina.

In the aftermath of the decision, the ACC ruled any school that "considers it inadvisable" for its basketball team to play at South Carolina may attempt to reschedule the game on a neutral court. Should it not be possible to arrange that, the league ruled, the game would be canceled by mutual consent.

On Dec. 13, 1966, Duke and South Carolina agreed to cancel its two scheduled games that season.

"We are not mad," said Duke's Cameron, "but it is the feeling of the Duke administration that this incident has grown out of proportion and a cooling off period is desirable."

On Jan. 9, 1967, the NCAA completed its investigation of the South Carolina athletic program and declared Grosso ineligible. The NCAA cited USC for the following infractions:

- During the year 1965-66, Marvin Bass, the university's director of athletics and head football coach, provided money to three players who were academically ineligible.
- From the fall of 1965 through the first semester of 1966-67, Mike Grosso's expenses "were paid by a corporation upon which he was neither naturally, nor legally dependent."
- In July, 1965, a representative of South Carolina's athletic department arranged a game in which four prospects were given a tryout.

The NCAA placed South Carolina on probation for two years and prohibited the Gamecocks from participating in any television program subject to control of the NCAA.

The biggest loss, as far as McGuire was concerned, was Grosso's eligibility.

"There's no doubt how much he would have helped us," McGuire said. "He'd have been our leader, the fellow who wins those tight games for you, like Larry Miller does for North Carolina . . . He is like an Art Heyman, or a Wilt Chamberlain or a Billy Cunningham as far as his value to the team is concerned."

Grosso, with encouragement from McGuire, transferred to Louisville, where he led the Cardinals to the NIT two straight seasons. While at Louisville, Grosso injured his knee and was never a dominant player. Grosso eventually had an undistinguished career in the American Basketball Association, playing 25 games for the Pittsburgh Condors in 1972.

Just as he had during his UNC days, McGuire helped promote rivalries. At UNC, the most heated rivalries were with N.C. State, Duke and Wake Forest. At South Carolina, the war was with Clemson.

During the 1966 game at Clemson, Gamecock and Tiger players had engaged in a brief exchange of punches. McGuire, who claimed he was taunted by Clemson football players behind his bench, challenged any and all of them to a fight following the game.

When Clemson played at South Carolina in 1967, the Tigers

ACC BASKETBALL / THE '60s

were showered by paper cups. At one point, referee Joe Mills was hit in the head by a bag of peanuts. Referee Charlie Eckman threatened twice to clear Carolina Field House of spectators if the throwing of debris continued.

Donnie Walsh, coaching South Carolina while McGuire was in Houston pleading Grosso's case to the NCAA Council, appealed to Eckman not to clear the Coliseum.

"On second thought, I decided I couldn't do that to Donnie," Eckman said. "Donnie had been a perfect gentleman on the bench and hadn't said a word to me all night. For Donnie's sake, I had a change of heart.

"But you can't imagine how bad those students were. Man, they threw everything on the floor—peanuts, ice, fruit, paper cups, money—you name it, they threw it out there. But the worst thing of all were their remarks from the stands . . . They were yelling something about (Vic) Bubas and he wasn't even there. Can you imagine that?"

The incidents of unrest were not limited to South Carolina during 1967. In January, officials George Conley and Roy Owen left the Maryland playing floor with 1:15 remaining in the game and declared the Terps a winner over N.C. State.

Maryland led 59-55 when Conley called a double technical foul on State Coach Norm Sloan. After Maryland's Jay McMillen made one of the two technical free throws, Conley walked to the scorer's table, put down the ball and said the game was over and the 60-55 score would stand.

When McMillen missed the second technical foul shot, Sloan reportedly said to Conley, "Isn't that too bad?"

Sloan reportedly went to the officials' locker room following the game, in violation of ACC rules, and confronted Conley, a former Kentucky state senator. ACC Commissioner Jim Weaver investigated the incident but took no action against Sloan.

A few days later, minutes after UNC defeated N.C. State 79-78 in Chapel Hill, a fight broke out involving players and spectators. Nick Trifunovich of State and Bob Lewis of UNC exchanged punches, then players from both teams poured onto the court, as well as fans. Chapel Hill police quickly restored order and no arrests were made.

"We haven't had anything like this happen around here in a long time and I'm sure it's not going to happen again," UNC Coach Smith said. "It wouldn't have happened this time if the students hadn't rushed out on the floor to congratulate our players. Before anyone knew it, they became involved in the incident."

In late February, Clemson and UNC were involved in a brief flurry of fisticuffs near the end of a game at the Charlotte Coliseum. One week later at Clemson, tempers flared early in the Tigers' game against Virginia. With 8:17 remaining in the first half, referee Joe Mills ejected Virginia Coach Bill Gibson.

The league's unrest helped lead to the resignation of official Charlie Eckman after 20 years in the ACC.

"The players and coaches have been great, the best in my 20 years in the league," Eckman said, "but the crowd behavior has been the worst ever.

"We've had to take a lot of abuse from students and fans this year. It doesn't bother me. I'm used to it. But I don't see how some of the other guys stand it. Something has to be done about the crowds. It's just up to the school presidents to control the students, but so far they haven't done it.

"Look, I don't mind the booing and all that. It's part of the game, part of the color and atmosphere. What I mind is the things they throw: Beer cans, hot dogs, soda bottles, rolled-up programs, hot pennies . . . Yeah, hot pennies. The kids at Duke—high-class kids—heat pennies with matches and throw them at opposing players. At Maryland, when they don't like a call they throw rubber balls out of the stands."

Commissioner Weaver stepped in, directing the league's officials to strictly enforce the rules regarding coaches' conduct. He also asked the league's athletic directors to help control crowd behavior.

The signal that Duke's reign over the league was ending came in the opening weeks of the season. First, the Blue Devils had a return engagement with UCLA. After defeating the No. 1-ranked Bruins in Durham and Charlotte the previous season, Duke had to play UCLA twice in Los Angeles. The Bruins were again the nation's top-ranked team and featured 7-1 sophomore Lew Alcindor, who opened his college career by scoring 56 points against Southern California.

"I don't mind the booing and all that. It's part of the game, part of the color and atmosphere. What I mind is the things they throw: Beer cans, hot dogs, soda bottles, rolled-up programs, hot pennies . . ."

☐ **Official Charlie Eckman**

For psychological reasons, Duke coach Vic Bubas told his Blue Devils that Alcindor was "6-foot-13, not 7-foot-1."

No psychological warfare would have worked for Duke against UCLA, which blasted the Blue Devils 88-54 and 107-87. Alcindor had 19 points and 16 rebounds in the first game, followed by a 38-point, 22-rebound effort.

Duke won only half of its first eight games, then faced Penn State without nine players who were suspended for breaking curfew. Starters Mike Lewis, Tim Kolodziej, Dave Golden and Bob Riedy, plus reserves Warren Chapman, Tony Barone, Jim Liccardo, Ron Wendelin and Joe Kennedy were not allowed to suit up for the game at Duke Indoor Stadium.

Bob Verga scored 38 points in Duke's 89-84 victory. Stuart McKaig, Steve Vandenberg, Fred Lind and C.B. Claiborne all started for the first time in their careers. The only substitute Duke used was Bob Francis, who suited up for the first time after practicing with the team all season. Dale Stubbs was recruited from the student body, but did not play. Bob Matheson, an All-America football player at Duke, had agreed to suit up at halftime if the seven players dressed ran into foul trouble. But he was not needed.

Duke's slippage in 1967 could be attributed to its difficult non-conference schedule and the rise of North Carolina as a power. The Blue Devils dropped non-league games to Virginia Tech, Ohio State and UCLA twice. Two of their three league losses were to the Tar Heels.

Bubas actually made light of Duke's slide when he said at midseason, "If you ever hang me in effigy, please hang me near the library . . . It's more academic that way."

UNC's rise to the top of the ACC was most surprising since Smith began the season with sophomores Rusty Clark, Dick Grubar and Bill Bunting in the starting lineup. As the season would prove, however, these were not ordinary sophomores teaming with senior Bob Lewis and junior Larry Miller.

How does a Demon Deacon spell fun? H-A-M.

The '60s

Wake Forest

Perhaps the biggest upset in the history of Wake Forest basketball was the one time Bones McKinney was at a loss for words against Princeton in the 1963 Kentucky Invitational.

He had no time to stop and talk. Kicking his foot high in the air, McKinney's loafer flew off and landed at the foul line at Kentucky's Memorial Coliseum. Luckily, McKinney's Demon Deacons had the ball at the other end of the court.

If his team could have practiced what McKinney always preached—"Pass the ball, look for the good shot," he'd say—he would have had time to sneak onto the court, retrieve the shoe and return to the bench without anyone noticing. But as he ran out to pick up the shoe, a ballpoint pen dropped from his shirt pocket. Tucking the shoe under one arm and grabbing the pen, he looked up to see two Princeton players headed toward him on a fast break.

McKinney crouched into the same defensive stance he taught his players and turned the Princeton fast break into a 2-on-1 situation. Princeton scored the basket, and McKinney was assessed a technical foul. But he added a literal footnote to the history of ACC basketball.

"Sometimes I hate myself for all those antics on the bench," McKinney once said. "Some people think I rehearse them, but if that were so I'd be in Hollywood. I just want to win. That's the whole story."

For eight seasons (1958-65) as head coach at Wake Forest, McKinney not only established himself as the ACC's original showman but also produced winning basketball teams.

McKinney's sideline antics were worth the price of admission. He always sported bright red socks and a bow tie for good luck, and placed a bucket of water and dipper beneath his seat to keep his thirst quenched. A gangly man of 6-foot-6, he towered over other coaches, officials and often his players.

He occasionally peeled his sport coat and tossed it into the stands. He was known to throw a clipboard on the floor, race to the scorer's table several times a game, leap to his feet to protest an official's call, carry on conversations with fans and cheerleaders and shout until he was hoarse.

"Getting off the bench is a spontaneous action with me," McKinney said during the 1964 season. "That's not good—and I'm going to try to stop it. I'll put a seatbelt on, and I'll buckle it, at least for home games. I've taken a look at myself and this is what I want to do. It's tough to be honest with yourself, but sometimes you have to do it."

McKinney wore the seatbelt in Wake Forest's game against Maryland on Jan. 20, 1964. But when Wake Forest lost a 12-point lead in the first half, he unbuckled for good.

Against St. Bonaventure in the 1961 NCAA East Regional semifinals in Charlotte, McKinney was the Deacons' sixth man. Early in the game, the ball rolled out of bounds in front of the Wake Forest bench. McKinney picked it up and threw it downcourt to Billy Packer, who dribbled to the foul line and sank a jump shot. Amazingly, the play went unnoticed by the two officials and contributed to Wake's 72-67 victory.

Despite his flair for the dramatic, McKinney's talent was best reflected by his teams that were drilled in the fundamentals of strong defense and fast-break offense. He was recognized by colleagues as the master strategist in the early days of the ACC, first as an assistant to Wake Coach Murray Greason for five seasons, then as the Deacons' head man. He produced Wake Forest's ACC Tournament championships in 1961 and 1962, with the Deacons advancing to the NCAA Final Four in '62.

Along the way, McKinney captured the fancy of an entire league. What else was expected of someone who was born on New Year's Day (1919), married on Christmas Day (1941) and delighted in telling people his initials were HAM?

Horace Albert McKinney was born in tiny Lowland, N.C., but moved to Durham at age 5. He dropped out of high school after the 10th grade and for two years worked in a Durham silk mill, hung out at the corner drugstore and played basketball at the YMCA.

"When the late Paul Sykes convinced me to go back to school, it turned my life around," said McKinney, who was an honor student when he graduated from Durham High School in 1940.

By McKinney's senior year he was also 6-5 and the star on a team that won 73 straight games from 1937 through 1941. Several of those victories were against college freshman squads, and others were in regional and national tournaments.

During the 1940 Eastern Interscholastic High and Prep School Tournament in Glens Falls, N.Y., McKinney began displaying his talents—as a player and showman. When a foul was called against him, McKinney got down on his knees to beg. The fans went wild, but when the official turned to see what was happening, McKinney was tying his shoes. At the conclusion of the tournament, McKinney was presented a trophy with the inscription, "The Clown Prince of Basketball."

McKinney's nickname did not come from his slender build. Rather, he was cast as "Beau Brummel Bones" in a school-play version of "A Midsummer Night's Dream," and "Bones" stuck. McKinney kept the nickname because he said Horace sounded too much like "horrors."

Following high school, McKinney headed off to N.C. State University on a scholarship for "deserving boys of Durham County."

McKinney proved himself deserving when, as a sophomore in 1942, he was All-Southern Conference and led the league in scoring. McKinney often thanked referees for calls against him, checked with the scorekeeper to make sure he was given credit for a basket, gave himself audible pep talks while running down the floor and made faces at officials. He often yelled out "swish" just before a shot went into

McKinney's antics resulted from one simple urge: "I just want to win."

the basket.

McKinney was drafted into the Army late in 1942. By the time he enrolled at the University of North Carolina four years later, his jersey No. 5 was retired at Fort Bragg, N.C. He was an instant star at UNC, joining the Tar Heels in January of '46 and leading them to the NCAA championship game, a 43-40 loss to Oklahoma A&M.

He then took a shot at professional basketball with the Washington Capitals and served as player-coach in 1951 until the team was disbanded. He was picked up by the Boston Celtics and played with them two years. In six NBA seasons, McKinney averaged 9.8 points and 3.5 rebounds.

McKinney, of course, left his mark on the NBA in other ways. SPORT magazine once featured him as "Bones McKinney—Magnificent Screwball." In one of his first games with Washington, McKinney attempted and missed a shot, then complained that the ball was warped. Unable to convince the officials, McKinney grabbed the ball and rolled it the length of the court. Sure enough, to the delight of McKinney and the fans, the ball was lopsided.

After being reared a couple of miles from Duke University in Durham and attending N.C. State and UNC, it seemed only natural that McKinney completed his swing of the Big Four schools by coaching at Wake Forest.

McKinney retired from pro ball following the 1952 season, entered the Southeastern Baptist Seminary at Wake Forest, N.C., and assisted Greason as coach of the Demon Deacons. He eventually was ordained a Baptist minister and often preached at churches in the Wake Forest and Raleigh area. He once excused himself from a postgame press conference by saying, "Excuse me, fellas, but I have a wedding to conduct tonight."

As a coach, McKinney always sought an edge.

When Wake Forest played in South Carolina's old gymnasium, McKinney rarely gave a halftime talk to his players. "The walls were so thin, we just got real quiet and listened to what the South Carolina coach was saying," McKinney says. He was known to save a timeout by intentionally spilling water from his bucket onto the playing floor. As play was stopped to wipe up the water, his team rested.

Seeking more time with his wife, Edna, and his six children, McKinney left Wake Forest following the 1965 season with a 122-94 career record.

"I don't think we called it burnout back then, but that's what it was," McKinney said years later. "You get tired of going out there (recruiting) and it starts to show."

McKinney left, of course, with a quip and a smile that he brought back as coach of the Carolina Cougars in the old American Basketball Association and, later, as a TV commentator for ACC games. He settled in Hickory, N.C.

"I had a lifetime contract at Wake Forest," said McKinney, laughing about an agreement he had with former Wake Forest President Dr. Harold Tribble. "Then Dr. Tribble called me one day, pronounced me dead and fired me."

ACC BASKETBALL / THE '60s

East Carolina and his brother was a student at North Carolina. His new Tar Heel teammates were happy to have him aboard. They called Bunting "Pronto" because he was so quick.

A pivotal game for UNC in 1967 came on Jan. 7 in Durham when the Tar Heels escaped with a 59-56 victory over Duke. The game was tied at 56 in the final seconds as Smith frantically signaled for his team to call a timeout.

"I tried to call time so that we could set up one last shot," Smith said. "Then I saw Rusty Clark looking toward the basket and Larry Miller breaking under for a layup. I can't tell you how much I was hoping nobody had seen my timeout signal and fortunately they hadn't."

Miller made the layup, and Duke called for a timeout. The Blue Devils were out of timeouts, and a technical foul was called. UNC's Lewis then sank the technical to account for the final three-point margin.

Other than that close call, the Tar Heels virtually breezed through the regular season, stumbling in the conference only against Clemson in Charlotte and at South Carolina.

The Gamecocks and Duke were UNC's biggest challenges and were seeded second and third, respectively, in the ACC Tournament. Once South Carolina slipped past Maryland and Duke routed Virginia in the first round, the stage was set for a meeting between the two schools who refused to play each other during the regular season.

"We've been looking to Duke for a long time," South Carolina's McGuire said.

Added South Carolina player Al Salvadori: "We want to beat Duke for Mike Grosso. We feel that Grosso got a raw deal and we're going to win this one for big Mike."

In a game that was close throughout, Duke rode the 21-point performance of Bob Verga to a 69-66 victory.

"There was a lot of emotion out there. You know all that," Bubas said. "But the game was clean. We played hard. Both teams, both coaches. But it was a good game."

UNC, meanwhile, defeated N.C. State 56-53 and Wake Forest 89-79 to reach the championship game. Smith had his Tar Heels play volleyball during practice on Monday before the Tournament in an effort to relax them.

"I even got in there and played, too," Smith said. "And I made sure to have Rusty Clark on my side. He's some volleyball player."

UNC's tandem of Lewis and Miller led the Tar Heels to an 82-73 victory over Duke in the championship game. Lewis had 26 points and five rebounds, while Miller scored 32 to go with 11 rebounds. Miller, who had been in a late-season shooting slump, made 13 of 14 field goal attempts in the final.

All was not lost for Duke, which became the first team to represent the ACC in the National Invitational Tournament. Virginia had played in the NIT in 1941 and N.C. State participated in the postseason tournament in 1947, 1948 and 1951, when both schools were members of the Southern Conference. When the ACC was formed in 1953, league members decided that the ACC Tournament champion would be represented in the NCAA Tournament and no other school would be allowed to play in the postseason.

In December of 1966, the ACC Basketball Committee voted unanimously to allow the ACC Tournament runnerup to participate in the NIT, if invited. Cameron, head of the ACC Committee, said the NIT gained favor with the committee because of better supervision and more representative fields in recent years. Speculation existed that Bubas, who was being wooed by the University of Illinois, used his influence to have the rule changed.

Senior Bob Lewis (22) and junior Larry Miller (44) teamed to hoist UNC to the '67 ACC title and Final Four.

Clark, a 6-11 center, was considered the first major in-state recruit for Smith. "I used to follow the feats of York Larese and Doug Moe in those days and I just hoped that one day I could tag along in their footsteps," said the Fayetteville, N.C., native, who stepped in and averaged 13.9 points and 10.3 rebounds a game.

Of Grubar, a 6-3 guard from Schenectady, N.Y., Smith said, "It's like having a coach out there when he's on the floor. He's a good quarterback, our leader."

Bunting, a 6-8 forward from New Bern, N.C., had a difficult time in selecting a school to attend. His father and uncle were graduated athletes from Duke, his mother was a graduate of

UNC's Dean Smith stalks off court at Duke Indoor Stadium in '68 game amid cries from the crowd for a "T."

Duke was extended an invitation to the NIT following its championship loss to UNC and accepted. The Blue Devils' first opponent was Southern Illinois, which was led by All-America guard Walt Frazier. The Salukis won their 17th straight game and 22nd in 24 overall with a 72-63 decision over Duke at Madison Square Garden. Frazier scored 17 points and eventually led Southern Illinois to the NIT title.

Meanwhile, Smith had the Tar Heels playing volleyball again as they prepared to meet Princeton in the NCAA Tournament at College Park, Md. "I'm not superstitious," Smith said of the volleyball practice, "but then again I don't intend to fight it."

The Tar Heels had to fight for their lives against Princeton before winning 78-70 in overtime. UNC led by eight points with seven minutes remaining in regulation, but its Four Corners offense faltered and Princeton forced overtime. The Tar Heels continued to use their delay offense in overtime and made all 11 of their free throw attempts, including six by Grubar, to win.

"It took a lot of courage to lose the lead the way we did and then come back strong in overtime," Smith said.

Boston College, coached by Bob Cousy, was UNC's next opponent.

"I was scared in the early minutes of the first half," Smith said. "I thought Cousy himself was leading their fast break."

UNC survived an early surge by Boston College, got 31 points from Bob Lewis and turned back the Eagles, 96-80.

On Monday following the Saturday victory over Boston College, the Tar Heels were back on the Carmichael Auditorium practice floor . . . playing volleyball. "We've done the same the thing the past two weeks and we won," Smith said, "so we'll just continue that ritual."

As UNC prepared to meet Dayton in the Final Four in Louisville, much was made of the Tar Heels' possible matchup against powerful UCLA, which was to play Houston in the other semifinal game.

"I saw UCLA on TV when it played its first game with Duke on the West Coast," said Larry Miller. "How do you beat them? Ask Coach Smith. Would we slow it down? Perhaps. I'd give anything to get a chance at them."

That chance never came. UCLA held up its end of the bargain by defeating Houston and then topped Dayton for the national championship. Dayton, which got 34 points from Don May, rolled to the final with a 76-62 victory over the Tar Heels.

"Perhaps the prospect of meeting UCLA was in the back of our team's mind, although everything was done to prevent that kind of thinking," Smith said.

The letdown of losing to Dayton carried over to UNC's third-place game, and the Tar Heels lost 84-62 to Houston, which got 23 points and 16 rebounds from Elvin Hayes.

119

'68

With four starters returning from a team that just missed playing unbeaten UCLA for the national championship, North Carolina prepared again in 1968 to take aim at the Bruins. UCLA, which returned all five starters, including 7-foot-1 Lew Alcindor, was a good bet to repeat as national champs.

At UNC, the lone missing link from '67 was Bob Lewis. But the Tar Heels had an able replacement in sophomore guard Charlie Scott, the first black scholarship athlete at UNC. Thus, instead of Miller and Lewis, opponents had to deal with Miller and Scott.

"You want to know what flashes through my mind when we are doing a pretty good job of containing Larry Miller and Scott is tearing us apart?" asked Duke Coach Vic Bubas. "I'm thinking, we're getting Superman coverage and Zorro is killing us."

"Zorro" was the target of a most interesting and intense recruiting struggle between Smith and Davidson Coach Lefty Driesell. They both badly wanted Scott, who was extremely quick, an excellent passer and an outstanding shooter. Former Virginia Tech Coach Chuck Noe said of Scott's play on defense, "He'd make a fortune as a pickpocket in New York."

Scott, a native of New York City, did his prep schooling at Laurinburg Institute in North Carolina. His basketball skills were such that more than 100 college coaches recruited him. By the end of his junior year at Laurinburg, Scott had taken a special liking to Driesell and decided he would attend Davidson College.

Only after Scott committed to Davidson did Smith enter the recruiting process. Bill Currie, UNC's radio announcer at the time, recommended that Smith go to Laurinburg and watch Scott play. Smith liked what he saw, and, upon finding that Scott was an excellent student, began wooing the talented guard.

Scott's recruiting visit to Chapel Hill and an incident at a Davidson restaurant eventually led to his change of heart—

Rusty Clark, shooting over Duke's Mike Lewis, was one of four Tar Heel starters returning in 1968.

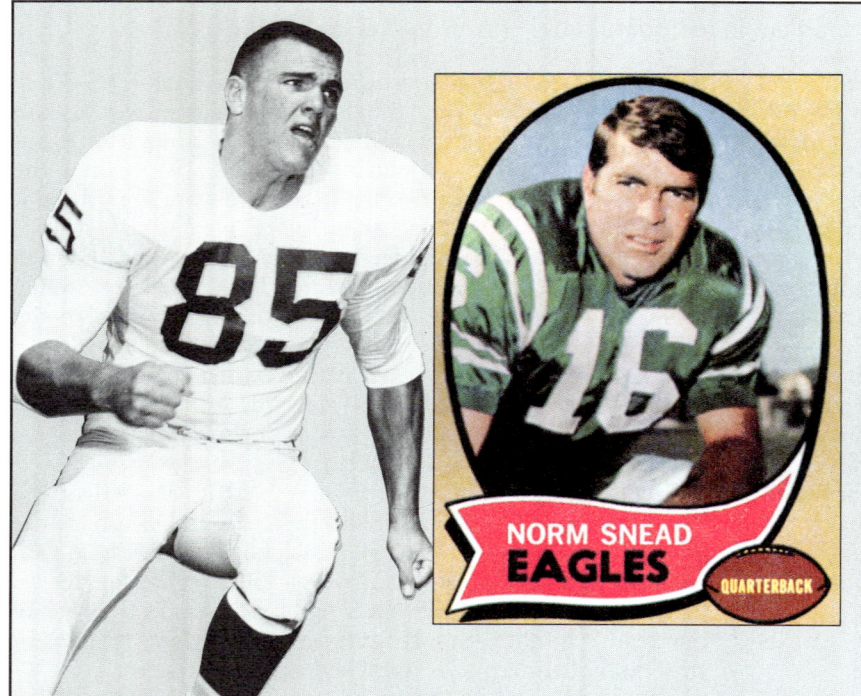

Two-Sport Deacons

Wake Forest's 1961 basketball roster included two players who later played in the National Football League. Norman Snead played four games in December of 1960 but left the team to play in the Blue-Gray and Senior Bowl all-star football games. Snead threw four TD passes in the Senior Bowl and never returned to hoops, moving on to an all-star career in Washington, Philadelphia and Minnesota. Bill Hull, meanwhile, averaged nearly 10 points and 10 rebounds during his junior season, and a year later was drafted by the Chicago Bears. The 6-6, 220-pounder set up the winning field goal with an interception for the Dallas Texans in their 20-17 win over Houston in the 1962 AFL championship game.

ACC BASKETBALL / THE '60s

State's Bill Kretzer dribbles during 14-minute lull against Duke in the '68 ACC semifinals while Coach Norm Sloan (background) rests his eyes.

and schools. Scott visited UNC during Chapel Hill's Jubilee Weekend.

"Looking back on it," Scott told *Carolina Court,* "I should have known that any school having the Temptations and Smokey Robinson and the Miracles for a weekend had a good shot at getting me."

Later, Frank McDuffie and his wife, Sammie, paid a visit to Davidson Assistant Coach Terry Holland in Davidson. McDuffie was Scott's basketball coach at Laurinburg, and his wife was an administrator at the school.

"Coach Holland took us to a restaurant there but they wouldn't serve us because we were black," Mrs. McDuffie said. "I think when Charlie heard about that, things turned more toward Chapel Hill."

Driesell didn't like Scott's decision. Scott tells of the time he was walking to a movie in Laurinburg and Driesell jumped out from behind some bushes to plead with Scott.

UNC downed Kentucky in the season's fourth game to give Smith a 4-1 record against Wildcat Coach Adolph Rupp, whose club ended the season ranked in the top 10. The 84-77 win sent the Tar Heels on a 20-game win streak, the school's longest since the 1957 club went unbeaten en route to the national championship, and the longest in the ACC since Duke won 20 straight in 1963.

Interest in UNC basketball was at a new peak. For the first time, there was no public sale of tickets to Tar Heel games. Those who were fortunate enough to have tickets saw Rusty Clark grab a school-record 30 rebounds, to go with 27 points, in an 83-60 victory over Maryland. Clark broke Billy Cunningham's school record of 28 rebounds and left the game with five minutes remaining.

UNC fans also saw the Tar Heels wear sweat bands for the first time, much like tennis players of the day. Smith ordered them after several players had difficulty handling the ball in preseason games.

South Carolina had the Tar Heels sweating all the way to the conclusion of their late February game in Carmichael Auditorium. South Carolina Coach Frank McGuire fielded a team known as the "Four Horsemen and A Pony." The Horsemen were seniors Skip Harlicka, Gary Gregor, Frank Standard and Jack Thompson, all of whom averaged in double figures. The Pony was sophomore forward Bobby Cremins, whom UNC's Smith said "is all basketball player. He's all hustle."

Cremins, a 59 percent shooter from the foul line, made 13 of 16 in the game and six of seven in the final 1:27 to lead South Carolina to an 87-86 victory in Larry Miller's last home game.

Three days later, UNC dropped a three-overtime decision at Duke by the same 87-86 score in a game that made seldom-used reserve Fred Lind a hero forever to Blue Devil fans.

Lind had scored only 11 points in six games as a sophomore and 12 points in 13 games prior to the UNC game in his junior season. But when Duke's Mike Lewis fouled out with 3:54 remaining in regulation, Bubas played a hunch and inserted Lind, who'd seen only brief action so far.

"Coach Bubas told me during the week that he might use me more in this one," Lind said. "I certainly didn't want to let him down."

Lind responded with an incredible performance. He played 31 of the game's 55 minutes, including all three overtime periods. By game's end, Lind had 16 points and nine rebounds. He sank two free throws to tie the game at 65 at the end of regulation and followed with a basket in the final seconds of the first overtime to tie the game. "It was a lucky shot," Lind

121

ACC BASKETBALL / THE '60s

Silk ties and pocket hankies aside, McGuire was a scrapper, turning dormant programs at UNC and USC into national powers.

McGuire a double dose of fun and fury.

Frank McGuire was dubbed "The Irishman" when he began coaching at St. John's five decades ago. His hair was a red tint, he dressed impeccably and he had all of the eloquent mannerisms of a dapper dandy.

During his nine seasons at North Carolina and 16 later at South Carolina, he still adjusted the cuffs on his shirt and straightened his tie the same way. He was a legend in his two stints in the ACC.

Just weeks before his magnificent home in Columbia, S.C., was destroyed by fire late in 1987, he showed a visitor the priceless memorabilia that marked his storied coaching career. Trophies, plaques, pictures and old film . . . all lost forever.

In one room was a closet filled with suits and sport jackets he wore only on trips "home" to New York, where he served as a consultant for Madison Square Garden after retiring from coaching. In another room was a closet of lighter weight suits and sport jackets worn only in Columbia. All were tailored to fit the man once selected one of the 10 best-dressed men in America.

McGuire, also popularly considered among the best-dressed coaches in the history of college basketball, was recognized as National Coach of the Year three times at three different schools. In 41 years of coaching, his teams won 725 games, including 550 at the college level. He coached St. John's to a second-place finish in the 1952 NCAA Tournament, led UNC to a national championship in 1957 and had South Carolina atop the national polls in 1970 and 1971. He was inducted into the National Basketball Hall of Fame in 1976.

Along the way, McGuire also became one of the most controversial figures in ACC history. His actions, and those of his teams, often provided a stark contrast to his high-class image, and that of his programs. McGuire teams were often involved in on-court fights. He exchanged heated words with athletic officials throughout the league. Many believe McGuire was partly responsible for South Carolina's secession from the ACC.

"At every school," McGuire once said of the ACC, "I knew the doorman, the janitors, the holdover students." He said he also knew well the words "drop dead."

McGuire will long be remembered for bringing big-time basketball to UNC and USC. He found success in the South quite simply. He tapped the bottomless reservoir of basketball talent in New York city, using his charm and charisma as his chief recruiting tools. When he visited high school players in New York, McGuire often took along a Roman Catholic priest. McGuire wanted to assure parents that priests practiced in the South and that their sons would attend a Catholic church every Sunday.

McGuire had a way with parents. A young prep player

The '60s

South Carolina

122

ACC BASKETBALL / THE '60s

named Billy Cunningham lived on East 10th Street in Brooklyn, the same street where McGuire was reared as the youngest of 13 children. McGuire's brother-in-law was a police officer in that district, and young Cunningham's father was a fire chief. The two often talked basketball over beer after work. When McGuire made an official recruiting visit to Cunningham's house, he said hello to the youngster in the living room, then walked straight to the kitchen for a 30-minute chat with the Cunningham parents. The conversation finished, McGuire walked through the living room, shook hands with the recruit and said, "I'll see you in Chapel Hill."

McGuire also assured parents that he was in charge of a first-class operation. Blazers were ordered so players would look presentable on road trips. Haircuts were mandatory for players the day of every game. No player practiced unless he was clean-shaven. Lennie Rosenbluth, an All-America for UNC in '57, missed several practices that season because he failed to shave.

Although a strict disciplinarian, McGuire was willing to bend rules on occasion. When he coached the Philadelphia Warriors of the NBA in 1962, he agreed that star center Wilt Chamberlain looked better with a mustache than without. Players at UNC and USC were allowed to drink beer and smoke cigarettes, if their parents consented and it wasn't done in McGuire's presence.

When McGuire came to UNC in 1952 he learned that most ACC teams traveled by automobile. Coaches supplemented their modest salaries by collecting travel expenses. McGuire insisted his teams travel only by chartered bus. They also stayed in hotels, not rooms in the gymnasium provided by the home team.

When McGuire wanted something badly enough, he was often cold and demanding. He wanted to take friends along on recruiting trips at the school's expense. He wanted parties thrown for members of the press, also at the school's expense. If the school balked, McGuire was known to make his side of the story public.

But there was also a very warm side to McGuire.

Once, McGuire was kidded in a radio interview about most of his UNC players coming from New York City. The announcer said unwittingly that the North Carolina air was probably invigorating for the running and playing of McGuire's own son. McGuire explained that the boy was an invalid and, when the announcer blundered an embarrassed apology, added, "You don't have to apologize . . . We feel God has singled us out for an extra responsibility and we're proud to be able to accept it."

Son Frankie, not basketball, was actually the reason McGuire moved to the South. McGuire made that known throughout his stays at UNC and USC, thus giving the impression that he never considered the South his home. He liked youngsters from New York, both as personalities and players.

"I coach nationalities," McGuire said. "There are ways to motivate Jewish players and Italian players. A lot of people didn't think of that, but I was born and raised with them. I know how to get them mad and how to get the most out of them.

"The boys have tremendous competition, they are brought up on basketball in playgrounds and under good high school coaches and summer camps. They play day and night, 12 months a year. Only the best can survive the competition . . . I am not foolish enough to think, of course, that boys from the City can run any faster or jump any higher than others, but I understand them better, and what is even more important is they understand me."

In return, McGuire was never really embraced by the South. He used an "us against the world" philosophy to motivate his players. McGuire appealed to his Catholics to beat the Southern Baptists on other ACC squads and to his New Yorkers to show that the rugged city game was better than the finesse style played in the South.

Such tactics caused problems at UNC and at USC. He engaged in a verbal war with N.C. State Coach Everett Case that lasted several seasons, even though McGuire says the two were actually close friends. He criticized fans around the league for their poor behavior. He challenged the commissioner of the ACC when two of his UNC players were ruled ineligible for fighting.

Fighting seemed to be part of the game for McGuire's ACC teams. "I think Frank was probably a very, very good motivator," former Maryland Coach Lefty Driesell says. "When he was at South Carolina . . . I think he kind of turned his team, which was smart on his part, against the whole league. I don't know why (all the fighting), maybe he just had aggressive players."

McGuire thinks otherwise.

"They used to talk about Catholic guys fighting Baptists all the time. But actually there would be Catholic guys on both teams, or Baptist guys on both teams fighting," McGuire says. "It had nothing to do with that . . . We saw each other so often, the rivalries built year-in and year-out . . . The people who accused me of starting fights didn't understand I didn't want fights on the court. I told my players, if they want to fight, go downstairs or somewhere but don't be fighting on the basketball court."

McGuire's strong suit was motivation. Near the end of McGuire's stay at UNC, Assistant Coach Dean Smith took over practice when the boss went on a recruiting trip. McGuire didn't return until just before the next game, walked into the locker room, erased the match-ups Smith had diagrammed on the chalkboard and sent the team out to victory with a rousing pep talk.

McGuire was most loyal to his assistants and players. Buck Freeman coached McGuire at St. John's, then served as McGuire's assistant at UNC and USC. McGuire fought for the eligibility of Mike Grosso for two seasons at South Carolina. When the ACC ruled Grosso ineligible for not meeting league entrance requirements, McGuire arranged for him to transfer to Louisville.

A picture of Grosso that hung in McGuire's living room perished along with pictures of friends Nat King Cole, George Steinbrenner and Frank Sinatra. The fire left him with only memories.

"Sometimes you say, 'It's a tough life,' " McGuire said of coaching. "Well, it's a good life. It's what you make out of it. Nobody makes you coach. In other words, they don't hold a gun to your head and say you have to coach. I enjoyed it and had a good time." ∎

UNC was all business in the Final Four semifinals against Ohio State—Miller (44 above) scoring 20 and Bunting (31 opposite) adding 17—but Alcindor and UCLA chopped them to size during a 78-55 championship rout (inset).

said. "I knew there wasn't much time left and I had to shoot. I don't recall seeing the basket. I just shot, and luckily it went in."

Lind's final rebound with 19 seconds remaining in the third overtime led to a layup basket by Steve Vanderberg that gave Duke an 87-84 lead and the victory.

Duke and South Carolina renewed their home-and-home series after the one-year cooling-off period. Despite fear of an incident when the teams met first in Columbia and then in Durham, both crowds were well-behaved. South Carolina won both games, 83-80 and 56-50, costing Duke a chance to finish first in the regular season as the Blue Devils finished one game behind UNC. Duke thought it had one more crack at the Tar Heels during the ACC Tournament, which was held in the Charlotte Coliseum for the first time.

N.C. State, 9-5 in the regular season, had other ideas. When the Wolfpack met Duke in the semifinals, N.C. State Coach Norm Sloan thought it best to hold the ball and pull Duke out of its zone defense. The idea was to bring Duke center Mike Lewis away from the basket.

"The fact that we went out in this configuration and he stayed underneath the basket is what generated the slowdown," said State forward Vann Williford. "We never talked about it, never practiced it, or never considered it until the game actually started."

The Wolfpack's Bill Kretzer was assigned to hold the ball near midcourt, and he did so for most of the first half. At one point, he held the ball for 14 minutes without advancing it. At halftime, Duke led 4-2.

"I accept full responsiblity for choosing to do it that way," Bubas said. "The truth of the matter is, we couldn't pressure a team of grandmothers. Regardless of what anyone says, I knew we couldn't press."

The game was tied at 8 with 2:30 remaining. A missed free throw by Duke's Dave Golden allowed State's Dick Braucher to make a clinching free throw with three seconds left and give the Wolfpack a two-point victory. The game has been known ever since as "The 12-10 Game" and sparked Bill Currie, UNC's radio announcer, to tell his audience the game was as "exciting as artificial insemination."

The championship game was hardly a match as UNC rolled past State 87-50, the largest victory margin in a title game. Leading 31-26 at halftime, UNC Coach Smith left his team's dressing quarters just a few minutes early and said, "You fellows talk it over among yourselves. Hold a sort of 'truth' meeting with yourselves." The Tar Heels responded by scoring more points (56) in the second half than State scored in the entire game. Balance was again the key for UNC, which got 21 points and seven rebounds from Miller, 16 and 10 from Scott, 12 and 11 from Clark, 11 and five from Grubar, and nine and 11 from Bunting.

Duke again accepted the ACC's invitation to the NIT, rolled past Oklahoma City 97-81 in the first round and then lost to St. Peter's 100-71 in the second round. The Blue Devils led Oklahoma City 49-28 at halftime when Chief Coach Abe Lemons kept his team on the floor to play a shirts-and-skins scrimmage game during intermission in Madison Square Garden.

UNC, meanwhile, faced unbeaten (23-0) and third-ranked St. Bonaventure with 6-11, 265-pound center Bob Lanier in the first round of the NCAA East Regional in Raleigh. The Tar Heels ganged up on Lanier, who still managed 23 points and

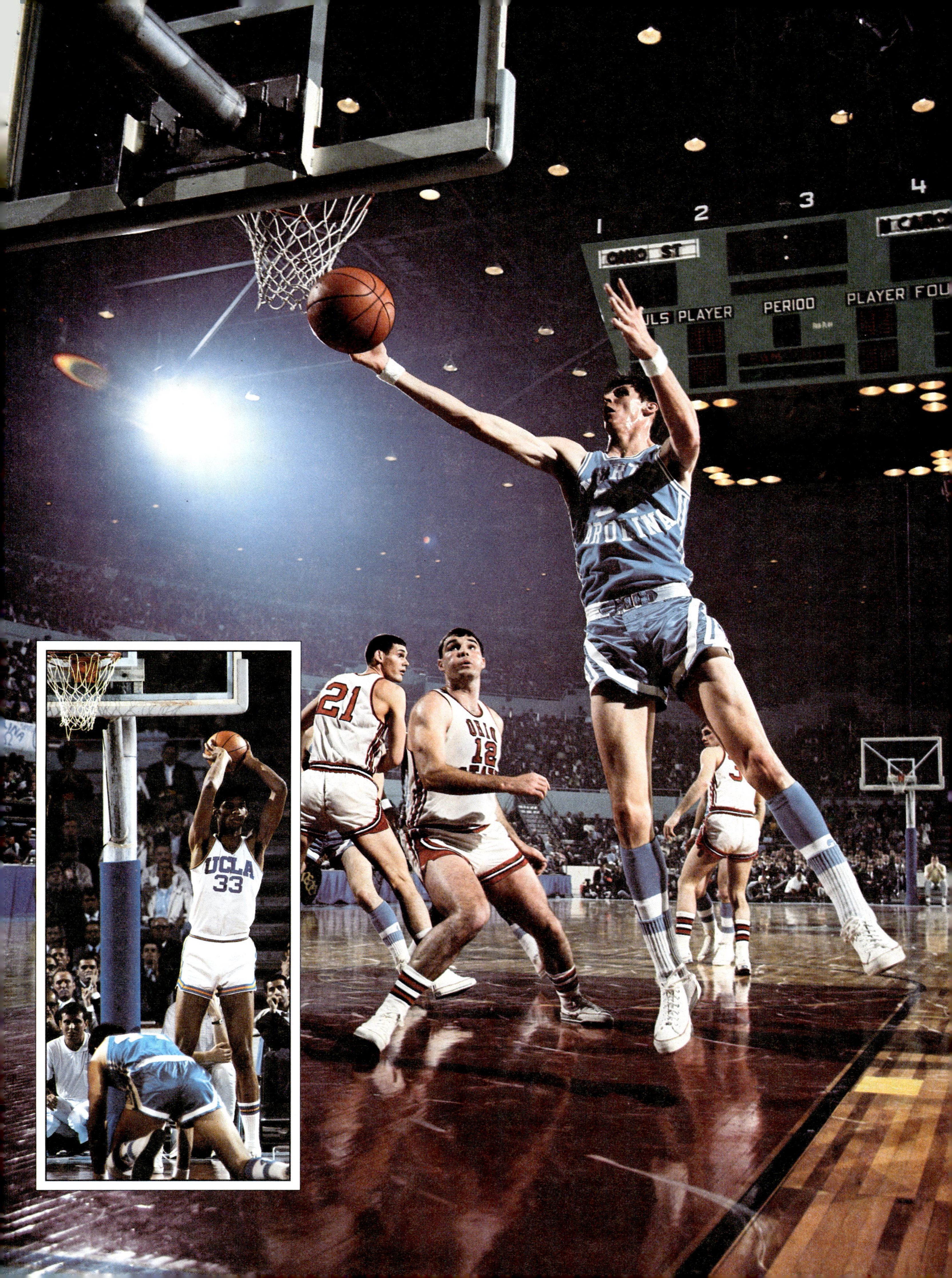
1 2 3 4
OHIO ST
PERIOD
21
12
UCLA
33

ACC BASKETBALL / THE '60s

nine rebounds, to post a 91-72 victory. Miller was at his best with game-high totals of 27 points and 16 rebounds.

Next up for UNC was Davidson on the same Reynolds Coliseum court.

The Wildcats built a six-point halftime lead, but UNC picked up its defensive pressure in the second half and limited Davidson to 29.4 percent shooting from the field. The Tar Heels, with a 22-point, 17-rebound performance from Rusty Clark, took a nine-point lead in the final minutes and ended with a 70-66 victory.

"I'm 35 years old and one day before I die I'm going to be up there in the national finals," said Davidson Coach Driesell.

Smith said: "I believe this is a better Carolina team than the one last year. As you know, that team was one of the greatest in Carolina's history."

There was no looking ahead to UCLA when the Tar Heels arrived in Los Angeles to face Ohio State in the NCAA semifinals. Having learned a valuable lesson in 1967 when it lost to Dayton, UNC was in top form and defeated Ohio State 80-66.

All five starters scored in double figures with Miller's 20 points leading the way. Bunting had one of his better games of the season with 17 points and 12 rebounds.

Following the game, Smith allowed his team to watch part of UCLA's 101-69 victory over undefeated Houston in a rematch of their much-ballyhooed, regular-season meeting in the Astrodome. It marked the last time Smith allowed one of his teams to view an opponent prior to an NCAA Tournament meeting.

"Awesome," Smith said in evaluating UCLA. "Even without Lew Alcindor, the Bruins would be one of the top teams in the nation."

UCLA had Alcindor for the championship game and proved why it was easily the nation's best team with a 78-55 thrashing of UNC. The margin of victory was the largest in an NCAA title game to that date.

The Tar Heels controlled the game's tempo early with a variation of the Four Corners offense and trailed 13-12 with 10 minutes remaining in the first half. But Alcindor blocked two shots and accounted for eight points in a 10-2 UCLA spree that paced the Bruins to a 32-22 halftime lead. UCLA had scoring bursts of seven, eight and nine points in the second half.

Alcindor scored 34 points and had 16 rebounds as UCLA outrebounded UNC 39-25 and made 51.7 percent of its field goal attempts, compared to 34.9 percent for the Tar Heels.

"UCLA has got to be the greatest basketball team ever assembled," Smith said.

'69

Finishing second to UCLA wasn't so bad. UNC fans were appreciative of Coach Dean Smith's efforts and awarded him with a 1968 Cadillac convertible following the season. But Smith's work with the class of 1969 was hardly complete.

Rusty Clark was the most highly recruited of the class that also included Joe Brown, Bill Bunting, Dick Grubar, Gerald Tuttle and Joe Brown. In getting the 6-foot-10 Clark, Smith had made a major breakthrough in recruiting by beating Duke's Vic Bubas, State's Press Maravich and Wake Forest's Bones McKinney. The 6-8 Bunting came aboard because he figured, with Clark at center, he could play forward. For much the same reason Grubar, a 6-3 center in high school, thought he could play in the backcourt at UNC.

Tuttle and Brown were valuable reserves. The 6-foot Tuttle wanted to play for the University of Kentucky, but the London, Ky., native was never offered a chance by his home-state school. He selected UNC because his older brother had known Tar Heel Assistant Coach Larry Brown. The 6-5 Brown came out of the North Carolina mountains for academics more than basketball, although he was an all-state player in Valdese.

The trio of Clark, Bunting and Grubar gave Smith the nucleus of his best recruiting class since taking over for Frank McGuire in 1961. During a freshman-varsity game in 1966, Smith came to realize the uniqueness of the class of '69. The varsity, with talented sophomores Larry Miller and Bob Lewis, finished third in the ACC and had a 16-11 record. But they lost that intrasquad game to the freshmen.

"It's just not like Coach Smith to allow something like that to happen," Bunting later said. "But it made us feel very special to win that game and the feeling lasted."

Smith never allowed another freshman team to play against the varsity. He also never had a class quite like that of 1969. In three years of varsity competition, that class became the first in ACC history to finish first in the regular season, win the ACC Tournament and advance to the Final Four all three seasons. From 1967 through 1969, the Tar Heels were 81-15 overall and 45-6 against ACC competition. One-third of the 15 losses were in the Final Four.

The trip to a third straight Final Four was not an easy one for UNC, which had an early season game at third-ranked Kentucky and a possible meeting with No. 1-ranked and two-time defending national champion UCLA in New York's Holiday Festival.

The Tar Heels, ranked second nationally, got double-figure scoring off the bench from junior guard Eddie Fogler and sophomore forward Lee Dedmon and cruised past Kentucky, 87-77. But the meeting with UCLA in the Holiday Festival championship was foiled by St. John's, which turned back the Tar Heels 72-70.

UNC bounced back and reeled off 11 straight victories before meeting South Carolina in the annual North-South Doubleheaders in Charlotte. The Gamecocks were emerging as a force under McGuire, who had nursed his program along since 1965 with records of 6-17, 11-13, 16-7 and 15-7.

All of South Carolina's players were McGuire recruits by 1969, and not surprisingly most were from the New York City area. Whereas the "Underground Railroad" ran from New York City to Chapel Hill for McGuire in the 1950s, it made one additional stop in Columbia, S.C. Six of the 10 players, including four of the five starters, on the '69 Gamecock roster hailed from the New York area.

Along with New Yorkers, McGuire also brought controversy. It was probably no coincidence that on-court fighting returned to the ACC along with McGuire. South Carolina's rise to near the top of the ACC standings also coincided with a rash of fisticuffs in the league.

When South Carolina guard Billy Walsh engaged in a shoving match with Virginia center Norm Carmichael early in the season, Gamecock center John Ribock intervened and belted Carmichael with his fist. A week later, South Carolina guard Bobby Cremins and Davidson's Doug Cook were ejected for fighting.

Then, in a late January game at Florida State, McGuire pulled his team off the floor with 1:57 remaining and the Gamecocks behind 87-76. "I've been in this game too many years not to know what was happening out there," McGuire said following the forfeit. "They just kicked the heck out of us physically. Thank God we didn't have any serious injuries."

Those incidents occurred in South Carolina's three losses

prior to its meeting with UNC in the North-South Doubleheaders. The Gamecocks were a tough bunch known to their fans as the "Iron Five." The starting five of Cremins, Walsh, Ribock, John Roche and Tom Owens scored 96 percent of the team's points that season and had 86 percent of the rebounds.

Using only those five players, South Carolina defeated UNC 68-66. Roche led the winners with 30 points and prompted UNC's Smith to say, "If he could play that well all the time, South Carolina could beat UCLA." Smith also proclaimed the Gamecocks as the league favorites during the regular season. But when UNC avenged the loss with a 68-62 victory at South Carolina, the Tar Heels clinched first place in the regular season. A charging foul against Roche with 55 seconds remaining sealed the UNC win after South Carolina had pulled within two points.

While UNC and USC were on the rise, Duke was continuing to fall. A stretch of losses to Michigan, Virginia, East Tennessee and Wake Forest was the longest for a Bubas-coached team at Duke. On the afternoon of the Dec. 11 game at Virginia, Bubas called a meeting with Assistant Coaches Chuck Daly and Hubie Brown. In that meeting, Bubas said he would retire at the end of the season. It was later reported in the media, and Bubas confirmed it.

Following the loss to East Tennessee, Bubas met with his team and said: "We have disgraced ourselves by the way we played. There will have to be some drastic changes made." Then, prior to the game against Wake Forest, Bubas told the team of his retirement plans.

By the time the regular season came to a close, the Blue Devils had regrouped and were ready to give Bubas a fond farewell. In the regular-season finale in Durham, Duke got an unexpected 33 points from Steve Vandenberg and defeated the Tar Heels 87-81. Vandenberg, who averaged 8.3 points a game for the season, made 10 of 14 field goal attempts and all 13 of his free throws and had 12 rebounds.

"Precious," Bubas said of the win. "This one is precious to me because it is my last game in Duke Indoor Stadium."

Playing a hunch, Bubas started Vandenberg. It was a page right out of the coaching book of Everett Case, whom Bubas had served for eight years as an assistant coach at N.C. State prior to his 10 years at Duke.

Duke continued to play well in the ACC Tournament when it defeated a dissension-racked Virginia team in the first round, then stunned South Carolina in the semifinals.

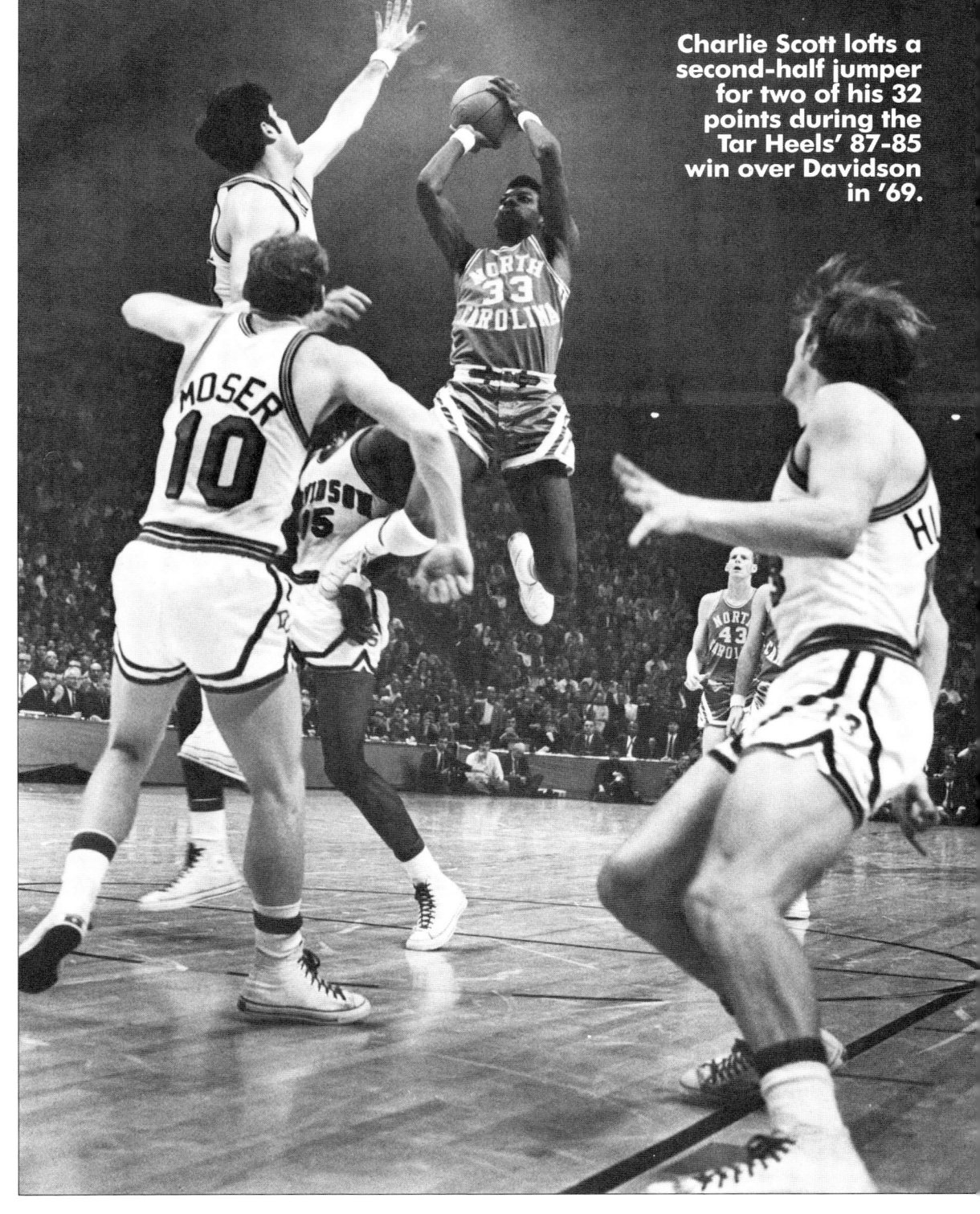

On the Monday prior to the ACC Tournament, Virginia players presented a list of grievances against Coach Bill Gibson to Athletic Director Steve Sebo. On Tuesday, the players issued the following statement to the media: "We apologize for the manner in which the situation has been handled, and we are genuinely repentant for any discredit which our actions have brought upon the University. We do, however, feel that there exists a number of justifiable grievances which were catalytic to the premature exposure of certain team members' feelings. It is regrettable that the discontent was expressed in such a vein." On Wednesday, five players and the faculty athletic committee met for five hours, and Sebo issued a public statement the following day in support of Gibson.

Those circumstances led to the 99-86 thrashing by Duke, which then limited Roche to 4-of-15 shooting to post a 68-59

Charlie Scott lofts a second-half jumper for two of his 32 points during the Tar Heels' 87-85 win over Davidson in '69.

ACC BASKETBALL / THE '60s

A Class Above
These five members of the UNC class of 1969 accomplished something no other class has ever done in ACC basketball: They won three straight regular-season titles, three ACC Tournaments and went to three Final Fours. From left to right above are Gerald Tuttle, Rusty Clark, Bill Bunting and Joe Brown; at right is Dick Grubar.

victory over South Carolina. That set up a championship meeting against UNC, which had breezed by Clemson 94-70 and struggled past Wake Forest 80-72 in the first two rounds.

Duke led the championship game by nine points at halftime and by 11 early in the second half when UNC guard Charlie Scott took charge. He scored 28 of his 40 points in the second half and rallied the Tar Heels to an 85-74 victory. Scott made 17 of 23 shots from the floor.

"I looked down at the Carolina bench, and I felt that everybody except Charlie Scott looked like the thing was over," Bubas said. "He was yelling, 'Give the ball to me, I'll win the game.' And I'm afraid that's what happened. But when a guy hits 30-foot jump shots going to his left, falling into the crowd, and makes 40 points, the only thing you can say is 'nice going.'"

Smith said, "It was one of the great individual displays you've ever seen."

Scott took up the slack after his backcourt mate, Grubar, went down with a sprained knee in the first half. The injury would sideline Grubar for the NCAA playoffs.

Without Grubar, UNC squeezed past Duquesne 79-78 on a brilliant pass from Scott to Dedmon for the decisive basket in the final seconds. For the second straight season, the Tar Heels' opponent in the East Regional final was Davidson. Instead of Raleigh, this year's meeting was in College Park, Md.

Lefty Driesell, who would become Maryland's coach after the game, gave the Washington media a preview of his candor when he said, "I'd rather die than lose to North Carolina again."

Scott's basket tied the game at 85 with 1:30 remaining. As Davidson held for a final shot, the Wildcats' Jerry Kroll charged into Tuttle. UNC then ran the clock down to 13 seconds and called a timeout. The final play was set, and Scott's 15-footer with two seconds remaining gave the Tar Heels the East Regional championship for a third straight season, 87-85.

"One man stood out," Smith said of Scott, who led all scorers with 32 points.

"I'm disappointed for the boys, but we have a good many boys returning and maybe Davidson can get here next year," said Driesell, who resigned the following day to accept Maryland's offer.

Prior to the NCAA semifinals in Louisville, Scott criticized the media after he finished second to South Carolina's Roche for ACC Player of the Year honors, charging that the voting was racially biased. Scott then took out his frustration on the basketball court during the NCAA Tournament. That was evident in victories over Duquesne and Davidson, but it was not enough to carry UNC against Rick Mount, Bill Keller and Purdue in the NCAA semifinals. The Tar Heels missed the defense of the injured Grubar and were almost helpless as Mount scored 36 points and Keller added 20 in a 92-65 rout.

"We kind of looked ahead to UCLA and took Purdue lightly," Scott said. "They were a lot tougher than we thought they were. They were on and we were off."

Despite a 35-point performance by Scott in the consolation game, UNC fell to Drake 104-84, then watched UCLA win another national championship with an 92-72 victory over Purdue. Thus closed a unique chapter in ACC history, one that may never be matched again, when one team advanced to the Final Four three straight seasons.

ACC BASKETBALL / THE '60s

SPOTLIGHT

Vic Bubas

"I appreciate the total job he did as a coach. Bobby Knight says a coach should be the best teacher. Coach Bubas was the best professor."

By DICK HERBERT

ACC BASKETBALL / THE '60s

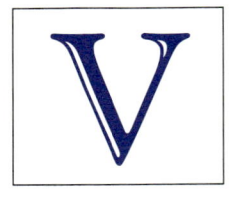

Vic Bubas sat upstairs at Duke Indoor Stadium in October of 1968, watching his Blue Devils scrimmage the freshman team. He had lost from the previous year's team six seniors, including All-America Mike Lewis, and he knew four sophomores would have to play prominent roles.

Perhaps he also knew this would be his last season as Duke's head basketball coach.

Bubas blew his whistle and disappeared through a portal. He was coming down to the court, and he had something to say.

Sending the freshman team to the far baseline, Bubas gathered the varsity around him and started to pace.

"I can tell most of you are really playing hard," he began, still pacing. "I can tell that many of you are giving me 100 percent.

"But the five guys who play for me . . . the five guys who start for me . . . have got to give me MORE than 100 percent."

Bubas stopped pacing, crouched into a defensive stance and clenched his fists. His face turned blood red.

"I . . . WANT . . . PASSION!" he boomed all over the old gym.

•

From motivation to organization, Bubas took coaching to another level in the ACC. He often called his the era of the "executive coach." Perhaps realizing that bench coaching alone could no longer sustain a school's program, Bubas was the first to make his profession a business. His business was selling Duke basketball.

He faced an unusual situation at Duke, a private institution located in a city heavily populated with fans of the nearby Tar Heels of North Carolina. To win the support of the Durham community, Bubas went out to meet its people. He stopped for gas at different service stations, took his clothes to different cleaners and shopped at a variety of department stores, introducing himself to as many people as possible. He conducted basketball clinics for men, women and children; he spoke to anyone who would listen, from church groups to sewing clubs.

His most intensive sales pitch was to high school prospects across the country. He was one of the first coaches to court not only prep seniors, but juniors as well, keeping detailed files on every known prospect in the country. Assistant coaches were assigned a section of the country to scour for prospective players. No scouting trip was too great a distance for Bubas or one of his aides.

Not far into Bubas' first season at Duke, 1960, tickets to home games became increasingly difficult to secure. A year later, Bubas had the first of six straight 20-win seasons, and his program was on the way to being among the best in the country.

What Bubas accomplished in one decade at Duke clearly makes him the "Coach of the '60s" in the ACC. Only the legendary John Wooden of UCLA had a better record in that period.

His Duke teams won 213 games and lost only 67, a .761 winning percentage that ranked 10th among all-time NCAA Division I coaches as late as 1987. His 128-38 record against league competition netted a .771 winning percentage, still unmatched in ACC history. Bubas' teams finished first in the ACC's regular-season race four seasons, won four ACC Tournaments and reached the NCAA Final Four three times.

Nine of Bubas' players graduated to professional basketball. A man of high principles, Bubas believed it was most important for his players to succeed in the classroom. Of the 33 players he brought to Duke, 29 earned diplomas.

He also succeeded in earning the high regard of his players, assistants and associates. Many of his rivals in coaching held him in the same esteem. Duke University made him a vice president to keep him on campus following his decision to leave coaching after the '69 season.

Through all of his successes at Duke, and those as commissioner of the thriving Sun Belt Conference since its inception in 1976, Bubas has retained the same modesty and humility that have long marked his character.

"My father came to this country as an immigrant from Yugoslavia," Bubas said upon his induction to the North Carolina Sports Hall of Fame in 1976. "He couldn't speak English, didn't have any money and wore a sign around his neck telling where he was going. He became one of the most successful businessmen in Northern Indiana.

"When you compare his start, his handicaps and his achievements to mine . . . that keeps everything in the proper perspective."

Bubas' success at Duke came after four years as a player and eight as an assistant to N.C. State's Everett Case, a giant in the profession. Although he holds State and Case in the highest regard, Bubas never intended to succeed Case there.

"The program there was established," he says. "What could I do to improve it? I

Bubas had plenty to smile about with likes of Bob Verga (L) and Mike Lewis, two pillars of his '66 Final Four team.

wanted to build a program that was my own."

Prior to the end of the 1959 season at State, Bubas decided his career was at a crossroads and he would leave the Wolfpack. If he did not get a head-coaching job he liked, Bubas planned to attend graduate school at the University of Florida. He was disappointed when he lost out at the University of New Mexico, which elected to promote Assistant Coach Robert Sweeney.

Shortly afterward, Hal Bradley left Duke to become head coach at the University of Texas. Bubas made no formal application at Duke, but Athletic Director Eddie Cameron learned through a mutual friend that Bubas was very interested. Cameron screened more than 135 candidates over a six-week period but never interviewed Bubas.

"It wasn't necessary," Cameron says today. "I knew what he could do. I knew he would be a success at anything, and he was."

On Thursday night, May 1, 1959, Bubas was told by the same mutual friend that Cameron would recommend him to the Duke Athletic Council at its Monday meeting. The announcement of the new coach would be made Tuesday, if the Council approved the recommendation.

Cameron phoned Bubas Monday morning and asked him to meet at a restaurant near the Raleigh-Durham Airport.

"I walked in," Bubas recalls, "shook hands with Eddie and Carl James, assistant athletic director, and Eddie says, 'Don't you think it's time to go recruiting?'"

There was little talk about contract or salary. At a reported $9,000, Bubas wound up making $500 a year less than he made at State. Contract negotiations were never a problem for Duke with Bubas, who worked under year-to-year, verbal agreements with Cameron.

"At the end of the season," Bubas says, "we would have a 15-second discussion and then a handshake. That's all it took. I had told Eddie, 'You pay me what you want to, but what I make on the side is mine if it is honorable.' He agreed and defended me when there were complaints about my making too much from our basketball school. Eddie told them I was paying exactly the same (for rent and facilities) as other camps at Duke were paying."

That afternoon, Bubas chartered a plane to Princeton, W. Va., to visit Rod Thorn, one of the nation's top prospects. Thorn wanted to play baseball and study medicine, so Bubas took with him Ace Parker, Duke's baseball coach, and Dr. Lenox Baker, the Blue Devils' team physician and an internationally known physician.

Home-state pressure prevailed, and Thorn went to West Virginia. But that hardly slowed Bubas, who was intent on making Duke every bit the basketball power of his alma mater, N.C. State.

The following day in Durham, the 31-year-old Bubas was introduced to the media as Duke's new basketball coach. The presentation was made in front of the Indoor Stadium as students crowded around to listen.

"Gentlemen, this is Vic Bubas, our new basketball coach," Cameron said. "We hope he is our basketball coach forever."

Members of the media were delighted because they knew Bubas would be cooperative, and they were rarely disappointed in his 10 seasons. That was just one of the many ways he sold his program to the public.

On Wednesday, Bubas met with Art Heyman, the highly coveted high school senior from Long Island, in New York's Manhattan Motel. Heyman liked the new Duke coach and would later become ACC Player of the Year as a Blue Devil.

"He had a steely set, and you knew what he wanted. He didn't have to scream and holler," aide Bucky Waters says.

Despite a fast start with the media and recruits, Bubas was not welcomed by all at Duke. Many Blue Devil supporters were disappointed the school did not hire an alumnus or someone previously connected to the Duke program. Further questions were raised about hiring an assistant coach, especially one from N.C. State.

"There was some thought that if N.C. State were not a basketball factory, it certainly was not the citadel of Southern education that Duke University was," says Bucky Waters, whom Bubas hired as an assistant coach at age 22.

In support of Bubas' hiring, State's Case told *The Raleigh Times*: "Vic was always a keener student of the game than

ACC BASKETBALL / THE '60s

most. He studied basketball with the idea in mind that someday he would coach it. You could always trust his judgment . . . Vic is a fine strategist and has a knack for getting close to his players. He is a relentless worker and has a great desire for winning."

As much as anything, Bubas' organizational skills made him a success.

"When I try to analyze the various factors," says Dr. Baker, "the word 'organized' is the first to come to mind. Every approach had its place. He was a born executive with the power of assigning duties and responsibilities, plus seeing that everyone does his job on time—all this without raising his voice."

Organization to Bubas meant doing everything—from recruiting to coaching—in a first-class manner. When hired at Duke, he immediately remodeled the basketball office with new carpet and furniture. When an assistant coach came to work one day in a sports shirt, Bubas told him such dress did not fit his idea of corporate management.

No detail was too small. Bubas upgraded parking for regular fans attending games at Duke Indoor Stadium. Believing fans did not want to watch games with coats in their laps, Bubas hired smiling coeds to check garments at the door.

He was a fan of major league baseball owner and promoter Bill Veeck and often recommended his autobiography, *Veeck As In Wreck*, to friends and associates. Taking a page from Veeck's book, Bubas paid special attention to the upkeep of the women's restrooms at the Indoor Stadium. He also encouraged women to come onto the court following the game and mingle with players, get autographs and take pictures. He also instituted a family section in the end zones, selling $10 season tickets.

"He made it so a season ticket was a social event," Waters says. "You didn't just roll out in blue jeans and cruise into the game. He created an atmosphere to see and be seen."

When Duke was scheduled to play out of town, Bubas sent

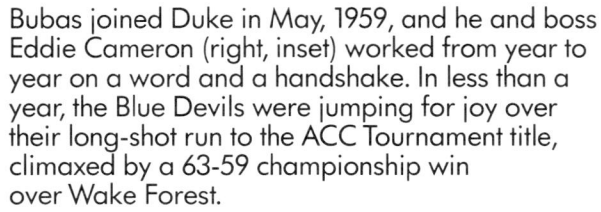

Bubas joined Duke in May, 1959, and he and boss Eddie Cameron (right, inset) worked from year to year on a word and a handshake. In less than a year, the Blue Devils were jumping for joy over their long-shot run to the ACC Tournament title, climaxed by a 63-59 championship win over Wake Forest.

132

ACC BASKETBALL / THE '60s

an assistant to scout out the best hotels. He was mostly concerned about a hotel's kitchen. When his No. 1-ranked Blue Devils were listless and lost to Duquesne in the first round of the 1962 Steel Bowl, Bubas was convinced someone had fooled with the team's pregame meal. From then on, Duke carried high-energy supplements for road games and used them with pregame meals.

During the 1964 NCAA championship game, Bubas noticed the enthusiasm created by UCLA's pep band and dancing girls. He got film and music of the UCLA routines and suggested the Duke cheerleaders borrow some ideas. He also patterned the Duke pep band—outfitted in straw hats and striped shirts—after the University of California band.

In preparation for a series of games against UCLA during the 1966 and 1967 seasons, Bubas sent his assistant coaches to several clinics given by Wooden with the hope of picking up something from the Bruin coach.

"We also scouted Lew Alcindor in freshman games," says Chuck Daly, an assistant to Bubas for six years and later a successful head coach with the NBA Detroit Pistons. "It was regular procedure to observe how other coaches conducted practice . . . Vic was incredibly thorough. He told us not to leave a stone unturned in what we were to do."

Bubas' organization was best reflected in the quality of his assistant coaches. Besides Daly and Waters, Bubas also hired Fred Shabel, Tom Carmody and Hubie Brown as assistants at Duke.

All agree Bubas helped advance their careers, and each eventually became a head coach at either the college or professional level. Shabel coached at Connecticut, Waters at West Virginia and Duke and Carmody at Rhode Island. Brown coached teams in the ABA and NBA, while Daly coached in the NBA.

"Many coaches and executives do not do this, but he truly supported us," says Shabel, who was the chief assistant to Hal Bradley and was retained by Bubas. After four seasons with Bubas, Shabel became head coach at Connecticut. Later he was athletic director at the University of Pennsylvania and then chairman of Spectacor, a company that manages the Spectrum in Philadelphia and several other arenas.

When Shabel was being considered at Connecticut, Bubas offered to fly there to offer a personal recommendation.

"I consider Vic as my mentor," Shabel says. "When one labels a person as his 'mentor,' you know he is positive. Vic is the most management-oriented person I have ever met. I have been in three positions since Duke and I have never met anyone so management-oriented.

"He sort of gave us a mode of organization for everything we did. In many respects I have followed the model he set. He delegated a lot. It was like he was the general partner and the assistants were limited partners. He was always involved, on top of it with total knowledge."

Waters succeeded Bubas at Duke after a successful head-coaching stint at West Virginia and held the job through 1973. He is now a fund raiser for the Duke Medical Center and a television commentator on basketball.

Waters says Bubas was a superb planner—a puzzle solver.

"He would fit people and plans toward an objective with great clarity, and he could do it for the long range. He knew how to take apart and put together players and coaches. He was always logical and so patient. He was the most organized man I ever knew.

"Coach Case was well organized, but Vic took it to a higher dimension. He had a total plan. Seldom did he raise his voice. He had a steely set, and you knew what he wanted. He didn't have to scream and holler. If there was an outburst, it carried more power. Whatever field he would have gone into he would have been a success."

Bubas' success can probably be traced to a work ethic from his father, who was born in Vukovagorica, a village outside Zagreb, Yugoslavia. The elder Bubas (pronounced Boo-bosh in his native country) came to the United States in 1915 at age 20 and went to Omaha, Neb., to join relatives and work in the stockyards. He then went to Chicago to work in the steel mills.

"He was nearly killed three times by cranes," the younger Bubas recalls. "Safety standards were not very good then."

A newer mill was built in Gary, Ind., and that is where the Bubas family settled. Bubas' father opened a hardware store with just $50 capital, but by the time his son went to college, the store was among the most successful in Northern Indiana. When he wasn't in school, Bubas worked in the hardware store.

"Making me work was one of the finest things ever to happen to me," Bubas says. "Just meeting the public, having to sell things. It taught me a lot—a lot about people."

Baseball and basketball took hold in the eighth grade, and from then on he practiced day and night and learned all he could about the games. Bubas' father often complained that his son knew the batting average of Chicago Cub first baseman

State was 111-24 and won four Southern Conference championships during Bubas' days from 1948-51.

133

Coach and players celebrate 71-66 triumph over State in '66 ACC final before eventual third-place NCAA finish.

Phil Cavaretta, but couldn't remember the price of a nail in the hardware store.

He played varsity basketball his senior year at Lew Wallace High School in Gary and then joined the Army in 1944 as World War II was drawing to a close. He was sent to Germany after the surrender there and was supposed to go into Army police duty for the 1st Infantry Division.

"We rode a cattle car in bitter cold for three days getting into Germany," he says. "When I arrived I saw a friend from Gary who said his team needed a player. To keep the morale up, there was an extensive sports program. I did well in the first game, 6-for-8 shooting from outside, and the commanding officer pulled my records and I did not do police work."

When Bubas left the Army in 1945, he returned to Gary to work in the hardware store and play AAU basketball. There he was recommended to Case in the spring of 1946.

"I came to Raleigh and visited with Coach Case," says Bubas, who had considered another scholarship offer from the University of Southern California. "In my conversations with him, I told him that, more than anything, I wanted to be a basketball coach. I told him that I would sacrifice a chance to join my father's prosperous hardware store if I could coach.

"He told me to enter State, achieve good grades, act as a gentleman at all times and fight hard on the basketball court. He said if I did that, he would fight just as hard to help me land a coaching job."

The 6-foot-2, 175-pound Bubas went to Raleigh for the 1948 season and was a reserve guard behind Eddie Bartels and Leo Katkaveck. He later earned All-Southern Conference honors twice and played on teams that compiled a 111-24 record, won four league championships and advanced to the NCAA Final Four in 1951.

One highlight of his playing career was scoring the first basket in the new Reynolds Coliseum on a follow shot against Washington & Lee on Dec. 2, 1949.

"Almost every day I had gone over to see how the Coliseum was growing," Bubas says. "I couldn't wait for it to be completed. In recruiting me, Coach Case had talked about the great place it would become after completion.

"The opening tap usually went back to me, and I wasn't about to pass the ball off. I drove in, missed the shot but got the rebound. Again I missed, but got the ball and put it in."

As a junior, Bubas was joined in the State backcourt by Lee Terrill, who would follow his path as freshman coach and then chief assistant to Case.

"Vic always was a knowledgeable basketball student," Terrill says. "He was always watching carefully what others

134

were doing, paying very close attention to weaknesses of his team and very willing to innovate and institute new ideas right into his offensive or defensive methodology."

As a sophomore at State, Bubas married Tootie Boldt of Gary, Ind., a high school friend he dated seriously after returning from Germany. Sammy Ranzino, a teammate all four seasons at State, was Bubas' best man in the wedding.

Despite being one of only 12 State seniors in 1951 to be named to the Golden Chain, a leadership and scholarship fraternity, Bubas remained intent on a coaching career. Tootie (nicknamed in her childhood when other children could not pronounce her given name of Marcelyn), knew well of her husband's passion for basketball.

"I can remember dates (in high school) when we would pack a lunch and sit through eight high school playoff games in one day," she says.

Case held to his word and hired Bubas as his freshman coach following the 1951 season. In four seasons, Bubas' frosh teams were 64-10. When he became Case's top assistant n 1955, Bubas was often placed in charge of the team in practice as well as in games. So close were Bubas and Case, State players called the two, "Pete and Repeat."

"In my senior year (1959), we lost a tough overtime game at Kansas State and were playing at Kansas the next night," says Lou Pucillo, whom Bubas recruited to State out of Philadelphia. "We were playing very poorly. Vic was calling the plays and making the substitutions. He called one play that didn't work, and a substitution resulted in a stupid foul. Everything he tried failed, and each time Coach Case reminded him it didn't work.

"Finally, Coach Case asked him, 'What should we do?'

"Vic replied, 'I don't know.'

"Case said, 'I don't pay you not to know.'

"Vic was disturbed at this and replied, 'What do you want me to do, pull a rabbit out of the hat?'

"Case looked at him and said, 'You're damn right I do if that's what it takes to win this game.'"

Bubas couldn't pull a rabbit from his hat in that game, but he did help Case in the art of zone defenses. Case's knowledge was based upon man-to-man and basic zones like the 2-1-2. Bubas' strength was teaching matchup zones.

Bones McKinney, when he was an assistant to Murray Greason at Wake Forest, had become a close friend of Bubas, and often they exchanged information. When Bubas was at State, he became very interested in a 1-3-1 zone defense the Deacons had used against North Carolina's national championship team of 1957.

"We used to compare notes on ballclubs we both played," McKinney says. "Vic came over to old Wake Forest and wanted to know about pivot play. We went through all our drills, most of which I had learned from Easy Ed Macauley and George Mikan in the NBA."

Bubas incorporated what he learned from different sources and developed practice sessions at Duke that were like clinics. His teams were well-versed in multiple offenses and defenses. Practices usually lasted two hours or less, with emphasis on 1-on-1 and 2-on-2 drills under game situations. Extensive attention to detail, such as making players step off the line after shooting every free throw just as they would in a game, was simply for "peace of mind," according to Bubas.

Halftime talks were equally as clinical. Bubas allowed each assistant coach one minute to speak about a particular phase of the game. When they were finished, Bubas spoke for only a couple of minutes and rarely raised his voice.

"He never cursed," Waters says. "He knew how to nip at someone without cursing or raising his voice. If someone was not rebounding, Vic would say something like, 'If you want to continue to play forward in a tuxedo out there, do know I appreciate the fact we won't have to send yours to the cleaners.'"

Bubas did everything with dignity.

"There was one of his expressions that has had a tremendous impact on me: 'The hardest thing to do in life is to bite your tongue,' " Daly says. "I learned that was true in personal life and in coaching—knowing when to back off and not say anything."

When he did speak, Bubas usually had something worthwhile to say. Of his general philosophy on coaching, Bubas once said: "Certainly an important facet is the actual process of aiding the boys in the development of their skills and to mold them into a smoothly functioning team, but there is much more to it.

"You might divide coaching up into three very broad areas: First you have to recruit the boy; then you must make sure that he remains with you; and finally you get around to actually coaching him. Each of these areas of the coaching job is equally important. If you slack off anywhere your chances of

135

producing a championship team drop considerably."

Bubas' strong suit was probably recruiting.

Dean Smith, the North Carolina coach since 1962 who went head-to-head with Bubas in recruiting through the 1969 season, says: "Vic taught us how to recruit. We had been starting on prospects in the fall of their senior year, like almost everybody. But Vic was working on them in their junior year. For a while all of us were trying to catch up with him."

Because of Duke's academic standards, Daly says, Bubas recognized the importance of targeting only those prospects who could be admitted to the school.

"We couldn't go around the country like chickens with their heads cut off," Daly says. "We had to be organized and start early. It's not difficult to learn who are the good players. We had to know more than that. Thus, we had to know about the juniors in high school."

Bubas required his assistants to project the chances of an athlete staying in school once he was admitted.

> "Vic taught us how to recruit. We had been starting on prospects in the fall of their senior year, like almost everybody. But Vic was working on them in their junior year. For a while all of us were trying to catch up with him."
>
> ☐ **UNC Coach Dean Smith**

"There were some who did not qualify under the normal entrance requirement," Bubas says. "I knew there were some non-athletes admitted as exceptions, so I went to the admissions office and asked that I could have one admitted. I said if that one did not work out, I wouldn't ask them again. That put a lot of pressure on the coaches. But, you know, the admissions office once told me they wished they had as good a record as I did in judging prospects."

After the assistant coaches provided all the information about a prospect they could find, Bubas went to the home for the clincher.

"He was overpowering," says Waters, who admits he was more impressed by Bubas than Case when recruited by N.C. State. "He especially impressed the mothers. He had everything a mother wanted her son to be. No one can copy it . . . He made a tremendous first impression. The set of his jaw, his measured articulation and eye contact that was not intimidating but held your concentration. You felt a real sense of sincerity."

Prospects were often brought to Bubas' home, where they enjoyed the family atmosphere. Bubas made players, coaches and administrators aware of his family's importance in his life, often taking his wife and children along on road trips. His players were especially close to his family, which includes daughters Sandy, Vikki and Karen. One player, Stu Yarborough, married Sandy.

Although he signed a top prospect like Heyman after taking the Duke job, Bubas had some early disappointments during the 1960 season before his first recruiting class became eligible as sophomores. His home-opener, a 10-point loss to Georgia Tech, was a blow. So were three lopsided losses to North Carolina and two to Wake Forest. The '60 regular season brought a 7-7 record and fourth-place finish in the league.

That set the stage for one of the greatest upsets in ACC Tournament history. After losing to UNC by 22, 26 and 25 points during the regular season, Duke defeated the Tar Heels 71-69 in the semifinals. Then the Blue Devils, who lost to Wake Forest by 17 and 19 points earlier, beat the Demon Deacons 63-59 for the championship, Duke's first.

The title sent Duke on its way to becoming a national power. Bubas' recruiting success landed the likes of Jay Buckley, Buzzy Harrison and Jeff Mullins in 1960; Hack Tison in 1961; Jack Marin and Steve Vacendak in 1962; Bob Verga in 1963; and Mike Lewis in 1964. Lewis was from Missoula, Mont.

"It was Vic's conviction that trying to beat North Carolina in the state was always going to be very tough," Waters says. "He had ultimate belief in Duke and its image. He believed we were capable of going out and getting the best anywhere, from Minnesota or Montana. He just thought big."

The consistent haul of big talent led Duke to consecutive seasons of 22-6, 20-5, 27-3, 26-5, 20-5, 26-4, 18-9 and 22-6. The Blue Devils finished first in the ACC's regular-season race four straight years from 1963 through 1966, won the ACC Tournament in 1963, 1964 and 1966 and reached the NCAA Final Four all three of those seasons. Duke lost to eventual national champion Loyola of Chicago in the 1963 NCAA semifinals, to UCLA in the 1964 national championship game and to Kentucky in the national semifinals in 1966 when Verga was sick with the flu.

"I appreciate the total job he did as a coach," says Mullins, who went on to play professionally and coach collegiately. "Bobby Knight says a coach should be the best teacher. Coach Bubas was the best professor."

Bubas has always said his '66 club was the strongest. Of all his players, Bubas considers Heyman his best in the clutch, Marin the best fundamentally, Verga the top long-range shooter, Mullins best at medium range, Lewis the best big man and Vacendak the fiercest competitor.

One who would have been among his best players at Duke was Larry Miller, whom Smith lured to UNC in a recruiting war against Bubas and Duke in 1964. That recruiting loss perhaps signaled the beginning of the end for Bubas, who then had average recruiting seasons in 1965, 1966 and 1968.

"That may have been the death knell as far as his zest for recruiting," Waters says of Miller's decision. "He just got tired. He said: 'The thought of getting on another airplane to go chase another teenage kid just was overwhelming. It was a battle to do that.'"

In the 1967 ACC Tournament championship game against Duke, Miller made 13 of 14 shots and scored 32 points in a Tar Heel victory that ended the Blue Devil dominance of the '60s.

The decision to leave Duke after 10 years was not a hasty one for Bubas, who mulled it over for nearly a year.

"Toward the end, I took longer to dress for practice," he said after retiring. "You wonder, should you see one more film, one more kid? At the end, I didn't. It wasn't fair to the team. You owe your recruits the best chance to win the championship. I found myself starting to slip. I had to weigh it all—and I found myself losing interest. I'd done this for 18 years, how about something else?"

In early December of 1968, Bubas informed his assistant coaches of his decision to quit at the end of that season. When he told his players prior to a game against Wake Forest

ACC BASKETBALL / THE '60s

Assistant Coach Bucky Waters (R) was more impressed as a recruit by Bubas than the legendary Everett Case.

at mid-season, they responded with a 122-93 victory.

"It's not surprising he left Duke after 10 years," Waters says. "People with that capacity to learn need to be continually challenged with the next puzzle."

Upon Bubas' decision, Duke President Douglas Knight asked him to become a member of the administration. The position offered was vice president for community relations. When Knight was succeeded by former North Carolina Governor Terry Sanford, Bubas remained and became an important aide.

"I have told Tootie, 'How lucky can you get to have worked for three giants in their field—Everett Case, Eddie Cameron and Terry Sanford?'" Bubas says. He was particularly close to Cameron, and the two continued their friendship at the Bubas home in Tampa, Fla., and at the family's summer cottage in North Carolina on Kerr Reservoir.

Despite the glittering accomplishments of his basketball teams, Bubas believes the greatest contribution he made to Duke was his work in building a student union.

"It took four years and a lot of work," says Bubas, who was chairman of the committee handling the project. "But the Bryan Center will stand there as long as there is a Duke University."

Also standing forever at Duke will be the many accomplishments of Bubas as the school's basketball coach. It was only fitting that he closed out his coaching career at the Indoor Stadium with a victory. The Blue Devils, who were 87-13 at home under Bubas, stunned second-ranked North Carolina 87-81 in early March of 1969.

"What I'll miss most," Bubas said before his last home game, "is the people. The fantastic association of being with young people, sweating together, smiling together, crying together. You're in that arena, and you look around, and there's no place to hide. You do it, or you don't. I don't think anything else can approach it—except maybe war."

Following that game, Bubas was carried off the floor by students and then thrown into the shower by his players. His suit drenched and his hair matted down from the dunking, Bubas then sat down for a press conference in his office. Two reasons for his retirement, daughters Vikki and Karen, jumped in his lap.

"Last night, I was sitting up in the stands watching the freshman game and I started to feel nostalgic," Bubas said as his daughters cried. "It's hard to leave something in which you have become so emotionally involved.

"But then I'm looking forward to my new position, so this was it. There will be no (Vince) Lombardi comeback for me. This is the way to go out, a winner."

ACC

'He's something special.'

Two decades ago, three ACC coaches coveted a basketball fortune named Tom McMillen. The battle for his services, chronicled in this bizarre tale, introduced the ACC to big-time recruiting.

Coverboy McMillen said his heart was in Chapel Hill, but a telegram to Dean Smith confirmed that family ties and the Terrapins had prevailed.

An Overdose of Squa

The Saga

By BILL MILLSAPS
Reprinted from the *Richmond Times-Dispatch*, November 29, 1970

Even in a warmup drill before a freshman game, there is an unmistakable intensity about the tall, pale, dark-haired young man in the white uniform.

A gangly 18-year-old who stands 6 feet, 11 inches, he goes about his pregame preparations with a fierce purpose, as if the game he's about to play is much more than a game.

His name is Tom McMillen, and his skills at the game of basketball are such that he could one day lead the University of Maryland to the national collegiate basketball championship.

McMillen has yet to play a varsity game for the Terrapins, but already he is one of America's best-

Continued on page 140

TOM McMILLEN
..an incredible summer..

DEAN SMITH
.."letter was fraud

---

western union Telegram

==AA23 PC03C

P WSA005 PDF=MANSFIELD PENN 10 855AEDT=
=COACH DEAN SMITH DLR AFTER TWO PM=
AND STAFF=CARE BASKETBALL OFC=UNIV OF NCAR=
CHAPPELHILLNCAR

=(931)
1970 SEP 10 AM 10

=VERY VERY SORRY HOPE YOU UNDERSTAND GOING TO MARYLAND FOR REASONS YOU KNOW=
TOM MCMILLEN=

WU 1201 (R 5-69)

known sports figures. As a senior at Mansfield (Pa.) High School last year, he made the cover of *Sports Illustrated,* and only two other high school athletes—Lew Alcindor and Rick Mount—have been so recognized.

One of five children and the son of a Mansfield dentist, McMillen has accomplished much at this early stage. In four high school years, McMillen scored 3,068 points, an average of 35.3 points a game. In 1969-70, his senior season, he averaged 47.7 points, and 22 rebounds a game.

McMillen was president of the student body, valedictorian of his senior class, a prize-winning debater and an altar boy. Last fall, he was named by President Nixon to the 15-member President's Council on Physical Fitness and Sports.

With these credits, it is no wonder that McMillen became the focal point of what is probably the most intense, the most publicized and the most misunderstood recruiting battle ever waged for a high school athlete.

Nearly every school in America that gives basketball scholarships wanted McMillen, but the fight to get him ultimately narrowed to Maryland, the University of North Carolina and the University of Virginia, all members of the Atlantic Coast Conference.

When McMillen finally entered Maryland on Sept. 11, he left behind three years of recruiting pressure, two extremely disappointed coaches and a five-month-long crisis within his family.

Before explaining all that, it is necesssary to understand why the war to gain McMillen's services was so bitterly fought.

To build a winning football program, a coach must recruit a large number of good athletes, since two-platoon football requires 22 starting players, 11 for both offense and defense. No one great individual player ever made an otherwise mediocre team a champion.

The very fact that basketball requires only five starters and two or three capable players on the bench makes the recruiting of athletes to play the sport more concentrated. Since fewer good players are needed, the "great ones" are avidly sought.

A basketball coach can feel fairly sure that an outstanding high school basketball player will be outstanding in college, too. Football coaches cannot, because career-ending injuries and academic attrition seem to hit that sport harder than they do basketball.

So when a high school player like Alcindor or McMillen comes along with both academic and athletic skill, there is virtually no limit to college coaches' zeal in trying to recruit them.

How McMillen finally wound up at Maryland is a bizarre tale that, in its central aspects, involves three disparate personalities—Dean Smith, basketball coach at North Carolina; Bill Gibson, basketball coach at Virginia, and Lefty Driesell, basketball coach at Maryland.

Smith is a suave, usually soft-spoken graduate of the University of Kansas who has an abiding interest in theological history. He is generally acknowledged by his peers to be a great recruiter, and his skills in the department enabled North Carolina to win three straight ACC championships. But he saw that current talent was not up to the Tar Heels' usual standard. He needed McMillen, in fact, had to have him, to keep North Carolina's basketball program at a high level of efficiency.

Gibson is a little more rough-hewn, a blunt-spoken Pennsylvanian who came to Virginia in 1962 and has tried, without success until this season, to produce a winning basketball team. With the players the Cavaliers had on hand, Gibson believed that UVa was only one player away from collegiate basketball greatness. That one player was Tom McMillen.

Driesell, a Norfolk native who graduated from Duke, exudes an enormous personal force. He is known to work his associates to the breaking point, and the only reason he manages to keep them is that they know Driesell works himself to the limit. A man given both to coarse, country-boy good humor and towering rages, Driesell has said that he wants to "make Maryland the UCLA of the East." With McMillen, he knew he could make a giant leap in that direction.

The other major characters in the story are Dr. Jim McMillen (Tom's father), Mrs. Margaret McMillen (his mother), Jay McMillen (his brother and a player at Maryland from 1965 to 1967) and Joe Harrington (a close friend and teammate of Jay's at Maryland and now an assistant coach under Driesell).

O f the three coaches most heavily involved in the fight for McMillen, Gibson had the longest and closest personal relationship with the boy.

"I've known Tommy since he was just a little kid," said Gibson. "While I was coach at Mansfield State (1956-1962), I became friends with the McMillen family. We remained close even after I came to Virginia in 1962."

But McMillen's talents with a basketball were not readily apparent until after his ninth-grade year.

"By then we could see it coming," said Gibson. "It wasn't hard to see that this boy was going to be a super player."

Dean Smith "saw it coming" even before that.

"I first heard of Tommy from Sal Esposito, a professor of physical education at North Carolina," said Smith. "Sal told me I should invite both Jay and Tommy down to my basketball camp in the summer of 1964, the summer after Tommy's eighth-grade year.

"When Tommy arrived, I was shocked at his size. He was 14 years old, and already he was 6-4."

"We put Tommy in the group with the 14-year-olds and pretty soon Doug Moe, one of my camp counselors, came to me and said, 'You've got to get this kid out of the 14s and put him in with the 17s. He's much too good for the 14s.'"

"McMillen came back to Smith's basketball camp two other summers (once as a counselor), and twice he attended Gibson's basketball summer camp in Gettysburg, Pa.

"He's an unbelievable kid," said Gibson. "I remember having to chase him off the courts during rest periods. He was supposed to be resting, and there he would be, out on the court, doing something with the basketball. He's the most dedicated kid I've ever seen."

In December of 1968, Smith sent Bill Guthridge, then a UNC assistant coach, to Mansfield to watch McMillen play a game, and in May of 1969, Smith was the guest speaker at the Mansfield High School basketball banquet. That August he went to Mansfield to visit with the McMillens, and by this time, the North Carolina coach and the prospect were close friends. Later this friendship would prove to be so close as to provoke a family crisis.

By September 1969, McMillen had cut his list of colleges to 15 (one school he eliminated because the coach did not attend church), and by November, he had it down to five— Pennsylvania (his sister, Shela, is a junior there now), Duke,

ACC BASKETBALL / THE '60s

The Cast Of Characters
Dean Smith (L) had been to three Final Fours, but he needed McMillen to keep his baby blue machine clicking on all cylinders. Bill Gibson (C) was eight years into his quest to take Virginia into the ACC's upper crust, and McMillen was his missing link. Lefty Driesell (R) promised a "UCLA of the East" at Maryland, and a player like McMillen could help him deliver.

Virginia, North Carolina and Maryland.

McMillen's parents wrote all the other schools who had expressed interest in their son and asked them not to contact him further except through the family or his coach at Mansfield, Rich Miller.

Finally, McMillen decided he would visit only four schools—Virginia, Maryland, Duke and North Carolina. Each naturally went out of its way to present a favorable impression, but Virginia came up with a novel idea, considering McMillen's ambition to become a doctor. Gibson arranged for McMillen to watch Dr. Frank McCue, an orthopedic surgeon at the University Hospital, perform knee surgery.

"He watched it all," said McCue, "and after it was over, he asked some of the most intelligent questions I've ever heard a layman ask about a surgical procedure. He impressed me as a brillant kid."

Meanwhile, two events occurred of more than passing importance. Jay McMillen applied and was rejected for the North Carolina medical school (he's now in dental school at Maryland). And Paul McMillen, Tom's oldest brother, transferred from the Duquesne Law School to the UNC School. In October 1969, Paul left law school and went to work for a Chapel Hill bank.

In January 1970, Smith went to Mansfield again and he said that McMillen told him that "he would make an early decision to get out from under all the (recruiting) pressure."

By early April, McMillen had cut his list to three—Maryland, Virginia and North Carolina. His parents arranged for the coach of each school to sit down with their son and make one final pitch. Gibson made what he thought would be his final talk on April 10. Smith came up on the 11th. Driesell and Joe Harrington (who, while he was a Maryland player, had spent two summers as a McMillen house guest) had the 12th.

Smith described his April 11 session with McMillen:

"Tom and I sat at the kitchen table in the McMillen house, and I went over all the things that North Carolina could offer him. The McMillens were entertaining some guests at the time in another part of the house, but Mrs. McMillen periodically would come into the kitchen. Tom told her 'Mom go on now. We're talking basketball.'"

As it turned out, this incident was important in later developments.

On April 13, McMillen went into seclusion. He took with him all his literature and notes on each school and thought through his decision.

Around 11 on the night of April 14, McMillen called Smith in Chapel Hill "and he kind of talked around the thing," said Smith. "Finally, he said, 'Coach Smith, how will I look in Carolina blue?' My wife saw me getting visibly excited, and

141

McMillen scored 1,807 points, fifth best in Terp history.

she started jumping up and down.

"Tom told me that he wanted me to call Jack Williams (the UNC sports publicist) immediately to release the fact that he would sign with us, I called Jack, and the story broke minutes later."

Smith and young McMillen decided to hold a press conference in Mansfield the next afternoon (the 15th) and to hold the signing ceremonies at Pierce's Restaurant in Elmira, N.Y., 20 miles to the north. That, as it turned out, also became a key factor.

By the morning of the 15th, Smith had the first indication of dissension within the McMillen family. "Rich Miller called me early that morning and told me the press conference was off. He told me Tom's parents were opposed very much to his decision. Later, I told Tommy, 'If your parents still feel this way in September, just forget it.' I think that was the right thing to say, but as a recruiting statement, it was stupid."

These developments provided encouragement for Driesell, Harrington and Gibson, who kept in almost daily touch with either Tom or his parents all through the next few months.

Between April 15 and mid-June, Smith also talked several times with McMillen and his parents, "although Dr. and Mrs. McMillen became increasingly cold toward me," said Smith.

During this period, McMillen was trying to decide whether to play in the Dapper Dan Classic, a high school all-star game in Pittsburgh. Smith advised him to play. "I told him, 'Tom, you're the best. Go to Pittsburgh and prove it.'" McMillen's parents did not want him to play in the Dapper Dan, and this also proved crucial later.

On June 23, McMillen called Smith again and told him he was ready to sign despite the opposition of his parents. Smith went to Mansfield on June 24, and that afternoon met McMillen at Pierce's Restaurant in Elmira.

Smith had a national letter-of-intent for McMillen to sign, "but I just had Tom sign his first name. I knew it was not a valid letter-of-intent without his parents' signatures." Neither Dr. nor Mrs. McMillen was present for the "signing."

Said Smith, "I thought that if the story came out like 'McMillen signs with UNC' that it might take some of the heat off Tommy."

On the morning of June 25, Ladd Baucom, sports editor of the Greensboro Record, called Dr. and Mrs. McMillen at 6:30. They leveled what is now a famous blast at Smith, charging that the coach had abrogated their parental authority, that recruiting was "a nasty, dirty business" and that they had "valid reasons" for not wanting their son to attend North Carolina.

The words "valid reasons" carried the aroma of possible recruiting violations on the part of North Carolina, and indeed at one point, Gibson came right to the edge of such a charge against Smith.

In mid-June, Gibson asked Virginia's athletic director, Steve Sebo, to set up a meeting with Jim Weaver, the late ACC commissioner. Sebo scheduled the meeting — secretly in a Charlottesville motel, but Gibson called it off. "I thought I had North Carolina dead to rights," he said, "but I needed some corroboration from certain people who decided they didn't want to get involved."

Gibson will not now discuss either his charges or the people who refused to furnish corroboration.

Smith was naturally upset by the phrase "valid reasons." On June 26, Tom McMillen called the North Carolina coach and asked him to come to Mansfield to "square things away

142

with his parents," Smith said.

"I went to Mansfield on the 27th and met with them. We talked, and Dr. and Mrs. McMillen decided to release to *Sports Illustrated* what the 'valid reasons' were.

"I thought that by listing what the reasons were, it would clear my name and Tommy's. So they agreed, and I played secretary. They got the statement worded just as they wanted."

The "valid reasons," as listed by Smith:

(1) THE KITCHEN EPISODE—Mrs. McMillen thought Smith was trying to keep her away from listening to the final recruiting talk. Smith said it was entirely Tom's wish that the two be alone.

(2) THE DAPPER DAN—Dr. and Mrs. McMillen did not want Tom to play in the game. Smith did. Tom played.

(3) THE SIGNING PLACE—Dr. and Mrs. McMillen wanted their son to sign in Mansfield. Smith and McMillen had met several times previously at Pierce's Restaurant, had liked it and had selected the place without second thoughts as the "signing" site.

"We were waiting for a call from Curry Kirkpatrick of *Sports Illustrated*," said Smith. "Just before he was supposed to call, Jay telephoned his parents, and they read him the statement. Jay told them to forget releasing anything like that to *Sports Illustrated*. He told Dr. and Mrs. McMillen, 'It'll just make Coach Smith look bad.' I still don't know what Jay's motives were in giving that advice.

"Curry finally called and I told him there would be no statement. Just before I left, Tommy said, 'C'mon, coach, kiss Mom.' So I did. You know, like kiss-and-make-up. I thought everything had pretty much been ironed out."

The next day, back in Chapel Hill, Smith wrote the McMillens a letter saying he was glad that the situation had been patched up. "I received a return letter from Mrs. McMillen which indicated that they were still very much opposed to me personally and to North Carolina."

From that point until early August, Smith said he experienced great difficulty in reaching Tom by telephone in Mansfield.

On Aug. 7, Smith said he received "an angry call from Mrs. McMillen over a letter Tommy had received. She had been opening Tommy's mail while he was out in Colorado playing for the Olympic development team, and she said Tom had received a letter from someone named Mike Johnston, president of 'The Tar Heel Club' in Chapel Hill. The letter said something like, 'as previously explained to you by Coach Smith, you'll have several credit cards and a $100 per month stipend when you come to UNC. Glad to have you with us.'

"I told Mrs. McMillen that the letter was an obvious fraud. I told her that I had promised Tommy nothing beyond that which the NCAA allows."

There is no Mike Johnston listed in the Chapel Hill telephone book. Neither is there a "Tar Heel Club" in Chapel Hill. There is a Tar Heel Club in Durham, but its roster of members does not list a Mike Johnston. All the rest of the UNC booster clubs carry the name "foundation." Smith said he had no idea who sent the letter.

"I still do not believe that I completely convinced Mrs. McMillen that the letter was fraudulent," said Smith.

By mid-August, McMillen was in Europe touring with the Olympic development team, and shortly after he returned, Dean Smith went to Europe to conduct basketball clinics.

Smith said he had a trans-Atlantic phone conversation with McMillen and told him if the situation became tough again, he would return immediately from Europe.

After McMillen came back to Mansfield, Dr. McMillen contracted pneumonia just before taking the family on a planned vacation to Maine.

After a short hospital stay, Dr. McMillen went with Tom, Jay and Joe Harrington to Ocean City, Md., for the long Labor Day weekend. It was during this time that Smith believes McMillen's resolve to attend North Carolina weakened. He could no longer place himself in the position of being diametrically opposed to his parents' wishes.

"Dr. McMillen, do you have a violent objection if Tommy goes to Virginia? He said, 'No,' and I looked at Tommy and his face just lit up. Right then, I figured I held all the aces."

☐ **Virginia's Bill Gibson**

At this juncture, Virginia's Gibson entered the picture in a key role for the first time since mid-April.

"I returned to Charlottesville from a basketball tour of Japan on Saturday, Sept. 5," said Gibson, "On the night of the 6th, I received a phone call from a friend of mine in Mansfield. He told me that Tommy definitely wasn't going to North Carolina and for me to get up there on the double.

"I went up on Tuesday. Wednesday morning, the 9th, Tommy and I had breakfast together. That night, Mrs. McMillen had scheduled a lawn party at their home, and I figured to make my last pitch to Tommy there.

"That night, Mrs. McMillen guided Dr. McMillen, Tommy and myself into the living room. She said, 'You have something to discuss.' We kind of hemmed and hawed around, and finally I said, 'Dr. McMillen, do you have a violent objection if Tommy goes to Virginia?' He said, 'No,' and I looked at Tommy and his face just lit up.

"Right then, I figured I held all the aces. Later on that night, Tommy asked me questions about stuff he would need for school. I knew we were in.

"Well, at 1 a.m. on the 10th, Jay came walking into the house. A friend had driven him up from College Park. I don't know how Jay found out how touch-and-go the situation was, but he did.

"I left at 1:30 a.m. and went to a friend's house to spend the night. At exactly eight minutes after 9 that morning, Mrs. McMillen called me and said, 'Jay and Tommy have left for College Park.' I later found out that Jay and Dr. McMillen had Tom up until 6 o'clock that morning hashing over the whole thing. It must have been pretty rough."

Smith was still in Europe that morning when Tom McMillen sent a wire to Chapel Hill: "Coach Smith, going to Maryland for reasons you know."

In addition to getting what Gibson calls "a helluva boy," Driesell had a moment of sweet revenge. In 1965, a New York boy named Charles Scott came to Laurinburg (N.C.) Prep School for a year of academic seasoning. He was a great high school player, and Driesell, then coach at Davidson, had received a commitment from Scott to attend the Southern

ACC BASKETBALL / THE '60s

Conference School.

After his year at Laurinburg, Scott decided to attend North Carolina. Later, he became a two-time All-American, and now he is the star rookie for the Virginia Squires of the American Basketball Association.

In mid-November, Dr. McMillen told this reporter that he would be willing to discuss the recruiting of his son. He originally agreed, but he had a change of mind after discussing the situation with Tommy, his wife and Coach Driesell.

On the night of Dec. 8, just after the Maryland freshmen played the Lehigh freshmen, Dr. McMillen reversed himself to certain extent.

"I think it should be made clear that Tommy never signed with North Carolina," said Dr. McMillen. "And the idea that he went to Maryland because of his mother's insistence is preposterous. My wife wanted him to go to Virginia.

"North Carolina had it going all their way, but then they really messed it up.

"Tommy got some really terrible letters after he came to Maryland. They were from what you might call North Carolina 'fans.' Some of them contained outright threats against him, and none of those were signed. One man wrote a letter containing some veiled threats and was stupid enough to sign his name to it. If we had wanted, I think we could have prosecuted him."

Dr. McMillen said his wife, now recuperating from a broken hip in a Blossburg, Pa., hospital, is planning to write a book on her son.

In a brief interview, Tom McMillen said that he hasn't regretted his decision.

"I haven't tried to put last summer out of my mind," he said. "It's there, and you just can't forget it. But I like it here. The academic work is interesting (so far, McMillen has had nothing but A's on test papers), and this school is big enough (35,000 students) for me to kind of get lost in it sometimes. That has its bad and good aspects."

Earlier this month, McMillen told a *Washington Post* reporter, Paul Attner, that he did consider the sentiments of his family when he made his decision to come to Maryland. "But the ultimate choice was mine. You have to consider everyone's feelings when you do something like this and maybe I didn't do that at first."

Attner wrote, "Yet, he seems destined to play his college ball under the stigma of being a 6-foot-11 momma's boy, an impression, he says, 'which is entirely wrong.' Correct or not, fans at North Carolina, Duke and other Atlantic Coast Conference strongholds are not about to let him forget the controversy surrounding his belated decision to attend Maryland."

In his short talk with this reporter, McMillen said, "I think they treat me normally here. They don't overwhelm me and they don't neglect me."

McMillen, who is so organized he plans his activities for each day on three-by-five index cards, will never have any worries along that line.

Russ Potts, a member of the Maryland athletic publicity staff, said, "McMillen is a super kid, but he's *so* naive. He thinks that he's just like you and me. But he's not. He's something special. He always will be."

ACC

Congressman Tom McMillen (D-Maryland) agrees with the basic content of Bill Millsaps' story on his recruitment. However, through correspondence with the editors of *ACC Basketball: An Illustrated History*, Congressman McMillen wants to clarify several inaccuracies in the article, which was first published in the *Richmond-Times Dispatch* Nov. 29, 1970.

In addition to making official recruiting trips to Virginia, Maryland, Duke and North Carolina, McMillen said he visited Pennsylvania, Princeton and Kentucky. McMillen also said his father, who died Dec. 29, 1973, was not sick with pneumonia during the recruiting process and that the McMillen family vacation that summer was in Rehobeth, Del., not Ocean City, Md.

In reflecting, Congressman McMillen said the recruiting process was trying but was one of the most enjoyable periods of his life. McMillen was a three-time member of the All-ACC team at Maryland and remains the school's all-time leading scorer (1,807 points) for a three-year career. He was a member of the 1972 U.S. Olympic basketball team.

McMillen delayed his professional career for one year of study at Oxford as a Rhodes Scholar. He then played 11 seasons in the NBA with the Buffalo Braves, Atlanta Hawks, New York Knicks and Washington Bullets before winning a seat as the Fourth District Congressman from Maryland.

Jay McMillen, now a practicing doctor in St. Joseph's, Mo., said he never applied to the University of North Carolina Medical School, as reported in the story. He graduated from the University of Maryland Medical School in 1974.

Aftermath

U.S. Rep. Tom McMillen

Dr. McMillen said, if he had it to do over again, he wouldn't have gotten so involved in his brother's recruitment.

"One of the traits of Scotch-Irish is their loyalty in the face of reason," Dr. McMillen said. "I think that surfaced in this recruiting. For a lot of reasons, my father and myself had allegiences to Maryland. We thought Tom ought to go to Maryland and do what he eventually did . . .

"The only thing I didn't like about it was I felt responsible for Tom all the while he was at Maryland because I helped him make the decision. In the long run, he was probably better off at Maryland because he was one of a few, but would have been one of many at North Carolina."

Margaret McMillen, Tom's mother, never wrote the book about her son's recruiting that she mentioned. She remarried following her husband's death and now lives in Mansfield during the summer and in Florida during the winter.

Joe Harrington remained at Maryland as an assistant until 1979 before moving on to become head coach at George Mason and later Long Beach State.

Bill Gibson coached 11 seasons at Virginia, through 1974, and one at South Florida. He died of a heart attack in July of 1975.

Lefty Driesell coached at Maryland for 15 seasons, through 1986, and went on to work for the school's educational foundation in a fund-raising capacity. Then in April, 1988, Driesell accepted the head coaching position at James Madison University in Harrisonburg, Va.

Dean Smith continues to coach at North Carolina.

— Editors

THE '70s

THE '70s

Amen, Amen, Amen.

N.C. State took a page from Maryland's song book in a 103-100 win in the '74 ACC final, the league's greatest game.

John Lucas bounded across the Greensboro Coliseum court and into the Maryland huddle. Any possible fatigue from three consecutive nights of grueling basketball was lost with the prospect of winning an ACC championship.

"I want to take it," Lucas screamed to Coach Lefty Driesell above the din of delirious fans. "I want to take it. Give me the ball. I'm taking this shot and we're winning this game."

For 39 minutes and 51 seconds, two of the nation's best basketball teams ran up and down the Coliseum court at a furious pace. There may have been an equal collection of talented athletes on the court for a previous ACC Tournament game, but never had so many stars performed at such a high level. Never mind that it was also a championship, one determining the league's lone representative to the 1974 NCAA Tournament.

The 15,451 fans on hand, plus a regional television audience, were drained. Intense action, combined with unseasonably warm, 65-degree weather outside, created sauna-like conditions inside. Exactly 141 tins of aspirin were sold during Thursday's opening round, and the Coliseum's supply was depleted by Saturday's championship.

Maryland was trying to dethrone State, a team that went unbeaten in 27 games the previous season but stayed home during the NCAAs to serve a one-year probation. Only an early season loss to UCLA kept the Wolfpack from another undefeated season. Against ACC opponents, State had not been beaten in 31 straight games.

Yet when Maryland center Len Elmore banked in a shot near the basket with 1:12 remaining, State's drive to a national championship was up in the air. The Coliseum scoreboard registered the fifth tie of the game. Both teams had 97 points.

Fueled by a snubbing in All-ACC voting, State's Burleson towered over the Terps for 38 points.

State got the first crack at a final game-winning shot, and the Wolfpack called time out with 57 seconds remaining. As Coach Norm Sloan sketched a final play, guard Monte Towe sat, exhausted and legs outstretched, at the end of the bench. Moments earlier, Towe had limped to the sideline with leg cramps and was being attended to by trainer Herman Bunch.

Mark Moeller rushed to the scorer's table to check in for Towe. Moeller wasn't the ball handler that Towe was, but the 6-3 junior was an aggressive and dedicated player whose eight points contributed to State's 76-74 ACC championship victory over Maryland the year before.

Twenty-five seconds remained when an errant pass by Moeller was intercepted by Maryland forward Tom McMillen. State fans shook their heads in disbelief, thinking all the while that a case of leg cramps was going to keep the Wolfpack from winning the ACC and ultimately the national championship.

Maryland ran the clock to nine seconds, then called time out to set a final play. The timeout allowed Towe, who shook off his cramps, to return to the lineup.

Having listened to Lucas' plea, Driesell turned to his assistant coaches for help. There was confusion, no doubt. But Lefty knew the ball should be in Lucas' hands on the final play. Lucas was a clutch performer, confident to the point of being cocky. He welcomed any chance to take charge in a pressure situation, having won city and state tennis championships since grammar school before thousands of spectators.

"We're better athletes," Driesell said as the horn sounded and Maryland broke its huddle. "Just take it, Luke. Take it and go."

At the other end of the court, Sloan knew exactly what he wanted from his team. State's freelance style of play for most of the game allowed Sloan to concentrate on end-of-game situations.

Regardless of who received Maryland's inbounds pass, Sloan wanted his defender to go for a steal even if it meant fouling. With only four team fouls in the second half, State could commit two more before sending Maryland to the free throw line.

"Concentrate, pressure the ball and keep them from getting a good shot," Sloan said as he knelt before his team. He then turned to guard Moe Rivers for special instruction.

"Don't let Lucas drive the lane. Moe, you've done it for us all year, force Lucas to one side of the court. He'll want to go to his left, you know that. That's okay, force him to his left."

State broke its huddle confident it could prevent Maryland from taking a good shot. Lucas carried enough confidence for the rest of the Maryland team as the Terps returned to the court.

"I'll win this thing. Don't worry, Coach," Lucas said.

Before Lucas could catch the inbounds pass from Mo Howard, Rivers went for the steal and fouled. One of Maryland's precious nine remaining seconds had vanished.

On the second inbounds try, Howard passed to Lucas, who caught the ball and attempted to dribble down the lane. Lucas was left-handed, rarely dribbling with his right hand. But he made up for the deficiency with superior quickness.

Rivers, considered State's best defender, slapped at the ball with his quick hands and forced Lucas to pick up his dribble just to the left of the key.

Rivers had done his job.

Lucas then spotted Howard open, 18 feet to the left of the basket. Towe, in an attempt to help Rivers keep Lucas from penetrating the lane, had left Howard alone.

Lucas passed to Howard as the clock ran to four seconds. Howard, who had made 10 of his previous 13 shots in the game, was open. Maryland's chances for winning the ACC championship and shaking five straight frustrating losses to State over the past two seasons rested in Howard's hands.

"He could have stuck it right off the glass that he so loved," Terp Assistant Coach Dave Pritchett said 14 years later.

Howard, like the rest of the Maryland team, was geared to thinking Lucas would take the final shot. For one fateful second, maybe less than a second, he surveyed the court. In that instant, Towe recovered his defensive position and darted toward Howard to contest the shot. State center Tom Burleson, all 7-4 of him, was also running, arms extended, toward Howard.

Instead of shooting, Howard turned and passed the ball back to Lucas.

Some 25 feet from the basket, Lucas heaved the ball.

It didn't come close as time expired.

The State players charged back to the sidelines in celebration. They had executed Sloan's plan perfectly and were rewarded with an overtime.

The Maryland players hung their heads as they walked back to map strategy for five more minutes of overtime.

"You had to win that one to get to the NCAAs," Burleson was to say later, "and that game was just so incredible."

●

Tom Burleson couldn't sit still the day of a big game. He burned off nervous energy during a morning shooting session at the Coliseum, then did some shopping with his sister.

Preparing Burleson's pysche was an important part of Sloan's planning for State's championship game against Maryland. Burleson had a competitive edge like no other member of that '74 State team. Give him enough incentive to win and he was likely to respond with a spectacular performance.

"Knock him down and he was like a big bag of bones getting thrown into a corner," said State Assistant Coach Eddie Biedenbach years later. "But he'd jump up with cuts and bruises and play right on. Nobody realizes how tough Tommy is."

Sloan had plenty of wood to stoke Burleson's fire for the championship. Earlier in the week, Burleson was not named to the All-ACC first team, finishing sixth in the voting behind Maryland's Len Elmore.

However unfair it was, Burleson probably lost his spot on the first team during State's 80-74 victory over Maryland on Super Bowl Sunday in Raleigh. He made only three of 19 shots and was generally embarrassed by Elmore, who went on to wrestle the ACC's rebounding title away from Burleson for the first time in three years.

Elmore talked as big a game as he played that season. Following the game in Raleigh, he told a reporter to tell Burleson, "I'm the best center in the ACC."

Sloan clipped the quote from the newspaper and tucked it in his wallet. He removed it on the morning of State's championship game against Maryland and taped it to Burleson's locker.

Following the morning shooting session, the Wolfpack returned to the Albert Pick Hotel near the Greensboro Regional Airport. The team gathered again at 4 o'clock for a pregame meal of steak and potatoes in the hotel ballroom. A can of Ken-L Ration dog food was placed on Burleson's plate.

The can meant Sloan had deemed Burleson's play against Virginia (15 points, 11 rebounds) in the Tournament semifinals to be the most valuable on the team. Even though David Thompson

ACC BASKETBALL / THE '70s

scored 37 points in State's 87-66 victory, the choice of Burleson was one more ploy by Sloan to psych his center.

Prior to the season, Curry Kirkpatrick of *Sports Illustrated* wrote that the Wolfpack deserved the "Ken-L Ration Award" for having the nation's biggest "dog" schedule of non-conference opponents. Following every win in '74 — even those over Chihuahuas Vermont and East Carolina — Sloan designated a winner of the dog food. By season's end, Ken-L Ration had learned of Sloan's award and sent a case of dog food to State, as well as a trophy to the team MVP at the end of the season.

"It makes me sick. I see who is getting bids to this NCAA Tournament. I know that we and Carolina and State are better than most teams. But only one of us is going. It's not fair."

☐ **Maryland Coach Lefty Driesell**

So as the chartered Greyhound bus carrying the N.C. State team rolled down Lee Street toward the Greensboro Coliseum, Burleson was consumed with how he could dominate Elmore.

Meanwhile, as the Maryland team entered the back side of the Greensboro Coliseum, a strange feeling ran through the team. The Terps were back for a third straight year and were a little tired of having to beat a team from North Carolina on Tobacco Road for the title. The prospect of losing to State, then watching the likes of Creighton, Pittsburgh and South Carolina play in the NCAA Tournament, irritated Driesell.

"It makes me sick," Driesell said. "I see who is getting bids to this NCAA Tournament and I know that we and Carolina and State are better than most of the teams. But only one of us is going. It's not fair."

The feeling was a little different for State players and coaches as they arrived at the Coliseum. Hundreds of fans were already in the parking lot — three hours before tipoff — seeking extra tickets. Sloan walked his players through the crowd of fans. He wanted them to take note of the interest in the championship game, as well as the Tournament.

The ACC Tournament was special to Sloan because he played under Coach Everett Case in the late '40s at State. Case loved any kind of tournament, whether it was the old Southern Conference, the ACC or the Dixie Classic.

"The Tournament is a banquet and every game is a feast," Sloan often quoted Case as saying.

There was little festivity in the State locker room prior to the '74 championship game. Burleson read the quote from Elmore, then read it again. Sloan mentioned to the team that it was important to "grind it out." Otherwise, the players knew what to do as they dressed in their home uniforms — white with red piping.

Driesell, likewise, had few instructions for his club. Defensive assignments were posted on a chalkboard, but little was different from previous meetings against State.

"No strategy is going to win or lose this game," Driesell told his team, which sported red V-neck jerseys with white trim. "We've just got to play better than they do."

Across the Coliseum, officials Jim Hernjak and Hank Nichols went through their usual pregame rituals. Hernjak was the veteran of the team and was calling his fourth ACC Tournament. Nichols was the league's rising star, calling the championship game in each of his first two ACC seasons.

The crowd formed a sea of red all around the Coliseum, which had added a second deck four years earlier to increase its capacity by 7,000. Not a seat was empty when Hernjak walked to center court and tossed the ball into the air for Burleson and McMillen.

The game's first two possessions were a clear indication of things to come.

Burleson won the opening jump and Towe gained possession in the backcourt. Towe dribbled the ball four times and quickly passed to Tim Stoddard in the corner. Without hesitating, Stoddard fired a 20-footer that missed. It wasn't the kind of shot State wanted, and for the moment Sloan probably wished Stoddard had stuck to playing baseball.

Stoddard was State's third choice off the Hammond (Ind.) High School team of 1971. Guard Pete Trgovich headed to UCLA, and forward Junior Bridgeman chose Louisville. So State landed Stoddard because Assistant Coach Sam Esposito, who doubled as the baseball coach, knew the 6-7 forward threw his 230 pounds around a basketball floor as well as he threw a fastball from a pitching mound. He would pitch Esposito's Wolfpack to ACC baseball titles in '73, '74 and '75.

But Stoddard was not State's best shooter, and Lucas grabbed the missed shot and advanced it past halfcourt with five dribbles. He quickly shot a pass to the corner, where McMillen aimed a 20-footer at the basket and missed.

Fifteen seconds had elapsed, and the teams had already traveled the length of the court twice and attempted two long jump shots.

Owen Brown rebounded McMillen's miss and sank a 5-foot hook shot. Whatever Brown contributed on offense was a bonus to Maryland. A broken foot in preseason slowed Brown, but he gained a starting spot at midseason and now was given the unenviable task of guarding Thompson. Brown replaced Tom Roy in the starting lineup following State's Super Sunday win over the Terps. That's when Thompson scored 41 points against Roy, who fouled out in 15 minutes, Brown and Jap Trimble.

For two seasons, Maryland tried everything and everyone to stop Thompson, who was the ACC's Player of the Year for a second season. Thompson offered a unique problem for the Terps, and most other opponents. He was an exceptional outside shooter, ranking third in the league with a 54.7 shooting percentage that season. "In our rating system, the highest number is five," said Boston Celtic Coach Tom Heinsohn. "Thompson gets 10 on his shooting alone."

The Wolfpack ran one basic play throughout most of the '73 and '74 seasons, geared of course to Thompson's shooting and leaping abilities. Towe handled the ball from his point guard position, and Rivers played one wing. Towe's first pass was usually to Stoddard on the other wing, with Burleson posted down low on the same side of the court. Stoddard first looked to get the ball inside to Burleson. Meanwhile, Thompson posted at the opposite baseline and then moved to the top of the key.

That's where Thompson was most dangerous. He could shoot over any size player because of his vertical leap. He was also lightning quick and could drive past a defender to the basket.

"You had to decide if you wanted to give Thompson the ball at the top of the key or near the free throw line," Driesell said. "If you denied the pass from Stoddard to Thompson, look out."

If Thompson was denied the pass, he would break to the basket and jump for an alley-oop pass from Stoddard. Only a

ACC BASKETBALL / THE '70s

no-dunk rule prevented the lob pass from being a sure two points. Even so, it was about 90 percent certain that Thompson would drop in any pass near the basket for two points. The sight of Thompson breaking down the lane to time his leap and snare a high-arcing pass was absolutely spectacular.

"Sometimes I catch myself just standing and watching him," Towe said. "He's just amazing."

By the ACC Tournament, Driesell had decided to let Thompson get the ball at the top of the key and hope he would have a poor shooting night. Brown was to guard Thompson because, at 6-8, he was 4 inches taller than the State forward.

Brown's follow shot in the game's early seconds was the first of six straight field goals for the Terps, who bolted to a 14-5 lead in less than four minutes.

Maryland's "special stack" offense worked to perfection in the early minutes. Throughout the season, the Terps also used only one set play on offense. Elmore and McMillen set up on one side of the lane, then Elmore cleared to the opposite side. When Lucas dribbled to McMillen's side of the court, they played a two-on-two game with the opponent. Both could drive as well as shoot from outside.

Maryland once thought about clearing one side of the court for Howard, who was 6-3, to work against Towe. But opponents soon learned that Burleson and Thompson looked after their little buddy inside. In return, Towe bought a pizza for any teammate who blocked one of his man's shots.

Maryland's offense gave State trouble because Burleson guarded McMillen. If McMillen cleared to the corner, Burleson followed and it left the basket virtually unguarded, except for Thompson. But State did not want Thompson guarding the basket for fear of foul trouble.

State, which played only man-to-man defense, countered Maryland's attack by having Towe leave Howard on occasion to help Rivers guard Lucas. That left open jump shots for Howard, who was dangerous because he was a streak shooter. Howard made his first four attempts, and with six minutes expired, Maryland had made 12 of 14 shots for a 25-12 advantage.

Howard was highly recruited out of St. Joseph's Prep School, where he was the Philadelphia player of the year his senior year. Although he played center in high school, Howard fit into Maryland's plans as a shooting guard because of Lucas' ball-handling skills at point guard. Howard was also content to be a role player and made himself a defensive specialist.

When the teams met in late January in College Park, Howard's play was instrumental in Maryland building a 67-59 lead with nine minutes remaining.

"You don't really worry, though," Towe said after Thompson scored 31 of his 39 points in the second half as State rallied for an 86-80 victory. "At times like that, you just turn it over to David. Wouldn't you?"

Thompson's athletic ability and Burleson's determination to beat Elmore 1-on-1 kept State from getting blown out by Maryland in the first half of the championship game. In one sequence, Thompson rebounded a McMillen miss, dribbled the length of the court, missed a short jump shot, rebounded it and banked in a shot from 8 feet. On another play, Burleson rebounded a shot and dropped the ball back over his head into the basket.

Burleson and Thompson each had 10 points, but the Wolfpack still trailed Maryland 37-26 with 7:26 left until halftime. State was a difficult team to put away. Only UCLA had done that, outscoring the Wolfpack 30-12 over the final 10 minutes for an 84-66 victory on Dec. 15 in St. Louis.

"That defeat caused all of us to stop and take stock of ourselves, to seriously re-evaluate ourselves," Sloan said.

Down to Maryland by 11, State took stock again and rallied. Thompson was fouled when he missed an alley-oop attempt on a pass from Stoddard and made one free throw. When Thompson missed the second free throw, Stoddard rebounded and made a reverse layup to give State its first lead, 42-41, with 3:11 until halftime.

Maryland quickly responded with a 15-footer from Lucas, a steal and fast-break layup by Lucas and an 8-foot hook shot by McMillen on which Thompson was called for goaltending as he knocked the ball high into the stands.

The first half ended with Maryland leading 55-50.

"Truthfully, I don't mind being behind a point, two or three at the half," Driesell said later. "If you're behind, you can come in at halftime and raise a little Cain, criticize people and tell them they've got to do this or that."

As it was, Maryland needed to make no changes at halftime. The Terps continued their torrid Tournament shooting, making 63.4 percent of their 41 first-half attempts after hitting 52.7 percent against Duke in the first round and 63.3 percent against UNC in the semifinals.

Maryland stayed with its plan to let Thompson catch the ball at the top of the key. Even though he scored 21 points by halftime, Thompson missed eight of 15 shots. Despite a 14-point first half by Burleson, Driesell told his guards not to sag back on the State center. Driesell was confident that Elmore could stop Burleson, and his guards needed to keep a hand in the face of Towe and Rivers.

Driesell's only concern at halftime was foul trouble. Brown had three in his attempts to stop Thompson. Elmore, Lucas and Roy each had two. Roy had played the final three minutes of the half; otherwise, Driesell made no substitutions.

"Push the ball up the floor," Driesell told his team. "Jam the lane defensively and no second shots for Thompson, Burleson and Stoddard."

State got several baskets via offensive rebounds and, like Maryland, had only four turnovers in the first half. The Wolfpack made half of its 42 shot attempts.

Sloan made a significant switch at halftime, putting the quicker and more agile Phil Spence on McMillen, who had missed only two of 10 shots and had 16 points. Spence was quick enough to play in front of McMillen and deny the pass inside from Lucas.

"They can't keep shooting like they are," Sloan said as he removed the garish plaid jacket that had become his trademark since he wore it for State's Super Sunday TV game in 1973.

"Keep grinding it out," Sloan said. "Get a hand in their face on every jump shot. They won't shoot 60 percent this half. Grind it out. Take your time and stay with it. Make them earn everything. Don't let them get things too easily."

Everything seemed to fall apart for the Terps in the first six minutes of the second half. A 16-6 run gave State a 66-61 lead. Maryland emphasized slowing State's fast break, but the Wolfpack got three breakaway layups during the stretch. State also got a basket from Towe on a shot attempted from beyond the line that marked three-point range for the Carolina Cougars, who played many of their American Basketball Association home games at the Coliseum. The circle was 23 feet, 9 inches from the basket.

If things weren't bad enough for the Terps, Lucas picked up an unnecessary third foul when he reached around Towe from

The offense of Burleson (L) and defense of Thompson (R) proved too much for Elmore and the Terps.

ACC BASKETBALL / THE '70s

behind. Then Brown got his fourth when he swung his elbows after a rebound and brushed Burleson, who collapsed to the floor. Nichols rewarded Burleson's acting with the foul call.

Just as the crowd began to sense that State was ready for the kill, Maryland rallied behind Lucas and Howard. Watching Maryland's semifinal victory over UNC, Burleson had noticed that the Terps got excellent outlet passes from Elmore and McMillen. So Burleson took it upon himself to guard the Maryland rebounder on each State miss. His arm waving in the faces of Elmore and McMillen prevented any quick outlet passes by the Terps.

But Burleson couldn't stop Maryland's guards from making steals. First Lucas hit a jumper, made a steal and converted it into a fast break layup. Then Howard made a steal, a breakaway layup, then two more layups off State mistakes. All of a sudden, Maryland led 77-72 with 11:40 remaining.

The fast-paced action and the lead swings made both coaches feel they had no control over the action. There was so much talent on the floor, no strategic move was going to stop either team.

Both coaches had actually modified their styles for this season.

Driesell abandoned his usual gimmicks, such as holding a couple of late-night practices and letting a dance expert teach his team agility exercises. Driesell didn't conduct a midnight practice to open the season as he did in his first four years at Maryland. By his fifth ACC Tournament, Driesell had built the Maryland program to a point where he didn't need gimmicks.

Sloan, who managed ACC Tournament slowdown upsets of Duke (1968 semifinals) and South Carolina (1970 championship) with inferior talent, committed to doing less coaching with his '74 squad.

"It's difficult for the players when you have an intense, uptight coach," said Sloan. "I was as intense and uptight as they come . . . If you have the superior team, go out and play. Most of the time you'll win."

Sloan could afford to do that since he had Thompson, whom he had lured out of Shelby, N.C., after a recruiting battle with UNC. But Thompson had a bad second half, making only three of nine shots, so Burleson took it upon himself to score. Over the middle seven minutes, Burleson scored on two hook shots and two tip-ins of Thompson misses. State pulled back even at 89 when Spence made one of two free throws.

In addition to tying the score, Spence drew a fourth foul on Lucas. Now the Terps were in serious foul trouble: Brown and Roy already had four each, and Elmore had three. For that reason, State probably did Maryland a favor when it went to its Tease offense with 4:25 remaining and the score tied at 91.

The Tease was essentially the same as UNC's Four Corners, but Sloan was not about to give Tar Heel Coach Dean Smith credit for devising such a successful offense.

The rivalry between Sloan and Smith was only one of many among the coaches in the ACC. They often carried them off the court, into recruiting.

UNC, Maryland and Virginia fought to the bitter end for McMillen. State and Duke were placed on one-year probations for illegally recruiting Thompson, and a public spat developed later when State coaches indirectly accused UNC's Smith of turning the Wolfpack in to the NCAA. Burleson was wooed by State, Maryland and UNC. He chose State because he liked the Raleigh campus during a 4-H visit in junior high. He and Thompson also made a pact during a summer camp to attend the same school.

Lucas attracted attention from UNC, Duke, State and Maryland in an unusual way. No coach was certain Lucas could play in the ACC. He did not have a jump shot and used only his left hand. At one point, Duke Assistant Coach Hubie Brown said Lucas would never be more than a reserve for the Blue Devils. UNC's Smith said Lucas would have to sit while George Karl played.

But Driesell took to the charisma of Lucas, who was a standout at Hillside High School in Durham, N.C. Driesell also came to realize that no player moved the ball downcourt and into the right player's hands better than Lucas. He was like a hockey player, maneuvering at a breakneck pace.

But as soon as Towe stopped and signalled for State to run its "tease" offense, Lucas was no longer in control of the action. The ball was now in the hands of Towe, who three years earlier was considered a better prospect as a jockey than a major college basketball player.

Dick Dickey, an All-America at State from 1948 through 1950, saw Towe play at Converse (Ind.) High School and recommended him to the State coaches. A few years earlier, Dickey had recommended Rich Yunkus to Sloan, then John Mengelt. Yunkus went to Georgia Tech and Mengelt to Auburn before both landed in the NBA.

Sloan decided to take Dickey's advice on Towe and sent Biedenbach to take a look. From the outset, Biedenbach was skeptical. But he was impressed with Towe's long-range shooting and athletic skills. Towe quarterbacked Converse to consecutive state football championships.

Towe made up for his lack of size with incredible quickness and ball-handling skills. He was the first player that forced UNC's Smith to abandon full-court pressure because Towe simply dribbled through it.

If the defense denied Stoddard's pass, Thompson would take off toward the basket, soaring into alley-oop position.

ACC BASKETBALL / THE '70s

Towe was at his best in the center of State's "tease," where he could dribble around and through the defense. He was remarkable at spotting an open teammate for a basket, or pulling the ball out to midcourt to run time off the clock.

His lob to Burleson gave State a 93-91 lead, but McMillen's 8-foot baseline turnaround tied the game. Then Spence scored on a layup with 2:58 remaining on a brilliant pass from Burleson that bounced between McMillen's legs near the basket.

After McMillen turned the ball over to State, Burleson followed a miss by Towe and was fouled by Brown, his fifth. Driesell inserted guard Billy Hahn into the game. Although Brown was valuable to Maryland, Hahn actually helped the Terps on defense because, at 5-11, he was better able to chase Towe.

Burleson made both free throws and State led 97-93 with 2:12 remaining.

In less than a minute, Maryland got clutch bank shots from Roy and Elmore to tie the game at 97. Roy's basket surprised State because he was not much of a threat on offense. Roy was a rebounder and defensive specialist who earlier in the season held Larry Fogle of Canisius to 20 points, or 13 below his nation-leading average. Roy gained a reputation around the league as a roughneck player, drawing the wrath of fans, especially those at Duke.

"I don't mind being thought of as a bad guy," Roy said. "You get a little respect from the players on the floor."

Elmore had earned that respect in other ways. He was highly recruited out of Brooklyn's Power Memorial High School, where he played after Lew Alcindor left for UCLA. Like Alcindor, Elmore was intelligent as a player and student. But not until his junior year did Elmore take basketball seriously. He was more interested in studying for law school. Once he made a commitment to basketball, Elmore became an exceptional rebounder and scorer.

Elmore worked Maryland into a tie and ultimately into a position to win the ACC championship at the end of regulation. But Howard passed up the potential game-winning shot and the teams headed to overtime.

The previous two nights were beginning to take a toll on the Terps. In Maryland's 85-66 opening-round win over Duke, Driesell rested McMillen and Lucas for six minutes apiece and Elmore only four. In the 105-85 semifinal win over UNC, Brown, Elmore and Howard played the entire game. Lucas and McMillen each got only two minutes rest.

Driesell kept his starters in the game against UNC to the very end. He wanted to savor every last second of such a lopsided decision, the worst loss in the Tournament for UNC since 1959.

"That was a hate game," Pritchett recalled of the semifinal. "That was a vicious game. We were going to beat their butts as bad as we could beat them."

In retrospect, Driesell probably should have stored those precious few minutes of rest for his starters. Instead, he faced overtime against State with McMillen, Elmore, Lucas and Howard having played every second against State.

State, on the other hand, was well-rested. Since there were only seven teams in the league, the Wolfpack received a first-round bye for finishing first in the regular season. A 21-point decision over Virginia in the semifinals allowed Sloan to get 54 minutes, or 27 percent, of the action from his bench. Against Maryland, Sloan gave each of his starters at least a two-minute breather in each half.

State controlled the tip in overtime, but Howard and Hahn forced Thompson into a turnover and Elmore converted one

State's Monte Towe (top) made up for his lack of size with extraordinary ball-handling skills, giving Terps John Lucas (L) and Tom McMillen plenty of problems to discuss.

of two free throws at the other end for a 98-97 lead. Burleson countered with a 5-foot hook across the lane.

After each team turned the ball over, Howard was fouled and made two free throws. Thompson then missed an 8-foot shot, McMillen rebounded and Lucas was fouled.

Lucas toed the free throw line for a 1-and-1 with Maryland leading 100-99 and 2:16 remaining. A 75 percent free throw shooter for the season, Lucas missed his first attempt.

"He was just exhausted," Driesell said later in defense of Lucas.

The miss was the break State needed, and Towe whipped a pass through Maryland's defense. The pass landed in Spence's

Terp Coach Lefty Driesell stalks off the floor after shaking hands with State Coach Norm Sloan following another bitter ACC Tournament championship loss.

hands, and his layup gave the Wolfpack a 101-100 lead with 2:04 left.

Burleson blocked Howard's 5-footer from the baseline, but Rivers missed a 1-and-1 attempt with 1:21 left. Driesell then decided to go for broke and play for a final shot. Rivers quickly forced a jump ball when he tied up Lucas, but Maryland retained possession on the jump.

The clock ticked below 30 seconds when Lucas dribbled to the right wing and spotted Elmore cutting from the baseline toward the opposite side of the foul line. Lucas jumped to throw the cross-court pass over Rivers' head. But the pass sailed several feet over Elmore's head. Elmore, thinking the pass was intended for a teammate behind him, pulled his hands down to his side and the ball went out of bounds. It was that far overthrown.

"I've never forgotten that pass," Lucas said years later.

Maryland was then forced to foul, and Hahn hacked Towe with six seconds remaining. Towe, who was once timed to have released the ball less than a second after getting it from the official on free throws, rapidly made both attempts, and State led by the final score of 103-100.

Following Towe's free throws, Maryland advanced the ball to midcourt and called a timeout. But the Terps could only get off a long, meaningless shot by Hahn that missed at the buzzer, and N.C. State won the ACC championship.

"I never thought we'd lose until I heard the horn go off," said Lucas, who buried his face in a towel for 10 minutes following the game. He then cried openly.

Sloan and Driesell met at the scorer's table where they abruptly shook hands, both drained with emotion. Driesell was momentarily stunned by the loss and shook his head in disgust, as Sloan slapped his hands together in jubilation and joined his team on the court.

Much of the crowd stood dazed, knowing they had just witnessed an incredible game. The 203 points were the most for an ACC championship game. Maryland made 61 percent of its field goal attempts. State sank 55 percent of its attempts. Few of the game's 29 turnovers were unforced.

Maryland's attack was balanced with McMillen and Howard scoring 22 apiece, Elmore and Lucas getting 18 each and Brown scoring 14. Elmore also had 13 rebounds, and Lucas 10 assists.

No Maryland player had a poor performance, making it more difficult to accept the second-place trophy. With State fans singing *Amen, Amen*—the Maryland victory song in Cole Field House—Driesell first ordered his team to the locker room. But Maryland Athletic Director Jim Kehoe intercepted the team and asked it to remain on the court for the awards ceremony.

Thompson was always the first State player to clip the championship nets. He scored 29 points, but his performance was not among his best. He missed 14 of 24 shots, had six turnovers and only five rebounds. Towe was spectacular with 17 points,

ACC BASKETBALL / THE '70s

eight assists and only one turnover in 41 minutes.

Then there was Burleson.

"He's a great ballplayer, but 38 points against me is unbelievable," Elmore said. "Nobody has ever done that to me and I just can't believe it."

Burleson got a career high by making 18 of 25 shots. He also had 13 rebounds. If he wanted to convince the skeptics, Elmore among them, then Burleson did more than enough.

"We tried everything we could to stop the guy," Driesell said. "He just had a fabulous, fabulous night. He was super fired up."

Driesell then walked to the State locker room, found Burleson and said, "Tommy, that was the best game I have ever seen a big man play."

Often maligned and not always appreciated throughout his career, Burleson was recognized for at least one night as the reason State won the ACC championship. He graciously accepted a second straight Everett Case Award as the Tournament's MVP, then continued a ritual he had started early that season.

He walked to each cubicle in the State dressing room and shook hands with every player. "Thanks, you made me another $100,000 tonight," said Burleson, who figured his NBA stock could reach $1 million if State won the NCAA Championship.

Across the room, Sloan was talking to a horde of writers.

"That was one of the greatest college games that has ever been played," Sloan said. "And I think we beat the second best team in the nation tonight."

That was no consolation to Maryland and Driesell, who answered every last question from reporters outside the deathly silent Terps' dressing room.

Driesell then took one long gulp of a soft drink and said, "It's a hard way to make a living."

•

Maryland, claiming it had nothing else to prove, refused a bid to play in the National Invitational Tournament.

Two days following the ACC championship, McMillen said the Terps should withdraw from the ACC. "We're the outcasts," he said. "Just for once I'd like to see the roles reversed. I'd like to see everything going for us with the crowd behind us and see what they would do. It's got to make a difference."

State went on to win the NCAA Championship on the same Greensboro Coliseum court two weeks later. The Wolfpack stopped UCLA's streak of seven straight titles with a thrilling, double-overtime victory in the national semifinals, then defeated Marquette in an anticlimactic championship game.

NCAA Tournament history is filled with lore about the greatest games of all-time — North Carolina's triple-overtime win over Kansas in 1957, Loyola's dethroning of two-time champion Cincinnati in 1963, Villanova's upset of Georgetown in 1985, to mention three.

But in ACC annals, there is only one.

The greatness of the 1974 ACC Tournament championship grew to mythical proportions over the years. Sloan said in the early '80s that he recalled only a handful of turnovers in the game. Others distinctly remember two, and sometimes three, overtime periods. And although only 15,451 witnessed the game, many thousands more tell friends they were at the Greensboro Coliseum on Saturday night, March 9, 1974.

Myths aside, the game has maintained its place as the greatest ever played in the Atlantic Coast Conference.

'70

On October 15, 1969, more than 8,000 basketball fans filed into Carolina Coliseum on the University of South Carolina campus. They came to witness the arrival of the South's newest college basketball power. This was the first day of practice for the 1970 season, and the Gamecocks of South Carolina were the nation's No. 1-ranked team. *Sports Illustrated* said so, as did *Sport, Basketball News, Basketball Weekly, Basketball Yearbook, Time* and The Associated Press.

South Carolina Coach Frank McGuire had been there before. He was hired at North Carolina in the early '50s to challenge Coach Everett Case and his N.C. State Wolfpack. Once McGuire had led UNC to a national championship in 1957, the Tar Heels were crowned king of the ACC.

McGuire aimed to do the same at South Carolina, and 1970 was the season he expected to sweep through the ACC and on to the NCAA Championship. A UCLA team without Lew Alcindor was not expected to win a fourth straight national title. South Carolina, which returned its top four players from a team that was 21-7 in 1969, was a natural choice to win the ACC. Since the league sent seven teams to the Final Four in the previous decade, it was reasonable to expect the ACC to have another challenger for the national crown.

The lone player lost from the previous season was guard Billy Walsh, who was declared academically ineligible for the first semester and was eventually sidelined for the season. With Walsh in South Carolina's fold, the Gamecocks could have employed a three-guard offense and relied on 6-foot-2 Bobby Cremins to help with the rebounding.

Without Walsh, Cremins and John Roche, the ACC Player of the Year the previous season as a sophomore, worked in the backcourt. That allowed 6-10 sophomore Tom Riker, who had averaged 26.6 points and 18.3 rebounds for the South Carolina freshman team the previous season, to play on the front line along with 6-8 John Ribock and 6-10 Tom Owens.

The lineup change was most noticeable in rebounding. South Carolina outrebounded its opponents by almost two per game in 1969. With Owens getting 14 rebounds a game, Riker nine and Ribock 6.8, the Gamecocks outrebounded their opponents by 13.1 a game in 1970.

This South Carolina team proved to be one of the best in ACC history. It swept through the conference season without a loss, a feat previously accomplished only by UNC in 1957 and Duke in 1963. The Gamecocks were rarely challenged during the regular season, winning by an average margin of 18.1 points. Against ACC competition, the Gamecocks' winning margin was 16.2 points.

"This is the smartest team I've ever had," McGuire said. "Ever."

The Gamecocks were also one of McGuire's toughest teams. From the season's outset, South Carolina played like it meant business. Roche and Ribock were involved in first-half scuffles in the Gamecocks' season opener against Auburn, and McGuire and Auburn Coach Bill Lyon exchanged heated words.

Throughout 1957, when McGuire guided North Carolina to an undefeated season, he said a loss would help take the pressure of a winning streak off his team. The pressure was released from McGuire's 1970 team early when the Gamecocks were stunned by Tennessee, 55-54, in Columbia.

"It was bad losing to Tennessee, but I'd rather we lose to Tennessee than to North Carolina," Roche said.

Roche and the Gamecocks got a chance to defeat North

155

ACC BASKETBALL / THE '70s

Carolina, posting a victory in the midst of a 17-game winning streak. The Gamecocks were 8-1 and ranked third nationally, while the Tar Heels were 9-1 and ranked fourth when the teams met in Columbia on Jan. 5. UNC Coach Dean Smith elected to slow the game's tempo, but the strategy backfired and South Carolina came away with a 65-52 victory.

The Tar Heels, after three straight trips to the NCAA Final Four, slipped to 18-9. Two of the losses were to Wake Forest, which had not beaten UNC twice in one season since 1965 and had dropped 11 straight games to the Tar Heels. A season-ending loss to Duke, followed by a loss to Virginia in the ACC Tournament and another to Manhattan in the NIT, left UNC with three straight losses for the first time since 1966.

One of South Carolina's two losses during the regular season was to Davidson. Led by first-year Coach Terry Holland, Davidson upset the second-ranked Gamecocks 68-62 in Columbia as guard Bryan Adrian scored 26 points.

"I have a funny feeling Bryan felt he had something to prove, and he did," Holland said of Adrian, who wanted to transfer to South Carolina following his freshman year at Davidson but was denied the chance by McGuire.

Wins at State, UNC and Wake Forest in a six-day span, plus an earlier victory at Duke, gave the Gamecocks a sweep of Big Four schools in North Carolina. No ACC team had previously accomplished that feat and only Maryland in 1975 has done it since.

While South Carolina was stealing most of the headlines around the league in 1970, there were other newsworthy events. Lefty Driesell's arrival as coach at Maryland meant that at least two of the non-Big Four schools were making serious attempts to have representative programs.

"I'm glad to see Lefty come into the ACC," South Carolina's McGuire said. "He'll stir things up."

Driesell said his first team would be lucky to win 10 games. It actually went 13-13. More importantly, Driesell made things more exciting at Cole Field House. The pep band played *Hail To The Chief* as he walked onto the floor. Driesell flashed "V" signs for victory to the students, who responded with loud cheers.

When forward Will Hetzel sank a 40-foot shot at the buzzer to beat Duke 52-50, fans stormed onto the court in celebration. They lifted Driesell to their shoulders and paraded him around Cole Field House.

Bucky Waters was also in his first season at Duke, returning to an unsettled situation where he was once an assistant coach. Just prior to the season opener, the Duke Faculty Committee for Athletics recommended the school leave the ACC. The Committee cited differences with the ACC in academic standards, programs and aims as the chief reasons why Duke should withdraw from the league. One week later, Duke reversed its stand and said it planned to remain in the ACC with no de-emphasis of athletics.

Waters did very well in his first year, as the Blue Devils were 17-9 and earned a berth in the NIT, where they dropped an opening-round decision to Utah, 78-75.

Duke and UNC accepted bids to the NIT immediately after losing to Wake Forest and Virginia, respectively, in the first round of the ACC Tournament in Charlotte. N.C. State beat Maryland in another first-round game spiced by Wolfpack Coach Norm Sloan yelling to Driesell several times to "shut up." The tourney had opened with South Carolina surviving a Clemson slowdown to win 34-33 on two free throws by Roche with eight seconds remaining.

In the semifinals, Roche twisted an ankle in a collision with Wake Forest guard John Lewkowicz with 11 minutes remaining in the game. The Gamecocks defeated the Deacons 79-63, but Roche was doubtful to play against N.C. State in the championship game. State had reached the title game when Rick Anheuser's follow shot with 39 seconds remaining gave the Wolfpack a 67-66 victory over Virginia.

Anheuser was part of what was known as a "bargain basement" team. He was a transfer from Bradley University. Guard Al Heartley, the valedictorian of his high school class in Clayton, N.C., and the first black to play for the Wolfpack, was a walk-on before earning a scholarship. Guard Joe Dunning hailed from a small school in Delaware and had so much trouble gaining confidence in front of ACC crowds that Sloan gave him a copy of *Psycho Cybernetics*, which dealt with the power of positive thinking. Forward Vann Williford was originally headed to Pfeiffer College before Sloan gambled a scholarship on him at State. New Jersey guard Ed Leftwich was the only highly recruited player on the roster.

By the time of the ACC Tournament, Sloan had his bargain boys playing excellent basketball. They took a 21-6 record into the championship game against South Carolina, and Sloan had an excellent game plan laid out. The Wolfpack planned to control the tempo, which it did to near perfection. South Carolina, with Roche slowed by his ankle sprain, was slightly out of sync.

Roche was not effective. He made only four of 17 shots and finished with nine points. Also, McGuire elected to play a 2-1-2 zone defense, which allowed the Wolfpack to hold the ball out and play a slower tempo.

South Carolina built an 11-point lead with two minutes left in the first half, but State trimmed it to 24-17 by halftime.

"We had two fouls on three of our starters," Sloan said. "I just didn't really feel like we had anybody that we could take off the bench and put in. So I said, 'Look, when you get the basketball and South Carolina is zoning, let's just hold it.' I just thought by holding the basketball we would protect ourselves from fouling somebody out.

"It just turned out we held the ball for something like six minutes, and Frank gave them the signal at that point to come get us. In coming to get us, they left a man open under the basket. I think it was Williford and he knocked in a quick basket, we intercepted the inbounds pass and instead of being down 11 and everybody turning on us for making it a dull game, we were now down seven, had scored two quick baskets and the momentum switched."

On the shooting of Williford and the rebounding of Anheuser, State battled back to tie the game at the end of regulation, 35-35. Roche missed a jump shot that would have won it at the buzzer and missed again at the end of the first overtime.

With 22 seconds left in the second overtime, Cremins dribbled past midcourt and looked to pass. Leftwich slapped the ball away from him and drove for what proved to be the game-winning basket. Anheuser then added two free throws to account for the 42-39 final. McGuire chased referee Steve Honzo off the Charlotte Coliseum court, claiming that Leftwich had fouled Cremins on the crucial steal.

"I thought Cremins was fouled on that steal by Leftwich," McGuire said. "Cremins had a sprained finger. If Roche was healthy he'd have made those shots. He doesn't normally miss them.

"It's a pattern of things that go against me in the tourney. Another case of playing Russian Roulette. Even the fans threw things at me and my players as we walked off the court."

Dead-eye Davis doomed Deacon defenders.

Charlie Davis was pigeon-toed and looked like he was worn to a shadow. He spread a mere 145 pounds over his 6-foot-1 frame. So thin was Davis that, at one point during his days at Wake Forest, he went on a bananas-and-beer diet to gain weight.

"When I came out on the court I wore a size 12 (shoe), was awfully thin and I didn't look like a player," Davis says. "I don't know if it's true or not, but I think I got eight or 10 points before people realized, 'Hey, he really can play.'"

The '70s
Wake Forest

Once he let fly with the first jump shot, there was no doubt that Charlie Davis could play. More often than not, a Davis shot would settle into the basket like a pillow tossed onto a bed. He made 46 percent of his field goal attempts in a three-year career. The percentage is remarkable on two counts. First, Davis' shooting range often exceeded 20 feet. Secondly, he was often double-teamed as the result of being the focus of Wake Forest's offense.

But Davis was more than a jump shooter. That he attempted more than 200 free throws in each of his three seasons says something about his ability to drive to the basket. From the foul line, Davis was a dead-eye shooter.

Though almost 15 years has passed since he left the ACC, he remains the league's all-time best free throw shooter with an .873 career percentage. He is the only player to ever lead the ACC in that category three straight seasons.

Davis was accorded All-ACC honors each of his three varsity seasons. He was a unanimous choice to the all-conference team as a senior when he was also Player of the Year by an 86-30 voting margin over South Carolina guard John Roche. When Davis left Wake Forest with a school-record scoring average of 24.9, the athletic department retired his jersey No. 12.

"I've seen a lot of players," says Gil McGregor, a teammate of Davis from 1969 through 1971, and currently Wake Forest's academic advisor for athletes. "There have been a lot of good players at Wake Forest, some that I've played with and others I've watched. But I've never been around a better player than Charlie Davis."

Find a pickup game in Harlem in the mid-'60s and the same thing was likely to have been said about Davis. His shooting displays on the playgrounds of Manhattan were legendary. By Davis' account, there was only one player in the history of New York City street games who was a better shooter. That was Charlie Davis, Sr.

Charlie's father was a left-hander who played for the Harlem Yankees, a minor league equivalent to the Harlem Globetrotters. Young Charlie shot right-handed, but he learned all the other tricks of the basketball trade from his father.

By his junior year at Brooklyn Tech, Davis was considered as good as any guard coming out of New York City. Seeking revenge on the poor fellow who held him to 16 points in an earlier meeting, Davis once scored 57 of his team's 72 points. Several other times he topped 50 points for Brooklyn Tech.

But his grades were suffering, and Davis went off to Laurinburg (N.C.) Institute midway through his senior year of high school at the suggestion of Wake Forest coaches.

While at Laurinburg, Davis was contacted by one of his Harlem buddies, Norwood Todmann, who was the first black player at Wake Forest. Secure in knowing that Wake Forest was "all right" for blacks, according to Todmann, Davis decided to attend the Winston-Salem school.

Coach Jack McCloskey welcomed Davis to Wake Forest with open arms. McCloskey's Deacons were 5-21 prior to Davis' arrival on the varsity, then he posted records of 18-9, 14-13 and 16-10.

Charlie Davis.

Davis usually saved his best effort for the University of North Carolina. In seven games against the Tar Heels, Davis averaged 30.6 points. The Demon Deacons defeated UNC twice during the 1970 season with Davis scoring 34 and 41 points.

"The way Dean's (Smith) teams play defense, it was made for me," Davis says. "His teams don't play a trap unless you pick up the ball. If you just take a step backwards, it will always break their pressure. We also took the first open jump shot instead of driving to the basket."

Although Davis led the league in scoring as a senior, his Wake Forest team failed to advance past the ACC Tournament semifinals for a third straight season. He was once described as the Ernie Banks of basketball, an unselfish superstar who never played on a winner—just like the Chicago Cubs legend who never played in the World Series.

"When it was all over, I looked for a ring and didn't have one," Davis said. "I'd trade a lot of those points for a chance to have been in the (NCAA) Tournament."

Davis played for two seasons in the NBA with Cleveland, then Portland, but his small build was not suited for the rugged pro game. So Davis returned to Winston-Salem and entered private business under the name Charles Davis.

"I wanted to make sure I got judged as Charles Davis the businessman, not Charlie Davis the basketball player," he said.

South Carolina's John Roche (11) was ineffective on a gimpy ankle in the '70 ACC final, shooting just 4-of-17 against State's Ed Leftwich (30).

Roche said: "The shots wouldn't drop. I lost the game for us, nobody else. I blew it."

McGuire kept his team in the locker room following the game and did not permit it to accept the second-place trophy. McGuire, who had coached 14 teams in the ACC Tournament and took four to the championship game, said he did not know his team was supposed to be present for the awards ceremonies.

The loss was crushing to South Carolina, and reports circulated soon after that McGuire was campaigning to have the school secede from the ACC. Cremins left school and went into hiding in the mountains of North Carolina. The remaining members of the team only became more angered at the dominance the Big Four teams held over the ACC. It didn't help that most of the crowd of 11,666 at the Charlotte Coliseum had pulled for State to upset the Gamecocks.

Adding insult to injury, South Carolina could not be invited to the NIT because the Gamecocks were hosting the East Regional. NCAA rules then prohibited a school from playing in the NIT if it was hosting a regional.

"This is one of the best teams I've ever coached," McGuire said. "I think it's the best team in the nation. I hope State does well in the regionals."

The Wolfpack had spent itself by the time it met St. Bonaventure in the East Regional in Columbia. Bob Lanier scored 24 points and had 19 rebounds as the Bonnies defeated State 80-68 despite a 35-point, 12-rebound effort by "Moving" Vann Williford.

State's loss to St. Bonaventure infuriated South Carolina even further.

"Our boys could play St. Bonaventure anywhere they want to be played," McGuire said. "John Ribock is strong physically. Tom Owens can block shots. Bless John Roche's heart. He is now in a cast. If we could have gotten by State, we could have gone all the way."

Pack's Burleson overloaded with height and heart.

The '70s
N.C. State

After more than 10 years away, Tommy Burleson went home to the mountains of North Carolina and bought a place atop Rhoney's View, about three miles up the hill from Newland.

Not much about the "Newland Needle" changed since the day he went off to play basketball at N.C. State in 1970 . . . just a big old country boy who went away to college for a few years.

He was phenomenon then, a 7-foot-4 center whose fierce competitiveness made him one of the best centers in Atlantic Coast Conference history.

In December of 1971, when Burleson was still on the freshman team, N.C. State Coach Norm Sloan described his developing center to the *Greensboro Daily News*: "Besides his physical ability—the great hands and the soft shooting touch—he has an excellent mental approach to the game. He is a fierce competitor who has learned to relax and maintain his poise at the same time. He is confident and ambitious, but humble."

Put quite simply, Burleson was a winner.

State was 73-11 during Burleson's three years at center. The Wolfpack did not lose a game his junior season and lost only once his senior year en route to the 1974 NCAA championship. Twice he led the ACC in rebounding, twice he was named to the all-league first team and twice he was the ACC Tournament's Most Valuable Player.

Burleson sometimes looked awkward playing the game. His hips looked too large for the rest of his frail frame. His upper body was particularly slender, giving Burleson the appearance of Ichabod Crane on stilts.

But there was also something graceful about Burleson. He was agile and possessed unusually soft hands for such a large man. Combining the two traits, Burleson perfected a sweeping hook shot that was virtually unstoppable, and he had a knack for snatching missed shots out of the air.

Prior to his first appearance in a varsity uniform, Burleson had appeared on the cover of *Sports Illustrated* as part of the "Year Of The New Giants" feature story. He immediately proved worthy of celebrity status with a 23-point, 16-rebound performance in the 1972 season opener. Burleson followed that with a 37-point, 21-rebound showing against Georgia when he scored 15 of N.C. State's final 20 points after the game was tied at 72. The Wolfpack won, 92-81.

By the end of his sophomore season, Burleson was the ACC's leading rebounder (14 a game) and second-leading

ACC BASKETBALL / THE '70s

"Newland Needle" sports victory nets and big grin after beating Marquette in 1974 NCAA title game.

scorer (21.3 average to 21.6 by Virginia's Barry Parkhill). He was impressive enough to become the youngest and tallest member of the 1972 U.S. Olympic team that won a silver medal in Munich. The Olympic experience proved the most rewarding, yet disappointing, of Burleson's basketball career.

"I was taught that losing builds character and enables you to win," Burleson says of the USA's disputed defeat to the Soviet Union in the gold medal game. "I felt like we should be able to face the fact that we lost."

Burleson never could accept that defeat, nor any other. He grew up in a competitive atmosphere, whether working in cabbage patches, raising crops or showing livestock as a member of 4-H.

Burleson was big at birth, weighing 10 pounds, 3 ounces and measuring 23 inches long. He was 5-8 in the sixth grade, 6-4 in the eighth and 7-feet in the 10th. His parents had to order special pants, with a 29-inch waist and 37-inch inseam, from a clothing store in Massachusetts. About that time, an aunt sat down with Burleson and offered a few precious words of wisdom that stayed with Burleson.

"When you're that tall, throw your shoulders back, don't stoop your shoulders," she told young Tommy. "So be proud, walk tall."

Burleson has always been proud of his height. That pride peaked when he could take advantage of his height on the basketball floor. The barn behind the Burleson home became Tommy's playground. He learned to shoot with a flat trajectory because of the barn's low ceiling. But mostly, he just learned to shoot. Often he would hold a private shooting session for an hour, then head to town for a high school game.

At Avery County High School, Burleson was fortunate to have a coach dedicated to making him a great player. Roger Banks worked Burleson into one of the nation's best prepsters. Burleson ran laps with a 50-pound weighted jacket. He wore ankle weights and lifted weights. Banks ordered Kenny Church, the strongest and meanest kid in school, to beat on Burleson during practices.

"I pushed him to the breaking point every day," Banks told the *Greensboro Record*. "I ran him until tears came into his eyes."

The work paid off, and Burleson was forever grateful to Banks. Avery County had a 112-10 record in Burleson's four years, and Burleson caught the eye of more than 300 college coaches. N.C. State won Burleson's services primarily because of its outstanding agriculture program.

When David Thompson and Monte Towe joined Burleson on the Wolfpack varsity for the 1973 season, State was unbeatable. But the Pack was also unable to participate in the NCAA Tournament because of violations in the recruiting of Thompson. With State winning all 27 games in '73, Burleson established a trend of playing his best in big games.

Although Thompson made the winning basket in State's Super Bowl Sunday victory over Maryland in '73, it was Burleson's 20 points and 15 rebounds that carried the Wolfpack. A year later, when State defeated Maryland to win the ACC Tournament, Burleson had the finest game of his career, scoring 38 points on 18-of-25 shooting and pulling down 13 rebounds. It is considered among the best performances in Tournament history.

Then, when the Wolfpack downed UCLA in the NCAA semifinals, Burleson neutralized Bruin center Bill Walton with 20 points and 14 rebounds. His final college game was a victory over Marquette for the national championship.

"I was a self-made player to the point that I developed some skills," Burleson said years later. "But God gave me the physical ability and he gave me a big heart and the desire to want to go out there and win. That's something you can't teach."

Burleson took his big heart and desire to the NBA, where he played for seven seasons with Seattle, Kansas City and Atlanta. By the end of his second season, when he averaged 15 points and nine rebounds for the SuperSonics, Burleson was considered the third-best center in the NBA behind Kareem Abdul-Jabbar and Dave Cowens.

A knee injury in 1979 spelled the eventual end to Burleson's career. Four years later, he sold a restaurant he owned in Seattle and returned to Newland to co-own and operate a lighting and electrical supply company, raise a family and satisfy his competitive drive by racing speedboats.

Burleson is never very far from basketball, serving as an assistant coach for the Avery County High School team. He wanted to stay close to the game and have access to the school gymnasium, for himself and his two sons.

And just as his father helped his gawky kid learn coordination through juggling, Burleson started his sons working with oranges, apples, and, eventually, basketballs. ■

ACC BASKETBALL / THE '70s

'71

South Carolina had visions of a national championship in 1971. Again, the Gamecocks were figured to be among the nation's top teams with most publications tabbing them second best to defending champion UCLA.

The only loss off the 1970 squad was guard Bobby Cremins. In his place, the Gamecocks had sophomore Kevin Joyce, an immensely talented athlete. In the New York City Catholic League championship game during his senior season, Joyce psyched himself up by shaving his head. He then scored 53 points and earned recognition in *Sports Illustrated's* Faces In The Crowd.

Just as in 1970, South Carolina had a multi-talented starting lineup of Joyce, John Roche, Tom Owens, Tom Riker and John Ribock, a lineup blessed with speed, shooting and size. This team also had depth in guard Bobby Carver and forward Rick Aydlett. So excited were South Carolina's fans about the prospects of the 1971 season, 12,456 packed Carolina Coliseum for the team's preseason intrasquad game.

This was to be the last hurrah for Roche, Owens and Ribock, a trio which had taken South Carolina from obscurity to the national spotlight in their two varsity years. Yet the trio still had not won an ACC championship, nor had it played in an NCAA Tournament.

During the Roche era, South Carolina had become the most disliked team in the ACC. Most of the Gamecock players hailed from New York, just as Coach Frank McGuire used imports at UNC in the '50s. But while McGuire's Tar Heels were relatively controversy free, his Gamecocks found themselves in one spat after another with ACC opponents.

Just three games into the new season, the Gamecocks were back in the soup. Before South Carolina's game against Duke started in Columbia, Ribock elbowed the Blue Devil mascot during warm-up drills. Later, when Duke guard Dick DeVenzio drew a charge from Roche, the two players tumbled to the floor and Roche kicked at the Duke guard as they were getting up.

Then, on Dec. 16 in Columbia, a wild fight broke loose in the final five minutes of South Carolina's game against Maryland. USC's Aydlett and Maryland's Jay Flowers came to blows under the Gamecock basket with 4:52 remaining and South Carolina leading 96-70.

"It was like a bomb explosion," McGuire said. "Some spark set it off and then who really knows what happened after that?"

Soon Ribock was fighting Maryland's Jack Neal while Roche and Carver were teaming up against Maryland's Howard White. Before long, Maryland Coach Lefty Driesell was on the floor attempting to break up the melee. As Driesell approached Ribock, South Carolina's Jimmy Powell bear-hugged the Maryland coach from behind. Ribock then swung and landed a punch to Driesell's face. The picture of Powell holding Driesell as Ribock swung with his right fist ran in newspapers across the country the following day.

Officials Gene Conley and Joe Agee called the game off at that point and declared South Carolina a winner.

"I would like for somebody to research how many times this South Carolina team has been involved in fights over the last two seasons," Driesell said. "There is no excuse for a team that has this much basketball talent fighting when they have a 30-point lead. I don't think it should be tolerated.

"I'm out there trying to break up the fight and McGuire's standing over there smiling and straightening his tie. He isn't going to get by, I'll tell you that. If I was McGuire I wouldn't

Heated words and scuffles like these exchanges with Duke marked South Carolina's stormy reign among ACC kingpins in the early '70s.

160

ACC BASKETBALL / THE '70s

bring my team to College Park."

After watching films of the fight, McGuire claimed that Ribock did not hit Driesell.

"The best we can find out from looking at the films is that Lefty was swinging away and hit himself in the mouth," McGuire said. "That's what it looked like."

Driesell responded: "That's ridiculous. The films have been on TV. I know I've got a split lip, and I know I didn't swing at anyone. That's a lie."

Maryland and South Carolina officials discussed the possibility of canceling the Jan. 9 rematch in College Park. But the ACC ruled that the game would be played. Norvall Neve, acting as ACC commissioner after the July 11, 1970, death of Jim Weaver, added that McGuire "is smart enough and has been around long enough to know what the consequences would be" if South Carolina refused to play Maryland.

"The consequences (of playing the game) might be 15 or 20 people killed," McGuire said. "I honestly don't think the game should be played under any conditions."

After a victory over Clemson extended their ACC regular-season win streak to 17, the second-ranked and unbeaten Gamecocks faced three road games at North Carolina, Maryland and Virginia with only a home game against non-conference foe Temple in between. The Gamecocks lost all three ACC games and were involved in several incidents.

In Chapel Hill, the 20th-ranked Tar Heels stunned South Carolina with surprising ease, 79-64.

True to form, McGuire could not accept defeat.

"Older men should have more poise," McGuire said of officials Jim Hernjak and Otis Almond, who called three technical fouls on South Carolina. "I was displeased with the officiating, and I think it went both ways."

McGuire then took a shot at UNC's fans.

"There were things said tonight behind our bench that should not be said," McGuire said. "It has been said that our crowd is bad, but our crowd is 1,000 percent better than any other in the Atlantic Coast Conference."

After an 84-71 victory over Temple, McGuire prepared his team for the worst when it traveled to Maryland, where Terrapin Athletic Director Jim Kehoe assured the ACC and South Carolina that the game would be played without incident. Ticket demands were the highest at Cole Field House since Maryland played top-ranked North Carolina, coached by McGuire, in 1958.

Maryland's strategy was to stall and pull South Carolina out of its vaunted 2-1-2 zone defense. North Carolina had employed the same strategy, and the Gamecocks elected to play man-to-man defense. Against Maryland, McGuire ordered his team to remain in a zone defense.

Maryland held possession of the ball for all but 20 seconds of the first half. After 20 minutes, the Gamecocks led 4-3. Maryland picked up the pace some in the second half, and at the end of regulation the game was tied at 23.

South Carolina looked as if it would escape when the Gamecocks forged to a 30-25 lead with 16 seconds remaining in overtime. But Maryland's Jim O'Brien scored on a layup, the Terps intercepted the inbounds pass and Dick Stobaugh scored for Maryland. Suddenly, South Carolina's lead was 30-29 with eight seconds remaining.

Maryland's Bob Bodell intercepted another inbounds pass to set up a short bank shot by O'Brien that gave the Terps a 31-30 victory.

"The good Lord had to be with us, the way we did it," said Driesell, who was paraded around the floor on the shoulders of celebrating fans.

McGuire fumed.

"My boys got jostled, pushed and punched going off the court," he said. "It may have been by people who didn't mean anything, but we were promised protection. Where was it? This would have never happened in Columbia. I was hit on the back four times."

Two nights later, McGuire was still angry when South Carolina played at Virginia. The Cavaliers were the surprise of the ACC, winning their first six games and eight of their first 10. They also elected to play slowdown, and the strategy worked when Barry Parkhill sank a 15-foot jump shot with seven seconds remaining for a 50-49 Virginia victory.

"There were things said tonight behind our bench that should not be said. It has been said that our crowd is bad, but our crowd is 1,000 percent better than any other in the ACC."
☐ **South Carolina Coach Frank McGuire**

"I know it was a gamble to hold the ball and go for the last shot with us one point down," said Virginia Coach Bill Gibson, whose club stalled the last 2:10 of the game. "But we had confidence in Barry."

During the game, McGuire got into a hassle with a member of the press corps, and Riker engaged a photographer in a shoving match. A University Hall-record crowd of 9,550 watched as McGuire confronted John Hedberg of *The Staunton Leader*. McGuire said Hedberg had been "abusing me" during the game. In the brief encounter that followed, Riker shoved John Atkins, a photographer for the Charlottesville (Va.) *Daily Progress*.

A technical foul was called on McGuire, but one was also called on the Virginia fans for throwing paper and other objects onto the floor.

By this time, even South Carolina followers had grown tired of McGuire's antics. Herman Helms, sports editor of *The State* in Columbia and a long-time friend of McGuire's, perhaps best summed up the feelings of ACC fans when he wrote in January of '71: "McGuire does not lose with dignity. The true fiber of a man is revealed not by how he wins but how he loses. The predictable conduct of McGuire in times of defeat is beginning to take the flavor and thrill out of victories. It is time the coach got rid of his persecution complex, stopped making excuses and faced the fact that the Gamecocks are only human."

The Gamecocks' 82-71 loss at Duke, their fourth in the league, essentially eliminated them from the ACC's regular-season race.

Despite not being in the running for first place, South Carolina still had a score to settle with North Carolina when the Tar Heels visited Columbia in late February.

"It was our best game in a long time," said Roche, who scored 32 points in the Gamecocks' 72-66 victory. The game featured 57 personal fouls, six player disqualifications and 84 free throw attempts. UNC Coach Dean Smith was whistled for two technical fouls.

Once again, South Carolina was involved in a couple of

Gamecocks' pests poisoned by Roche killer.

Twice he was ACC Player of the Year. Three times he was first-team All-ACC. His 56-point outburst in one game was a league and school record. His name appeared on most All-America teams in 1970 and, again, in 1971.

John Roche did it all for South Carolina. He led the Gamecocks through an unbeaten ACC season in '70 and to the ACC Tournament title a year later. For helping make South Carolina a national basketball power, school athletic officials retired his jersey.

The '70s

South Carolina

Yet when Roche peeled off jersey No. 11 for the final time, he was hardly content with his college career. Roche left South Carolina and the ACC as a bitter young man.

"Yes, I am glad to leave," Roche said following South Carolina's loss to Fordham in the NCAA East Regional at Raleigh's Reynolds Coliseum in late March of 1971. "It has been hard to play in this league under the circumstances . . . There is so much hate throughout the ACC, especially among the fans."

Roche went on to play five seasons in the American Basketball Association and another four in the NBA before going on to practice law in Denver.

"My memories now of the ACC and college ball are very favorable," Roche said recently. "I think I didn't enjoy my senior year much, but I enjoyed my first two years very much. I don't harbor any negative feelings about my college career in any way. In fact, those were very enjoyable days."

•

The star recruit off Roche's La Salle Academy team in New York City was Tom Owens, a towering 6-foot-10 center. Every school wanted Owens, who was a strong rebounder yet very mobile. Many recruiters were not so sure about Roche, an intelligent player, excellent shooter and outstanding student. They were concerned he was a little slow afoot. South Carolina Coach Frank McGuire thought Owens needed Roche, and vice versa. As long as the two wanted to attend the same school, McGuire figured they made a nice package.

This "Mutt and Jeff" team learned the fundamentals of basketball under La Salle Coach Danny Buckley, who, coincidentally, had learned under McGuire at St. John's. Along the way, Owens had also developed a close friendship in New York with Bobby Cremins, who had gone off to South Carolina the previous year. Through Buckley and Cremins, the prep pair learned of McGuire's style, on and off the court.

During their visit to the Columbia, S.C., campus, Owens and Roche were introduced by McGuire to South Carolina Governor Robert E. McNair. They also learned that McGuire believed wholeheartedly in allowing his players to dictate style of play. McGuire let it be known that Roche and Owens would be the nucleus for taking South Carolina to the top, just as Tommy Kearns and Lennie Rosenbluth had come out of New York City to do it for him at North Carolina in 1957.

By their junior season at USC, Roche and Owens had taken South Carolina to No. 1. The Gamecocks were the consensus pick as the nation's top team before the 1970 season based on the return of their entire starting lineup from a team that was 21-7 in 1969.

Roche was one of four sophomore starters on the '69 team. Owens, John Ribock and Billy Walsh were the others. But Roche was the standout of the four.

In his first varsity game, Roche sank a 25-footer with two seconds left to beat Auburn, 51-49. He scored a tournament-record 38 points on 17-of-23 shooting as USC shocked second-ranked North Carolina in the North-South Double-headers at Charlotte. He was the MVP of the Quaker City Tournament in Philadelphia when the Gamecocks handed La Salle, a team on NCAA probation, its only loss of the season.

"When we beat them, that's when we felt we could play the style we did and compete with anyone," Roche says.

That style called for Roche to handle the ball as much as 75 percent of the time, and for USC to make up for a lack of quickness on defense by employing a tight 2-3 zone. The play usually began and ended with Roche, which is the way McGuire wanted it. Clemson Coach Tates Locke once said Roche should not only be the league's Player of the Year but its Coach of the Year as well.

Roche was a master at knifing his way through a defense, pulling up for a jump shot or passing off to an open teammate. At 6-3, Roche was big enough to post up against smaller guards near the basket. His ball-handling skills were so good he could dribble on the perimeter without fear of theft, just as he did up and down the stairs of his three-story home as a youngster. He was meticulous in his work on the court: He kept index cards of every practice so he could chart his progress.

Because of its style, South Carolina soon was vulnerable on two counts. A team could either stop Roche, which was very difficult, and have a chance to win. Or a team could take its chances with a slowdown game, knowing full well that the Gamecocks could not, and would not, chase.

"That was the most appropriate style for our team when I was a sophomore. I don't think there is any disputing that," Roche said. "When I was a junior and senior there were more legitimate questions raised as to whether we should have changed . . . A lot of people felt we should run more and press more. I'm not sure our team was capable of doing that, but we'll never know."

It's difficult to dispute the results, particularly in 1970. The Gamecocks followed UNC in 1957 and Duke in 1963 as the third team to go unbeaten within the ACC. Roche, of course, was the leader. He had 27 points and 13 assists in one game against Maryland, then scored 31 points in the second half of a game against Temple. Twice he topped 30 against N.C. State.

With Roche's and South Carolina's success came much controversy. The Gamecocks were the first ACC team out-

Roche gained a measure of pleasure when Commissioner Bob James presented him with the '71 ACC championship trophy after a last-second win over UNC.

side the state of North Carolina to sustain success within the league. They posed a clear threat to the Big Four's supremacy, and fans in North Carolina seemed to resent that.

USC was also involved in numerous fracases. A fight, however small, broke out in each of the Gamecocks' first three losses of 1969, and *Sports Illustrated* characterized the Gamecocks as a bunch of "bullies" in a January, 1971, story.

"That article had a great deal of influence on how people looked at our team," Roche said years later. "I think 'bullies' was unfair. We did have some incidents, but they were really relatively few. People seem to remember them as more than a few."

Roche received bags of hate mail. Once, at Wake Forest, students held a mock flushing of Roche down a commode. When Roche was injured in the semifinals of the 1970 ACC Tournament against Wake Forest, some in the Charlotte Coliseum crowd cheered. The injury meant Roche was not at full strength when the Gamecocks met N.C. State in the championship.

"I felt then, and now in reflection, that was easily the best team I played on at South Carolina," Roche says. "The East Regional was on our home court that year and we really felt that was the year for us to win the national championship.

"It was disappointing when we lost (in two overtimes to the Wolfpack), but it would have still been difficult to win the Regional because my injury took six weeks to heal. But I still thought we could come back the next year and win it."

Roche said the 1971 team, with Kevin Joyce replacing Cremins in the backcourt, was much more suited to a fast-paced game. But McGuire stayed with what made the Gamecocks successful the previous two seasons.

"There's no secret to our strategy," McGuire said. "It's what it has always been—when in trouble, go to Roche."

Roche was as spectacular as ever, scoring 32 points in a win at Notre Dame and making 21 of 34 field goals in his 56-point effort against Furman. But Roche admittedly got caught up in the anti-South Carolina sentiment as well as the mumbling among his underclassmen teammates that he controlled too much of the action.

He was accused of kicking Dick DeVenzio when the Duke guard was on the floor and, on another occasion, kneeing Steve Previs of North Carolina. He even exchanged words with UNC Coach Dean Smith. The Gamecocks were also involved in a wild free-for-all against Maryland.

"By the time our team was seniors, I don't think I was alone in feeling that we had had about enough of playing in the ACC," Roche said. "Some of that frustration and feeling showed in our performance as players and as people. So we contributed to those feelings against us."

Roche was three times All-ACC and twice ACC Player of the Year, finishing second to Wake's Charlie Davis his senior year. As fine a season as Davis enjoyed, no doubt some of the lopsided 86-30 vote total in his favor resulted from the controversy surrounding Roche.

But Roche and South Carolina got somewhat of a last laugh when they won the 1971 ACC Tournament, beating North Carolina on a last-second basket by Owens.

"I think it was very important to the people of South Carolina and to us not to go through our career without winning the ACC Tournament," Roche says. "Once we got to South Carolina, we recognized how difficult that was, so we considered that a significant accomplishment. But I think we would have preferred to win it our junior year because we had a better team and we were in a position to go a little further."

The Gamecocks lost in their first game of the NCAA Tournament in 1971, and Roche walked away a bitter man. "Basketball is more than just a game in this league," he said. ∎

ACC BASKETBALL / THE '70s

Gamecock Coach Frank McGuire assembles Riker, Owens and troops during timeout of '71 ACC title win over North Carolina.

ugly incidents. When UNC guard George Karl ran into a Ribock pick, he fell to the floor where he was kicked at by Ribock. At one point, Roche passed by the UNC bench and reportedly cursed at Smith.

Prior to his final game at South Carolina, Roche's No. 11 jersey was retired. Only jersey No. 42, worn by Grady Wallace in 1956 and 1957, had previously been retired at South Carolina.

Roche was hardly ready to retire as a college basketball player. His aim, and that of the Gamecocks, was to win an ACC championship. The Tournament featured one of its strongest fields with N.C. State (12-14) and Clemson (9-16), playing under first-year coach Tates Locke, as the only teams with losing records.

The Gamecocks rolled to a 71-63 victory over Maryland in the first round, followed by an easy 69-56 victory over N.C. State in the semifinals. North Carolina, meanwhile, defeated Clemson 76-41 and Virginia 78-68 to reach the championship game.

The title game, not particularly well played by either squad, came down to a jump ball with six seconds remaining. UNC led 51-50 with 6-10 Tar Heel center Lee Dedmon set to jump against 6-3 Gamecock guard Kevin Joyce in front of the South Carolina basket.

"I thought all along we were going to win until there were only six seconds to play," Roche said. "(Then) I thought, 'Well, it's going to take a miracle now.'"

The "miracle" happened when Joyce outjumped Dedmon and tipped the ball to teammate Owens, who laid the ball in the basket for a 52-51 South Carolina victory.

"It happened so fast," Owens said, "I really didn't have time to think about anything. All of a sudden the ball was there and I shot it. I think if I would have had time to think about it, I might have blown it. I would have thought, 'Wow, there's a lot of pressure.'"

The Tar Heels, who made only 15 of 28 free throws, were shocked afterward.

"How could we lose?" asked Karl. "They were beaten."

"That play did not beat us," said UNC's Smith. "We had our chances to win the game at the foul line and we let it get away. We feel we should have won, but we were beaten by a very fine team. One play didn't make the difference."

South Carolina had finally gotten what it wanted: An ACC championship. The Gamecocks' participation in the NCAA Tournament the following week was almost insignificant by comparison. That showed in their play as they dropped a 79-64 decision to Pennsylvania and then fell to Fordham 100-90 in the consolation game of the East Regional.

While South Carolina returned to Columbia in a hurry, North Carolina and Duke carried the ACC flag proudly in the NIT. The Tar Heels, who wore blue shoes for the first time in 1971, turned back Duke 73-67 in the semifinals, then won the championship with an 84-66 victory over Georgia Tech. Bill Chamberlain was named the tournament's MVP after scoring a career-high 34 points in the championship game.

The 1971 season brought to an end the three-year run for South Carolina and the controversial Roche. Under his direction, the Gamecocks were 69-16, including a 41-9 record against ACC competition. While Roche was leading the Gamecocks through three glorious years of basketball, he also carried on feuds with opposing players, coaches and fans.

"Yes, I am glad to leave the Atlantic Coast Conference," Roche said. "It has been hard to play in this league under these circumstances. The outside influences have hurt the team this year. There is so much hate throughout the ACC, especially among the fans.

"By the end of the year, our team felt disgust at some of the things that happened during the season. It is shocking to think of some of things that were said to us by grown men.

"I would like to give somebody the mail I get, and it is more than just two or three letters a day. I'm speaking of typed letters from businessmen, from doctors and lawyers. Many of them say things like, 'The happiest moment of my life was when you were injured in the ACC Tournament.'

"Basketball is more than just a game in this league."

ACC BASKETBALL / THE '70s

'72

By the end of the 1971 basketball season, rumors that South Carolina and Clemson were prepared to leave the ACC grew stronger. Neither school was happy with the league's admission standards for athletes, which they claimed kept them from competing with other schools around the country in all sports.

In early March, the ACC voted to continue its rule of requiring both an 800 SAT score and a 1.6-grade point projection (based on the student's high school grade point average) for athletic eligibility. However, a provision was added for students who scored between 700 and 799. They could be admitted if they had a projected grade point average of 1.75.

Trustees of Clemson and South Carolina wanted to recruit student-athletes under the NCAA's guidelines, which required only a projected 1.6 grade point average.

Clemson decided to play a wait-and-see game with the ACC. South Carolina decided on March 29, 1971, to withdraw from the league effective August 15 of that year.

Ironically, the ACC dropped its SAT score requirements within a year after being threatened with a lawsuit by two prospective Clemson soccer players.

The relationship between USC and the remaining seven schools continued in football. But no ACC schools cared to continue a basketball series with South Carolina, primarily because of the feud between Gamecock Coach Frank McGuire and several other league members.

From a basketball standpoint, South Carolina's departure from the league was damaging. The Gamecocks were the first school to offer a sustained challenge to the Big Four stronghold on ACC championships. In the league's first 18 years, Maryland (1958) and South Carolina (1971) were the only non-Big Four schools to win the ACC Tournament. Only South Carolina in 1970 finished first in the regular season among those schools located outside the state of North Carolina.

With McGuire and South Carolina gone, many wondered if any school would ever again challenge the Big Four's domination. That question was quickly answered in 1972 as both Maryland and Virginia proved worthy challengers to North Carolina for first place in the regular season.

In 1971, Virginia won 11 of its first 13 games and gained a national ranking for the first time in the school's history. The Cavaliers climbed to 15th in the rankings but fell flat and lost six of their last seven games.

The outlook for Virginia was bright with four starters, including leading scorer Barry Parkhill, returning for 1972. Parkhill was sensational from the outset, scoring a school-record 51 points in one early season victory over Baldwin-Wallace. But few expected the Cavaliers to win their first 12 games and 18 of their first 19 as they did.

By mid-January, Virginia had won at Duke for the first time since 1927 and at Wake Forest for the first time since 1959. The Cavaliers were ranked eighth nationally and primed for a meeting in Charlottesville with third-ranked North Carolina.

A University Hall crowd that included Virginia Governor Linwood Holton was disappointed as the Tar Heels posted an 85-79 victory. But the Cavaliers rebounded to have their first-ever winning season against ACC competition. Virginia finished 8-4 in the league, good enough for a second-place tie with Maryland.

No one enjoyed Virginia's success more than Coach Bill "Hoot" Gibson, who three years earlier was the target of much criticism from players, students and fans. Those who once wore "Boot The Hoot" buttons on the Virginia campus were now shouting "Hoot, Hoot, Hoot!" to salute their head coach.

There was no secret to Maryland's sudden rise in the ACC standings. Coach Lefty Driesell brought in one of the top recruiting classes in the country in 1970: 6-foot-11 Tom McMillen, 6-11 Mark Cartwright, 6-9 Len Elmore, 6-3 Jap Trimble, 6-3 Stan Swetnam and 6-0 Rich Porac.

They formed what was perhaps the best freshman team in ACC history, going unbeaten in 16 games in 1971 and winning by an average of 34 points. The Terp frosh scored more than 100 points in nine games and averaged 99.8 points for the season. They also played the last 10 games without Elmore, who was sidelined with a knee injury.

McMillen showed he was every bit the superstar Driesell envisioned, averaging 29.3 points and 15.4 rebounds for the freshman team. He scored 48 points in a game against Georgetown and later scored 38 and had 31 rebounds in a win over West Virginia.

McMillen, from Mansfield, Pa., was the most highly recruited prep basketball player in the country. He was the third high school athlete to be featured on the cover of *Sports Illustrated* after he scored 4,000 points in his prep career and was touted as the "next Lew Alcindor." His Mansfield High School jersey was retired to the Basketball Hall of Fame in Springfield, Mass. More than an athlete, he finished first in his class academically, was president of the student council, played the first trombone in the school band and was a prize-winning orator.

McMillen first committed to play for Dean Smith at North Carolina, reportedly against the wishes of his parents. But upon returning from playing for the U.S. Olympic Development team in Europe prior to his freshman year, McMillen changed his mind and decided to attend Maryland.

"The final decision was mine," McMillen said in a press conference at Maryland. "My parents had their son's best interest at heart and they felt my interests could best be suited by a place they were familiar with."

So talented were McMillen and Elmore, they might have scared away senior Barry Yates. He decided to forego his final season, turned pro and played one season with the Philadelphia 76ers. Thus, Yates was the first ACC player to declare hardship and turn pro before his college eligibility expired. At Maryland, fans joked that Yates was good enough to play for the 76ers but not for the Terps.

Those freshmen had graduated to the varsity for the 1972 season.

Other than a surprise blowout at Virginia and a two-point loss at Clemson, Maryland had performed up to expectations by the time it faced North Carolina in Chapel Hill in late January. First place in the ACC standings was at stake, but even more attention was paid to McMillen's first game in Chapel Hill, where he originally intended to play.

Fearing the worst kind of reception for McMillen, UNC's Smith appealed to students prior to the game to be on their best behavior. During the introduction of players, McMillen was actually given a standing ovation by the crowd at Carmichael Auditorium.

"Maybe they set an example for the Atlantic Coast Conference with their sportsmanship today," Smith said of the crowd.

McMillen scored 20 points and had 13 rebounds, but it was not enough as UNC managed a 92-72 victory. It was Smith's seventh straight win without a loss over Driesell, two of them

165

coming in NCAA Regional play while Driesell coached Davidson.

That streak ended two weeks later. A crowd of 15,287, the largest ever at Cole Field House and a record for an ACC game, saw Howard White make two free throws with seven seconds remaining as Maryland stunned North Carolina 79-77.

"It isn't nothing that special to me that I beat Carolina," said Driesell, who nonetheless joined his team in cutting down the nets following the game.

In all four of UNC's regular-season losses—road games at Princeton, Duke, Maryland, and N.C. State—the opposing team cut down the nets. A victory over the Tar Heels in 1972 was reason to celebrate. With the addition of Bob McAdoo, a Greensboro native who transferred from Vincennes (Ind.) Junior College, Carolina had a team talented enough to challenge for the national championship.

McAdoo was Smith's first junior college recruit. Before attending UNC, McAdoo was offered a contract of $800,000 to sign with the NBA's Atlanta Hawks. By season's end, McAdoo was also drafted by the Virginia Squires of the ABA, and rumors persisted that the 6-9 center would play only one season with the Tar Heels.

Alongside McAdoo on the front line were forwards Dennis Wuycik and Bill Chamberlain and sophomore reserve Bobby Jones. McAdoo and Jones were both fantastic leapers, having won back-to-back North Carolina prep high jump championships.

Jones, as he would do successfully for many years in the pro ranks, often played the sixth-man role for the Tar Heels. He substituted on the front line for McAdoo, Wuycik or Chamberlain. Wuycik was well-schooled in the fundamentals of basketball under Chuck DeVenzio at Ambridge (Pa.) High School. DeVenzio also coached his son Dick, who played at Duke. (Another player on that Ambridge team was Frank Kauffman, who helped lead Purdue past UNC in the semifinals of the 1969 NCAA Tournament.) Chamberlain, after being named the NIT's Most Valuable Player the previous season, entertained thoughts of turning pro but decided to stay at UNC for his senior season.

Chamberlain stayed because he believed the addition of McAdoo made the Tar Heels a championship contender. With George Karl, Steve Previs and Kim Huband in the backcourt, UNC had the ball handlers and outside shooters to complement a talented front line.

Except for a few rough spots, the season was pretty much clear sailing for the Tar Heels. One exception was their game at Duke, when the Tar Heels were stunned when Robbie West made a 20-foot jump shot with three seconds remaining for a 76-74 Blue Devil victory. The game followed the official renaming of Duke Indoor Stadium in honor of the school's athletic director, Eddie Cameron.

The win over UNC was one of few highlights for Duke in an otherwise tumultuous season. Despite 17-9 and 20-10 records in his first two seasons, Bucky Waters was under fire as head coach. In those two years, five highly touted players had left school, and much-respected Assistant Coach Jack Schalow left the business.

Waters was not alone in being pressured by alumni and fans to produce wins and championships. At Wake Forest, rumors persisted that an alumnus wanted to buy out the final two years on Coach Jack McCloskey's contract. Wake fans claimed McCloskey could not recruit. In six seasons, his lone big catch was Charlie Davis. McCloskey had just missed landing Geoff Petrie, who attended Princeton, and Artis Gilmore, who first attended Gardner-Webb, then led Jacksonville to the Final Four in 1970.

McCloskey lasted through the '72 season, but when the Demon Deacons finished 8-18, he departed Wake for the NBA as a coach, then later became a general manager. McCloskey was 70-89 in six seasons at Wake.

At N.C. State, Coach Norm Sloan was not concerned about job security. Instead, Sloan lobbied for freshman eligibility. Sloan said the NCAA rule which prohibited freshmen from participating in varsity athletics was one designed for football. In basketball, he claimed, freshmen could compete at the varsity level. Sloan was certain that freshman David Thompson from Shelby, N.C., could help his varsity squad that finished 16-10 in 1972.

In February, the NCAA voted to make freshmen eligible to play football and basketball for the 1972-73 school year upon approval by individual conferences. One week later, the ACC ratified the NCAA ruling.

Until Thompson became eligible for the 1973 season, UNC was the team to beat in the ACC. By placing first in the regular season for the second straight season and fifth time in the previous six, the Tar Heels were again the favorite to win the ACC Tournament.

Best Ever At Virginia
Virginia's basketball program reached new heights in 1972 behind the prowess of leading scorer Barry Parkhill. The Cavaliers were ranked as high as eighth nationally and enjoyed their first-ever winning season within the ACC, going 8-4. Parkhill averaged 21.6 points and was named ACC Player of the Year.

The addition in '72 of Robert McAdoo (35) to a front line already formidable with Dennis Wuycik (44) gave UNC reason to shoot for No. 1. Steve Previs (13 above) and Bill Chamberlain joined in the celebration following a 73-59 win over Penn in the East Regional final.

77-78
DUKE
GUEST
TIME OUT
PERIOD 3 4
BONUS
FOULS
PLAYER
FOULS
It's the real thing
Coke

DUKE
13:56
GUEST
BONUS
PERIOD 3 4
FOULS
PLAYER
FOULS
It's the real thing.
Coke.
IRON DUKES
SPANARKEL
34
22

STATE
50

24

ACC SCRAPBOOK

Until the advent of the 45-second clock in college basketball, the stall was an equalizing mechanism that allowed weaker teams to effectively shorten a ballgame, thus improving their chances to win, or to try to draw a team out of a zone defense. Here are some noteworthy scenes from stall ball (clockwise from opposite): Dudley Bradley of UNC holds the ball against Duke as the Tar Heels stall away most of the first half of their 1979 game at Duke; the Blue Devils led 7-0 at the half and went on to a 47-40 win. ■ State's Bill Kretzer (50) idles the evening away during the Wolfpack's 12-10 upset of Duke in the '68 ACC Tourney semifinals. ■ South Carolina lost four ACC road games in 1971, two of them when UNC and George Karl (22) held the ball and later when Duke and guard Dick DeVenzio spread it out.

ACC BASKETBALL / THE '70s

After not having to play the first day, the Tar Heels breezed past Duke 63-48 in the semifinals before facing Maryland in the championship.

The match-up continued a friendly wager made between Driesell and UNC guard George Karl, who picked the Tar Heels over the Terps in recruiting. After turning down the scholarship offer from Maryland, Karl made a gentleman's bet with Driesell about head-to-head competition. Karl ran his record against Maryland and Driesell to 4-1 when the Tar Heels defeated the Terps 73-64 for the ACC crown.

Following the Tournament, Maryland and Virginia immediately accepted invitations to the NIT. The Cavaliers were eliminated in the first round by Lafayette, 72-71. But the Terps won the title with a string of victories over St. Joseph's 67-55, Syracuse 71-65, Jacksonville 91-77 and Niagara 100-69.

McMillen, who scored 19 points and had 10 rebounds in the championship game, was named the NIT's Most Valuable Player.

"This is the greatest game I've ever had because it's the first national championship I've ever had," Driesell said.

While Maryland was winning one national title, UNC was competing for the other. The Tar Heels' first-round opponent in the NCAA Tournament in Morgantown, W. Va., was South Carolina, which was 23-4 in its first season as an independent.

"Sure, we remembered our loss to South Carolina last year," said guard Steve Previs of the Tar Heels' 1971 ACC Tournament championship loss to the Gamecocks. "We blew it. But we didn't hold anything personal against Frank McGuire. He didn't play."

Karl's 18 points led UNC in a 92-69 victory.

Pennsylvania was little challenge to the Tar Heels in the NCAA East Regional championship as MVP Wuycik scored 18 in a 73-59 victory. The win gave UNC its first trip to the Final Four since 1969.

Wuycik and the Tar Heels wanted a shot at UCLA, but they needed to hurdle Florida State in the semifinals to meet the winner of UCLA's game against Louisville in the championship.

Florida State was a seven-point underdog in Los Angeles, but the Seminoles used the quickness and ball handling of 5-8 guard Otto Petty to break through UNC's pressure defense and build a 45-32 halftime lead. Florida State's lead eventually reached 23 points before UNC put on a furious rally and closed to within three points in the final minute.

The Seminoles held on to win 79-75 in what Smith said was "the longest night I ever had in coaching."

The Tar Heels started the game without Chamberlain, who was on the bench for arriving late to the pregame meal after visiting with former UNC player Charlie Scott. Chamberlain's penalty for being seven minutes late to the meal was to sit out the first seven minutes of the game.

"I'm just so sorry it was my indiscretion that had hurt the team," Chamberlain said.

In his place, Jones played well, but the Tar Heels fell into too big of a hole.

"I believe I personally was guilty of looking ahead to UCLA," Karl said. "We will always believe we could have given UCLA a run for its money. Always."

Florida State gave UCLA a run for the NCAA title before falling, 81-76. UNC rebounded in the third-place game to defeat Louisville, 105-91.

"I'm sad we didn't get to the finals, for I'll always believe we would have had a chance against UCLA," McAdoo said. "I am going back home feeling we still can beat anyone. And anyone includes UCLA."

'73

North Carolina's Bob McAdoo gave into the financial lure of pro basketball and signed a lucrative contract with the Buffalo Braves of the NBA in the summer of 1972. UNC, Maryland and N.C. State were all ranked in The Associated Press preseason Top 20, and all proved worthy of their rankings by season's end.

By the first week in January, UCLA was the nation's top-ranked team, followed in order by N.C. State, Maryland and UNC. Of the ACC trio, State was the most formidable. With 7-foot-4 junior Tom Burleson in the post, 6-4 sophomore sensation David Thompson at one forward and 5-7 sophomore guard Monte Towe in the backcourt, the Wolfpack had the nucleus of one of the great teams in league history.

Unfortunately for State, the NCAA stepped in and prevented it from participating in postseason play. The Wolfpack was on probation for recruiting violations, most of which centered around the wooing of Thompson, and could not participate in the 1973 NCAA Tournament.

The NCAA found that Assistant Coach Eddie Biedenbach participated in an informal basketball game with five prospective athletes. Also, the NCAA said two prospects were given financial aid to attend a summer school session and a prospect was housed for free in a dormitory that was used by camp counselors. Finally, the NCAA found that three prospects were hired as counselors for Coach Norm Sloan's summer basketball camp.

"The one-year NCAA probation levied on us was a personal embarrassment for me," Sloan said. "But I feel certain it will have no effect on our morale or our record."

Those findings were made known in October. Three months earlier, the NCAA had placed Duke on a similar one-year probation that prevented the Blue Devils from participating in postseason tournaments. Duke also was penalized for its recruiting of Thompson.

A statement by Duke Chancellor John B. Blackburn shed light on the matter when he said, "In the spring of 1971, a friend of the university, who, under the NCAA interpretation of its rules, was a representative of the university's interests, took a high school senior (Thompson) whom the university was attempting to recruit for its basketball program, and his high school coach to the ACC Tournament.

"He also purchased a sports coat and trousers for the young man, without the knowledge of anyone in the university. The NCAA has determined that these actions constitute a violation of its rules. The young man did not enroll at Duke."

Duke Coach Bucky Waters said the probation was "an injustice."

Not far into the season, rumors circulated that UNC Coach Dean Smith, who also recruited Thompson, had turned N.C. State into the NCAA.

"It is the most wildly rumored thing I've heard in North Carolina. I hear it everywhere," Smith said. "We solemnly swear we did not report North Carolina State."

In addition to the probations placed on Duke and State, two rule changes were significant. Previously, one free throw attempt was awarded for the first five non-shooting fouls against a team and then the 1-and-1 bonus went into effect on the sixth. Under the new rule, a team retained possession of the ball without a free throw on the first six non-shooting fouls by the opponent. The other rule change, allowing freshmen to compete at the varsity level, had long-range impact.

Lefty Driesell was introduced in the spring of '69 as Maryland's new coach and made his widely circulated "UCLA of the East" remark. Two years later, ecstatic fans paraded Driesell around Cole Field House after upsetting South Carolina.

For 1973, the only ACC freshmen to land a spot in their teams' starting lineups were Lee Foye of Wake Forest, Wally Walker of Virginia and John Lucas of Maryland. Lucas, with a 14.2 average, and Walker, at 13.7 points a game, were the only freshmen to average in double figures.

Lucas was far and away the most prominent freshman in the ACC. His presence in the Maryland lineup gave the Terps leadership in the backcourt to go with a tremendous front line of Tom McMillen, Len Elmore and Jim O'Brien. With senior Bob Bodell in the backcourt and depth provided by 6-8 Owen Brown, 6-9 Tom Roy, 6-6 Darrell Brown and 6-3 Mo Howard, Maryland quickly established itself as one of the nation's top teams.

"My goal is to be No. 1," said Maryland Coach Lefty Driesell. "I know I'm one of the few coaches honest enough to admit it, but I want to win it (NCAA title) once, and then maybe I'll get out of this stupid racket."

The Terps played like NCAA champions as they won their first 10 games by an average margin of 23 points.

That set up a Super Bowl Sunday showdown against N.C. State, which had won its first 11 games by an average of 31 points. On the afternoon of Jan. 14, 1973, the Miami Dolphins defeated the Washington Redskins 14-7 to complete a 17-0 NFL season. The 3:30 p.m. Super Bowl kickoff gave Castleman D. Chesley of Philadelphia the idea of staging a college basketball game for national television earlier in the day.

Chesley, who had been producing regional ACC basketball telecasts since 1958, suggested to ACC athletic directors in May of 1972 that N.C. State and Maryland play prior to the football classic. The ACC approved the move, and Chesley added national coverage to his original 16-station network. But even Chesley did not dream that the game would pit two undefeated teams against each other with Maryland ranked second in the country and N.C. State ranked third.

Chesley and the estimated TV audience of 25 million could not have asked for more. State called time out with 12 seconds remaining and the game tied at 85. It was perhaps only fitting that the Wolfpack had no set play in the final seconds . . . that's the way Sloan liked his team to play.

Sloan said in the preseason: "We'll seek constant motion as a freelance team without a single organized play. I may be criticized for a lack of organization eventually, but so far it looks awfully good to me."

That's the way it looked to the national TV audience when Thompson soared above McMillen and Elmore to tip in Burleson's miss at the buzzer for an 87-85 victory. It capped a 37-point performance by Thompson and set off a wild celebration on the State campus in Raleigh. That was just the beginning.

In addition to the obvious talents of the Thompson-Burleson-Towe triumvirate, the Wolfpack was blessed with depth. Rick Holdt and Tim Stoddard were the other starters with Joe Cafferky, Greg Hawkins, Mark Moeller and Steve Nuce coming off the bench. The size, quickness and depth of State led to an average of 92.9 points a game, a 21.8-point average margin of victory and 10 games in which the Wolfpack topped 100 points. Those three figures were league records.

There were relatively few scares for the Wolfpack as it followed UNC in 1957, Duke in 1963 and South Carolina in 1970 as the only teams to remain unbeaten within the league during the regular season. The Tar Heels in '57 and the Wolfpack in '73 were the first to have a perfect record in all games.

Any N.C. State meeting with Maryland became special. The return match in Raleigh on the last day of January was as entertaining as the Super Sunday game in College Park. Thompson's seven straight points midway through the second half and 24 total, along with 11 rebounds, helped the Wolfpack to an 89-78 victory. Students flooded the court in celebration and cut down both nets.

"If we can go all the way unbeaten, that will be as good as getting a crack at UCLA," said Thompson of State's inability to compete in the NCAA Tournament because of probation.

The Wolfpack had a few close calls en route to a 27-0 season.

171

Thompson soars to alter McMillen shot during '73 Super Sunday shootout.

State managed narrow home-court wins over Virginia, 64-59, and UNC, 76-73. Against UNC, the Wolfpack needed an 18-foot jump shot by Mark Moeller with 47 seconds left for a 74-73 lead. UNC then committed two turnovers before Thompson made two free throws with three seconds left.

"We are tired," Thompson admitted. "Virginia and North Carolina used the spread-out offense against us. And we've been playing a lot lately."

UNC was the stiffest challenge to State during the regular season. But this was an erratic Tar Heel team, one that climbed as high as fourth in the national rankings when State was second and Maryland was third. UNC kept the ranking with a victory over Maryland and a 91-79 win over Florida State that helped avenge the '72 NCAA semifinal loss. But the Tar Heels fell in the rankings when they were stunned by Miami of Ohio, 102-92, in Carmichael.

UNC's best chance of beating State came on Feb. 27 in Chapel Hill. The Wolfpack had not won in its seven previous tries at Carmichael Auditorium, and UNC had lost only three regular-season finales at home in Coach Dean Smith's 11 years.

UNC stayed within striking distance of the Wolfpack throughout the game and cut the State lead to two with one second left. Burleson's basket at the buzzer accounted for the final 82-78 score. Since then, UNC has not lost its final home game of the season.

"I'd have said it was ridiculous," Sloan said when asked if he thought the Wolfpack could go 24-0 during the regular season. "Matter of fact, I still say it's ridiculous. You just don't go on the road to places like Duke and College Park and Chapel Hill and expect to come out with a win."

The ACC faced an unusual situation as the league Tournament approached. State received a first-round bye for its first-place finish during the regular season. But the Wolfpack and Duke were unable to represent the ACC in the NCAA Tournament due to probations. That left only five teams qualified to play in the NIT or NCAA tournaments.

The ACC met and decided that the runner-up in the ACC Tournament would advance to the NCAAs. If State and Duke met for the league championship, the two semifinal losers would play to determine a representative in the NCAAs. That game would be played on Sunday night following the Saturday night championship game.

The latter alternative was not necessary because Duke dropped a 59-55 decision to Virginia in the first round. The first round also featured one of the biggest upsets in the history of the Tournament when Wake Forest stunned North Carolina 54-52. Wake Forest scored on a last-second, length-of-the-court pass and short jump shot by Lee Foye to force overtime. Then the Deacons scored on a layup by seldom-used reserve Phil Perry with one second remaining in overtime for the win.

The Demon Deacons, who finished 11-14 during the regular season, defeated the eighth-ranked Tar Heels and became the first bottom-seeded team to ever win in the Tournament. Only Virginia in 1977 has done it since.

Maryland, despite playing without injured center Len Elmore, reached the championship game and a third meeting against N.C. State. Once again, the Wolfpack had the magic in the end. Two free throws by Thompson with 10 seconds remaining clinched the 76-74 victory and gave N.C. State a perfect 27-0 record.

"It's a happy feeling, but an empty one," said Tournament MVP Tommy Burleson, who showed he deserved first-team All-ACC by scoring 14 and getting 11 rebounds in the semifinals against Virginia, then having a 14-point, 14-rebound performance against Maryland.

While the Wolfpack stayed home, Maryland represented the ACC in the NCAA field and North Carolina went to the NIT.

UNC turned back Oral Roberts 82-65 and Massachusetts 73-63, but the Tar Heels failed to give the ACC a third straight NIT title when Notre Dame prevailed 78-71 in the semifinals.

Maryland, meanwhile, defeated Syracuse in the NCAA East Regional as Elmore returned to the lineup to score 10 points and get 14 rebounds in a 91-75 victory. The Terps missed a trip to the Final Four when Providence got 30 points from Ernie DiGregorio in a 103-89 victory in the East Regional championship in Charlotte. DiGregorio fouled out with 11:37 to play, but Kevin Stacom scored 24 to save the win.

ACC BASKETBALL / THE '70s

'74

As UCLA's string of national championships stretched, the chase to dethrone the Bruins became more frustrating. With each approaching season, the list of contenders seemed to grow. The ACC usually produced one serious threat, but only North Carolina in 1968 got a first-hand chance to knock off the Bruins.

For the 1974 season, the ACC appeared to have three contenders for the national championship. N.C. State, of course, was the chief challenger with three starters returning from the Wolfpack's unbeaten team of 1973. North Carolina returned the nucleus of a team that won 25 games in '73. Then there was Maryland, which returned six of its top nine players from a 23-7 team the previous season.

If there ever was a chance for Maryland to back Coach Lefty Driesell's claim of becoming the "UCLA of the East," it was in 1974. The Terps opened the season against the defending national champs.

Maryland was ranked No. 4 in national preseason polls. UCLA carried a 76-game win streak into the meeting in Los Angeles and was again atop the rankings.

A last-second steal by UCLA's Dave Meyers preserved the Bruins' 65-64 victory. Maryland guard John Lucas lost control of the ball as he moved into position to shoot with four seconds remaining. Meyers stepped in to gain possession and UCLA, a 20-point favorite, had the victory.

"I've never been more proud of any aggregation than I am of this one," Driesell said. "It ain't got a 'W' after it, but I sure am proud."

Maryland went on to have its finest season ever. The Terps won 23 of 28 games, with three of the losses coming to N.C. State. The combination of guards Lucas and Mo Howard, forwards Tom McMillen and Owen Brown and center Len Elmore meshed to make Maryland one of the top teams in league history.

North Carolina was in much the same predicament as Maryland. The Tar Heels fielded one of their better teams with Bobby Jones, Walter Davis, Mitch Kupchak and Tommy LaGarde

Most Incredible Comeback
UNC's Tar Heels staged the ACC's most remarkable comeback on March 2, 1974, when they rallied from eight points down with 17 seconds remaining to tie Duke and force overtime. This 30-foot jump shot by freshman Walter Davis just beat the buzzer and tied the game, and the Tar Heels went on to win, 96-92.

ACC BASKETBALL / THE '70s

in the lineup. Unfortunately, they did so in a season when N.C. State was dominant. UNC lost only six games—two to Maryland, one to Purdue in the opening round of the NIT and three to N.C. State.

The Wolfpack was on a mission from the outset of the '74 season. NCAA probation prohibited State from challenging UCLA for the national title a year earlier. Now, nothing could stand in the Wolfpack's way.

Season-opening victories over East Carolina and Vermont prepared State for a showdown with UCLA on Dec. 15. The made-for-TV matchup netted each school $125,000. Since neither school would agree to play on the other's home court, they decided to play in St. Louis.

The Bruins' win streak had reached 78 games by the time they arrived in St. Louis. State also had a win streak, one that stretched to 29 games.

In the end, Keith Wilkes was too much for State. The smooth UCLA forward scored 27 points and had six assists. He also held the Wolfpack's David Thompson to 17 points on 7-of-20 shooting. The key stretch came when UCLA's Bill Walton sat on the bench for 21 minutes with four fouls. State could not take advantage of Walton's absence, and when he re-entered the game with 9:30 remaining, the score was tied at 54. He immediately led the Bruins on scoring streaks of nine and 10 points, and UCLA coasted down the stretch to an 84-66 victory.

"We kind of eased up because Walton was out," Thompson admitted.

"I hope we're better than this," said State Coach Norm Sloan. "We'll just have to wait and see . . . The defeat can be traced to me. Back when we played the Red and White (preseason intrasquad) game, I didn't feel good about our team. We were too slow. We were waiting for something to happen rather than making it happen. We didn't have enough motion.

"I was reluctant to make any major changes, though, because of the fact that we finished unbeaten last year. I just didn't have enough courage to do it. I now view it as a mistake on my part."

Sloan said he needed to better take advantage of the talents of guard Moe Rivers, who was a penetrator on offense. Rivers replaced Joe Cafferky, who was more of an outside shooter for the Wolfpack the previous season. Rivers, a transfer from Gulf Coast (Fla.) Junior College, was recruited specifically to be the Wolfpack's starting second guard.

The rest of the lineup was set from the previous season. Monte Towe was again the playmaking guard who, at 5-7, was the darling of N.C. State, as well as ACC, fans. Towe was the perfect complement to towering Tommy Burleson, a 7-4 stringbean affectionately known to State fans as the "Newland Needle."

When Burleson needed help on the boards, he could turn to either of State's forwards. Tim Stoddard was often an immovable object inside at 6-7 and 230 pounds. He had split time the previous season with the since-graduated Rick Holdt.

Thompson was the ACC's first three-time Player of the Year. Twice he was national Player of the Year. More than anything, he was usually the edge State needed in close games.

The Wolfpack had quite a few close calls as it went through a second straight unbeaten season in the ACC. The first narrow escape came in the opening round of the Big Four Tournament, when the fifth-ranked Wolfpack edged fourth-rated North Carolina 78-77, as the Tar Heels' Ed Stahl missed a shot with three seconds remaining.

The next test came on Super Bowl Sunday. For the second straight season, the opponent for the nationally televised contest was third-ranked Maryland. This time, the scene shifted to Reynolds Coliseum. But the results were much the same as in 1973. Thompson again stole the show with 41 points in the Wolfpack's 80-74 victory.

State's next test came in Chapel Hill, where the Tar Heels were primed to end the Wolfpack's ACC win streak. State's freelance style of play again gave the precision Tar Heels fits, and the Wolfpack got away with an 83-80 win.

While State was walking a tightrope through the ACC, UCLA's record 88-game win streak was stopped at Notre Dame. When the Bruins lost back-to-back games at Oregon and Oregon State in mid-February, State became the nation's top-rated team for the first time since 1959.

State's home finale belonged to Burleson, who was presented the game ball by his teammates following an 83-72 victory over UNC. Burleson scored 19 points and had nine rebounds as the Wolfpack won its 29th straight game against ACC opponents, breaking the mark of 28 established by Duke in 1963 and 1964.

Only All-ACC Frosh

Skip Wise of Clemson holds the distinction of having been the only freshman to ever make All-ACC first team, averaging 18.5 points for the Tigers in 1975. Wise was noted for a chest-high dribble and exceptional quickness. "He was always telling himself he was going to be the best basketball player that ever played," teammate Tree Rollins says. "I have never seen a guy practice as much as he did or work on his game as much as he did. He was the best. He was a helluva player."

ACC BASKETBALL / THE '70s

When State closed out the regular season with a 72-63 victory over Wake Forest, the Wolfpack became the first and only team to go unbeaten in the ACC two straight seasons.

Still, to qualify for the NCAA Tournament, the Wolfpack had to win the ACC Tournament. Again, the stiffest challenges were expected to come from North Carolina and Maryland.

UNC Coach Dean Smith prepared his team for the Tournament after a miracle win over Duke in the regular-season finale at Carmichael Auditorium. The Tar Heels overcame an eight-point deficit in the final 17 seconds of regulation to win 96-92 in overtime.

Trailing 86-78, UNC got two free throws from Bobby Jones. Walter Davis stole the Duke inbounds pass and scored, and John Kuester did the same to make it 86-82. Another inbounds pass was swiped, and Jones hit a rebound layup with six seconds remaining.

Duke's Pete Kramer was fouled by Kuester, but Kramer missed the front end of a 1-and-1. Stahl rebounded for UNC and called time out with three seconds left. Davis caught the inbounds pass, took two dribbles and banked in the tying basket from 30 feet away at the buzzer.

"I wasn't trying to bank it," Davis sheepishly admitted.

Duke took a three-point lead in overtime, but UNC rallied to win.

The loss was particularly devastating to Blue Devil Coach Neill McGeachy, who was elevated from assistant when Bucky Waters quit suddenly the previous September. During Waters' four seasons, students and fans repeatedly called for his ouster despite a 63-45 record.

The Blue Devils were 10-16 under McGeachy, who was never certain whether he would be retained as coach beyond one season. He was hired after Duke officials made a pitch to get retired Kentucky coach Adolph Rupp to come to Durham. McGeachy was never given a vote of confidence by Duke officials.

Duke hired Bill Foster away from the University of Utah and gave him a long-term contract, clarifying that McGeachy had been an interim coach who was given consideration for the permanent post.

Maryland, meanwhile, dismantled North Carolina 105-85 in the ACC Tournament semifinals to earn a final shot at N.C. State. The Wolfpack reached the championship with an 87-66 victory over Virginia in the final ACC game for Cavalier Coach Bill Gibson, who later resigned and left for South Florida.

Prior to the championship game, Driesell clamored for a change in the NCAA Tournament format that allowed only one team from each conference to make the field.

"I think you should pick the best teams to play for the national championship," Driesell said. "It would make a much better playoff. I just don't think every conference champion should get an automatic bid."

That left one spot for the ACC champion in the NCAA Tournament and perhaps two others for league representatives in the NIT. The winner of the State-Maryland game in Greensboro would advance to the NCAA Tournament, with the East Regional to be played in Raleigh.

In what is generally considered the greatest game ever played in the ACC, and perhaps in college basketball, State defeated Maryland 103-100 in overtime.

"The team we beat tonight is the No. 2 team in the country," Sloan said.

Maryland had a chance to win at the end of regulation when it had possession of the ball with nine seconds left and

State dominated UNC during the Burleson era, with the Pack thwarting efforts from Tar Heels like Mitch Kupchak for nine straight wins from 1972 to '75.

the game tied at 97. But the best shot the Terps could get was a desperation 25-footer by Lucas as time expired. It missed and State took charge in overtime.

The Wolfpack's Burleson did the most damage, scoring 38 points on 18-of-25 shooting and collecting 13 rebounds. But it was Towe who made the kill with two free throws with six seconds left in overtime to clinch the victory.

The loss was the third straight in the championship game for the Terps, who were discouraged and angry. They declined an invitation to play in the NIT.

State had more home-court support in the East Regional in Raleigh. Thompson was a one-man show in the opening round as he scored 40 points and had 10 rebounds in the Wolfpack's 92-78 victory over Providence.

With 10:17 remaining in the first half of the East Regional championship against Pittsburgh, Thompson soared through the foul lane in an attempt to block a shot by Panther Keith Starr. Thompson climbed the back of teammate Phil Spence, flipped head over heels and landed on his head.

Thompson was unconscious for about four minutes. The 12,400 fans at Reynolds Coliseum and a regional TV audience held its breath as the nation's top player lay motionless. Finally, he was carried off the floor on a stretcher and rushed to nearby Rex Hospital.

At halftime, with State leading 47-41, Sloan told his team to win the game for Thompson. With 6:51 remaining in the game and the Wolfpack leading 79-59, Thompson returned to the court with a 3-inch bandage around his head. The crowd, informed that Thompson was okay, cheered madly. The Wolfpack then went on to a 100-72 victory and began preparation for the Final Four in Greensboro.

The NCAA semifinals pitted Marquette against Kansas in one bracket with State to face UCLA in the other. Neither

175

ACC BASKETBALL / THE '70s

the Wolfpack, which had won 26 straight games since its early season loss to UCLA, nor the Bruins, which carried a 25-3 record to Greensboro, had forgotten their earlier meeting.

"I want North Carolina State to remember that we beat them by 18 points on a neutral floor with Bill Walton playing only half the game," UCLA Coach John Wooden said. "I don't know if that's a psychological edge or not. But I want them to think about it."

State had changed, and improved considerably since its first meeting with UCLA. First, Rivers now fit better into his role as a second guard with Towe as the point guard. Also, Spence, a transfer from Vincennes (Ind.) Junior College, gave the Wolfpack depth on the front line. When Thompson sat out 30 minutes of the East Regional final against Pittsburgh, Spence scored 10 points and had 14 rebounds.

Just two weeks after State went into overtime to defeat Maryland in a college basketball classic, the Wolfpack needed two overtimes to defeat seven-time defending champion UCLA 80-77 in the NCAA semifinals.

State rallied twice from apparent defeat. The Wolfpack trailed by 11 in the second half, yet recovered to tie the game at 65 and force overtime. State also trailed 74-67 with 3:27 left in the second overtime. But Towe made two free throws and then drew a crucial charging foul on UCLA's Tommy Curtis. Two State baskets and a Burleson free throw cut the Bruins' lead to 75-74 with 1:38 left.

Thompson, who finished with 28 points and 10 rebounds, then went to work. He first made a 12-foot jump shot after UCLA's Dave Meyers missed a free throw. Then Thompson rebounded a missed jumper by Bruin Greg Lee and was fouled with 34 seconds left. Thompson made both free throws for a 78-75 lead that clinched the State victory.

"I thought we had the game well in hand a couple of times," Wooden said. "But we made some mistakes that cost us."

State's Sloan said: "Before the season began last fall I told our team we had a chance to be one of the greatest basketball teams of all time. I'm not making that claim now, but we beat one of the greatest of all time."

The loss was the first after 38 straight NCAA Tournament victories for UCLA, which got 29 points and 10 rebounds from Walton. But he was neutralized by Burleson, who had 20 points and 14 rebounds.

"Our greatest victory ever?" Towe said. "No, we've had some great ones the last two seasons. If we win Monday, that will be our greatest."

Monday's game was for the national championship against a Marquette team that had disposed of Kansas, 64-51. But the finale was almost anti-climactic because State effectively won the national crown with the semifinal victory over UCLA.

Two technical fouls against Marquette Coach Al McGuire late in the first half sent State on a 10-point spree in 53 seconds and a 39-30 halftime lead. When State went on a 12-2 run to open the second half, the Wolfpack was well on its way to a 76-64 victory and the championship.

"We wanted it so badly," Sloan said. "The players deserved to be national champions. I would have been heartbroken if they hadn't won."

There had been much speculation that Thompson, who scored 21 points to earn the Tournament's MVP Award, would forego his senior year to sign a professional contract. But he announced after the game that he would return to State for another season.

"Already, I'm hoping we can be No. 1 again," Thompson said.

176

ACC BASKETBALL / THE '70s

Title-bound Triumvirate
N.C. State dethroned seven-time defending NCAA champion UCLA and Bill Walton and captured the 1974 title behind the play of three key players: Forward David Thompson (opposite); center Tommy Burleson (R) shown blocking a Walton jump shot; and guard Monte Towe (inset).

'75

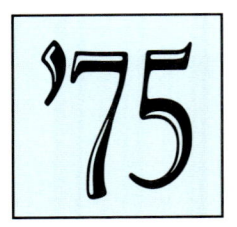

N.C. State began the 1975 season as the nation's No. 1-ranked team, but the magic of the previous two years was missing. Without 7-foot-4 center Tom Burleson in the middle, opponents quickly learned that zone defenses could contain the Wolfpack.

Wake Forest was the first to knock off the Wolfpack en route to the Deacons' first Big Four title in January of 1975. The Demon Deacons got 25 points from guard Skip Brown in the opening round of the Big Four Tournament to post an 83-78 upset victory. Wake Forest's 2-3 zone defense limited State to 34.9 percent field goal shooting, including a 5-for-20 performance by Thompson.

The loss snapped a 37-game win streak for State, including 34 straight against ACC opponents that dated to March of 1972.

By the conclusion of the Big Four Tournament, followers of the ACC began to notice the exceptional talent within the freshman class. The frosh of 1975 had a greater impact on the league than any one class before or since.

State's undefeated season in 1973, its NCAA championship in 1974 and subsequent exposure for the league on national TV probably helped ACC schools lure the top high school players in the land.

At the top of the 1975 freshman class was Clemson's Skip Wise, a 6-4 guard from Baltimore. In only his second game, Wise scored 38 points against Pennsylvania. By season's end, he averaged 18.5 points, which was the highest average by an ACC freshman until Georgia Tech's Mark Price scored 20.3 points a game in 1983.

Wise became the only freshman in league history to make the All-ACC first team. He edged teammate Tree Rollins by two votes to gain first-team honors. Wise, however, turned out to be one of the saddest stories in ACC history. He signed a five-year, $750,000 contract to play professional basketball with the Baltimore Claws of the American Basketball Association following the season. The Claws folded a few weeks after Wise left Clemson, starting him down a path of rejection by other teams and scrapes with the law. Soon after the Claws folded, Wise had tryouts with the San Antonio Spurs and Golden State Warriors, but he was cut by both teams. Less than a year later, Wise was sentenced to 12 years in prison for possession and distribution of heroine.

Although Wise only played two games of professional basketball with the Spurs of the ABA, four others in the ACC freshman class of '75 had distinguished pro careers: Maryland's Brad Davis, North Carolina's Phil Ford, N.C. State's Kenny Carr and Virginia's Marc Iavaroni.

There are still other ways to gauge the strength of that freshman class. In addition to Wise, Davis, Ford, Carr and Iavaroni, Clemson's Stan Rome and Wake Forest's Rod Griffin gave the freshman class seven players who averaged scoring in double figures. Only the 1978 freshman class (six players in double figures), and the 1977 and 1983 class (five each) have come close to matching that mark.

Also, 1975 was the only season in which every ACC team had at least one freshman starting in the ACC Tournament, although Duke started freshman Ken Young because of an injury to guard Tate Armstrong. Ford became the first freshman to win the Everett Case MVP award in the Tournament.

With nearly every ACC team landing at least one top prep player for 1975, the league quickly developed true balance.

Maryland's Magic Magid

Ask any ACC coach who the best pure shooter in league annals has been, and the answer will likely be Brian Magid. He played two years at Maryland from 1976-77 and developed a fan following known as Magid's Mob; they cheered his every move and screamed for Coach Lefty Driesell to play him more. Driesell, however, felt Magid was a defensive liability, and Magid transferred to George Washington after two years, having scored only 168 points. Prior to games at Duke, students would place dollar bills on spots of the court from which they wanted Magid to shoot. More often than not, Magid would pocket the money after making the shot.

N.C. State, Maryland and North Carolina had established programs, while Wise and Rome quickly moved Clemson into the league's upper echelon. Virginia, the only team in the league to finish below .500 (12-13), and Duke appeared headed in the right direction with first-year coaches Terry Holland and Bill Foster, respectively. Back-to-back strong recruiting classes by third-year Wake Forest Coach Carl Tacy also had Wake Forest on the right track.

"I've never seen the ACC better," said former Duke Coach Vic Bubas, then a vice president at Duke. "In the past, we often had one or two good teams and the fans got carried away and said the ACC was the best conference. I never made that statement as coach, as I recall. And I don't think we could have truthfully made that statement until a couple of years

ACC BASKETBALL / THE '70s

ago. Now, though, I really believe ACC basketball is the best."

The ACC's strength at the top, with three teams winning at least 20 games for four straight seasons, forced the NCAA to reconsider its tournament selection policy. For the 1975 NCAA Tournament, the field was expanded from 25 to 32 teams and could include two selections from a single conference.

The expanded field placed a greater importance on the ACC's regular-season race. The ACC Tournament champion would still qualify for the NCAA field. But the second pick from the league was likely to be the team that finished first in the regular season, should it not win the ACC Tournament.

N.C. State, of course, was again the favorite to place first in the regular season for a third straight time. Thompson got the Wolfpack off to a fast start when he scored an ACC-record 57 points in the third game of the season. In just 34 minutes, Thompson made 27 of 37 field goal attempts and had 17 rebounds as the Wolfpack scored a league-record 144 points in a 56-point victory over Buffalo State. Previous scoring highs were by South Carolina's John Roche (56) and State's Ronnie Shavlik (55).

Thompson finished his career with more points (2,309) than any player in ACC history who played only three seasons, and his 26.8 career scoring average was the third highest behind Virginia's Buzz Wilkinson (28.6) and UNC's Lennie Rosenbluth (26.9). Thompson was the first to be three-time ACC Player of the Year before Virginia's Ralph Sampson (1981-83) joined him. Thompson also became the only player to be a unanimous pick for Player of the Year.

Prior to his final appearance at Reynolds Coliseum, Thompson's No. 44 jersey was retired. He then scored 36 points in a 103-80 victory over UNC-Charlotte. He would have scored 38, but a slam dunk was disallowed because dunking was illegal. The sellout crowd of 12,400 was nonetheless thrilled to see Thompson cap his home career in such a manner.

Despite Thompson's heroics, other league teams began to catch up with State in 1975. North Carolina ended a nine-game losing streak to the Wolfpack with a 76-74 victory in the Tar Heels' home finale. Maryland also ended a six-game skid against State when the Terps defeated the Wolfpack twice during the regular season, 103-85 in College Park and 98-97 in Raleigh.

Maryland's only regular-season league losses were at Clemson and at home against UNC. The Terps also dropped a home game to UCLA in December. Otherwise, Maryland had little trouble while employing an unusual three-guard lineup. Terp Coach Lefty Driesell was forced into the alignment when guard John Lucas broke his collarbone in the season opener against Richmond. Freshman Brad Davis played well in his place. When Lucas returned, Driesell continued to play Davis along with guards Lucas and Mo Howard.

Driesell rotated Owen Brown, Steve Sheppard and Tom Roy inside. As a result, Maryland became the only team in league history to have six players average scoring in double figures. The Terps were so solid they became only the second team to sweep Tobacco Road, winning at Duke, Wake Forest, UNC and State just as South Carolina had done in 1970.

Maryland, which ranked among the nation's top 10 teams throughout the season, could have been even better. When the Terps played at Clemson, a Tiger fan waved a sign that read: "Lefty, we have Abraham. Where's Moses?" Abraham was Clemson freshman forward Colon Abraham. Moses was a 6-11 center from Petersburg, Va., named Moses Malone. He first signed with Maryland, then opted to play with the Utah Stars of the ABA instead of going to college.

"I'm sure we probably would win the national championship with Moses, but we couldn't possibly have this much fun playing basketball," said Maryland's Davis.

Maryland's first-place finish at 10-2 virtually ensured a bid to the NCAA Tournament. But Driesell still wanted badly to win the ACC Tournament, something Maryland had done only in 1958. If he ever won the Tournament, Driesell said, he would use the championship trophy as a hood ornament and drive his car around the state of North Carolina to show it off.

For the third straight season, State derailed Lefty's joy ride. The Wolfpack, determined to avenge itself for a subpar showing during the regular season, defeated Virginia in the first round 91-85 and advanced to the championship game with an 87-85 victory over the second-ranked Terps.

State played the final 10 minutes without Thompson, who was sidelined with severe leg cramps. The Wolfpack feared Thompson would be slowed by the cramps in the championship against North Carolina, which needed a most unusual play to defeat Wake Forest in overtime, then needed another overtime to turn back Clemson in the semifinals.

Against Wake Forest, the Tar Heels trailed by eight points with 56 seconds left in regulation but quickly cut that lead in half. The Demon Deacons thought they had iced the win when Jerry Schellenberg threw a length-of-the-court pass to Skip Brown, who was fouled by UNC's Dave Hanners. But referee Fred Hikel ruled the pass grazed the overhanging scoreboard in the Greensboro Coliseum and awarded the ball to UNC.

"If the ref had some doubt that it hit the scoreboard it never should have been called," said Wake Forest Coach Tacy.

Walter Davis hit a corner jumpshot, Wake Forest missed two 1-and-1s and UNC's Brad Hoffman made a 12-footer with one second remaining to tie the game at 90 and force overtime. Then Wake Forest was given a technical foul for not forcing the action on defense; UNC converted its free throws and escaped with a 101-100 victory.

Clemson, which advanced past the first round of the ACC Tournament for the first time since 1964 and for only the third time in school history with a 78-76 win over Duke, proved another difficult test for UNC. The Tar Heels used the ball handling of freshman Ford to run their Four Corners offense over the final 11:30 of regulation, which ended in a tie at 64. Ten of UNC's 12 points in overtime came from the foul line during the delay offense, and the Tar Heels won 76-71.

Capping off a splendid season for freshmen, Ford was named the Tournament MVP after scoring 24 points to lead the Tar Heels in a 70-66 victory over State for the championship. The rest of the All-Tournament team included freshmen Wise and Carr, as well as Mitch Kupchak and Thompson.

The ACC could have had four representatives in postseason play for the first time, but State rejected a bid to the NIT. Thompson was one of the Wolfpack players who voted against playing in the NIT, which he labeled "a loser's tournament."

Clemson was more than happy to accept a bid to the NIT, the first postseason tournament appearance in school history. But the Tigers exited quickly with a 91-86 loss to Providence. Clemson Coach Tates Locke said he was pleased with the Tigers' 17-11 record but was leery of an investigation of his program by the NCAA. Two weeks later, Locke resigned, perhaps aware that a probationary sentence was coming from the NCAA. Locke had just completed the final year of a five-year contract.

Attention focused on the league's two representatives in the

179

UNC used freshman Phil Ford's ball handling from the Four Corners to eliminate Clemson in the '75 ACC semifinals.

NCAA Tournament. The Tar Heels were the first to fall. They defeated New Mexico State in the first round 93-69 but lost to Syracuse 78-76 when Jimmy Lee swished a fallaway jump shot from 20 feet with three seconds remaining.

Maryland advanced to the championship of the Midwest Regional with an 83-79 victory over Creighton, followed by an 83-71 decision over Notre Dame. But the hot-shooting Terps turned cold in a 96-82 loss to Louisville. Maryland, which entered the game as the nation's top field goal shooting team at 55 percent, hit only 43 percent of its attempts against Louisville.

For the sixth time in seven years, the ACC did not send a member to the NCAA Championship game. The league's credibility was shattered even further in October of 1975 when the NCAA placed Clemson on probation for three years. The sanctions prohibited Clemson from participating in postseason play for three seasons and from appearing on any NCAA television games. Clemson was also permitted only two basketball grant-in-aids for the 1976-77 season and three for 1977-78.

Wally reveled in wonderful '76 title run.

The '70s

Virginia

Three championship rings rest in the trophy case of Wally Walker's home. He played on NBA title teams with Portland in 1977 and Seattle in 1979. Those two rings are much larger than the third, but they hardly measure in importance to the one he earned at the University of Virginia in 1976.

"Hands down, it's the most meaningful," Walker says of the Cavaliers' lone ACC championship. "I loved being part of the pro championship teams, but I just wasn't emotionally tied to a community like I was to the institution at Virginia.

"In pro sports, winning is the ultimate, but it's still a business . . . College is a great feeling. It was a team, and I had a little more to do with it at Virginia than I did as a pro."

Walker understates the case. His performance in leading Virginia past three nationally ranked teams was one of the most outstanding in ACC Tournament history.

"I was just in a zone the whole tournament," Walker says. "I was surprised if I didn't make a shot. If it didn't go in the basket, I was dumbfounded."

In wins over N.C. State (ranked 17th in the country), Maryland (No. 9) and North Carolina (No. 3), Walker scored 73 points on 28-of-41 shooting from the floor. He missed only one of 18 free throw attempts and led Virginia with 21 rebounds. His defense limited Maryland's John Lucas to 5-of-15 shooting and 12 points in the semifinals and UNC's Walter Davis to 5-of-13 shooting and 10 points in the championship, a 67-62 triumph.

Walker was a unanimous choice as the Everett Case Award winner. He remains the lone Cavalier to be so named as the ACC Tournament's most valuable player.

The seeds for Walker's performance and Virginia's championship were planted long before the Cavaliers carried the title trophy out of the Capital Centre in Landover, Md.

Prior to the 1975 season, first-year Coach Terry Holland put his team through a rigorous conditioning program that Walker described as "boot camp." Two principles changed from Walker's first two years under Coach Bill Gibson: The Cavaliers would now be one of the best-conditioned teams in the ACC and they would play nothing but man-to-man defense.

Walker had emerged as a star under Gibson because he was allowed to display his immense offensive skills. He averaged 14 points a game as a freshman and 17.5 as a sophomore while becoming affectionately known to

180

ACC BASKETBALL / THE '70s

Walker shoots over UNC's Mitch Kupchak (21) and Walter Davis during Cavaliers' 67-62 upset in the '76 ACC championship game.

Virginia fans as Wonderful Wally. He made 12 of 13 field goals in a game at UNC during his first season, helping the Cavaliers win in Chapel Hill for the first time since 1919.

Not even three knee operations in his first two seasons could slow Walker's offensive production. That was until Holland came aboard.

"Wally was utilizing his talents for his own benefit; he wasn't benefiting the other players," Holland says in *Cavaliers!*, a history book of Virginia basketball. "He was never a rebel or anything like that. He was a great kid . . . I remember sitting him down one day and telling him, 'Wally, I know this sounds silly but you're not one of our two best forwards right now.'"

Those were harsh words to a 6-foot-7 forward who had averaged 31 points and 21 rebounds at Penn Manor High School in Millersville, Pa., and thereby could choose any ACC school he wished to attend. About the only thing that stood in Walker's way at Virginia was Barry Parkhill, and that was only because the Cavalier All-America already wore jersey No. 40 when Walker arrived. Walker took his second choice, No. 41, and Parkhill elected to take his new teammate under his wing.

During the summer prior to his sophomore season, Walker moved in with the Parkhill family in University Park, Pa., and practiced basketball daily at Penn State University. Before the summer was out, Walker was recovering from knee surgery. So it was for good reason that Holland wondered what Walker was all about after watching a gimpy-legged forward who could not play defense.

"I didn't think I was playing bad defense, but in fact I was," Walker recalled. "It was up to me to adjust to what he was doing. To a degree, that was true for the entire team, but more so for me."

With Walker improving, Virginia made the necessary adjustments and became an outstanding defensive team by the end of his junior season. When the Cavaliers lost a one-point decision at UNC late in Walker's senior year, Holland told them they were the best team in the ACC.

His players, not so convinced, made plans to spend spring break in Ft. Lauderdale, Fla., immediately following the ACC Tournament. But Wally spoiled those plans by turning truly wonderful for three straight nights.

"It was so much fun," said Walker. "It was as if we didn't know how to act because it was the first thing we had ever won. It was just so emotional to be part of that."

After retiring from the NBA, Walker completed business school at Stanford and joined an investment firm, all the while carrying with him memories from that wonderful weekend of '76. ∎

Tar Heels' 'Ford Corners' scourge of ACC.

Despite being among 21,000 students, he was lonely. College courses in Chapel Hill were much more difficult than those at Rocky Mount High School. Playing college basketball was even worse. He made only five of his first 25 field goal attempts and occasionally got burned by opponents on defense.

"I called home crying," Phil Ford said of his first semester at the University of North Carolina. "It was the first time in my life that basketball was hard. I got to Carolina and realized there were guys my size, smaller than me and bigger than me who could play basketball a lot better than I could."

The '70s
North Carolina

That changed quickly. Ford became the first freshman to be named MVP of the ACC Tournament. Three times he would earn All-ACC first-team honors, including a unanimous selection his senior season. By then, no one played college basketball better than Phil Ford. He was voted the best in the ACC and named National Player of the Year in 1978.

Ford loved being the center of attention on a basketball court, and there was no better situation for him than as director of Coach Dean Smith's Four Corners offense. Some simply called it the "Ford Corners." When Ford crossed midcourt and held four fingers above his head late in a game, he might as well have been smoking UNC's victory cigar.

"I admit," Smith would say years later, "it (Four Corners) was unfair with Ford. He hit the foul shots, he could drive, he could take it in, bring it out and pass it off. He was unstoppable."

With Ford running the show, UNC finished first in the ACC's regular-season race three times. Twice the Tar Heels won the ACC Tournament, and in 1977 they finished as runner-up to Marquette in the NCAA Tournament. UNC was 99-25 in Ford's four seasons, including a 50-17 record against ACC competition.

When the Tar Heels lost to San Francisco in the opening round of the 1978 NCAA Tournament, Ford's illustrious career came to an end. Two weeks later, Ford still wore the tape around his ankles from his last college game.

"I just didn't want it to end," he said.

Ford went on to play seven seasons in the NBA, where he earned Rookie of the Year honors in 1979 and was an all-star in 1980. But a serious eye injury and a bout with alcoholism cut short his pro career.

"I abused alcohol and there's no excuse," said Ford, who went into the banking business in Raleigh, N.C. "It was a mistake. I have to live up to that mistake. It's something I wish had not happened, but I've made some bad decisions in my life and I've made some great decisions."

One of Ford's best decisions was to concentrate on basketball rather than football or baseball while growing up in Rocky Mount, an eastern North Carolina tobacco city of 50,000. Baseball and football were Ford's first choices. But basketball was what he played best, ever since his father cut out the bottom of a barrel and constructed an 8-foot goal in the family's backyard.

Ford learned to bribe the older kids with a handful of cookies to stay around and play more basketball. He needed an edge because Ford was probably a little short on natural talent. Most of the older kids could dunk a basketball, a distinct advantage on Ford in games of H-O-R-S-E. Though he was never able to dunk at 6-foot-1, Ford learned to leave the ground, spin 360 degrees in the air and shoot a layup.

"I had to think of the wildest thing I could do," he said.

Ford was the first player known for the "360" in the ACC and it soon became part of his repertoire, along with a delicate jump shot and clever ball handling. More than anything, Ford used keen decision-making from his point guard position. Only once in four years can he remember calling a play that was not to Smith's liking.

"If I had to choose the ideal qualities I'd want in a guard, the result would be Phil Ford," Smith told the *Greensboro Daily News*. "Because of his special blend of talent and desire, I don't know of any guard anywhere in the world who is as suited to the role."

In addition to his extraordinary skills, Ford also possessed a special savvy and enthusiasm for the game.

"He was the fiercest competitor I've ever seen in the ACC," said long-time Maryland Coach Lefty Driesell. "If you could get every player to play as hard as Phil Ford did, you'd never lose a game."

Ford was tagged with the nickname "Bunny Rabbit," first by high school teammates because he lost two front teeth playing basketball, then again by his college teammates because of the bounce he carried in his walk and his run.

"Basketball was just really fun," Ford said. "I can't think of anything that has been more fun than playing basketball. It was something I loved to do. That was just my personality that showed. With Walter (Davis) and Bruce (Buckley), they were just as excited and pumped up to play as I was. But they aren't the type to go out and jump up and down and start crying and pat guys on the butt. But somebody like me, if I get excited, there's no telling what I might do."

What Ford did was become the first freshman to start for Smith at the beginning of a season, help UNC end a nine-game losing streak against N.C. State as a freshman and average 26 points in three games of the ACC Tournament to earn MVP honors. As a sophomore, Ford played on what he has called his best team at UNC with Davis, Mitch Kupchak, Tom LaGarde, and John Kuester in the starting lineup. The Tar Heels lost only four times in 29 games. The most difficult defeat was to Alabama in the opening round of the NCAA Tournament when Ford was hobbled by an injury he sustained during a pickup game in Rocky Mount.

His injured knee was well enough to lead the U.S. Olympic team to a gold medal in Montreal in the summer of 1976. Then he helped march UNC to the national championship game in '77.

Ford's play out of the Four Corners was particularly instru-

ACC BASKETBALL / THE '70s

Four fingers from No. 12 generally meant another win for UNC from 1975-78; "I admit, it was unfair with Ford," Coach Dean Smith says.

mental in UNC's drive to the '77 Final Four. He hyper-extended his elbow in the Tar Heels' East Regional semifinal victory over Notre Dame, then played only sparingly in the final against Kentucky. Still unable to extend his arm fully, Ford continued to feed freshman Mike O'Koren (31 points) from the Four Corners as UNC beat Nevada-Las Vegas in the national semifinals.

Ford's injury probably caught up with him, and UNC, in the championship game against Marquette. Unable to shoot properly, Ford was limited to six points on 3-of-10 shooting as the Tar Heels lost a 67-59 decision to Al McGuire's Warriors.

Approaching his senior season, Ford said he aimed to play the perfect game. He came close in his home finale at Carmichael Auditorium in 1978. With first place in the regular season on the line, UNC defeated Duke 87-83 as Ford scored a career-high 34 points. He also had two steals, five assists and only three turnovers in 40 minutes. Remarkably, Ford played the game with a bruised knee and a sprained left wrist.

"He was just taking it down and spinning it off his feet or under his legs or hooking it," said Duke Coach Bill Foster. "We didn't have any defense for that."

In Ford's four seasons, few found a defense for him. He finished as the school's all-time leading scorer with 2,290 points. He was also the career leader in assists with 559 until Kenny Smith passed him in 1987.

Perhaps no player in UNC or ACC history surpassed Ford in enthusiasm. Certainly, no player struck fear in the hearts of opposing coaches as much as Ford when he held those four outstretched fingers above his head. ∎

ACC BASKETBALL / THE '70s

'76

The NCAA decided during the winter of 1975 that teams could dress a maximum of 13 players for home games and only 10 on the road. The idea was for teams to save money, said the NCAA.

Before the Big Four Tournament of the 1975-76 season, the participating teams were all claiming the Greensboro Coliseum as a home court. Finally, the NCAA rescinded the rule and allowed teams to dress all of their scholarship players for home and road games. The decision was made prior to the Big Four Tournament.

When Wake Forest took its second straight Big Four championship and ran its season-opening win streak to 10 games with victories over fifth-ranked UNC and 13th-ranked N.C. State, the unranked Demon Deacons made a statement that the ACC was deeper than ever in talent. Wake immediately jumped to seventh in the rankings, Maryland was second, UNC sixth and State 11th.

Wake Forest followed the Big Four with a victory over Maryland, giving the Deacons three wins over unbeaten and ranked teams in one week and stopping the Terps' 11-game win streak to start the season. But Wake Forest quickly faded and left the regular-season race to favorites UNC, Maryland and State.

UNC showed its strength outside the league when the Tar Heels blasted seventh-ranked Kentucky 90-77 early in the season at Charlotte. Later, they clinched a sixth straight 20-win season with a 113-106, four-overtime victory over Tulane in a game that lasted more than three hours in the Louisiana Superdome. "It was an epic, a classic," said UNC Coach Dean Smith.

Within the league, two games proved most pivotal. The third Super Bowl Sunday game for national television pitted State against UNC in Chapel Hill. The Wolfpack rallied from a five-point halftime deficit to defeat the Tar Heels 68-67 when Al Green, a transfer from Western Arizona Junior College, sank a free throw with no time remaining on the clock.

The league's other pivotal game was also played in Chapel Hill as the Tar Heels narrowly escaped with a 95-93 overtime victory over Maryland. The game featured 54 personal fouls, but it was one no-call by the officials with 20 seconds

Big Four Feast

Despite never winning the ACC Tournament during the '70s, Wake Forest was a beast in the Big Four Tournament, which ran in December for 11 years from 1970 to 1980 at the Greensboro Coliseum. The Deacons won it four times, more than anyone, and freshman Frank Johnson (L) and senior Skip Brown were all smiles after a 97-96 win in overtime over Carolina in the 1976 tournament.

Tree planted seeds of Tigers' hoops growth.

Wayne "Tree" Rollins was perhaps the most significant basketball signee in the history of the Clemson program.

As a high school All-America in Cordele, Ga., Rollins was recruited by more than 200 schools. He visited 11 before selecting the Tigers, instantly making them a threat to win the ACC championship for the first time.

Four years later, Rollins had taken Clemson out of the ACC's basement and into its upper echelon. Although the Tigers failed to win a league crown, Rollins left Clemson as the best center in the school's history and one of the best ever in the ACC.

The '70s

Clemson

In 110 games from 1974 through 1977, Rollins averaged 13.3 points and 11.9 rebounds. Through the 1988 season, an ACC player blocked 100 or more shots in a season only eight times. Amazingly, Rollins did it all four seasons at Clemson. Twice he led the ACC in rebounding and three times he was second-team All-ACC.

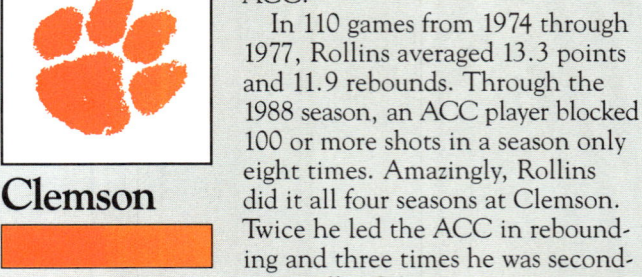

Before Rollins departed Clemson for a lengthy career in the NBA, his jersey No. 30 was the first retired by the school. His 1,311 career rebounds and 450 blocked shots remain school records.

"More than basketball, the biggest thing about him was that he was such an unselfish guy and had such a great attitude," says Bill Foster, who succeeded Tates Locke as Clemson's coach for Rollins' final two seasons. "He's a super person, just a fine guy."

Those qualities were quickly apparent to the coaches who flocked to see Rollins play basketball at Crisp County High School in Cordele.

"It's like something out of *Aesop's Fables* . . . a 7-footer with heart and ambition and shooting touch, with a mother who is trying to be honest," Locke said during the recruiting process.

Rollins' mother, Wilma Robinson, a staunch Baptist who was an instructor at the Cordele Retardation Center, kept a close watch on the recruiting that stretched as far as Hawaii and UCLA. Those were among the trips made by Rollins in the days when unlimited visits were allowed by the NCAA.

"That was an exciting time," says Rollins, who once was crafty enough to schedule visits to Florida State and Clemson on the same weekend. "Each weekend I could go somewhere different. For a high school guy to travel that way was a tremendous educational experience."

In the end, Rollins chose Clemson because of his

ACC BASKETBALL / THE '70s

liking for Locke and because Clemson was a short drive from Cordele. He admits to being recruited illegally by many schools, including Clemson. But he insists that Locke never violated an NCAA rule with him.

"We had some pretty aggressive alumni and it wasn't Tates' fault that they were so aggressive," Rollins says. "Still, the people at Clemson were great to me. It was a nice, small town and just a great experience for me."

The best of times for Rollins and Clemson came before the NCAA handed down a three-year probation the summer before the 1976 season. Rollins, who averaged 25 points, 18 rebounds and eight blocked shots during his senior year of high school, was an immediate force in the ACC.

In his second game, Rollins scored 22 points to go with 20 rebounds and nine blocked shots against St. John's. From the outset, Rollins was an intimidator. He picked up the nickname "Tree" as a 6-8 junior high student and continued to stand out like a tree both on and off the court at Clemson.

"If someone shouted, 'Hey, Wayne,' on campus, I probably wouldn't even turn around," Rollins said.

The only area in which Rollins did not stand out was on offense. He scored 20 or more points in a game 19 times at Clemson, and three times ranked among the ACC's top 10 field goal shooters. But Rollins barely averaged 10 field goal attempts a game for his career.

His forte was rebounding and blocking shots, and nobody did that better than the kid with a 42-inch sleeve. He registered the only statistical triple-doubles (double figures in three categories) in Clemson history with 20 points, 14 rebounds and 10 blocked shots against Presbyterian as a junior, and 16, 15 and 10 against Duke as a senior.

Rollins' play was instrumental in taking Clemson basketball to new heights. The Tigers had their first winning season (14-12) since 1967 when Rollins was a freshman. Then they were 17-11, 18-10 and 22-6 from 1975 through 1977, marking the first time in more than 50 years that Clemson had four consecutive winning seasons.

Within the ACC, Rollins' presence made Clemson a title contender. The Tigers finished tied for second in 1975 and 1977 and came within inches of reaching the title game of the '75 ACC Tournament. A follow shot by Rollins missed at the end of regulation, and Clemson dropped a 76-71 overtime decision to UNC in the semifinals.

"It rolled around the rim and out," Rollins says. "It actually went in, but wouldn't stay down."

Shortly after that loss, Clemson accepted its first postseason tournament bid but lost to Providence in the first round of the NIT.

"We just weren't able to win the big one when I was there," says Rollins, whose easygoing nature and broad smile have won the admiration of his NBA teammates in over 10 years with Atlanta. "Even when we went to the NIT, we went up to New York with the attitude that it was second best."

Not long after the NIT trip, Locke and Clemson learned of the NCAA probation. Later that summer, Locke was replaced by Foster.

"When I got there I didn't know what to expect because there had been so many rumblings about all the problems with probation," Foster says. "But basically what I found in Tree was a very unselfish kid who didn't have a big ego."

Foster talks at length of Rollins' rebounding and shot-blocking abilities. But his most vivid memory of Rollins is that of a senior in 1977 who was the first to help the freshmen carry the team luggage on road trips.

"He was very coachable," Foster says. "His attitude was just unbelievably good." ∎

Rollins' 1,311 rebounds and 450 blocked shots remain Clemson records.

ACC BASKETBALL / THE '70s

William Carey & William Edwin

There have been only 40 men named to head coaching positions in the ACC's 35-year history. What must the odds be, then, of two of them with the same name coaching in the same league at the same time? No matter how far-fetched, Bill Foster was the head man at Clemson from 1976-84 and Duke from 1975-80. That's William Carey of the Tigers on the left and William Edwin of the Blue Devils on the right. The latter moved to South Carolina for the '81 season, furthering the long odds by giving that state two BFs. Sports fans kept them straight by calling the Gamecocks' coach "Chicken Foster" and the Tigers' coach "Clem Foster."

---

remaining that caused most of the fury. As Maryland's John Lucas advanced the ball past midcourt for an attempt at a tying basket, he appeared to be tripped by UNC's Phil Ford. Lucas lost control of the ball, and time expired before Maryland could attempt a shot.

Maryland coaches Lefty Driesell and Joe Harrington, as well as several Maryland players, argued vehemently with officials Jim Howell and John Moreau. Driesell pumped a fist at the taunting UNC student body and Harrington almost came to blows with two fans. Harrington then passed Moreau in the corridor beneath the stands and shouted, "No damn guts" to the official.

The following day, Howell resigned after seven years as an official in the ACC. He had been an official for 13 years and was the first black to call the NCAA final, in 1973 and 1974.

"I'm not talking about the coaches and players," Howell told *The Washington Post*. "I'm responsible for how much they can get away with during a game. I can control some of that. I have no ill feelings toward any of them. It's the spectators, the things they say during and after a game. You bite your tongue . . . Nothing in the ACC is easy."

Despite the loss, Maryland was thought to have the best chance among the non-Big Four schools to win the ACC Tournament. Not only did the Terps finish tied for second in the regular season, they also had somewhat of a home-court advantage with the Tournament being played at the Capital Centre in Landover, Md.

By moving the Tournament outside the Tar Heel State for the first time, ACC officials believed Maryland, Virginia and Clemson might have better chances to win. In the first 22 years of the Tournament, only Maryland in 1958 and South Carolina in 1971 had broken the Big Four schools' stronghold on the league title.

The second-seeded Terps barely survived a scare in the first round with an 80-78 overtime victory over Duke. The Blue Devils missed the front end of three 1-and-1s in the final 13 seconds of regulation.

In the semifinals, Maryland faced a Virginia team that had finished 15-11 overall and sixth in the ACC race with a 4-8 record. One of those late-season losses was a 73-71 decision to third-ranked UNC in Chapel Hill when Mitch Kupchak made a follow shot at the buzzer.

Following the game, second-year Virginia Coach Terry Holland told his team he believed it was the best in the conference and should win the Tournament. The Cavaliers' 75-63 victory over third-seeded and 17th-ranked N.C. State in the opening round opened some eyes. A 73-65 triumph over ninth-ranked Maryland in the semifinals had the Cavaliers believing what Holland said.

"Coming into the Tournament, I felt our team was playing well enough that if we played anybody for 120 minutes we would probably come out on top," Holland said. "In other words, we were playing percentage basketball at that time and I felt like the percentages were in our favor over the long haul."

Virginia, the underdog in the first two rounds, was given even less of a chance to defeat fourth-ranked UNC in the championship. The Tar Heels entered with a 25-2 record and a 13-game win streak. Undaunted, the Cavaliers controlled the game's tempo, refused to wilt against UNC's defensive and offensive pressure and beat the Tar Heels at their own slowdown tactics in the final four minutes. Virginia got 21 points from Tournament MVP Wally Walker in a 67-62 victory.

"We all had made plans to go to Florida next week for spring vacation," Walker said. "But we'll gladly change that."

Virginia apparently exhausted itself while defeating three nationally ranked teams in three days, because the Cavaliers were flat in the first round of the NCAA Tournament and were eliminated by DePaul 69-60 in Charlotte.

UNC was also eliminated by Alabama 79-64 in the first round of the Mideast Regional. The Tar Heels got only 28 minutes and two points out of Ford because of a knee injury. Ford, visiting his family earlier in the week, had twisted his knee during a pickup game at his old Rocky Mount High School gym.

That left only N.C. State to represent the ACC in postseason play. The Wolfpack rolled past Holy Cross in its first NIT game, but fell 80-79 to a UNC-Charlotte team led by Cedric Maxwell in the semifinals in New York.

Perhaps giving an indication of the kind of pressure ACC teams were now facing in the postseason, UNC-Charlotte Coach Lee Rose said: "This is the first time we've beaten an ACC team. I think this should really put us on the map."

ACC BASKETBALL / THE '70s

'77

When both ACC representatives in the 1976 NCAA Tournament failed to escape their first games, talk throughout college basketball centered around whether the league was indeed the best in the country. The ACC had a remarkable 82-13 record (an .863 winning percentage that set a league record) against outside competition in '76. Yet the league failed miserably in postseason play.

"If I'm a Pac-8 or Big Ten fan and you tell me the ACC's the best basketball conference in the country, I'm gonna laugh at you until you prove it," said Maryland Coach Lefty Driesell. "I don't know if the ACC is as strong as the reputation it has around here because our teams have done so poorly in the playoffs.

"I don't think we can say we're so great when Frank McGuire (UNC in 1957) and Norm Sloan (N.C. State in 1974) are the only ones to win the national championship from our league. And we get so few teams to the Final Four in the national playoffs to have so many ranked in the top 10."

Actually, Driesell had not done his homework. In its first 23 seasons, the ACC had sent 10 teams representing four schools to the Final Four. *Basketball Weekly*, a national tabloid, rated the ACC as the nation's top league in 10 of the previous 11 seasons.

Sloan said only UCLA of the Pac-8 Conference kept the ACC from being the most dominant league in the country. The Bruins had won the NCAA championship 10 of the previous 13 seasons with title game victories over Duke in '64 and UNC in '68.

All agreed that another trip by an ACC team to the Final Four in 1977 was necessary to uphold the league's image as the nation's best. North Carolina came to the rescue when the Tar Heels advanced to the championship game before losing to Marquette. It also helped the league's image when Wake Forest reached the Midwest Regional championship, where it was also eliminated by Marquette.

The league was once again strong from top to bottom. Only Virginia (12-17) had a losing record. ACC teams lost only 16 games to outside competition in 1977, three of them to eventual national champion Marquette and two others to NCAA Tournament teams, Notre Dame and Hofstra.

One indication that the league had established stability was the absence of coaching changes for the 1977 season. There had been a head coaching change in the ACC every year since 1972, but another change would not be made until the 1981 season when Jim Valvano replaced Norm Sloan at N.C. State and Mike Krzyzewski took over for Bill Foster at Duke.

Foster's Blue Devils made significant strides in 1977. They posted their first winning season (14-13) since 1972, ended a 27-game road losing streak against ACC teams and stunned 15th-ranked Tennessee early in the season. But Duke's chance to challenge for the league title was lost when guard Tate Armstrong broke his wrist in mid-January.

Armstrong was one of seven ACC players who represented the United States in a gold medal performance in the 1976 Olympics. Kenny Carr of N.C. State, Steve Sheppard of Maryland, and Walter Davis, Phil Ford, Mitch Kupchak and Tom LaGarde of UNC were all members of the 12-man team, which was coached by the Tar Heels' Dean Smith.

The United States avenged the 1972 loss to the Soviet Union in the 1976 championship by downing Yugoslavia by 21 points for the Olympic gold medal at Montreal. Smith also selected a team without top-notch players Robert Parrish, Leon Douglas and John Lucas, all of whom signed professional contracts. Smith came under much criticism before and during the Olympics for his selection of seven ACC players, including four Tar Heels.

Wally Walker of Virginia was unhappy that he was left off the '76 Olympic squad, and Cavalier fans cried foul. The criticism even carried over to the 1977 season. When guard Jerry Schellenberg led Wake Forest to the Big Four Tournament championship over UNC and was named MVP, he made it known to Smith that he did not appreciate being passed over during the Olympic team selections.

One week earlier, Smith had been ejected from an ACC game for the second time in his coaching career. Referee Jack Manton of Cumming, Ga., a first-time referee in the ACC, called two of three technical fouls against Smith in the first half against Clemson. A crowd of 15,200 at the Greensboro Coliseum was stunned by Smith's automatic ejection, then watched the Tar Heels roll to a 91-63 victory over the 16th-ranked Tigers. (Manton surfaced years later as the agent for NFL running back Herschel Walker.)

Not only did the dunk return to college basketball in 1977, so did on-court fighting. N.C. State's Carr was ejected from a game against Virginia and carried a few stitches in his lip after exchanging blows with Cavalier Ed Schetlick. A melee erupted during Maryland's early season game against Richmond in College Park. The Terps' front line of Mike Davis, Larry Gibson and Lawrence Boston was ejected from the game along with Mike Dow of Richmond.

Action wasn't limited to the ACC court. Clemson agreed to a 10-year contract to play two games a year against South Carolina beginning with the 1977-78 season. No other ACC team had played a regular-season game against South Carolina since the Gamecocks withdrew from the league in 1971. Clemson and South Carolina had not met since the 1971-72 campaign.

At Maryland, Driesell was the Terps' first casualty of the season. In late November, while playing a pickup game against his teenage son, Chuck, Driesell tore the Achilles tendon in his right foot. He wore a cast on the foot through most of the season.

So hot was the action during the regular season, Wake Forest began to take note of the temperature during games played at UNC's Carmichael Auditorium. One of the old wives' tales in the ACC was that Smith turned up the thermostat in Carmichael before home games. The heat, opponents reasoned, helped UNC because the Tar Heels usually had depth and employed a fast-paced style of play.

"The heat there is a real factor," said Wake Forest Coach Carl Tacy.

"It's probably the hottest place to play in the conference," said Wake Forest forward Rod Griffin. "In fact, it's probably the hottest place I've ever played in."

Smith found the charges against him humorous.

"I wish it were cooler," Smith said. "You know, I've never been able to wear a wool suit because of that."

Smith and the fourth-ranked Tar Heels were cool customers as they built a 15-point lead over 10th-ranked Wake Forest during a late January game in Carmichael. But the Demon Deacons rallied back to win 67-66 when Schellenberg, despite hoots from the UNC crowd because of his earlier statements to Smith, made two free throws with 14 seconds remaining.

The victory not only snapped a 12-game losing streak in the regular season against UNC but also made Wake Forest

ACC BASKETBALL / **THE '70s**

Key possession of '77 NCAA title game: O'Koren waits at scorer's table while Kuester holds ball in Four Corners...

the front-runner in the ACC race. At that point, the Deacons were 5-1 in the league and 15-2 overall. When Wake Forest won its next three games, the Deacons jumped to fourth in the polls.

Wake was brought down by losses to Clemson and Maryland, but the Demon Deacons still had a chance to place first in the regular season for the first time since 1962. Wake needed a victory at N.C. State for at least a share of first place. A win, coupled with a UNC loss at Duke, would have given Wake first place outright and the top seed in the ACC Tournament.

Neither happened. Wake Forest lost to N.C. State 91-85, and UNC claimed sole possession of first place with a 9-3 record following an 84-71 win over Duke.

The Tar Heels were once again one of the nation's most talented and deepest teams. Besides the starting lineup of Ford, Davis, LaGarde, John Kuester and freshman Mike O'Koren, UNC had depth in guard Tom Zaliagiris, swingmen in Dudley Bradley and John Virgil and frontcourt backups in frosh Rich Yonakor, Steve Krafcisin and Jeff Wolf.

As it turned out, UNC needed the depth.

In February, LaGarde injured his knee in practice and was

ACC BASKETBALL / THE '70s

...Moments later, Ellis blocks Buckley's layup attempt, the Warriors retake the lead and never look back.

lost to the Tar Heels at least through the ACC Tournament. At the time, LaGarde was third on the team in scoring with 15.1 points a game and tops in rebounding with 7.4 per game. In his place, Smith turned to a trio of freshmen known as "Yonwolfsin." Together, the trio averaged nine points and six rebounds a game and went unbeaten in their first 12 games in place of LaGarde.

One of those wins was a 70-56 decision over N.C. State in the semifinals of the ACC Tournament. That set up a rematch in the championship with Virginia, which was seeking another miracle story after being seeded seventh. The Cavaliers, 10-16, stunned Wake Forest 59-57 in the opening round on a 5-foot bank shot by Marc Iavaroni in the closing seconds. Then they bombed Clemson in the semifinals, 72-60.

UNC entered the championship game not certain Davis would play. The All-ACC forward broke the index finger on his shooting hand in the Tar Heels' semifinal victory over State. Davis, whose broken finger was heavily taped, did not start and went scoreless in eight minutes of second-half action against Virginia.

Virginia appeared primed to take advantage of UNC's injuries and led 64-56 with seven minutes remaining. The Tar Heels

Walter Davis (R) comforts Mike O'Koren while Marquette players collect NCAA title trophies.

cut Virginia's lead to three in the next minute, but Ford fouled out. Down the stretch, O'Koren also fouled out. But UNC's depth continued to wear on Virginia and the Tar Heels survived for a 75-69 victory.

"I don't like to compare teams but, no, I can't remember ever winning a game like this," said Smith. "It was a gutsy effort. I looked over on the bench toward the end and saw Ford, O'Koren, Davis and LaGarde sitting there."

The championship sent UNC to the NCAA East Regional. Wake Forest was the second NCAA Tournament choice from the ACC and went to the Midwest Regional. Maryland was initially offered a bid to play Old Dominion in the first round of the NIT, but the Terps preferred a meeting with Georgetown. The NIT then withdrew its bid and invited Villanova.

Wake Forest, entering the NCAA Tournament for the first time since 1962 in the throes of a four-game losing streak, rebounded to knock off Arkansas 86-60 and Southern Illinois 86-81. The Deacons ended an 18-game Arkansas win streak in the first round, then made 22 of 24 second-half free throws to match the school record for wins (22) with an 86-81 decision over Southern Illinois.

In the Midwest championship, Wake Forest led Marquette 43-40 with 16 minutes remaining. But the Demon Deacons went cold and the Warriors advanced to the Final Four with an 82-68 victory. Bernard Toone, who averaged only 3.8 points a game during the regular season, scored 18 points in 24 minutes to lead Marquette.

UNC, meanwhile, got past Purdue 69-66 in the opening round of the East Regional without Davis, who had undergone surgery on his broken finger. Then, with Davis back in the lineup, the Tar Heels turned back Notre Dame 79-77 in the next round. They rallied from 14 points down in the second half to defeat the Irish, who lost their lead while attempting to run the Four Corners offense in the game's final minutes.

The victory was costly to UNC, however, as Ford injured his elbow. Prior to the East Regional championship game, LaGarde appeared ready to return from his injury. But he reinjured his knee in practice and his college career was ended.

With Ford limited to 15 minutes and two points in the East Regional championship, the Tar Heels struggled to a 79-72 victory over Kentucky. Kuester directed UNC's offense in place of Ford, scored 19 points and matched his ACC Tournament MVP award with the East Regional trophy.

"Kuester was the one who beat us," said Kentucky's Rick Robey. "He kept their team together all day."

So the Tar Heels—with many of their fans taping two fingers together in honor of Davis' injury—limped into the national semifinals for the fifth time under Smith and the first time since 1972. It was the first of Smith's trips to the Final Four that UCLA was not in the field.

Instead, UNC faced the Runnin' Rebels of Nevada-Las Vegas. The Tar Heels' plan was to get a lead over UNLV in the second half and attempt to slow the Runnin' Rebs to a crawl. UNC trailed 49-43 following a run-and-shoot first half, came back to hold a 59-55 advantage with 15 minutes remaining and then called on Ford to run the Four Corners the rest of the way. It worked as UNC hung on for a 84-83 victory.

The leader for UNC was freshman O'Koren, who scored 31 points on 14-of-19 shooting and had eight rebounds against UNLV. O'Koren's next matchup was with an old schoolyard friend, Marquette's Jim Boylan. UNC's Davis had sought a championship meeting against his nephew, UNC-Charlotte's Lew Massey, but the 49ers' Cinderella story came to a close with Marquette's 51-49 semifinal victory.

The NCAA championship in Atlanta had all the makings of a classic. Marquette Coach Al McGuire had announced earlier in the season that he would be retiring. But it was UNC's O'Koren who stole the spotlight during a press conference on Sunday prior to Monday night's title game.

When asked if his 31-point effort against UNLV was a career high, O'Koren said, "So far." When asked how he was such an excellent rebounder, the 6-foot-7 native of Jersey City, N.J., said, "If you don't rebound in the schoolyard, they throw you through the fence."

UNC took a 15-game win streak into the title game but spotted Marquette a 39-27 halftime lead. The Tar Heels scored 14 of the first 16 points in the second half to tie the game at 41. UNC then went to its Four Corners spread and Marquette watched the Tar Heels hold the ball for three minutes, refusing to abandon its 2-3 zone defense.

"They had us playing their game. Then they went to the Four Corners," said Marquette's Boylan. "It slowed them down and allowed us to get our momentum back. It might have been over for us if they had not gone to it."

While UNC was holding the ball, O'Koren sat at the scorer's table, unable to enter the game. Before he could get into the game, the Tar Heels lost possession when Bruce Buckley's shot was blocked by Marquette's Bo Ellis. Marquette used a delay game of its own, eventually scored to take a lead it never lost, then hit 12 straight free throws down the stretch for a 67-59 victory.

"I took my jersey off and just looked at it," said Davis, a senior. "Every time I've put it on, I felt we could win. I'll think more of this season than any other I've had here. All the injuries we had and all the people that counted us out."

ACC BASKETBALL / THE '70s

'78

Duke was counted out of the ACC regular-season race in 1977 when senior guard Tate Armstrong went down with a broken wrist. The Blue Devils had an 11-3 record at the time, then won only three of their final 13 games to finish at 14-13.

Despite the collapse, there were signs in '77 that Coach Bill Foster was building a solid base for an outstanding program in his fourth season. Jim Spanarkel, a splendid 6-foot-5 guard, had been the ACC Rookie of the Year in 1976, and 6-11 center Mike Gminski, only 17 years old during his first season at Duke, was the league's top freshman in 1977. The incoming freshmen included Philadelphia's 6-7 forward Gene Banks, considered by many the top prep prospect in the country the previous year; and Kenny Dennard, a 6-7 forward from King, N.C., and one of the state's top prospects.

Banks displayed the exuberance of the young Blue Devils when he said prior to a Big Four Tournament meeting with No. 1-ranked North Carolina: "It's going to be just like going to heaven, something you always dream of doing. It will be like getting a pair of wings. It will be ecstasy."

Ecstasy for Duke players had long been performing in front of vocal crowds at Cameron Indoor Stadium. For the 1978 season, Duke had completed a major renovation of the building, which was then 37 years old. The original playing floor was ripped out and replaced by a shining maple wood surface. All new bleacher seats were placed in the lower arena and a fresh coat of paint was splashed throughout.

Something that had not changed at Cameron were the zany students who annually provided support for the Blue Devils. There long rested a common belief that Duke fans—or at least a loud contingent of them—were unique to the ACC, if not college basketball.

The arena lent itself to fan participation, and Duke students took advantage of their proximity to the court. No other school in the conference allowed its students to occupy the bottom 10 rows of seats on both sides and the bottom 15 to 20 rows in the end zones.

Sitting in those seats was one thing, using them to intimidate game officials and opposing teams was quite another.

Frank McGuire was quick to recognize the wrath of Duke students. Following one of his North Carolina team's losses at Duke in the late '50s, McGuire refused to leave the court without a police escort. While his team waited, McGuire was pelted with apple cores.

Later, one of McGuire's stars at South Carolina, John Roche, became perhaps the only player in ACC history to retaliate against the Duke students. He once threw an entire cooler of Gatorade into the student section.

But Duke students generally have had the last word. Through the years, they have been the most clever, brainy, resourceful and ingenious in the league. From the time the pep band strides into a stepped-up version of Mitch Ryder and the Detroit Wheels' 1966 hit *Devil With The Blue Dress On* until the game's final seconds tick off, insanity replaces serenity among some Dukies.

Duke students have been particularly harsh on N.C. State and Maryland.

They once pelted the court with aspirin when the Wolfpack's Moe Rivers, charged with stealing aspirin at a Raleigh drugstore, was introduced. They showered the court with underwear when State players Tony Warren and Tiny Pinder, charged with altering price tags on underwear at a Raleigh discount store, were introduced. A sign in the student section read, "Warren, Pinder: You Can't Switch The Numbers On The Scoreboard." For Tom Burleson, once arrested for breaking into a pinball machine, the pep band struck up a rendition of *Pinball Wizard*.

Duke fans have also paid special attention to every move made by Norm Sloan, the State coach from 1966-80. Claiming he wanted to minimize the crowd's influence because Duke students usually arrived "drunk," Sloan once played a slowdown game at Cameron. Whenever Sloan visited Cameron, students chanted, "Have A Drink Norman Sloan, Have A Drink (clap, clap)!"

Once, a male Duke student dressed as a tall, broad-shouldered lady in a pink sweater carried a baton and microphone to halfcourt prior to the Blue Devils' game against State with "MRS. NORM SLOAN" inscribed on his back. To Sloan's wife, who sang the national anthem at State home games during her husband's stint as coach, it was no joke. From then on, Cameron was the only gymnasium in the ACC where she would not attend a game.

Maryland Coach Lefty Driesell, a reserve player on the Duke teams of 1953-54, and former President Richard M. Nixon, a 1937 graduate of the Duke Law School, were once depicted on a placard as being "Duke's Two Mistakes."

Duke students often wore bald-head caps to mock Driesell's hairless head and sometimes sought the Maryland coach's autograph on them. When Driesell had to hobble the sidelines in a cast during the 1977 season after he tore the Achilles tendon in his right foot, six Duke students showed up behind the Maryland bench in coats, ties and plastic casts on one foot.

When Jim "Bozo" O'Brien played at Maryland, a Duke student dressed in a "Bozo The Clown" costume jumped out of the stands and joined the Terps' shooting line during warmup drills. When *The Washington Star* reported during the 1978 season that several Maryland players would have to raise their grades to remain eligible to play basketball the following season, Duke students came prepared. They sat behind the Maryland bench in dunce caps.

Officials have often been the target of Duke students. One student used to carry a rubber chicken dressed in stripes on a stick and wave it furiously at the officials. Students once borrowed judging cards from the Duke swim coach and rated each call.

Once, a TV camera panned the Duke crowd and zoomed in on a student holding a sign that read, innocently, "Pilot Life," referring to the longtime sponsor of ACC basketball. The student quickly flipped the placard to reveal a profane verb about the company. The sponsor was upset and so was producer C.D. Chesley, who became more careful about crowd shots.

During a nationally televised game in 1979 between Duke and Marquette from Cameron, the NBC crew was prepared to switch the game off the air on a moment's notice if the crowd "got out of hand." The crowd remained in control, although NBC officials called it the most raucous they had encountered.

It was obvious early in the '78 season that Duke fans would have a lot to cheer about during the 1978 season. UNC Coach Dean Smith said, "I expect Duke to make a run for the ACC championship and national championship."

The Blue Devils got a boost after Christmas when Bob Bender, a transfer from Indiana who had played on the Hoosiers' national championship team of 1976, became eligible and

ACC BASKETBALL / THE '70s

Duke allows its students to occupy the bleacher seats on all sides of the court, creating a cauldron of frenzy unmatched anywhere in the league.

joined Spanarkel and John Harrell in the backcourt.

Bender became eligible for the Blue Devils on Jan. 9. Five days later, he came off the bench to score 11 points as Duke defeated second-ranked UNC 92-84. For the first time in almost a decade, Duke was atop the ACC standings and its students celebrated by clipping the nets at Cameron Indoor Stadium.

Bender was the last piece in Duke's puzzle, one that captured the fancy of ACC fans because of the Blue Devils' youth. Banks, Dennard and reserve Jim Suddath were freshmen. Gminski, Bender and Harrell were sophomores. Spanarkel and reserves Scott Goetsch and Harold Morrison were juniors. The lone senior was seldom-used reserve Bruce Bell.

The youthful Blue Devils were a happy-go-lucky lot. They were also a superstitious group. Bender traditionally took the last warmup shot. Banks, known to Duke fans as "Tinkerbell," carried a stuffed dog with him to every game and put it in his locker.

Banks also wore the same pair of socks the entire season. Dennard brushed his teeth just before he took the court for each game. "I hate to burp and taste food when I'm playing," said Dennard.

The Blue Devils were led in their rituals by Foster, who wore the same brown suit through a five-game winning streak in February. When Duke rampaged through the ACC Tournament and all the way to the NCAA Championship game, Foster stuck with the same navy blue jacket, blue vest and plaid pants with a light blue shirt and solid blue tie.

"These guys are looser and more confident than any team in the past," said veteran Duke trainer Max Crowder, who was with the Blue Devils during their 1960s glory years.

Duke rolled into the end-of-the-season showdown with North Carolina for first place. Each team entered the game in Chapel Hill with an 8-3 record. At stake was not only the first-round bye in the ACC Tournament but a possible NCAA Tournament berth. The team that finished first during the regular season, should it not win the ACC Tournament, could be expected to receive the league's second NCAA Tournament berth.

It was also the final home game for UNC guard Phil Ford. Earlier in the season, in a game against Clemson, Ford had broken Lennie Rosenbluth's career scoring record of 2,045 points. He was to build even further on that record with a spectacular closing performance at Carmichael.

"He was not only inspired, he was just taking it down and spinning it off his feet or under his legs or hooking it," Foster said. "We didn't have any defense for that."

Ford finished with a career-high 34 points in UNC's 87-83 victory. He played the entire game, made 13 of 19 field goals and had five assists. His performance offset the trio of Banks, Spanarkel and Gminski, who scored 25, 23 and 21 points, respectively.

Ford's finale and the first-place finish climaxed an unusual season for the Tar Heels. On the heels of their fine showing in the previous NCAA Tournament, UNC was expected to again challenge for the national title in '78.

Championships in the Big Four Tournament and Rainbow

ACC BASKETBALL / THE '70s

Danger zone: Duke's trademark in '78 was a 2-1-2 zone defense anchored in the middle by Gminski (43).

Classic were certainly convincing evidence early. But the Tar Heels also suffered stunning losses, including a 78-75 upset at William & Mary. The Indians made 14 of 16 second-half shots and dedicated the game to teammate John Kratzer, a senior guard who was being treated for stomach cancer. Another upset came in the North-South Double-headers in Charlotte where Furman scored 18 straight points in the second half en route to an 89-83 victory.

Ten days following the loss at William & Mary, UNC defeated Cincinnati in Greensboro. To help boost the television audience in Cincinnati, Bearcats' Coach Gale Catlett agreed to be wired for sound during the game. When Catlett engaged in a discussion with an official, they were joined by UNC's Smith. Catlett yelled an obscenity at Smith that was aired in Cincinnati.

The incident received national attention. Virginia Coach Terry Holland was quoted by the *Richmond-Times Dispatch* as saying there is "a gap between the man (Smith) and the image the man tries to project." Holland referred to an incident in the 1977 ACC Tournament in which UNC defeated Virginia for the championship. Holland said that Smith, en route to the dressing room at halftime, allegedly grabbed Cavalier forward Marc Iavaroni and accused him of being "a dirty player."

Smith's response was to say that Holland "doesn't know me from Adam."

The season marked the first time in ACC history that every team finished the season above .500. That depth made for an interesting ACC Tournament, which had a couple of new wrinkles. For the first time, outside officials were hired to call the Tournament. Commissioner Bob James said the move was made to respond to concerns of coaches who believed the style of officiating in conference games hurt ACC teams in NCAA play. At the time, the ACC was considered a touch-foul, or finesse, league.

Jim Hernjak, an ACC official for 11 years, called the decision a "real slap in the face."

A national TV audience watched the ACC Tournament championship game for the first time. ABC, as part of its *Wide World of Sports* program, arranged national coverage of the championship on Saturday afternoon from Greensboro. Concerned that a Saturday afternoon final after Friday night semifinals would result in a sloppy and fatigued championship, the first two rounds were played on Wednesday and Thursday with no games on Friday.

"It'll be a snowy day in Greensboro before Duke plays in the ACC championship," said Duke's Bill Foster, realizing fully that snow was predicted for Greensboro that weekend.

It did snow in Greensboro, and Duke did reach the championship. The Blue Devils defeated Clemson 83-72 in the first round and Maryland 81-69 in the semifinals.

Duke's big three of Gminski, Banks and Spanarkel proved to be too much in the championship for Wake Forest, which ousted Virginia 72-61 and UNC 82-77 in the opening rounds. Gminski had 25 points and 16 rebounds. Banks had 22 and 10, and Spanarkel finished with 20 points as Duke won its first ACC championship since 1966, 85-77.

"I really felt I had let the university down for three years by leaving this tournament after one day," Foster said. "Now

Devildom ruled by Sir Tinkerbell Banks.

Bill Foster was so eager to have Gene Banks at Duke, he was willing to tamper with the U.S. Postal Service. Foster needed Banks' signature on a national letter-of-intent in April of 1977, but the coach had used up the three visits with Banks allowed under NCAA rules. Still, Foster did not want to risk having Uncle Sam lose Banks' valuable autograph in the mail.

"I signed the letter, put it in the mailbox and went on to school," Banks says. "Then he came by the house and took it out of the mailbox."

The '70s
Duke

Foster checked Banks' signature, tucked the letter into his jacket pocket and quickly headed to the Philadelphia airport for a happy return trip to Durham. After hearing two months of rumors that Banks had changed his mind and might go elsewhere, Foster finally knew Duke had landed one of the nation's best high school players as well as one of its most charismatic.

For the next four years, Duke and its fans, the city of Durham and an entire basketball league shared Foster's joy. "Tinkerbell," as Banks became known throughout the ACC, won the hearts of fans with a presence as formidable in street clothes as in a basketball uniform.

Banks was instrumental in Duke's winning two ACC Tournament championships, finishing second in the NCAA Tournament and compiling a 90-37 record from 1978 through 1981. He relished his status as Duke's first black superstar and added an enthusiasm for the game that ran through the Blue Devils and into the student body like it had in the school's glory days of the late '60s.

"If things go well and I have God's grace," Banks said not long after arriving at Duke in August of 1977, "I think I can finish up as the most versatile, complete, exciting, flamboyant, hustling player that ever played for Duke."

Few argued that Banks was all of that. He was versatile enough to shoot from 15 feet as well as mix it up beneath the basket, thanks to a perfectly sculptured, 6-foot-7, 205-pound body. That versatility fit well on a front line in 1978 that included the power of forward Kenny Dennard and center Mike Gminski.

Gminski, a sophomore, and the freshman tandem of Dennard and Banks took Duke on a youthful joyride in '78 that culminated with an ACC championship and NCAA title game matchup against Kentucky.

Prior to a 22-point, eight-rebound performance in Duke's 94-88 loss to Kentucky, Banks' life was threatened through a message delivered to the Duke coaching staff.

When informed of the threat following the game, Banks shrugged and said, "When I was 13, a guy chased me with a gun."

Banks was the second of eight children who were shuffled to 10 different homes by the time he was a senior at West Philadelphia High School. He found stability through basketball and became the most heralded Philadelphia prep player since Wilt Chamberlain in the mid-'50s.

"I will take Gene Banks over any high school player I've ever seen, except Wilt Chamberlain." said longtime West Philly Coach Joe Goldenberg, "and that would be a toss-up."

Banks averaged nearly 20 points and 20 rebounds a game in leading the West Philly Speedboys to an unprecedented three straight city titles and a 79-2 record. When he scored 31 points and had 23 rebounds in the city championship game as a senior, Banks was named the tournament's MVP for a third time.

Duke then won Banks' services following an intense recruiting battle. UCLA had Chamberlain and Los Angeles Mayor Tom Bradley telephone Banks on its behalf. NBA player George McGinnis urged Banks to attend Villanova. Among Philadelphia's Big Five schools, Pennsylvania had the inside track. But an Ivy League rule that prevented freshmen from playing on the varsity had Banks leaning toward Duke.

On the surface, Duke was the most unlikely of choices for Banks. The Blue Devils were a forgotten power of the '60s and had finished last in the ACC the previous four seasons. The school was academically difficult, socially conservative and overwhelmingly white.

But Banks liked those kind of challenges.

"I really felt that once the smoke cleared, I could make them a national power," Banks said.

Foster had an early connection with Banks, whose high school coach, Goldenberg, had played for Harry Litwack at Temple. Foster and Litwack owned a summer camp together in the Pocono Mountains.

During his official recruiting visit to Duke, Banks sneaked away from his Hilton Hotel room and investigated the campus and the city of Durham on his own. He found a diverse community, one he would eventually touch through frequent visits to the predominantly black campus of North Carolina Central University as well as trips to a downtown hamburger stand.

"I spent time in the black community and the white community," Banks says. "I just loved meeting people. It didn't matter who you were: White, black, or whatever. To me, Durham was my home for awhile. I engulfed Durham as well as it engulfed me. I wasn't a guy who came down there and couldn't talk. I knew what I was saying and what I wanted to say."

Banks says his immense exposure by the Philadelphia media in high school prepared him for Duke and the ACC. While a photograph of Muhammad Ali hung in his dorm room, Banks' gift for gab became as legendary around the league as Ali's did in boxing circles. From the outset, Banks was a dream for the media. When he was through talking with the press, Banks would often head for Mannella's restaurant in Durham, grab a microphone from the band and sing to the crowd.

"I was always doing something, being seen," Banks says. "Duke needed that breath of fresh air, that new thing that was happening. We were in magazines and on television . . .

Banks' presence was imposing on the basketball floor and in the Durham community. "I engulfed Durham as well as it engulfed me," he said.

I was the one to do a lot of that. I knew what was going on. Coach Foster saw that in me and never put tight reins on me."

Foster knew how to control Banks. When the two talked, the practical joking coach sometimes sprayed his office with a can of aerosol labeled "Bull."

By the end of his freshman season, Banks had already played himself onto the cover of *Sports Illustrated*. But his charm wore off somewhat during his sophomore year. The Blue Devils lost their No. 1-ranking early in the 1979 season, eventually lost the ACC championship game to North Carolina and fell in the first round of the NCAA Tournament. Banks didn't endear himself to Duke fans when he said, "Some people are going to get hurt falling off the bandwagon."

His junior season was marred by the death of his younger sister Venesse, charges of selling marijuana to an undercover policeman, rumors that Foster was leaving Duke for South Carolina and reports that Banks would forego his senior season to play professional basketball.

The drug-selling charges were eventually dropped, and Banks decided to stay four years at Duke after first announcing intentions to leave early. His friendship with Foster continued to grow. When Banks returned to Philadelphia for Vennesse's funeral, Foster stayed by his star player's side.

Foster insisted that Banks remain in Philadelphia following the funeral and miss Duke's game against N.C. State. But Banks left immediately after the funeral service and was met at the Raleigh-Durham Airport by Duke Assistant Coach Steve Steinwedel. Banks changed into his Duke uniform on the way to State's Reynolds Coliseum, listened to the national anthem on the car radio and made the game by tipoff.

Duke lost that late-season game to State, but rebounded to capture the ACC Tournament title. The Blue Devils also won an NCAA Regional game at Kentucky before losing in the Mideast championship to Purdue in the Duke coaching finale for Foster.

Duke struggled under Coach Mike Krzyzewski during Banks' senior season. But the Blue Devils did make the NIT, and when Banks was forced to miss a second-round game against Alabama with a broken hand, he sat on the Duke bench wearing a tuxedo.

Banks left Duke as its second-leading scorer. He was known for his consistent play, averaging 16.7 points and 7.9 rebounds a game over his career. Banks was the ACC's top freshman in 1978 and was a first-team All-ACC selection in 1981 when he became the first Duke player since Bob Verga in 1967 to lead the conference in scoring.

Despite his success, Banks generally played in the shadow of teammate Gminski, who was an All-ACC selection three times, ACC Player of the Year in 1979 and had his jersey No. 43 retired by Duke.

Gminski could not match Banks when it came to flair, though, and that was never more evident than in Banks' home finale. Just as he had done at his last game for West Philadelphia High School, Banks tossed red roses to the Cameron Indoor Stadium crowd prior to meeting North Carolina. Then he sank an 18-foot turnaround jump shot at the buzzer to force overtime. His follow shot with 12 seconds left in overtime clinched Duke's 66-65 victory.

Afterward, Duke students lifted Banks on their shoulders and paraded him around Cameron. Banks then grabbed a microphone and signaled for his mother to come out of the stands.

"That was the closest I have ever been to being in heaven," Banks says. "When they saw me pointing to my mother, no cop was needed, the fans just parted right out of the way and she walked right down like the parting of the Red Sea."

Banks did not leave Duke without first earning a degree in history, then giving the commencement address to the class of 1981. It was a significant accomplishment for Banks, who did not score 700 on his Scholastic Aptitude Test in high school.

"It's not what the instrument looks like," Banks said in the five-minute speech entitled "I Believe in Music."

"It's the note that it plays, and how well it blends in, and helps create a melody."

this is the greatest thing that's ever happened to me in basketball because I didn't know we'd ever get here."

The route to greatness for Duke was certainly unusual. Only Banks among the regular players was highly recruited. Wake Forest thought it had Dennard wrapped up before he signed with Duke. The Blue Devils pulled a coup when they got Gminski out of Monroe, Conn. He was academically prepared, and eligible, to pass up his senior year of high school to attend Duke at age 17. Spanarkel, from Jersey City, N.J., was not recruited seriously by any other ACC school.

Yet those players formed a team strong enough to win the ACC Tournament over a field with four other postseason tournament participants. UNC got the league's other NCAA Tournament bid but bowed out in the first round of the West Regional to San Francisco, 68-64.

That left N.C. State and Duke. The Wolfpack, taking advantage of the NIT's new regional format, defeated South Carolina 82-70 and Detroit 84-77 in games played at Reynolds Coliseum. In the semifinals at Madison Square Garden in New York, Clyde "The Glide" Austin sank a halfcourt shot at the buzzer to give State an 86-85 overtime victory over Georgetown and send the Wolfpack into the championship game. State spotted Texas a 15-point halftime lead and fell 101-93 in the final.

Duke, meanwhile, struggled past Rhode Island 63-62 in the first round of the NCAA Tournament East Regional in Charlotte and edged Pennsylvania 84-80 in the second round in Providence, R.I. After the first two struggles, Duke exploded past Villanova for the Regional championship, 90-72, in Providence.

"I can't say enough about the way we put it all together today," Foster said. "A lot was said about our lack of quickness, but today we got out and ran the ball. We didn't want to play tentative. Our running game has to come from defense, then rebounding, then passing before we can score. If any of the four don't work, then it all breaks down."

Following Duke's second-round win, Penn Coach Bob Weinhauer said the Blue Devils were slow. He predicted they would lose in the East championship game to Villanova. Weinhauer's comments served as motivation for Duke against Villanova and carried over to the Final Four in St. Louis, where the Blue Devils faced Notre Dame in one semifinal.

With their 2-3 zone helping to contain Notre Dame's strong inside game, the Blue Devils got their running game going and raced to a 43-29 halftime lead. Duke led 80-68 with just over three minutes to play, and a national championship date for the first time since 1964 appeared imminent.

But Notre Dame staged a furious rally in the closing minutes and had a chance to tie with 18 seconds remaining. Duck Williams missed a 20-footer, and Duke's John Harrell was fouled as he rebounded the ball. Harrell, a transfer from North Carolina Central in his hometown of Durham, made two free throws with nine seconds left to clinch the Blue Devils' 90-86 victory.

Besides Harrell's clutch free throws, Duke got 29 points from Gminski, 22 points and 12 rebounds from Banks, 20 points from Spanarkel and seven points to go with seven rebounds from Dennard.

"Our confidence won't fall," Dennard said. "It will be right up there at 9 o'clock (the time of the championship game). Yes, I believe in teams of destiny. I also believe in personal destiny, too. I have to think we can't lose now."

The national championship game matched youthful and spirited Duke against veteran and venerable Kentucky, which advanced to the title game with a 64-59 semifinal victory over

Cocky and quick, Lucas a winner on two courts.

The '70s

Maryland

Freshman John Lucas didn't just walk onto the Cole Field House floor in November of 1972 for Maryland's opening game against Brown. He strutted, the familiar flat-footed strut ACC fans came to know.

Lucas was confident in himself, certain of his ability to take care of the task at hand and bound to make all others take notice.

Lucas was in the first freshman class to compete in varsity competition within the ACC. That was of no big concern to Lucas. He competed under similar circumstances six years earlier at age 12.

That's when he took the Southeastern Junior Tennis Tournament by storm, winning the 14-and-under singles competition, as well as the 16-and-under title. He finally lost the 18-and-under championship match, although exhaustion caught up with him as much as the talent level. Two years later, he won seven events in the Durham (N.C.) City-County Tournament. He was a member of the U.S. Junior Davis Cup team by his junior year in high school.

"I was already like a senior in college because I already knew what it was like to play in front of 15,000 people, all by myself," Lucas said of his first college basketball game. "I was used to being in control because I knew how to be in control of my tennis matches."

On the first play of the game, a Brown guard shot by Lucas toward the basket. When Lucas' teammate, Len Elmore, swatted the shot away, Lucas retrieved it and missed a set shot at the other end of the court. He did not miss another in four attempts that game, then made all eight of his attempts in the next game against Richmond.

By making 12 straight shots over his first two college games, Lucas sounded a warning to the rest of the ACC: Freshmen could play in this league, and he was out to prove it. Wally Walker of Virginia, Mitch Kupchak of North Carolina and Lee Foye of Wake Forest also proved worthy of first-year eligibility that season. But none displayed the brashness of Lefty Driesell's lefty guard.

Lucas, just as much as any undisciplined player who learned the game on the playgrounds, was a product of his environment. He was from a prominent, middle-class family in Durham. His father was a high school principal and his mother was a schoolteacher. Education came first in the Lucas household, then athletics.

"I was just bound and determined to win," Lucas said. "That was just something I got from my dad. I just had

ACC BASKETBALL / THE '70s

Lucas' reach-around steals led to dozens of fast breaks during 110 Maryland games from 1973-76.

Lucas' father, John Sr., that Lucas probably would not beat out returning guard George Karl for a starting position.

Driesell sought a second opinion, this time from Assistant Coach Joe Harrington, and decided to go after Lucas. When Driesell offered Lucas a shake with his left hand, the two might as well have signed a contract for life.

In many ways, Lucas became an extension of his coach at Maryland. Driesell said Maryland would someday be the "UCLA of the East." Lucas said he would be the best guard in the country. When he was switched to forward during his junior season, Lucas said: "I used to be the best guard, now I'm the best forward. If I have to be, I'll be the best center."

Lucas *was* among the ACC's best guards because of his quickness. He was a master at leading a fast-break and getting the ball into the proper hands. On defense, his reach-around steals were often predictable but, more often than not, unstoppable. Beyond that, Driesell said, "John was a great competitor, a super competitor. He was a great leader, a smart player from the first day of practice."

Lucas was a starter for every one of his 110 games over four years at Maryland. He led the Terps into the NCAA Tournament twice, to a first-place finish in the ACC's regular season in 1975 and to a four-year record of 92-23. He was the first Maryland player to make first-team All-ACC three straight seasons. He finished as the school's all-time leader in scoring (2,015 points) and assists (514), although his records have since been broken.

Lucas was a consensus All-America in 1975 and 1976, the same two years he won the ACC singles tennis championship. After the Houston Rockets made him the first selection in the 1976 NBA draft, Lucas signed a $1.9 million contract and became a pro standout for more than a decade. Simultaneous to his signing with Houston, Lucas signed with the Golden Gators and played World Team Tennis during the league's short existence.

"He was just a tremendous athlete," Driesell said.

Lucas agreed.

a competitive edge. I always could find a way to win."

That determination made up for a few deficiencies in Lucas' basketball game. Left-handed almost to a fault, Lucas would turn a driving layup from the right side of the basket into a twisting left-handed shot. Lucas also did not have a jump shot. When Driesell sent Assistant Coach George Raveling to scout Lucas, Raveling told Driesell, "Lucas can't play."

Raveling was not alone in his thinking. N.C. State made a passing attempt to recruit Lucas, but ultimately backed away. Duke wanted Lucas, more because the Blue Devils feared losing a Durham player to another school than because of his talent. North Carolina Coach Dean Smith told

197

Gminski (L) taps in two points for Duke while Spanarkel fights through a foul during 1978 ACC title game.

Arkansas. Duke, unranked in the preseason after a last-place finish in the ACC in 1977, started three players less than 20 years old. Kentucky, ranked No. 1 throughout the season and the pre-tournament favorite, started four seniors.

Duke's improbable dream season was shattered in a 94-88 defeat by Kentucky before a crowd of 18,721 at the Checkerdome. Kentucky forward Jack "Goose" Givens scored 41 points, just three shy of the championship scoring record set by UCLA's Bill Walton in 1973. Givens had 23 points by halftime, including the Wildcats' last 16, as Kentucky built a 45-38 lead. He then led the Wildcats on a second-half surge that resulted in an insurmountable 66-50 advantage with 13 minutes remaining.

"I took one shot in the second half and it hit the side of the backboard and went in," Givens said. "That's the kind of night I was having."

Duke played well in defeat. Banks scored 22 points. Spanarkel had 21, Gminski had 20 and 12 rebounds and Dennard added 10 points. Not until after the game was Banks informed that his life had been threatened twice in telephone calls prior to the game.

That incident, more than the loss, marred the end of a Duke season that included an ACC championship and 27 victories. With the entire starting unit returning for the 1979 season, there were few hung heads in the Duke locker room following the championship loss.

"We'll be back," said Banks, echoing the sentiments of his teammates.

'79

On one hand, Duke's trip to the 1978 championship game spoke well of the ACC. The league now had been represented in the Final Four 11 times in the past 17 seasons. On the other hand, only N.C. State had returned from a Final Four trip with a national championship during that period.

Before the league would begin another quest for a national title in 1979, it agreed to accept a new member. In March of 1978, the ACC admitted Georgia Tech as its eighth member.

"Geographically, it opens up some two million people and strengthens our conference tremendously," said Duke Athletic Director Tom Butters.

Although Georgia Tech was admitted to the league in the fall of 1978, the Yellow Jackets were not eligible for competition in basketball until the 1980 season.

Before Tech's admission, ACC schools had an issue to settle during the 1979 season. Six ACC teams came in with high hopes. Duke and North Carolina were thought to be contenders for the national championship.

They had the opportunity to test their mettle early in the annual Big Four Tournament. The event was started in 1970, less than a decade after the annual Dixie Classic had folded in the wake of point-shaving scandals.

From the day the Dixie Classic went under until the opening

198

tap of the Big Four Tournament, there seemed to always be talk of reviving a holiday tournament for North Carolina's ACC representatives. In between, Duke and UNC hosted a double-header in Greensboro, N.C. State and Duke hosted one in Raleigh, and N.C. State was in something called the Lafayette Tournament at Ft. Bragg, N.C. None were successful.

The Big Four Tournament was founded in part because of an expansion of the Greensboro Coliseum, which added an upper deck and increased its seating capacity from 9,000 to 15,000. By splitting tickets five ways, with the Coliseum getting one share and each school getting another, the tournament figured to be a big success, certainly a near sellout.

The first tournament drew more than 11,000 spectators each night.

"The only thing that surprised me was that it wasn't an overnight success," said Wake Forest Athletic Director Gene Hooks. Not until 1974, when David Thompson led once-beaten and second-ranked N.C. State, did each school sell its full allotment of tickets. Even then, some tickets were available at the door. Finally, in 1975, the event was sold out before the first game was played. Every remaining game in the tournament's history was a sellout.

As attendance increased, the tournament became more profitable for the participating schools. Each received $45,000 following the 1973 event. Two years later, each received a $60,000 check.

Despite the sellouts, and the annual payoff to each school, only N.C. State's Norm Sloan among the coaches seemed to like the event.

"It is great for the fans and for us," Sloan said. "As coaches we strive to develop interest in our programs and interest is at its greatest when the Big Four teams play each other. If we lose two, we've gained valuable experience under pressure conditions. If we win two, we've gained confidence and experience. And if we split, it is still a great experience. There is always added excitement when the Big Four teams meet and that includes the coaches, players and fans. Besides, we all make money to support our programs."

UNC's Dean Smith, Duke's Bill Foster and Wake Forest's Carl Tacy hardly shared Sloan's view. They simply saw no point in playing two more games each season against Big Four opposition.

Smith said: "I would rather have games with Indiana and UCLA, one home and one away, than the Big Four. But that's wishful thinking. The Big Four is here to stay."

Smith made those comments in 1976. The Big Four was actually to stay only five more seasons. By 1981, UNC had decided to drop out and had plans for a 20,000-plus seat arena, which if filled for a non-conference game, could net a bigger payoff than two nights in the Big Four. When UNC announced its plans to withdraw, the Big Four was doomed.

Wake Forest then wrote a fitting epitaph to the Big Four Tournament. The Demon Deacons won the finale in December of 1980 with an 82-71 decision over 10th-ranked UNC. The championship was Wake Forest's fourth in the tournament's 11-year history. N.C. State took the title three times, while UNC and Duke each won it twice.

When Duke won the Big Four Tournament early in the 1979 season, the Blue Devils retained their No. 1 ranking in both national polls. Duke returned the same lineup of Gene Banks, Kenny Dennard, Mike Gminski, Jim Spanarkel, John Harrell and Bob Bender that had helped it finish second nationally the previous season.

Six games into the season, there was no reason to believe Duke did not deserve its No. 1 ranking. But the Blue Devils

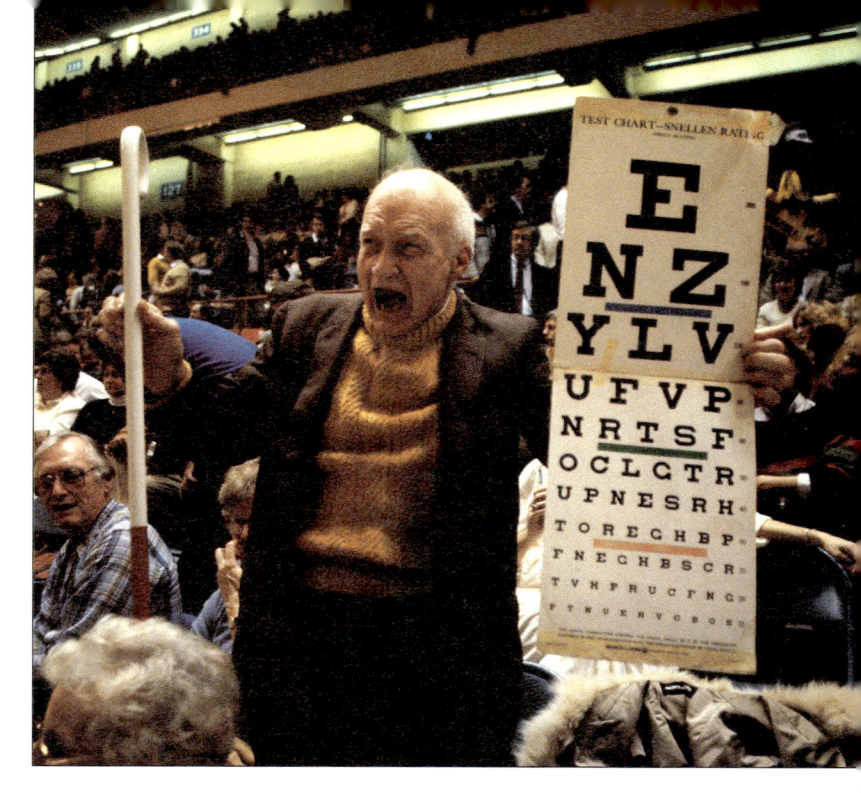

The Big Four Tournament was a fan's delight and spurred many to extremes: One Wake Forest supporter brought along an eye chart for the refs while a UNC flutist stuck her foot in her face.

ran into trouble in the ECAC Holiday Festival in New York. They lost a 90-84 overtime decision to Ohio State after leading by 17 with 13 minutes to play. The next night, Duke dropped a 69-64 decision to St. John's after blowing another big lead.

Within the ACC, the chief challengers to Duke were Maryland, Virginia and North Carolina. Early in the season, guard Ernest Graham scored a school-record 44 points on 18-of-26 shooting from the floor as he led Maryland to a wild 124-110 victory over N.C. State in College Park, Md. Later in the season, Larry Gibson's three-point play with one second remaining gave Maryland a 67-66 victory over No. 1-ranked Notre Dame.

Virginia won 11 of its first 15 games, including a 106-68 rout of Providence that represented the most lopsided game in the 41-year history of the Sugar Bowl Tournament. The Cavaliers also won at Wake Forest to snap the Deacons' 16-game home-court win streak and defeated N.C. State when the

Dudley Bradley slams home game winner with seven seconds remaining after stripping State's Clyde Austin (R) as Tar Heels collect 70-69 win.

Wolfpack was ranked eighth. But for the first time under Coach Terry Holland, Virginia was outrebounded for the season and the Cavaliers' lack of board strength cost them in league play.

Duke and UNC relied on inside strength and were often able to overpower their opponents. The Tar Heels' most impressive wins came over Michigan State at home and N.C. State in Raleigh.

UNC defeated third-ranked and eventual national champion Michigan State 70-69 in Chapel Hill when the Spartans' Jay Vincent missed a 10-foot jump shot at the buzzer. Earvin "Magic" Johnson had 18 points, six rebounds and six assists for Michigan State.

Dudley Bradley proved to be the magic man in the Tar Heels' victory over N.C. State. He caught the Wolfpack's Clyde Austin with his back turned, stole the ball near midcourt and went in for an emphatic dunk with seven seconds remaining to give UNC a 70-69 victory in a stunned Reynolds Coliseum. State had erased all of UNC's 40-19 halftime lead prior to Bradley's steal.

That win helped put UNC in position to finish first in the regular-season race when the Tar Heels and Blue Devils met in the finale at Duke's Cameron Indoor Stadium. A UNC victory would have given the Tar Heels first place. A Duke win would have left the teams tied for first with 9-3 league records.

After 20 minutes of "action," Duke held a 7-0 lead.

"It should have been 2-0 or something like that at the half," said UNC's Smith. "I wanted to win the game 2-0. That's just as good as 82-80."

Following a tip-in basket by Duke's Vince Taylor 33 seconds into the game, UNC held the ball for 12 minutes and 25 seconds. The strategy backfired when Rich Yonakor shot from the left baseline and missed the basket entirely. Yonakor's shot spurred the now-famous chant of "Air Ball, Air Ball" around the league.

UNC only attempted one other shot in the first half. Duke, meanwhile, was getting baskets from Gminski and Spanarkel for the seven-point advantage. UNC abandoned the stall tactics in the second half, and the Blue Devils stretched their lead to 36-22 with 2:45 remaining.

With 30 seconds left, Gminski swung an elbow following a rebound and belted UNC's Al Wood in the face. A dazed Wood left the game and Gminski was ejected. Gminski's ejection proved incidental when Duke held on for a 47-40 victory.

Exactly one week later, UNC got revenge on Duke for the "7-0" game. The Tar Heels' Bradley again stole the show as UNC defeated the Blue Devils 71-63 for the ACC Tournament championship. Bradley hit seven of 11 shots, scored 16 points, passed for four assists and had seven steals.

"Coach should get as much credit for this game as he got abuse for that one," UNC's Mike O'Koren said of the two Duke games.

Duke and UNC were the obvious selections to represent the ACC in the NCAA Tournament. Both teams received a first-round bye, then were scheduled for a second-round game in the East Regional in Raleigh. With the East finals scheduled for Greensboro, ACC fans envisioned one of the two teams advancing to the Final Four.

But a funny thing happened on the ACC's road to the Final Four in Salt Lake City. On what was to become known around the ACC as Black Sunday, Penn stunned UNC 72-71 in the first game at Reynolds Coliseum, then St. John's upset Duke 80-78.

"It's a big jump for the East," said St. John's guard Bernard Rencher, "because nobody thinks we're as tough as the ACEC . . . or whatever you want to call it."

Black Sunday quickly turned to Blue Monday the following day when Clemson, Virginia and Maryland all lost in the second round of the NIT.

It was a disappointing closing to what had otherwise been an illustrious decade for the ACC, one in which N.C. State had had an undefeated season (1973) and an NCAA championship (1974), and UNC (1977) and Duke (1978) had national second-place finishes.

200

ACC BASKETBALL / THE '70s

SPOTLIGHT

David Thompson

"He just will not let them lose. If State needs something, Thompson will get it for them. He's just the best I've ever been around."

By BARRY JACOBS

ACC BASKETBALL / THE '70s

Rarely have man and moment conspired to better effect than on that afternoon in January of 1973 when Maryland, the nation's second-ranked basketball team, met N.C. State, No. 3.

The first ACC contest ever televised nationally, the game was presented as a prelude to Super Bowl VII, pitting the undefeated Miami Dolphins against President Richard Nixon's favorite team, the Washington Redskins. As things turned out, it was the basketball that was super, the football anticlimactic. Miami bested Washington in typically conservative NFL fashion, allowing only a gift touchdown courtesy of panicked Dolphin placekicker Garo Yepremian. But Maryland and State played furiously to the buzzer in a game featuring two outstanding teams and four all-conference players, including a nascent talent whose emergence would forever change the shape of the Atlantic Coast Conference.

What's more, and the two cannot be separated, the greatest star in the ACC pantheon, an exemplary youth by any standards, burst to the fore just when accepted American heroes were in shortest supply.

It was the murky dawn of an era of national confusion. Protracted American involvement in the Vietnam War had spawned equally protracted, and escalating, protest at home, especially on college campuses. Simultaneously, federally mandated integration transformed a begrudging South; women struggled militantly for equal opportunity; ecological alarm led to creation of the U.S. Environmental Protection Agency; the well-chronicled search for personal freedom widened into a thousand avenues of enlightenment and excess.

The turmoil gradually filtered into the relatively stable world of ACC basketball. At Duke, Bucky Waters' crewcut approach led to player rebellion and, soon enough, a new coach. Virginia and Clemson finally integrated their basketball squads even as North Carolina's Charlie Scott complained of being bypassed as conference player of the year because he was black. South Carolina withdrew from the league, the only defection in ACC history.

And then came Super Sunday, 1973, when the most romantic of athletic dreams took wing before the nation's eyes in the form of a 6-foot-4 forward from Shelby, N.C.

The score was tied at 85 with 1:45 remaining when Maryland's Tom McMillen misfired and State grabbed the rebound. In those pre-shot clock days, teams often stalled for minutes before taking a final shot, especially when playing on the road. The Wolfpack proceeded to do just that behind the ball-handling legerdemain of its tough sophomore floor leader, 5-7 Monte Towe.

But, like the Wolfpack, the Terps were an excellent defensive squad and would not yield a clear inside opportunity. Finally, with 12 seconds remaining and no set play called, the Wolfpack's all-conference center, 7-4 Tom Burleson, fired and missed from well beyond his normal range.

Enter David Thompson.

Thompson had already scored 35 points in the game, which he began as the ACC's leading scorer and from which he went on to become only the second sophomore (after Clemson's Butch Zatezalo) to pace conference scoring. This was no surprise after a debut in which Thompson led State's freshman team to a 15-1 record, averaging 35.6 points and 13.6 rebounds per game.

In fact, aficionados of the game were so enamored of his skills that, even before Thompson played a varsity contest, Fred Schaus, former coach of the Los Angeles Lakers, boldly asserted: "Thompson is better right now than when Jerry West was as a college senior. Thompson is one of the 10 best basketball players in the nation, pros included."

But early in his sophomore year, strained knee ligaments limited Thompson's lateral movement. Even though the Wolfpack opened with 11 straight wins, skeptics surfaced to question Thompson's talents. "I wasn't moving on offense and wasn't getting to the boards like I should have," Thompson explained later. "I was playing adequate, but not super."

Then came Maryland, Burleson's misfire, and a human eagle soaring from nowhere to grab the errant shot and guide it into the basket for the winning points. It was a stunning move, a stunning moment. The game's first well-rounded, above-the-rim performer had arrived. "It seemed," said awed teammate Phil Spence, "like gravity didn't affect him."

Thompson played tenacious and thoughtful defense. He could shoot deftly to today's 3-point range. He passed well, was unselfish with the ball. He hated to lose. He knew the game, knew his talents, yet worked as hard on his last day of college practice as he did the first. But above all he did two things best: He jumped impossible distances, and, like Elgin Baylor, remained airborne long beyond the capabilities of mere mortals. He also regularly reached deep into his reservoir of talents to make whatever play his team needed most. "He just will not let them lose," said Bobby Jones, North Carolina's all-conference forward. "If State needs something, Thompson will get it for them. He's just the best I've ever been around."

Recalls teammate Mark Moeller: "He just captured everyone's fancy about the game. Because of his abilities and his love for the game, he would bring us up to another level."

Or, as one ACC coach lamented about facing the Wolfpack, "When they get into trouble, they just go to Superman."

Writers scrambled to come up with suitable nicknames: Skywalker, Dazzling Dave, King David. They called Thompson the eighth wonder of the world, claimed he was born on the planet Krypton, that he killed a bear when he was only 3.

Rarely have modern sports pages been filled with rhapsodies such as those occasioned by Thompson's play. Larry Keech of the *Greensboro Daily News* wrote of his "graceful majesty." Bob Lipper of Norfolk's *Virginian-Pilot* commented almost plaintively: "Words—no matter how flowery, how precise, how flattering—cannot do justice to his artistry." *The Charlotte News'* Ron Green wrote, "He can hit from anywhere inside the city limits, climb the backboard without benefit of a ladder and he's learning to dribble 'Flight of the Bumblebee' on the piano with a basketball."

Even Thompson's descriptions of his talents seemed almost awed. "Sometimes I go up to block a shot and I feel like the ball is just a little out of my reach," he told an interviewer. "It seems like I can feel my arm growing. It's coming right out of my shoulder. And all of a sudden I can stretch and reach the ball."

Similarly, all of a sudden that day at College Park, with Thompson leading them, State's players realized they could stretch and reach any goal.

"David is the one who made it all happen," says Towe. "I'm not sure we felt we were that good or knew we were that good until his tip-in of the basket our sophomore year at Maryland. I think that win and that play seemed to spur us on for the next three years, the next two years in particular."

In those two seasons—commencing in the fall of 1972 and

Once in practice, Monte Towe made a bad pass which Thompson leaped for and laid gently in the basket. Thus was born No. 44's signature, the alley oop.

extending to the spring of 1974—N.C. State enjoyed the greatest prosperity in ACC history. Over that span, the Wolfpack was 57-1, along the way becoming the only team ever to manage consecutive undefeated ACC campaigns. Over Thompson's three varsity seasons, State was 79-7.

That year of Thompson's Super Sunday debut the Wolfpack was undefeated, stopped finally not by an oncourt opponent but by an NCAA probation. The next season, probation ended, N.C. State lost but once in 31 outings. "That team had the perfect blend of personalities and talents," recalls Norm Sloan, the N.C. State coach who left for the University of Florida in 1980. "We had so much confidence in each other," says Spence, who went on to be a high school coach in Cary, N.C. "It was a great group of guys. It was just all for one, one for all. If David scored, we scored. If I got a rebound, we got a rebound."

"We were good and we were lucky," says Towe, who became Sloan's assistant at Florida. "I think we played as a unit, we played within ourselves. We had role players who understood what each one of us was supposed to carry out on the court."

And the Wolfpack had David Thompson, three-time ACC Player of the Year, three-time unanimous first-team All-America, twice (1974 and 1975) national Player of the Year. For 12 seasons after he left, N.C. State reserved a page in its basketball press guide devoted to "The Remarkable David Thompson."

Perhaps most remarkable of all, and a key ingredient in transforming the unassuming Thompson into a figure of heroic proportion, he was by all accounts as special a person as he was a player. "God didn't give many players David's talent," said Sloan, "but he didn't give any others the personality and humility to go with it, like he did David."

"David always had time for you," says Moeller. "He was absolutely deluged with autograph seekers and people wanting him to come and do things, and David was always very gracious about that." It was years later that Thompson succumbed to addictive drugs, perhaps overwhelmed by the pressures accompanying a trend-setting $800,000 per year professional contract.

In fact, the burden of expectations weighed heavily upon Thompson, even at State. "I know people expect too much from me," he told Paul Attner of *The Washington Post*. "I have to be great every game or they are disappointed. It's just going to happen that way. I just have to guard against pressing too much."

Yet, throughout his college days, Thompson readily donned a role model's mantel, voluntarily visiting prisoners and hospitalized children and maintaining a Boy Scout image. "David always gave of himself. He wanted to be that role model," says Spence. "David just loved being loved. He loved people enjoying him and looking up to him."

Away from the public eye, according to Moeller, "DT" was just one of the guys, a follower who enjoyed hanging out with his friends. "When he's in a room full of people he knows and is comfortable with, he's not real quiet," says Moeller. "But he's not going to be the ringleader, either."

•

The youngest of 11 children, David Thompson grew up in a homebuilt cinderblock house down a country lane nine miles from the town of Shelby in the foothills of southwestern North Carolina. His parents, Vellie and Ida Thompson, were a quiet, working-class couple of extremely modest means, folks to whom actions spoke far louder than words. "I just don't have much to say," David's father, Vellie, told *The Charlotte News* reporter Bob Padecky that winter of 1973. "I guess all of us are like that . . . We like to be calm outside. Inside we are burning. It's just that we don't show it."

Early on, David did show his feelings by running off and crying if older boys, his three brothers included, prevented him from joining basketball games on the dirt court in the Thompson's yard. "Lordy, I remember that basketball," said his father, a church deacon. "He used to do that more than anything. I remember he used to turn on my car's headlights and play in the dark. He sure loved that basketball. I had to whup him for that every now and then to keep him straight."

At age 13 Thompson made the junior varsity at Shelby's newly integrated and consolidated Crest High School, and so excelled that he was invited to join the varsity by Christmas. But, out of a sense of loyalty to his JV teammates, the shy freshman declined the offer of advancement.

Sometimes on defense, Thompson once said, "It seems like I can feel my arm growing."

The next year Thompson not only made the varsity, but held his own in pickup games at nearby Gardner-Webb College with the likes of small college stars Artis Gilmore and George Adams. Nicknamed "Head" by his Crest teammates because of his skull size, Thompson modeled himself after Charlie Scott, the first black varsity basketball player at UNC. He certainly possessed Scott's innate athletic gifts, plus an ability, says Ed Peeler, his coach at Crest, "to be in the right place. You don't have to coach those things."

So Peeler set out to teach the slender wing forward the basics of defense. A solid "C" student, Thompson had no

204

ACC BASKETBALL / THE '70s

trouble mastering his court lessons, leading a losing team to the district final. Following that first varsity season, Thompson attended Dean Smith's summer basketball camp in Chapel Hill. "Of course, we thought we had David all along," says Smith. "He had been a Carolina fan."

Back then summer all-star camps and prep player ratings weren't the rage they would become, and Thompson remained relatively unknown, in part because he enrolled in public school at a younger age than most children and was only 15 as a high school junior. "He was just starting to grow, so he couldn't be a dominant player," says State's chief recruiter in those days, Eddie Biedenbach, who first heard of Thompson while recruiting Burleson.

Thompson grew leaner and developed the long arms (38½-inch sleeves), huge hands and outstanding jumping ability (44-inch vertical leap from a standing start) that would become his trademarks. Still, after watching a film highlighting Thompson's talents, Biedenbach wasn't impressed. Then he saw Crest in action. "They came out for warmups, and I was amazed that David had so much spring and explosion even warming up," Biedenbach says. During the game Thompson won the recruiter's heart by scoring three baskets "with guys all over him. It doesn't take you long to decide to recruit a guy who can do that," says Biedenbach.

Amidst the pressures of a 32-game winning streak that ended with the only loss of his senior season, along with a surge of recruiting interest, Thompson remained immutably himself. Eager to share his good fortune, each time he was invited to visit a campus he took along a different teammate. "He never took the same one," says Peeler. "I'll always remember that about him."

Soon only three schools—State, UNC and Gardner-Webb—were in the running, though not before an apparently well-meaning Duke alum gave Thompson a sports jacket, pants and 1970 ACC Tournament tickets, earning that school a year's probation. Dean Smith spoke at Thompson's high school basketball banquet in the spring of 1971, but in June Thompson signed with State, in part because of Burleson's towering presence at center. Despite NCAA and ACC investigations into the recruitment of Thompson, Sloan was ecstatic. Told of the coup while playing golf, he "jumped up and down like a little kid," according to Biedenbach.

By the time Thompson enrolled in college that fall, rumors of imminent probation swirled around the basketball program. Meanwhile, the prize recruit told *The Technician*, State's student newspaper, that the campus "is bigger than I thought it was. When I came here at night and saw all the lights, it scared me at first. I thought to myself, 'What am I doing here?'"

The answer to that question came quickly enough.

Typical was the experience of Moeller, a fellow freshman from Ohio. In his first scrimmage involving Thompson, Moeller went up for what he thought was an uncontested corner jumpshot. "I saw this guy under the basket, but he was far away. All of a sudden it was like the lights were turned off, and this black arm came up and the ball went sailing over my head . . . It got more amazing as time went on. Every day he'd do something that was more amazing."

In Thompson's third game as a freshman he scored 54 points, a Reynolds Coliseum record. (He eclipsed that mark three years later with 57, also the ACC scoring record, in a home game against Buffalo State.)

But at Carmichael Auditorium in Chapel Hill the Wolflets, comfortably ahead at halftime, lost 95-83 to the Tar Babies after big man Tim Stoddard fouled out. "It affected us tremendously, and particularly David," recalls Towe. Thompson had chosen State over UNC and wanted to prove that he, and not Tar Heel recruit Ray Harrison of Greensboro, was the best freshman in the state. When the teams met for a rematch in Raleigh, "David came out and went absolutely bananas, and at one point had like 13 points in a row," remembers Moeller, who became a commercial real estate broker in Raleigh. State won by 26, with Thompson scoring 49.

As the 1972-73 season approached, expectations were high for Wolfpack basketball in general and for the 18-year-old Thompson, a supposed cross between Oscar Robertson and Julius Erving, in particular. "No matter what you say about David, you can't exaggerate," opined Sloan.

> "God didn't give many players David's talent. But he didn't give any other the personality and humility to go with it, like he did David."
> ☐ **State Coach Norm Sloan**

But even as the squad was engaged in preseason practice, the NCAA slapped the program with a one-year probation, barring it from postseason play. A number of violations cited by the NCAA did not involve Thompson. Those that did—his illegal transportation to, and lodging on campus; participation by Biedenbach in a pickup game with Thompson and other prospective students—took place subsequent to his recruitment. Both ACC Commissioner Bob James and N.C. State Chancellor John Caldwell determined that the violations were the result of inadvertent errors, a position Sloan vehemently defends to this day. "It was all stupid stuff," he says. "When people accuse us of intentionally going on probation to win a national championship"—a charge repeatedly made by Indiana Coach Bob Knight and others—"it's untrue and it's unfair."

Thompson, an especially sensitive person, taped to his dorm room door a headline that blared: "State Placed On Probation For Recruiting Violations." Each time he exited his room the headline reminded him to play harder. "I owe that much to the fans," he explained.

Joining a 16-10 squad that featured Burleson and seniors Rick Holdt and Joe Cafferky, Thompson was quick to begin repayment of his imaginary debt. The first victim, an Appalachian State squad coached by former Wolfpack Coach Press Maravich, endured a 130-53 shellacking in which Thompson led his team with 33 points and 13 rebounds. "We worked for this game for six weeks," said Maravich, "and it was just awful."

Maravich also had to watch helplessly as the Pack unveiled its signature alley-oop pass from Towe or Stoddard to Thompson, which invariably brought down the house. State came up with the move in practice one day when Thompson made a backdoor cut, grabbed a pass that playmaker Towe said "looked like it was going out of the gym," and easily laid it in the basket. "Coach Sloan said that looked pretty good," Towe relates with a smile, "and why didn't we try to put that in our offense?"

Back then the dunk was illegal, banned to protect backboards from shattering and to limit the dominance of big

ACC BASKETBALL / THE '70s

men such as UCLA's Lew Alcindor (later to become Kareem Abdul-Jabbar). Some believe it was because of Thompson that the dunk was returned to the game in 1976. "We would have seen some unbelievable dunks," muses Moeller.

Thompson's high-flying handiwork wasn't all that impressed observers. Following a 125-88 rout by State, South Florida Coach Don Williams said: "Nobody can handle Thompson alone. Sometimes three men can't." Which is exactly what Maryland's Lefty Driesell discovered when Bob Bodell, Owen Brown and Jim O'Brien tried in vain to slow Thompson during their Super Sunday showdown at College Park.

The Wolfpack had other close calls along the way to achieving the sole perfect record in school history, among them Sloan's first pair of regular-season defeats of UNC, a rally from a late seven-point deficit against Clemson and a 76-74 victory over Maryland in the ACC Tournament final. "I can remember everyone talking about making the ACC Tournament our NCAA Tournament," says Moeller.

And then abruptly, painfully, the season was over, halted by probation. "I thought we got a raw deal," said Thompson. "At the end of the season I felt empty."

That summer he and Burleson played for the United States in the World University Games in Moscow, which the Americans won. His team's leading scorer, Thompson received an ovation from the Soviet team when awarded his medal. As they had during the season, again the pros came calling, this time with a reported $2 million offer as the ABA and NBA continued a price war for talent. Again Thompson said no.

Probation ended, and in 1974 the Wolfpack was clearly aiming for the national title, won in '73 by UCLA for the seventh consecutive season and ninth time in 10 years. Eager to make its mark, State agreed to play the Bill Walton-led Bruins in a made-for-television matchup on a neutral court in mid-December. But after 30 minutes of close play, UCLA broke the game open and rolled to an 84-66 victory. Thompson went 7-of-20 and scored only 17 points against Bruin All-America forward Keith Wilkes.

Soon afterward, Thompson, Spence and several others were walking along a Raleigh street when a stranger accosted Thompson about his showing against UCLA. "David just broke down and told the guy, 'I tried to do my best,'" recalls Spence, a 6-8 junior college All-America who, like solid second-guard Moe Rivers, transferred to State for the 1974 season. "Me, I would have told him where to go. David wanted people to love him. He told the guy he was sorry. It was coming from his heart."

The UCLA loss proved a galvanizing experience for the entire Wolfpack. "We were, like, possessed," says Spence. Adds Moeller: "It let us know we needed to do some improving. I can honestly say from that game on, we got better and

Thompson won three player of the year awards in the league and two in the nation, sparking State to a 79-7 mark from 1973 to '75.

ACC BASKETBALL / THE '70s

better, and by the end of the season we were playing our best basketball. That's the way it's supposed to be."

State recovered to beat North Carolina—featuring Jones, Walter Davis and Mitch Kupchak—three times, including a 78-77 win in the early season Big Four Tournament. Soon after achieving the top rating in the national polls, State rallied from 15 points down in the second half to win at Purdue.

And, led by Thompson, the Pack repeatedly subdued Driesell's great Maryland team of McMillen, John Lucas, Len Elmore, Mo Howard and company. The Terps brought out the best in Thompson: In their nine career meetings, he averaged 22.1 shots, 6.6 rebounds and a whopping 31.2 points per game.

Depending on the size and quickness of the defender he faced, Thompson would either shoot over him, or maneuver him close to the basket and then jump over him. For the prince of lightness, it was that maddeningly simple.

During the '74 season, in a Super Sunday rematch at Raleigh with the higher-rated Terps, he scored 41 with eight rebounds and three steals to lead State to victory. "There was nothing you could do to stop him," said Tom Roy, one of two Terps to foul out while guarding Thompson. Later in the year Thompson scored 31 second-half points to rally the Pack to a win at Cole Field House. Departing slightly from his ordinarily reserved, deferential manner, Thompson said afterward: "That crowd was having too much fun. I had to do something to quiet them down."

The teams met a third time in the 1974 ACC Tournament final. Only one squad could advance to the NCAAs; in that pre-expansion era, second-best wasn't good enough. The Wolfpack felt that Maryland was its chief roadblock to winning a national title.

Burleson turned in the best game of his career, perhaps the best single-game performance in league annals (38 points, 13 rebounds), and earned tournament MVP honors. Spence contained McMillen and scored several key baskets in the late going. Thompson had 29 points, Towe 17. Still, the Terps hit 61 percent of their shots with every starter in double figures. The game stretched into overtime. And finally the Wolfpack won, 103-100, in what became the most celebrated contest in ACC history.

N.C. State opened its NCAA title quest in the East Regional in Raleigh, defeating No. 5 Providence, led by All-America Marvin Barnes. Thompson had 40 but, when asked, admitted he'd played better against Maryland. "He's played better?" asked a disbelieving Friar starter. "How? . . . My mind isn't programmed to believe something like that."

In the regional final, State faced No. 8 Pittsburgh, and quickly established a lead it would never relinquish. Midway through the first half, Thompson had a shot deflected and thought he was fouled. Angered, he raced upcourt, sprinted across the lane and leaped impossibly, characteristically high to harass a Panther shot. But, as he went up his foot caught Spence's shoulder, and with a great thud Thompson fell, landing head first on the Reynolds Coliseum floor.

Reynolds Coliseum went silent as Thompson lay unconscious. "All of a sudden, basketball became meaningless," teammate Mark Moeller said. But after being diagnosed with a mild concussion, Thompson returned to watch the second half alongside Sloan.

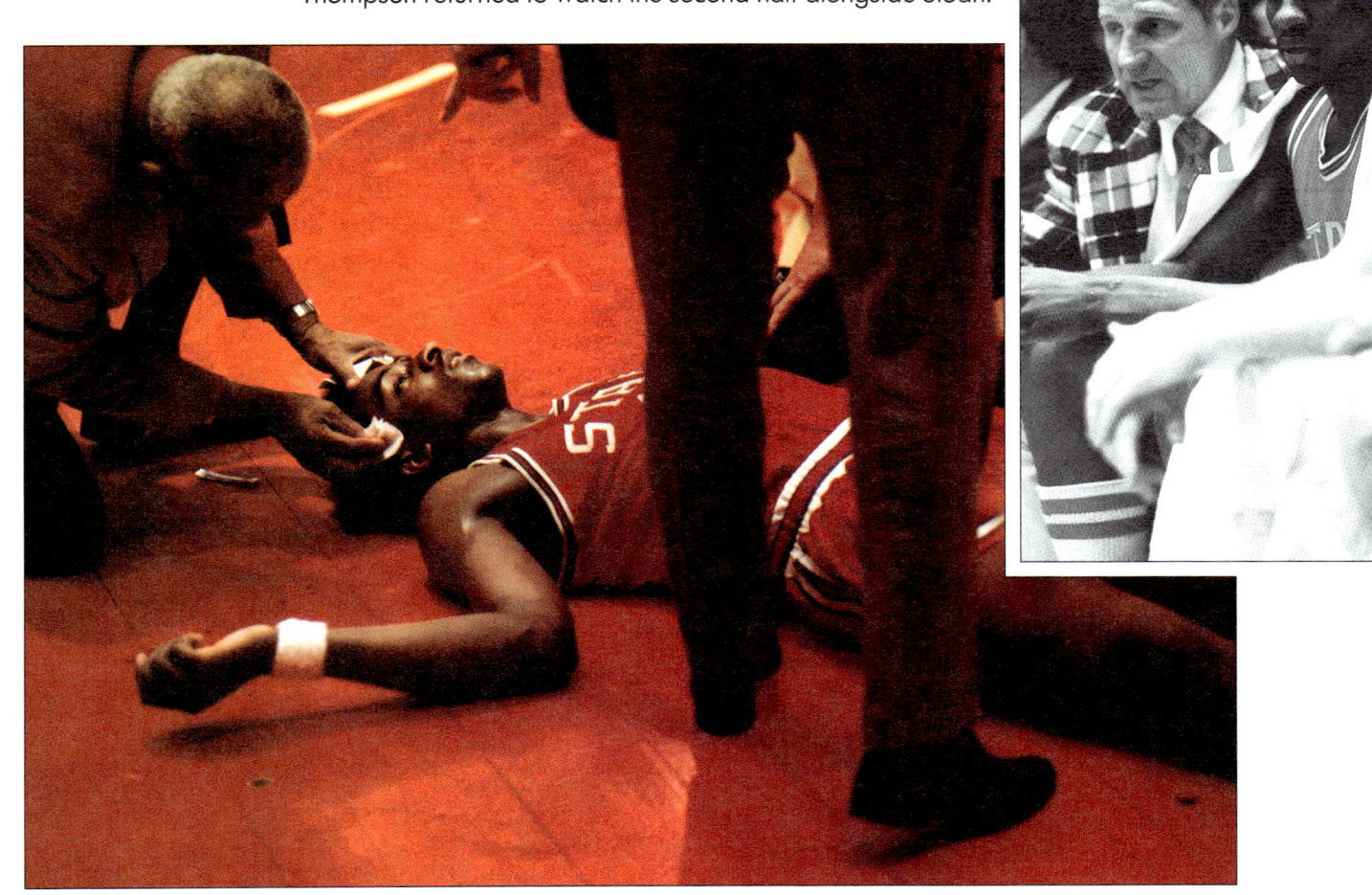

ACC BASKETBALL / THE '70s

The place went silent. For nearly four minutes Thompson lay unconscious. Many thought he was dead. People cried. Teammates and coaches felt sick. "All of a sudden basketball became meaningless," recalls Moeller.

Thompson was rushed to Rex Hospital while the team prayed silently at halftime for his recovery. Before the second half, word came that he'd suffered a mild concussion and was all right. After receiving 15 stitches in the back of his head, a heavily bandaged Thompson returned to Reynolds to a warm ovation.

Thompson returned to form in State's next game, against No. 2 UCLA in the Final Four in Greensboro, with 28 points and 20 rebounds. Down by 11 points in the second half, State rallied to send that game into overtime. In the second extra period, UCLA forged ahead 74-67 with 3:27 left. But two minutes and 34 seconds later, State led 76-75 and went on to win 80-77.

A relatively easy 76-64 victory two days later over No. 3 Marquette captured the title, the first in N.C. State history and the first for an ACC team in 17 seasons.

Again the pros came calling. Again Thompson elected to stay in school. "You can only drive one car and wear one suit at a time, and you can only eat three meals a day," he said in an oft-quoted remark.

So, adoring fans were treated to an encore performance, though this time by a State squad lacking Burleson. Without the big man, the defense was not as formidable nor the chemistry as good. There was a 22-point, late-season loss at Clemson that the squad found tough to swallow, followed by a minor player rebellion during halftime of a loss at UNC.

In all, the '75 season saw six losses, including a 70-66 defeat by UNC in the ACC Tournament final while Thompson suffered severe leg cramps. Invited to the NIT, State's seniors voted to stay home and call it quits.

By that time Thompson had won every major individual award, becoming the ACC's reigning career scoring leader and the Pack's leading scorer ever. But beyond numbers and games, beyond limitations of race or social status, he won something more precious still, as Larry Brown, his coach during Thompson's early pro career, noted when the Denver Nuggets visited North Carolina: "People were waiting around the bus just to touch him—children, mothers with kids. It was something that was mind-boggling. I remember the players on our team couldn't believe it . . . I grew up with Carolina. I thought that was a special program, but this was something else."

In a way, Thompson's career, with its impossible beauty and its barriers overcome, was every fan's dream come true, inspiring a generation of athletes who, like Michael Jordan, grew up rooting for him and N.C. State. "There are teams who have stars. They win, but people really don't relish the idea of them winning," says Towe. "I think that people, even the most typical rivals, enjoyed seeing David and the team win a national championship because of the way he represented himself and the way he carried himself. And I think it rubbed off on everyone."

Thompson (third from left) and the Wolfpack at their pinnacle of success: The 1974 NCAA Championship.

THE '80s

THE '80s

Lights, Camera, Action.

Coaches once fretted that TV would spoil their gate. Now the ACC's bouncing ball is a nationwide wheel of fortune.

The action was frantic. Pandemonium reigned.

With 20 seconds left in the 35th ACC Tournament championship game on March 13, 1988, North Carolina guard Jeff Lebo stripped the ball from Duke forward Danny Ferry and headed off on a 2-on-1 fast break with teammate King Rice. Duke's Quin Snyder backpedaled, attempting to guard both Lebo and Rice at the same time. Rice took the initiative and drove to the basket against Snyder, but his shot caromed off the backboard glass, bounced on the rim, then off.

Duke's Kevin Strickland grabbed the missed shot as Lebo, trying to draw a charging foul, went sprawling backward to the floor. UNC Coach Dean Smith jumped and pleaded for an official's whistle as Strickland dribbled to the corner and looked downcourt.

Ten seconds were left when Strickland fired a long pass to wide-open teammate Robert Brickey at the opposite end of the court. Brickey caught the ball at the top of the key and drove for a layup that would have given Duke a 65-61 lead and the championship.

But, racing in from behind, UNC's Steve Bucknall contested Brickey's shot and forced a miss. Strickland, following the play, slipped and went sliding beneath the basket and out of bounds as the ball bounced off the rim.

Snyder, also alertly following the play, rebounded the Brickey miss and frantically dribbled away from the basket toward the Duke bench. UNC's Scott Williams tried in vain to foul Snyder, who continued to dribble along the sideline.

Five seconds were left when Snyder threw the ball to Ferry across the court and collided chest-to-chest with Lebo. Snyder and Lebo both fell backward in opposite directions.

The old guard: C.D. Chesley (R) and his mid-'70s ACC crew (L-R) of Bones McKinney, Billy Packer and Jim Thacker.

Today's regime: Raycom/Jefferson-Pilot cameras catch the action, described at the '88 ACC Tournament by play-by-play man Mike Patrick (L) and analyst Lefty Driesell.

ACC BASKETBALL / THE '80s

The action was almost too fast for the fans, most of whom were screaming at the top of their lungs by the time official Joe Forte blew his whistle and approached Snyder and Lebo, still flat on their backs.

Thirty-one years earlier a similar block/charge call in the final seconds determined whether North Carolina would defeat Wake Forest in the ACC Tournament semifinals. Only the 12,400 fans at N.C. State's Reynolds Coliseum got to see official Jim Mills call a blocking foul against Wake Forest's Wendell Carr that sent UNC's Lennie Rosenbluth to the free throw line and the Tar Heels on their way to ACC and NCAA titles.

The 16,500 fans in the Greensboro Coliseum on this day, however, were hardly alone. When Forte raised his right fist and pointed his left hand at Lebo for blocking, millions of basketball fans across the country watched via NBC television. Hundreds of thousands of others in the ACC area saw not only the play, but several replays of the final seconds, via the Raycom/Jefferson-Pilot regional telecast.

Quin Snyder's mother, at her home in Mercer Island, Wash., watched her son sink two free throws to clinch Duke's 65-61 victory and the ACC championship. And Rosenbluth, whose free throw secured UNC's victory over Wake Forest in the 1957 ACC Tournament semifinals, suffered the agony of defeat with his old school as he watched from his home outside Miami, Fla.

Sitting in the Greensboro Coliseum stands were Rick and Dee Ray, the chief executive officer and president, respectively, of Raycom Sports and proud parents of ACC television broadcasts since 1983. They smiled at each other, knowing that an audience of fans across the ACC states was again treated to a classic finish of a championship game. They also knew that ACC TV sponsors, paying into the millions for precious minutes of advertising, were again pleased to have their products associated with ACC basketball.

Prior to the Tournament, Raycom/Jefferson-Pilot had negotiated a deal to pay the league more than an estimated $8 million a year for regional television rights to ACC basketball games through the 1994 season. Less than 10 years earlier, the ACC was getting less than $500,000 a season for its TV rights.

•

In many ways, the progress of TV coverage for ACC basketball parallels the advancement of the game itself. When radio was the only broadcast vehicle for ACC fans to follow games, the two-hand set shot was still a valuable weapon for any college team.

But just as the slam dunk replaced the set shot, so too did regional and national television replace radio as the primary medium for ACC fans to follow games they could not attend. By 1988, UNC center J.R. Reid was as recognizable to basketball fans in Cheyenne as Charlotte.

That's a far cry from when television first hit the ACC scene in 1955. Back then, most basketball fans in Wyoming didn't know the name Dickie Hemric nor that his Wake Forest team played in the ACC.

The ACC took tentative steps into the unknown world of TV in '55. With much reservation, Commissioner Jim Weaver and league officials agreed to let WUNC-TV, Channel 4 in Chapel Hill, televise one game that season. The public TV station requested and received approval from University of North Carolina officials and those at Wake Forest University to provide a non-commercial telecast of the Jan. 8 game between the two teams from UNC's Woollen Gym.

With the ACC's approval, the game was seen by fans on a signal that carried over a 50-mile radius from Chapel Hill. UNC won the game 95-78, and the reaction to the telecast was mixed.

Dee and Rick Ray ended the 1979 basketball season with $16.40 and no credit...

"Basketball is real good on TV, next to boxing, I would say," said Wake Forest Assistant Coach Bones McKinney. "But whether it is good for the game, well, that's something else. You can't convince me that TV will not hurt the attendance. It's so easy to stay home in the comfort of your own parlor to see a game, rather than go out on a cold or rainy night and fight the crowd.

"Yes, the telecasts of basketball in this area must be handled with kid gloves. Otherwise, somebody is going to suffer."

ACC TV was nearly grounded before it got on the air. The UNC-Wake Forest telecast was a test for TV's effect on attendance; while the Tar Heels and Demon Deacons played before a sellout crowd, Duke and N.C. State played at the same time in nearby Durham.

"Why all the empty seats?" State Coach Everett Case asked rhetorically of the crowd that was 2,000 shy of capacity at

ACC BASKETBALL / THE '80s

Duke Indoor Stadium. "Too many people stayed home to watch the Carolina-Wake Forest game on television. You can't tell me TV doesn't hurt attendance. This is the first time in five years we haven't drawn a capacity crowd in Duke Gym. You can say what you want, but I blame it on TV."

Duke Coach Hal Bradley agreed with Case and said, "If there's a conflict, and one of the games is on TV, you'll feel it at the gate."

UNC Coach Frank McGuire, usually one to take an opposing view, saw the benefits of television. He also showed great foresight.

"I guess we had an audience of 50,000 or more," McGuire said of the first telecast. "There is no doubt that the sport is in for a change. Whether this change will be good or bad, from the standpoint of attendance, I do not know.

"I do know, however, that the game will become more popular. More youngsters will be permitted to stay up at night to see the telecasts. And even the younger girls seem to like it. We already have started receiving letters from the girls asking for pictures of our players."

Prior to that first telecast, ACC fans relied on radio play-by-play provided by Ray Reeve. In the early days of the league, Reeve formed the Tobacco Sports Network, which transmitted the games on a delayed basis so as not to affect attendance. Later on, Reeve provided live broadcasts of as many as six ACC games a week. His gravel-voiced delivery became as much a part of ACC basketball in the early '50s as Ronnie Shavlik's hook shot. Some historians have suggested that Reeve's broadcasts contributed to the ACC's early growth as much as any player, coach or administrator.

The emergence of TV into the ACC picture most upset the radio stations, which feared the loss of an audience for their commercial broadcasts.

"The University, aware of its status as a tax-supported institution, is determined not to compete with private enterprise unnecessarily," said Billy Carmichael Jr., vice president and finance officer for UNC. "It wishes to protect the radio industry of the state from competition by WUNC-TV in respect to presenting basketball games on the air."

A unique agreement was made between WUNC-TV and a number of radio stations. Three UNC games of 1956 were broadcast over certain cooperating radio stations, and shown simultaneously on WUNC-TV without sound. The venture was known as Broadvision.

The first three Broadvision games were UNC vs. Maryland on Jan. 16, UNC vs. N.C. State on Jan. 18 and UNC vs. Wake Forest on Feb. 15. All three were selected to avoid conflicts with Duke and N.C. State home games, as well as with area high school games.

UNC won the first Broadvision game, 64-55, over Maryland. The "radiocast" was well received by fans, as well as by TV and radio officials. However, there were necessary adjustments to be made. For instance, TV viewers needed more access to the scoreboard and time clock. UNC solved that problem by placing a wooden, hand-operated scoreboard in one corner opposite the camera.

When commercial telecasts rendered Broadvision useless in 1958, the hand-operated scoreboard remained on the Woollen Gym sideline as an aid to the UNC coaching staff when reviewing films of the games. The scoreboard was retained when UNC later moved to Carmichael Auditorium and then to the Smith Center.

Broadvision ultimately gave way to the vision of Castleman De-Tolley Chesley.

C.D. Chesley worked within the sports divisions of the ABC, NBC and Dumont Networks during the early days of television. He experimented with the TV broadcasts of Notre Dame football games, which were shown to a national audience on a delayed basis. The voice of Lindsey Nelson saying, "After an exchange of punts, we go to further action in the third quarter," became familiar to college football fans every Sunday morning.

As coordinator of the NCAA's college football package for NBC and ABC, Chesley fostered the idea of regional telecasts. A one-time UNC football player, Chesley selected ACC football for his first regional experiment in 1956. He approached athletic directors Eddie Cameron of Duke, Chuck Erickson of North Carolina and Rex Enright of South Carolina about the regional telecasts of three ACC football games for the 1956 season. Chesley offered the ACC $75,000 for the rights.

The response to those telecasts was not overwhelming, but the league respected Chesley's interest. A year later, after watching UNC win the ACC Tournament in basketball, Chesley was convinced that the Tar Heels would be appealing to a TV audience in North Carolina. When they advanced to

...today they preside over a company that employs 45 and bills some $50 million a year.

213

the NCAA semifinals in Kansas City, Chesley paid the NCAA rights fee and set up a five-station network to carry the UNC games back in North Carolina. In less than one week, Chesley secured the necessary equipment for the telecasts from Kansas City, found sponsors and announcers and arranged telephone lines.

Fans across North Carolina watched nervously from their homes as the Tar Heels went three overtimes to defeat Michigan State in the semifinals. The championship game also went three overtimes with fans staying up past midnight to watch UNC defeat Wilt Chamberlain and Kansas.

"They were renting TV sets for hospitals (in North Carolina)," Chesley told the *Greensboro Daily News*. "It was the damnedest thing you ever heard of.

"I knew right then and there that ACC basketball could be as popular as any TV show that was shown in North Carolina. We didn't know how it had gone over back here in North Carolina. The game started so late in the East that we wondered if anyone had stayed up to watch it.

"The next day (Sunday) we found out that almost everybody had stayed up. We got letters from fans thanking us for two years after about that one game against Kansas."

Chesley's stroke of genius, and his incredible luck in televising two remarkable games, led to the formation of the C.D. Chesley Network and ultimately to a package of regionally televised ACC games for the 1958 season.

In May of '57, Chesley sold the ACC on the idea of televising 12 league games on stations from Maryland to South Carolina. The eight member schools decided to divide all receipts from broadcasts rights.

Chesley then drove his Ford station wagon throughout North Carolina, Virginia, Maryland and South Carolina seeking TV stations to carry the games. Twenty stations liked the idea, but only if Chesley was able to find sponsors for the telecasts.

Chesley enlisted the help of Duke's Cameron, as well as coaches Case and McGuire, who spoke at several promotional luncheons on behalf of the proposed TV package.

"I have a feeling it might help college athletics in the long run," Cameron said. "I may be wrong. Time will tell. But it helps the public to know our athletes and to see what we've got to offer. I'd rather for the fans to be watching an ACC contest than Mickey Mouse or some cowboy show."

Pilot Life Insurance Co. was the first advertiser to support Chesley's project. When Chesley had trouble selling out the first year of telecasts, Pilot Life bought six minutes of advertising—half the commerical allotment—for all 12 games. (ACC fans have been sailing with the Pilot through league telecasts ever since.)

Soon Chesley and his network became fixtures in the ACC.

"I think he was very proud that he made ACC basketball," Ruth Chesley said upon her late husband's induction into the North Carolina Sports Hall of Fame in 1987. "He knew he made the ACC what it is today."

Chesley ran the company out of his home in Linville, N.C., although an associate and a secretary worked out of Philadelphia. Chesley rented equipment for the telecasts and hired all personnel on a part-time basis. Yet what appeared to be a small-time operation gained the utmost respect from the ACC.

"Chez was always above board," said Skeeter Francis, the long-time public relations director for the ACC. "He was straightforward. He knew the technical side and he produced. When his check was due in the league office, it was there."

"Make a mistake and he would tell you," said Frank Slingland, who produced ACC games for 22 years and later became the producer of *NBC Nightly News*. "I remember a game when I missed a couple of inbounds plays because I'd cut away to the cheerleaders or something. Chez didn't like it. 'Knock it off,' he told me. He was right, of course."

Chesley was the product of a prep school background in the Washington, D.C., area. After leaving UNC, he graduated from the University of Pennsylvania and attended the prestigious Wharton School of Business and Finance at Penn. He served as an intelligence officer during World War II, then as an assistant athletic director at Penn before going into TV.

In his second year of televising ACC games, Chesley was stricken with throat cancer and underwent surgical removal of part of his voice box. Despite the surgery, Chesley learned to talk again, using esophageal speech. He often visited patients with similar problems and taught them how to speak. People who have such an operation are not supposed to be able to swim or whistle, but Chesley learned to do both.

That same kind of determination carried over to his work. Chesley's motto from the outset was, "Do it right, or don't do it." He insisted that ACC telecasts be of the same quality—or better—as national network productions.

From the outset, Chesley hired quality announcers. Jim Simpson of NBC was the first play-by-play announcer, and he was joined in the booth by Charlie Harville. Chesley also employed such announcers as former Duke standout Jeff Mullins, former ACC coaches McKinney and Bobby Roberts, and Woody Durham. Later, the team of play-by-play man Jim Thacker and color commentator Billy Packer was a staple on ACC broadcasts into the '80s.

Chesley was an innovator. For football telecasts, he had a member of the TV crew stand on the sideline and wave an orange hat to the officials when a timeout was needed for a commercial. He was the first to have two cameras located at midcourt in basketball and the first to have a camera on the floor, beneath a basket. He once experimented with a wireless microphone on a basketball official during a telecast.

Despite the success of the telecasts in the ACC region, Chesley and the league were always cautious of too much exposure. Chesley's package included only nine games as late as 1964. That was a pittance compared to the 40 games televised by the mid-'80s, but the first national telecast of a college basketball game didn't come until 1968, when UCLA played Houston in the Astrodome.

There was always the prospect of expanding his network to other conferences, but Chesley remained devoted to the ACC.

Chesley once told *The News and Observer* of Raleigh: "Lindsey Nelson, who broadcasts Notre Dame football for me, once said to me that there are four sports events you ought to see before you kick the bucket—the Masters, the Kentucky Derby, a Notre Dame home game and the World Series. Those are all great events. But the atmosphere and the enthusiasm at an ACC Tournament are better than the World Series ever thought about being."

By 1964, Chesley convinced the league to televise the ACC Tournament championship game on the first Saturday night in March. To accommodate the network, the game's tipoff was first moved from 8 p.m. to 9 o'clock, then changed to 8:30. Critics said the ACC was showing its greed for the new TV dollar by changing the game's starting time.

"That's absurd," said Roy Clogston, N.C. State's athletic director and a member of the ACC TV Committee. "The money we get out of it doesn't amount to peanuts. The committee met five times before reaching a decision. We will

ACC BASKETBALL / THE '80s

receive between $7,500 and $8,000 for telecast rights, and after you split this eight ways among our eight members, it means each school will get less than $1,000."

As late as 1969, athletic officials around the league were still concerned that TV games hurt attendance. In December of 1968, only 3,000 fans attended the ill-fated Triangle Classic at State's Reynolds Coliseum, where N.C. State played Navy and Wake Forest played Washington. At the same time, UNC's game against Villanova in the semifinals of New York's Holiday Festival was televised back to North Carolina.

"It's killing us," said State Athletic Director Willis Casey. "I don't know what, if anything, can be done about it, but something must be done to protect regular-scheduled games at our home bases. Otherwise, we are going to hurt ourselves beyond recovery."

While schools scheduled more carefully to avoid conflicts with televised games, video coverage continued to expand.

By 1971, both the ACC Tournament semifinals and championship were televised live, which meant $35,000 in rights fees to the ACC. The league also got $120,000 for the rights to the TV package that included 14 regular-season games. The home team received 40 percent of the per-game rights fee and the other seven league members divided the remaining 60 percent.

The ACC was becoming a special event for fans every Saturday afternoon and Wednesday evening. Bedtimes were extended throughout the ACC area so school children could watch the conclusion of the 9 o'clock games.

Then came the Super Bowl Sunday game of 1973. Again, Chesley's foresight, mixed with a lot of luck, took ACC TV to another level. Chesley proposed to ACC athletic directors the idea of an N.C. State-Maryland game prior to football's Super Bowl. The league liked the idea, and Chesley added a national feed to his 16-station regional network. But even Chesley did not dream that the game would pit two undefeated teams. Maryland ranked No. 2 in the country and State No. 3.

That national TV audience got a taste of ACC basketball in grand style. State Coach Norm Sloan wore bright yellow pants and a black-and-orange checked sport coat just for TV. Wolfpack guard Monte Towe wore a mask to protect a broken nose he suffered in an earlier game. Maryland, of course, had foot-stomping Coach Lefty Driesell.

The game also featured college basketball's best player, State forward David Thompson, who tipped in a missed shot with three seconds remaining to give the Wolfpack an 87-85 victory in College Park, Md.

Fans across the nation saw why ACC basketball was so special.

The following season, 1974, the ACC televised 13 games during the regular season and the entire ACC Tournament for the first time. Athletic directors were a little concerned that four TV games in one day was too much for even the die-hard fans. Once again, ACC fans could not get enough basketball as portable television sets popped up in offices and classrooms from Clemson to College Park.

Several independent TV producers were also watching the furor over college basketball along the Atlantic seaboard. Just as Chesley had the idea to televise a few games each season, independent producers in Atlanta, Washington and Charlotte thought maybe the market could be expanded.

Washington TV station WMAL produced a few Maryland games in the late '70s, and Ted Turner's WTBS experimented with several ACC games on his national cable network in the early '80s. In each instance, the ACC and Chesley played hardball and attempted to keep independent stations from producing games. The league claimed that it did not want the market to be saturated, and that Chesley had exclusive rights to the games.

Enter Rick Ray, Dee Birke and a fledgling company named Raycom Sports.

Prior to the 1979 season, Ray arranged to televise a package of ACC games in North Carolina. The package included all of N.C. State's games in Alaska's Seawolf Classic and seven UNC road games. Ray paid UNC $84,000 for the rights to the Tar Heel games.

"Yes, we were a little nervous," Ray recalled. "That was the biggest debt I'd ever run up. I thought I'd have to work forever to pay it off."

To better promote the telecasts, Ray convinced Alaska officials to change the tournament name to the Great Alaska Shootout, a name it retained as it eventually became one of the nation's top early season tournaments.

Ray was in charge of producing the games that season, and Birke sold the commercials. He previously worked as a station manager for WCCB in Charlotte and she owned Birke Advertising. This was before the two were married, and Ray agreed to pay Dee 10 percent of her gross sales each year.

"The first year, that was just wonderful," she said. "That was only $26,000. The second year he owed me $89,000 and we were married by then. Then we went to where he owed me $130,000, then $900,000."

Ray added: "Now I owe her $14 million dollars. I feel like Ronald Reagan."

In order to sell the first year's telecasts, Dee cut a deal with Gulf Oil to sponsor each game of the package. For $40,000—a 50 percent discount—Gulf got two minutes of advertising on each game. By 1988, the same two minutes would cost Gulf, or anyone else, "millions," according to the Rays.

Following each round of games, the Rays set their alarm for 2 a.m. in Alaska. Advertising for UNC games later in the season needed to be sold. With a six-hour time difference back to the East Coast, that was the only time the Rays could contact potential advertisers.

There were a few other problems with the first live telecasts from Alaska. A control room had to be built on the University of Alaska campus. Color cameras had to be shipped to Anchorage from Seattle, Wash.

Ray also hired an Alaska native to handle the graphics to be displayed on the screen. At game time, Dee discovered that the man had never seen a basketball game and did not know how to type. Dee Ray became Raycom's first graphics technician for one night.

Despite being televised late in the evening to North Carolina, the telecasts from Alaska were very well received. The UNC road games of 1979 got an even better reception. The Tar Heels' game at Maryland drew a 33 rating in North Carolina, making it one of the most viewed TV shows for the entire year in the state.

The Rays were thrilled with the results, even though it was a financial struggle. They put 58,000 miles on their BMW that first season. (The car was still with the company in 1988, with 220,000 miles on it.) Twice the Rays ran out of fuel in their Charlotte home and had to sleep by the fireplace. They ended the 1979 season with every credit card used to the limit and $16.40 in their pockets.

"But, we had $230,000 in receivables," Ray said. "That was

enough to pay all the bills, pay the schools and it gave us a little bit of money to live on and operate on the next year."

Chesley was not as happy about the goings-on.

Late in the '79 season, Ray received a telephone call at home from Chesley.

"Rick, we've worked together for a long time," Ray recalls Chesley saying. "But I want you to know that this ACC is my pie. I own the pie and you can't have a piece of it."

It was too late. Chesley's pie was being divided many ways. For the 1979 season, the ACC granted NBC rights to televise the North Carolina-Arkansas, Maryland-Notre Dame, Duke-Marquette and Louisville-Duke games. The previous season, ABC televised the ACC Tournament championship on *Wide World of Sports*.

Chesley continued to fight for exclusive rights to ACC telecasts. With some concern about overexposure, and perhaps more as a statement of allegiance to Chesley, the ACC granted exclusive rights to the Chesley Network for the 1981 season. The new contract required all ACC schools to get approval from both the league and Chesley before it televised a game on its own.

Although the ACC and Chesley blocked most regional telecasts for the 1981 season, they gave way to national offers. After NBC was outbid by CBS for the rights to future NCAA Tournaments, it assembled a regular-season package of games. NBC met with ACC Commissioner Bob James in New York and agreed to a deal that would pay the ACC $1.35 million for six national and three regional TV appearances by league teams. Chesley, meanwhile, paid the ACC $1 million for 36 regional games.

The ACC's and Chesley's control over the rights did not sit well with independent networks in the region.

"We don't think it was appropriate for them to negotiate an exclusive agreement without opening it to bidding when there's another company in the marketplace with signed contracts (for UNC games)," Ray told the *Greensboro Daily News*.

Finally, Raycom filed an antitrust suit against the ACC and Chesley. According to the suit, the exclusive contract kept a large number of ACC games off TV, and that constituted "warehousing."

Before the suit was brought to court, the ACC opened for bidding the rights to telecasts for the 1982 season. That forced Chesley's retirement. He died a year later at age 69.

"He was one of the pioneers in the telecasting of conference programs and his programs served as a model for many conferences later," James said.

While they retained the utmost respect for Chesley and the quality of telecasts he provided the ACC over the years, the Rays also believed that TV coverage of ACC basketball could be expanded and better marketed.

The ACC took 16 bids for rights to the 1982 package of games. MetroSports of Washington, D.C., was the highest bidder at $3 million and was granted exclusive rights by the ACC. Even though MetroSports turned a $350,000 profit that season, there were problems.

"Chesley was such a legend to follow," Rick Ray says. "MetroSports really had to take all the hard knocks that first year after Chesley. They were the ones who had to raise the advertising rates. Really, it was a blessing that we did not have the highest bid that year."

The following year, Raycom teamed with Jefferson-Pilot Teleproductions of Charlotte to make a bid. The combination presented a strong sales package by the Raycom group, as well as a strong production force by Jefferson-Pilot. Not only did the Raycom/Jefferson-Pilot team offer the ACC $18 million over three years, it also campaigned for the package. When the league athletic directors met at the Holiday Inn Four Seasons in Greensboro, they were greeted by a production truck outside. Signs hung from the truck that read: ACC On The Road With Raycom/Jefferson-Pilot.

After two days of negotiations, Clemson Athletic Director Bill McLellan called the Rays into the meeting of athletic directors.

"Rick, I want you to know that from now on when you get a cut, you can't just bleed Carolina blue," McLellan said to Ray, a UNC graduate. "Now, you've got to bleed eight different colors."

For the 1983 season, Raycom had a nine-man staff and $10 million in billings. By 1987, Raycom had a staff of 45 and approximately $50 million in billings. Along the way, Raycom expanded to include basketball coverage of the Pac-10, Big Eight, Southwest, PCAA and Metro conferences. In football, Raycom handled the SWC, the University of Miami, the Kickoff Classic, Liberty Bowl and the All-American Bowl in '87.

Raycom televised 250 events live in 1988, more than any of the three major networks. The Raycom network included 160 stations, 90 percent of which were affiliated with ABC, NBC or CBS. More than 60 sponsors were included in Raycom's 1988 package of regional telecasts.

The rapid growth and success was not without some setbacks. Raycom offered a package of pay TV games during the 1984 season. Although the games were offered in addition to the regular package of ACC games, fans balked at the the ill-fated "Season Ticket" idea, and it was scrapped at midseason.

"We just misread the public," Dee says. "We did not do a good job of explaining to the viewers that these were not games coming off the other package. They thought we were holding the ACC hostage."

Aside from the pay TV blunder, the ACC and Raycom/Jefferson-Pilot have had a happy marriage. When their original contract expired following the 1985 season, the two parties agreed on another five-year deal reportedly at a cost of $8 million per year. Following the third season of that contract, ACC Commissioner Gene Corrigan renegotiated a new, six-year agreement between the league and Raycom/Jefferson-Pilot.

ACC basketball has long been considered the plum of regional telecasts in the country. The quality of the league's basketball, as well as a top-rate TV production, a strong network of affiliated stations and the league's history have all played into its success.

"When Rick was training me, he told me the national networks are losing shares and people are going to look more toward regional networks," Dee Ray said. "And that's exactly what's happened. Our ratings in 1987 in basketball were better than ABC's, and nearly the same as NBC's."

•

Rick and Dee Ray each drive shiny new Mercedes throughout the ACC. In addition to their home in Charlotte, they have an East Side condo in New York City and a beach home on Hilton Head Island, S.C.

Their goal is to make Raycom Sports Inc. a $100 million business by 1990.

"Could you ever imagine anything like this when you took off for Alaska 10 years ago?" they were asked.

"You do envision these things," Dee Ray said. "Otherwise, they wouldn't come true."

ACC BASKETBALL / THE '80s

'80

As the ACC entered a fourth decade, it continued to claim superiority over all of college basketball. Two national championships, several teams annually ranked among the nation's best and perhaps the most fanatical following of fans backed the boast.

There were skeptics, however.

"As a group, our little teams in the Pac-8 year in and year out would kick the ACC's rear end," said Southern California Coach Bob Boyd.

Boyd based his challenge on the fact that a Pac-8 Conference representative won the NCAA championship 10 times from 1964 through 1975. Of course, UCLA was that representative on each occasion.

"The ACC hasn't helped itself in the postseason tournament play," UCLA Coach John Wooden told the *Greensboro Daily News*. "The schools have been engrossed in building up their own conference from within and self-publicizing themselves. It hasn't made them the best in the competition that counts—the NCAA."

What hurt the ACC most in NCAA Tournament play was probably the same thing that helped it most in creating competitive balance and fan interest: The ACC Tournament. Ten times in the league's first 26 years, the regular season winner—and presumably the best team—failed to win the ACC Tournament and qualify for the NCAA Tournament.

Of the 16 teams that won the regular season and survived the ACC Tournament, three were on probation (N.C. State in 1955, 1959 and 1973) and unable to compete in the NCAA Tournament. Of the remaining 13 ACC champions, 12 advanced to the semifinals of the NCAAs by winning a regional tournament. The only team among that group that did not reach the NCAA semifinals was N.C. State, which lost a four-overtime decision to Canisius in the 1956 NCAAs.

In its favor, the ACC also had an impressive decade in the '70s. North Carolina won the NIT championship in 1971 and Maryland did the same in 1972 when that title carried some prestige. N.C. State went unbeaten in 1973 but was ineligible for postseason play because of NCAA probation. The Wolfpack came back the following season to win the NCAA championship. UNC lost the NCAA championship game to Marquette in 1977, and Duke lost to Kentucky in the 1978 NCAA final.

Black Sunday, that dreadful day (to ACC fans) in 1979 when Duke and UNC lost East Regional Tournament games in Raleigh, was long forgotten by mid-January of 1980. By then, five of the nation's Top 20 teams were from the ACC. No fewer than six ACC teams were ranked in the Top 20 at some point during the 1980 season.

Those six schools each won at least 20 games, and all six were invited to postseason tournaments. Virginia won the NIT, while Duke and Clemson advanced to NCAA Regional Tournament finals before losing.

There were two welcome arrivals to the ACC to open the '80s, and by season's end there were two departures. Georgia Tech officially entered the league as its eighth member, essentially replacing South Carolina, which had dropped from the league in 1972. Meanwhile, Virginia welcomed 7-foot-4 center Ralph Sampson, probably the most sought-after prep player since Moses Malone in 1974. The departures were Coach Norm Sloan, who left N.C. State for Florida, and Coach Bill Foster, who left Duke for South Carolina.

Globetrotters, ACC Style

Several players have gone from the ACC to the Harlem Globetrotters and one has even gone from the Globetrotters to the ACC. Clyde "The Glide" Austin (C) and Kendal "Tiny" Pinder (R) joined the Globetrotters after their careers at N.C. State and dribbled and clowned their way around the world with the likes of Twiggy Sanders (L). Austin, a starter for four years at State from 1977-1980, was still a member of the Globetrotters in 1988. Jimmy Hebron (inset), an assistant coach with Bobby Cremins at Georgia Tech since 1982, played from 1974-76 for the Washington Generals, the team that travels with the Globetrotters and serves as their laugh-a-minute punching bag. Hebron's job was to guard Curly Neal, the Globetrotters' famous ball handler. "We played 280 games a year against them, so if you didn't get along with the person you guarded, you could have problems," Hebron says. "Curly Neal was really good people. We got along fine."

217

ACC BASKETBALL / THE '80s

Georgia Tech experienced the kind of problems any newcomer to a powerful league would expect. The Yellow Jackets were short-handed and outmanned. They won only eight of 26 games under Coach Dwane Morrison, whom ACC fans remembered as an interim coach at South Carolina for part of the 1964 season. Although short on talent, Morrison's team hardly proved to be a pushover. It employed a slowdown style of play designed to shorten the length of the game.

"It's like in football," Morrison said. "You have to establish the ground game. It's three yards and a cloud of dust, unless you're on Astroturf. Then it's three yards and a burnt elbow."

The Yellow Jackets' deliberate style drove ACC opponents and fans crazy. It helped Tech take ninth-ranked UNC to the wire in Greensboro before losing 54-53 when Lenny Horton's 3-footer rimmed out at the buzzer. Later, in Atlanta, the Yellow Jackets stunned 18th-ranked Virginia 62-61 when Brook Steppe made two free throws with eight seconds remaining.

Virginia lost despite getting 29 points and six rebounds from Sampson, who by then was being touted as the next Lew Alcindor. Sampson ended an intense recruiting battle on May 31, 1979, when he announced at his Harrisonburg (Va.) High School gymnasium that he would attend Virginia, choosing the Cavaliers over Virginia Tech, North Carolina and Kentucky.

Sampson made an immediate impact on the Virginia program. Even before he played a game, the Cavaliers had catapulted into most Top 20 polls. But just as Sampson experienced growing pains as a player, so did Virginia as a team. The Cavaliers were brilliant at times, defeating Duke twice and North Carolina once. At other times, Virginia was merely mortal. The Cavaliers not only lost to Georgia Tech, but also dropped a decision to San Jose State.

The pressures of playing under a microscope apparently caught up to Virginia by season's end. After struggling to a late-season win over William & Mary, Coach Terry Holland announced that he and his players would not talk to the media for the remainder of the regular season. That period included a loss to Maryland, then a defeat at the hands of Clemson in the first round of the ACC Tournament.

Virginia regrouped to win the NIT with victories over Lafayette 67-56, Boston College 57-55, Michigan 78-69, Nevada-Las Vegas 90-71 and Minnesota 58-55. Sampson led the championship win with 15 points and 15 rebounds against a Minnesota team that featured 7-foot Randy Breuer and 6-10 Kevin McHale. Sampson scored 96 points in the five tournament games, had 69 rebounds and 26 blocked shots as he became the first freshman MVP in the NIT's 43-year history.

While Sampson was just making his presence known in the ACC, coaches Sloan and Foster were seeking new horizons. Despite a 20-8 record, it was a tumultuous year for Sloan and the Wolfpack, which lost four straight ACC games at midseason to drop out of the race. State fell to Duke in the first round of the ACC Tournament and then lost to Iowa in the opening round of the NCAA Tournament.

Much of the N.C. State season was spent answering questions about the two cars owned by star guard Clyde "The Glide" Austin. *The News and Observer* of Raleigh reported that two cars, a 1980 Cadillac sedan and a 1976 MG, were registered in Austin's name. Austin said his fiancee was making payments on the Cadillac and a friend from his hometown of Richmond, Va., was making payments on the MG. The ACC investigated Austin's situation, and he was eventually cleared of any wrongdoing.

When all questions were answered concerning Austin's situation, Sloan began fielding queries about his possible move to Florida. Sloan said years later that the shadow of Coach Dean Smith and his success at North Carolina proved too much for him at State.

"If you're in a beauty contest, you want to win," Sloan said. "But when the same contestant always wins, it's time to find a new contest."

Sloan announced his decision immediately following the regular season.

Foster waited a week longer—the day following his Blue Devils' ACC Tournament championship victory over Maryland—to announce his move from Duke to South Carolina. The change had been rumored since mid-February but denied by Foster until the announcement.

Foster left Duke in a blaze of glory. The Blue Devils were ranked No. 1 in the preseason and lived up to that billing with titles in the Big Four, Industrial and Iron Duke tourna-

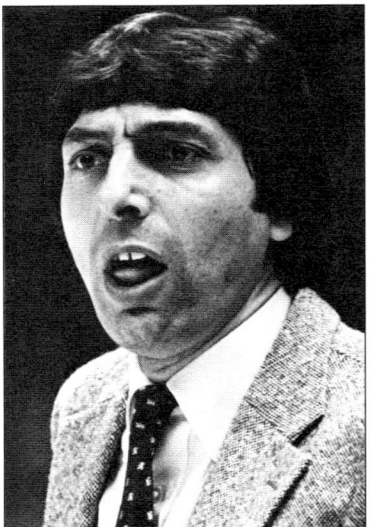

Bill Foster (top left) and Norm Sloan (top right) departed the ACC following the 1980 season, Foster leaving Duke for South Carolina and Sloan departing N.C. State for Florida. Mike Krzyzewski (bottom left) became the new coach at Duke, Jim Valvano the new man at State.

ACC BASKETBALL / THE '80s

ments. A 12-0 start kept Duke atop the national rankings until Clemson registered perhaps the biggest victory in the school's history. The Tigers defeated the Blue Devils 87-82 in an overtime game that was watched by a Littlejohn Coliseum crowd of 13,500.

The loss sent Duke into a tailspin in which it dropped eight of 15 games to close the regular season. The Blue Devils did survive an overtime game against Clemson in the home finale of center Mike Gminski, who had his uniform No. 43 retired before he scored 29 points and had 19 rebounds.

Prior to Gminski's farewell speech in Cameron Indoor Stadium, teammate Gene Banks grabbed the microphone and announced that he, too, was leaving. Banks told the crowd he would forego his senior season to play professional basketball. One week later, Banks changed his mind and decided to stay for another season at Duke.

With Banks, Gminski and Kenny Dennard on top of their games, the Blue Devils charged past State 68-62 and UNC 75-61 to reach the ACC Tournament championship game. Maryland, which was top-seeded after losing only three conference games during the regular season, defeated Georgia Tech 51-49 in overtime and Clemson 91-85 to reach the title game.

In Buck Williams, Albert King and Ernest Graham, Maryland had assembled one of the league's best front lines to counter the Banks-Gminski-Dennard trio. The championship was an epic struggle in which the two teams missed just 14 shots combined in the second half. Only 10,392 fans braved a blizzard to watch the game at the Greensboro Coliseum. They saw Duke miss four shots in the second half, three of which were tipped back in, including one by Gminski with eight seconds remaining.

Gminski's tip gave Duke a 73-72 lead before King missed a hurried 20-foot shot, and Williams was unable to control the rebound as the basketball hung delicately on the rim for a split second. Williams was taken out of the play on a body block by Duke's Dennard that went unnoticed by the officials.

Despite his missed last shot, King was named the Everett Case Award winner after he scored 16, 38 and 27 points in the three Tournament games.

With the NCAA Tournament field expanded to 48 teams and the limit on the number of representatives from any conference dropped, the ACC was extended five invitations. A testimony to the ACC's strength was the fact that all five teams were seeded sixth or higher in their respective regions.

UNC was the first to be eliminated. The Tar Heels were third-seeded in the Midwest but fell to Texas A&M in two overtimes, 78-61. Although UNC won 11 of 15 games after freshman forward James Worthy was lost with two broken bones above his right ankle in a January game against Maryland, the Tar Heels were never quite the same team without their leading rebounder and top inside scorer.

Maryland, second-seeded in the East, defeated Tennessee 86-75 before bowing out to Georgetown, 74-68. With N.C. State, seeded fourth in the East and already eliminated by Iowa 77-64, only Clemson and Duke were left.

Clemson enjoyed one of its finest seasons and was seeded sixth in the West Regional. The Tigers, behind Larry Nance, defeated Utah State 76-73, Brigham Young 71-66, and Lamar 74-66 before losing to UCLA in the West Regional championship, 85-74.

Duke, seeded fourth in the Mideast, defeated Penn 52-42, then stunned Kentucky on its home court in Lexington. Banks' free throw with 22 seconds remaining gave the Blue Devils a 55-54 lead and the win as Kyle Macy's jump shot with three seconds left bounced off the rim.

Duke was not so fortunate two nights later as Joe Barry Carroll and Purdue dealt the Blue Devils a 68-60 defeat. Following the loss, Gminski and Foster bid adieu to the Duke team.

"Most of it shouldn't be in the newspapers, but what he said touched us very much," Banks said. "I'm sure we'll get a good coach, but he'll never be another Coach Foster."

Long before Foster's official announcement that he was leaving, Duke Athletic Director Tom Butters began a search for a new coach. He wanted the best coach in the country, so he called Indiana's Bob Knight and made an offer. Some 10 years earlier, Knight had been offered the head coaching position at Maryland. Knight accepted that offer, then changed his mind within 24 hours and remained at Army. When Butters called, Knight said he was not interested in going to Duke, but he recommended a 33-year-old coach at Army named Mike Krzyzewski.

Three days following Duke's NCAA loss to Purdue, Krzyzewski was named head coach of the Blue Devils. He was the least known of the three other final candidates for the position: Bob Weltlich of Mississippi, Paul Webb of Old Dominion and Bob Wenzel, an assistant under Foster at Duke. But Krzyzewski was the one most sought by Butters.

"I met with Mike and just couldn't get him out of my mind," Butters said.

Down the road in Raleigh, N.C. State first offered its coaching position to Morgan Wootten, the famed coach at DeMatha High School in Washington, D.C. But when Wootten turned down a lucrative, five-year offer, State Athletic Director Willis Casey turned to 34-year-old Jim Valvano of Iona (N.Y.) College.

"I made a ridiculous statement when I went to North Carolina State that basketball isn't a life or death thing," Valvano said later, "but I found out different. It's worse."

Albert King won the '80 ACC Tournament MVP award, but the championship trophy went to Duke in a thriller.

Talent, charisma equal fresh Air Jordan.

By his fourth season in the National Basketball Association, Michael Jordan was the highest-paid team sport athlete in the world. His contract with the Chicago Bulls was worth between $4 million and $7 million, which represented less than 20 percent of Jordan's net worth.

He owned the Nike Air Jordan line of shoes and clothing. He was paid handsomely for endorsing Chevrolet, Coca-Cola, McDonald's, MacGregor NBA products, hair and skin care from Johnson, Wilson basketballs and his own line of watches.

The '80s

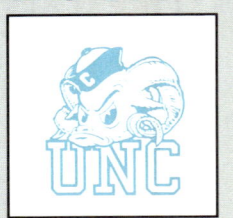

North Carolina

"He's just the most marketable athlete in the United States, if not the world," said David Brenner, the Bulls' promotion manager. "He has that combination of talent, excitement and flair on the court, and charisma off the court."

An all-star in each of his first four NBA seasons who became the highest-scoring guard in pro history in 1987 by averaging more than 37 points a game, Michael Jordan was arguably the best basketball player in the world just seven years after not being sure he could play in the ACC.

"I didn't know I could play big-time basketball," says Jordan when asked about scholarship offers from North Carolina and South Carolina during his senior year of high school. "I was getting an opportunity to play Division I basketball. Nobody from Wilmington, North Carolina, gets that kind of opportunity.

"I didn't want to pass it up, but a lot of people back home wanted me to pass it up. They wanted me to go to a school where they felt I could play, like UNC-Wilmington or Appalachian State. My (high school) principal wanted me to go to the Air Force Academy so I would have a job after I got out."

Jordan had good reason not to believe in his game. He was cut from his junior high school team, then did not make the varsity as a sophomore at Wilmington Laney High School. As a junior, Jordan still did not attract much attention from college recruiters.

Exercising his "Cedric Maxwell Rule," whereby any and every prospect in North Carolina deserves at least one look, UNC Coach Dean Smith sent Assistant Bill Guthridge to scout Jordan. Guthridge was the only ACC coach to see him as a junior, thereby assuring that UNC would not overlook Jordan as the Tar Heels did Maxwell, who went from Kinston, N.C., to UNC-Charlotte en route to the NBA.

Then Smith visited the Jordan family.

"He didn't talk basketball first," Jordan said. "He talked academics. I was sitting there with a basketball in my hand during the whole conversation. I finally put the ball down and I listened, and my parents really got involved. Finally, he started talking basketball, I picked the ball back up and started moving it around."

Even then, Smith was not convinced that Jordan would be an outstanding college basketball player, or at least not the star he was to become. But Wilmington Laney Coach Pop Herring was convinced.

"Dean Smith will win his first national championship during Michael's four years," Herring said when Jordan announced he was going to UNC.

Jordan was not so confident in his abilities.

"Going into my freshman year, I thought I just wanted to play a couple of minutes and get more minutes the next year and just increase those minutes each year," Jordan says. "I was geared up for coming off the bench and just contributing. That's all I wanted to do."

Jordan was slowed in practice prior to his freshman season by a broken blood vessel in his hand. He missed two weeks of practice, putting him further behind fundamentally than junior guard Jimmy Braddock. But when Smith wrote the Tar Heels' starting lineup on the locker room chalkboard at the Charlotte Coliseum prior to UNC's 1982 season-opener against Kansas, "Jordan" was the fifth name listed.

"I was nervous, I didn't know what to say," Jordan says of being in the same group with Phil Ford, Mike O'Koren and James Worthy as the only freshmen—at that time—to start for Smith in their first varsity game. "I never really thought I could do it."

Jordan scored UNC's first basket against Kansas. He also scored the Tar Heels' final basket of the 1982 season, an 18-footer with 17 seconds remaining to give UNC a 63-62 victory over Georgetown and the national championship.

"He was calm as ever," Jordan said of Smith's setting up the game-winning shot during a timeout. "He said Georgetown was ignoring me because I was the youngest guy out there. Georgetown really didn't think the ball would come to me at all. I didn't think so, either, until Coach Smith said, 'If the inside game is not there, swing it around to Michael's side. Either he will have the shot or he can penetrate.'

"I'm saying to myself, 'My goodness, either you're the hero or the goat.' When I broke the huddle, I just took a deep breath."

As Jordan headed back to the playing floor, Smith said, "Knock it in, Michael."

"When the ball swung back to me, I didn't think," Jordan said. "I felt I was open, squared up to the basket, followed through and it felt good. I closed my eyes. I did not see it go in. My initial reaction was to follow the shot, so I took a step to follow the shot, then I saw it go in."

Riding on the bus to the Louisiana Superdome, Jordan envisioned himself making the shot to win the national championship. "But I never really thought it would come true," he said.

Immediately following the game, Jordan's father, James, was pretending to kick an object down the hallway outside the UNC locker room. "It's the monkey off Coach Smith's back," he said.

Despite giving Smith his first national title, and UNC its first since 1957, Jordan was still a little dumbfounded by the

ACC BASKETBALL / THE '80s

"Knock it in, Michael," Dean Smith told his cool freshman, who did just that, giving UNC its 1982 NCAA championship.

whole experience. He sat in the UNC locker room with his father and watched as teammates James Worthy, Sam Perkins, Matt Doherty and Jimmy Black celebrated wildly.

"I didn't know what was going on," Jordan said. "I was sitting there thinking there was another game afterward. I was that naive about it. I didn't really know what a national championship meant to a college team."

Jordan also didn't fathom what the game-winning shot would mean to him.

"That moment started my career," Jordan said. "That gave me confidence to work and be something special. It gave me confidence to know that I could play that game. When I came back my sophomore year, I was ready to play."

Jordan grew two inches to 6-foot-6 and gained 15 pounds to 196 during the summer before his sophomore season. Smith said he was quicker, could jump higher and was a smarter player.

"That's when I said, 'Hey, we've got a great player here,'" Smith said.

Although he was the ACC Rookie of the Year in '82, it wasn't until his junior season that Jordan exploded into the national spotlight. He was a unanimous All-ACC selection in '83 and '84 and was the league's Player of the Year as a junior, winning in a landslide (113 votes to 15 for teammate Perkins). He was second in the ACC in scoring (20.0 average) as a sophomore and topped the league (19.6 average) as a junior when he was also national Player of the Year.

More than putting numbers on the board, Jordan brought a special charisma to the game that had not been seen at UNC since the days of Charlie Scott. His trademark was a tongue that would curl out the side of his mouth when he shot.

"It takes a special kid to have that kind of talent, plus that type of enthusiasm," said Georgia Tech Coach Bobby Cremins. "You don't find that combination very often. Magic Johnson has it . . . You watch Michael play defense. How many kids of that caliber play defense like he does?"

Jordan also had a flair for the dramatic that even he couldn't explain.

"I really don't like to be put in a situation where you win or lose a ball game because there is always the chance you might lose," Jordan said. "It's just that everything has turned my way. Everything is coming up roses."

During the 1983 season, Tulane led UNC by two points and had the ball with four seconds remaining. But two Tulane players collided on the inbounds pass and the ball bounced free. Jordan grabbed it with his back to the basket, spun and threw in a 24-footer that tied the game. The Tar Heels won in triple overtime.

That same season, Maryland's Chuck Driesell was going for an unguarded layup at the buzzer that would have won the game when Jordan, charging from the top of the key, swatted the ball out of bounds to preserve the victory.

Later that season, Jordan's steal in the backcourt and dunk capped an incredible 11-point rally in the final four minutes of UNC's victory over Virginia at Carmichael Auditorium.

Jordan's play was instrumental in UNC's finishing in at least a tie for first place in the ACC regular-season race three straight seasons. The Tar Heels were 88-13 during Jordan's career, including a 43-6 mark against ACC teams.

Following his junior season, Smith recommended that Jordan turn pro. The Chicago Bulls drafted him after Houston and Portland had selected 7-footers Akeem Olajuwon of Houston and Sam Bowie of Kentucky, respectively. Before signing with the Bulls, Jordan was the leading scorer as the U.S. Olympic team captured a gold medal in Los Angeles.

Even though he found fame and fortune in the NBA, Jordan remains uncomfortable with life in the fast lane. He does not drink or smoke and campaigns against drug use.

Jordan wears a pair of gray UNC shorts under his Bulls uniform during games to remind him of his roots. During the off-season, he treasures the time he can sit on a Franklin Street bench in Chapel Hill, where his game-winning shot against Georgetown in 1982 seems to grow in importance with each passing ACC season. ∎

ACC BASKETBALL / THE '80s

'81

New coaches Jim Valvano at N.C. State and Mike Krzyzewski at Duke found the going tough in their first ACC seasons. State finished 14-13 but managed only four wins against league competition. The Wolfpack did capture the Holiday Festival championship at New York's Madison Square Garden in a homecoming for Valvano.

Duke, meanwhile, finished 17-13 and fared better in the ACC with a 6-8 record. The highlight of Duke's season was an emotional farewell to seniors Gene Banks and Kenny Dennard in their home finale at Cameron Indoor Stadium. Banks first passed out roses to the crowd prior to the game, then sank a miracle turnaround jump shot from 18 feet to tie the game at the end of regulation. His basket with 12 seconds remaining in overtime gave the Blue Devils a 66-65 victory over North Carolina.

Banks then broke his wrist in Duke's first-round, 79-69 NIT victory over North Carolina A&T. The Blue Devils defeated Alabama 75-70 without Banks but were eliminated by Purdue in the third round, 81-69.

While Krzyzewski and Valvano were getting their feet wet in the ACC, Dean Smith at UNC and Terry Holland at Virginia had firmly established their programs as the best in the league and among the best in the nation. The matchups of those two basketball giants proved to be the focal point of the 1981 ACC season.

By the time of the first meeting on Jan. 10 in Charlottesville, Virginia was third-ranked, unbeaten through 10 games and had extended its two-year win streak to 15 games. Center Ralph Sampson was getting ample help inside from teammates Lee Raker and Craig Robinson, while the Cavaliers' backcourt of Jeff Lamp, Jeff Jones and Othell Wilson was the best in the league.

UNC, meanwhile, was ranked 16th. The Tar Heels had won the Great Alaska Shootout and defeated eventual national-champion Indiana 65-56 in Chapel Hill, despite playing without freshman forward Matt Doherty. But UNC had also lost the Big Four championship to Wake Forest, 82-71, and the Winston Tire Holiday Classic title game to Minnesota, 76-60, in Los Angeles. A 56-55 setback at the hands of Kansas dropped the Tar Heels further in the national rankings.

The presence of freshman center Sam Perkins, along with James Worthy and Al Wood, gave UNC a formidable front line.

For 30 minutes, Virginia attempted to pound the ball inside to Sampson despite UNC's matchup-zone defense to prevent such tactics. As a result, the Tar Heels led 47-36, and Virginia's streak appeared to be at an end. But Virginia changed gears over the final 10 minutes, virtually ignored Sampson on offense and began shooting from the outside.

The Cavaliers made 11 of their final 12 shots from the field. The one shot Virginia missed during that stretch, Sampson was there to tap the ball in as the Cavaliers scored on each of their final 14 possessions. That tap of a Raker miss with 3:04 remaining gave Virginia a 52-51 lead, its first since 2-0.

Sampson then sealed the victory with an 8-footer from the baseline and two free throws for a 56-51 Virginia lead.

UNC had led 49-44 with 8:29 remaining when UNC's Smith ordered his team into the Four Corners offense. The strategy backfired when UNC committed several turnovers and went cold shooting from the floor.

"That was a good offense when Phil Ford was there," Sampson said.

The regular-season rematch was on Feb. 3 in Chapel Hill. By then, Virginia was still unbeaten through 18 games, had run its winning streak over two seasons to 23 and was the nation's No. 1-ranked team. UNC had won six straight games since the loss to Virginia and was 16-4.

For the second time in three weeks, Virginia made a miracle comeback to win. The Cavaliers came from 16 points down in the second half to force overtime, then escaped Carmichael Auditorium with an 80-79 victory in a game that ended with a shoving match between the two teams.

"A couple of times I thought they could have blown us out," said Lamp. "But this team just doesn't want to lose."

Said UNC's Wood, "I've seen this old movie and I hate it."

The Virginia victory brought order to the ACC standings as the Cavaliers walked away with their only first-place finish in league history. But Virginia had not seen the last of UNC; the two teams were to meet again in the NCAA Final Four in Philadelphia.

Prior to that meeting, Virginia extended its winning streak to 23 games on the season and 28 over two seasons. Notre Dame brought it to a halt with a 57-56 victory over the Cavaliers in Chicago. Virginia then lost a chance to go unbeaten in the ACC when it dropped a 73-66 overtime decision at Wake Forest, a team that earlier that season had won the Big Four championship over UNC.

Virginia lost to Maryland in the semifinals of the ACC Tournament when the 20th-ranked Terps exploded for an 85-62 victory. UNC, meanwhile, reached the championship game with victories over N.C. State, 69-54, and Wake Forest, 58-57. When UNC defeated Maryland 61-60 for the championship, it marked the Tar Heels' ninth ACC title as Maryland lost the championship game for the fifth time in 10 years.

The ACC season was played with a different system for officials. For the first time, three officials were used in all league games. Also, two Southwest Conference officials were employed for all weekend ACC games as part of a tradeoff with the SWC.

The use of three officials was generally considered a sound move by league coaches. On the other hand, the tradeoff of officials for weekend games was considered unnecessary and costly. ACC schools were paying approximately $1,250 for each SWC official because of added travel expenses, compared to only about $250 for an ACC ref.

Timo! Timo!
North Carolina fans took a liking to a 6-10 center from Finland named Timo Makkonen from 1981-85 and would shout for his entry into the late stages of UNC routs. Makkonen was the ultimate human victory cigar: UNC won all 41 games in which he played.

Part of the thinking in using outside officials for some ACC games was to give teams a look at different styles of officiating. Thus, ACC teams would be better prepared for postseason play.

Four ACC teams were invited to the NCAA Tournament and another two went to the NIT. Duke, which bowed out in the third round, and Clemson represented the ACC in the NIT. The Tigers had a second straight 20-win season, including a 58-57 victory over Indiana early in the season. But they fell to Temple, 90-82, in the opening round of the NIT.

Maryland defeated Tennessee-Chattanooga, then was soundly whipped by Indiana 99-64 in the NCAA Tournament. Wake Forest lost its first game, 67-64 to Boston College.

That left Virginia and UNC. The Cavaliers were the top-seeded team in the East Regional and rolled past Villanova 54-50, Tennessee 62-48, and Brigham Young 74-60 to reach the Final Four. UNC was second-seeded in the West and reached the NCAA semifinals with victories over Pittsburgh 74-57, Utah 61-56, and Kansas State 81-68.

Only in 1976, when Indiana and Michigan met for the national championship, had one conference sent two representatives to the Final Four. This time, Virginia and UNC were matched in one bracket while Indiana and LSU were paired in the other.

No one figured UNC's Wood would have one of the most spectacular games in NCAA Tournament history. At least five Virginia players attempted to slow Wood, but he made 14 of 19 field goals and 11 of 13 free throws. His 39 points broke by one the NCAA semifinal record set by West Virginia's Jerry West in 1959 as UNC took a 78-65 win.

"We got beat by a great player having a great day," Holland said.

Over one 10:30 stretch of the second half, Wood outscored Virginia 22-21 as UNC went from a 39-37 lead to a 74-58 advantage. While Wood was dominating on one end of the court, Perkins was closing out Sampson in every way possible on the other. Perkins' defense prevented Sampson from getting the ball in scoring position, and the Virginia center managed only 11 points.

"They can have those two regular-season wins. We'll take this one," said Wood, who would lead UNC into its fifth national title game. The Tar Heels won it in 1957 and took second in '46, '68 and '77.

The championship was nearly postponed when President Ronald Reagan was shot the afternoon of the game by John Hinckley. NCAA and network TV officials debated until just before game time whether to play the game as scheduled, but when word arrived that Reagan would survive the shooting, postponement was deemed unnecessary.

UNC and Indiana battled on even terms for 20 minutes with the Hoosiers taking their first lead just before halftime, 27-26. But Indiana picked up its man-to-man pressure early in the second half, bolted to a 39-30 lead and never looked back en route to a 63-50 victory and the championship.

Indiana outscored UNC 36-24 in a second half in which Wood and Perkins were limited to five field goals and five rebounds between them by the Hoosiers' Jim Thomas and Landon Turner. Indiana's Ray Tolbert held Worthy to three field goals before the UNC forward fouled out with 5:07 to play. In the backcourt, Indiana's Isiah Thomas made seven of 10 field goal attempts in the second half and finished with a game-high 23 points, 11 more than UNC got from its backcourt.

"They just hound you," Worthy said of Indiana. "I haven't seen a man-to-man defense like that all season."

Al Wood, UNC's smooth, sharp-shooting forward, led the Tar Heels to the '81 Final Four and then into the title game with a 39-point performance against Virginia.

ACC BASKETBALL / THE '80s

'82

James Worthy was back in 1982 to help UNC take another crack at winning the national championship. So was Sam Perkins, as well as Matt Doherty and Jimmy Black. With the addition of hotshot freshman Michael Jordan of Wilmington, N.C., the Tar Heels were tabbed as the nation's top team in the preseason. Virginia, with Ralph Sampson and most of his supporting cast returning, was ranked third in most polls.

The Tar Heels wasted no time jumping into the fire of stiff competition with a meeting against No. 2-ranked Kentucky in the sixth game of the season. Worthy scored 26 to lead UNC to an 82-69 victory in East Rutherford, N.J.

With Kentucky out of the way, the focus of the league's attention once again was on the monumental matchups between UNC and Virginia. The Cavaliers ripped off 12 straight wins, including a 63-61 decision over Brigham Young in the annual Tip-Off Classic in Springfield, Mass., and an 87-54 rout of Notre Dame.

There was other news around the league, though. Georgia Tech was playing its first season under Coach Bobby Cremins. Dwane Morrison resigned prior to the ACC Tournament in 1981 with one year remaining on his contract. Morrison's undoing was a 4-23 season in '81, a year in which the Yellow Jackets became the first team since Clemson in 1954 and 1955 to go winless within the league.

"He's one of the best basketball coaches in the country as far as teaching fundamentals," Georgia Tech guard Brook Steppe said of Morrison. "But we don't have a whole lot of talent. That's a handicap, but that's where recruiting fits in."

Enter Cremins, a master recruiter in six years at Appalachian State. At age 33, Cremins immediately injected enthusiasm into a program that had hit rock bottom. All Cremins asked was for Georgia Tech fans to be patient; they had to be as Tech went 10-16 in 1982.

The patience of Duke fans was also tested as the Blue Devils suffered through a 10-17 season, their poorest in 55 years. Clemson also slipped to 14-14 after eight straight winning seasons. Meanwhile, Maryland used a slowdown attack to salvage a 16-13 season, and N.C. State climbed to 22-10.

Wake Forest surged to 21-9 and finished third in the ACC with a 9-5 record. For the first time, the Demon Deacons played all their home conference games at the 15,700-seat Greensboro Coliseum. Wake Forest had long sought an alternative to playing in 8,200-seat Winston-Salem Memorial Coliseum, which had become a drafty eyesore.

"It will make our basketball program more regionally oriented to the Triad," said Wake Forest Athletic Director Gene Hooks of the Greensboro-High Point-Winston-Salem area. "This is a calculated gamble on our part, but we feel we need to give this thing a try."

The Deacons made their biggest mark, however, on the road in Chapel Hill, ruining UNC's unbeaten record and No. 1 ranking with a 55-48 victory at Carmichael Auditorium. Jim Johnstone led the way for Wake Forest with 16 points and 10 rebounds against a UNC club that played without Perkins, who was sidelined with a virus.

Perkins had been at full strength 12 days earlier when UNC, unbeaten through 10 games and top-ranked nationally, squared off against No. 2 Virginia, also unbeaten through 12 games. The Tar Heels beat Virginia 65-60 for the second straight time, but Perkins, Worthy, Doherty, Jordan and the rest of the Tar Heels could not stop Sampson. The Virginia center showed why he was the national Player of the Year in 1981 with a 30-point, 19-rebound performance.

The rematch in Charlottesville was three weeks later on Feb. 3. This time, UNC was 16-1 and ranked second, while Virginia was 20-1 and ranked third. The one-man team Virginia took to Chapel Hill had turned into an army by the time the teams met in Charlottesville. Sampson was still the Cavaliers' leader with 18 points and 12 rebounds, but this time he got plenty of help from teammates Othell Wilson (20 points, five assists) and Craig Robinson (14 points) as Virginia blitzed UNC 74-58.

"Tonight everybody contributed," Sampson said. "Everybody else did their part and I did my part."

With the victory, Virginia was in the driver's seat to claim first place in the regular season. The Cavaliers rolled over five more conference opponents and needed just a victory at Maryland in the regular-season finale to claim sole possession of the top spot for a second straight season.

Maryland stuck to its slowdown attack, stayed within striking distance of Virginia, then got a 12-foot, lean-in jumper from Adrian Branch in overtime to defeat the Cavaliers 47-46. Meanwhile, in Chapel Hill, UNC and Duke waited 70 minutes after a blown circuit caused a power failure early in the Tar Heels' meeting with Duke at Carmichael Auditorium. When play resumed, UNC handled the Blue Devils easily, 84-66.

UNC's win, coupled with Virginia's loss, left the teams in a tie for first place with 12-2 records and facing, in all likelihood, a rubber match in the ACC final.

That matchup became reality after UNC brushed past Georgia Tech 55-39 and N.C. State 58-46, while Virginia survived scares to post wins over Clemson, 56-54, and Wake Forest, 51-49, in overtime. Clemson fell when Horace Wyatt's shot at the buzzer missed. Then Ricky Stokes picked up a loose ball and fired in a 10-foot bank shot as time expired to lift the Cavaliers over Wake Forest.

The first-round game between Maryland and N.C. State proved to be of little significance other than it was one of the worst-played games in the Tournament's history. When the Wolfpack took a 13-11 lead at halftime, the Greensboro Coliseum crowd of 16,034 stood and booed in unison. "I was embarrassed," Maryland guard Jeff Adkins said of N.C. State's 40-28 victory. "I've seen high school practices better than that."

Even though neither team deliberately played a stall game, the low-scoring affair was evidence enough to suggest that ACC basketball needed a shot clock. That became even more obvious when UNC met Virginia for the ACC championship before a national TV audience.

The Tar Heels led 44-43 with 7:30 remaining in a game that was as fast-paced and action-packed as the two previous meetings between the teams. At that point, however, UNC Coach Dean Smith ordered the Tar Heels to play keep away. The plan was to draw Sampson from under the basket. Virginia Coach Terry Holland opted not to chase, and six minutes ran off the clock with UNC retaining possession of the ball.

"It takes two to have a slower game," Smith said. "If a 7-4 guy wants to stay under the basket, fine."

When Virginia began to chase UNC with two minutes remaining, the Cavaliers were forced to foul. They committed five fouls in less than a minute to put the Tar Heels in the bonus and on the foul line. With 28 seconds remaining, UNC's

Doherty made one of two free throws to give the Tar Heels a 45-43 lead. Over the next 15 seconds, UNC fouled Virginia twice, but the Tar Heels had only six team fouls and did not send the Cavaliers to the free throw line.

Finally, Virginia's Jimmy Miller lost the ball out of bounds with three seconds left. Doherty was fouled again by Virginia and made two free throws. Sampson's dunk at the buzzer was inconsequential in UNC's 47-45 victory.

"A coach thinks about winning the basketball game under the present rules," Smith said when asked about a shot clock. "I worry about our players being happy right now."

UNC's Black was told that fans in the Greensboro Coliseum and those watching on TV probably thought the last 7:30 was boring.

"Boring?" Black said. "I'm sorry, we're out there to win the game."

The win gave UNC the top seed in the NCAA East Regional and allowed the Tar Heels to play their first-round game in Charlotte and the next two rounds in Raleigh. Virginia was top-seeded in the Mideast, Wake Forest was seventh-seeded in the East and N.C. State was likewise in the Mideast.

Maryland defeated Richmond 66-50 in the first round of the NIT, but fell to Georgia 83-69 in the second round. Clemson dropped a first-round NIT decision to Mississippi, 53-49.

Of the NCAA Tournament teams, State went down first with a 58-51 loss to Tennessee-Chattanooga. Wake Forest defeated Old Dominion 74-57 in the East but fell to Memphis State, 56-55. Virginia, meanwhile, defeated Tennessee 54-51 before losing to Alabama-Birmingham, 68-66, on UAB's home court.

That left UNC, which marched all the way to the national championship. The Tar Heels survived a scare in their first NCAA game from James Madison as Worthy had a three-point play, drew a charge and made two key free throws in the final minute of a 52-50 victory.

In Raleigh, UNC placed all five starters in double figures to turn back Alabama 74-69, then did the same in a 70-60 victory over Villanova to reach the Final Four.

UNC's ninth trip to the Final Four fell on the 25th anniversary of the Tar Heels' national championship in 1957. UNC's '82 edition had much the same makeup of the '57 five.

The ACC's focus in '82 was on UNC and Virginia; here James Worthy lofts a shot over the long arm of Cavalier Ralph Sampson during the Tar Heels' 65-60 win.

The common denominator between the two was the prominence of the "underground railroad" from New York to Chapel Hill.

Frank McGuire opened that railroad when he moved from St. John's to UNC in 1953. In his nine-year stay as coach of the Tar Heels, McGuire wooed 34 players from the New York area to Chapel Hill. The '57 starting lineup included three New Yorkers—Lennie Rosenbluth, Joe Quigg and Bob Cunningham—and one, Tommy Kearns, from nearby Bergenfield, N.J.

Of the '82 Tar Heels in the starting lineup, three hailed

225

Sampson ushered Cavs into hoops fishbowl.

The story goes that Virginia Center Ralph Sampson was standing in the locker room corner pulling on his length-43 pants when he was approached by an innocent reporter.

"Ralph's not ready yet," said Jerry Glover, a Virginia football player who served as Sampson's bodyguard in post-game interview sessions.

"Ready for what?" asked the reporter.

"Ready to talk to everyone," Glover said.

The reporter smiled. "Who does he think he is, the President of the United States?"

The '80s

Virginia

Truth is, in Charlottesville, Va., 7-foot-4, 215-pound Ralph Sampson was not just larger than the President. Sampson was also bigger in legend. Few in Charlottesville would have argued that Sampson's impact on that city and the University of Virginia from 1979 through 1983 was greater than anyone's since Thomas Jefferson, who founded the school.

Sampson's presence probably had more impact on a school than any player in ACC history.

Most of Sampson's legend was made on the University Hall basketball floor, where he was generally believed to be the most graceful college center since Lew Alcindor played for UCLA. Like Alcindor, now known as Kareem-Abdul Jabbar, Sampson started as a superstar and made steady improvement through his four-year career.

He left Virginia as a three-time national Player of the Year and three-time ACC Player of the Year. He missed by one vote being a unanimous All-ACC choice in 1981, then garnered every vote each of the following two seasons. More importantly, Sampson led Virginia to an NIT championship in 1980, to the Final Four in '81, to No. 1 rankings in '82 and '83 and to a 112-23 record over four seasons. Three times Sampson and Virginia either shared or finished first in the ACC's regular season.

Despite rules that encouraged teams to box two and sometimes three opponents around him in zone defenses, Sampson averaged 16.9 points and 11.4 rebounds for his career. He was Virginia's all-time leading rebounder with 1,511 and blocked shots with 462. His No. 50 jersey was retired.

Off the court, Sampson established himself as a solid student and graduated with a degree in speech communications. But he was hardly the average student at Virginia.

"Every time you pick up a magazine or a national publication, he's got his picture in it," said Joe Mark of Virginia's Student Athletic Foundation, which surpassed the $1 million mark in contributions one year prior to Sampson's arrival and reached $1.5 million by his junior season. "Every time you turn on the TV, there he is."

Although Virginia previously had standout players such as Buzz Wilkinson, Barry Parkhill, Wally Walker and Jeff Lamp, none came close to gaining the national recognition of Sampson. The widespread recognition was probably the result of Sampson's immense talents being displayed during a boom in TV and print coverage of college basketball.

Within a five-day span during Sampson's junior season, he had interview requests from 30 daily newspapers, all three TV networks and countless magazines. Correspondents from *Sports Illustrated, Time, Newsweek* and *US* magazines all visited Charlottesville. When the Cavaliers played in New York during the 1981 season, Sampson appeared live on *Good Morning America*.

Before Sampson planted his size 17 shoes on the Virginia campus, no Cavalier basketball game had been televised nationally. By his senior season, fans across the country were accustomed to seeing Sampson play on TV. Many games, such as an 89-73 victory over Ohio State in 1981 when Sampson had 40 points and 16 rebounds, were arranged specifically for national TV.

The biggest made-for-TV matchup in Virginia history was Sampson's confrontation with Georgetown's celebrated center, Patrick Ewing, in December of 1982. Sampson, with 23 points and 16 rebounds in Virginia's 68-63 victory, got the best of Ewing, who had 16 points and eight rebounds. Virginia netted about $85,000 after it split TV rights with the other ACC schools.

The demands on Sampson went beyond the playing floor. He participated in public service announcements and granted hundreds of interviews, photo sessions and autographs during his career. Sampson did all that, despite being a painfully shy 18-year-old when he brought an 8-foot bed in his father's pickup truck from nearby Harrisonburg, Va., in 1979.

From the outset, it was apparent that Charlottesville would never be the same once Sampson arrived. Giddy students painted "Ralph's House" on the dome of University Hall. They gawked when he walked across campus, and generally made it difficult for Sampson to live a normal life as a student. As a way to better deal with the situation, Sampson lived in the basement of Coach Terry Holland's home for one year.

"You got people coming by to bang on his door at midnight or 2 o'clock in the morning," Holland said. "Then there were times they think they can find him in, and have a chance to take his picture.

"It was very difficult to explain to people. We'd have 10 to 15 calls a day and people would say, 'We'd like to come over and just take a picture of Ralph.' And we would say, 'Well, it's like he's an animal in a zoo. He's not an exhibit all day long.'"

Sampson *was* on exhibit on the basketball floor. Fans flocked to University Hall, and season tickets became valuable commodities. Nearly every Virginia game over his four seasons was sold out.

Virginia fans saw "Stick" hit double figures in scoring, rebounding and blocked shots twice in his first 10 games of his freshman season. His 15-point, 15-rebound performance in the 58-55 NIT championship victory over Minnesota made Sampson the tournament's first freshman MVP.

ACC BASKETBALL / THE '80s

Because of his size, Sampson was naturally able to dominate play around the basket. But he was also also an excellent ball handler and had a soft jump shot that was effective to 18 feet.

"There ought to be a law against him," said Brigham Young Coach Frank Arnold. "When a guy 7-4 goes out and shoots from where he does and makes 'em, it's criminal."

When Sampson led Virginia to the Final Four during his sophomore year, then to the NCAA Tournament his junior and senior seasons, the mania over basketball in Virginia was at an all-time high.

"The (Virginia) sports information office calls and says CBS is in town and wants some T-shirts," said Bobby Mincer, operator of Mincer's Pipe Shop where he sold Sampson memorabilia on the Virginia campus. "So we pack it up and get it over to them. Three years ago we didn't have those requests. But three years ago we didn't have the spirit that we have around here."

Because it was a violation of NCAA rules, the Virginia athletic department had to chase Ralph T-shirts off the market. No item could picture Sampson. Yet, a week after Virginia won a recruiting battle against UNC to sign Sampson, a light blue T-shirt hit the streets with his picture and the slogan: "Carolina Blue It." It was quickly smothered. So was the T-shirt that pictured Sampson and claimed: "Good News For The Hoos, Ralph's Back." That came on the heels of Sampson's decision to remain at Virginia for his senior season after spurning a $1 million-a-year offer to play for the Los Angeles Lakers of the NBA.

Sampson could have also taken a $400,000 offer from the Boston Celtics following his freshman season, or an $800,000 offer from either Detroit or Dallas after his sophomore year.

Instead, he chose to remain in Charlottesville where the most marketable shirt in town was a Virginia jersey with Sampson's No. 50 on the front and back. The most popular bumper sticker was one that simply read "RALPH!" And the most popular sandwich at Littlejohn's, a restaurant near campus, was the Ralph Sampson.

Sampson's stature was not tarnished in the least despite Virginia's failure to win either an ACC or an NCAA championship. He closed out his home career with a spinning, turnaround jump shot from the free throw line that gave Virginia an 83-81 victory over Maryland.

"His teams won more games over a four-year period than any other team in the country," Holland said of Sampson, who was the first player selected in the 1983 NBA draft, by the Houston Rockets. "I think that simply is the mark of the man. He played well individually, he played well collectively and he played to help us win games."

"There ought to be a law against him," one frustrated coach groused after a Sampson exhibition.

ACC BASKETBALL / THE '80s

from the New York area: Doherty was from Long Island, Black from The Bronx and Perkins from Brooklyn. While McGuire recruited New York in the '50s and '60s out of necessity, Smith wooed talent out of the Big Apple only when it was available. Smith preferred to take the top players from North Carolina, where he found Worthy and Jordan.

Doherty, an Irish Catholic, was thought to be headed to Notre Dame. But after an official visit to Chapel Hill in October of 1979, he canceled a scheduled visit to South Bend and became UNC's earliest commitment ever in basketball. The NCAA had just passed a rule allowing schools to sign high school seniors before their final seasons.

Black was headed to Iona in 1978 to play under Coach Jim Valvano when UNC entered the picture. The Tar Heel coaching staff was relying on a recommendation from Jack Curran, the coach at Archbishop Molloy High School in New York. Curran liked what he saw when his team played Black and Cardinal Hayes High School, and thought UNC would like him as well. UNC Assistant Coach Bill Guthridge thought Black was "the motor we need" to replace Phil Ford.

Perkins was reared in Brooklyn by his grandmother, Martha. She was most interested in her grandson being a Jehovah's Witness, and Perkins did not play basketball until his sophomore year at Tilden High School. That's where he met Herb Crossman, a recreation-league coach who befriended Perkins and took on the father-figure role Perkins had never known. When Crossman moved to a new position in Latham, N.Y., he persuaded Perkins' grandmother to allow Sam to move with him. Crossman became Perkins' legal guardian and eventually steered him to UNC.

Each starter fit into a role on the '82 Tar Heels, Doherty as the small forward who could both rebound and score, Black as the quintessential playmaker and Perkins as the center who could mix it up near the basket or shoot jump shots from the high post. With Worthy, the perfect power forward, and Jordan, an electrifying freshman who could shoot the 18-footer as well as play above the rim, UNC seemed to have the perfect combination.

The Tar Heels' mix was simply too much for Houston in the NCAA semifinals. UNC scored the game's first 14 points and led 31-29 at halftime. With Perkins getting 25 points, Jordan 18 and Worthy 14, the Tar Heels held off Houston, 68-63. One of the keys to winning was the defensive play of Black, who held Houston guard Rob Williams without a field goal in eight attempts.

The showdown for the national championship with Georgetown pitted freshman center Patrick Ewing against UNC's front line, Worthy against Gastonia, N.C., hometown friend Sleepy Floyd and John Thompson against his coaching friend Dean Smith.

The championship game was the fourth for Smith as coach without a title, and his players vowed to get the runner-up monkey off his back before a national TV audience and 61,612 fans in the Louisiana Superdome in New Orleans. What followed was one of the most exciting and well-played national championships ever.

The two powerhouses battled toe-to-toe from tap to buzzer.

The game's early minutes were dominated by the play of Ewing, who scored on one end of the court and blocked nearly every UNC shot on the other. Unfortunately for Ewing, five of his first-half blocks were goal-tends. Thompson had instructed Ewing to block everything in the early going in an attempt to intimidate the Tar Heels and force them away from the basket.

Nothing Could Be Finer
Twenty-five years after its first NCAA title, UNC collected a second with a 63-62 win over Georgetown in 1982. The starting five of (L-R) Sam Perkins, Jimmy Black, Michael Jordan, Matt Doherty and James Worthy laugh it up for TV's Billy Packer moments after Worthy dribbled off (R) with Freddie Brown's misguided pass.

228

ACC BASKETBALL / **THE '80s**

UNC did not back down. Despite trailing 32-31 at halftime, the Tar Heels were encouraged. They had not allowed the Hoyas a fast-break layup, a tip-in or a follow shot.

UNC gained the lead in the opening seconds of the second half on a backdoor layup by Doherty. But the lead would change hands another 12 times in the second half. Georgetown could never increase its lead to more than four points, while UNC failed six times to increase its largest lead of three points.

As the intensity of the game increased, the action became more physical. Ewing threw an elbow at Worthy while running downcourt. Black and Floyd got in a shoving match in front of the Georgetown bench. Then Worthy and Mike Hancock had to be separated by the officials on an inbounds play.

After Georgetown sent UNC into the bonus with over nine minutes to play, the Tar Heels forged a one-point lead on a pair of dunks by Worthy. With a 57-56 lead and 5:30 to play, UNC spread the court and went to its "4-C" offense, a variation of the Four Corners.

But Georgetown took advantage of some poor free throw shooting by UNC, stayed alive on short jumpers by Ewing and Floyd and led 62-61 with less than one minute to play. UNC then called time out with 32 seconds left to set up a final play.

Figuring the Hoyas would surround Worthy and Perkins with a zone, Smith thought UNC could swing the ball around to Jordan for an open jumper. "Knock it in, Michael," Smith told Jordan as they broke the huddle. "Everybody get on the board," he told the others.

Worthy dunks for two.

Just as the play was diagrammed, the ball swung around to Jordan. The freshman calmly sank an 18-footer with 17 seconds remaining and UNC had a 63-62 lead.

"I thought about something like that when I was coming over on the bus," Jordan said. "It (the ball) just happened to come my way."

Georgetown still had time to get off a final shot. But guard Fred Brown, perhaps confused by UNC's scrambling defense or perhaps engulfed by the intensity of the moment, threw the ball directly into the hands of Worthy.

"I was pretty surprised because it hit me right in the chest," said Worthy, who missed two ensuing free throws but still earned MVP honors with a career-high 28 points.

When Georgetown's Floyd missed on a 50-foot heave at the buzzer, UNC was the national champion.

"This is the only year it would have bothered me (if UNC had lost) in that we had the best basketball team, I thought," Smith said.

So confident was Smith about his team's chances, he told them before they took the court against Georgetown, "If you win this game, I'll run wind sprints after our first practice next fall."

The following October, the then 51-year-old Smith ran sprints following practice as the remaining members of his national championship squad watched.

'83

As predictable as things were in 1982, they were equally unpredictable in 1983. Perhaps an omen came before the season, when the ACC adopted two experimental rules: A 30-second shot clock and a 3-point basket from the relatively short distance of 19 feet from the back of the rim.

The first indication of the season's wackiness was the inauspicious start for the defending national champions. UNC lost to St. John's and Missouri to open the season 0-2 for the first time since 1929. A miracle throw-in from 25 feet by Michael Jordan at the buzzer forced the first of three overtimes and saved the Tar Heels from a third straight defeat in a 70-68 decision over Tulane. Then UNC was outscored 21-9 in the first half against LSU before rallying to win 47-43.

By Christmas, the unusual in the ACC was suddenly the norm. Maryland, which struggled to defeat Towson State nine days earlier, defeated third-ranked UCLA in two overtimes. Then Chaminade, an NAIA school which was fielding a basketball team for only the seventh season, stunned top-ranked and unbeaten Virginia 77-72 in Hawaii.

Wagner College also engineered a stunner. Wagner coaches borrowed film from Duke the morning of their early January game, planned a scouting report, then went out and defeated the Blue Devils in Durham, 84-77.

In his senior season, Virginia's Ralph Sampson was the focus of attention much the way David Thompson was at N.C. State in 1975. It was the classic case of the league's most dominant player having to face constant harassment on defense by opponents. Like Thompson, Sampson usually took his frustrations out by playing excellent basketball.

Sampson's first challenge of his final season at Virginia was posed by Georgetown's Patrick Ewing. The battle of the giants in Washington's Capital Centre on Dec. 11, 1982, was the most ballyhooed regular-season game since UCLA played N.C. State in St. Louis early in the 1974 season. It drew comparisons to the meeting between UCLA's Lew Alcindor and Houston's Elvin Hayes in the Houston Astrodome 15 years earlier.

Sampson, with 23 points and 16 rebounds, got the best of Ewing (16 and eight) as Virginia won, 68-63.

Sampson was back for his senior season after turning down lucrative offers from NBA teams for the second straight year. As long as Sampson was around, the ACC was again a two-team race between his Cavaliers and North Carolina. The final two matchups between those two teams were classics, just as the previous eight meetings were.

In the first game, at Charlottesville, UNC bolted to an 85-62 lead with 9:41 remaining. But Virginia made an incredible comeback, and Sampson's 3-point basket with 50 seconds remaining brought the Cavaliers within two at 97-95. UNC's Jimmy Braddock and Michael Jordan made four points on 1-and-1 free throws to account for the Tar Heels' 101-95 victory, which ended Virginia's 34-game home-court winning streak.

The rematch in Chapel Hill saw Virginia build a 16-point lead with 8:43 remaining and hold to a 10-point lead with 4:12 left. But UNC rallied this time and trailed 63-60 with 1:20 left. After Sampson missed the front end of a 1-and-1, UNC's Jordan tipped in a missed shot, then stole the ball from Rick Carlisle in the backcourt and drove for a dunk that gave the No. 1-ranked Tar Heels a 64-63 victory.

The two victories over Virginia also put the Tar Heels in

ACC BASKETBALL / THE '80s

position to claim first place in the ACC's regular-season race. But UNC faltered in consecutive late-season conference games to finish in a tie for the top spot with Virginia. Tacked on to a nationally televised home upset to Villanova, UNC had lost three straight games for the first time since 1970 and three consecutive in the regular season for the first time since 1966.

The first of UNC's two league losses was at Maryland, 106-94. The second was at N.C. State three days later. The Wolfpack carried a 14-8 record into the game and was playing without senior guard Dereck Whittenburg, who had broken his foot a month earlier against Virginia.

State took a 37-36 halftime lead, then pulled away from the Tar Heels in the second half. Thurl Bailey's dunk with eight seconds remaining gave the Wolfpack a 70-63 victory and sparked a wild celebration at Reynolds Coliseum. State fans toasted the Pack's first win over UNC in eight tries with Jim Valvano as coach.

Valvano, in his third season as head coach, was rewarded earlier in the season with a 10-year contract. He said then that his plans were to one day guide the Wolfpack to a national championship. No one, not even Valvano, expected that title to come in 1983.

The win over UNC, the ultimate return of Whittenburg for the Wolfpack's final three regular-season games and the experimental rules used in ACC games all contributed to State's run to the national crown.

Although the Wolfpack lost to Virginia and Maryland in Whittenburg's first two games back, State rebounded to wallop Wake Forest 130-89 in the regular-season finale. Whittenburg and Terry Gannon led N.C. State's scoring with 25 points each. Not surprisingly, Gannon made seven baskets from beyond the 3-point circle and Whittenburg had four. The higher scoring was also the result of the 30-second clock that was used for all but the final four minutes in ACC games.

The average number of points scored in an ACC game jumped from 59.3 per team in 1982 to 78.2 per team in 1983. Only two teams scored more than 90 points in a conference game in '82. The 100 mark was topped by ACC teams on 23 occasions in '83.

"We're getting a lot of money from TV and the fans are paying a lot and the game was getting boring," Georgia Tech's Bobby Cremins said of the experimental rules. "I think coaches suddenly realized they were overcoaching and there was a need to give the game back to the players."

Not all coaches cottoned to the experimental rules.

"I heard people say . . . that it gave a guy like (Clemson guard) Marc Campbell a chance to neutralize a guy like Ralph Sampson in a game," said Duke Coach Mike Krzyzewski. "I think that's a bunch of baloney. Is that the purpose? I think the beauty of upsets is to see a team neutralize a good player, not with one guy who gets hot from 19 feet, but with a team effort."

No ACC team took advantage of the experimental rules as much as N.C. State. The Wolfpack attempted 381 shots from 3-point range (79 more than the next highest total by UNC) and made 43.7 percent of them. More importantly, the Wolfpack made the longer shot an integral part of its offense, and that carried over to the NCAA Tournament, even though it was played without a shot clock and without a 3-point basket.

With a 17-10 record during the regular season, it appeared State would have to win at least two games in the ACC

From Coach To Caddie

Dwane Morrison left his coaching job at Georgia Tech following the 1981 season and a year later could be found on the PGA Tour, carrying the golf bag of longtime friend J.C. Snead. Morrison, who ended each of his press conferences by saying, "Bless you, brother," caddied for Snead for several months in 1982. Contacted at his home in Atlanta in 1988, Morrison said he was active as a stockbroker, and, true to form, ended the conversation, "Bless you, brother."

ACC BASKETBALL / THE '80s

ACC BASKETBALL / **THE '80s**

'Bound Heard 'Round The World

Dereck Whittenburg's last-ditch shot to beat Houston (above) was so bad it was good — it missed short and to the right, where Lorenzo Charles leaped, caught it and and stuffed it through, sending Coach Jim Valvano and the Pack into a dizzy celebration.

Tournament in Atlanta to receive a bid from the NCAA Tournament Committee. A free throw by Lorenzo Charles with three seconds remaining gave the Wolfpack a 71-70 win over Wake Forest in the opening round, then State came from six points down in overtime to defeat UNC, 91-84.

Virginia stood in the way of State's ACC championship. The Cavaliers appeared primed to win a league title for Sampson. He had closed his home career in storybook fashion by sinking a 14-footer with four seconds remaining for an 83-81 win over Maryland. Then the Cavaliers ripped Duke 109-66, the most lopsided defeat in Blue Devil and ACC Tournament history, before handling Georgia Tech 96-67 in the semifinals.

Virginia played the championship game without sophomore forward Tim Mullen, who strained ligaments in his left knee during the victory over Georgia Tech. With Sidney Lowe (18 points for the game), Whittenburg (15) and Gannon (12 on four 3-pointers) bombing from outside, and Bailey (24 points) and Charles (12 rebounds) working inside, N.C. State managed a 71-66 lead despite an outstanding 24-point, 12-rebound effort by Sampson.

At that point, Virginia Assistant Coach Jim Larranaga questioned an official's call and was whistled for a technical foul. Whittenburg made two free throws and followed with a driving shot over Sampson for a 75-66 N.C. State lead that was eventually whittled to the final margin of three, 81-78.

"We rose to the occasion," Bailey said. "The type of ballclubs we played were very good and now we learned how good we are."

The championship gave State a berth in the NCAA Tournament, which also extended invitations to Virginia, UNC and Maryland. Wake Forest went to the NIT and defeated Murray State 87-80, Vanderbilt 75-68 and South Carolina 78-61 before losing to Fresno State 86-62 in the semifinals.

Maryland defeated Tennessee-Chattanooga 52-51 in the Midwest Regional before losing to Houston, 60-50. UNC was seeded second in the East Regional and defeated James Madison 68-49 and Ohio State 64-51 before falling to Georgia, 82-77, foiling the ACC's chance to place two teams in the Final Four.

Virginia and N.C. State were sent to the West Regional, where the Cavaliers were top-seeded and the Wolfpack was seeded sixth. Virginia made quick work of Washington State 54-49 and Boston College 95-92 to reach the West final in Ogden, Utah.

The real story was developing in Corvallis, Ore., where the Wolfpack needed two overtimes and a lot of help from Pepperdine to post a 69-67 victory in the first round. State trailed by six points with one minute remaining in the first overtime when Dane Suttle, the third best field goal shooter in Division I, twice missed 1-and-1s. A dunk by Bailey and a follow shot by Cozell McQueen tied the game. Whittenburg's free throw shooting in the second overtime allowed N.C. State to advance.

"Hey, we may be destined to win this thing," Valvano told his team in the locker room afterwards.

Next for the Wolfpack was Nevada-Las Vegas, which built a 12-point lead midway through the second half. Again, State charged back and won 71-70 on Bailey's follow shot with four seconds remaining. Bailey scored 25 points and had nine rebounds after reading in the previous day's newspaper that UNLV forward Sidney Green said, "He (Bailey) doesn't show me much."

The Wolfpack used a more conventional style to defeat Utah in the third round in Ogden, Utah. State trailed 32-30 early in the second half, but 79 percent field goal shooting over the final 20 minutes accounted for a 75-56 victory and sent the

Wolfpack into the West Regional final game against Virginia.

The Wolfpack returned to previous tournament form when it spotted Virginia leads of 10 points in the first half and seven with 7:30 remaining. State came back to tie the game at 61 on a 22-footer by Whittenburg, who was 11-of-16 shooting for the game and finished with 24 points.

Two free throws by Charles with 23 seconds remaining ultimately sealed State's 63-62 victory, but not before Mullen's 18-footer and Othell Wilson's 6-footer missed in the final seconds for Virginia. The Cavaliers could not get the ball to Sampson on the final play.

"I feel bad for myself," Virginia's Wilson said. "But I feel worse for Ralph."

Sampson thus concluded a brilliant college career without an ACC or NCAA championship despite 112 wins against only 23 losses.

N.C. State, meanwhile, prepared to meet Georgia in the NCAA semifinals in Albuquerque, N.M. The Wolfpack and Bulldogs were considered underdogs in the Final Four field, with the winner of the other semifinal matchup between powerhouses Houston and Louisville expected to win the national crown.

By this time, State had a magnificent blend of talent. Lowe and Whittenburg formed one of the best backcourts in league history. The duo played on the same DeMatha (Washington, D.C.) High School teams, then became roommates at State and starters for their final three seasons with the Wolfpack. Lowe, although not an outstanding shooter, was an excellent ball handler and playmaker. Whittenburg's strength was his outside shooting as well as his ability to post opposing guards near the basket and back in for easy shots.

On the front line, State had three diamonds in the rough. Bailey honed his skills, which included an excellent baseline jump shot and precise timing to block shots, and ultimately led the Wolfpack in scoring and rebounding for three straight seasons.

Charles was not highly recruited out of New York City and did not develop into a force inside until late in the '83 season. Prior to the season, Charles was arrested and charged with stealing a pizza from a delivery man in Raleigh. "If anything, that incident helped Lorenzo focus on a number of things," Valvano said.

McQueen may have been the unsung hero of the bunch. After splitting playing time with Chuck Nevitt as a freshman, the 6-foot-11 McQueen emerged as a strong defensive player and rebounder during his sophomore season.

Off the bench, the Wolfpack had Terry Gannon, an uncanny shooter from long distance who made 58.9 percent of his 3-point attempts in '83. State also had Ernie Myers, who averaged 11.2 points in place of Whittenburg at midseason, then accepted his role as a reserve when Whittenburg returned.

In retrospect, State's drive to the Final Four was not as much a fluke as it appeared to be. Because of the misfortune earlier in the season, the Wolfpack was forced to became a multidimensional team. Whittenburg's injury forced State to develop an inside game. When Whittenburg returned, the Wolfpack could score from anywhere on the floor and spread defenses thin.

In the Final Four semifinals, State shot 54 percent from the floor in the first half while holding Georgia to 28 percent shooting. Then the Wolfpack stretched a 33-22 halftime lead to 59-41 with six minutes to play. Georgia rallied, but State held on to win, 67-60.

"We should be able to milk a lead like the one we had. After all we are an agricultural school," Valvano said.

Jordan's steal and slam dunk against Virginia were the crowning touches in a 64-63 win for the No. 1 Tar Heels.

ACC BASKETBALL / THE '80s

Valvano's loose approach helped as State prepared to meet No. 1-ranked Houston. Valvano played up the idea that the Wolfpack's best chance at winning was to hold the ball against Houston, which featured 7-foot center Akeem Olajuwon.

Valvano's plan was to use Gannon as much as possible off the bench in a three-guard alignment that would move Houston's defense away from the basket. He wanted the Wolfpack to run only if the opportunity was there to do so. He wanted to keep Houston from running and prevent the Phi Slamma Jamma fraternity, as the Cougars liked to call themselves, from getting a dunk. Mostly, Valvano wanted a game in the 50s.

"We're going to go out there and play our butts off," Valvano told his team in the locker room prior to the game, according to his book about the national championship season, *Too Soon To Quit*. "Yeah, we're going to control tempo. We'll run when we want to run. We'll stop when we want to stop, and all I ask, all I ever ask, is to be in a position to win the game at the end. Not only are you going to have your best day, but I'm ready, and I'm going to have my best game, too.

"We're going to represent N.C. State University, the ACC and ourselves. And we're going home with the second national championship in N.C. State's history."

The Wolfpack played what Valvano later termed a "perfect" first half and led Houston 33-25. But Houston came out for the second half and outscored the Wolfpack 17-2 and took a 42-35 lead with 10 minutes remaining. Then Houston Coach Guy Lewis decided to run some time off the clock.

But the strategy backfired. As the Wolfpack had done throughout its run to the championship, it elected to foul the opponent and make it win the game at the foul line. Houston, just like Pepperdine in the first round and UNLV in the third round, could not make free throws down the stretch, and State pulled into a tie at 52 with 1:05 remaining.

The Wolfpack then fouled Houston guard Alvin Franklin, and he missed the front end of a 1-and-1. State rebounded and called time out with 44 seconds remaining to set up a final shot. The play was designed for Lowe to penetrate the Houston defense, then either drive to the basket, seek out Gannon or Whittenburg on the wings or Bailey in one corner.

Houston's trapping defense prevented Lowe from driving, and with 10 seconds left, he threw the ball far outside to Whittenburg. Not knowing how much time remained, Whittenburg launched a 30-foot shot that was short of the basket. Charles saw that the shot was going to be short, jumped, caught the ball and dunked it.

N.C. State was the national champion, 54-52.

"I can't put my emotions in words right now," Gannon said. "Maybe 10 years from now I'll be able to put this in perspective in my life. I can't see anything, if I live to be 100, that could top this moment."

Gannon was one of the backcourt trio that was chiefly responsible for the championship. None of the three had a turnover in the game, and each helped State control the game's tempo and keep the game in the 50s. Whittenburg with 14 points and Bailey with 15 led the scoring. Olajuwon had 20 points and 18 rebounds, but got little help from the rest of the Houston front line. McQueen (four points, 12 rebounds), Charles (two and seven) and Bailey (15 and five) totaled 21 points and 24 rebounds compared to Houston's front-line totals of 28 and 26.

"This morning the whole team picked up the papers and saw where everyone gave us no chance," Whittenburg said. "How wrong they were. It made us play a little harder. Finally we can take off the Cinderella pumps and be champs."

'84

With consecutive national championships, the ACC could stake claim to being the nation's best without much argument. Attendance was soaring throughout the league, and television ratings were at an all-time high.

Non-conference teams were now beginning to seek a piece of the ACC's financial pie. One way for non-league teams to get into the action was by scheduling nationally televised games, such as Louisville's meeting with N.C. State in Raleigh early in the 1984 season. Another way was for the smaller schools to schedule games on the home court of ACC schools and secure a nice financial guarantee.

But outside opponents found that ACC teams rarely lost at home to non-conference teams. N.C. State was the only ACC team to lose a home game to a non-league opponent during the 1984 season, losing to Louisville and dropping an NIT first-round game to Florida State in Reynolds Coliseum. The rest of the league's seven teams combined to win 49 games without a home loss to outside competition.

That sort of record was not unique to the 1984 season. By the time North Carolina closed the doors two years later after 21 seasons of play at Carmichael Auditorium, the Tar Heels had lost only four games to non-conference opponents in that building: Virginia Tech in 1966, Princeton in 1967, Miami of Ohio in 1973 and Villanova in 1983.

Even Georgia Tech, whose program was at rock bottom when it joined the ACC in 1979, had posted a 31-6 record against non-league teams at the school's Alexander Memorial Coliseum by the end of the 1984 season.

All totaled, ACC teams had won 88.6 percent (859-111 record) of their home games against outside competition since they began playing in the facilities in use in 1984.

"It's not an easy thing to do (win on an ACC court)," South Florida Coach Lee Rose said after his team lost at Duke in '84. "To do it, you have to play a great, great game."

Not many of the nation's top teams were playing on ACC courts. Louisville at State in 1984 and Villanova at UNC in 1983 were exceptions. The ACC's record against non-conference opposition had much to do with scheduling. A look at the 1984 schedules saw ACC teams playing home games against non-Division I teams Flagler, Randolph-Macon, Johns Hopkins and Alabama A&M. By playing the lesser opponents, ACC teams built confidence while padding their won-loss records.

ACC teams have always scheduled what might be considered borderline non-conference opponents, including East Carolina, Western Carolina, Appalachian State, South Florida, James Madison and Furman. Those schools have had much to gain even in a loss on an ACC school's home court.

"If you're going to go on the road, why not play against a good team in a good atmosphere?" ECU Coach Charlie Harrison said. "If something good happens, it's a great experience for your program. It's going to benefit us either in recruiting or in the media if we win. And even if we lose, we have gained something from the experience."

Part of the experience for non-conference teams was usually in dealing with ACC crowds, whether it be the Duke students leaning into the opponents' huddle during a timeout; the N.C. State pep band playing its fight song in the face of the opposing coaches prior to the game; the Maryland crowd standing and cheering as the Terps' pep band played *Hail To The Chief* when Coach Lefty Driesell entered the court or the Virginia fans waving their hands behind the basket during an opponent's free throw attempt.

"The thing we found was that there seems to be a very powerful distracting influence on visiting teams," said UNC sports psychologist John Silva, who conducted a 10-year study on the effects of home crowds during ACC games. "For teams coming in playing against nationally powerful teams . . . and if they are at all unsure of themselves, then I think the crowd would have even more of an influence.

"If a team comes in and they believe they can play with you, then the crowd effects are minimized. If a team comes in and does not believe they can play with you, then the crowd effects are maximized."

So how does a non-conference team win on an ACC court?

"The main thing is, you've got to be better than the other guy," South Florida's Rose said.

That usually has not been the case over the years and certainly was not in 1984. Aside from its 57-2 record against non-conference opponents at home, the ACC was 51-16 outside the league for an overall mark of 108-18, an .857 winning percentage that ranked second to the .863 percentage outside the league in 1976.

Two non-conference games involving North Carolina were particularly significant during the 1984 season. The Tar Heels won 16 straight games to open the season, including championships in the Stanford Invitational and Holiday Festival, and were ranked No. 1 in the country when they faced LSU in Chapel Hill on Jan. 29. Although UNC extended its winning streak with a 90-79 victory, the Tar Heels lost freshman guard Kenny Smith with a broken left wrist.

Less than two weeks later, UNC faced Arkansas in a nationally televised game at Pine Bluff, Ark. With 21 wins, the Tar Heels had the fourth longest winning streak to open a season in ACC history. The 1957 Tar Heels won all 32 of their games and the 1973 N.C. State team went unbeaten in 27 games. Virginia won its first 23 games in 1981.

UNC's streak of '84, which was matched again in 1986, came to an end at Arkansas when Charles Balentine's 5-foot baseline jumper with five seconds remaining gave the Razorbacks a 65-64 win.

Prior to Smith's injury and UNC's subsequent loss to Arkansas, there was talk about this being Coach Dean Smith's best Tar Heel team. It had a front line perhaps unmatched in college basketball with Michael Jordan, Brad Daugherty and Sam Perkins, all of whom were eventual first-round NBA draft picks. It also had senior Matt Doherty and freshman guard Smith in the backcourt, with Joe Wolf, Dave Popson, Buzz Peterson and Steve Hale for depth.

Yet the injury to Smith seemed to upset the apple cart, and UNC faltered down the stretch. The Tar Heels struggled to a two-overtime victory over Duke in the regular-season finale in Chapel Hill. Matt Doherty's running 12-footer with one second remaining sent the game into the first overtime, and UNC finally won 96-83 in the second overtime. The Tar Heels became the sixth team (UNC in 1957, Duke in '63, South Carolina in '70, N.C. State in '73 and '74) to go unbeaten within the league.

The Tar Heels were expected to challenge for the national championship upon Smith's late-season return to the lineup, but they didn't. Playing with a protective cast on his left wrist, Smith never matched his early season form, and UNC was stunned by Indiana in the East Regional semifinals, 72-68.

"The reason it was disappointing," Coach Smith said of the loss, "(was because) it was the third time I thought we had

Pack's Jimmy V: One NCAA title, a million laughs.

Not long after Jim Valvano was introduced as N.C. State's 15th basketball coach in March of 1980, someone asked him why he talks so fast.

"We had three minutes to make our point," Valvano said of his days growing up in New York. "That's how long it was before the next train came along."

Valvano was then asked if his wife, Pam, sang the national anthem as Norm Sloan's wife did when Sloan coached the Wolfpack.

The '80s

N.C. State

"No she doesn't," Valvano said. "But she does do a very clever tap routine to the national anthem. Unfortunately, it doesn't come across real well on the radio."

With that, Valvano was off and running as the most colorful and quotable coach in the ACC since Bones McKinney at Wake Forest in the early '60s.

Along the way, Valvano also became one of the league's most successful coaches. His first eight teams at State averaged more than 20 wins a season, reached the NCAA Tournament final round of eight teams on three occasions and won two ACC Tournament championships.

The apex of Valvano's coaching career came in 1983 when the Wolfpack marched to the NCAA championship, defeating Houston 54-52 for the title on a last-second dunk by Lorenzo Charles.

That Wolfpack team captured the fancy of fans across the country with its dogged determination, just as Valvano has won over ACC fans as a funny, flamboyant, fast-talking Yankee.

The best of Jim Valvano:

"My mother said I was vaccinated with the Victrola. I haven't shut up since."

"In America, I am an Italian. Down South, I'm an EYE-talian. I had to go to Italy to become an American."

On Southern California coach and close friend George Raveling: "George has many interests and is a great reader. Says he reads a book a week. I don't know where he gets all those comics."

"When football coaches started to break down films, it really started their problems with a sense of humor. How can a coach, after his team loses 47-3, say he needs to check the films to explain the defeat? I could tell him why he lost. He just got kicked. Whoever started that film stuff must have been named Kodak."

"There is a certain amount of weight in the world and that doesn't change. So in order for you to lose weight, somebody else has to gain it. Have you ever tried

"If I were really Joe Namath, they'd say I was ruggedly handsome," Valvano says. "But since I'm not, they say I've got a big nose."

your best to diet but couldn't lose any weight? That's because somebody else in the world has probably lost 100 pounds and that hurts all of us."

"At one Wolfpack Club meeting, this guy comes up and said, 'Coach, you know we love you.' I said, 'That's great, but will you still love me if we're 8-22 next season?' He said, 'Coach, we'll love you . . . and we'll miss you.'"

A caller on Valvano's weekly radio show asked, "What should I do about a painful knee?" Valvano responded, "Limp."

Another caller asked, "Who's going to the Super Bowl?" Valvano responded, "My uncle Bruno, he's got tickets."

"I don't know when I'm going to beat him, but I know I'm going to outlive him," Valvano said after losing his first six meetings with UNC and Coach Dean Smith.

"People down here want me to hunt and fish. I tell them I'm from New York. What are you going to do in New York—fly cast at a fire hydrant?"

"After a loss this year, somebody asked me what I was going to do. I told him I was going to stop off and get a six-pack of Miller Lite and go home. Well, Miller sent me a year's supply of beer. Why didn't I say I was going to drive there in my Mercedes?"

"I'm going to have two of my players guard one of the officials one time. Can you see that? Two-on-one all over the floor. Maybe draw a charge one time. But they'd probably blow that call, too."

"Bowling played a big part in my life," Valvano once told the Bowling Proprietors Association annual convention. "I'm Italian, you know, and three things Italians do are shoot, kill and go bowling."

On the ACC using officials from the Southwest Conference in 1981, "I knew I was in trouble before our first game when one of the officials came up to me and said, 'Howdy, pardner.' I thought Gene Autry was going to referee."

"I asked a ref if he could give me a technical for thinking bad things about him and he said, 'Of course not.' I said, 'Well, I think you stink.' And he gave me a technical. You can't trust 'em."

"Who made up this schedule anyway, the Marquis de Sade? I've traveled so much, I feel like I'm on a USO Tour."

"When my wife heard about the new NCAA rule that prohibits a coach from leaving his college campus to recruit high school athletes the entire month of August, she looked at me and said, 'Good, that means I can make love 30 times in August.' I said, 'Good, put me down for two.'"

On his marriage to Pam Levine: "She was the first girl I dated that didn't have a mustache. She saw my nose and thought I was Jewish. I saw her name and thought it ended in 'i'. It was three years before we realized we had a mixed marriage."

On a reported bed check conducted during the 1983 NCAA Tournament: "Yeah, we had one. I checked and all the beds were there."

On State's underdog status against Houston for the '83 national championship, "Even my mother is taking Houston and laying seven points."

President Ronald Reagan asked Valvano, "Is it Val-vah-no or Val-vane-o?" Valvano replied, "I don't know, is it Ree-gun or Ray-gun?"

"I don't like the coaches' box. To be very low key about this and to not go out on a limb, I think it is the dumbest rule in the history of sport, starting with the Olympic Games when they made them take the fig leaf off. I think I'm going to go home and yell at my wife and kids a lot more because it's a stupid rule. If I wanted to be in a coaches' box, I could be a baseball coach. I'd be the third base coach here at State."

"People sometimes confuse me with Joe Namath. If I were really Joe Namath, they'd say I was ruggedly handsome. But since I'm not, they say I've got a big nose."

"My dad coached for 30 years. My uncle coached. My older brother is a coach. If my dad had let my mother out of the house, she would have probably been a coach. As it is, she is the head coach of the home."

On playing at Cameron Indoor Stadium, "If we lose there, it's because of (Danny) Ferry, (Kevin) Strickland and (Mike) Krzyzewski and not because of some kid from Jersey sitting behind me calling me a putz."

Tall Tales

Chuck Nevitt (L) and Martin Nessley lived life among the skyscrapers, Nevitt standing 7-foot-5 when he left N.C. State in 1982 and Nessley measuring 7-2 when his Duke career ended in 1987. Each had a weight problem—Nevitt couldn't put enough weight on, Nessley couldn't take enough off. "I could sit down and eat two whole pizzas," the 212-pound Nevitt once said. "It really got to be a chore to eat. I got to where I was tired of eating." Nessley was known as an excellent cook among his teammates, and his weight often flirted with 300 pounds. Although neither excelled in college basketball, Nevitt found places on the NBA rosters of Houston, the LA Lakers and Detroit through 1988, and Nessley played for the LA Clippers and Sacramento Kings in '88.

---

the best team in the country." Smith said his 1977 team was the best until injuries struck, and the Tar Heels finished runner-up in the NCAA Tournament. He also thought his 1982 national championship team was the nation's best.

UNC's feat of going unbeaten within the conference was most remarkable because of the league's balance in 1984. Besides UNC, which finished 28-3, Maryland, Duke, Wake Forest and Virginia all won at least 20 games. N.C. State managed 19 wins, Georgia Tech had 18 and Clemson was a .500 club with 14 wins.

Each ACC team seemed to have a particular highlight in a season when an experimental 45-second clock ran throughout the game:

■ Clemson defeated Marquette 66-61 to win its season-opening IPTAY Tournament in the last hurrah for Coach Bill Foster, who left following the season to start a new program at Miami.

■ Duke stormed to 14 wins in its first 15 games, then lost four straight conference games. One of those losses was a 78-73 decision at Cameron Indoor Stadium to UNC. Twice during the game, UNC Coach Smith left the bench area and pounded his fist on the scorer's table. Following the game, Duke Coach Mike Krzyzewski charged that there was a "double standard" in the ACC with one set of rules for Smith and another for the rest of the league's coaches.

Within the next week, Fred Barakat, the ACC's supervisor of officials, found that there was no "double standard" as Krzyzewski charged. The day following Barakat's report, Krzyzewski was awarded a new five-year contract by Duke.

Krzyzewski and Duke then got the last laugh when the Blue Devils defeated UNC 77-75 in the semifinals of the ACC Tournament.

■ Georgia Tech got off to a 14-2 start that included a wild and crazy 72-71, three-overtime decision over Virginia in Atlanta. The game was televised in the ACC area and lasted past midnight.

The Ramblin' Wreck was invited to the NIT for its first postseason appearance since losing to UNC in the final of the 1971 NIT. This time, Georgia Tech fell in the first round at Virginia Tech, 77-74.

■ N.C. State stretched its two-year winning streak to 15 games before losing to Virginia Tech in Greensboro, 89-65. The Wolfpack put together a nine-game winning streak near the end of the regular season and earned a berth in the NIT. But it fell to Florida State in the opening round in Raleigh, 74-71 in overtime.

■ Wake Forest posted its fourth straight 20-win season and nearly reached the NCAA Final Four. The Demon Deacons were seeded fourth in the Midwest Regional, where they defeated Kansas 69-59, then ended the 42-year coaching career of DePaul Coach Ray Meyer with a 73-71 overtime victory. Delaney Rudd's 20-footer at the buzzer forced the extra period. But Wake Forest was not so fortunate in the Midwest final, where it dropped a 68-63 decision to Houston.

■ Maryland had a topsy-turvy season. Near the end of January, starting guard Adrian Branch and reserve Steve Rivers were charged with possession of marijuana and dismissed from the team. The incident came one season after forward Herman Veal was suspended from the team for allegedly making improper sexual advancements on a Maryland coed.

But Veal returned to the team for the 1984 season, as did Branch late in the season. Driesell then managed to guide the Terps to a second-place finish in the regular season and past N.C. State 69-63 and Wake Forest 66-64 to the ACC championship game.

In his sixth attempt at winning the title, Driesell finally succeeded. The Terps went on a 14-point scoring spree behind the outstanding play of Tournament MVP Len Bias and defeated Duke 74-62 for the championship.

"Back when I first started out I wanted to win that thing real bad," Driesell said of the title. "I said, 'If we win that thing I'm going to have my car in here and I'm going to get that trophy and screw it on the hood and ride all around the state of North Carolina for a week.' I really was going to do that. Now, I'm too old for that. I've got to get home and get some sleep."

Littlejohn Grant's Tomb to Clemson foes.

Virtually inseparable since birth, twins Horace and Harvey Grant had finally parted ways. They played high school basketball together, and both went off to Clemson University. That's where the symbiosis ended.

Harvey, unwilling to dedicate himself to schoolwork and wanting to establish his own identity, headed off to Independence (Kan.) Junior College and eventually to the University of Oklahoma.

That left Horace to make a name for himself during his final two years at Clemson.

The '80s

Clemson

Mission accomplished. When he became the first player in ACC history to lead the league in scoring (21.0 average), rebounding (9.6) and field goal shooting (70.8 percent) in 1987, Littlejohn Coliseum was known to Tiger opponents as Grant's Tomb. For his spectacular season, Grant was named as Clemson's first ACC Player of the Year.

"It was an honor," Grant said a year later as a member of the NBA's Chicago Bulls. "I think it proved that if you work hard, good things come to you. At the time, it didn't mean a great deal to me. But after the fact, it means a lot because no Clemson player had ever done that."

Although Clemson Coach Bill Foster saw immense potential in Horace, and Harvey, as high school players in Sparta, Ga., even he did not envision that either would eventually be the ACC's top player.

"We went down to Sparta the night before we signed them and spent the night in a motel," says Foster, who left Clemson following Horace's freshman season to coach at the University of Miami. "It's hard to believe now, but Clemson, Georgia Southern and Southern University were the only schools that wanted them. We're talking about two first-round NBA draft choices."

Finding diamonds in the rough was certainly nothing new to Foster. He had done the same with Cedric Maxwell at UNC-Charlotte and with Larry Nance at Clemson. Both were unheralded out of high school but developed into outstanding college players and professional stars.

"After Maxwell and Nance, every time we showed up around other guys, everybody would take a look at who we were recruiting," Foster says. "So, with the Grants, we never went down to Sparta much. We just kind of laid back and hoped nobody would notice them."

Foster had actually spotted the twins at a summer basketball camp in Milledgeville, Ga., which is just 19 miles down Highway 22 from Sparta. In the Grants, Foster and Assistant Coach Dwight Rainey saw a couple of skinny, 6-foot-8 kids who were mostly arms and legs. Like Maxwell and Nance, the Grants had exceptionally good hands and coordination.

Sensing he had unearthed a couple of gems, Foster agreed to offer both of the Grants a scholarship if they promised not to tell a soul until signing day. Meanwhile, Foster kept forwarding Clemson posters to the towering twins.

"The whole thing was such a secret," Foster says. "The first time I went into their home was when we signed them. They had Clemson paraphernalia wall-to-wall."

What Foster got in the Grants was a pair of fierce competitors.

"When Harvey and I were growing up, we were the only guys our size," Horace says. "We really thrived on the competition between the two of us."

Horace Grant

At Clemson, Harvey was red-shirted his first season. Horace sometimes wondered if maybe he, too, should have used an extra year on the sidelines to nurture his game. In his first games at UNC and N.C. State, Horace managed only a field goal in each.

"Right then I knew I was in for a long battle," Horace says. "I told myself that I had to improve, had to work a little harder, which I did."

Horace became more dedicated in the weight room. Not only did he bulk up to 220 pounds, he also grew to 6-10 by his sophomore year. He also developed a more well-rounded game by playing away from the basket as a forward under Foster, then playing more of a back-to-the-basket, inside game under Coach Cliff Ellis.

Perhaps the key to Horace's development, though, was Harvey's departure.

Horace said: "Many people consider Harvey and I as one. We're twins but we want our own identity. Harvey didn't want to be in Horace Grant's shadow. His leaving did us both a lot of good. Now people know me as Horace Grant, not the twin brother of Harvey."

Horace had made his mark by the end of his junior year (16.4 points, 10.5 rebounds, 72.5 percent field goal shooting), then spurred himself and the Tigers even higher in 1987. Under his leadership, Clemson finished second in the ACC for the first time with a 10-4 record. The Tigers earned a Top 10 ranking and 25 wins (against six losses) were the most ever for a Clemson team.

When Clemson broke the school record with its 24th victory, an 87-71 decision over Wake Forest at Littlejohn, the Tigers clipped the nets. Ellis intended for the nets to be retired to Clemson's trophy case. "Uh, uh," Horace said. "These are going to my apartment. I'm going to have to call Harvey and brag about it."

The rest didn't help Maryland much in the NCAA Tournament. The Terps defeated West Virginia 102-77 in the second round of the Mideast Regional, then lost to Illinois, 72-70.

■ Virginia may have had the most unusual season of all ACC teams. The Cavaliers played their first three games without senior guard Othell Wilson, who was suspended from the team for preseason altercations with Coach Terry Holland and guard Rick Carlisle.

When Wilson returned, Virginia continued to ride a 10-game winning streak. But the wheels fell off for the Cavaliers at midseason and they dropped nine of 13 games at one point.

After losing in the first round of the ACC Tournament to Wake Forest 63-51, there was some doubt whether Virginia would be invited to the NCAA Tournament with a 17-11 record. Playing its first season without center Ralph Sampson, the Cavaliers were not a particularly attractive team.

But Virginia got the invitation and was seeded seventh in the East Regional. Holland had a new way of preparing his team for the NCAA Tournament. Prior to the opening-round victory over Iona, Holland has his team meet in a hotel suite with Bob Rotella, a Virginia professor of sports psychology.

Rotella put the players in a trance and asked them to visualize themselves doing good things on the basketball court.

The Cavaliers proceeded to surprise everyone, including themselves, by defeating Iona 58-57, Arkansas 53-51 in overtime, Syracuse 63-55 and Indiana 50-48 to advance to the Final Four.

"We've started every year thinking of the Final Four," Wilson said. "But this year I don't think we really believed it. This year, we were concerned with our ACC games. I'm surprised where we are, I admit it."

Said Holland: "Personally, I am very happy. I know people will talk about us making it this year and not when Sampson was here. I am not as good a coach as I will be made out to be for this accomplishment and not as bad a coach as I was made out to be last year when we did not go."

Without Sampson, Virginia relied on the inside play of seniors Kenton Edelin (6.4 rebounds a game) and Jim Miller (10.8 points) as well as that of freshman Olden Polynice (7.7 points, 5.6 rebounds). The guards included seniors Wilson (13.8 points) and Carlisle (11.1 points). The Cavaliers' strength might have been their depth, with capable reserves in freshman Tom Sheehey, senior Ricky Stokes, junior Dan Merrifield and junior Tim Mullen.

All that was not enough as Virginia fell to Houston, 49-47 in overtime, at the Final Four played in Seattle. Despite the loss, Virginia represented the ACC well. The Cavaliers became the fifth league team in the '80s to reach the Final Four, joining UNC in '81 and '82, Virginia in '81 and State in '83.

Lefty Driesell finally claimed his long-coveted ACC tournament title in 1984 after five losses in the championship game.

ACC BASKETBALL / THE '80s

'85

"There's just tremendous balance in college basketball, but even more so in the ACC," UNC Coach Dean Smith said prior to the 1985 season. "Can you imagine the balance we had last year with Virginia seeded sixth in the ACC Tournament to be in the Final Four?

"That's a real tribute to the balance in the league and there's even more balance this year."

Until the 1980s, there had long been a dominant team in the ACC, one that had to fend off challenges. In the league's early years, Everett Case's N.C. State Wolfpack dominated, then Vic Bubas and his Duke Blue Devils had a lock on the top spot in the mid-1960s.

Then came UNC's Smith, and his Tar Heels were top dogs through the '70s and into the '80s. They met challenges from South Carolina in the early '70s, Maryland and N.C. State in the mid-'70s, Duke in the late '70s and Virginia in the early '80s. The challengers occasionally finished first and won titles. But UNC never dropped below at least a tie for second place in the regular-season standings.

Heading into the 1985 season, instead of teams taking turns at challenging for the top spot, it appeared they were ganging up. The result? Sustained balance.

By the end of the 1985 regular season, UNC, Georgia Tech and N.C. State were tied for first place in the ACC with 9-5 records. Duke and Maryland were right behind with 8-6 records. It marked the first time that five losses within the league still qualified for first place. No team had ever finished atop the standings with four losses, and only nine times in the league's first 32 years had three losses meant first place.

Never before had so many teams been bunched so close to first place, although four were within one win of first place in 1956 and again in 1965.

None of the eight teams finished with losing overall records for a second straight season. In fact, for only the second time in league history (the other year was 1978), all teams had winning records, although Clemson (16-13), Wake Forest (15-14) and Virginia (17-16) barely made it.

Another telling factor in the league's overall balance was a diminishing home-court advantage against ACC opponents. For the first time in league history, every team lost at least two ACC home games.

"Most of the time, the ACC has got eight of the top 25 to 30 teams in the country, top to bottom," said Maryland Coach Lefty Driesell. "All these teams are well coached. You win an ACC game, I don't care whether it's home or on the road, you've done a night's work."

There were any number of reasons how all this came about:

■ Relaxed admission standards.

"The talent pool is much greater since 1973," said UNC's Smith in reference to an NCAA change that altered admission requirements for athletes. Instead of having to project a 1.6 freshman grade point average based on a combination of high school grades and college entrance exam scores, the NCAA allowed athletes to be admitted solely on a 2.0 grade-point average obtained from high school courses.

■ Emergence of talented black players.

M.L. Carr, Lloyd Free, Artis Gilmore, John Drew, Henry Logan and Earl Monroe all played at small colleges in North Carolina before going into professional basketball. Those players were either not recruited by ACC schools before blacks played in the league, or they were recruited and turned down the ACC.

By 1970 there were still only nine black players among 105 (8.6 percent) in the ACC. Of the 101 players in 1985, 63 (62.4 percent) were black. More significantly, 28 of the 40 regular starters were black.

■ Greater coaching security.

An ACC coach was no longer rushed to produce a winning team by fear that he might lose his job. New coaches such as Mike Krzyzewski at Duke, Bobby Cremins at Georgia Tech and Jim Valvano at N.C. State opted for building solid foundations that netted long-term success.

It helped that coaches were getting long-term contracts. Smith, Driesell and Valvano were all working under 10-year deals. Krzyzewski, Cremins, Virginia's Terry Holland and Wake Forest's Carl Tacy were all known to have five-year contracts. Cliff Ellis was in his first season at Clemson under a three-year agreement.

Georgia Tech Coach Dwane Morrison, who departed following the 1981 season, was the last to be fired in the ACC.

■ Athletes turning pro early.

Although it had not had a great effect by 1985, it would prove to be a significant factor later. Athletes who chose to turn professional prior to their senior year of college made the league even more balanced. The first such instance came in 1983 when UNC played without James Worthy, the first draft choice of the Los Angeles Lakers after his junior season. Then, after his junior year in 1984, Michael Jordan turned pro and joined the Chicago Bulls.

Two other prominent ACC players were missing early in the 1985 season. Center Olden Polynice left the Virginia team prior to its December game at Duke. Polynice had just been acquitted in an honor trial, even though he admitted to violating the school's honor code by turning in someone else's term paper as his own. Polynice returned to the team following the Duke game, but Virginia could still manage only three conference wins for the season. The Cavaliers' 17-16 overall record was the poorest under Holland since the 1977 season.

Two weeks after Polynice left the team, freshman center Chris Washburn was charged with second-degree burglary and dismissed from the N.C. State team. Washburn was later convicted of stealing stereo equipment from a State dormitory room. At 6-foot-11, Washburn was one of the nation's most touted high school players. Without Washburn, the Wolfpack still managed a 23-10 record and nearly reached the Final Four.

While those two ACC big men were in the headlines, the smallest player in league history was getting his share of attention as well. Tyrone Bogues, a 5-3 sophomore from Baltimore, not only proved he could play in the nation's best basketball conference but also that he could be a star. In one midseason game at Duke, playing under a death threat from a fan in Winston-Salem, Bogues had 12 points, seven assists and four steals in Wake Forest's overtime victory. He also held Johnny Dawkins to eight points, stopping the Duke guard's double-figure scoring streak at 51 games.

Although Duke dropped that game, the Blue Devils showed they were challengers for the league title when they went into UNC's Carmichael Auditorium and defeated the Tar Heels 93-77. The victory was Duke's first in Carmichael since 1966, a streak of 18 straight UNC wins.

"We had not won here in a while?" deadpanned Krzyzewski. "I did not know that."

Georgia Tech terrorized the ACC in '85 with the front-line power of Yvon Joseph (L) and John Salley.

The Tar Heels would have needed a miracle finish to defeat Duke in that game, but they had already used one to beat Maryland earlier. UNC trailed Maryland by three points with 23 seconds remaining and the Terps at the foul line. Two missed free throws by the Terps, a steal of an inbounds pass by UNC's Curtis Hunter and six straight Tar Heel points left UNC with a 75-74 victory.

All of UNC's magic at Carmichael was scheduled to end when the Tar Heels played Clemson on Feb. 27. With the Dean E. Smith Student Activities Center slated to open for the 1985-86 season, the game against Clemson was to be the finale at Carmichael. UNC easily handled the Tigers 84-50, but the game was not the last at "Blue Heaven" after all. When the Smith Center was not ready for play, the Tar Heels opened the 1985-86 season at Carmichael.

The ACC's regular-season race came down to a season-ending meeting between UNC and Duke in Durham. UNC needed a win to finish in a three-way tie with Georgia Tech and N.C. State for first place and extend the Tar Heels' streak of not having finished lower than second place to 19 years.

"I know some people don't think finishing first in the regular season means a lot any more, but it is important," said Smith following the Tar Heels' 78-68 victory. "The Tournament is three games and the regular season is 14."

The ACC Tournament played in Atlanta was as wide open as it had ever been. Typical of the first-round play was UNC's overtime victory over Wake Forest. The Demon Deacons led 47-43 late in regulation when center Charlie Thomas was called for hanging on the rim in an effort to prevent an injury. Thomas was assessed a technical foul, which resulted in a five-point swing in UNC's favor. The turn of events led to the overtime and ultimately to UNC's 72-61 victory.

The Tar Heels and Georgia Tech advanced to the championship game. While it was the first such title game for the Ramblin' Wreck, it was the 15th appearance for UNC. Tech climaxed a six-year odyssey from disgrace to respectability by defeating UNC 57-54 for the championship, its third win over UNC that season.

"I'm so proud and I'm so happy," said Georgia Tech Coach Bobby Cremins, whose club won the championship he coveted as a player at South Carolina. Having played on the losing end of South Carolina's championship game against N.C. State in 1970, Cremins was redeemed. "I feel like we have accomplished something that is very difficult to accomplish," Cremins said.

For the first time, every ACC team was invited to postseason play. In the NIT, Wake Forest lost in the first round to South Florida, 77-66; Clemson fell in the first round to Tennessee-Chattanooga, 67-65; and Virginia advanced to the quarterfinals with wins over West Virginia, 56-55, and St. Joseph's, 68-61. But the Cavaliers lost to Tennessee, 61-54.

Two of the five representatives in the NCAA were eliminated early. After defeating Pepperdine 75-62 in the Midwest Regional, Duke lost a 74-73 decision to Boston College. Maryland, which earlier in the season had posted the 500th career win for Driesell, defeated Miami of Ohio 69-68 in overtime and Navy 64-59 in the Southeast Regional before losing to eventual national champion Villanova, 46-43, in Birmingham.

The remaining three ACC teams advanced to the final of their respective regional before losing. All lost in the final to teams from the Big East Conference.

North Carolina, seeded second in the Southeast Regional, defeated Middle Tennessee State 76-57, Notre Dame 60-58 on the Fighting Irish's home court and Auburn 62-56. UNC, playing without guard Steve Hale, who suffered a separated shoulder in the Tar Heels' victory over Middle Tennessee State, fell to Villanova in the Regional final, 56-44.

Georgia Tech, seeded second in the East Regional, rolled past Mercer 65-58, Syracuse 70-53 and Illinois 61-53 before losing to No. 1-ranked Georgetown, 60-54, in Providence when sharpshooter Mark Price made only three of 16 field goal attempts.

N.C. State was probably the surprise representative from the ACC. The Wolfpack, seeded third in the West, defeated Nevada-Reno 65-56, Texas-El Paso 86-73 and Alabama 61-55. But the Wolfpack did not have enough firepower for Chris Mullin-led St. John's and fell to the Redmen, 69-60, in Denver.

ACC BASKETBALL / THE '80s

'86

Duke quickly got the ACC back in line for national championship honors when it advanced to the NCAA Final Four in 1986. The Blue Devils stormed to a first-place finish in the ACC's regular season, took the Tournament title, then reached the NCAA title game before losing to Louisville.

Along the way, Duke registered an NCAA-record 37 victories against only three losses. But the Blue Devils were not alone among ACC teams in grabbing national headlines. In fact, Duke was joined near the top of national polls throughout the season by ACC counterparts Georgia Tech and North Carolina. One of those three schools held the No. 1 national ranking in both wire service polls throughout the regular season.

Once Duke climbed into the top five following a Big Apple NIT championship victory over Kansas, the ACC's top three teams remained ranked fifth or better throughout the season. The lofty national rankings made the race for king of the hill in the ACC even more intriguing.

That three-team race developed into the one of the most interesting in league history. Over a seven-week period from mid-January to the first week of March there were seven meetings among the three teams:

■ Jan. 18—The first match between Duke and North Carolina was a momentous occasion. The game marked the official opening of the Dean E. Smith Student Activities Center, a mammoth 21,444-seat arena that was built primarily to house the UNC basketball team. The game also brought together two unbeaten teams. UNC was ranked No. 1 nationally with a 17-0 record. Duke was ranked No. 3 with a 16-0 record. Michigan was No. 2, but had lost earlier in the week to Minnesota.

"It was like being in the main event, like a big boxing match," said Duke guard Billy King. "You're down on that floor and the lights are all on you with everybody watching."

A packed house watched as a key technical foul call against Duke Coach Mike Krzyzewski led to six straight UNC points in the first half. Then guard Steve Hale (28 points on 10-of-12 shooting) led a 16-5 charge in the second half as the Tar Heels prevailed, 95-92.

■ Jan. 21—Both teams had 15-1 records with Duke ranked second nationally and Georgia Tech third when they met in Atlanta. Mark Price scored 25 points and Bruce Dalrymple 21 as Tech handed Duke its second straight loss.

■ Jan. 25—Top-ranked and unbeaten (19-0) UNC ended a three-game losing streak against Georgia Tech by defeating the fourth-ranked Ramblin' Wreck 85-77 in Chapel Hill. UNC's tall inside tandem of 6-11 Brad Daugherty (23 points, 11 rebounds) and 6-foot-11 Joe Wolf (22 points) was too much for Tech.

■ Feb. 4—The Tar Heels were still top-ranked and now 22-1 when they met Tech, 17-2 and No. 2. Down by 13 points with 12 minutes to go, UNC rallied to win a classic overtime thriller, 78-77. "It was a great basketball game," said Tech Coach Bobby Cremins. "What more can you ask? It was just a super, super basketball game."

■ Feb. 9—Duke was fourth in the national polls with a 21-2 record, and Tech was ranked third with an 18-3 record when the teams met in Durham. The rematch went to the Blue Devils, 75-59, as Mark Alarie scored 24 points and Johnny Dawkins added 22. "They were psyched up this go-round," said Tech forward Duane Ferrell.

■ March 2—Much was at stake when top-ranked Duke (28-2) faced third-ranked UNC (26-3) in the regular-season finale at Durham. A UNC win meant a three-way tie for first place among the Tar Heels, Duke and Georgia Tech. A Duke victory meant an outright first-place finish for the Blue Devils and a third-place finish for the Tar Heels.

Behind 27 points from forward David Henderson and 21 from Dawkins, Duke clinched its first outright first-place finish since 1966, which was the last time UNC failed to finish first or second in the conference.

In the process, Dawkins passed Mike Gminski (2,323 points) to become Duke's all-time career scoring leader.

"I'm not going to talk about what lies ahead," Krzyzewski said. "For four damn years we've worked for this. We're going to enjoy it."

"It was like being in the main event, like a big boxing match. You're down on that floor and the lights are all on you with everybody watching."
☐ Duke's Billy King

■ Duke also got to enjoy the ACC Tournament championship. In the final, and most important, meeting between two of the league's top three teams, the top-rated Blue Devils held off fifth-ranked Georgia Tech 68-67 at the Greensboro Coliseum.

Craig Neal missed an 18-foot shot in the closing seconds, Dawkins rebounded it and made two free throws to seal the victory and Duke's first championship since 1980.

"One by one we've accomplished all our goals this season," said Duke senior center Jay Bilas.

While the rest of the league's teams came up short in the end, they certainly were not short of noteworthy accomplishments.

At Maryland, the season of senior forward Len Bias was representative of the team's up and down year. In one mid-season game at Duke, Bias scored 41 points. Later, following a win at N.C. State, Bias and teammates Jeff Baxter and John Johnson broke curfew and were suspended by Coach Lefty Driesell. Never were Bias and the Terps better than when he scored 35 points and Maryland handed UNC its first loss in the Smith Center, 77-72 in overtime.

"If Len Bias ain't the player of the world," Driesell said, "then there ain't no players."

The loss started UNC into a tailspin that resulted in five defeats over the Tar Heels' final eight games. Prior to that point, UNC probably had as many highlights as Duke.

The Tar Heels opened the season with a convincing 107-70 victory over UCLA as Daugherty made all 13 of his field goal attempts. In the midst of a 21-game win streak to open the season, UNC defeated Nevada-Las Vegas to capture the Alaska Shootout championship and whipped Manhattan by an ACC-record 84-point margin (129-45) en route to the Orange Bowl Classic title. Also included in that streak was a 66-64 victory at Marquette, when the Tar Heels overcame a nine-point deficit in the final 4:17, and a 90-79 triumph over N.C. State to officially close—for the second time—Carmichael Auditorium to men's basketball.

UNC teams posted an eye-opening 169-20 record in games

Cremins trades goat's horns for hero's halo.

Bobby Cremins stood outside the Georgia Tech locker room in Atlanta's Omni on March 10, 1985, his shirt soaked in perspiration and his silver hair in disarray. Yet with all the disorder, everything was quite in order for Cremins. His Georgia Tech Yellow Jackets had just won the ACC Tournament with a 57-54 victory over North Carolina.

Georgia Tech's six-year odyssey from obscurity to respectability was complete, as was Cremins' 15-year longing to exchange goat horns for a hero's halo.

"This means so much to me," Cremins said. "I've always wanted to come back and win this thing."

The '80s

Georgia Tech

Fifteen years earlier, a young, dark-headed Cremins sat dejected in the South Carolina locker room and listened as N.C. State celebrated an ACC championship. The Gamecocks had gone through the regular season undefeated but needed to win the Tournament to vie for the national championship.

Minutes earlier, in the second overtime, Cremins had advanced the ball past midcourt in the Charlotte Coliseum only to have it stolen by the Wolfpack's Ed Leftwich. Cremins chased behind helplessly as Leftwich drove for an uncontested layup that gave State a 42-39 victory.

"I didn't think I'd ever get over that," Cremins says. The loss was such a bitter pill for Cremins to swallow, he escaped to a friend's cabin in the mountains of North Carolina and stayed for three weeks trying to figure out what to do with his life.

Cremins had been at such crossroads numerous times before as he went from being teenage hoodlum to basketball star to bellhop to graduate student, and, finally, to basketball coach.

He was the third of four children to Irish immigrants. His father was a longshoreman, his mother a housewife. Their son was trouble. By age 15, he had joined a New York City street gang, the Gladiators. There would be car thefts, muggings and robberies.

"One night," Cremins once told the *Atlanta Journal-Constitution*, "I got lowered down from the roof inside a grocery store and was going to get the cash register. They were lowering me down, and one of those big dogs, you know, like Rin Tin Tin, came running out barking at me. I started screaming, and they pulled me up, and we ran."

Fortunately, Cremins developed as much a liking for basketball at a young age as he did for gang life. He won a basketball scholarship to All Hallows High School, but failed to meet the academic standards during his junior year and was suspended from school. After repeating his junior year, Cremins broke his collarbone while playing football.

When his All Hallows teammates headed to a tournament in Schenectady, N.Y., Cremins stayed home to nurse his injury. Seven of his teammates were caught drinking on the trip and suspended from the team. Although still slowed by the injury, Cremins returned to the team and finished the season as the team's leader in scoring, rebounds and assists. Only 6-feet tall, Cremins often had to play center and once matched up against Power Memorial's Lew Alcindor.

Cremins was ruled ineligible for basketball the following season because he was a fifth-year student. So All Hallows Coach Bill Kenney recommended that Cremins attend Fredrick Military Academy in Portsmouth, Va. As luck would have it, South Carolina Coach Frank McGuire spotted Cremins while scouting another Fredrick Academy player. After Cremins scored 27 points in the game, McGuire offered him a scholarship.

Cremins first needed to score 800 on the college entrance exam. With one point to spare, he was off to Columbia, S.C., in August of 1966, wearing the three-piece wool suit his mother had bought him for college. He also carried a brown paper bag stuffed with clothes and a pool cue.

Adjusting to college basketball was easy for Cremins; college life was another matter. Not knowing the complicated procedure to register for classes, Cremins simply signed up for 10 courses, including chemistry, physics and French. The coaching staff quickly altered his schedule, but they forgot to tell Cremins he needed to purchase books. It wasn't until mid-semester grades were published and showed Cremins with four Fs and one D that the coaches realized the oversight.

Despite his new environs, Cremins was all South Bronx. When McGuire first had the team over to his home for a barbecue, Cremins walked directly up to the coach and said, "Hey, Frank, nice pad you got here!" Only a few days after arriving in Columbia, Cremins hopped on the rear bumper of a bus to return to campus from a movie in downtown Columbia. After a lengthy chase, the police nabbed Cremins and arrested him. Cremins was not fazed. He figured a mode of transportation used in New York was good enough for Columbia. Another time, when showing a recruit the town, Cremins drove a teammate's car through the front of a house. Cremins did not have a driver's license. The car was damaged. The house was demolished.

Known to his South Carolina teammates as "Cakes" because as a youngster he always had dirty ears, Cremins played basketball with the same kind of reckless abandon. He was 6-2, 165 pounds and full of drive and energy. He was an intense player on defense, more often than not taking the opponents' top shooter. It helped that Cremins had long arms, enabling him to touch his kneecaps with his fingertips without bending his waist. Cremins was also hard-nosed around the basket, averaging 6.8 rebounds a game for his career. Although he was not a particularly gifted shooter, Cremins managed to find ways to score and averaged 7.6 points a game.

More than anything, Cremins was a competitor. He was at his best as a sophomore when he scored 23 points, including six straight free throws (he was only a 57 percent shooter for his career) in the closing seconds, to help South Carolina upset nationally ranked North Carolina 87-86 in Chapel Hill.

ACC BASKETBALL / THE '80s

"He was all heart," McGuire says. "He had guts and he proved it in Chapel Hill when he got on the foul line in the last minute. He didn't have the ability of the other fellas, but he was better. He would get the job done."

When Cremins left South Carolina he did so without the one thing he treasured most: An ACC championship. He also left without a college degree, having fallen some 12 hours short. He was cut by the Pittsburgh Condors and the Carolina Cougars of the American Basketball Association.

He then faced another crossroad as he sat on a highway in Laurinburg, N.C., not knowing in which direction to hitchhike. He headed south to Columbia, played some AAU basketball, then was off to Italy for a year of hoops. When he returned to the United States, Cremins had no money in his pocket, and his basketball playing career was at the end of the line. He took a job at the Waldorf-Astoria Hotel in New York as a bellhop.

Six months of carrying luggage was enough to send Cremins back to Columbia, where he completed his undergraduate work and earned a degree in marketing. Basketball remained his love, and Cremins became an assistant coach, first at Point Park College in Pittsburgh, then under McGuire at South Carolina.

When Cremins took the head-coaching reins at Appalachian State, he knew very few Xs and Os. He did know something about recruiting, taking after McGuire in establishing a pipeline between New York City and North Carolina, this time to Boone instead of Chapel Hill. Six years at Appalachian netted three Southern Conference championships.

When Georgia Tech, which had recently joined the ACC, sought a new coach to build a program capable of contending with its new rivals, the school looked to Cremins. Who better to tackle what appeared to be insurmountable odds?

Cremins first asked Tech students and fans for patience. The Yellow Jackets were 1-27 against ACC competition the two seasons before Cremins arrived and 12-41 overall. A major rebuilding task was at hand.

Cremins' teams finished 10-16 and 13-15 in his first two seasons. But those faithful also saw a light at the end of Tech's dark tunnel. The light was Cremins' ability to recruit.

"A decision we made in recruiting was we wanted to go after the top-ranked players," Cremins says. "We didn't want to settle for second best, not in this league. The way we decided to go about it was to just work our butts off and hope that something good would happen."

Guard Mark Price of Enid, Okla., was the first big catch, and Cremins landed him only because the Oklahoma schools were after Wayman Tisdale, and the other ACC schools were after Steve Hale. Both were Oklahoma products.

With Price on hand and with the lure of Tech, Atlanta and the ACC, Cremins slowly began to catch other top players. John Salley and Yvon Joseph followed. Then there were Bruce Dalrymple, Duane Ferrell and Tom Hammonds, all of whom like Price were ACC Rookie of the Year.

By Cremins' fourth season at Tech, the Ramblin' Wreck was a reflection of its coach. Tech played with heart and scrapped for every loose ball, every rebound, every edge. It swept powerful North Carolina during the regular season and defeated the Tar Heels in the final of the 1985 ACC Tournament.

With that, Bobby Cremins had finally won the ACC championship that eluded him 15 years earlier. ∎

After Cremins corralled Price (25) out of Oklahoma, the likes of Salley, Dalrymple and Hammonds were soon to follow.

ACC SCRAPBOOK

Think of the basketball programs at North Carolina under Dean Smith and at Duke under Mike Krzyzewski and one word always comes to mind: Defense. The Tar Heels' reputation for trapping, half-court pressure—the kind applied at left by Steve Hale and Buzz Peterson in 1985—preceeds them, while Duke raced to Final Fours in 1986 and '88 on the strength of suffocating man-to-man pressure. Three players in ACC history have been known for their outstanding efforts on defense: Doug Moe (lower left) for UNC from 1959-60; Dudley Bradley (below) for the Tar Heels from 1976-79; and Billy King of Duke (R) from 1985-88. UNC Coach Frank McGuire once said of Moe: "His performance on defense is one of the greatest attractions in the game." Former Duke

Coach Bucky Waters added: "Moe was the most dominating defensive player that I have seen in this league. He was an absolute contract on defense." Bradley became known as UNC's "Secretary of Defense." After Arkansas All-America Sidney Moncrief made only six of 15 shots in one game against Bradley in 1979, Moncrief said, "He is the best defensive player I've ever seen." No ACC player has topped the 97 steals he made during the 1979 season. King's prowess was instrumental in Duke's run to the 1988 Final Four and included several noteworthy performances. He held Notre Dame's David Rivers to 3-of-17 shooting and drew several crucial charges (right); he limited UNC's Jeff Lebo to 2-of-14 shooting in a one-point Duke victory in February; and he reduced Temple's Mark Macon to 6-for-29 shooting in Duke's East Regional final win.

covering 22 seasons at Carmichael. N.C. State's Nate McMillan officially scored the final basket in the building. Wolfpack Coach Jim Valvano—always the ham—didn't want to come away empty-handed so he made a layup immediately following the game. Valvano took on additional duties for N.C. State this season, being named athletic director.

Wake Forest never got such satisfaction in its first season under Coach Bob Staak. He replaced Carl Tacy, whose surprise retirement after 13 seasons came on the heels of forward Kenny Green's departure for the NBA prior to his senior season. Wake Forest Athletic Director Gene Hooks first offered the job to Boston College Coach Gary Williams, who once played at Maryland. But when Williams turned down Wake Forest, Hooks turned to Staak, who was coaching at Xavier of Ohio.

Staak found the ways of the ACC difficult in his first season. The Demon Deacons became only the fourth team to go without a win against ACC competition. They followed in the footsteps, however small, of Clemson in 1954 and 1955 and Georgia Tech in 1981.

But Duke held the ACC spotlight in '86. All season long the Blue Devils seemed to find ways to win. They were an experienced group, one with four seniors and a junior in the starting lineup. If ever there was a team built around one recruiting class, it was this Duke squad.

His third recruiting class was Krzyzewski's nirvana. The class of Dawkins, Alarie, Henderson, Bilas, Weldon Williams and Bill Jackman was rated by most as the best in the country. The group entered Duke under unique circumstances. Jackman would eventually transfer to Nebraska, but four of the remaining five formed the nucleus of Duke's starting lineup as freshmen in 1983.

As a result of being thrown immediately into the ACC fire, the group suffered growing pains. An 84-77 loss to lowly Wagner in 1983 and a 109-66 thrashing by Virginia in the first round of the '83 ACC Tournament were forever reminders of where this class of athletes started.

Fans taunted the group that season and called for Krzyzewski's job. Both players and coach remained patient, interested more in long-term rewards than short-term results. An 11-17 record in 1983 turned to 24-10 in 1984 and 23-8 in 1985. The more the group played together, the better it got. By the end of four seasons, the seniors were not just a class but a class act. How they got to be such a unique group is a story in itself.

Dawkins was the ringleader. So important was Dawkins to Krzyzewski's recruiting haul, the Duke coach passed over two other potential superstars to land the 6-2 guard out of Washington, D.C. With quick, darting moves to the basket and a soft left-handed jump shot, the pencil-thin Dawkins was best suited for playing an off-guard position. But since he was called on to quarterback the team from the point guard position as a freshman, he learned better ball-handling skills and improved as a player.

By the time Dawkins left Duke, he was one of the best players in school history, and his No. 24 jersey was retired. He scored more points (2,556) than any player in Blue Devil history. He was Duke's first two-time consensus All-America, twice made all-ACC and won the Everett Case Award as the ACC Tournament MVP in '86.

The next biggest catch for Krzyzewski was Alarie, who more than being one of the nation's best prep forwards was also a straight-A student in high school. No longer using its academic standards as an excuse in recruiting, Krzyzewski used them as a tool in landing Alarie out of Scottsdale, Ariz.

As a player, Alarie could often be overlooked. His performance was rarely spectacular, but consistently good. Like Dawkins, Alarie first had to learn a position foreign to him. As a freshman, the 6-8 Alarie played center for Duke despite giving away several inches to most opponents. The season as a center helped Alarie develop power moves to the basket, made him a better rebounder and improved his defensive skills. When he moved to a forward position for his final three seasons, Alarie developed an excellent outside shooting touch, became one of the league's most versatile players and was All-ACC as a senior.

The one who seemed to add an intangible element to the group was Henderson. He was not particularly tall (6-6), strong, talented or a great shooter. But Henderson was a fierce competitor and had a will to win like perhaps no other member of the group. He was often the player Duke turned to in crucial situations, and more often than not he scored the big basket or grabbed the important rebound.

Krzyzewski went to Rolling Hills, Calif., for the 6-8, 210-bound Bilas. To play center in the ACC, Bilas eventually had to add 25 pounds to his frame, and his hulk-like appearance eventually earned him the nickname "Arnold," as in Schwarzenegger. Bilas proved to be an able rebounder and strong defensive player.

Williams' strength was as a practice player.

"It might be like the light man in a Broadway show," Williams said, "or the third-seat trombonist. Without it, there's no unity."

The final link in Duke's unity was point guard Tommy Amaker, who was recruited a year later out of Woodbridge, Va. With Amaker in charge of the offense, Dawkins was allowed to play at shooting guard. For depth, Krzyzewski called on freshman Danny Ferry, who the previous season was considered the top high school player in the country, and Billy King, a superb defender who could play guard as well as forward.

So perfect was the combination, Duke was expected to represent the ACC in the Final Four. Only N.C. State among the other four ACC representatives in the NCAA Tournament threatened to reach the NCAA semifinals. State, which lost

Carl Tacy's Wake Forest teams were always competitive during his 13 seasons at the Deacon helm (222-149 record), but he retired after the 1985 season to enter private business.

its sixth of seven games in a first-round defeat to Virginia in the ACC Tournament, recovered to down Iowa 66-64, Arkansas-Little Rock 80-66 in two overtimes, and Iowa State 70-66 in the NCAA Tournament. The Wolfpack appeared headed to Dallas and the Final Four when it led Kansas 57-52 with nine minutes remaining in the Midwest Regional final at Kansas City. But the Jayhawks rallied behind 10 straight points by Danny Manning to win, 75-67.

The Blue Devils, top-seeded in the East Regional, struggled past Mississippi Valley State 85-78 in the first round, then reeled off victories over Old Dominion, 89-61, and DePaul, 74-67, to reach the East final against Navy.

Navy featured 6-11 David Robinson, who posed a rebounding problem for the smaller Blue Devils. But Bilas matched Robinson's rebound total of 10, and Duke out-rebounded the Midshipmen 49-29 en route to a 71-50 victory.

In the NCAA semifinals in Dallas, Duke matched its 36-2 record against the 35-3 record of Kansas, which had lost to Duke 92-86 in the first Big Apple NIT championship early in the season. Again, Duke faced a size problem. Kansas featured 7-1 Greg Dreiling and the 6-11 Manning.

As always, Duke made up for lack of size with aggressive, man-to-man pressure that made each Kansas pass difficult. Still, Kansas led 65-61 with 4:23 to play. From that point, Duke shifted its defensive pressure into high gear and outscored the Jayhawks 10-2 the rest of the way for a 71-67 victory.

In the championship game, Duke faced a Louisville club that featured 18-year-old freshman center Pervis Ellison. He earned MVP honors with 25 points and 11 rebounds. Herbert Crook had 12 rebounds for the Cardinals, leading them to a significant 39-27 rebounding edge over the Blue Devils. Louisville also made 58 percent of its field goal attempts, compared to 40.3 percent for Duke.

Those two factors added up to a 72-69 victory and the national championship for Louisville.

"I don't want our guys hanging their heads," Krzyzewski said. "They've had an excellent season, and it's been an excellent four years for the seniors."

Two members of Duke's prized '82 recruiting class, Mark Alarie (L) and Jay Bilas (inset), helped propel the Blue Devils into the '86 Final Four.

Bias story one of triumph and tragedy.

Lorenzo Charles worked all over the Cole Field House court in an attempt to contain Maryland forward Len Bias. The N.C. State forward was then informed that Bias wore a gold necklace with a Superman insignia around his neck.

"Superman?" Charles asked. "I don't know about that, but sometimes he doesn't seem human."

For parts of four seasons (1983-86), Len Bias was a superhuman basketball player in the Atlantic Coast Conference. Twice he was the league's Player of the Year. Twice he led the conference in scoring. More than once he was compared to some of the game's best all-time players.

The '80s
Maryland

"When you think of Bias, you think of (Michael) Jordan," Virginia Coach Terry Holland once said in reference to the former North Carolina All-America. "Few thought anybody would achieve that status around here for a long time, but Bias has come as close as you can get, if he's not there already. He can go inside and out. He's certainly that type of player."

George Karl, a former UNC player and later coach of the Golden State Warriors in the NBA, once told *USA Today*: "He has great body strength. The comparison is to Dominique Wilkins—not as explosive but he shoots better. The pro game will enhance him."

Tragically, Bias never played a pro game.

In the early morning of June 19, 1986, two days after being selected by the Boston Celtics as the second pick in the NBA draft, Len Bias was dead. While at a private party in room 1103 of the Washington Hall dormitory on the University of Maryland campus, Bias ingested a lethal dose of cocaine.

One of the ACC's best basketball players ever, and certainly one of its better athletes, was dead at age 22. His death stunned an entire nation of college basketball fans. It also helped open the nation's eyes to the harmful effects of cocaine.

"This is perhaps the saddest day in the history of the University of Maryland," said Maryland Chancellor John B. Slaughter at a news conference following Bias' death.

Bias had as great an impact on ACC basketball as any player in league history. In the wake of Bias' death, Maryland Coach Lefty Driesell was forced to resign, and Athletic Director Dick Dull stepped down. Bias' death led to a lengthy investigation of the Maryland athletic department. When it was found that he was 21 hours shy of graduation after four years of eligibility, stricter guidelines were established for Maryland student-athletes. The internal investigation by Maryland also led to a closer look at programs by other ACC schools.

"We're all shocked to hear of his death," N.C. State Athletic Director and Basketball Coach Jim Valvano said, speaking in essence for the entire ACC. "We choose, though, to remember him as a truly great basketball player in the college ranks and as a very fine young man."

Bias emerged as a force with 56 points and MVP honors in leading the Terps to the '84 ACC title.

That Bias was such an exemplary role model was perhaps what made his death so tragic. He was the oldest of four children to James and Lonise Bias. To his family, Len was known as "Frosty," because when he was born, "he had one little white layer of skin on him, and he peeled a lot," Lonise said. He was reared in a deeply religious, middle-class family in Landover, Md., on the outskirts of Washington, D.C. Prior to his senior season at Maryland, Bias became a born-again Christian, confirming his faith once again at the Pilgrim AME Church in Washington.

"As my wife said, 'He's in a better position than we are—he's at home with the Lord,'" Driesell said following Bias' death. "I'm sad but I'm not worried because I know he's in heaven . . . I love him and I'll miss him."

Driesell watched Bias progress from a gangly freshman who was uncomfortable with his skills to a polished senior who was confident to the point of being cocky.

Point guard Keith Gatlin, who roomed with Bias on road trips, once told *The Washington Post*: "We had this thing when we turned out the light. Len would say, 'Who you going to throw the ball to?'

'You, big fella.'

'Okay, now I can sleep.'"

As a freshman, Bias was neither a particularly sound

ball handler nor an outstanding shooter. He averaged only 22 minutes and seven points a game in 1983. But an important part of Bias' development came during the summer following his freshman season, when he took a job as a custodian and security guard at an elementary school near his home in Landover. Bored with his work, Bias took advantage of the school's gymnasium. He soon developed a better shooting touch and improved his ball handling.

Bias won an NCAA Tournament game for Maryland against Tennessee-Chattanooga with a last-second shot his freshman season. But it wasn't until he scored 56 points on 26-of-43 shooting and had 18 rebounds in three games of the 1984 ACC Tournament that Bias emerged as a star. He earned Tournament MVP honors in leading Maryland to its first ACC title since 1958.

As a junior, he led the league in scoring with a 19-point average and was selected the league's Player of the Year. His string of 52 straight games scoring in double figures ended when Maryland lost to Villanova in the NCAA Tournament.

Bias then opted for summer school instead of the U.S. Olympic Trials, and turned down lucrative offers to turn pro. He was prepared to showcase his wares during his senior season. His 41-point performance at Duke was a career high and the second highest total in Maryland history. Never was Bias better than during a 35-point effort in an overtime victory at North Carolina, the Tar Heels' first loss in the Smith Center. Late in overtime, Bias stole an inbounds pass and converted it into a dunk shot, then blocked the shot of UNC's Kenny Smith as he drove down the lane.

"If Bias is not the player of the world, then people just don't know basketball," Driesell said afterward.

Bias was a unanimous selection to the All-ACC team and was a decisive choice as the league's Player of the Year over Duke's Johnny Dawkins. Bias improved his all-around game to the point where he led the league in scoring (23.2 average) and free throw shooting (86.4 percent), ranked fourth in rebounding (7.0 a game) and eighth in field goal shooting (54.4 percent).

"I think if I did anything else in life, I could have become successful at it," Bias once told *The Baltimore Sun*. "I just want to be better than anybody thought I could become. Whenever anybody has criticized me, I've worked harder. When people said I couldn't shoot, I worked on my shot. When they said I wasn't a ball handler, I worked on that."

His work made him a professional prospect. When he was selected behind UNC's Brad Daugherty in the first round of the NBA draft, Bias said it was a "dream within a dream" to not only play professionally but to also play for the Boston Celtics.

He met with Celtics officials the day following the draft and also signed a $1.6 million endorsement contract with Reebok shoes. Less than 24 hours later, Bias was dead.

"Len Bias was a gifted, special person," Bias' father, James, told *USA Today*. "I don't know if he ever realized his gift or how special he really was." ∎

'87

A dark cloud hung over the ACC long before the 1987 season began. For some five months the league remained in a state of shock over the tragic death of Maryland basketball star Len Bias.

Bias was the ACC's Player of the Year in 1985 and again in 1986. He was All-America both of those seasons. At 6-foot-8, Bias was the model basketball player. He was a finely tuned athlete who seemed to draw as much pleasure out of playing the game as fans throughout the league derived in watching him play.

His MVP performance in 1984 led Maryland to its first ACC Tournament championship in 26 years. His 35-point performance in 1986 was instrumental in Maryland handing North Carolina its first loss in the new Smith Activities Center.

In four seasons at Maryland, Bias matured on the basketball court from a shy freshman who was unsure of his abilities to a standout senior who believed he was as good as any player in the country. Bias' development so impressed pro scouts that he was the second player selected in the 1986 NBA draft. The Boston Celtics picked Bias with the belief that he would help them to a second straight world championship.

On June 19, two days after the draft, Len Bias was dead.

First reports indicated Bias died of a mysterious seizure inside a dormitory on the Maryland campus. A lengthy police investigation followed and found that Bias had died of cocaine intoxication while in the company of several teammates.

Further investigation revealed that Bias was attending summer school at the time and was woefully deficient in his academic standing with the university. That launched an investigation of the Maryland athletic department, particularly the basketball program, under the direction of Maryland Chancellor John D. Slaughter.

As a result of the investigation, Maryland officials called for drug tests of its athletes and closer monitoring of their academic progress. The 1987 Maryland season was cut short, with the season opener held back until January.

Before the summer was over, Dick Dull had resigned as Maryland's athletic director. Then Coach Lefty Driesell, who in 17 seasons had built one of the nation's strongest basketball programs, reluctantly resigned at the request of Slaughter to take another position in the athletic department.

Slaughter then replaced Driesell with 41-year-old Bob Wade, who in 11 seasons as coach at Dunbar High School in Baltimore produced a 272-24 record, three No. 1 national rankings, nine state championships and 36 major-college players. Wade became the first black head coach in the ACC.

"I don't look at it as a color situation," Wade said. "I don't think Coach (Mike) Krzyzewski at Duke thought of himself as the first of his ethnic group. It's just an opportunity to coach at the college level.

"(The media) makes this out to be a challenge, but I treat this as my job. We've got to get off the front page and into the sports page. That is my job, my profession, my livelihood."

The late-season start for Maryland, and the loss of its four leading scorers plus seven of 11 scholarship players, made Wade's livelihood difficult for the 1987 season. The only returning player with considerable playing experience was center Derrick Lewis.

The Terps were competitive in many games against ACC opponents, but more often than not they were outmanned. Maryland joined the Clemson teams of 1954 and 1955, Georgia Tech of 1981 and Wake Forest of 1986 as the only clubs to go

251

winless in the ACC. The Terps managed a 9-17 record that included one midseason upset of West Virginia.

At the expense of Maryland, Wake Forest managed to end the second longest losing streak against ACC opponents in league history. The Deacons fell three short of Clemson's 28-game losing streak against ACC opponents from 1954 through 1956. Wake's streak ended at 25 with a 69-58 victory over Maryland at the Winston-Salem Coliseum at midseason. Later in the season, Wake defeated Maryland again, 75-68.

Clemson Coach Cliff Ellis could certainly relate to the rebuilding job Wade was doing at Maryland and Coach Bob Staak was experiencing at Wake Forest. By his third season, Ellis had his Tigers in position not only to establish respectability, but also to challenge for the ACC championship.

A soft early season schedule led to most of Clemson's first 17 wins, including a 112-39 decision over Armstrong State that represented the largest margin (73 points) of victory for the Tigers since 1911. Another early season win came at Georgia Tech, as Clemson served notice to the rest of the league that it was for real. Two losses each to Duke and UNC prevented the Tigers from finishing first in the regular season.

Nevertheless, Clemson's 10-4 record within the league was its best ever and accounted for the Tigers' second-place finish. Only two other Clemson teams (1975 and '77) had managed such a standing, and only six other Tiger teams had posted winning records within the league. Clemson won 25 games for the first time in school history.

"We believe in our team," Ellis said.

Mostly, Ellis believed in 6-10 center Horace Grant, the ACC Player of the Year. Grant became the seventh player in history to lead the league in scoring (21.0 average) and rebounding (9.6).

Only another superb season by UNC took some of the shine off Clemson's outstanding year. The Tar Heels dominated the regular season like few teams had done in ACC history. They went unbeaten in the ACC, just as UNC did in 1957, Duke in 1963, South Carolina in 1970, N.C. State in 1973 and 1974, and UNC in 1984.

Only an early season loss at UCLA and a midseason defeat at Notre Dame stood between UNC and a perfect regular season. Otherwise, the Tar Heels were ranked No. 1 in the country most of the way. They handled such notable non-league opponents as No. 2 Purdue and No. 5 Illinois. Key games within the league included a 108-99 win at Clemson when a 41-point effort by guard Kenny Smith overcame a 50-38 halftime deficit; a 94-85 decision over Wake Forest on Feb. 11 that marked the 600th win of Coach Dean Smith's career; and a 96-80 triumph over Clemson in Chapel Hill that assured UNC of a first-place finish for the 14th time in Smith's 26 years at the helm.

The Tar Heels fully utilized the rules adopted for all of college basketball in 1987. UNC played its usual fast-paced game with pressure defense to take advantage of the 45-second clock. The Tar Heels also took great liberties in shooting from 3-point range, which was 19 feet, 9 inches from the basket.

As a result, UNC fell just short of N.C. State's ACC scoring record average of 92.9 points in 1973. The Tar Heels averaged 91.3 points a game.

Fans and players seemed to like the new rules. Coaches were not so sure. They all liked the shot clock, but ACC coaches were split over the 3-point basket. Ellis, Smith, Wade and N.C. State's Jim Valvano favored the 3-pointer. Duke's Mike Krzyzewski, Georgia Tech's Bobby Cremins and Wake Forest's Bob Staak were against it. Virginia's Terry Holland took the

ACC defenses mere mincemeat to minute Muggsy.

The '80s
Wake Forest

Nate McMillan quickly surveyed the open court ahead of him, making certain that Tyrone "Muggsy" Bogues was nowhere in sight. McMillan, N.C. State's steady point guard, was fully aware of Coach Jim Valvano's Muggsy Rule.

"If you don't see that little sucker in front of you, never, never dribble the basketball," Valvano said over and over again prior to the Wolfpack's meeting with Wake Forest during the 1987 season. "Make sure Bogues is in front of you before you put the ball on the floor."

McMillan was near midcourt and saw an open path to the State basket. He figured there was no way Bogues could swipe the ball this time, and quickly dribbled full-speed to the basket. McMillan had again underestimated the quickness of Bogues, who sneaked behind him, swiped the ball, reversed directions and headed toward the Wake Forest basket.

McMillan looked to Valvano and shook his head. Valvano threw up his arms in despair. They weren't the first to be awed by Muggsy, a 5-foot-3 blur in sneakers.

"We never bring the ball up against Muggsy," said Maryland Coach Lefty Driesell. "I ain't that dumb. I saw Muggsy play in high school for two, three years and he'd steal the ball off Houdini."

From 1983 through 1987 Bogues was the Houdini of ACC basketball. But in addition to being the league's most entertaining player, Bogues was one of its most outstanding. By starring for underdog Wake Forest, Bogues also won the hearts of ACC players, coaches and fans. His electrifying quickness, ball-handling skills and reckless style of play made him one of the Deacons' all-time best players.

When Wake Coach Carl Tacy signed Bogues out of Baltimore's Dunbar High School, skeptics were aplenty. Monte Towe could have eaten a bowl of cereal right off the top of Bogues' head, the skeptics said. No way someone smaller than Towe, the 5-7 former State point guard, could play in the ACC. Four years later, Bogues was among the league's top point guards. He was a first-team All-ACC selection in 1987 and had his jersey No. 14 retired by Wake Forest prior to his last home game.

"I proved that you shouldn't judge a person by his size," Bogues said. "Judge him by his ability."

Bogues' dogged determination to overcome his height was evident to his mother from an early age.

"Whenever Tyrone wanted to do something, he was

ACC BASKETBALL / THE '80s

At 5-foot-3, Bogues (14) survived in a land of the giants by robbing dribblers of their bounce: "He can strip them at halfcourt in front of God and the world."

going to do it come hell or high water," Elaine Bogues told the *Greensboro News & Record*. "Like when I told him he was too little to walk downstairs by himself. One day he got away from me, and I found him outside the ground floor. He's like that. When somebody tells him he can't do something, he works that much harder to do it."

Bogues was told often as a youngster that he could not play with the taller boys on the courts near the Lafayette Court housing project where he was reared. But Bogues persisted, and soon he was recognized for his exceptional skills, much like Skip Wise was more than a decade earlier.

"I think he pretty much set the pace for the guys in Baltimore and in the city," Bogues says of Wise, who was an All-ACC player in 1975 at Clemson before heading down an ill-fated road that led to prison. "Skip was a legend as a basketball player in Baltimore. We all grew up in the streets. We saw the illegal things going on, but what happened to Skip got us to realize that wasn't a way out. That helped us to get our minds straight."

At Dunbar High School, Bogues played on teams that included David Wingate (who later played at Georgetown), Reggie Lewis (Northeastern), Gary Graham (Nevada-Las Vegas), Keith James (UNLV) and Michael Brown (Clemson).

Bogues was voted the team's most valuable player as it went 59-0 over his final two seasons and was ranked as the nation's No. 1 prep team.

"I predict Muggsy will rewrite the ACC records in steals and assists," said Dunbar Coach Bob Wade when Bogues signed with Wake Forest. When Wade later coached at Maryland, he had to face Bogues.

Bogues the freshman waited his turn as senior guard Danny Young led Wake Forest to the NCAA Tournament's round of 16. Once he got the chance to run Wake Forest's show as a sophomore in 1985, Bogues became an instant attraction around the ACC.

Most teenagers who crowded him for autographs were taller than Bogues. Muggsy—nicknamed after the Bowery Boys character who was the leader of a gang of street kids—could relate to the youngsters because he was still buying clothes in the boys' department. What made him different, however, was his strength and quickness. Bogues was a solid 145 pounds, and opponents often swore he had more than two hands.

"I don't know how you could steal the ball from him, unless you're a groundhog," said Temple Coach John Chaney.

"You try to trap that little dude, and you'll go bonkers," said Clemson guard Grayson Marshall. "We tried that and he made mincemeat out of us."

Bogues was even more intimidating when the opponent had the ball. Every opponent altered its offense to keep the ball away from Bogues.

"He activates a primal fear in guards he faces," Wake Forest Assistant Coach Ernie Nestor told *The Washington Post*. "They know he can strip them at halfcourt in front of God and the world."

Bogues gained national recognition as a sophomore for his 20-point, 10-assist performance against N.C. State in Greensboro. Wake's 91-64 victory was shown on national TV.

"In 40 years, I've never seen a player dominate a game the way Muggsy Bogues did," NBC's Al McGuire said.

By his senior season, Bogues was a co-captain for the Deacons. He led the team in scoring (14.8 average) in 1987 and led the ACC in assists, steals and minutes played for a third straight season.

"A lot of people just didn't understand the kind of impact he can have in a basketball game," Nestor said. "The barometer on which they judged him was how big he was, and that's a poor barometer. If I remember my history right, Napoleon wasn't much bigger, and he almost conquered the world."

After conquering the ACC, Bogues was the 12th player selected in the 1987 NBA draft. He became the shortest player in NBA history. During his rookie season with the Washington Bullets, he sat courtside one afternoon in Atlanta and reflected on his days at Wake Forest.

"I hope that something like 20 years from now, maybe someone will remember that a 5-3 guy played with the guys who were supposed to be the stars," Bogues said. "There was no doubt at all that I could play. I always thought I was capable of playing on any level. It was just a matter of proving to the rest of the people that a guy my size can compete. That's what I was out to do, not only to those people, but to myself."

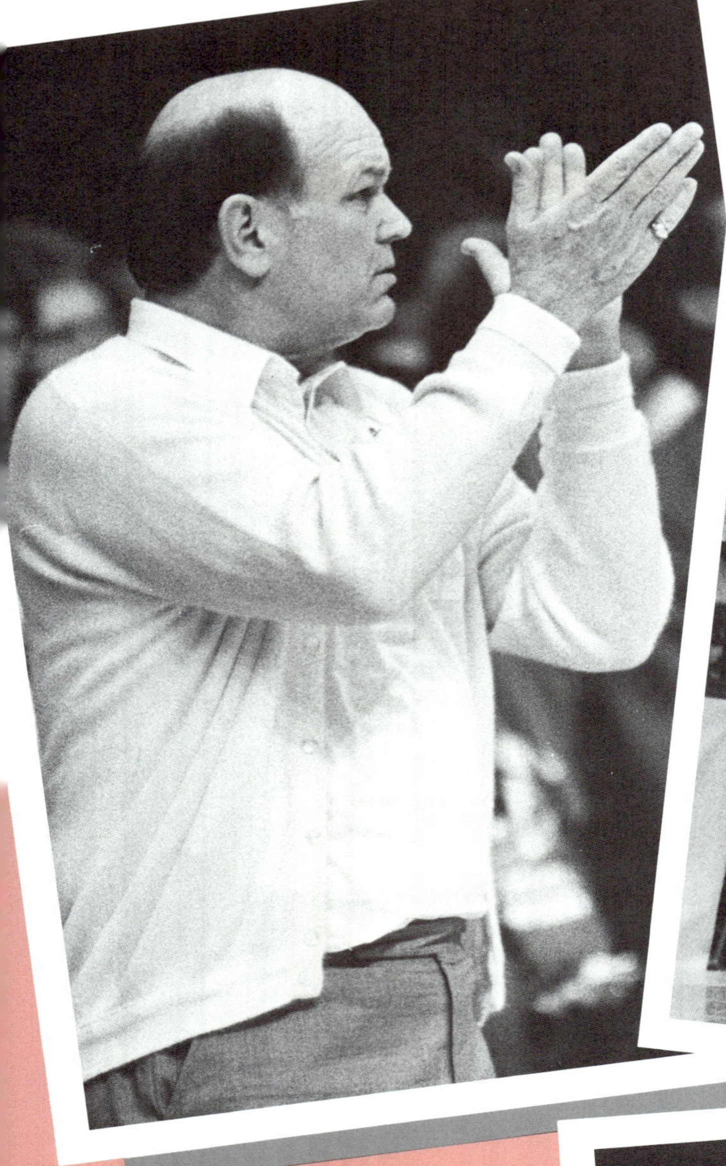

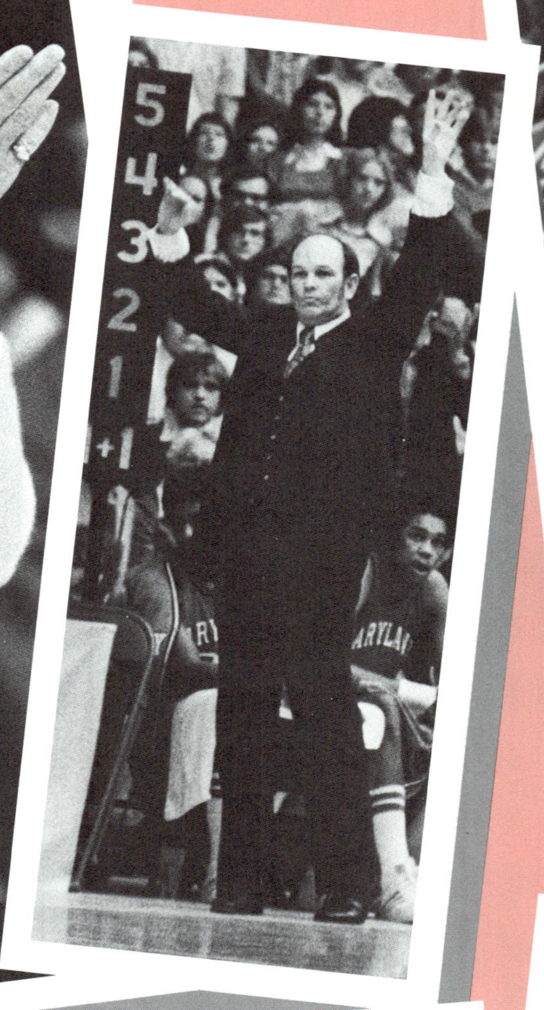
5
4
3
2
1
+1

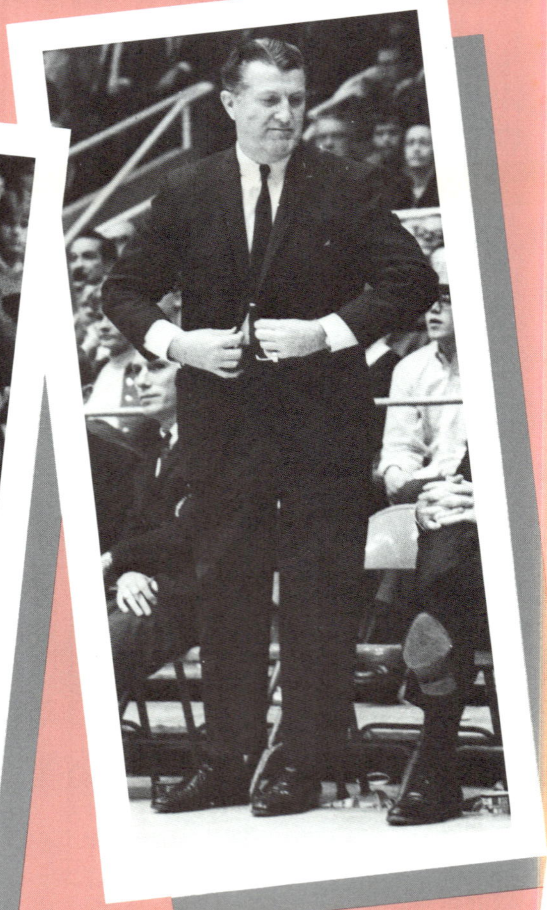

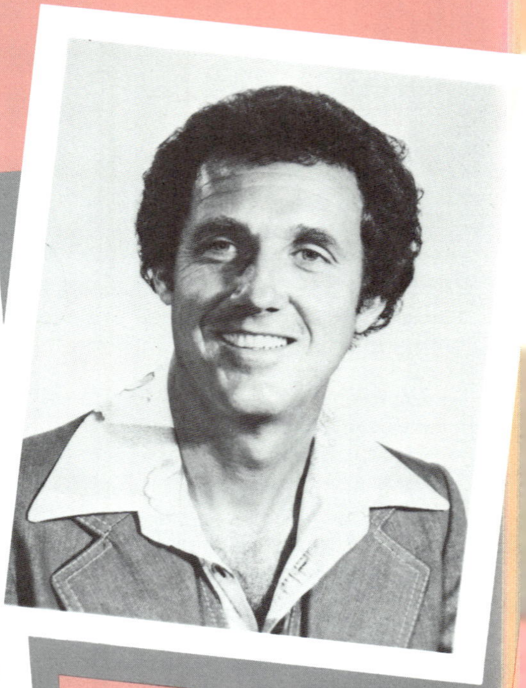

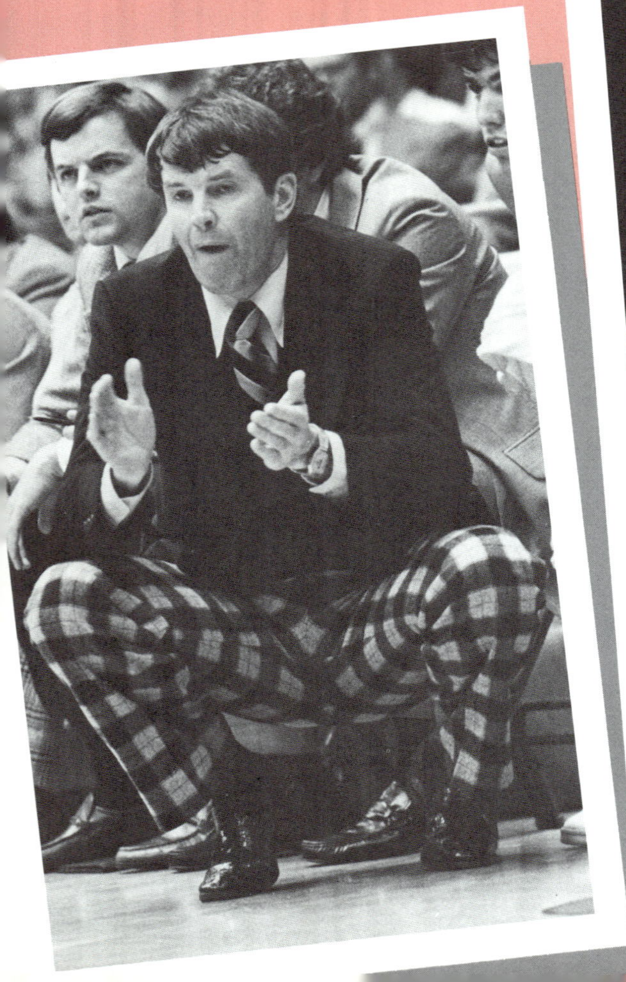

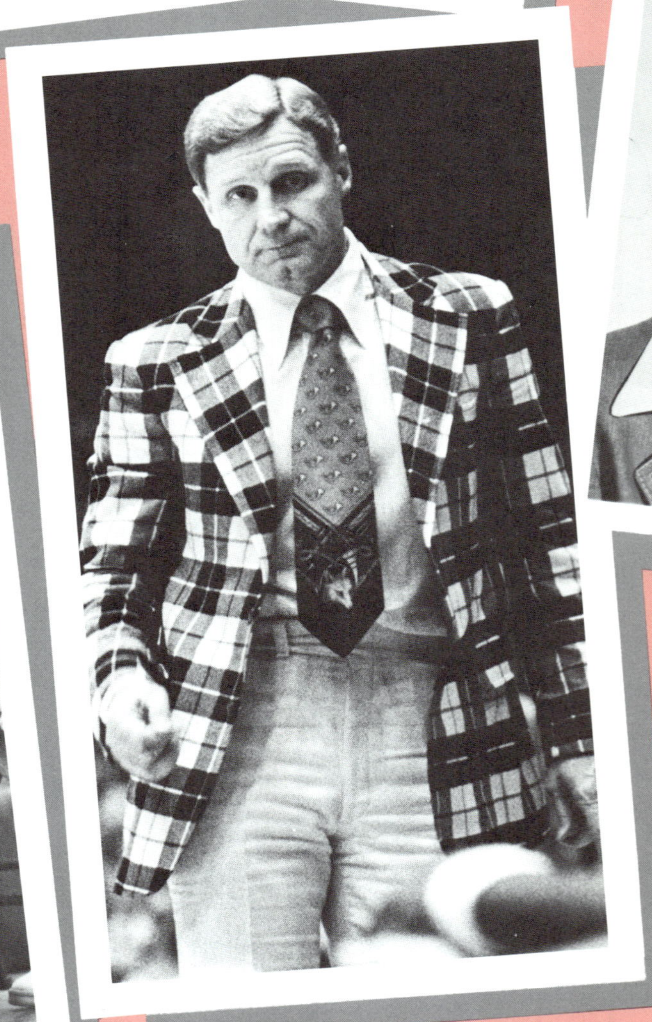

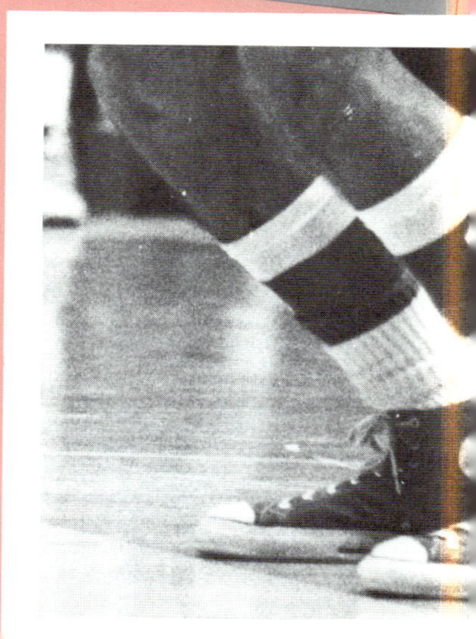

ACC SCRAPBOOK

From the GQ guide to ACC fashion (clockwise from left): A crew-cutted row of UNC Tar Heels watches from the bench in 1959 in their heavy, hooded warm-ups, while Clemson's Rock Stone models his full-sleeved jersey (circa 1956). ■ The Tar Heels led the league in '72 in wins and odd stares with their baby blue shoes and numbered stockings. ■ Bill Foster of Clemson collared best-dressed awards with his mid-'70s leisure suit, while N.C. State's Norman Sloan and Duke's Bill Foster felt these threads from their psychedelic haberdashers were good luck charms during Final Four runs in '74 and '78. ■ Maryland's Lefty Driesell felt more comfortable in a golf shirt and sweater in the mid-'80s after enduring the three-piece suit era of the late-'70s, while Frank McGuire, first at UNC and later at South Carolina, set the standards with carefully knotted ties and buttoned jackets. ■ Tar Heel Coach Dean Smith reflects the signs of the times with skinny lapels and shiny hair in the '60s, fat lapels and a kaleidoscope tie in the '70s, and the polished chairman of the board look of the '80s.

middle ground.

"Years from now," Smith said, "we'll look back and wonder what all the controversy was about. It'll be like the center jump being done away with after each goal."

Cremins said of the 3-pointer, "We should move it back or eliminate it."

N.C. State entered the ACC Tournament needing a championship to gain a berth in the NCAA after a 17-14 regular season. Playing without center Chris Washburn, who skipped his final two seasons to turn pro, State at one point lost six straight games. The Wolfpack defeated Duke 71-64 in the first round and Wake Forest 77-73 in the semifinals. State needed one overtime to down Duke, and two to get by Wake Forest. For the championship in Landover, Md., State met second-ranked UNC, which had downed Maryland 82-63 in the first round and Virginia 84-82 in another two-overtime semifinal game.

State stunned UNC 68-67 behind the MVP performance of Vinny Del Negro. A reserve during much of the regular season, Del Negro made two free throws to clinch the victory with 14 seconds remaining.

The State victory avenged losses of 18 and 17 points to UNC in the regular season.

State's game plan was simple: Prevent UNC's backcourt from scoring and beat the Tar Heels on the boards. The Wolfpack was good on both counts as UNC guards Smith and Jeff Lebo combined for 17 points on 7-of-19 shooting, while Chucky Brown's 10 rebounds led State to a 30-20 edge on the boards.

With State gaining the automatic invitation to the NCAA Tournament, the ACC was represented in postseason play by six teams. But it was not a particularly successful tournament for the league as four teams fell in the opening round.

Clemson, slowed in the ACC Tournament by an ankle injury to guard Grayson Marshall, fell to Southwest Missouri State 65-60 in the Southeast Regional. Georgia Tech lost in the opening round of the Midwest Regional, 85-79 to LSU; and Virginia quickly dropped out of the West Regional, 64-60 at the hands of Wyoming. In a first-round matchup, State lost 82-70 to former Wolfpack Coach Norm Sloan and his Florida team in the East Regional.

Just as it did during the regular season, Duke continued to surprise in the NCAA Tournament. The Blue Devils, who lost four starters to graduation following their NCAA runner-up finish in 1986, were expected to drop to the middle of the ACC pack in '87. Instead, they rebounded and finished third in the regular season with a 9-5 record.

In the NCAA Tournament, youthful Duke first defeated Texas A&M 58-51, then Xavier, 65-60. But eventual NCAA champion Indiana was too much for the Blue Devils, who fell 88-82 in the semifinals of the Midwest Regional at Indianapolis. It marked the first time that one of Krzyzewski's teams had faced an Indiana team coached by his mentor, Bob Knight.

With senior guard Kenny Smith leading the way, UNC averaged 91.3 points a game in '87.

UNC was the top-seeded team in the East Regional, and the Tar Heels appeared to be headed to the Final Four with a 113-82 win over Pennsylvania followed by a 109-97 victory over Michigan in Charlotte. UNC got revenge for an mid-season loss to Notre Dame with a 74-68 victory in the East Regional semifinals at East Rutherford, N.J.

But Syracuse used its superior quickness and a 42-32 rebounding margin to stun UNC 79-75 for the East Regional championship and a trip to the Final Four.

"This has been a great North Carolina team, one of the best we've ever had," Smith said of his 32-4 Tar Heels. "But I know you have to be lucky and you have to be good (to reach the Final Four)."

ACC BASKETBALL / THE '80s

'88

Even during what was generally considered a down season for the ACC, four teams were ranked in the Top 20 at least once, five received bids to the NCAA Tournament, another went to the NIT and Duke reached the Final Four.

Still, there was a telltale indicator that the league was not as strong as usual. The ACC's record against non-conference opponents slipped to 93-33, a .738 percentage that was the lowest since a .724 winning percentage in 1970. By comparison, the league won 86.3 percent of its games against non-conference teams in 1976.

Perhaps the slip resulted from more balance throughout college basketball or from the scheduling of more difficult non-conference games by ACC teams. But there were other reasons.

The ACC's slide probably started four years earlier with a poor recruiting class for almost the entire league. Next came a coaching change at Wake Forest following the 1985 season, then the tragic death of Maryland star Len Bias following the 1986 season.

The bottom fell out of the league's balance with the latter two incidents. Wake went winless within the league in 1986 and Maryland did the same in '87. Previously, only three ACC teams went winless within the league: Clemson in 1954 and 1955 and Georgia Tech in 1981, its first ACC season.

When Carl Tacy departed after 13 seasons at Wake Forest, he left the cupboard bare for new Coach Bob Staak. By 1988, Staak was still building a foundation for the Demon Deacons and they were beginning to reap rewards.

Although it finished in last place for the second time in three seasons under Staak, Wake registered stunning upsets over N.C. State and North Carolina within an eight-day period in late January. The Deacons first defeated the 20th-ranked Wolfpack, 71-68, then downed the third-ranked Tar Heels, 83-80.

The turnaround at Maryland was even more dramatic. The death of Bias eventually meant the end of Lefty Driesell's 17-year coaching career at Maryland and a reduced schedule for 1987. But new Coach Bob Wade did a remarkable job in getting the program back on its feet in less than two seasons.

Maryland managed six wins within the league, 18 overall and advanced to the second round of the NCAA Tournament before losing to No. 6 Kentucky, 91-80.

Clemson, with its youngest team ever and Grayson Marshall as its only senior, fell to 14-15 for the season after losing to Southern Mississippi, 74-69, in the opening round of the NIT.

Clemson's youth was representative of the entire league as four teams had only one senior: Marshall at Clemson, Derrick Lewis at Maryland, Ranzino Smith at UNC and Mitch Cullin at Wake Forest. The disastrous recruiting season of 1984 helped explain why the ACC was so young in '88.

Of the 26 players signed by ACC schools as the freshman class of 1985, only 13 remained in the league by the conclusion of the '88 season. Of those 13 not a single one was considered a superstar by ACC standards and only N.C. State guard Vinny Del Negro was a first-team All-ACC selection. Seniors Duane Ferrell of Georgia Tech, Mel Kennedy of Virginia and Lewis of Maryland were all second-team selections.

State, Virginia and Georgia Tech were thought to have had excellent recruiting years in 1984. But the Wolfpack's big prize that year, center Chris Washburn, left after only two seasons for the NBA. With Del Negro providing the leadership, State was 24-8 overall in '88 and finished second in the league with

Coaches Bob Staak (top) at Wake Forest and Bob Wade at Maryland began to reap the rewards of their rebuilding efforts in 1988.

a 10-4 record. But the Wolfpack bowed out in the first round of the NCAA Tournament with a 78-75 upset loss to Murray State. Following the loss, State Coach Jim Valvano interviewed for the UCLA head coaching job and was reported to have taken it. But Valvano said family considerations prevented him from taking the job, and he remained at State.

Virginia's senior class remained intact with Kennedy, John Johnson, Darrick Simms, John Dyslin and Tim Martin. But Kennedy was suspended for academic reasons and missed the first eight games of '88, then Johnson was suspended when he failed a drug test and missed the Cavaliers' final six games. The unrest resulted in a 13-18 record for Virginia, its first losing season since 1977.

Georgia Tech's recruiting class of '84 fell apart as Bud Adams, Willie Reese and Antoine Ford all left the program. With Dennis Scott winning a fifth ACC Rookie of the Year award for Tech in six seasons, the Yellow Jackets went 22-10 before losing in the second round of the NCAA Tournament, 59-55 to Richmond. Scott's 3-pointer from 24 feet at the buzzer gave Tech a 71-70 victory over DePaul in early February and sent the Yellow Jackets on a seven-game win streak that vaulted them into the Top 20.

Sports Illustrated
LA IS THE CHAMP
ALT HAZZARD DRIVES
HROUGH DUKE

Sports Illustrated
JANUARY 4, 1971 60 CENTS
CHALLENGE FROM THE SOUTH
Hard-driving John Roche

COLLEGE BASKETBALL
Sports Illustrated
YEAR OF THE NEW GIANTS
7'4" Tom Burleson of North Carolina State

COLLEGE BASKE
Sports Illustrat
North Carolina State's David Thompson Threatens UCLA

Sports Illustrated
DECEMBER 10, 1973 60 CENTS
UCLA BY A WHISKER
Maryland's Len Elmore Battles Bill Walton

BABE RUTH Part 2
Sports Illustrated
MARCH 25, 1974 60 CENTS
THIS TIME IT'S FOR KEEPS
UCLA vs. North Carolina State

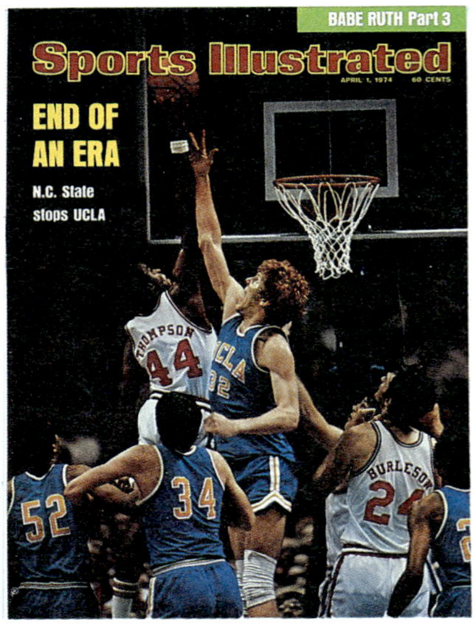
BABE RUTH Part 3
Sports Illustrated
APRIL 1, 1974 60 CENTS
END OF AN ERA
N.C. State stops UCLA

Sports Illustrat
UPSET IN THE ACC
Phil Ford Kicks Up His Tar Heels

Sports Illustrated
APRIL 4, 1977 ONE DOLLAR
MARQUETTE MAKES ITS MARK
Butch Lee Burns Carolina in the NCAAs

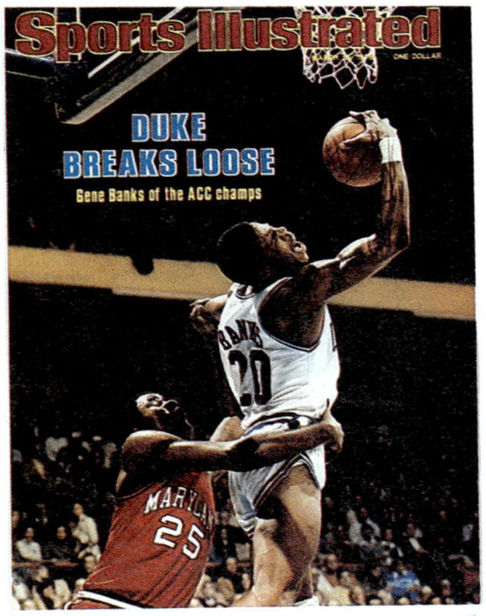
Sports Illustrated
ONE DOLLAR
DUKE BREAKS LOOSE
Gene Banks of the ACC champs

Sports Illustrated
STEALING THE ACC TITLE
Dudley Bradley Dunks Duke

Sports Illustrat
DECEMBER
LADIES AND GENTLEMEN,INTRO
THE ONE AND ONLY RALPH SA
HE DUNKS! HE BLOCKS
HE DRIBBLES BEHIND HI
HE'S 7'4" --AND STILL GR

COLLEGE BASKETBALL ISSUE
Sports Illustrated
DECEMBER 1, 1980 $1.50
That Old School Spirit
Ralph Sampson Virginia
Albert King, Maryland
Mark Aguirre, DePaul

Sports Illustrated
MARCH 30, 1981 $1.50
AND NOW, THE FINAL FOUR
Ralph Sampson Of Virginia Reaches for the Top

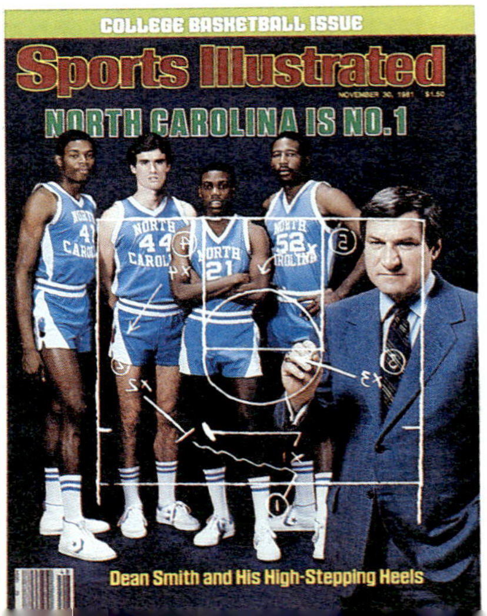
COLLEGE BASKETBALL ISSUE
Sports Illustrated
NOVEMBER 30, 1981 $1.50
NORTH CAROLINA IS NO.1
Dean Smith and His High-Stepping Heels

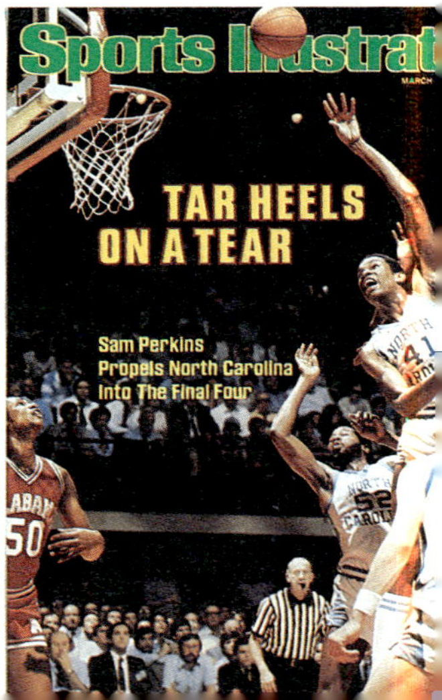
Sports Illustrat
MARCH
TAR HEELS ON A TEAR
Sam Perkins Propels North Carolina Into The Final Four

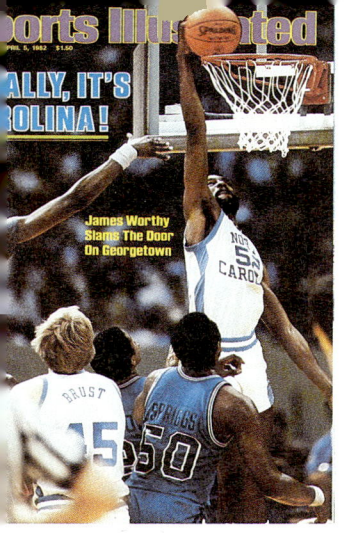

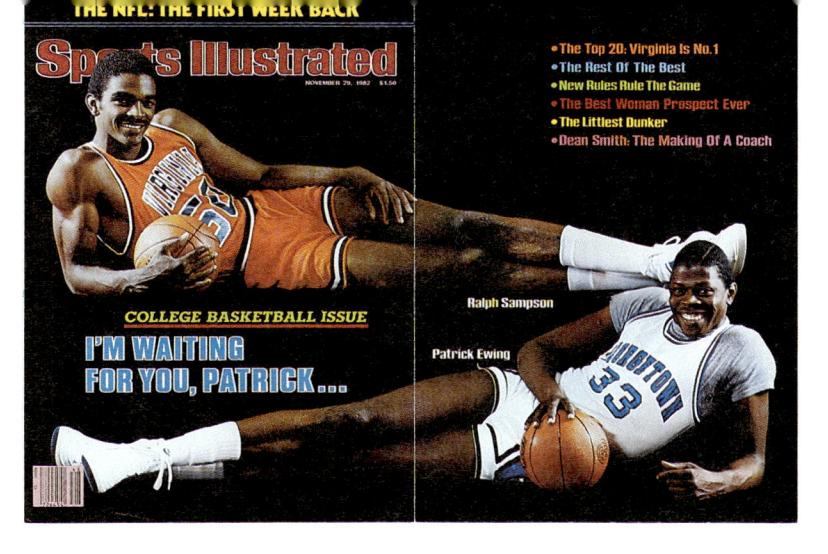

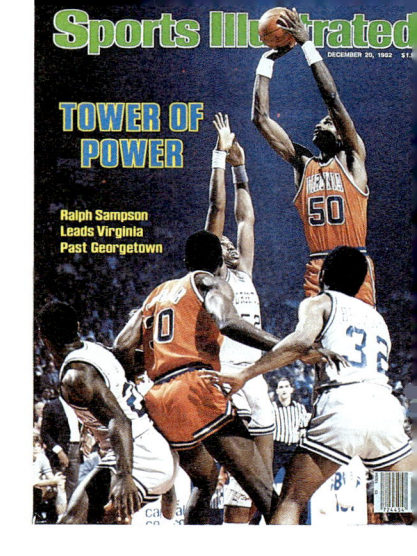

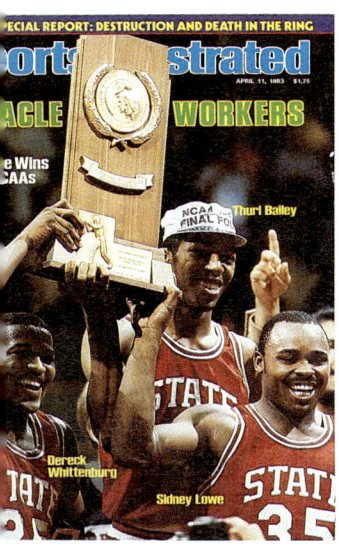

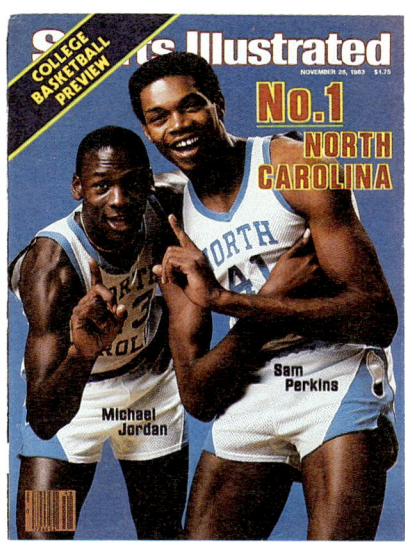

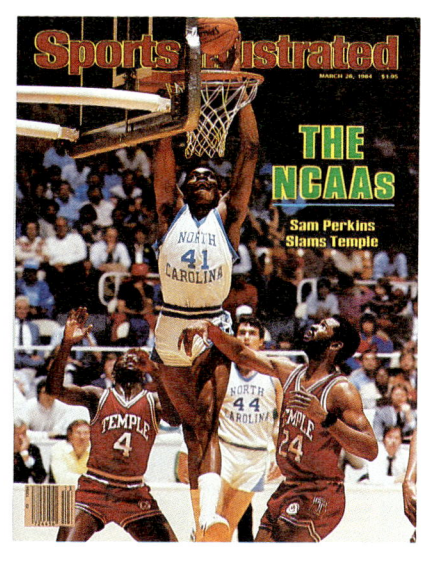

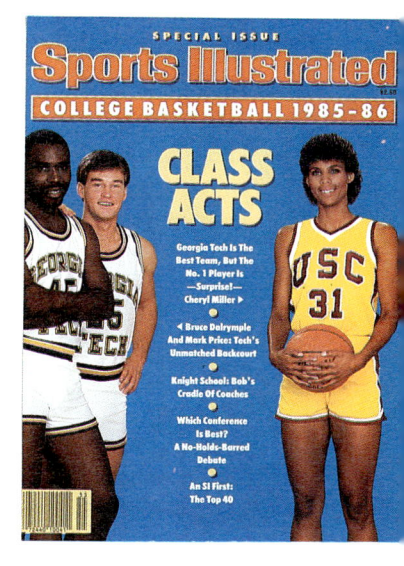

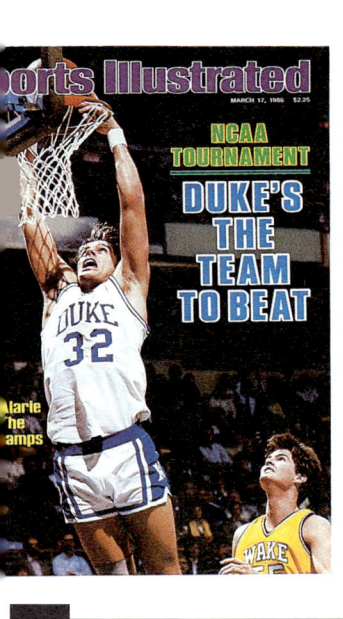

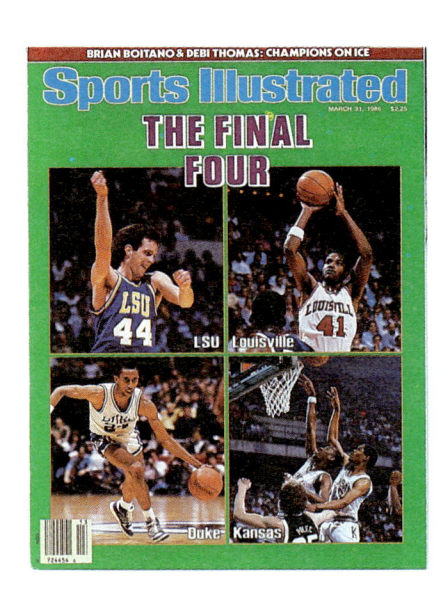

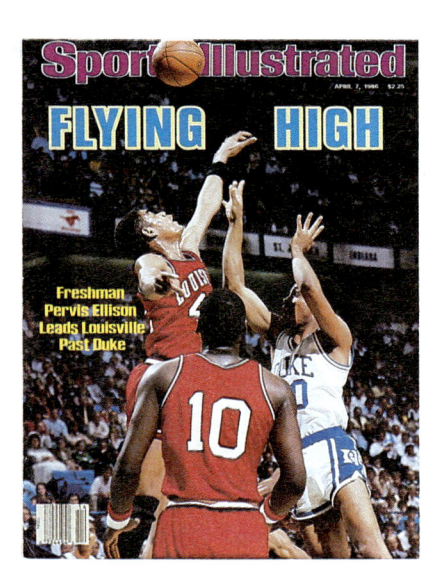

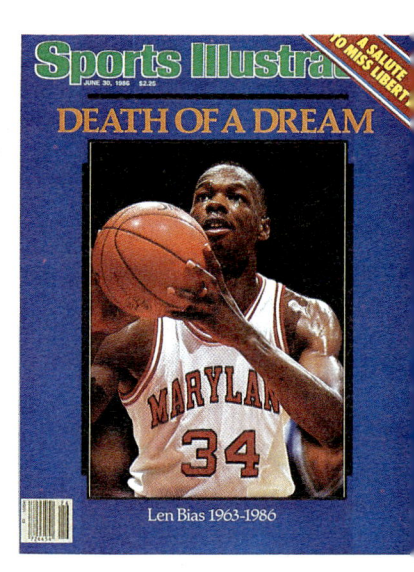

ACC SCRAPBOOK

ACC Basketball has graced the covers of 28 issues of *Sports Illustrated* magazine. Three of the covers have celebrated national titles (N.C. State in 1974 and '83 and UNC in '82), while opponents of ACC teams in national finals have been the focus three times (UCLA in '64, Marquette in '77 and Louisville in '86). Whether there exists an "SI Cover Jinx" is open to debate, but four teams might believe there does: John Roche's cover was dated Jan. 4, 1971; that day, the top-ranked Gamecocks fell to UNC, 79-64. ■ Tar Heel Dudley Bradley dunked on Duke in the issue of March 12, 1979; on March 11, Penn stunned UNC 72-71 in the NCAAs. ■ On March 30, 1981, Ralph Sampson was a coverboy; his Cavaliers fell to UNC, 78-65, in the Final Four that weekend. ■ And Tar Heel Sam Perkins appeared on the cover of the March 26, 1984 issue that came out just as Indiana ousted UNC 72-68 from the NCAAs.

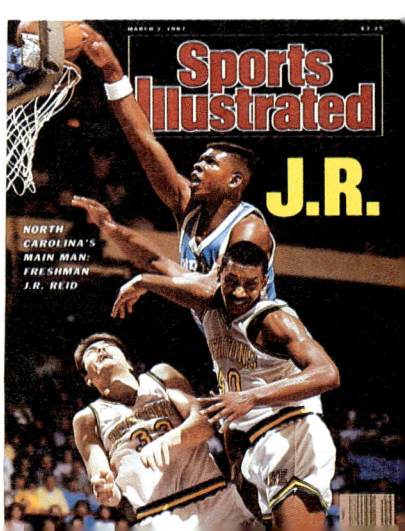

ACC BASKETBALL / THE '80s

Other than Tech's and N.C. State's occasional fling at Top 20 status, the focus of the league was on Duke and North Carolina for most of the season.

The Tar Heels opened the season without All-America J.R. Reid and Steve Bucknall, who were suspended for the Hall of Fame Tip-Off Classic against No. 1-ranked Syracuse. Reid and Bucknall were left in Chapel Hill after being charged with, and eventually pleading guilty to, assault on an N.C. State student in a Raleigh nightclub.

Without Reid and Bucknall, the third-ranked Tar Heels still managed a 96-93 victory over Syracuse, the team that ousted UNC from the NCAA Tournament the previous season in the East Regional final.

Following the win over Syracuse, UNC was ranked No. 1 in the country but retained that ranking for only one week. The Tar Heels lost at Vanderbilt in the fifth game of the season and later dropped a non-conference game to No. 1-ranked Temple, falling 83-66 in Chapel Hill.

Besides the upset loss to Wake Forest, the Tar Heels only stumbled twice in the ACC, both times to Duke. An 11-3 record within the league was good enough for a first-place finish, UNC's second straight and 19th in league history.

Two significant wins for the Tar Heels came against Georgia Tech. In Chapel Hill, guard Jeff Lebo hit five consecutive 3-pointers over the final 4:08 to give UNC a 73-71 victory. In Atlanta, the Tar Heels snapped Tech's seven-game win streak and clinched first place with a 97-80 victory.

Duke, meanwhile, wound up third in the regular-season race with a 9-5 mark after a three-game losing streak late in the season. The Blue Devils lost 89-78 at home to N.C. State, 91-87 at Georgia Tech, and 79-77 at Clemson.

On the bus ride back from Clemson, Duke Coach Mike Krzyzewski held a team meeting that seemed to turn the Blue Devils' tide. Krzyzewski said the subject of that meeting was changing the "me's" to "we's."

"It just seemed they had gotten to thinking more about improving their games than our game," Krzyzewski said. "They got away from the focus that if you reach team goals, you will reach individual goals."

Duke immediately turned things around and handed UNC a 96-81 whipping at Cameron Indoor Stadium to close the regular season. Earlier, in Chapel Hill, the Blue Devils defeated the Tar Heels 70-69 when center Robert Brickey blocked Lebo's 15-footer at the buzzer.

When Duke played as it did during the two wins over UNC, it was one of the nation's best teams. The Blue Devils were noted for a suffocating man-to-man defense that denied passing lanes and forced opponents out of their offense. It was a versatile group of players who could be used at any position. Brickey, although only 6-5, was listed as the team's center. Danny Ferry, at 6-10, could play guard as well as forward and center. Billy King, Kevin Strickland, John Smith and Alaa Abdelnaby were interchangeable, with Quin Snyder as the team's point guard.

"They are awesome," Georgia Tech Coach Bobby Cremins said at midseason. "Duke's defense is the best I've seen in years."

Following a 101-63 loss to Duke in early February, fourth-year Clemson Coach Cliff Ellis said, "I think they're probably the best team I've seen in the ACC since I've been in the league."

When the Blue Devils defeated Virginia 60-48 to open the ACC Tournament and avenged two regular-season losses to N.C. State with a 73-71 victory, they were matched against UNC for the championship. UNC defeated Wake Forest 83-62 and Maryland 74-64 to reach the title game.

'Shuh-shef-skee' sound of success for Duke hoops.

The '80s — Duke

The focus on Mike Krzyzewski's coaching career became crystal clear as he addressed the media prior to the 1988 Final Four in Kansas City. For the second time in three years, Krzyzewski had taken his Duke team to college basketball's grand ball.

It was significant that Krzyzewski's Blue Devils were in Kansas City, while Bobby Knight's Indiana Hoosiers and Dean Smith's North Carolina Tar Heels were home watching the Final Four on TV. For eight seasons as Duke's head coach, Krzyzewski was known first as a disciple of Bobby Knight, then as an excellent teacher. During that same period, whatever success Krzyzewski and his teams enjoyed was usually measured against the lofty standards set by Smith and his teams in the ACC.

But by taking a Duke team, one that was considered less talented than his 1986 national runnerup, back to the Final Four, Krzyzewski had been recognized across the nation as one of the game's brightest and most successful coaches. He had established his identity in the coaching profession.

"I think when you think of the elite programs, the ones that are successful, Duke is one of the programs you think of," Krzyzewski said. "A certain amount of the credit for that should go to the coach."

Building Duke's program to one of the nation's elite has been a step-by-step process for Krzyzewski. The blocks in that building process included his upbringing in Chicago, his plebe days at the United States Military Academy, an apprenticeship under Knight as a player at Army and coach at Indiana, and a five-year head coaching stint at Army.

Krzyzewski was reared in a Polish neighborhood in downtown Chicago, a neighborhood of two-family homes. His immediate family lived upstairs, some cousins lived downstairs. Both sets of his grandparents came to America from Poland. Krzyzewski's father worked as an elevator operator. His mother cleaned the Chicago Athletic Club.

Although some relatives shortened their last name to Kross, Krzyzewski had an uncle who insisted that he take pride in his Polish name. At age 4, young Mike was learning to say "Shuh-shef-skee, Shuh-shef-skee." By high school, college basketball recruiters knew not only how to pronounce Krzyzewski's name, but also how to spell it.

"I don't think my mom went to high school," Krzyzewski told The News and Observer of Raleigh. "My dad finished two years. But they came up with pretty intelli-

260

ACC BASKETBALL / THE '80s

Two ACC titles and Final Fours now on Coach K's resume.

gent decisions. And it was: 'You're going to go (to West Point).' I went, basically, because they said I should. I'm happy I did it, but I wouldn't have made that decision."

Krzyzewski entered Knight's program at Army as one of the team's weakest defensive players and left as one of its strongest. Knight considered Krzyzewski, who was captain of the Cadets in 1969 when they went to the NIT, one of the smartest players he has ever coached.

As much as learning a few things about basketball, Krzyzewski learned a few lessons about life, which would help him as a coach.

"They used to have these things (called) clothing formations," Krzyzewski says of his Army days. "They would say, 'Okay, you all have to be out here in two minutes in a new uniform.' Well, there is no way in the world that you're going to do it . . . When you're 18, it's stupid at that time. You wonder what the hell you're doing there. I could be on the beach or something. It's just an emotional time. You hate your parents for putting you there.

"But what it teaches you is, one, don't give up. You plan, organize and be ready to accept criticism. I'm not a real big military man, or anything like that. I don't believe in a lot of that stuff. But I was lucky to have gone through that . . . They want you to come up with a plan and stick to it. Take people's suggestions and be flexible, but stick to your basic plan."

Krzyzewski took the lesson to heart at Duke.

Inheriting a program that needed a new foundation, Krzyzewski endured much criticism about his insistence on making Duke players learn to play his style of basketball. His teams learned the Bob Knight principles of man-to-man defense, whatever the cost. Void of talent to match the North Carolinas and Virginias of the ACC, Krzyzewski's teams were 38-47 in his first three seasons.

Not once did he sacrifice the future for the present. If anything, it was the other way around. He retained his belief that his system would work, particularly at Duke.

"I was fortunate to have coached at West Point," said Krzyzewski, whose five Army teams were 73-59, including a 20-win season in 1977 and a trip to the NIT in 1978. "That gave me great training as far as national recruiting and what would appeal to young men throughout the country. The schools are very similar in that they're great academic schools. A lot of selling points we used at West Point we could use at Duke. Now, we had the opportunity to add ACC basketball, Duke's tradition, graduation rates, job placement and pro basketball possibilities to the sales package."

In his first recruiting season, Krzyzewski finished second in every case as he attempted to land prep stars Bill Wennington, Chris Mullin, Rodney Williams, Uwe Blab and Jim Miller. Undaunted, Krzyzewski came back the next season and landed Johnny Dawkins, Mark Alarie, Jay Bilas, David Henderson, Weldon Williams and Bill Jackman. That group, minus Jackman who ultimately transferred to Nebraska, helped turn the program around.

"I think he's a cross between Jim Valvano and Bobby Knight," Alarie once said of Krzyzewski. "He's somewhere in between. He combines a very friendly, loose atmosphere with an ability to get players to respond. He's a disciplinarian, but it's a very loose environment. It provides a nice atmosphere for hard workers."

That atmosphere helped Alarie's recruiting class establish an identity in 1983, but not without suffering growing pains. Duke was 11-17 in '83 and ended the season with a 109-66 defeat to Virginia in the ACC Tournament.

The Blue Devils did not soon forget that humiliating loss. Prior to playing at Virginia early the next season, Krzyzewski had his team practice in Cameron Indoor Stadium with 109-66 in lights on the scoreboard. Duke's 78-72 win over Virginia was a turning point for the program.

"We went into the season feeling we could compete with anyone," Krzyzewski said. "After that, we knew we could win against anyone."

After a 24-10 record in '84, Duke went 23-8 in '85 and 37-3 in '86, a year in which the Blue Devils won the ACC Tournament and advanced to the national championship game before losing to Louisville. When Duke went 24-9 in 1987, then 28-7 (including three wins over UNC for the first time in 22 years) en route to the Final Four in 1988, Krzyzewski had made his mark as an outstanding coach. He was no longer viewed as a disciple of Knight, and he faced fewer comparisons to Smith.

"I want to win every game, whether it's against Carolina or William & Mary," Krzyzewski said. "It's like looking at your neighbor and saying, 'He's got a Mercedes; I've got to have a Mercedes,' when I'd be just as happy with a station wagon as long as it's a nice station wagon.

"We can both be good. I've never had a goal to overtake any school. I respect Dean . . . He's good at what he does, and the way he does it. If I did it exactly the way he did it, I wouldn't be as good. Same with Coach Knight." ∎

UNC's J.R. Reid and Duke's Danny Ferry (L) jockeyed for position as the ACC's top player in '88 while their teams battled for the league supremacy. The Blue Devils edged the Tar Heels 65-61 for the ACC title, setting off a sea of celebration at the Greensboro Coliseum around Ferry and Robert Brickey.

ACC BASKETBALL / THE '80s

Duke's defense completely shut down UNC's offense during the final 11:45 of the championship game in the Greensboro Coliseum, which was hosting the Tournament for what was believed to be the final time. During that period, UNC made only one of 12 field goal attempts and had six turnovers.

On offense, the Blue Devils got clutch play from Ferry, the ACC Player of the Year and the Tournament's Everett Case Award winner. Ferry had 19 points and 10 rebounds. His offensive rebound and follow shot after Billy King's missed free throw with 1:28 remaining gave Duke a 63-59 lead.

After Kevin Madden made two free throws for UNC with 57 seconds left, the Tar Heels made a steal but failed to convert a fast-break opportunity. Snyder sealed the 65-61 victory with two free throws with four seconds left.

The championship was Duke's second in three years and gave the Blue Devils three victories over UNC in one season for the first time since 1966. It also gave Duke a top seed in the NCAA East Regional in Chapel Hill. Playing in the strange surroundings of the Smith Center, Duke rolled past Boston University 85-69 and SMU 94-79 in the first two rounds.

Duke's Billy King bottled up Temple sharpshooter Mark Macon in the East Regional final, holding him to 13 points on 6-of-29 shooting.

At The Top

Three men have guided the ACC from its infancy to its pre-eminent place in college basketball today. Jim Weaver (L) was commissioner of the league from 1953-70, Bob James (C) from 1970-87, Gene Corrigan from 1987-present.

ACC BASKETBALL / THE '80s

In East Rutherford, N.J., the Blue Devils edged Rhode Island 73-72 before facing No. 1-ranked Temple for the East Regional championship. Typical of Duke's play most of the season, the Blue Devils shut down the opposing team's top scoring threat and charged to a 63-53 victory.

Doing most of the damage on defense was King, a 6-foot-6 senior who became as acclaimed a defensive specialist as any ACC player since UNC's Dudley Bradley in the late '70s. Against Temple, King limited freshman guard sensation Mark Macon to 6-of-29 shooting and only 13 points.

UNC, meanwhile, had recovered from its ACC Tournament loss to Duke to reach the West Regional final by defeating North Texas State 83-65, Loyola Marymount 123-97, and Michigan 78-69. In the win over Loyola, UNC not only stopped the nation's longest winning streak at 25 games, the Tar Heels also set NCAA Tournament records for scoring and field goal percentage. Their 79 percent shooting was also a school record.

But for the fourth time in six seasons, UNC lost in a regional final. Second-ranked Arizona proved to be too much for the Tar Heels in the second half. The Wildcats trailed 28-26 at halftime before going on a 30-10 blitz to open the second half and coast to a 70-52 victory and trip to the Final Four.

Arizona joined Oklahoma, Kansas and Duke in Kansas City for the 50th Final Four. Duke's meeting with Kansas was a rematch of a regular-season game in Lawrence, Kan., one in which the Blue Devils rallied from a 23-8 deficit for a 74-70 victory in overtime.

Kansas featured Danny Manning, the national Player of the Year. The 6-11 Manning was probably a symbol of what happened to the ACC in its slip over the previous four seasons. He initially wanted to remain close to his Greensboro home and attend an ACC school. But former UNC player and Kansas Coach Larry Brown hired Manning's father, Ed, as an assistant coach and the Manning family moved to Lawrence, Kan., when Danny was a senior in high school. A year later, Manning elected to attend Kansas and play for the Jayhawks.

Manning then came back to haunt the ACC and Duke in the national semifinals. He scored 25 points and had 10 rebounds in the Jayhawks' 66-59 victory. Kansas scored the game's first 14 points, built an early 24-6 lead and held on for the win.

The loss did not detract, however, from Duke's excellent season. The Blue Devils finished 28-7 and gave the ACC its seventh representative in the Final Four in the '80s.

"We knew we weren't a great basketball team (in the preseason), but we always felt we were a real good basketball team that could keep getting better," Krzyzewski said. "We knew we were capable of getting to the Final Four."

NCAA Champ, Post ACC

Larry Brown set a new superlative in ACC annuals in 1988, becoming the first former ACC player to coach a team to the NCAA title. Brown played guard at North Carolina from 1961-63 and served as an assistant under Dean Smith in '66 and '67. Brown became head coach at Kansas in '83 and led the Jayhawks to an 83-79 win over Oklahoma for the '88 championship. Less than a week later, Brown rejected the head coaching position at UCLA.

264

ACC BASKETBALL / THE '80s

SPOTLIGHT

Dean Smith

"After '71, I think people everywhere realized the guy wasn't just a good recruiter. They realized he had a special talent for coaching."

By JOHN FEINSTEIN

One strand of net remained and, as he stood among a sea of celebrants and well-wishers, Dean Smith felt someone pushing a pair of scissors into his hands. "The last one's for you, coach," a voice said, and Smith found himself being half-pushed, half-carried towards the dangling net.

For a moment, he didn't fight the surging mass of hysterical fans. He had willingly taken a cut at the other end of the court, and now it seemed he would take the last one at this end. It was only right. After all, he had waited 21 years for this night and then had to sweat until the very last frantic seconds before Michael Jordan's jumper and Fred Brown's misguided pass had become part of college basketball history. Only then did he have the national championship he had so long been denied.

And so, with the scoreboard in the Louisiana Superdome still telling the story in giant lights—North Carolina 63, Georgetown 62—all that remained to complete the giddy evening in 1982 was for Smith to cut that last piece of net.

But he wouldn't do it. He got to within a few steps of the basket and stopped. "Where's Jimmy?" he shouted, the firmness in that nasal Kansas twang bringing everyone to a skidding halt. "Where's Jimmy Black? I want him to have the last cut."

Someone pointed out that Jimmy Black, the senior point guard, had already taken his turn with the scissors, that he had not been deprived. Smith was unmoved. "I want him to have the last cut," he said.

They went and found Jimmy Black, and Dean Smith handed him the scissors and stood by and watched Black drape the net around his neck. Why, he was asked later that night, was it so important that Black, not Smith, cut the net down?

"Because," Dean Smith answered, "he's a senior. He'll never have a chance to win a national championship again. I hope I will."

Even in what had to be the most euphoric moment of his career, Smith barely paused for breath. He was thinking ahead—to the next game, the next season, the next championship. For others, the joy lingered. For Smith, lingering is the same as malingering. He has to keep pushing forward—even when there is a net waiting to be cut down.

"When I go through a summer without wanting to sit down and plan for next season, that's when I'll know it's time to quit," he said during the summer of 1987, prior to his 27th season as North Carolina's basketball coach. "As long as the next challenge still excites me, I'll still coach."

That is the way it is with Dean Smith. He always wants to know what is next. How will today affect tomorrow? And why do people always ask him about yesterday?

•

Even if the past makes him uncomfortable—especially discussing his own past—one cannot understand the Dean Smith of today, a man who is quite literally a living legend in the state of North Carolina, without looking backward.

Dean Edwards Smith was born February 28, 1931, the second child and first son of Alfred and Vesta Smith of Emporia, Kan. His mother taught a total of 35 years in child development courses at Emporia State College and, later, in Topeka grade schools. His father was a minister's son, a coach in football, basketball, baseball and track. He coached Emporia High School to the 1934 state basketball championship. But more significant in terms of what his son would become, he coached what is believed to be the first integrated high school teams in Kansas.

"Sports were always important to Dean for as long as I can remember," says his older sister, Joan Ewing. "He always had this tremendous drive. I can remember sitting on our porch with him and he would be squeezing a softball to try and strengthen the muscles in his hands. He was always thinking like that."

Smith's father took him to games and often took him on trips. When Dean was old enough, they talked strategy. By the time he was 12, Dean Smith was fascinated with the concepts of coaching. "I was always interested in the Xs and Os, especially in football," Smith said. "I remember drawing up my first play and my dad showing me why it wasn't any good. It was a double-wing play but I forgot to block somebody."

As an athlete, Smith always played the positions that made him the leader, the organizer: Quarterback in football, point guard in basketball, catcher in baseball. He can still remember playing football in vacant lots and drawing all the plays for his team.

There are few things Smith does not remember. Casually, he will mention that a counselor from Columbia University came to Topeka High School when he was a senior to talk to 13 members of the class. Not about a dozen, or 10 to 15, but 13. He never forgets a name or a face or a bad call by an official.

The Tar Heels under Smith have had plenty to cheer about over the years—638 wins in 820 games.

"Dean has always been that way," Ewing said. "I think he gets that from our mother, his creativity and imagination from our father."

Ewing remembers one of the first times she noticed both her brother's ability to handle pressure and his attention to detail. "It was when he was in high school, playing for the mythical state championship, and it was a very cold, windy night. In the fourth quarter, the wind blew the ball several yards off the line of scrimmage. One of the key running backs on the team, also named Dean, ran over, picked it up and took it over to the referee.

"Dean started yelling at him not to do that. 'Save your strength, let the referee get the ball himself, we need you fresh.' He was always thinking that way. A few plays later, Dean, the running back, scored the winning touchdown."

Smith was a good student and was accepted at the University of Kansas on an academic scholarship, majoring in math. He played freshman football, varsity basketball and baseball. His Kansas teammates called him "Smiles" because Smith always had one on his face.

Even then, there was little doubt that Smith should go into coaching. As a junior on the Kansas team coached by the legendary Phog Allen, Smith would work the junior varsity team on one end of the court while the varsity practiced on the other.

"He was a good outside shooter, and, of course, a heck of a defensive man," said Bill Lienhard, a teammate of Smith's. "But even at that time it was kind of apparent to everybody that he was gonna make a heck of a coach."

In 1952, Smith was a reserve guard on the Kansas team that won the national championship.

It was 30 years before he was associated with another national champion, but Smith never doubted it would happen. One year before Carolina won the national title, he talked about what was then the one void in his coaching record: "I wouldn't trade our program the last 15 years for anyone's," he said. "Winning the national championship is a matter of skill and luck. We've had the skill, but not yet the luck. It usually comes down to one play, one inch. I'm sure one day we'll get that inch."

One year later, they did.

After graduating from Kansas, Smith went into the Air Force, eventually landing at the Air Force Academy as an assistant coach. He headed into coaching against the advice of Allen, among others. Allen and Dr. John Davidson, a Topeka optometrist, urged Smith to seek a medical degree.

In 1958, Frank McGuire, then the coach at North Carolina, arrived at the Final Four looking for an assistant. Sitting around one night with Air Force Coach Bob Spear, he mentioned the vacancy.

"I remember Bob telling me, 'If you want someone young and aggressive, I've got the guy for you.'" recalled McGuire, who had met Smith the previous year in Kansas City when North Carolina defeated Kansas in the national championship game. "He told me about Dean, and that was good enough for me."

267

Smith moved to Chapel Hill to work for McGuire in the fall of '58. Although the two men have remained friends for 30 years, their styles as coaches could not be more different. McGuire, using the so-called underground railroad between New York and Chapel Hill, was a great believer in rolling the ball out and letting the talent produce. Smith not only believed in teaching, he believed in discipline and detail. He respected McGuire when he worked for him, but he chafed under his leadership.

"Dean always wanted to do more," McGuire said. "He always thought there was more we could do to prepare, more we could do to teach them. I understood. That was his way. But I was in charge and we did things my way."

Smith's boldest action during his apprenticeship had nothing to do with basketball. Smith was 28 and in his second year as McGuire's assistant in 1959. The year before Smith had been a charter member of the Binkley Baptist Church, a liberal spinoff from the town's First Baptist Church.

Segregation was still an accepted fact of life in the South — a fact of life that disturbed the church pastor, Dr. Robert Seymour. When a black theological student came to spend the summer on the church staff, Seymour decided it was time for action. He wanted to take the students to a segregated restaurant.

"All of us in the church knew that the time had come to separate the men from the boys on social issues, especially civil rights," Seymour said. "Dean was completely aware of the situation."

Seymour called Smith. In a small college town Seymour was aware the assistant coach of the home team was a known and respected person. "I told Dean that if he came with us to the restaurant I was almost certain we would be served," Seymour said. "He was eager to do it."

The three men walked into the restaurant that night and sat down. Not a word was said. Orders were taken and the food was served. That was among the first steps toward integration in Chapel Hill.

This is not the kind of thing Smith likes to talk about. He wants to be respected, but he is uncomfortable with adulation. "Dean has never been one for going around saying, 'I did this, I did that,'" said Georgetown Coach John Thompson, his friend and coaching pupil. "He never told me about the restaurant incident. If he did, I would be shocked. To Dean, that's all part of being a human being. He doesn't think you ought to be patted on the back for being a human being."

Smith just shrugged at the mention of the incident.

"The way I was taught," he said softly, "freedom is for everyone, not just for some."

In 1961, he won his freedom from McGuire when the veteran coach left North Carolina to become coach of the NBA's Philadelphia Warriors. Smith became the coach, but it was not exactly a dream job. Although the Tar Heels had been national champions in 1957, the program had been put on probation for the 1962 season because of recruiting violations. UNC was limited to a 17-game schedule and to recruiting only ACC-area players in the aftermath of the point-shaving scandals. It was not an auspicious way to begin for an ambitious 30-year-old coach.

Smith's best players that first year were Larry Brown and Donnie Walsh, both of whom later coached on the college and professional levels. But it was not a good team. And it was McGuire's team, used to his methods, his personality.

"It was a real adjustment for all of us," Brown said. "Frank had all this charisma. He just kind of told us to go get 'em. Dean was completely the opposite. He was always teaching. Every minute of every practice was planned. He seemed conscious of every move we made. He was everywhere at once. But when it came time to play he just told us to play as hard as we could."

Smith remembers his first game vividly, an 80-46 victory over Virginia. "I was so organized, I had thought of every little thing," he said. "Then we got ready for the opening tap and the referee turned to me and said, 'Dean, where's the ball?' I had been so wrapped up in everything else I forgot to tell someone to bring the basketball out of the locker room. I had to send our head manager, Elliott Murnick (the name rolls off his tongue without hesitation), back to get it."

Brown remembers something else about that game. "He had told us to go all out and if we got tired, give him the clenched fist as the tired sign. Walsh and I kept giving him the sign and each time he would shake his fist back and say, 'Yeah, yeah, way to go, keep it up.'"

"It's true," Smith laughed. "I forgot my own tired signal."

It is difficult now to picture Smith as a wide-eyed kid coach. But it has been a turbulent 27 years. Walk by the bust of him in the lower lobby of the Dean E. Smith Student Activities Center and remember that once they burned him in effigy outside Woollen Gym, the team's home before Carmichael Auditorium.

That was in 1965, Smith's fourth year as Carolina coach. The first three teams had been fair, but not great, certainly not nearly as good as Carolina fans were accustomed to. On the night of Jan. 6, 1965, the Tar Heels were routed 107-85 at Wake Forest. When the bus pulled up to Woollen Gym, students were burning Smith in effigy. Billy Cunningham, a senior on that team, roared off the bus and ripped the effigy down. Smith never forgot the incident — the burning or Cunningham's act.

"You don't forget something like that," he said. "But I learned a lot from that season."

During that season, for the first and last time, Smith wondered if he had perhaps chosen the wrong profession. He turned inward, reading a lot, finding a passion for theology. But the book that he says changed him was one sent to him by his sister, Catherine Marshall's *Beyond Our Selves*. The key chapter for Smith was one called, "The Power of Helplessness."

Worry about only what you can control, Marshall wrote. Smith took that to heart and can still cite from the chapter. "I stopped worrying about all the external things that had affected me in the past," he said. "That whole period changed my attitude toward my vocation."

As he spoke, the voice lacked its usual urgency. "I'm uncomfortable talking about this. It's personal to me. I really don't enjoy talking about it."

But why this almost obsessive craving for privacy? The man lives in a house that can't be seen from the dead-end road because of all the trees around it.

"I don't consider myself that much of a private person," he said. "I don't like it, though, when I'm cast as some kind of an expert on the subjects that I'm not expert on. I'm just another human being with beliefs. People might listen to me because I'm a coach and I don't think that's right . . .

"I want my friends to be my friends because of me, not because of what I believe or because I'm a coach. I'm not one for sitting in a restaurant and holding court and talking basketball.

"When I'm not with my team or with other coaches, I really don't want to talk basketball. I do it for a living all day long. I don't need to talk about it with my friends."

If he ever did talk publicly about some of his non-basketball thinking, Smith might shock some of his constituents. The man is a closet liberal. He signed anti-war petitions during the Vietnam conflict. He won't talk about how he feels about the Moral Majority because he knows once he starts talking about how uncomfortable it makes him, he might have trouble stopping. He advised Charles Waddell, a Carolina football and basketball star, not to get into football coaching because he thinks blacks aren't given a fair shake. He has trouble justifying the $30 million recreation center (read, basketball arena) built with his name on it.

Despite some soul searching, Smith survived the 1965 season, finishing with a 15-9 record. In 1966 Carolina was 16-11. But quality players were beginning to arrive in Chapel Hill: Bob Lewis, Larry Miller, Rusty Clark, Dick Grubar, Bill Bunting, Charlie Scott.

Even when the Tar Heels were struggling on the court during those early years, they were making rapid progress off the court. Smith learned a lot about recruiting by closely watching Vic Bubas, then the Duke coach, and adopting many of his methods. Smith eventually used them to beat Bubas to key players, most notably Miller.

"Vic was way ahead of everyone," Smith said. "He modernized coaching, not just in terms of recruiting but in terms of making it a business, showing people how to commercialize themselves and make money off the court."

By 1967, Smith had put a powerhouse together. The Tar Heels reached the Final Four three straight years, losing the 1968 final to UCLA and Lew Alcindor. Smith remembers one thing about that 1968 final. "When I told the players we were going to open in the Four Corners, there was just the slightest bit of doubt in their eyes. I'm not sure they were sure it was the best thing."

That may have been the last time one of Dean Smith's teams doubted him. In 1971, picked to finish fifth in the ACC, the Tar Heels won the regular season and lost the Tournament to a McGuire-coached South Carolina team on a fluke play at the buzzer. The Tar Heels went on to win the NIT and no one ever questioned Smith's coaching ability again.

"Before that season I think some people thought the three Final Four teams were the result of great talent," says Eddie Fogler, who played for Smith and then coached under him for 13 years before becoming the coach at Wichita State in 1986. "After '71, though, I think people everywhere realized the guy wasn't just a good recruiter. They realized he had a special talent for coaching."

Now, Smith knows that if he told his players to play standing on their heads, they would do it.

"Eddie (Fogler) keeps telling me that I've mellowed, that I let the players get away with little things in practice, that I'm not as tough as I once was," Smith says. "Maybe that's true, maybe it's just a part of getting older, maturing. I'm not sure."

"He doesn't have to be as tough now," Fogler says. "Before he had won all the championships he might have to shout or say something twice to get it done. Now, when he says something to a player, it gets done. Immediately."

When Smith blows his whistle to start practice, every player drops his basketball at his feet and runs full speed to the center jump circle, stopping with his feet on the circle.

Throughout the practice the only sounds other than squeaking sneakers and bouncing basketballs are Smith's voice and Smith's whistle. He talks almost non-stop, instructing, correcting and sometimes scolding. Occasionally he will stop play to quiz a player on his role in a certain offense or defense. There is no room for daydreaming.

"Order. When you think of Dean, you think of order. He not only knows basketball, but he knows just how to communicate what he knows. He's articulate about it."

☐ **Georgetown's John Thompson**

Rich Clarkson, a photographer for the Topeka (Kan.) *Capital-Journal*, once casually walked onto the court during a practice session to talk with Smith. "He said, 'Rich, I can't talk to you now, we're in practice. Please leave the court,'" Clarkson recalled. "And this is an old classmate. We used to room together on road trips (at Kansas)."

Each practice has an emphasis, a specific area of concentration. If anyone on the team makes a mistake in that area, everyone runs a sprint. Throughout practice the managers keep charts, marking down the good and the bad.

Taking a charge, setting up a steal and boxing out so someone else can get a rebound result in bonus points used by players to get out of sprints. Errors produce minus points and more sprints. Graduating seniors who have leftover bonus points can "will" them to players still in the program.

"Order. When you think of Dean, you think of order," said Georgetown's Thompson, Smith's assistant on the '76 Olympic team. "He not only knows basketball, but he knows just how to communicate what he knows. He's articulate about it."

How organized is Carolina? Watch the Tar Heels closely during a timeout. They form a perfect circle around Smith, players in the game seated in front of him, other players standing behind him, managers standing behind the bench. When the timeout is over, one manager goes down the row and wipes every seat off before anyone sits down.

"Saves us a lot on our cleaning bill," Smith said.

When Carolina travels, a plane is usually chartered. When the Tar Heels play at Maryland, they do not stay in the Quality Inn or the Holiday Inn in College Park. They stay at Washington's elegant Watergate Hotel.

Every move is planned. During warmups before a game, one of the managers charts the layup line. A miss means a sprint in practice the next day.

"That's always been one of my pet peeves with the pros," Smith once said. "The way they warm up would be like Jack Nicklaus going out to practice trick shots before a tournament or Roger Staubach throwing passes behind his back before a game.

"The disciplined person in society is the truly free person. We give our players discipline to make them free."

Carolina players are always neat and well-groomed. Several years ago Smith asked a student reporter who got on a bus

Spanning Four Decades...

'50s
as an assistant to Frank McGuire.

'60s
in '68 Final Four defeat by UCLA.

'70s
in '77 Final Four loss to Marquette.

'80s
in '82 NCAA title win over Georgetown.

without a tie if he owned one. "Because if you don't," he said, "I'll buy you one."

That organization, that attention to the smallest detail and that ability to control help explain Carolina's success year after year.

That success and Smith's legend prospered throughout the 1970s. Carolina had three great rivalries in the ACC during that decade: David Thompson teams at N.C. State; the John Lucas-Mo Howard-Brad Davis teams at Maryland and the Jim Spanarkel-Mike Gminski-Gene Banks teams at Duke. The Tar Heels won four ACC Tournaments during the '70s and reached the Final Four twice more: In 1972, led by Smith's first and last junior college star, Robert McAdoo, and in 1977.

It is ironic that the loss in the national championship game to Marquette in 1977 was one of the low points of Smith's career because the Tar Heel presence in that final certainly represented one of the high points.

That team may have been as talented as any Smith has ever coached. Three of the starters—Tom LaGarde, Walter Davis and Phil Ford—had been members of the '76 U.S. Olympic team. The other starters were the ever-cool senior John Kuester and brilliant freshman Mike O'Koren.

"Healthy, we were the best team that year," Smith said. "Unfortunately, we didn't stay healthy."

LaGarde went down in February, gone for the season. Davis was hurt in the ACC Tournament, Ford during the East Regional semifinals victory over Notre Dame. Injured and always behind, Carolina staged a remarkable series of comebacks, beginning with the ACC title game against Virginia. They came from behind to beat Purdue in the first round of the NCAAs and from way behind to beat Notre Dame. They led Kentucky all the way in the regional final, but again Kuester had to run the delay because Ford was hurt. When O'Koren scored 31 points to lead the Tar Heels from behind in the semifinals against Nevada-Las Vegas, only Marquette stood between Smith and the title.

It looked as if it was destined to be. But it wasn't. The final followed the same pattern as all the other games, Carolina down 12 and coming back to pull even with 12 minutes left.

Carolina basketball under Smith grew to proportions massive enough to support a 21,444-seat arena bearing the coach's name; the Dean E. Smith Student Activities Center opened in 1986.

But with the score tied and all that time left, Smith went to the Four Corners. He also ignored Fogler's suggestion to call time out to get O'Koren back into the game in place of reserve Bruce Buckley.

Even in a national championship game Smith would not change his style—Don't Call Time Out if You Don't Have To; Don't Sub for a Senior Until it is Time. He had lived by these rules. That night he died by them.

Buckley saw an opening in the defense and broke to the basket. Bo Ellis swooped over and blocked the shot. Marquette took the lead back, and Carolina never caught up again. Al McGuire might never have become a national hero if Smith hadn't gone to the Four Corners or Smith had called time.

"I wanted to spread the defense out, get their big man away from the basket," Smith said. "The delay had worked so well for us that year that we called it the Goose Gossage. It was our big man out of the bullpen at the end."

But this time, Smith went to the bullpen too soon. It was a loss, even coming at the end of a brilliant coaching run. That haunted him until Fred Brown's pass landed in the arms of a stunned James Worthy five years later.

By taking the Tar Heels to the Final Four in '77—the fifth time in 11 years—Smith had established himself as one of the nation's best college coaches. Along the way, he also carefully nurtured his image, one that has been called phony by other coaches and has frustrated the press.

Virginia Coach Terry Holland once questioned Smith's image as a gentleman after Smith engaged in a shouting match with Cavalier forward Marc Iavaroni during a 1977 ACC Tournament game. That same year, Smith charged onto the court to yell at Kentucky's Rick Robey after the 6-foot-10 center knocked the 6-2 Kuester flat. Robey said Smith cursed at him. Smith denied the charge.

"Dean Smith is a great coach," said Bill Foster, who lived in Smith's shadow for six years at Duke. "His record is excellent, and what's more he's won with good kids, the kind who graduate and go on to do things outside of basketball when they finish college.

"How can you knock that? I admire the guy a lot. I just think that sometimes people get tired of hearing he invented basketball."

In fact, when he was at Duke Foster often joked, "I thought it was Naismith who invented this game, not Dean Smith."

Former UNC players would probably debate that claim.

"People always say, 'Nobody can be that good,'" Larry Brown said. "They don't want to believe that someone can be that smart, that caring, that together. So they dismiss him as some kind of goody two shoes. But that's the way he is. Just a good, caring person."

"He is," said Fogler, "the best person I have ever known and no one else is even a close second."

Smith's former players and associates remain fiercely loyal, and he cultivates their friendship. Smith often refers to anyone who has passed through his program as being part of the "Carolina family."

"He does a lot of things for a lot of people that don't even play for him anymore," Miller says. "I could go back there today, and if I needed help in any way, I'm sure he'd provide it in any way he could. I think that's his greatest asset. My parents still get Christmas cards. And it's everybody that way, not just me."

Smith lays the groundwork for that relationship during the recruiting process. His emphasis in recruiting is education first, then team basketball. Of the 164 players who lettered under Smith through the 1987 season, 158 graduated. All of the 164 adapted to his team style of play.

"We ask them, 'What is your goal in college?'" Smith said. "If their goal is to get an education and become a better player, we feel we have a good chance (to sign the player). If they want to average 30 points as a freshman, we don't."

Smith's system, in which seniors are kings and freshmen are mere courtiers, regardless of ability, is one of the things that appeal to recruits. There is another side of Smith the public rarely sees. Sam Perkins said one of his major reasons for choosing Carolina was "because I felt comfortable sitting and talking with Coach Smith. He didn't try to impress me. He didn't say that a red carpet would be rolled out for me. We just had a conversation. I liked that."

Smith's reputation for treating everyone the same, star or scrub, also helps.

"My first few days of practice I was really surprised," said Brad Daugherty. "He was just as likely to get on Michael Jordan or Sam Perkins as on one of the freshmen."

Said Duke Coach Mike Krzyzewski: "He has never gone the junior college route (except for McAdoo) or the transfer route, so players know they'll get their turn. He has the longevity factor. And he's gotten ahead and stayed ahead."

Smith's program moved to an even higher plane of success and dominance in the '80s. After a 21-8 record in 1980, the Tar Heels began a streak in 1981 that has seen them win no fewer than 27 games in a single season. During that time they have won or shared first place in the ACC's regular season race six times, twice going 14-0 in conference play.

When UNC finished first in the ACC's regular season during the 1988 season, the Tar Heels extended their string of finishing among the league's top three teams to 24 seasons. For some perspective, consider that the next longest streak of top three finishes in league history was Duke's nine from 1961 through 1969.

Despite Smith's remarkable record, Carolina has been curiously vulnerable in postseason play since removing the national championship stigma from his head in 1982. Since then, the Tar Heels have been 28-8, 28-3, 27-9, 28-6, 32-4 and 27-7. In ACC regular-season play they are 70-14 during that period. But they have not once won the ACC Tournament—their record in Tournament play is a modest 8-6. They have reached the NCAA Sweet Sixteen a remarkable eight straight seasons but have not reached the Final Four since 1982. Suddenly, people are saying that Smith's teams choke in March.

That claim disturbs him, to say the least.

"I think our teams have played well in March," he said. "Was Syracuse a good team (in 1987)? Was Louisville good the year before? Villanova? We've had injuries, but I don't like to use them as excuses. But I thought we did remarkably well to get to the final eight in '85 without Steve Hale, just as one example."

His voice is calm and clinical as he talks. This is July in Chapel Hill, and the heat is stifling. Smith is in a suit, eating in a comfortable country kitchen. Still, for him, he is relaxed, talking about his golf, laughing easily at jokes.

But in the middle of the golfing conversation, he is suddenly reminded of a story. "You were talking before how competitive I am," he said. "I guess I am. I like to come down the 18th hole in a golf match with something on the line. The other day I was playing in a tournament and one of the guys in my foursome was a writer who had said we choked in March. We came to 18 and I said to my partner, 'Let's see who chokes now.' I hit an 8-iron about 5 feet (remember, exact details) from the hole and he didn't come close."

He smiled tightly. "I liked that."

Dean Smith always likes winning—especially against someone who has been critical of him or his team.

Still, the March record must disturb him. "Does it frustrate you?" he is asked. "Does anything frustrate you?"

"People who drive 45 in the left hand lane," he says.

In a sense, that is as it should be. He has lived a complicated 57-plus years. He has been married twice, with three grown children from his first marriage and two girls (9 and 7) from the second.

Smith and his wife Anne divorced in 1973 after a long separation. Smith remarried in 1976 to a doctor he met on an airplane when he noticed her reading *The Gospel According to Peanuts.*

But that is personal. Irrelevant, Smith would say, because it doesn't concern the team.

"If I had known years ago that coaching would involve the travel, the interview time and all the other things that go with it, I might not have become a coach," he said. "I stay in it because when I wake up every morning, I still look forward to going to work. I still enjoy seeing a group start on Oct. 15 with one goal in mind, trying to become a cohesive group trying to reach certain goals. I still enjoy that."

That may be the clue. This is a man who grew up with three main elements in his life: Coaching, teaching and religion. That has never changed. No one ever taught him about adulation or about criticism.

Certainly he enjoys winning far more than losing. But his joy comes in the teaching and it comes in those taut, tingling moments at the end of the most tense of games. Smith lives for those moments, and ACC fans have become accustomed to how they usually end. Down eight points with 17 seconds to play against Duke in 1974, UNC rallied to win in three overtimes. Behind by two points with Tulane in possession of the ball with four seconds left in 1982, UNC wins in three overtimes. Down nine points with 4:11 remaining at Marquette in 1986, UNC wins by two . . . the list of miracle comebacks is seemingly endless.

"You look at him with five seconds left and the score tied and you look for the tension," O'Koren said. "You look for the hands to shake, the voice to quiver. Never. He's always in complete control, always knows just what he wants, just what we need to do. He never hesitates."

When the game is over, the moment has passed for him.

Usually the moment has passed with Smith as a winner. His .778 winning percentage ranks fifth all-time among college coaches. His 638 wins make him one of only 15 to ever top the 600 mark, and ranks eighth all-time among Division I coaches. Yet Smith insists that's only because he's been around a long time.

He is right about that. He has coached through many generations and eras. He coached during the Vietnam War. He has coached during the age of nuclear proliferation and championed the cause of a nuclear freeze. He has coached during the Jesse Helms era in his home state and campaigned avidly for Jim Hunt in his Senatorial race against Helms in 1984.

"If Helms wins," he said on election day 1984, at least half-in-jest, "I might run against him in 1990."

Friends will tell you that won't happen. With all the victories and championships, there is still more for Smith to do. He is still challenged by those who challenge his dynasty and, March record aside, his program is most certainly a dynasty. For 20 years in the toughest league in America, it has been Carolina and someone else at the top of the conference. That is a dynasty.

"I can't see him not coaching," said his close friend, top assistant and alter-ego Bill Guthridge. "He likes to compete too much."

Of course that is the bottom line of Dean Smith, who was inducted into the Basketball Hall of Fame in 1982. Just to be competitive, he would deny it, but the fact is that he lives to compete. Mark Whicker, the nationally syndicated columnist who graduated from Carolina in 1973, once said, "Dean Smith is the only man I know who competes with you during an interview."

"I don't think I do that," Smith said. "Do I do that? What makes you competitive in an interview?"

Enough said.

He will never change. He will always win, he will always have a myriad of rules. He will always have managers charting the layup lines, players who watch everything they say and an ashtray full of cigarettes. He will always feel compelled every time he gets into his BMW with an outsider to explain that he drives it only because one of his ex-managers is a BMW dealer. He will always look for every angle and, most of the time, he will find it.

He is human. He makes mistakes. Sometimes he over-coaches, other times he over-preaches. But he's good, damn good and one final story tells just how good.

Several years ago as an ACC coaches' meeting was breaking up, former Maryland Coach Lefty Driesell, one of many arch-rivals over the years, gathered the other coaches in a room.

"Listen you guys," he said seriously. "We gotta do somethin' about Dean. We can't just keep lettin' him whip up on us all the time."

"What do you think we ought to do, Lefty," Jim Valvano asked, "loan each other players when we play him?"

Lefty thought about that one for a minute then laughed, "Well," he said, "that ain't the worst idea I've heard."

Only bouncing balls, squeaking shoes and Smith's voice are heard at practice.

HEY REF!!

Ref's charge: Start perfect, then get better.

Life's never been easy for officials in the ACC. They're expected by fans, players and coaches to be perfect for the season opener and improve every game thereafter.

"It takes a certain kind of guy to be a referee," said Charlie Eckman, an official for the first 15 years in the ACC. "He has to have personality, poise, guts. He has to be a bit of a psychiatrist, and a bit of a psychologist. But, most important, he has to have a feel for the game. Officiating is 90 percent guts and judgment and 10 percent rule book."

Eckman was one of the most colorful characters in ACC history. At age 16, he realized he could earn $1 a game as an official instead earning nothing by playing. He purchased a whistle and started calling. After working his way through the college ranks, Eckman eventually called NBA games.

During a late-night meeting with Fred Zollner, the millionaire owner of the Fort Wayne Pistons, Eckman made the statement that he could probably coach the team. Although Eckman's only experience as a coach was with a girls' volleyball team in Baltimore, Zollner took Eckman by surprise and hired him as the coach of the Pistons in 1954.

One of Eckman's players in Fort Wayne was Gene Shue, who played at Maryland when Eckman was an official in the ACC. When Zollner moved the Pistons from Fort Wayne to Detroit for the 1958 season, Eckman went along. But before the first season in Detroit ended, Eckman quit under fire.

Eckman returned to Glen Burnie, Md., where he scouted baseball for the Philadelphia Phillies, officiated ACC basketball games, served as a public relations man for two race tracks and was the chief judge of Orphans' Court in Anne Arundel (Md.) County.

Eckman was known throughout the ACC for his terrific sense of humor and earned the nickname of "Jolly Cholly." Eckman's rapport with players was harmonious to the point that when he became sick in the middle '60s, Duke guard Steve Vacendak sent the official a get-well card.

Eckman was one of several officials in the '50s and '60s who were as recognizable to fans as ACC players and coaches. The Mills twins, Joe and Jim, called Southern Conference and ACC games from 1950 through 1968. Until 1960, the identical twins from Apex, N.C., were virtually inseparable. Even then, the split was involuntary.

"A lot of people said we protected each other," Jim says, "so they broke us up."

No ACC official was more colorful than Lou Bello, who provided a barrel of laughs over his 17 seasons. Bello would occasionally plop himself in the lap of a female cheerleader at one end of the court while the action was going on at the other. Once he scooped a paper airplane off the floor, raced downcourt like a kid and handed it to a UNC player on the bench. "Hold this for me 'til after the game," Bello said.

Officials have come from diverse backgrounds and primary occupations. Ralph Stout was the mayor of Mountain City, Tenn., during his officiating days. Lou Moser, whose son Mike later officiated in the ACC, was a deputy sherriff in New Castle (Ind.) County. Longtime official Jim Hernjak was the plant manager for Bethlehem Steel in Steelton, Pa.

One ACC ref who developed into a respected official throughout the country was Hank Nichols, the chairman of the Villanova University Education Department. He was hired by the NCAA in 1986 to evaluate officiating throughout the country.

Lenny Wirtz turned to officiating as an alternate route into athletics. At 5-foot-5, he was not a serious candidate for a spot on any basketball floor. Yet for 31 years, Wirtz was an official in college basketball as well as in the NBA. He also served as commissioner of the LPGA from 1961 through 1969.

By the 1980s, the ACC's 30 officials had come under the supervision of Fred Barakat and were considered among the best in the country. The 1983 NCAA championship game was called by three ACC officials: Nichols, Joe Forte and Paul Housman.

In 1988, officials were paid $350 a game plus a per diem for meals and travel to take abuse from fans and coaches. ∎

Three of the best-known ACC officials: Lou Bello (top), Hank Nichols (L) and Lenny Wirtz.

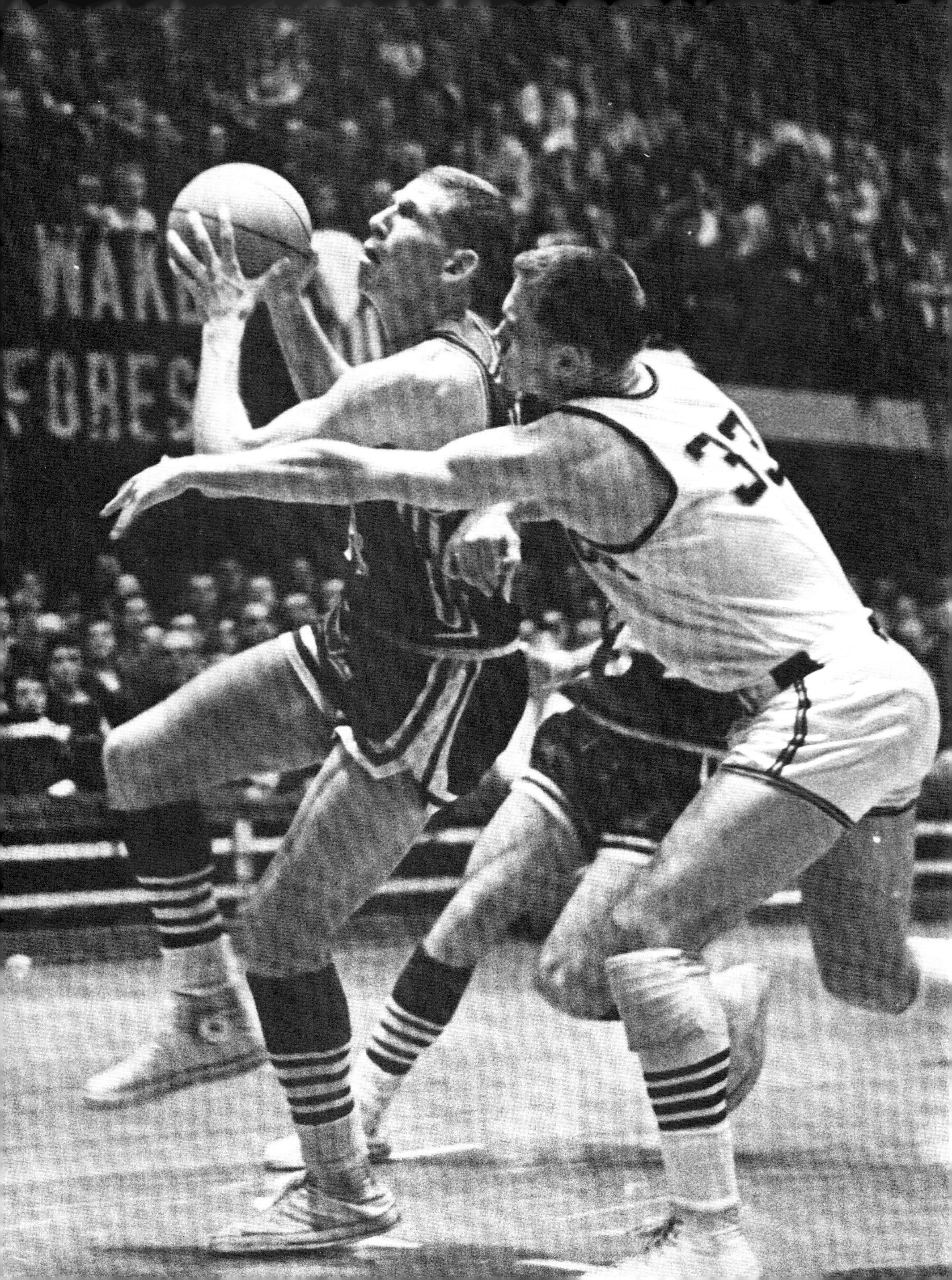
WAK
FORES

REFERENCE

'54

ACC Player of the Year
Dickie Hemric

1953-54 Final Standings

TEAM	Conf.	Overall	Ave.	Opp.
Duke	9-1	22-6	83.3	66.5
Maryland	7-2	23-7	65.3	55.7
Wake Forest	8-4	17-12	76.2	69.9
*N.C. State	5-3	26-7	81.1	68.4
North Carolina	5-6	11-10	68.5	63.6
South Carolina	2-8	10-16	65.1	69.8
Virginia	1-4	16-11	79.6	74.6
Clemson	0-9	5-18	62.3	78.3

*Won ACC Tournament

NCAA — N.C. STATE third in East Regional: beat George Washington 75-73, lost to La Salle 88-81, beat Cornell 65-54.

ACC Tournament

MARCH 4-6, 1954 AT RALEIGH, N.C.

FIRST ROUND: Wake Forest 58, South Carolina 57 (OT); Maryland 75, Clemson 59; Duke 96, Virginia 68; N.C. State 52, North Carolina 51. **SEMIFINALS:** N.C. State 79, Duke 75; Wake Forest 64, Maryland 56 (OT). **FINAL:** N.C. State 82, Wake Forest 80 (OT).
ALL-TOURNAMENT — FIRST TEAM: Dickie Hemric, Wake Forest; Gene Shue, Maryland; Mel Thompson, N.C. State; Ronnie Shavlik, N.C. State; Skippy Winstead, North Carolina. **SECOND TEAM:** Buzz Wilkinson, Virginia; Bernie Janicki, Duke; Rudy D'Emilio, Duke; Herb Applebaum, N.C. State; Lefty Davis, Wake Forest.

All-ACC

FIRST TEAM: *Dickie Hemric, Wake Forest (200 votes); Gene Shue, Maryland (190); Mel Thompson, N.C. State (181); Rudy D'Emilio, Duke (174); Buzz Wilkinson, Virginia (148). **SECOND TEAM:** Vic Molodet, N.C. State (91); Lefty Davis, Wake Forest (91); Joe Belmont, Duke (81); Jerry Vayda, North Carolina (80); Ronnie Mayer, Duke (65).
PLAYER OF THE YEAR: Hemric (18); Thompson (10); Shue (8); Ronnie Shavlik, N.C. State (4); Herb Applebaum, N.C. State (3).
COACH OF THE YEAR: Everett Case, N.C. State (13); Hal Bradley, Duke (11); Frank McGuire, North Carolina (8); Bud Millikan, Maryland (7); Murray Greason, Wake Forest (4).
*Unanimous Selection

Scoring, Rebounding Leaders

TOP TEN SCORERS

Player, School	G	FG	FT	TP	Ave.
Wilkinson, Virginia	27	288	238	814	30.1
Hemric, Wake Forest	28	225	230	680	24.3
Shue, Maryland	30	237	180	654	21.8
Thompson, N.C. State	33	207	201	615	18.6
Davis, Wake Forest	29	184	137	505	17.4
Vayda, North Carolina	21	123	111	357	17.0
Smith, South Carolina	26	147	137	431	16.6
McCarty, Virginia	27	176	77	429	15.9
Shavlik, N.C. State	33	204	115	523	15.8
Wells, Clemson	23	133	89	355	15.2

TOP TEN REBOUNDERS

Player, School	G	RBS.	Ave.
Hemric, Wake Forest	28	424	15.1
Shavlik, N.C. State	33	441	13.4
Smith, South Carolina	26	306	11.5
Gage, Clemson	23	261	11.3
Likins, North Carolina	21	228	10.9
L. Collins, South Carolina	26	270	10.3
Mayer, Duke	27	265	9.9
Thompson, N.C. State	33	316	9.6
Vayda, North Carolina	21	183	8.7
Gamble, Virginia	26	192	7.4

Rosters

CLEMSON

No.	Name	Hgt.	Yr.	Hometown
20	Ames Wells	5-8	Sr.	Columbia, SC
21	Doc Morgan	6-1	So.	Greenville, SC
22	Bill Yarborough	6-1	So.	Walhalla, SC
24	Barry Ryan	6-1	Jr.	Washington, DC
25	Bruce Holzschuh	6-2	So.	Teaneck, NJ
30	Billy Riser	6-7	So.	Bowman, SC
31	John Mikell	6-2	So.	Greenville, SC
32	Buddy Shook	6-3	So.	Liberty, SC
33	Tommy Smith	6-4	So.	Hendersonville, NC
34	Ben Crosland	5-11	So.	Greenville, SC
35	Charley Gage	6-4	Sr.	Clemson, SC

COACH: Banks McFadden

DUKE

No.	Name	Hgt.	Yr.	Hometown
13	Herky Lamley	6-4	Jr.	Havertown, PA
14	Don Tobin	6-5	So.	Avalon, PA
15	Rudy D'Emilio	5-11	Sr.	Philadelphia, PA
20	Bernie Janicki	6-3	Sr.	Ambridge, PA
21	Rudy Lacy	6-4	Sr.	Roanoke, VA
22	Marv Decker	6-5	Sr.	Bloomfield, NJ
23	Marty Doherty	6-9	So.	Pelham, NY
24	Tom Blackburn	6-0	So.	West Upton, MA
25	Don Sims	5-11	So.	Elizabeth, NJ
30	Joe Belmont	5-11	So.	Philadelphia, PA
32	Charlie Driesell	6-4	Sr.	Norfolk, VA
33	Junior Morgan	6-7	So.	Asheboro, NC
34	Fred Shabel	6-0	Sr.	Union City, NJ
35	Ronnie Mayer	6-4	So.	Avalon, PA
40	Jim Duncan	6-11	So.	River Forest, IL
42	Hal Turner	5-10	Jr.	Englewood, NJ

COACH: Hal Bradley
ASSISTANTS: Tony Drago, Dick Crowder

MARYLAND

No.	Name	Hgt.	Yr.	Hometown
22	Tom Young	6-0	Jr.	Natrona Heights, PA
23	Ken Atchinson	6-0	So.	Washington, DC
24	John Peterson	6-0	So.	Mineola, NY
25	Gene Shue	6-2	So.	Baltimore, MD
32	Marvin Long	6-4	So.	Salisbury, MD
33	Bob Kessler	6-3	So.	Alexandria, VA
34	Bob Dilworth	6-4	So.	East Orange, NJ
35	Dave Webster	6-1	So.	Washington, DC
40	Ronnie Brooks	6-0	So.	Washington, DC
42	Bill Martin	6-3	So.	Garden City, NY
43	John Sandbower	6-3	So.	Baltimore, MD
44	Ralph Greco	6-1	So.	Aliquippa, PA
45	Bob Everett	6-6	Jr.	Washington, DC

COACH: Bud Millikan

NORTH CAROLINA

No.	Name	Hgt.	Yr.	Hometown
20	Gene Glancy	6-0	So.	Belleville, NJ
21	Al Lifson	6-2	Jr.	Elizabeth, NJ
23	Skippy Winstead	6-2	So.	Roxboro, NC
25	Al Long	6-0	Jr.	Durham, NC
30	Cliff Walker	6-4	So.	Durham, NC
31	Gerry McCabe	6-3	So.	New York, NY
35	Cooper Taylor	5-10	Sr.	Raleigh, NC
40	Dick Kocornik	6-5	Sr.	West Orange, NJ
41	Paul Likins	6-9	Jr.	Elkhart, IN
42	Bud Maddie	6-4	Sr.	Bronx, NY
43	Jerry Vayda	6-4	So.	Bayonne, NJ
44	Tony Radovich	6-2	So.	Hoboken, NJ

COACH: Frank McGuire
ASSISTANT: Buck Freeman

N.C. STATE

No.	Name	Hgt.	Yr.	Hometown
71	Whitey Bell	6-0	So.	Warsaw, IN
72	Jim Stevenson	6-3	Sr.	Winston-Salem, NC
73	Vic Molodet	6-0	So.	East Chicago, IN
74	Dick Tyler	6-3	Sr.	Newburgh, NY
75	Dave Gotkin	6-0	Jr.	New York, NY
76	Bobby Adams	6-0	Sr.	Lexington, KY
78	Ronnie Scheffel	6-0	Sr.	Kingston, NY
79	David Kelley	6-2	So.	Shelbyville, IN
80	Philip DiNardo	6-4	So.	Philadelphia, PA
81	Herb Applebaum	6-3	Sr.	New York, NY
82	Doug Kincaid	6-0	Sr.	Greensboro, NC
83	Mel Thompson	6-3	Sr.	Richmond, IN
84	Ronnie Shavlik	6-7	So.	Denver, CO
85	Lou Dickman	6-3	So.	Batesville, IN
87	Cliff Dwyer	6-9	Jr.	Cincinnati, OH

COACH: Everett Case
ASSISTANTS: Butter Anderson, Vic Bubas

SOUTH CAROLINA

No.	Name	Hgt.	Yr.	Hometown
11	Jack Hufford	5-9	Jr.	Rossville, IN
12	Tommy Tarlton	5-11	So.	Columbia, SC
13	Tom Hofferth	6-3	Jr.	Hammond, IN
14	Joe Smith	6-3	Jr.	Lyman, SC
15	Bob Peterson	5-11	So.	Elkhart, IN
21	Al Hough	6-2	So.	Columbia, SC
22	Phil Spotts	6-1	So.	Newberry, SC
23	Paul Goldsmith	6-2	So.	Greenville, SC
24	Al Spotts	6-1	So.	Newberry, SC
32	David Neilson	6-4	So.	Aiken, SC
33	Mervin Rabinowitz	6-1	Sr.	Charleston, SC
34	Tom Collins	6-4	So.	Mullins, SC
35	Lee Collins	6-6	So.	Lancaster, SC

COACH: Frank Johnson

VIRGINIA

No.	Name	Hgt.	Yr.	Hometown
3/11	Bob McCarty	6-2	So.	Clarksburg, WV
5/22	Charlie Gamble	6-4	Sr.	Falls Church, VA
6/16	Larry Jenkins	6-4	So.	Richmond, VA
7/15	Bill Morris	6-0	Jr.	Washington, DC
9/19	John Middleton	6-1	Jr.	Charleston, WV
10/24	Austin Pearre	6-3	So.	Frederick, MD
11/21	Bill Casey	6-2	Sr.	Norfolk, VA
13	Dick Lotts	6-0	Jr.	Waynesboro, VA
14	Buzz Wilkinson	6-2	Jr.	Pineville, WV
16/18	George Grattan	6-4	Jr.	Harrisonburg, VA
17	Dave Cooke	6-1	Sr.	Charlottesville, VA

COACH: Bus Male

WAKE FOREST

No.	Name	Hgt.	Yr.	Hometown
10	Jim Kotecki	6-5	Jr.	Natrona, PA
11	Billy Lyles	5-11	Sr.	Fairmont, NC
12	Bill Livengood	6-0	Jr.	Dale, IN
13	Lefty Davis	6-2	So.	Johnston City, IL
14	Tom Preston	6-3	Jr.	Winston-Salem, NC
15	Maurice George	6-1	Jr.	Winston-Salem, NC
20	Graham Phillips	6-1	Jr.	Warsaw, NC
21	Bill Yarbrough	6-0	Sr.	Charlotte, NC
22	John DeVos	6-2	Jr.	Hinsdale, IL
23	Bob Weatherspoon	6-4	So.	Durham, NC
24	Dickie Hemric	6-6	Jr.	Jonesville, NC
25	Frank McRae	6-2	So.	Salisbury, NC
31	Al DePorter	6-1	Sr.	Paterson, NJ
33	Ray Lipstas	6-1	So.	Berlin, NJ

COACH: Murray Greason
ASSISTANT: Bones McKinney

All-America Teams

ASSOCIATED PRESS

FIRST TEAM: Frank Selvy, Furman; Don Schlundt, Indiana; Tom Gola, La Salle; Cliff Hagan, Kentucky; Bob Pettit, LSU. **SECOND TEAM:** Bevo Francis, Rio Grande; Bob Leonard, Indiana; Frank Ramsey, Kentucky; Dick Ricketts, Duquesne; Tom Marshall, Western Kentucky. **THIRD TEAM:** Togo Palazzi, Holy Cross; Arnold Short, Oklahoma City; Bob Mattick, Oklahoma A&M; Johnny Kerr, Illinois; **Dickie Hemric, Wake Forest.**

UNITED PRESS INTERNATIONAL

FIRST TEAM: Frank Selvy, Furman; Don Schlundt, Indiana; Tom Gola, La Salle; Cliff Hagan, Kentucky; Bob Pettit, LSU. **SECOND TEAM:** Bevo Francis, Rio Grande; Dick Ricketts, Duquesne; Frank Ramsey, Kentucky; Bob Leonard, Indiana; Tom Marshall, Western Kentucky. **THIRD TEAM:** Togo Palazzi, Holy Cross; Paul Ebert, Ohio State; Arnold Short, Oklahoma City; Bob Mattick, Oklahoma A&M; Johnny Kerr, Illinois.

Final Top 20 Polls

AP

1.	Kentucky	25-0
2.	La Salle	26-4
3.	Holy Cross	26-2
4.	Indiana	20-4
5.	Duquesne	26-3
6.	Notre Dame	22-3
7.	Bradley	19-3
8.	W. Kentucky	29-3
9.	Penn State	18-5
10.	Okla. A&M	24-5
11.	Southern Cal	19-14
12.	G. Washington	23-3
13.	Iowa	17-5
14.	LSU	21-5
15.	Duke	22-6
16.	Niagara	24-6
17.	Seattle	26-2
18.	Kansas	16-5
19.	Illinois	17-5
20.	Maryland	23-7

UPI

1.	Indiana	20-4
2.	Kentucky	25-0
3.	Duquesne	26-3
4.	Okla. A&M	24-5
5.	Notre Dame	22-3
6.	W. Kentucky	29-3
7.	Kansas	16-5
8.	LSU	21-5
9.	Holy Cross	26-2
10.	Iowa	17-5
11.	LaSalle	26-4
12.	Illinois	17-5
13.	Colo. A&M	22-7
14.	**N.C. State**	**28-7**
	Southern Cal	19-14
16.	Oregon State	19-10
17.	Seattle	26-2
	Dayton	25-7
19.	Rice	23-5
20.	Duke	22-6

La Salle beat Bradley 92-76 for NCAA title.

'55

Wake Forest's Dickie Hemric

1954-55 Final Standings

Team	Conf.	Overall	Ave.	Opp.
*N.C. State	12-2	28-4	88.7	76.5
Duke	11-3	20-8	85.2	72.8
Maryland	10-4	17-7	65.5	61.9
Wake Forest	8-6	17-10	85.7	79.2
North Carolina	8-6	10-11	75.8	76.1
Virginia	5-9	14-15	89.8	84.4
South Carolina	2-12	10-17	75.7	79.9
Clemson	0-14	2-21	73.7	93.3

*Won ACC Tournament

NCAA — DUKE represented ACC because of N.C. State's probation, lost in first round of East Regional to Villanova.

ACC Tournament
MARCH 3-5, 1955 AT RALEIGH, N.C.

FIRST ROUND: Virginia 68, Maryland 67 (OT); Duke 83, South Carolina 67; N.C. State 101, Clemson 76; Wake Forest 95, North Carolina 82. **SEMIFINALS:** Duke 90, Virginia 77 (OT); N.C. State 85, Wake Forest 70. **FINAL:** N.C. State 87, Duke 77.

ALL-TOURNAMENT — FIRST TEAM: Buzz Wilkinson, Virginia; Ronnie Shavlik, N.C. State; Ronnie Mayer, Duke; Dickie Hemric, Wake Forest; Lefty Davis, Wake Forest. **SECOND TEAM:** Bill Miller, Virginia; Bill Yarborough, Clemson; Vic Molodet, N.C. State; Joe Belmont, Duke; Phil DiNardo, N.C. State.

All-ACC

FIRST TEAM: *Dickie Hemric, Wake Forest (250 votes); *Ronnie Shavlik, N.C. State (250); Buzz Wilkinson, Virginia (248); Lennie Rosenbluth, North Carolina (250); Ronnie Mayer, Duke (219). **SECOND TEAM:** Bob Kessler, Maryland (161); Bill Yarborough, Clemson (150); Joe Belmont, Duke (123); Vic Molodet, N.C. State (123); Lefty Davis, Wake Forest (75).
PLAYER OF THE YEAR: Hemric (22); Shavlik (12); Wilkinson (11).
COACH OF THE YEAR: Everett Case, N.C. State (26); Bus Male, Virginia (12); Frank McGuire, North Carolina (5); Hal Bradley, Duke (1); Murray Greason, Wake Forest (1).
*Unanimous Selection

Scoring, Rebounding Leaders

TOP TEN SCORERS

Player, School	G	FG	FT	TP	Ave.
Wilkinson, Virginia	28	308	282	898	32.1
Yarborough, Clemson	23	247	157	651	28.3
Hemric, Wake Forest	27	222	302	746	27.6
Rosenbluth, North Carolina	21	189	158	536	25.5
Shavlik, N.C. State	32	260	187	707	22.1
Mayer, Duke	28	217	173	607	21.7
Kessler, Maryland	24	178	131	487	20.3
McCarty, Virginia	29	236	99	571	19.7
Davis, Wake Forest	27	194	133	521	19.3
L. Collins, South Carolina	27	155	125	435	16.1

TOP TEN REBOUNDERS

Player, School	G	Rbs.	Ave.
Hemric, Wake Forest	27	515	19.0
Shavlik, N.C. State	32	581	18.1
L. Collins, South Carolina	27	434	16.1
Mayer, Duke	28	348	12.4
Rosenbluth, North Carolina	21	246	11.7
Dwyer, N.C. State	28	324	11.6
Kessler, Maryland	24	263	11.0
J. Smith, South Carolina	26	279	10.7
T. Smith, Clemson	23	220	9.6
Morgan, Duke	28	255	9.1

Rosters

CLEMSON
No.	Name	Hgt.	Yr.	Hometown
21	Don Shealy	5-10	So.	Newberry, SC
22	Doc Morgan	6-1	Jr.	Greenville, SC
23	Bill Yarborough	6-0	Sr.	Walhalla, SC
24	Barry Ryan	6-1	Sr.	Washington, DC
25	Bruce Holzschuh	6-2	Jr.	Teaneck, NJ
32	Buddy Shook	6-4	Sr.	Liberty, SC
33	Tommy Smith	6-4	Jr.	Hendersonville, NC
34	Rock Stone	6-3	So.	Piedmont, SC
35	Red Landers	6-1	So.	Asheville, NC
40	Ben Crosland	6-0	Sr.	Greenville, SC
41	Bill Riser	6-7	Jr.	Bowman, SC
42	David Bauman	6-3	So.	Asheville, NC

COACH: Banks McFadden

DUKE
No.	Name	Hgt.	Yr.	Hometown
12	Bob Thuemmel	5-10	So.	Englewood, NJ
13	Herky Lamley	6-4	Sr.	Havertown, PA
14	Don Tobin	6-5	Jr.	Avalon, PA
15	Jim Rogers	6-1	So.	Athens, WV
20	Richard Rosenthal	6-5	So.	Durham, NC
22	Tom Blackburn	6-0	Jr.	West Upton, MA
23	Marty Doherty	6-9	Sr.	Pelham, NY
30	Joe Belmont	5-11	Sr.	Philadelphia, PA
32	Bob Lakata	6-6	So.	Johnson City, NY
33	Junior Morgan	6-7	Jr.	Asheboro, NC
34	Jack Kalbfus	6-3	So.	Greensburg, PA
35	Ronnie Mayer	6-4	Jr.	Avalon, PA
42	Hal Turner	5-10	Sr.	Englewood, NJ

COACH: Hal Bradley
ASSISTANT: Tony Drago

MARYLAND
No.	Name	Hgt.	Yr.	Hometown
22	Al Bleich	6-2	So.	Washington, DC
25	Jack Doane	5-11	So.	Silver Spring, MD
30	Robert Hardiman	6-3	So.	Salisbury, MD
33	Mark Vodopia	5-11	So.	New York, NY
34	Bob Dilworth	6-4	Sr.	East Orange, NJ
35	Bob O'Brien	6-4	So.	McMechen, WV
40	Hank Houck	6-2	So.	Greenbelt, MD
42	Dave Webster	6-2	Jr.	Washington, DC
43	John Sandbower	6-3	Jr.	Baltimore, MD
45	Robert Nardone	6-3	So.	Bloomfield, NJ
50	Bob Kessler	6-4	Jr.	Alexandria, VA
52	Robert Murray	6-5	Sr.	Washington, DC
54	Bob Everett	6-6	Sr.	Washington, DC
55	Frank Fuqua	6-7	So.	Washington, DC
60	Drew Schaufler	6-5	So.	Philadelphia, PA

COACH: Bud Millikan
ASSISTANT: Ralph Greco

NORTH CAROLINA
No.	Name	Hgt.	Yr.	Hometown
10	Lennie Rosenbluth	6-5	So.	New York, NY
11	Dick Ward	6-1	So.	Wilson, NC
15	Willis Henderson	6-3	So.	Charlotte, NC
20	Bob Young	6-6	So.	New York, NY
21	Al Lifson	6-2	Sr.	Elizabeth, NJ
22	Ed Sutton	6-1	So.	Cullowhee, NC
23	Buddy Clark	6-3	So.	Louisville, KY
32	Gerry McCabe	6-3	Jr.	New York, NY
34	Frank Goodwin	6-1	So.	Belleville, NC
41	Paul Likins	6-9	Sr.	Elkhart, IN
42	Hilliard Greene	6-5	Jr.	Zebulon, NC
43	Jerry Vayda	6-4	Jr.	Bayonne, NJ
44	Tony Radovich	6-2	Jr.	Hoboken, NJ

COACH: Frank McGuire
ASSISTANT: Buck Freeman

N.C. STATE
No.	Name	Hgt.	Yr.	Hometown
73	Vic Molodet	6-0	Jr.	East Chicago, IN
74	John Maglio	6-0	So.	Havertown, PA
75	Dave Gotkin	6-0	Sr.	New York, NY
76	Cliff Hafer	6-5	So.	Middletown, OH
78	Ronnie Scheffel	6-0	Sr.	Kingston, NY
80	Phil DiNardo	6-4	So.	Philadelphia, PA
82	Nick Pond	6-4	So.	Montclair, NJ
84	Ronnie Shavlik	6-7	Sr.	Denver, CO
85	Lou Dickman	6-3	Jr.	Batesville, IN
87	Cliff Dwyer	6-10	Sr.	Cincinnati, OH
88	Bob Seitz	6-10	So.	Oaklyn, NJ

COACH: Everett Case
ASSISTANTS: Butter Anderson, Vic Bubas

SOUTH CAROLINA
No.	Name	Hgt.	Yr.	Hometown
11	Jack Hufford	5-9	Sr	Rossville, IN
12	Jack Neeley	6-1	So.	Columbia, SC
13	Tom Hofferth	6-3	Sr.	Hammond, IN
14	Joe Smith	6-3	Sr.	Lyman, SC
21	Benny Fannin	6-0	Jr.	Betsy Layne, KY
22	Sol Richardson	6-0	Jr.	Carr Creek, KY
24	Woody Preston	6-3	Jr.	Pikeville, KY
31	Art Smejkal	6-3	So.	Lake Villa, IL
32	David Neilson	6-4	Jr.	Aiken, SC
33	Sam Smith	6-3	Jr.	Carr Creek, KY
34	Tom Collins	6-4	Jr.	Mullins, SC
35	Lee Collins	6-6	Jr.	Lancaster, SC

COACH: Frank Johnson

VIRGINIA
No.	Name	Hgt.	Yr.	Hometown
1/8	Anthony Genevese	5-8	So.	New York, NY
4	Douglas Waugh	6-2	Jr.	Arlington, VA
5	Bill Miller	5-9	So.	Bethlehem, PA
6	Bob McCarty	6-2	Jr.	Clarksburg, WV
7	Bill Morris	6-0	Sr.	Washington, DC
9	Cecil Underwood	6-3	So.	Newport News, VA
10	Austin Pearre	6-3	Jr.	Frederick, MD
11	Tucker McLaughlin	6-3	So.	Halifax, VA
12	Robert Gunderman	6-3	So.	Franklin, NJ
13	Dick Lotts	6-0	Sr.	Waynesboro, VA
14	Buzz Wilkinson	6-2	Sr.	Pineville, WV
15	Jerry Cooper	6-6	Sr.	Clarksburg, WV

COACH: Bus Male

WAKE FOREST
No.	Name	Hgt.	Yr.	Hometown
10	Ernie Wiggins	6-0	So.	London, KY
11	Kenneth Cox	6-3	So.	Marietta, SC
12	Jim Gilley	6-6	So.	Winston-Salem, NC
13	Lefty Davis	6-2	Sr.	Johnston City, IL
14	Tom Preston	6-3	Sr.	Winston-Salem, NC
15	Maurice George	6-1	Sr.	Winston-Salem, NC
20	Graham Phillips	6-1	Sr.	Warsaw, NC
22	Jim DeVos	6-4	So.	Hinsdale, IL
23	Joe Stepusin	6-4	So.	Rankin, PA
24	Dickie Hemric	6-6	Sr.	Jonesville, NC
25	John Kotecki	6-5	Sr.	Natrona, PA
31	Jackie Murdock	5-11	So.	Raleigh, NC
33	Jon Gerdes	6-4	So.	Wilmington, NC

COACH: Murray Greason
ASSISTANT: Bones McKinney

All-America Teams

ASSOCIATED PRESS
FIRST TEAM: *Tom Gola, La Salle; Robin Freeman, Ohio State; Bill Russell, San Francisco; Dick Ricketts, Duquesne; Darrell Floyd, Furman. **SECOND TEAM:** Don Schlundt, Indiana; **Dickie Hemric, Wake Forest**; Sihugo Green, Duquesne; Richard Garmaker, Minnesota; **Ronnie Shavlik, N.C. State**. **THIRD TEAM:** Tom Heinsohn, Holy Cross; **Buzz Wilkinson, Virginia**; Bob Burrow, Kentucky; Dick Boushka, St. Louis; Maurice Stokes, St. Francis (Pa.)

UNITED PRESS INTERNATIONAL
FIRST TEAM: *Tom Gola, La Salle; Bill Russell, San Francisco; Dick Garmaker, Minnesota; Sihugo Green, Duquesne; Dick Ricketts, Duquesne. **SECOND TEAM: Ronnie Shavlik, N.C. State; Dickie Hemric, Wake Forest**; Robin Freeman, Ohio State; Don Schlundt, Indiana; Darrell Floyd, Furman. **THIRD TEAM:** Jack Stephens, Notre Dame; John Horn, Dayton; Maurice Stokes, St. Francis (Pa.); Tom Heinsohn, Holy Cross; Ken Sears, Santa Clara.
*Player of the Year

Final Top 20 Polls

	AP			UPI	
1.	San Francisco	28-1	1.	San Francisco	28-1
2.	Kentucky	23-3	2.	Kentucky	23-3
3.	La Salle	26-5	3.	La Salle	26-5
4.	**N.C. State**	**28-4**	4.	Utah	24-4
5.	Iowa	19-7	5.	Iowa	19-7
6.	Duquesne	22-4	6.	**N.C. State**	**28-4**
7.	Utah	24-4	7.	Duquesne	22-4
8.	Marquette	24-3	8.	Oregon State	22-8
9.	Dayton	25-4	9.	Marquette	24-3
10.	Oregon State	22-8	10.	Dayton	25-4
11.	Minnesota	15-7	11.	Colorado	19-6
12.	Alabama	19-5	12.	UCLA	21-5
13.	UCLA	21-5	13.	Minnesota	15-7
14.	G. Washington	24-6	14.	Tulsa	21-7
15.	Colorado	19-6	15.	G. Washington	24-6
16.	Tulsa	21-7	16.	Illinois	17-5
17.	Vanderbilt	16-6	17.	Niagara	20-6
18.	Illinois	17-5	18.	St. Louis	20-8
19.	West Virginia	19-11	19.	Holy Cross	19-7
20.	St. Louis	20-8	20.	Cincinnati	21-8

San Francisco beat La Salle 77-63 for NCAA title.

ACC BASKETBALL / REFERENCE

'56

N.C. State's Ronnie Shavlik

1955-56 Final Standings

Team	Conf.	Overall	Avg.	Opp.
*N.C. State	11-3	24-4	82.8	70.5
North Carolina	11-3	18-5	80.0	71.0
Wake Forest	10-4	19-9	80.7	75.2
Duke	10-4	19-7	80.6	69.8
Maryland	7-7	14-10	66.7	64.8
Virginia	3-11	10-17	73.8	78.9
South Carolina	3-11	9-14	78.2	79.3
Clemson	1-13	9-17	86.0	90.8

*Won ACC Tournament

NCAA – N.C. STATE lost in first round of East Regional to Canisius 79-78 (4OT).

ACC Tournament
MARCH 1-3, 1956 AT RALEIGH, N.C.
FIRST ROUND: Wake Forest 79, South Carolina 64; North Carolina 81, Virginia 77; N.C. State 88, Clemson 84; Duke 94, Maryland 69. **SEMIFINALS:** N.C. State 91, Duke 79; Wake Forest 77, North Carolina 56. **FINAL:** N.C. State 76, Wake Forest 64.
ALL-TOURNAMENT—FIRST TEAM: Vic Molodet, N.C. State; Lennie Rosenbluth, North Carolina; Jackie Murdock, Wake Forest; Jack Williams, Wake Forest; John Maglio, N.C. State. **SECOND TEAM:** Ronnie Shavlik, N.C. State; Ronnie Mayer, Duke; Bob Kessler, Maryland; Bill Miller, Virginia; Bob McCarty, Virginia.

All-ACC
FIRST TEAM: *Ronnie Shavlik, N.C. State (235 votes); *Lennie Rosenbluth, North Carolina (235); Vic Molodet, N.C. State (220); Lefty Davis, Wake Forest (219); Joe Belmont, Duke (197). **SECOND TEAM:** Ronnie Mayer, Duke (168); Grady Wallace, South Carolina (109); Bill Yarborough, Clemson (94); Bob Kessler, Maryland (94); Jackie Murdock, Wake Forest (83).
PLAYER OF THE YEAR: Shavlik (31); Molodet (10); Rosenbluth (7).
COACH OF THE YEAR: Murray Greason, Wake Forest (33); Everett Case, N.C. State (11); Banks McFadden, Clemson (1); Frank McGuire, North Carolina (1); Evan J. Male, Virginia (1).
*Unanimous Selection

Scoring, Rebounding Leaders

TOP TEN SCORERS

Player, School	G	FG	FT	TP	Ave.
Rosenbluth, North Carolina	23	227	160	614	26.7
Wallace, South Carolina	23	217	116	550	23.9
McCarty, Virginia	27	231	163	625	23.1
Mayer, Duke	25	195	163	553	22.1
Yockel, Clemson	26	210	124	544	20.9
Kessler, Maryland	24	158	174	490	20.4
Davis, Wake Forest	28	196	146	538	19.2
Yarborough, Clemson	26	182	123	487	18.7
Shavlik, N.C. State	28	177	156	510	18.2
Molodet, N.C. State	27	162	167	491	18.2

TOP TEN REBOUNDERS

Player, School	G	RBS.	Ave.
Shavlik, N.C. State	28	545	19.5
Collins, South Carolina	23	404	17.6
Kessler, Maryland	24	336	14.0
Rosenbluth, North Carolina	23	264	11.4
DiNardo, N.C. State	28	313	11.2
Williams, Wake Forest	28	309	11.0
Wallace, South Carolina	23	250	10.9
Seay, Clemson	25	262	10.5
Morgan, Duke	26	256	9.8
Brennan, North Carolina	23	219	9.5

Rosters

CLEMSON

No.	Name	Hgt.	Yr.	Hometown
20	Dick Yeary	6-0	So.	Nicholasville, KY
21	Doc Morgan	6-1	Sr.	Greenville, SC
23	Bill Yarborough	6-0	Sr.	Walhalla, SC
25	Bruce Holzschuh	6-2	Sr.	Teaneck, NJ
30	Rock Stone	6-4	Jr.	Piedmont, SC
31	Vince Yockel	6-3	So.	Jersey City, NJ
33	Tommy Smith	6-4	Sr.	Hendersonville, NC
34	Ed Brinkley	6-6	So.	Asheville, NC
35	Tom Cameron	6-2	So.	Jersey City, NJ
40	Eddie Moncrief	6-4	So.	Moultrie, GA
41	Gene Seay	6-6	So.	Greenville, SC
42	Bill Riser	6-7	Sr.	Bowman, SC

COACH: Banks McFadden

DUKE

No.	Name	Hgt.	Yr.	Hometown
11	Don Cashman	6-4	So.	New York, NY
13	Tony Buhowsky	6-9	So.	Roselle Park, NJ
15	Paul Schmidt	6-4	So.	Johnstown, PA
20	Richard Rosenthal	6-5	Jr.	Durham, NC
21	Ed Bryson	6-2	So.	Durham, NC
22	Bobby Joe Harris	5-11	So.	King, NC
24	Jim Newcome	6-5	So.	Gary, IN
30	Joe Belmont	5-11	Sr.	Philadelphia, PA
31	Hayes Clement	6-6	So.	New Bern, NC
32	Bob Lakata	6-6	Jr.	Johnson City, NY
33	Junior Morgan	6-7	Jr.	Asheboro, NC
34	Jack Kalbfus	6-3	Jr.	Greensburg, PA
35	Ronnie Mayer	6-4	Sr.	Avalon, PA
40	Bucky Allen	6-1	So.	Durham, NC

COACH: Hal Bradley
ASSISTANT: Tony Drago

MARYLAND

No.	Name	Hgt.	Yr.	Hometown
20	Al Bleich	6-2	So.	Washington, DC
22	John Love	6-0	So.	Camden, NJ
25	Jack Doane	5-11	Jr.	Silver Spring, MD
30	Robert Hardiman	6-3	Jr.	Salisbury, MD
32	Nick Davis	6-1	So.	Rankin, PA
33	John Nacincik	6-3	So.	Brooklyn, NY
35	Bob O'Brien	6-3	Jr.	McMechen, WV
40	Curt Prins	6-2	So.	Bethesda, MD
42	Pat Clarke	6-3	So.	Washington, DC
43	John Sandbower	6-4	So.	Baltimore, MD
44	Wayne McGinnis	6-6	So.	Baltimore, MD
45	Bob Nardone	6-3	So.	Bloomfield, NJ
50	Bob Kessler	6-4	Sr.	Alexandria, VA
54	Perry Moore	6-4	So.	Belpre, OH
54	John Urbanik	6-7	So.	Elizabeth, NJ
55	Don Dunlap	6-5	So.	Washington, DC
60	Drew Schaufler	6-5	Jr.	Philadelphia, PA

COACH: Bud Millikan
ASSISTANT: Bob Everett

NORTH CAROLINA

No.	Name	Hgt.	Yr.	Hometown
10	Lennie Rosenbluth	6-5	Jr.	New York, NY
11	Ken Rosemond	5-8	Jr.	Hillsborough, NC
20	Bob Young	6-6	Jr.	New York, NY
22	Roy Searcy	6-4	So.	Draper, NC
23	Buddy Clark	6-3	Jr.	Louisville, KY
32	Bob Cunningham	6-4	So.	New York, NY
33	Gerry McCabe	6-3	Sr.	The Bronx, NY
34	Pete Brennan	6-6	So.	Brooklyn, NY
40	Tommy Kearns	5-11	So.	Bergenfield, NJ
41	Joe Quigg	6-8	So.	New York, NY
42	Hilliard Greene	6-5	Sr.	Zebulon, NC
43	Jerry Vayda	6-4	Sr.	Bayonne, NJ
44	Tony Radovich	6-4	Sr.	Hoboken, NJ

COACH: Frank McGuire
ASSISTANT: Buck Freeman

N.C. STATE

No.	Name	Hgt.	Yr.	Hometown
72	Marvin Kessler	5-11	So.	Brooklyn, NY
73	Vic Molodet	6-0	Sr.	East Chicago, IN
74	John Maglio	6-0	Jr.	Havertown, PA
75	Bucky Waters	6-2	So.	Collingswood, NJ
76	Cliff Hafer	6-5	Jr.	Middletown, OH
79	Tom Hopper	6-3	So.	Glen Rock, NJ
80	Phil DiNardo	6-4	Sr.	Philadelphia, PA
82	Nick Pond	6-4	Jr.	Montclair, NJ
83	George Stepanovich	6-4	So.	East Chicago, IN
84	Ronnie Shavlik	6-9	Sr.	Denver, CO
85	Lou Dickman	6-4	Sr.	Batesville, IN
86	Mike Miles	6-7	So.	Upper Darby, PA
88	Bob Seitz	6-11	Jr.	Oaklyn, NJ

COACH: Everett Case
ASSISTANTS: Vic Bubas, Lee Terrill

SOUTH CAROLINA

No.	Name	Hgt.	Yr.	Hometown
12	Jack Neeley	6-1	Jr.	Columbia, SC
13	Lee Anderson	6-1	So.	Rockford, IL
14	Dean Crain	6-2	So.	Greenville, SC
15	Joe Granger	6-4	Jr.	Greenville, SC
15	Russ Porter	5-10	So.	Pikesville, KY
21	Benny Fannin	6-0	Sr	Betsy Layne, KY
22	Sol Richardson	6-0	Sr.	Carr Creek, KY
25	Marshall Perkins	6-4	So.	Inman, SC
31	Art Smejkal	6-3	Jr.	Lake Villa, IL
32	David Neilson	6-4	Sr.	Aiken, SC
33	Sam Smith	6-3	Sr.	Carr Creek, KY
35	Lee Collins	6-6	Sr.	Lancaster, SC
42	Grady Wallace	6-4	Jr.	Mare Creek, KY

COACH: Frank Johnson
ASSISTANT: Walt Hambrick

VIRGINIA

No.	Name	Hgt.	Yr.	Hometown
4	William Berndt	6-3	So.	Baltimore, MD
5	Bill Miller	5-9	Jr.	Bethlehem, PA
3	James Moyer	6-0	So.	Waynesboro, VA
6	Bob McCarty	6-2	So.	Clarksburg, WV
7	Thomas Hockersmith	6-3	So.	Fairfax, VA
8	Kendall White	5-10	So.	Lynchburg, VA
9	Cecil Underwood	6-3	Jr.	Newport News, VA
11	Robert Hardy	6-0	Jr.	Richmond, VA
12	Wistar Nelligan	6-3	So.	Lynchburg, VA
16	Austin Pearre	6-3	Sr.	Frederick, MD
17	Jerry Cooper	6-6	Jr.	Clarksburg, WV
18	Glenn Mitchell	6-3	So.	Washington, DC
	Ashton Godley	6-7	So.	Charlottesville, VA
	Mike O'Bryan	6-5	Jr.	Richmond, VA
	Morton Boyd	6-1	So.	Prospect, KY
	Robert Hickson	6-2	So.	Lynchburg, VA

COACH: Bus Male

WAKE FOREST

No.	Name	Hgt.	Yr.	Hometown
10	Ernie Wiggins	6-0	Jr.	London, KY
11	Jim Campbell	5-11	Sr.	Buies Creek, NC
11	Bill Tucker	5-10	Jr.	Louisville, KY
12	Jim Gilley	6-6	Jr.	Winston-Salem, NC
13	Jack Williams	6-4	Jr.	Johnston City, IL
14	Kenneth Cox	6-3	So.	Marietta, SC
15	Joe Stepusin	6-4	Jr.	Rankin, PA
20	Don Scalf	5-10	Jr.	High Point, NC
21	George Austin	6-7	So.	Smithfield, NC
21	Jack Frauson	6-6	So.	Mahwah, NJ
22	Henry Bowers	6-3	So.	Knightdale, NC
25	Wendell Carr	6-5	So.	Muncie, IN
31	Jackie Murdock	5-11	Jr.	Raleigh, NC
33	Jon Gerdes	6-4	So.	Wilmington, NC
35	John Reed	6-7	So.	North, SC
43	Lefty Davis	6-2	Sr.	Johnston City, IL

COACH: Murray Greason
ASSISTANTS: Bones McKinney, Harold Barrow

All-America Teams

ASSOCIATED PRESS
FIRST TEAM: *Bill Russell, San Francisco; Robin Freeman, Ohio State; Sihugo Green, Duquesne; Darrell Floyd, Furman; Tom Heinsohn, Holy Cross. **SECOND TEAM:** Ronnie Shavlik, N.C. State; K.C. Jones, San Francisco; Rod Hundley, West Virginia; **Lennie Rosenbluth, North Carolina**; Bill Uhl, Dayton. **THIRD TEAM:** Joe Holup, George Washington; Julius McCoy, Michigan State; Bob Ridley, Illinois; Bob Burrow, Kentucky; Willie Naulls, UCLA.

UNITED PRESS INTERNATIONAL
FIRST TEAM: *Bill Russell, San Francisco; Sihugo Green, Duquesne; Robin Freeman, Ohio State; Darrell Floyd, Furman; K.C. Jones, San Francisco. **SECOND TEAM:** Ronnie Shavlik, N.C. State; Rod Hundley, West Virginia; Tom Heinsohn, Holy Cross; Bill Uhl, Dayton; **Lennie Rosenbluth, North Carolina**. **THIRD TEAM:** Willie Naulls, UCLA; Julius McCoy, Michigan State; Bill Ridley, Illinois; Bob Burrow, Kentucky; Paul Judson, Illinois.

*Player of the Year

Final Top 20 Polls

AP
1. San Francisco 29-0
2. **N.C. State** **24-4**
3. Dayton 25-4
4. Iowa 20-6
5. Alabama 21-3
6. Louisville 26-3
7. SMU 25-4
8. UCLA 22-6
9. Kentucky 20-6
10. Illinois 18-4
11. Oklahoma City 20-7
12. Vanderbilt 19-4
13. **North Carolina** **18-5**
14. Holy Cross 22-5
15. Temple 27-4
17. Wake Forest 19-9
17. Duke 19-7
18. Utah 22-6
19. Okla. A&M 18-9
20. West Virginia 21-9

UPI
1. San Francisco 29-0
2. **N.C. State** **24-4**
3. Dayton 25-4
4. Iowa 20-6
5. Alabama 21-3
6. SMU 25-4
7. Louisville 26-3
8. Illinois 18-4
9. UCLA 22-6
10. Vanderbilt 19-4
11. **North Carolina** **18-5**
12. Kentucky 20-6
13. Utah 22-6
14. Temple 27-4
15. Holy Cross 22-5
16. Okla. A&M 20-7
  St. Louis 18-7
18. Seattle 18-11
  Duke **19-7**
  Canisius 19-7

San Francisco beat Iowa 83-71 for NCAA title.

280

'57

North Carolina's Lennie Rosenbluth

1956-57 Final Standings

Team	Conf.	Overall	Ave.	Opp.
*North Carolina	14-0	32-0	79.3	65.6
Maryland	9-5	16-10	64.6	61.2
Duke	8-6	13-11	78.4	77.0
Wake Forest	7-7	19-9	68.4	62.6
N.C. State	7-7	15-11	75.8	74.3
South Carolina	5-9	17-12	81.9	78.3
Clemson	3-11	7-17	72.5	82.3
Virginia	3-11	6-19	68.6	74.4

*Won ACC Tournament

NCAA—NORTH CAROLINA won NCAA title: beat Yale 90-74, beat Canisius 87-75, beat Syracuse 67-58 in East Regional; beat Michigan State 74-70 (3OT), beat Kansas 54-53 (3OT) in Final Four.

ACC Tournament
MARCH 7-9, 1957 AT RALEIGH, N.C.

FIRST ROUND: South Carolina 84, Duke 81; Maryland 71, Virginia 68; North Carolina 81, Clemson 61; Wake Forest 66, N.C. State 57. **SEMIFINALS:** North Carolina 61, Wake Forest 59; South Carolina 74, Maryland 64. **FINAL:** North Carolina 95, South Carolina 75.
ALL-TOURNAMENT—FIRST TEAM: Lennie Rosenbluth, North Carolina; Grady Wallace, South Carolina; Jack Williams, Wake Forest; Pete Brennan, North Carolina; Jackie Murdock, Wake Forest. **SECOND TEAM:** Tommy Kearns, North Carolina; John Nacincik, Maryland; Ray Pericola, South Carolina; Joe Quigg, North Carolina; Bob Cunningham, North Carolina.

All-ACC
FIRST TEAM: *Lennie Rosenbluth, North Carolina (275 votes); *Grady Wallace, South Carolina (275); Jackie Murdock, Wake Forest (269); Tommy Kearns, North Carolina (222); Jack Williams, Wake Forest (166). **SECOND TEAM:** Bob O'Brien, Maryland (160); Pete Brennan, North Carolina (152); Jim Newsome, Duke (142); John Richter, N.C. State (123); Ernie Wiggins, Wake Forest (93).
PLAYER OF THE YEAR: Rosenbluth (43); Wallace (4). **COACH OF THE YEAR:** *Frank McGuire, North Carolina, (47).
*Unanimous Selection

Scoring, Rebounding Leaders

TOP TEN SCORERS

Player, School	G	FG	FT	TP	Ave.
Wallace, South Carolina	29	336	234	906	31.2
Rosenbluth, North Carolina	32	305	285	895	28.0
Busch, Virginia	10	55	88	198	19.8
Yockel, Clemson	24	178	118	474	19.8
Williams, Wake Forest	25	155	95	405	16.2
Richter, N.C. State	24	136	100	372	15.5
Murdock, Wake Forest	28	134	161	429	15.2
Hardy, Virginia	25	142	96	380	15.2
Pericola, South Carolina	29	166	102	434	14.9
Brennan, North Carolina	32	143	185	471	14.7

TOP TEN REBOUNDERS

Player, School	G	RBS.	Ave.
Wallace, South Carolina	29	419	14.4
Richter, N.C. State	24	305	12.7
Lentz, South Carolina	29	360	12.4
Newcome, Duke	24	273	11.4
Brennan, North Carolina	32	332	10.4
Busch, Virginia	10	97	9.7
Rosenbluth, North Carolina	32	280	8.8
Quigg, North Carolina	31	268	8.7
Williams, Wake Forest	25	206	8.2
Gilley, Wake Forest	28	225	8.0

Rosters

CLEMSON
No.	Name	Hgt.	Yr.	Hometown
20	Dick Yeary	6-0	Jr.	Nicholasville, KY
22	Doug Hoffman	6-2	So.	Gastonia, NC
23	Bill Yarborough	6-0	Sr.	Walhalla, SC
24	Bill Landers	6-0	Jr.	Asheville, NC
25	Junius Smith	5-11	So.	Greenville, SC
30	Bob Fisher	6-3	So.	Fairmont, NC
31	Vince Yockel	6-3	Jr.	Jersey City, NJ
32	Fred DeBerry	6-0	Sr.	Raleigh, NC
34	Ed Brinkley	6-6	Jr.	Asheville, NC
35	Tom Cameron	6-2	Jr.	Jersey City, NJ
40	Eddie Moncrief	6-4	So.	Moultrie, GA
41	Gene Seay	6-6	Sr.	Greenville, SC

COACH: Press Maravich
ASSISTANT: Rock Norman

DUKE
No.	Name	Hgt.	Yr.	Hometown
11	Bob Vernon	6-1	Jr.	Riverside, NJ
14	Jerry Robertson	6-6	So.	Burlington, NC
15	Paul Schmidt	6-4	Jr.	Johnstown, PA
20	Richard Rosenthal	6-5	Sr.	Durham, NC
21	Ed Bryson	6-2	Jr.	Durham, NC
22	Bill Watson	6-1	So.	Huntington, WV
23	Don Miller	6-4	So.	Miami Beach, FL
25	Joe Marcovecchio	6-2	So.	Atlanta, GA
30	Bobby Joe Harris	5-11	Jr.	King, NC
31	Hayes Clement	6-6	Jr.	New Bern, NC
33	Jim Newcome	6-5	Jr.	Gary, IN
35	George Barrett	6-4	So.	Wabash, IN
40	Bucky Allen	6-1	Jr.	Durham, NC

COACH: Hal Bradley
ASSISTANT: Tony Drago

MARYLAND
No.	Name	Hgt.	Yr.	Hometown
22	Bill Murphy	6-3	So.	Pittsburgh, PA
24	Bob Moorhead	6-4	So.	Tacoma, WA
25	Gene Danko	6-2	So.	McKeesport, PA
30	Robert Hardiman	6-3	Sr.	Salisbury, MD
32	Nick Davis	6-2	Jr.	Rankin, PA
33	John Nacincik	6-3	Jr.	Brooklyn, NY
35	Bob O'Brien	6-3	Sr.	McMechen, WV
40	Julian Weingarten	6-4	So.	Washington, DC
42	Wayne McGinnis	6-7	So.	Whitehall, MD
44	Jim Halleck	6-0	Sr.	Elizabeth, NJ
45	Perry Moore	6-4	Jr.	Belpre, OH

COACH: Bud Millikan
ASSISTANT: Roy Lester

NORTH CAROLINA
No.	Name	Hgt.	Yr.	Hometown
10	Lennie Rosenbluth	6-5	Sr.	New York, NY
11	Ken Rosemond	5-8	Jr.	Hillsborough, NC
20	Bob Young	6-6	Sr.	New York, NY
22	Roy Searcy	6-4	Jr.	Draper, NC
30	Bill Hathaway	6-11	So.	Long Beach, NY
31	Gehrmann Holland	6-3	So.	Beaufort, NC
32	Bob Cunningham	6-4	Jr.	New York, NY
34	Danny Lotz	6-7	So.	Northport, NY
35	Pete Brennan	6-6	Jr.	Brooklyn, NY
40	Tommy Kearns	5-11	Jr.	Bergenfield, NJ
41	Joe Quigg	6-9	Jr.	Brooklyn, NY
43	Stan Groll	6-0	Sr.	Brooklyn, NY
44	Tony Radovich	6-2	Sr.	Hoboken, NJ

COACH: Frank McGuire
ASSISTANTS: Buck Freeman, Vince Grimaldi

All-America Teams

ASSOCIATED PRESS
FIRST TEAM: *Wilt Chamberlain, Kansas; **Lennie Rosenbluth, North Carolina**; Rod Hundley, West Virginia; Gary Thompson, Iowa State; Chet Forte, Columbia. **SECOND TEAM:** Elgin Baylor, Seattle; Charles Tyra, Louisville; Jim Krebs, SMU; **Grady Wallace, South Carolina**; Frank Howard, Ohio State. **THIRD TEAM:** Guy Rodgers, Temple; Bill Ebben, Detroit; Jim Ashmore, Mississippi State; Archie Dees, Indiana; Larry Friend, California.

UNITED PRESS INTERNATIONAL
FIRST TEAM: Wilt Chamberlain, Kansas; *Chet Forte, Columbia; **Lennie Rosenbluth, North Carolina**; **Grady Wallace, South Carolina**; Rod Hundley, West Virginia. **SECOND TEAM:** Elgin Baylor, Seattle; Charles Tyra, Louisville; Jim Krebs, SMU; Gary Thompson, Iowa State; Joe Gibbon, Mississippi. **THIRD TEAM:** Archie Dees, Indiana; Frank Howard, Ohio State; Guy Rodgers, Temple; Johnny Cox, Kentucky; Jim Ashmore, Mississippi State.
*Player of the Year

N.C. STATE
No.	Name	Hgt.	Yr.	Hometown
71	Whitey Bell	6-0	Jr.	Warsaw, IN
72	Marvin Kessler	6-0	Jr.	Brooklyn, NY
73	Bob Goodrich	6-0	So.	Philadelphia, PA
74	John Maglio	6-0	Jr.	Havertown, PA
75	Bucky Waters	6-2	Jr.	Collingswood, NJ
76	Cliff Hafer	6-5	Sr.	Middletown, OH
78	Lou Pucillo	5-9	So.	Philadelphia, PA
79	Tom Hopper	6-3	Jr.	Glen Rock, NJ
80	Ken Clark	6-5	So.	Flushing, NY
81	Bob MacGillivray	6-4	So.	Dorchester, MA
82	Nick Pond	6-4	Sr.	Montclair, NJ
84	John Richter	6-8	So.	Philadelphia, PA
85	Dick Kelly	6-4	So.	Philadelphia, PA
88	Bob Seitz	6-11	Sr.	Oaklyn, NJ

COACH: Everett Case
ASSISTANTS: Vic Bubas, Lee Terrill

SOUTH CAROLINA
No.	Name	Hgt.	Yr.	Hometown
	Marshall Perkins	6-4	Jr.	Inman, SC
15	Joe Granger	6-3	Sr.	Greenville, SC
21	Ray Pericola	6-2	So.	Union City, NJ
22	Jim Cauthen	6-0	Sr.	Hartsville, SC
23	Lee Anderson	6-2	Jr.	Rockford, IL
24	Dean Crain	6-2	Jr.	Greenville, SC
31	Art Smejkal	6-4	Sr.	Lake Villa, IL
33	Bobby McCoy	6-0	Sr.	Pikeville, KY
35	Dick Hoffman	6-1	So.	Union City, NJ
42	Grady Wallace	6-4	Sr.	Mare Creek, KY
43	Don Goodroe	6-7	So.	Columbus, GA
44	Fred Lentz	6-8	So.	Asheville, NC

COACH: Frank Johnson
ASSISTANT: Walt Hambrick

VIRGINIA
No.	Name	Hgt.	Yr.	Hometown
	Ashton Godley	6-6	Jr.	Charlottesville, VA
	Robert Hickson	6-2	Jr.	Lynchburg, VA
	Robert Mortell	6-9	So.	Fairfield, CT
	Jake Berman	6-0	Sr.	Richmond, VA
	Mike O'Bryan	6-5	Jr.	Richmond, VA
3	John Butler	5-11	So.	Lakewood, OH
5	Bill Miller	5-9	Sr.	Bethlehem, PA
7	John Siewers	6-5	So.	Richmond, VA
9	Cecil Underwood	6-3	Sr.	Newport News, VA
10	Dick Stobbs	6-3	So.	Norfolk, VA
11	Robert Hardy	6-0	Sr.	Richmond, VA
12	Wistar Nelligan	6-3	Jr.	Lynchburg, VA
13	Bill Metzger	6-6	So.	Utica, NY
19	Jerry Cooper	6-6	Sr.	Clarksburg, WV
21	Herb Busch	6-7	So.	Short Hills, NJ

COACH: Bus Male

WAKE FOREST
No.	Name	Hgt.	Yr.	Hometown
10	Ernie Wiggins	6-0	Sr.	London, KY
11	Bill Tucker	5-10	Sr.	Louisville, KY
12	Jim Gilley	6-6	Sr.	Winston-Salem, NC
13	Jack Williams	6-4	Sr.	Johnston City, IL
14	Kenneth Cox	6-3	Jr.	Marietta, SC
15	Joe Stepusin	6-4	Sr.	Rankin, PA
20	Don Scalf	5-11	Jr.	High Point, NC
21	Joe Ladd	6-6	So.	Lowell, NC
22	Henry Bowers	6-3	Jr.	Knightdale, NC
25	Wendell Carr	6-5	Jr.	Muncie, IN
31	Jackie Murdock	5-11	Sr.	Raleigh, NC
33	Dickie Odom	6-6	So.	Ahoskie, NC
35	John Reed	6-8	Jr.	North, SC
43	Olin Broadway	6-3	So.	Raleigh, NC
55	Bill Greene	6-1	So.	Kingsport, TN

COACH: Murray Greason
ASSISTANTS: Bones McKinney, Al DePorter

Final Top 20 Polls

AP
1. North Carolina 32-0
2. Kansas 24-3
3. Kentucky 23-5
4. SMU 22-4
5. Seattle 24-3
6. Louisville 21-5
7. West Virginia 25-5
8. Vanderbilt 17-5
9. Oklahoma City 20-7
10. St. Louis 19-9
11. Michigan State 16-10
12. Memphis State 24-6
13. California 21-5
14. UCLA 22-4
15. Mississippi St. 17-8
16. Idaho State 25-4
17. Notre Dame 20-8
18. Wake Forest 19-9
19. Canisius 22-6
    Okla. A&M 17-9

UPI
1. North Carolina 32-0
2. Kansas 24-3
3. Kentucky 23-5
4. SMU 22-4
5. Seattle 24-3
6. California 21-5
7. Michigan State 16-10
8. Louisville 21-5
9. UCLA 22-4
    St. Louis 19-9
11. West Virginia 25-5
12. Dayton 19-9
13. Bradley 22-7
14. Brigham Young 19-9
15. Indiana 14-8
16. Vanderbilt 17-5
    Xavier (Ohio) 20-8
    Oklahoma City 20-7
19. Notre Dame 20-8
20. Kansas State 15-8

UNC beat Kansas 54-53 (3OT) for NCAA title.

281

'58

North Carolina's
Pete Brennan

1957-58 Final Standings

Team	Conf.	Overall	Ave.	Opp.
Duke	11-3	18-7	69.2	64.2
North Carolina	10-4	19-7	71.8	64.9
N.C. State	10-4	18-6	67.0	61.5
***Maryland**	9-5	22-7	69.1	57.6
Virginia	6-8	10-13	70.5	72.1
Clemson	4-10	8-16	68.8	71.8
South Carolina	3-11	5-19	66.3	77.8
Wake Forest	3-11	6-17	63.1	67.8

*Won ACC Tournament

NCAA—MARYLAND third in East Regional: beat Boston College 86-63, lost to Temple 71-67, beat Manhattan 59-55.

ACC Tournament

MARCH 6-8, 1958 AT RALEIGH, N.C.

FIRST ROUND: North Carolina 62, Clemson 51; N.C. State 66, South Carolina 61; Duke 51, Wake Forest 44; Maryland 70, Virginia 66. **SEMIFINALS:** Maryland 71, Duke 65 (OT); North Carolina 64, N.C. State 58. **FINAL:** Maryland 86, North Carolina 74.

ALL-TOURNAMENT—FIRST TEAM: Pete Brennan, North Carolina; Nick Davis, Maryland; Lou Pucillo, N.C. State; Charles McNeil, Maryland; Tommy Kearns, North Carolina. **SECOND TEAM:** Bucky Allen, Duke; Bob Vernon, Duke; Ray Stanley, North Carolina; Al Bunge, Mayland; Bobby Joe Harris, Duke.

All-ACC

FIRST TEAM: *Pete Brennan, North Carolina (370 votes); Lou Pucillo, N.C. State (313); Tommy Kearns, North Carolina (292); Jim Newcome, Duke (288); Herb Busch, Virginia (246). **SECOND TEAM:** Dave Budd, Wake Forest (173); John Richter, N.C. State (136); Paul Schmidt, Duke (121); John Nacincik, Maryland (114); Nick Davis, Maryland (112); Bucky Allen, Duke (112).

PLAYER OF THE YEAR: Brennan (56); Pucillo (2). **COACH OF THE YEAR:** Everett Case, N.C. State (24); Hal Bradley, Duke (23); Bud Millikan, Maryland (10); Frank McGuire, North Carolina (1).

*Unanimous Selection

Scoring, Rebounding Leaders

TOP TEN SCORERS

Player, School	G	FG	FT	TP	Ave.
Brennan, North Carolina	26	170	214	554	21.3
Busch, Virginia	23	115	135	365	15.9
Budd, Wake Forest	23	112	140	364	15.8
Pucillo, N.C. State	24	151	76	378	15.7
Pericola, South Carolina	24	131	101	363	15.1
Kearns, North Carolina	26	135	118	388	14.9
Adkins, Virginia	23	139	62	340	14.8
Bell, N.C. State	18	95	65	255	14.1
Yockel, Clemson	24	125	82	332	13.8
McNeil, Maryland	29	151	99	401	13.8

TOP TEN REBOUNDERS

Player, School	G	RBS.	Ave.
Brennan, North Carolina	26	303	11.7
Richter, N.C. State	24	261	10.8
Busch, Virginia	23	232	10.1
Newcome, Duke	25	237	9.5
Bunge, Maryland	29	265	9.1
Budd, Wake Forest	23	195	8.5
Siewers, Virginia	23	183	7.9
Schmidt, Duke	25	197	7.9
Callahan, South Carolina	24	182	7.6
Broadway, Wake Forest	23	162	7.0

Rosters

CLEMSON

No.	Name	Hgt.	Yr.	Hometown
31	Jim Lewis	6-3	So.	Aliquippa, PA
32	Jim Hudson	6-4	So.	Jersey City, NJ
33	Dutch Shample	6-0	So.	McKeesport, PA
34	Bill Warren	6-3	So.	Horning, PA
41	Tom Cameron	6-2	Sr.	Jersey City, NJ
42	Ed Brinkley	6-6	Sr.	Asheville, NC
43	Vince Yockel	6-3	Sr.	Jersey City, NJ
44	Doug Hoffman	6-2	Jr.	Gastonia, NC
50	Eddie Moncrief	6-4	Sr.	Moultrie, GA
52	George Krajack	6-3	So.	McKeesport, PA
53	Walt Gibbons	6-7	So.	McKeesport, PA
54	Frank Clarke	6-6	So.	Wadesboro, NC
55	Don Carver	6-4	So.	Elkins, WV

COACH: Press Maravich

DUKE

No.	Name	Hgt.	Yr.	Hometown
11	Bob Vernon	6-1	Sr.	Riverside, NJ
12	Jack Boyd	5-11	So.	Yeadon, PA
13	Don Miller	6-4	Jr.	Miami Beach, FL
14	Jerry Robertson	6-6	Jr.	Burlington, NC
15	Paul Schmidt	6-5	Sr.	Johnstown, PA
20	Larry Bateman	6-7	So.	Greensboro, NC
22	Bill Watson	6-1	Jr.	Huntington, WV
23	Bill Gilley	6-6	So.	Carlisle, KY
24	Marty Joyce	5-11	So.	Philadelphia, PA
25	Bob Wayand	6-6	So.	Scotia, NY
30	Bobby Joe Harris	5-11	So.	King, NC
31	Hayes Clement	6-7	Sr.	New Bern, NC
32	Bob Lakata	6-6	Sr.	Johnson City, NY
33	Jim Newcome	6-6	Sr.	Gary, IN
35	George Barrett	6-4	Jr.	Wabash, IN
40	Bucky Allen	6-2	Sr.	Durham, NC

COACH: Hal Bradley
ASSISTANT: Fred Shabel, Whit Cobb

MARYLAND

No.	Name	Hgt.	Yr.	Hometown
20	Cokey Robertson	5-10	So.	Lonaconing, MD
22	Bill Murphy	6-3	Jr.	Pittsburgh, PA
23	Ed O'Loughlin	6-2	So.	Brooklyn, NY
24	Dave Young	6-2	So.	Abington, PA
25	Gene Danko	6-2	Jr.	McKeesport, PA
30	Tom Young	6-1	Sr.	Natrona Heights, PA
32	Nick Davis	6-2	Sr.	Rankin, PA
33	John Nacincik	6-3	Sr.	Brooklyn, NY
34	Pete Krukar	6-1	So.	Ford City, PA
35	Jerry Bechtle	6-2	So.	Elizabeth, NJ
40	Julian Weingarten	6-4	Jr.	Washington, DC
42	Wayne McGinnis	6-7	Jr.	Whitehall, MD
44	Jim Halleck	6-0	Jr.	Elizabeth, NJ
45	Perry Moore	6-4	Sr.	Belpre, OH
50	Charles McNeil	6-6	So.	Pennsgrove, NJ
52	Carroll Johnson	6-3	So.	Hyattsville, MD
53	Jerry Shanahan	6-2	So.	Pittsburgh, PA
54	Al Bunge	6-8	So.	Palmyra, NJ
55	Bob Wilson	6-9	So.	Rochester, PA

COACH: Bud Millikan
ASSISTANTS: Roy Lester, Bob O'Brien, Don Newberry

NORTH CAROLINA

No.	Name	Hgt.	Yr.	Hometown
11	John Crotty	5-11	So.	Jersey City, NJ
20	Wallace Graham	6-1	So.	Miami, FL
22	Roy Searcy	6-4	Sr.	Draper, NC
30	Ray Stanley	6-4	So.	Brooklyn, NY
31	Gehrmann Holland	6-4	Jr.	Beaufort, NC
32	Bob Cunningham	6-4	Sr.	New York, NY
33	Danny Lotz	6-7	Jr.	Northport, NY
34	Dick Kepley	6-8	So.	Roanoke, VA
35	Pete Brennan	6-6	Sr.	Brooklyn, NY
40	Tommy Kearns	5-11	Sr.	Bergenfield, NJ
41	Joe Quigg	6-9	Sr.	Brooklyn, NY
42	Harvey Salz	6-1	So.	Brooklyn, NY
43	Lee Shaffer	6-7	So.	Pittsburgh, PA
44	Mike Steppe	6-3	So.	New York, NY
45	Grey Poole	6-6	So.	Raleigh, NC

COACH: Frank McGuire
ASSISTANTS: Buck Freeman, Ken Rosemond

N.C. STATE

No.	Name	Hgt.	Yr.	Hometown
10/11	Whitey Bell	6-0	Sr.	Warsaw, IN
12/13	Marvin Kessler	6-0	Sr.	Brooklyn, NY
14/15	Bucky Waters	6-2	Sr.	Collingswood, NJ
20/21	Lou Pucillo	5-9	Jr.	Philadelphia, PA
22/23	Bob MacGillivray	6-4	Jr.	Dorchester, MA
24/25	John Richter	6-8	Jr.	Philadelphia, PA
26/27	Harold Atkins	6-5	So.	Kernersville, NC
30/31	Ken Clark	6-5	Jr	Flushing, NY
32/33	Tom Hopper	6-3	Sr.	Glen Rock, NJ
34/35	Dan Englehardt	6-0	So.	Seymour, IN
42/43	Don Gallagher	6-4	So.	Binghamton, NY
44/45	Walter Bortko	6-3	So.	Chicago, IL
50/51	Harold Estis	5-10	So.	New York, NY
52/53	George Stepanovich	6-4	Jr.	East Chicago, IN
54/55	Willett Bennett	6-3	So.	Hendersonville, NC

COACH: Everett Case
ASSISTANTS: Vic Bubas, Lee Terrill

SOUTH CAROLINA

No.	Name	Hgt.	Yr.	Hometown
21	Ray Pericola	6-2	Jr.	Union City, NJ
22	Dan Morgan	5-10	So.	Enka, NC
23	Lee Anderson	6-2	Sr.	Rockford, IL
24	Fred Luigs	6-4	So.	Paducah, KY
25	Wayne Godfrey	6-0	Sr.	Greer, SC
31	Walt Hudson	6-5	So.	Columbia, SC
32	Bury Hudson	6-5	So.	Columbia, SC
33	Dickie Prater	6-3	Jr.	Pikeville, KY
34	Mike Callahan	6-6	So.	Sussex, NJ
35	Dick Hoffman	6-1	Jr.	Union City, NJ
41	Bob Frantz	6-7	So.	Glassboro, NJ
43	Don Goodroe	6-7	Jr.	Columbus, GA
44	Fred Lentz	6-8	Jr.	Asheville, NC
45	Larry Dial	6-10	So.	Fairforest, SC

COACH: Frank Johnson
ASSISTANT: Walt Hambrick

VIRGINIA

No.	Name	Hgt.	Yr.	Hometown
4/3	John Butler	5-11	Jr.	Lakewood, OH
10/11	Robert Mortell	6-9	Jr.	Fairfield, CT
20	Paul Adkins	6-0	So.	Branchland, WV
21	Herb Busch	6-7	Jr.	Short Hills, NJ
22/23	Dick Stobbs	6-3	Jr.	Norfolk, VA
24/25	Bill Metzger	6-6	Jr.	Utica, NY
30/31	John Siewers	6-5	Jr.	Richmond, VA
32/33	Bruce Michelson	6-5	So.	Stamford, CT
34	Mike O'Bryan	6-5	Sr.	Richmond, VA
40/41	George Baskerville	6-4	So.	Richmond, VA
42/43	Wistar Nelligan	6-3	Sr.	Lynchburg, VA
44/45	John Haner	6-3	So.	Madison, WV
	Ward Lambert	6-1	So.	Wilmington, DE

COACH: Billy McCann

WAKE FOREST

No.	Name	Hgt.	Yr.	Hometown
10	Jerry Mitchell	6-3	So.	Youngsville, NC
12	Dave Budd	6-6	So.	Woodbury, NJ
13	Winston Wiggins	6-6	So.	Youngsville, NC
14/11	George Ritchie	5-11	So.	Chattaroy, WV
15	Wendell Carr	6-5	Sr.	Muncie, IN
21/41	John Reed	6-8	Sr.	North, SC
22	Henry Bowers	6-3	Sr.	Knightdale, NC
25	Charles Forte	6-0	So.	Huntington, NY
31	Bill Greene	6-1	Jr.	Kingsport, TN
34/35	Dickie Odom	6-6	Jr.	Ahoskie, NC
35/33	Wayne Calloway	6-1	Sr.	Winston-Salem, NC
44/45	Olin Broadway	6-3	Jr.	Raleigh, NC
50/51	Kenneth Cox	6-3	Sr.	Marietta, SC

COACH: Bones McKinney
ASSISTANTS: Al DePorter, Charlie Bryant

All-America Teams

ASSOCIATED PRESS

FIRST TEAM: Wilt Chamberlain, Kansas; *Oscar Robertson, Cincinnati; Elgin Baylor, Seattle; Guy Rodgers, Temple; Don Hennon, Pittsburgh. **SECOND TEAM:** Bob Boozer, Kansas State; Archie Dees, Indiana; Bailey Howell, Mississippi State; Lloyd Sharrar, West Virginia; **Pete Brennan, North Carolina. THIRD TEAM:** Jerry West, West Virginia; **Tommy Kearns, North Carolina;** Mike Farmer, San Francisco; Johnny Green, Michigan State; Tom Hawkins, Notre Dame.

UNITED PRESS INTERNATIONAL

FIRST TEAM: Wilt Chamberlain, Kansas; *Oscar Robertson, Cincinnati; Elgin Baylor, Seattle; Guy Rodgers, Temple; Don Hennon, Pittsburgh. **SECOND TEAM:** Bob Boozer, Kansas State; Archie Dees, Indiana; Dave Gambee, Oregon State; Mike Farmer, San Francisco; Tom Hawkins, Notre Dame. **THIRD TEAM:** Lloyd Sharrar, West Virginia; Bailey Howell, Mississippi State; Jerry West, West Virginia; **Pete Brennan, North Carolina;** Johnny Green, Michigan State.

*Player of the Year

Final Top 20 Polls

AP		UPI	
1. West Virginia	26-2	1. West Virginia	26-2
2. Cincinnati	25-3	2. Cincinnati	25-3
3. Kansas State	22-5	3. San Francisco	25-2
4. San Francisco	25-2	4. Kansas State	22-5
5. Temple	27-3	5. Temple	27-3
6. Maryland	**22-7**	**6. Maryland**	**22-7**
7. Kansas	18-5	7. Notre Dame	24-5
8. Notre Dame	24-5	8. Kansas	18-5
9. Kentucky	23-6	9. Dayton	25-4
10. Duke	**18-7**	10. Indiana	13-11
11. Dayton	25-4	11. Bradley	20-7
12. Indiana	13-11	**12. North Carolina**	**19-7**
13. North Carolina	**19-7**	**13. Duke**	**18-7**
14. Bradley	20-7	14. Kentucky	23-6
15. Mississippi St.	20-5	15. Oklahoma St.	21-8
16. Auburn	16-6	16. Oregon State	20-6
17. Michigan St.	16-6	**N.C. State**	**18-6**
18. Seattle	24-7	18. St. Bonaventure	21-5
19. Oklahoma St.	21-8	19. Michigan St.	16-6
20. N.C. State	**18-6**	Wyoming	13-14
		Seattle	24-7

Kentucky beat Seattle 84-72 for NCAA title.

ACC BASKETBALL / REFERENCE

'59

N.C. State's Lou Pucillo

1958-59 Final Standings

Team	Conf.	Overall	Ave.	Opp.
*N.C. State	12-2	22-4	68.3	61.3
North Carolina	12-2	20-5	71.9	65.2
Duke	7-7	13-12	65.3	69.1
Maryland	7-7	10-13	59.3	56.3
Virginia	6-8	11-14	70.6	71.3
Wake Forest	5-9	10-14	65.4	66.2
Clemson	5-9	8-16	56.9	64.2
South Carolina	2-12	4-20	61.5	69.6

*Won ACC Tournament

NCAA—NORTH CAROLINA lost in first round of East Regional to Navy 76-63.

ACC Tournament

MARCH 5-7, 1959 AT RALEIGH, N.C.

FIRST ROUND: Duke 78, Wake Forest 71; North Carolina 93, Clemson 69; N.C. State 75, South Carolina 72 (OT); Virginia 66, Maryland 65. **SEMIFINALS:** N.C. State 66, Virginia 63; North Carolina 74, Duke 71. **FINAL:** N.C. State 80, North Carolina 56.

All-TOURNAMENT—FIRST TEAM: Lou Pucillo, N.C. State; John Richter, N.C. State; Lee Shaffer, North Carolina; Paul Adkins, Virginia; George Stepanovich, N.C. State. **SECOND TEAM:** Bob MacGillivray, N.C. State; Doug Moe, North Carolina; York Larese, North Carolina; Howard Hurt, Duke; Carroll Youngkin, Duke.

All-ACC

FIRST TEAM: Lou Pucillo, N.C. State (328 votes); York Larese, North Carolina (328); John Richter, N.C. State (318); Doug Moe, North Carolina (288); Carroll Youngkin, Duke (251). **SECOND TEAM:** Lee Shaffer, North Carolina (185); George Stepanovich, N.C. State (182); Howard Hurt, Duke (165); Paul Adkins, Virginia (132); Charles McNeil, Maryland (104).

PLAYER OF THE YEAR: Pucillo (43); Richter (25); Larese (2); Shaffer (1); Ray Pericola, South Carolina (1); Stepanovich (1); Bob MacGillivray, N.C. State (1). **COACH OF THE YEAR:** Hal Bradley, Duke, (32); Everett Case, N.C. State (27); Frank McGuire, North Carolina (12); Billy McCann, Virginia (3).

Scoring, Rebounding Leaders

TOP TEN SCORERS

Player, School	G	FG	FT	TP	Ave.
Richter, N.C. State	26	158	127	443	17.0
Adkins, Virginia	25	150	99	399	16.0
Youngkin, Duke	25	136	127	399	16.0
Hurt, Duke	24	134	108	376	15.7
Larese, North Carolina	25	141	96	378	15.1
McNeil, Maryland	21	111	89	311	14.8
Pucillo, N.C. State	26	160	62	382	14.7
Budd, Wake Forest	24	108	135	351	14.6
Ritchie, Wake Forest	24	134	54	322	13.4
Shaffer, North Carolina	25	128	74	330	13.2

TOP TEN REBOUNDERS

Player, School	G	RBS.	Ave.
Richter, N.C. State	26	370	14.2
Stepanovich, N.C. State	26	331	12.7
Youngkin, Duke	25	277	11.1
Callahan, South Carolina	24	253	10.5
Bunge, Maryland	23	241	10.5
Busch, Virginia	25	227	9.1
Kistler, Duke	25	225	9.0
Budd, Wake Forest	24	206	8.6
Siewers, Virginia	25	206	8.2
Hurt, Duke	24	197	8.2

Rosters

CLEMSON

No.	Name	Hgt.	Yr.	Hometown
31	Jim Lewis	6-3	Jr.	Aliquippa, PA
33	Dutch Shample	6-0	Jr.	McKeesport, PA
34	Bill Warren	6-3	Jr.	Horning, PA
41	William Bonzulak	6-0	So.	Dumont, NJ
42	Ed Krajack	6-4	So.	McKeesport, PA
43	Connie Berry	6-4	So.	Spartanburg, SC
44	Doug Hoffman	6-2	Sr.	Gastonia, NC
50	Earle Maxwell	6-7	So.	Greenville, SC
52	George Krajack	6-3	Jr.	McKeesport, PA
53	Walt Gibbons	6-7	Jr.	McKeesport, PA
54	Frank Clarke	6-7	Jr.	Wadesboro, NC
55	Don Carver	6-4	Jr.	Elkins, WV

COACH: Press Maravich
ASSISTANT: Bobby Roberts

DUKE

No.	Name	Hgt.	Yr.	Hometown
11	Johnny Morris	6-2	So.	Roxboro, NC
12	Jack Boyd	5-11	So.	Yeadon, PA
14	Jerry Robertson	6-6	Sr.	Burlington, NC
15	Fred Kast	6-7	So.	Rahway, NJ
20	Larry Bateman	6-7	Jr.	Greensboro, NC
21	Howard Hurt	6-3	So.	Beckley, WV
22	Bill Watson	6-2	Sr.	Huntington, WV
23	Carroll Youngkin	6-6	So.	Winston-Salem, NC
24	Marty Joyce	5-11	Jr.	Philadelphia, PA
25	Bob Wayand	6-6	So.	Scotia, NY
30	John Frye	6-0	So.	Huntington, WV
31	Doug Albright	6-5	So.	Greensboro, NC
32	Merrill Morgan	6-2	So.	Montclair, NJ
34	Doug Kistler	6-9	So.	Wayne, PA
35	George Barrett	6-4	Sr.	Wabash, IN
40	Jay Beal	5-10	So.	Wethersfield, CT

COACH: Hal Bradley
ASSISTANTS: Fred Shabel, Whit Cobb

MARYLAND

No.	Name	Hgt.	Yr.	Hometown
22	Bill Murphy	6-3	Sr.	Pittsburgh, PA
25	Gene Danko	6-2	Sr.	McKeesport, PA
32	Paul Jelus	6-2	So.	Camden, NJ
33	Bruce Kelleher	6-2	So.	Wilmington, DE
34	Pete Krukar	6-1	Jr.	Ford City, PA
35	Jerry Bechtle	6-2	Jr.	Elizabeth, NJ
40	Julian Weingarten	6-4	So.	Washington, DC
42	Ted Marshall	6-6	So.	Johnstown, PA
43	Bob McDonald	6-7	So.	Lansdowne, PA
44	Jim Halleck	6-0	Sr.	Elizabeth, NJ
50	Charles McNeil	6-6	Jr.	Pennsgrove, PA
53	Jerry Shanahan	6-2	Jr.	Pittsburgh, PA
54	Al Bunge	6-8	Jr.	Palmyra, NJ
55	Bob Wilson	6-9	So.	Freedom, PA

COACH: Bud Millikan
ASSISTANT: Perry Moore

NORTH CAROLINA

No.	Name	Hgt.	Yr.	Hometown
11	John Crotty	5-11	Jr.	Jersey City, NJ
12	Lee Shaffer	6-7	Jr.	Pittsburgh, PA
22	York Larese	6-4	So.	New York, NY
30	Ray Stanley	6-4	Jr.	Brooklyn, NY
31	Gehrmann Holland	6-4	Sr.	Beaufort, NC
32	Lou Brown	6-4	So.	Jersey City, NJ
33	Danny Lotz	6-7	Sr.	Northport, NY
34	Dick Kepley	6-8	Jr.	Roanoke, VA
35	Doug Moe	6-5	So.	Brooklyn, NY
41	Hugh Donahue	6-8	So.	New York, NY
42	Harvey Salz	6-1	Jr.	Brooklyn, NY
43	Grey Poole	6-6	Jr.	Raleigh, NC

COACH: Frank McGuire
ASSISTANTS: Dean Smith, Joe Quigg

N.C. STATE

No.	Name	Hgt.	Yr.	Hometown
10/11	Bob McCann	6-0	So.	Philadelphia, PA
12/13	Mark Reiner	5-11	So.	Brooklyn, NY
14/15	Dick Culler	6-0	So.	High Point, NC
20/21	Lou Pucillo	5-9	Sr.	Philadelphia, PA
22/23	Bob MacGillivray	6-4	Sr.	Dorchester, MA
24/25	John Richter	6-8	Sr.	Philadelphia, PA
30/31	Harold Atkins	6-5	So.	Kernersville, NC
32/33	Bruce Hoadley	6-6	So.	Raleigh, NC
34/35	Dan Englehardt	6-0	Jr.	Seymour, IN
40/41	Jon Ed Simbeck	6-3	So.	Du Bois, PA
42/43	Don Gallagher	6-4	Jr.	Binghamton, NY
44/45	Stan Niewierowski	6-4	So.	Brooklyn, NY
50/51	Larry Ranta	6-10	Sr.	Gary, IN
52/53	George Stepanovich	6-4	Sr.	East Chicago, IN
54/55	Bob DiStefano	6-6	So.	Philadelphia, PA

COACH: Everett Case
ASSISTANTS: Vic Bubas, Lee Terrill

SOUTH CAROLINA

No.	Name	Hgt.	Yr.	Hometown
21	Ray Pericola	6-2	Sr.	Union City, NJ
22	Dan Morgan	5-11	So.	Enka, NC
23	Everette Newman	6-2	So.	S. Charleston, WV
24	Fred Luigs	6-4	Jr.	Paducah, KY
25	Melvin Quick	6-2	Jr.	Columbia, SC
31	Walt Hudson	6-5	Jr.	Columbia, SC
32	Bury Hudson	6-5	So.	Columbia, SC
33	Dickie Prater	6-3	Sr.	Pikeville, Ky
34	Mike Callahan	6-6	Jr.	Sussex, NJ
35	Ronnie Johnson	6-2	So.	Rockford, IL
41	Bob Frantz	6-7	Jr.	Glassboro, NJ
44	Fred Lentz	6-8	Sr.	Asheville, NC
45	Larry Dial	6-10	Jr.	Fairforest, SC

COACH: Walt Hambrick
ASSISTANTS: Ken Rosemond

VIRGINIA

No.	Name	Hgt.	Yr.	Hometown
10/11	Robert Mortell	6-9	Sr.	Fairfield, CT
12	John Haner	6-3	Jr.	Madison, WV
13/33	Rex Davis	6-4	Jr.	Carney's Point, NJ
13/33	Charles Joseph	5-9	Sr.	Staunton, VA
20	Paul Adkins	6-0	Jr.	Branchland, WV
21	Herbert Busch	6-7	Sr.	Short Hills, NJ
22/31	John Siewers	6-5	Sr.	Richmond, VA
24	Dick Stobbs	6-3	Sr.	Norfolk, VA
30/23	Bill Metzger	6-6	Sr.	Utica, NY
32/25	Jay McKenzie	6-0	So.	Richwood, WV
40/51	Ward Lambert	6-1	Jr.	Wilmington, DE
44/22	Walter Densmore	6-5	So.	Alexandria, VA
50/55	George Baskerville	6-4	Jr.	Richmond, VA

COACH: Billy McCann

WAKE FOREST

No.	Name	Hgt.	Yr.	Hometown
11	Alley Hart	5-9	So.	Kinston, NC
12/43	Dave Budd	6-6	Jr.	Woodbury, NJ
13	Winston Wiggins	6-6	Jr.	Youngsville, NC
15	Bill Fennell	6-5	So.	Wilmington, NC
22	George Ritchie	6-0	Jr.	Chattaroy, WV
25	Charles Forte	6-0	Jr.	Huntington, NY
32/20	Bill Cullen	6-3	Jr.	Fairfield, CT
33	David Adkins	6-0	So.	Kinston, NC
34/35	Dickie Odom	6-6	Sr.	Ahoskie, NC
41	Jerry Steele	6-8	Sr.	Elkin, NC
44/45	Olin Broadway	6-3	Sr.	Raleigh, NC
50/31	Bill Greene	6-1	Sr.	Kingsport, TN
52/10	Jerry Mitchell	6-3	Jr.	Youngsville, NC

COACH: Bones McKinney
ASSISTANTS: Al DePorter, Charlie Bryant

All-America Teams

ASSOCIATED PRESS

FIRST TEAM: *Oscar Robertson, Cincinnati; Jerry West, West Virginia; Bob Boozer, Kansas State; Bailey Howell, Mississippi State; Johnny Cox, Kentucky. **SECOND TEAM:** Johnny Green, Michigan State; Tom Hawkins, Notre Dame; Leo Byrd, Marshall; Don Hennon, Pittsburgh; **Lou Pucillo, N.C. State. THIRD TEAM:** Jim Hagan, Tennessee Tech; Bob Ferry, St. Louis; Ron Johnson, Minnesota; Joe Rutlick, Northwestern; **York Larese, North Carolina.**

UNITED PRESS INTERNATIONAL

FIRST TEAM: *Oscar Robertson, Cincinnati; Bailey Howell, Mississippi State; Bob Boozer, Kansas State; Jerry West, West Virginia; Don Hennon, Pittsburgh. **SECOND TEAM:** Tom Hawkins, Notre Dame; Johnny Cox, Kentucky; Johnny Green, Michigan State; Leo Byrd, Marshall; Al Seiden, St. John's. **THIRD TEAM:** Walt Torrence, UCLA; Bob Ferry, St. Louis; Doug Smart, Washington; Charlie Brown, Seattle; **Lou Pucillo, N.C. State.**

*Player of the Year

Final Top 20 Polls

AP

1.	Kansas State	25-2
2.	Kentucky	24-3
3.	Mississippi St.	24-1
4.	Bradley	25-4
5.	Cincinnati	26-4
6.	**N.C. State**	**22-4**
7.	Michigan St.	19-4
8.	Auburn	20-2
9.	**North Carolina**	**20-5**
10.	West Virginia	29-5
11.	California	24-4
12.	St. Louis	20-6
13.	Seattle	23-6
14.	St. Joseph's	22-5
15.	St. Mary's (Cal.)	19-6
16.	Texas Christian	20-6
17.	Okla. City	20-7
18.	Utah	21-7
19.	St. Bonaventure	20-3
20.	Marquette	23-6

UPI

1.	Kansas State	25-2
2.	Kentucky	24-3
3.	Michigan St.	19-4
4.	Cincinnati	26-4
5.	**N.C. State**	**22-4**
6.	**North Carolina**	**20-5**
	Mississippi St.	24-1
8.	Bradley	25-4
9.	California	24-4
10.	Auburn	20-2
11.	West Virginia	29-5
12.	Texas Christian	20-6
13.	St. Louis	20-6
14.	Utah	21-7
15.	Marquette	23-6
16.	Tenn. Tech	16-9
17.	St. John's	20-6
18.	Navy	18-6
	St. Mary's (Cal.)	19-6
20.	St. Joseph's	22-5

California beat West Virginia 71-70 for NCAA title.

ACC BASKETBALL / REFERENCE

'60

North Carolina's Lee Shaffer

1959-60 Final Standings

Team	Conf.	Overall	Ave.	Opp.
North Carolina	12-2	18-6	73.1	62.3
Wake Forest	12-2	21-7	72.8	63.1
Maryland	9-5	15-8	65.0	61.2
*Duke	7-7	17-11	64.3	63.2
South Carolina	6-8	10-16	73.6	79.5
N.C. State	5-9	11-15	60.4	60.2
Clemson	4-10	10-16	64.2	70.7
Virginia	1-13	6-18	67.3	75.6

*Won ACC Tournament

NCAA — DUKE second in East Regional: beat Princeton 84-60, beat St. Joseph's 58-56, lost to NYU 74-59.

ACC Tournament
MARCH 3-5, 1960 AT RALEIGH, N.C.

FIRST ROUND: N.C. State 74, Maryland 58; Wake Forest 74, Clemson 59; North Carolina 84, Virginia 63; Duke 82, South Carolina 69. **SEMIFINALS:** Duke 71, North Carolina 69; Wake Forest 71, N.C. State 66. **FINAL:** Duke 63, Wake Forest 59.
ALL-TOURNAMENT—FIRST TEAM: Len Chappell, Wake Forest; Doug Kistler, Duke; Howard Hurt, Duke; Lee Shaffer, North Carolina; York Larese, North Carolina. **SECOND TEAM:** Carroll Youngkin, Duke; Dave Budd, Wake Forest; John Frye, Duke; Bob DiStefano, N.C. State; Paul Adkins, Virginia.

All-ACC
FIRST TEAM: Len Chappell, Wake Forest (136 votes); Lee Shaffer, North Carolina (133); Al Bunge, Maryland (133); York Larese, North Carolina (117); Choppy Patterson, Clemson (76). **SECOND TEAM:** Art Whisnant, South Carolina (64); Dave Budd, Wake Forest (50); Paul Adkins, Maryland (48); Billy Packer, Wake Forest (46); Bob DiStefano, N.C. State (41); Howard Hurt, Duke (41).
PLAYER OF THE YEAR: Shaffer (50); Chappell (16). **COACH OF THE YEAR:** Bones McKinney, Wake Forest (34); Vic Bubas, Duke (26).

Scoring, Rebounding Leaders

TOP TEN SCORERS
Player, School	G	FG	FT	TP	AVE.
Shaffer, North Carolina	24	169	99	437	18.2
Chappell, Wake Forest	28	166	156	488	17.4
Adkins, Virginia	24	151	109	411	17.1
Whisnant, South Carolina	26	143	155	441	17.0
Moe, North Carolina	12	60	80	202	16.8
Bunge, Maryland	23	130	123	383	16.6
Patterson, Clemson	26	151	125	427	16.4
Larese, North Carolina	24	123	131	377	15.7
Callahan, South Carolina	26	144	119	407	15.7
Hurt, Duke	28	146	84	376	13.4

TOP TEN REBOUNDERS
Player, School	G	RBS.	AVE.
Mortell, Virginia	24	350	14.6
Bunge, Maryland	23	289	12.6
Chappell, Wake Forest	28	350	12.5
Callahan, South Carolina	26	309	11.8
Moe, North Carolina	12	135	11.3
Shaffer, North Carolina	24	269	11.2
Whisnant, South Carolina	26	261	10.1
Budd, Wake Forest	28	281	10.0
Youngkin, Duke	28	275	9.9
Kistler, Duke	28	262	9.4

Rosters

CLEMSON
No.	Name	Hgt.	Yr.	Hometown
31	Bob Benson	6-2	So.	Greensburg, PA
33	Dutch Shample	6-0	Sr.	McKeesport, PA
34	Jim Leshock	6-3	So.	Greensburg, PA
41	Bill Bonzulak	6-0	So.	Dumont, NJ
42	Ed Krajack	6-4	Jr.	McKeesport, PA
43	Dave Wallace	6-6	So.	Spartanburg, SC
44	Choppy Patterson	6-0	So.	Piedmont, SC
50	Earle Maxwell	6-7	Jr.	Greenville, SC
52	George Krajack	6-3	Sr.	McKeesport, PA
53	Walt Gibbons	6-7	Sr.	McKeesport, PA
54	Tom Mahaffey	6-7	So.	La Grange, GA
55	Don Carver	6-4	Sr.	Elkins, WV

COACH: Press Maravich
ASSISTANT: Bobby Roberts

DUKE
No.	Name	Hgt.	Yr.	Hometown
15	Fred Kast	6-7	Jr.	Rahway, NJ
20	Larry Bateman	6-7	Sr.	Greensboro, NC
20	Jack Mullen	5-11	So.	Weissport, PA
21	Howard Hurt	6-3	Jr.	Beckley, WV
23	Carroll Youngkin	6-6	Jr.	Winston-Salem, NC
24	John Cantwell	5-9	So.	Shawano, WI
25	Bob Wayand	6-6	Jr.	Scotia, NY
25	C.B. Johnson	6-3	So.	New Orleans, LA
30	John Frye	6-0	Jr.	Huntington, WV
31	Doug Albright	6-5	Jr.	Greensboro, NC
32	Merrill Morgan	6-2	Jr.	Montclair, NJ
35	Buzz Mewhort	6-4	So.	Toledo, OH
40	Jay Beal	5-10	Jr.	Wethersfield, CT
41	Doug Kistler	6-9	Jr.	Wayne, PA

COACH: Vic Bubas
ASSISTANTS: Fred Shabel, Bucky Waters

MARYLAND
No.	Name	Hgt.	Yr.	Hometown
32	Paul Jelus	6-2	So.	Camden, NJ
33	Bruce Kelleher	6-2	So.	Wilmington, DE
34	Pete Krukar	6-1	Sr.	Ford City, PA
35	Jerry Bechtle	6-2	Sr.	Elizabeth, NJ
40	Dave Schroeder	6-1	So.	Media, PA
42	Ted Marshall	6-7	So.	Johnstown, PA
43	Bob McDonald	6-7	Jr.	Landsdowne, PA
44	Steve Alpert	6-2	So.	Brooklyn, NY
50	Charles McNeil	6-6	Sr.	Pennsgrove, NJ
52	Mike Nofsinger	5-7	So.	Westernport, MD
53	Jerry Shanahan	6-2	Sr.	Pittsburgh, PA
54	Al Bunge	6-8	Sr.	Palmyra, NJ
55	Bob Wilson	6-10	Jr.	Freedom, PA

COACH: Bud Millikan
ASSISTANTS: Perry Moore, Jim Halleck

NORTH CAROLINA
No.	Name	Hgt.	Yr.	Hometown
11	John Crotty	5-11	Sr.	Jersey City, NJ
12	Lee Shaffer	6-7	Sr.	Pittsburgh, PA
20	Don Walsh	6-0	So.	Riverdale, NY
22	York Larese	6-4	Jr.	New York, NY
30	Ray Stanley	6-4	Sr.	Brooklyn, NY
32	Lou Brown	6-3	Jr.	Jersey City, NJ
33	Jim Hudock	6-7	So.	Tunkhannock, PA
34	Dick Kepley	6-8	Sr.	Roanoke, VA
35	Doug Moe	6-5	Jr.	Brooklyn, NY
40	Yogi Poteet	6-1	So.	Hendersonville, NC
41	Hugh Donahue	6-8	Jr.	New York, NY
42	Harvey Salz	6-1	Sr.	Brooklyn, NY
43	Grey Poole	6-6	Sr.	Raleigh, NC

COACH: Frank McGuire
ASSISTANTS: Dean Smith, Ken Rosemond

N.C. STATE
No.	Name	Hgt.	Yr.	Hometown
10/11	Bob McCann	6-0	Jr.	Philadelphia, PA
12/13	George Finnegan	6-0	So.	Rye, NY
20/21	Denny Lutz	6-1	So.	Charlestown, IN
22/23	John Key	6-8	Sr.	Durham, NC
24/25	Ken Clark	6-5	Sr.	Flushing, NY
30/31	Russ Marvel	6-6	So.	Gary, IN
32/33	Bruce Hoadley	6-6	Jr.	Raleigh, NC
34/35	Dan Englehardt	6-0	Sr.	Seymour, IN
40/41	Jon Ed Simbeck	6-3	So.	Du Bois, PA
42/43	Don Gallagher	6-4	Sr.	Binghamton, NY
44/45	Stan Niewierowski	6-4	Jr.	Brooklyn, NY
50/51	Dan Wherry	6-3	So.	Columbus, OH
52/53	Anton Muehlbauer	6-2	So.	Brooklyn, NY
54/55	Bob DiStefano	6-6	Jr.	Philadelphia, PA

COACH: Everett Case
ASSISTANTS: Lee Terrill, George Pickett

SOUTH CAROLINA
No.	Name	Hgt.	Yr.	Hometown
21	Ad Grabenstetter	6-4	So.	Metuchen, NJ
22	Bobby Robinson	6-0	So.	Camden, NJ
23	Everette Newman	6-2	Jr.	S. Charleston, WV
23	Jimmy Howell	6-0	So.	Columbia, SC
24	Fred Luigs	6-4	Sr.	Paducah, KY
25	Melvin Quick	6-2	So.	Columbia, SC
31	Walt Hudson	6-5	Sr.	Columbia, SC
32	Bury Hudson	6-5	Jr.	Columbia, SC
33	Bud Cronin	6-3	So.	Parkersburg, WV
34	Mike Callahan	6-6	Sr.	Sussex, NJ
35	Ronnie Johnson	6-2	Jr.	Rockford, IL
41	Bob Frantz	6-7	So.	Glassboro, NJ
43	Bob Rebhan	6-4	So.	Parkersburg, WV
44	Art Whisnant	6-4	So.	Hildebran, NC
45	Larry Dial	6-10	Sr.	Fairforest, SC

COACH: Bob Stevens
ASSISTANT: Gordon Stauffer

VIRGINIA
No.	Name	Hgt.	Yr.	Hometown
10/45	Robert Mortell	6-9	Sr.	Fairfield, CT
12	John Haner	6-4	Sr.	Madison, WV
15/51	Rex Davis	6-4	Sr.	Carney's Point, NJ
20	Paul Adkins	6-0	Sr.	Branchland, WV
21/53	William Jackey	6-2	So.	Hempstead, NY
22/55	Terry Harwood	6-7	Jr.	Riderwood, MD
23/41	Anthony Laquintano	5-11	So.	Philadelphia, PA
24	Kenneth Sanders	6-5	So.	Arlington, VA
24	Wesley Westman	6-3	So.	Charlottesville, VA
25	Ronald Miller	6-1	So.	Brooklyn, NY
32	Bruce Michelson	6-5	So.	Glenbrook, CT
33/24	Louis Farina	6-1	So.	Paterson, NJ
44/35	Walter Densmore	6-5	Jr.	Alexandria, VA

COACH: Billy McCann

WAKE FOREST
No.	Name	Hgt.	Yr.	Hometown
10/11	Alley Hart	5-9	Jr.	Kinston, NC
12/13	Dave Budd	6-6	Sr.	Woodbury, NJ
14/15	Winston Wiggins	6-6	Sr.	Youngsville, NC
20/21	Frank Loeffler	6-5	So.	Huntington, NY
22/23	George Ritchie	6-0	Sr.	Chattaroy, WV
25	Bill Fennell	6-5	Jr.	Wilmington, NC
30/31	Tommy McCoy	6-2	So.	Portsmouth, VA
32/33	Bill Cullen	6-3	Sr.	Fairfield, CT
34/35	Billy Packer	5-10	So.	Bethlehem, PA
40/41	Jerry Steele	6-8	Jr.	Elkin, NC
42/43	David Adkins	6-0	Jr.	Kinston, NC
44/45	Gene Compton	6-7	So.	Mebane, NC
50/51	Len Chappell	6-8	So.	Portage, PA
52/53	Jerry Mitchell	6-3	Sr.	Youngsville, NC
54/55	Charles Forte	6-0	Sr.	Huntington, NC

COACH: Bones McKinney
ASSISTANTS: Al DePorter, Charlie Bryant

All-America Teams

ASSOCIATED PRESS
FIRST TEAM: *Oscar Robertson, Cincinnati; Jerry West, West Virginia; Jerry Lucas, Ohio State; Darrall Imhoff, California; Tony Jackson, St. John's. **SECOND TEAM:** Tom Stith, St. Bonaventure; Terry Dischinger, Purdue; Roger Kaiser, Georgia Tech; Chet Walker, Bradley; Len Wilkens, Providence. **THIRD TEAM:** Lee Shaffer, North Carolina; Billy McGill, Utah; Horace Kennedy, Temple; Dick Hickox, Miami (Fla.).

UNITED PRESS INTERNATIONAL
FIRST TEAM: *Oscar Robertson, Cincinnati; Jerry West, West Virginia; Jerry Lucas, Ohio State; Darrall Imhoff, California; Tom Stith, St. Bonaventure. **SECOND TEAM:** Terry Dischinger, Purdue; Tony Jackson, St. John's; Jimm Darrow, Bowling Green; Roger Kaiser, Georgia Tech; Chet Walker, Bradley. **THIRD TEAM:** Horace Walker, Michigan State; Dave DeBusschere, Detroit; Tom Sanders, NYU; Walt Bellamy, Indiana; **Lee Shaffer, North Carolina.**
*Player of the Year

Final Top 20 Polls

AP
1.	Cincinnati	28-2
2.	California	28-2
3.	Ohio State	25-3
4.	Bradley	27-2
5.	West Virginia	26-5
6.	Utah	26-3
7.	Indiana	20-4
8.	Utah State	24-5
9.	St. Bonaventure	21-5
10.	Miami (Fla.)	23-4
11.	Auburn	19-3
12.	NYU	22-5
13.	Georgia Tech	22-6
14.	Providence	24-5
15.	St. Louis	19-8
16.	Holy Cross	20-6
17.	Villanova	20-6
18.	**Duke**	**17-11**
19.	**Wake Forest**	**21-7**
20.	St. John's	17-8

UPI
1.	California	28-2
2.	Cincinnati	28-2
3.	Ohio State	25-3
4.	Bradley	27-2
5.	Utah	26-3
6.	West Virginia	26-5
7.	Utah State	24-5
8.	Georgia Tech	22-6
9.	Villanova	20-6
10.	Indiana	20-4
11.	St. Bonaventure	21-5
12.	NYU	22-5
13	Texas	18-8
14.	**North Carolina**	**18-6**
15.	**Duke**	**17-11**
16.	Kansas State	16-10
17.	Auburn	19-3
18.	Providence	24-5
19.	St. Louis	19-8
20.	Dayton	21-7

Ohio State beat California 75-55 for NCAA title.

'61

Wake Forest's
Len Chappell

1960-61 Final Standings

Team	Conf.	Overall	Ave.	Opp.
North Carolina	12-2	19-4	76.7	65.7
***Wake Forest**	11-3	19-11	82.9	76.5
Duke	10-4	22-6	81.5	71.2
N.C. State	8-6	16-9	77.3	72.3
Maryland	6-8	14-12	67.2	67.6
Clemson	5-9	10-16	67.0	70.5
South Carolina	2-12	9-17	77.5	86.8
Virginia	2-12	3-23	70.2	85.5

*Won ACC Tournament

NCAA—WAKE FOREST second in East Regional: beat St. John's 97-74, beat St. Bonaventure 78-73, lost to St. Joseph's 96-86.

ACC Tournament

MARCH 2-4, 1961 AT RALEIGH, N.C.

FIRST ROUND: Wake Forest, bye; Maryland 91, Clemson 75; South Carolina 80, N.C. State 78; Duke 89, Virginia 54. **SEMIFINALS:** Wake Forest 98, Maryland 76; Duke 92, South Carolina 75. **FINAL:** Wake Forest 96, Duke 81.

ALL-TOURNAMENT—FIRST TEAM: Len Chappell, Wake Forest; Art Heyman, Duke; Billy Packer, Wake Forest; John Frye, Duke; Art Whisnant, South Carolina. **SECOND TEAM:** Bill Stasiulatis, Maryland; Scotti Ward, South Carolina; Dave Wiedeman, Wake Forest; Carroll Youngkin, Duke; Choppy Patterson, Clemson.

All-ACC

FIRST TEAM: *Len Chappell, Wake Forest (142 votes); *Art Heyman, Duke (142); *York Larese, North Carolina (142); *Doug Moe, North Carolina (142); Billy Packer, Wake Forest (97). **SECOND TEAM:** Art Whisnant, South Carolina (50); Tony Laquintano, Virginia (46); Ken Rohloff, N.C. State (45); Choppy Patterson, Clemson (43); Howard Hurt, Duke (42); Bob McDonald, Maryland (42).

PLAYER OF THE YEAR: Chappell (50); Heyman (15); Moe and Larese also received votes. **COACH OF THE YEAR:** Bones McKinney, Wake Forest (37); Vic Bubas, Duke (24).

*Unanimous Selection

Scoring, Rebounding Leaders

TOP TEN SCORERS

Player, School	G	FG	FT	TP	Ave.
Chappell, Wake Forest	28	271	203	745	26.6
Heyman, Duke	25	229	263	629	25.2
Larese, North Carolina	23	204	124	532	23.1
Moe, North Carolina	23	163	143	469	20.4
Laquintano, Virginia	26	203	110	516	19.8
Whisnant, South Carolina	26	149	199	497	19.1
Patterson, Clemson	26	174	146	494	19.0
Packer, Wake Forest	30	208	99	515	17.2
Ward, South Carolina	26	147	69	375	14.4
Maxwell, Clemson	26	120	118	358	13.8

TOP TEN REBOUNDERS

Player, School	G	Rbs.	Ave.
Chappell, Wake Forest	28	393	14.0
Moe, North Carolina	23	321	14.0
Mahaffey, Clemson	26	293	11.3
Maxwell, Clemson	26	284	10.9
Heyman, Duke	25	272	10.9
McDonald, Maryland	26	279	10.7
Hull, Wake Forest	30	298	9.9
Youngkin, Duke	28	274	9.8
Engel, Virginia	25	242	9.7
Kistler, Duke	28	269	9.6

Rosters

CLEMSON

No.	Name	Hgt.	Yr.	Hometown
4/3	Choppy Patterson	6-0	Jr.	Piedmont, SC
14/15	Carl Ward	6-2	So.	S. Charleston, WV
20/21	Bill Warren	6-4	Sr.	Horning, PA
22/23	Larry Seitz	6-4	So.	Morrisonville, IL
24/25	Speight Bird	6-7	So.	Rock Hill, SC
30/31	Jim Leshock	6-3	Jr.	Greensburg, PA
32/33	Bill Bonzulak	6-0	Jr.	Dumont, NJ
34/35	Mike Bohonak	6-2	So.	Pittsburgh, PA
40/41	Chuck Narvin	6-2	So.	Pittsburgh, PA
42/43	Bob Benson	6-2	Jr.	Greensburg, PA
44/45	Dave Wallace	6-6	Jr.	Spartanburg, SC
50/53	Earle Maxwell	6-7	Sr.	Greenville, SC
52/51	Ed Krajack	6-5	Sr.	McKeesport, PA
54/55	Tom Mahaffey	6-7	Jr.	La Grange, GA

COACH: Press Maravich
ASSISTANT: Bobby Roberts

DUKE

No.	Name	Hgt.	Yr.	Hometown
11	Fred Schmidt	6-4	So.	Philadelphia, PA
14	Scott Williamson	6-5	So.	Sanford, NC
15	Fred Kast	6-6	So.	Rahway, NJ
20	Jack Mullen	5-11	Jr.	Weissport, PA
21	Howard Hurt	6-3	Sr.	Beckley, WV
23	Carroll Youngkin	6-6	Sr.	Winston-Salem, NC
24	John Cantwell	5-9	Jr.	Shawano, WI
25	Art Heyman	6-5	So.	Rockville Centre, NY
30	John Frye	6-0	Sr.	Huntington, WV
31	Doug Albright	6-5	Sr.	Greensboro, NC
32	Merrill Morgan	6-2	Sr.	Montclair, NJ
34	Fred Cox	6-6	So.	Pittsfield, MA
35	Buzz Mewhort	6-4	Jr.	Toledo, OH
40	Jay Beal	5-11	Sr.	Wethersfield, CT
41	Doug Kistler	6-9	Sr.	Wayne, PA

COACH: Vic Bubas
ASSISTANTS: Fred Shabel, Bucky Waters

MARYLAND

No.	Name	Hgt.	Yr.	Hometown
30	Robert Eicher	6-2	So.	Greensburg, PA
32	Paul Jelus	6-2	Jr.	Camden, NJ
33	Bruce Kelleher	6-2	Jr.	Wilmington, DE
34	George Hodor	5-10	So.	Flushing, NY
35	Connie Carpenter	6-4	So.	Norwalk, CT
40	Dave Schroeder	6-1	Jr.	Media, PA
42	Ted Marshall	6-7	Jr.	Johnstown, PA
43	Bob McDonald	6-7	Sr.	Landsdowne, PA
44	Jerry Greenspan	6-6	So.	Newark, NJ
45	Bill Stasiulatis	6-3	So.	Bayonne, NJ
50	Joseph Barton	6-6	So.	Beaverdale, PA
52	Mike Nofsinger	5-9	Jr.	Westernport, MD
55	Bob Wilson	6-10	Sr.	Freedom, PA

COACH: Bud Millikan
ASSISTANT: Perry Moore

NORTH CAROLINA

No.	Name	Hgt.	Yr.	Hometown
11	Larry Brown	5-11	So.	Long Beach, NY
12	Harry Jones	6-7	Jr.	Charlotte, NC
20	Don Walsh	6-0	Jr.	Riverdale, NY
22	York Larese	6-4	Sr.	New York, NY
30	Dieter Krause	6-5	So.	Norfolk, VA
31	Peppy Callahan	6-2	So.	Smithtown, NY
31	Ken McComb	6-6	So.	Ardsley, NY
32	Lou Brown	6-3	Sr.	Jersey City, NJ
33	Jim Hudock	6-7	Jr.	Tunkhannock, PA
34	Dick Kepley	6-9	Sr.	Roanoke, VA
35	Doug Moe	6-6	Sr.	Brooklyn, NY
40	Yogi Poteet	6-1	Jr.	Hendersonville, NC
41	Jim Donohue	6-8	So.	Yonkers, NY
42	Martin Conlon	6-7	So.	Bronx, NY

COACH: Frank McGuire
ASSISTANTS: Dean Smith, Ken Rosemond

N.C. STATE

No.	Name	Hgt.	Yr.	Hometown
10/11	Bob McCann	6-0	Sr.	Philadelphia, PA
12/13	Jim Whitfield	6-5	So.	Durham, NC
14/15	John Punger	6-4	So.	Rockville Centre, NY
20/21	Denny Lutz	6-1	Jr.	Charlestown, IN
22/23	John Key	6-8	Jr.	Durham, NC
24/25	Terry Litchfield	6-9	Jr.	Louisville, KY
30/31	Russ Marvel	6-6	Jr.	Gary, IN
32/33	Bruce Hoadley	6-6	Sr.	Raleigh, NC
34/35	Jon Speaks	6-0	So.	Lexington, KY
40/41	Ken Rohloff	6-0	So.	Paterson, NJ
42/43	Pete Auksel	6-6	So.	East Chicago, IN
44/45	Stan Niewierowski	6-4	Sr.	Brooklyn, NY
50/51	Dan Wherry	6-3	Jr.	Columbus, OH
52/53	Anton Muehlbauer	6-2	Jr.	Brooklyn, NY
54/55	Bob DiStefano	6-6	Sr.	Philadelphia, PA

COACH: Everett Case
ASSISTANTS: Lee Terrill, George Pickett

SOUTH CAROLINA

No.	Name	Hgt.	Yr.	Hometown
21	Ad Grabenstetter	6-4	Jr.	Metuchen, NJ
22	Bobby Robinson	6-0	Jr.	Camden, SC
23	Jimmy Collins	6-0	So.	Dumont, NJ
24	Joe Laird	6-0	So.	Columbia, SC
31	Bob Rebhan	6-2	Jr.	Parkersburg, WV
32	John Godbold	6-3	So.	Rock Hill, SC
33	Bud Cronin	6-4	Jr.	Parkersburg, WV
34	Scotti Ward	6-0	So.	Valparaiso, IN
35	Ronnie Johnson	6-2	Sr.	Rockford, IL
40	Dave Prevoznik	6-6	So.	Cleveland, OH
43	Bob Haney	6-3	So.	Lucasville, OH
44	Art Whisnant	6-5	Jr.	Hildebran, NC
45	Bob Swenson	6-4	So.	Syracuse, IN

COACH: Bob Stevens
ASSISTANT: Gordon Stauffer

VIRGINIA

No.	Name	Hgt.	Yr.	Hometown
3/24	Harry Conn	5-10	So.	Newport News, VA
21/31	William Jackey	6-2	So.	Hempstead, NY
22/44	Gene Engel	6-5	So.	Cranford, NJ
23/34	Tony Laquintano	5-11	Jr.	Philadelphia, PA
24/42	Steven Jarvis	6-4	So.	Madison, WV
25/3	Ronald Miller	6-2	Jr.	Brooklyn, NY
31/52	Gene Flamm	6-6	So.	Levittown, NY
32/40	Timothy Jones	6-2	So.	Greenville, SC
33	Louis Farina	6-1	Jr.	Paterson, NJ
35/32	Wallace Smith	6-2	So.	Richmond, VA
44/35	Walter Densmore	6-5	Sr.	Alexandria, VA
50	Albert Hansen	6-3	So.	Haddonfield, NJ
54	John Hasbrouck	5-10	So.	Manhasset, NY

COACH: Billy McCann
ASSISTANT: Al Morgan

WAKE FOREST

No.	Name	Hgt.	Yr.	Hometown
10/11	Alley Hart	5-10	Sr.	Kinston, NC
12/13	Bob Woollard	6-10	Sr.	Bloomfield, NJ
14/15	Ted Zawacki	6-4	So.	Linden, NJ
20/21	Bill Hull	6-6	Jr.	Tarboro, NC
21/20	Gene Jackson	6-3	So.	St. Paul, NC
21	Jackie Jensen	5-9	Sr.	Bloomfield, NJ
22/23	Dave Wiedeman	5-11	So.	Delanco, NJ
25	Bill Fennell	6-5	Sr.	Wilmington, NC
30/31	Tommy McCoy	6-3	Jr.	Portsmouth, VA
32/33	Bob Bryan	6-3	So.	Bethseda, MD
32/33	Norman Snead	6-4	Sr.	Warwick, VA
34/35	Billy Packer	5-11	Jr.	Bethlehem, PA
40/41	Jerry Steele	6-8	Sr.	Elkin, NC
42/43	Paul Caldwell	6-0	So.	Bristol, TN
50/51	Len Chappell	6-8	Jr.	Portage, PA
52/53	Al Koehler	6-2	So.	Rahway, NJ
54/55	Tom Weadock	6-5	Jr.	Lima, OH

COACH: Bones McKinney
ASSISTANTS: Charlie Bryant, Jackie Murdock

All-America Teams

ASSOCIATED PRESS

FIRST TEAM: *Jerry Lucas, Ohio State; Tom Stith, St. Bonaventure; Terry Dischinger, Purdue; Roger Kaiser, Georgia Tech; Chet Walker, Bradley. **SECOND TEAM:** Walt Bellamy, Indiana; Tony Jackson, St. John's; Frank Burgess, Gonzaga; Billy McGill, Utah; **Doug Moe, North Carolina. THIRD TEAM: Art Heyman, Duke; York Larese, North Carolina;** John Rudometkin, Southern Cal; John Havlicek, Ohio State; Larry Siegfried, Ohio State.

UNITED PRESS INTERNATIONAL

FIRST TEAM: *Jerry Lucas, Ohio State; Tom Stith, St. Bonaventure; Roger Kaiser, Georgia Tech; Terry Dischinger, Purdue; Chet Walker, Bradley. **SECOND TEAM:** Walt Bellamy, Indiana; Tony Jackson, St. John's; Billy McGill, Utah; John Rudometkin, Southern Cal; John Havlicek, Ohio State. **THIRD TEAM:** Larry Siegfried, Ohio State; Dave DeBusschere, Detroit; Frank Burgess, Gonzaga; **Art Heyman, Duke; York Larese, North Carolina.**

*Player of the Year

Final Top 20 Polls

AP			UPI		
1.	Ohio State	27-1	1.	Ohio State	27-1
2.	Cincinnati	27-3	2.	Cincinnati	27-3
3.	St. Bonaventure	24-4	3.	St. Bonaventure	24-4
4.	Kansas State	23-4	4.	Kansas State	23-4
5.	**North Carolina**	**19-4**	5.	Southern Cal	21-8
6.	Bradley	21-5	**6.**	**North Carolina**	**19-4**
7.	Southern Cal	21-8	7.	Bradley	21-5
8.	Iowa	18-6	8.	St. John's	20-5
9.	West Virginia	23-4	**9.**	**Duke**	**22-6**
10.	**Duke**	**22-6**	**10.**	**Wake Forest**	**19-11**
11.	Utah	23-8		Iowa	18-6
12.	Texas Tech	15-10	12.	West Virginia	23-4
13.	Niagara	16-5	13.	Utah	23-8
14.	Memphis State	20-3	14.	St. Louis	21-9
15.	**Wake Forest**	**19-11**	15.	Louisville	21-8
16.	St. John's	20-5	16.	St. Joseph's	25-5
17.	St. Joseph's	25-5	17.	Dayton	20-9
18.	Drake	19-7	18.	Kentucky	19-9
19.	Holy Cross	22-5		Texas Tech	15-10
20.	Kentucky	19-9	20.	Memphis State	20-3

Cincinnati beat Ohio State 70-65 for NCAA title.

'62

Wake Forest's Len Chappell

1961-62 Final Standings

Team	Conf.	Overall	Ave.	Opp.
*Wake Forest	12-2	22-9	81.4	74.3
Duke	11-3	20-5	82.0	67.9
N.C. State	10-4	11-6	71.2	66.9
South Carolina	7-7	15-12	78.3	76.7
North Carolina	7-7	8-9	72.4	72.6
Clemson	4-10	12-15	72.1	74.6
Maryland	3-11	8-17	69.9	72.2
Virginia	2-12	5-18	70.2	83.1

*Won ACC Tournament

NCAA — WAKE FOREST third in Final Four: beat Yale 92-82 (OT), beat St. Joseph's 96-85 (OT), beat Villanova 79-69 in East Regional; lost to Ohio State 84-68, beat UCLA 82-80 in Final Four.

ACC Tournament

MARCH 1-3, 1962 AT RALEIGH, N.C.
FIRST ROUND: Clemson 67, N.C. State 46; Duke 71, Maryland 58; Wake Forest 81, Virginia 58; South Carolina 57, North Carolina 55. **SEMIFINALS:** Wake Forest 88, South Carolina 75; Clemson 77, Duke 72. **FINAL:** Wake Forest 77, Clemson 66.
ALL-TOURNAMENT — FIRST TEAM: Len Chappell, Wake Forest; Jim Brennan, Clemson; Art Heyman, Duke; Jeff Mullins, Duke; Billy Packer, Wake Forest. **SECOND TEAM:** Dave Wiedeman, Wake Forest; Jerry Greenspan, Maryland; Bob Robinson, South Carolina; Ronnie Collins, South Carolina; Art Whisnant, South Carolina.

All-ACC

FIRST TEAM: *Len Chappell, Wake Forest (146 votes); *Art Heyman, Duke (146); Jeff Mullins, Duke (133); Art Whisnant, South Carolina (131); Jon Speaks, N.C. State (97). **SECOND TEAM:** Larry Brown, North Carolina (94); Dave Wiedeman, Wake Forest (47); John Punger, N.C. State (46); Tony Laquintano, Virginia (40); Jim Hudock, North Carolina (36).
PLAYER OF THE YEAR: Chappell (81); Heyman (3). **COACH OF THE YEAR:** Bob Stevens, South Carolina (36); Bones McKinney, Wake Forest (23); Vic Bubas, Duke (15).
*Unanimous Selection

Scoring, Rebounding Leaders

TOP TEN SCORERS

Player, School	G	FG	FT	TP	Ave.
Chappell, Wake Forest	31	327	278	932	30.1
Heyman, Duke	24	219	170	608	25.3
Mullins, Duke	25	214	98	530	21.2
Whisnant, South Carolina	27	177	213	567	21.0
Laquintano, Virginia	23	185	100	470	20.4
Speaks, N.C. State	17	110	76	296	17.4
Brennan, Clemson	27	183	95	461	17.1
Brown, North Carolina	17	90	101	281	16.5
Greenspan, Maryland	25	125	130	380	15.2
Conner, Virginia	23	144	60	348	15.1

TOP TEN REBOUNDERS

Player, School	G	Rbs.	Ave.
Chappell, Wake Forest	31	470	15.2
Heyman, Duke	24	269	11.2
Mullins, Duke	25	259	10.4
Hudock, North Carolina	17	171	10.1
Punger, N.C. State	17	162	9.5
Greenspan, Maryland	25	235	9.4
Conner, Virginia	23	212	9.2
Marvel, N.C. State	17	153	9.0
Engel, Virginia	23	175	7.6
Woollard, Wake Forest	31	228	7.4

Rosters

CLEMSON

No.	Name	Hgt.	Yr.	Hometown
4/3	Choppy Patterson	6-0	Sr.	Piedmont, SC
10/5	Woody Morgan	6-7	So.	Hartsville, SC
12/11	Nick Milasnovich	6-2	So.	Youngstown, OH
14/15	Mike Bohonak	6-2	So.	Pittsburgh, PA
20/21	Jim Brennan	6-2	So.	McKeesport, PA
22/23	Larry Seitz	6-4	Jr.	Morrisonville, IL
30/31	Jim Leshock	6-3	Sr.	Greensburg, PA
32/33	Richard Hall	5-11	So.	Savannah, GA
40/41	Chuck Narvin	6-2	Jr.	Pittsburgh, PA
42/43	Bob Benson	6-2	Sr.	Greensburg, PA
44/45	Donnie Mahaffey	6-8	So.	La Grange, GA
50/43	Manning Privette	6-8	So.	Hartsville, SC
52/51	Gary Burnisky	6-5	So.	Bridgeville, PA
54/55	Tom Mahaffey	6-7	Sr.	La Grange, GA

COACH: Press Maravich
ASSISTANT: Bobby Roberts

DUKE

No.	Name	Hgt.	Yr.	Hometown
11	Fred Schmidt	6-4	Jr.	Philadelphia, PA
14	Scott Williamson	6-5	So.	Sanford, NC
15	Fred Kast	6-7	So.	Rahway, NJ
20	Jack Mullen	5-11	Sr.	Weissport, PA
21	Roger Hamilton	6-3	So.	Westerly, RI
22	Jay Buckley	6-10	So.	Cheverly, MD
23	Ray Cox	6-0	So.	Durham, NC
25	Art Heyman	6-5	Jr.	Rockville Centre, NY
30	Buzzy Harrison	6-3	So.	S. Charleston, WV
33	Bob Jamieson	6-5	So.	Greensboro, NC
34	Steve Salisbury			
35	Buzz Mewhort	6-4	Sr.	Toledo, OH
40	Tom Gebbie	6-7	So.	Park Ridge, IL
43	Bill Ulrich	5-10	So.	Audubon, NJ
44	Jeff Mullins	6-4	So.	Lexington, KY

COACH: Vic Bubas
ASSISTANTS: Fred Shabel, Bucky Waters

MARYLAND

No.	Name	Hgt.	Yr.	Hometown
20	Robert Eicher	6-2	Jr.	Greensburg, PA
22	Bill Stasiulatis	6-3	Jr.	Bayonne, NJ
25	Jerry Greenspan	6-7	Jr.	Newark, NJ
32	Paul Jelus	6-2	Sr.	Camden, NJ
33	Bruce Kelleher	6-2	Sr.	Wilmington, DE
35	Connie Carpenter	6-4	Jr.	Norwalk, CT
42	Ted Marshall	6-7	Sr.	Johnstown, PA
43	John Maddox	6-4	So.	Silver Spring, MD
50	Joe Barton	6-7	So.	Beaverdale, PA
52	Mike Nofsinger	5-9	Sr.	Westernport, MD
54	Scott Ferguson	6-8	So.	Hanover, PA

COACH: Bud Millikan
ASSISTANT: Frank Fellows

NORTH CAROLINA

No.	Name	Hgt.	Yr.	Hometown
11	Larry Brown	5-11	Jr.	Long Beach, NY
12	Harry Jones	6-7	Sr.	Charlotte, NC
20	Don Walsh	6-0	Sr.	Riverdale, NY
22	Mike Cooke	6-2	So.	Mt. Airy, NC
30	Dieter Krause	6-5	Jr.	Norfolk, VA
31	Bruce Bowers	6-8	So.	Wellesley Hills, MA
32	Peppy Callahan	6-2	Jr.	Smithtown, NY
33	Jim Hudock	6-7	Sr.	Tunkhannock, PA
34	Richard Vinroot	6-7	So.	Charlotte, NC
35	Charlie Burns	6-2	Jr.	Wadesboro, NC
41	Jim Donohue	6-8	Jr.	Yonkers, NY
42	Charlie Shaffer	6-3	So.	Chapel Hill, NC
43	Art Katz	6-7	So.	Williston Park, NY
44	Bryan McSweeney	6-5	So.	Hewlett, NY

COACH: Dean Smith
ASSISTANT: Ken Rosemond

N.C. STATE

No.	Name	Hgt.	Yr.	Hometown
10/11	Bob Mayton	6-2	So.	Raleigh, NC
12/13	Jim Whitfield	6-5	Jr.	Durham, NC
14/15	John Punger	6-5	Jr.	Rockville Centre, NY
20/21	Denny Lutz	6-1	Sr.	Charlestown, IN
22/23	Ken Rohloff	6-0	Jr.	Paterson, NJ
24/25	John Key	6-8	Jr.	Durham, NC
30/31	Russ Marvel	6-6	Sr.	Gary, IN
32/33	Pom Sinnock	6-4	So.	New Castle, IN
34/35	Jon Speaks	6-0	Sr.	Lexington, KY
40/41	Smedes York	6-4	So.	Raleigh, NC
42/43	Les Robinson	6-0	So.	St. Albans, WV
44/45	Ron Gossell	6-9	So.	Harvard, IL
50/51	Dan Wherry	6-3	Sr.	Columbus, OH
52/53	Don Greiner	6-3	Jr.	Lancaster, PA
54/55	Pete Auksel	6-6	So.	East Chicago, IN

COACH: Everett Case
ASSISTANTS: George Pickett, Lou Pucillo

SOUTH CAROLINA

No.	Name	Hgt.	Yr.	Hometown
20	Ronnie Collins	6-3	Jr.	Winnsboro, SC
21	Jimmy Collins	6-1	So.	Dumont, NJ
22	Bobby Robinson	6-0	Sr.	Camden, SC
23	Terry Lucansky	6-0	So.	Massillon, OH
24	Joe Laird	5-11	Jr.	Columbia, SC
25	Bill Yarborough	6-3	So.	Charleston, SC
31	Bob Rebhan	6-4	Sr.	Parkersburg, WV
32	David Barrett	6-5	Sr.	Ft. Wayne, IN
33	Bud Cronin	6-3	Sr.	Parkersburg, WV
34	Scotti Ward	6-1	Jr.	Valparaiso, IN
35	Russell Littleton	6-1	So.	Mt. Sterling, KY
40	Dave Prevoznik	6-6	Jr.	Cleveland, OH
41	Tom Caughman	6-6	So.	Fairfield, CA
43	Bob Haney	6-4	Jr.	Lucasville, OH
44	Art Whisnant	6-5	Sr.	Hildebran, NC
45	James Podell	6-5	So.	Denham, IN

COACH: Bob Stevens
ASSISTANTS: Gordon Stauffer

VIRGINIA

No.	Name	Hgt.	Yr.	Hometown
3	Gary Spohn	6-4	So.	Elverson, PA
10	John Hasbrouck	5-10	Jr.	Manhasset, NY
13	Gene Flamm	6-6	Jr.	Levittown, NY
20	Jay Lambiotte	5-8	So.	Newport News, VA
22	Gene Engel	6-5	Jr.	Cranford, NJ
23	Tony Laquintano	5-11	Sr.	Philadelphia, PA
24	Richard Katstra	6-9	So.	Saddle Brook, NJ
25	Ronald Miller	6-2	Sr.	Brooklyn, NY
30	Michael Greenberg	5-11	So.	Brooklyn, NY
33	Steven Jarvis	6-4	Jr.	Madison, WV
35	John Eller	6-5	Jr.	Weaverville, NC
40	Chip Conner	6-4	So.	Clover, VA
41	Fletcher Arritt	6-0	So.	Fayetteville, NC
44	Tommy Johnson	6-5	Jr.	Bayside, VA
55	William Jackey	6-2	Sr.	Hempstead, NY
	Robert Roberson	6-2	So.	Petersburg, VA
	Paul Gregory	6-1	Jr.	Virginia Beach, VA

COACH: Billy McCann
ASSISTANTS: Gene Corrigan, Jim Moyer

WAKE FOREST

No.	Name	Hgt.	Yr.	Hometown
5	Trask Buxton			
10/11	Richard Carmichael	6-5	So.	High Point, NC
12/13	Bob Woollard	6-10	Jr.	Bloomfield, NJ
14/15	Ted Zawacki	6-4	Jr.	Linden, NJ
20/21	Bill Hull	6-6	Sr.	Tarboro, NC
22/23	Dave Wiedeman	5-11	Sr.	Delanco, NJ
30/31	Tommy McCoy	6-3	Sr.	Portsmouth, VA
34/35	Billy Packer	5-11	So.	Bethlehem, PA
40/41	Frank Christie	6-4	So.	Marietta, OH
42/43	Butch Hassell	5-11	So.	Beaufort, NC
44/45	Brad Brooks	6-7	So.	Chevy Chase, MD
50/51	Len Chappell	6-8	Sr.	Portage, PA
52/53	Al Koehler	6-2	Jr.	Rahway, NJ

COACH: Bones McKinney
ASSISTANTS: Charlie Bryant, Jackie Murdock

All-America Teams

ASSOCIATED PRESS
FIRST TEAM: *Jerry Lucas, Ohio State; Billy McGill, Utah; Terry Dischinger, Purdue; Chet Walker, Bradley; **Len Chappell, Wake Forest**. **SECOND TEAM:** John Havlicek, Ohio State; **Art Heyman, Duke**; Cotton Nash, Kentucky; John Rudometkin, Southern Cal; Rod Thorn, West Virginia. **THIRD TEAM:** Paul Hogue, Cincinnati; Don Nelson, Iowa; Jack Foley, Holy Cross; Jimmy Rayl, Indiana; Dave DeBusschere, Detroit.

UNITED PRESS INTERNATIONAL
FIRST TEAM: *Jerry Lucas, Ohio State; Billy McGill, Utah; Terry Dischinger, Purdue; Chet Walker, Bradley; John Havlicek, Ohio State. **SECOND TEAM:** Cotton Nash, Kentucky; Rod Thorn, West Virginia; **Len Chappell, Wake Forest; Art Heyman, Duke**; Jack Foley, Holy Cross. **THIRD TEAM:** Jimmy Rayl, Indiana; Dave DeBusschere, Detroit; Paul Hogue, Cincinnati; John Rudometkin, Southern Cal; Don Nelson, Iowa.

*Player of the Year

Final Top 20 Polls

AP
1. Ohio State 26-2
2. Cincinnati 29-2
3. Kentucky 23-3
4. Mississippi St. 24-1
5. Bradley 21-7
6. Kansas State 22-3
7. Utah 23-3
8. Bowling Green 21-4
9. Colorado 19-7
10. Duke 20-5
11. Loyola (Ill.) 23-4
12. St. John's 21-5
13. Wake Forest 22-9
14. Oregon State 24-5
15. West Virginia 24-6
16. Arizona State 23-4
17. Duquesne 22-7
18. Utah State 22-7
19. UCLA 18-11
20. Villanova 21-7

UPI
1. Ohio State 26-2
2. Cincinnati 29-2
3. Kentucky 23-3
4. Mississippi State 24-1
5. Kansas State 22-3
6. Bradley 21-7
7. Wake Forest 22-9
8. Colorado 19-7
9. Bowling Green 21-4
10. Utah 23-3
11. Oregon State 24-5
12. St. John's 21-5
13. Duke 20-5
14. Loyola (Ill.)
15. Arizona State 23-4
16. West Virginia 24-6
17. UCLA 18-11
18. Duquesne 22-7
19. Utah State 22-7
20. Villanova 21-7

Cincinnati beat Ohio State 71-59 for NCAA title.

'63

Duke's Art Heyman

1962-63 Final Standings

Team	Conf.	Overall	Ave.	Opp.
***Duke**	14-0	27-3	83.2	69.0
Wake Forest	11-3	16-10	71.3	68.8
North Carolina	10-4	15-6	76.6	70.8
Clemson	5-9	12-13	67.4	66.9
N.C. State	5-9	10-11	69.7	68.5
South Carolina	4-10	9-15	65.5	70.9
Maryland	4-10	8-13	64.2	71.6
Virginia	3-11	5-20	63.6	74.5

*Won ACC Tournament

NCAA—DUKE third in Final Four: beat NYU 81-76, beat St. Joseph's 73-59 in East Regional; lost to Loyola (Ill.) 94-75, beat Oregon State 85-63 in Final Four.

ACC Tournament

FEBRUARY 28-MARCH 2, 1963 AT RALEIGH, N.C.

FIRST ROUND: North Carolina 93, South Carolina 76; Wake Forest 80, Maryland 41; Duke 89, Virginia 70; N.C. State 79, Clemson 78. **SEMIFINALS:** Duke 82, N.C. State 65; Wake Forest 56, North Carolina 55. **FINAL:** Duke 68, Wake Forest 57.

ALL-TOURNAMENT—FIRST TEAM: Art Heyman, Duke; Jeff Mullins, Duke; Dave Wiedeman, Wake Forest; Billy Cunningham, North Carolina; Ken Rohloff, N.C. State. **SECOND TEAM:** Jay Buckley, Duke; Larry Brown, North Carolina; Bob Woollard, Wake Forest; Frank Christie, Wake Forest; Buzzy Harrison, Duke.

All-ACC

FIRST TEAM: *Billy Cunningham, North Carolina (158 votes); *Art Heyman, Duke (158); Jeff Mullins, Duke (156); Dave Wiedeman, Wake Forest (124); Larry Brown, North Carolina (112). **SECOND TEAM:** Scotti Ward, South Carolina (107); Gene Engel, Virginia (75); Jim Brennan, Clemson (51); Jerry Greenspan, Maryland (50); Ken Rohloff, N.C. State (24).

PLAYER OF THE YEAR: Heyman (88); Cunningham (5). **COACH OF THE YEAR:** Vic Bubas, Duke (51); Dean Smith, North Carolina (22); Chuck Noe, South Carolina (15).

*Unanimous Selection

Scoring, Rebounding Leaders

TOP TEN SCORERS

Player, School	G	FG	FT	TP	Ave.
Heyman, Duke	30	265	217	747	24.9
Cunningham, North Carolina	21	186	105	477	22.7
Mullins, Duke	30	256	96	608	20.3
Engel, Virginia	25	178	104	460	18.4
Ward, South Carolina	24	152	118	422	17.6
Greenspan, Maryland	21	111	143	365	17.4
Conner, Virginia	25	170	94	434	17.4
Brennan, Clemson	24	144	111	399	16.6
R. Collins, South Carolina	23	133	115	381	16.6
Brown, North Carolina	21	102	95	299	14.2

TOP TEN REBOUNDERS

Player, School	G	Rbs.	Ave.
Cunningham, North Carolina	21	339	16.1
Heyman, Duke	30	324	10.8
Mahaffey, Clemson	25	267	10.7
Buckley, Duke	30	298	9.9
Greenspan, Maryland	21	184	8.8
Woollard, Wake Forest	26	225	8.7
R. Collins, South Carolina	23	192	8.4
Caldwell, Virginia	25	206	8.2
Mullins, Duke	30	241	8.0
Conner, Virginia	25	196	7.8

Rosters

CLEMSON

No.	Name	Hgt.	Yr.	Hometown
10/11	Nick Milasnovich	6-1	Jr.	Youngstown, OH
14/15	Larry Seitz	6-4	Sr.	Morrisonville, IL
20/21	Jim Brennan	6-3	Jr.	McKeesport, PA
22/23	Rudy Antoncic	6-4	So.	McKeesport, PA
24/25	Sam Cohn	6-1	So.	Beckley, WV
30/31	Chuck Narvin	6-2	Sr.	Pittsburgh, PA
32/33	Richard Hall	5-11	Jr.	Savannah, GA
34/35	Mike Bohonak	6-2	Jr.	Pittsburgh, PA
40/41	Woody Morgan	6-7	Jr.	Hartsville, SC
42/43	Donnie Seitz	6-5	So.	Morrisonville, IL
44/45	Choppy Patterson	6-0	Sr.	Piedmont, SC
50/51	Gary Burnisky	6-6	Jr.	Bridgeville, PA
52/53	Manning Privette	6-8	Jr.	Hartsville, SC
54/55	Donnie Mahaffey	6-8	Jr.	La Grange, GA

COACH: Bobby Roberts
ASSISTANT: George Krajack

DUKE

No.	Name	Hgt.	Yr.	Hometown
11	Fred Schmidt	6-4	Sr.	Philadelphia, PA
13	Brent Kitching	6-6	So.	Sharon Hills, PA
14	Scott Williamson	6-5	Jr.	Sanford, NC
20	Denny Ferguson	6-0	So.	Springdale, PA
22	Jay Buckley	6-10	Jr.	Cheverly, MD
23	Ray Cox	6-0	Jr.	Durham, NC
25	Art Heyman	6-5	Sr.	Rockville Centre, NY
30	Buzzy Harrison	6-3	Jr.	S. Charleston, WV
31	Hack Tison	6-10	So.	Geneva, IL
33	Bob Jamieson	6-5	Jr.	Greensboro, NC
42	Fred Cox	6-5	Jr.	Pittsfield, MA
43	Bill Ulrich	5-10	Jr.	Audubon, NJ
44	Jeff Mullins	6-4	Jr.	Lexington, KY
45	Ted Mann	6-5	So.	Durham, NC
55	Ron Herbster	6-2	So.	Chester, PA

COACH: Vic Bubas
ASSISTANTS: Fred Shabel, Bucky Waters

MARYLAND

No.	Name	Hgt.	Yr.	Hometown
20	Robert Eicher	6-2	Sr.	Greensburg, PA
22	Bill Stasiulatis	6-3	Sr.	Bayonne, NJ
25	Jerry Greenspan	6-7	Sr.	Newark, NJ
32	Jerry Bynam	5-11	Jr.	Silver Spring, MD
34	Bob Lewis	6-4	So.	Silver Spring, MD
35	Connie Carpenter	6-4	Sr.	Norwalk, CT
40	Sam McWilliams	6-1	So.	Washington, DC
42	Bill Moore	6-4	So.	Westwood, NJ
44	Thomas Maxwell	5-10	So.	Lansdowne, PA
45	Phil Carlson	6-4	So.	Tacoma, WA
50	Joe Barton	6-7	Jr.	Beaverdale, PA
54	Scott Ferguson	6-8	Jr.	Hanover, PA
55	Rudy Shively	6-6	So.	Portsmouth, OH

COACH: Bud Millikan
ASSISTANT: Frank Fellows

NORTH CAROLINA

No.	Name	Hgt.	Yr.	Hometown
11	Larry Brown	5-11	Sr.	Long Beach, NY
12	Ray Respess	6-4	So.	Pantego, NC
20	Peppy Callahan	6-2	Sr.	Smithtown, NY
22	Mike Cooke	6-2	Jr.	Mt. Airy, NC
30	Dieter Krause	6-5	Sr.	Norfolk, VA
31	Charlie Burns	6-2	Sr.	Wadesboro, NC
31	Bill Taylor	5-11	So.	Cary, NC
32	Billy Cunningham	6-5	So.	Brooklyn, NY
33	Bill Brown	6-3	So.	Charlotte, NC
34	Bruce Bowers	6-8	Jr.	Wellesley Hills, MA
34	Richard Vinroot	6-8	Jr.	Charlotte, NC
35	Bill Galantai	6-5	So.	New York, NY
40	Yogi Poteet	6-1	Sr.	Hendersonville, NC
41	Terry Ronner	6-6	So.	Wilmington, NC
42	Charlie Shaffer	6-3	Jr.	Chapel Hill, NC
43	Art Katz	6-7	Jr.	Williston Park, NY
44	Bryan McSweeney	6-5	Jr.	Hewlett, NY

COACH: Dean Smith
ASSISTANT: Ken Rosemond

N.C. STATE

No.	Name	Hgt.	Yr.	Hometown
10/11	Bob Mayton	6-3	Jr.	Raleigh, NC
12/13	Jim Whitfield	6-5	Sr.	Durham, NC
14/15	Larry Lakins	6-6	So.	Nappanee, IN
20/21	Larry Worsley	6-5	So.	Oak City, NC
22/23	Ken Rohloff	6-0	Sr.	Paterson, NJ
24/25	John Key	6-8	Sr.	Durham, NC
30/31	Tommy Mattocks	6-2	So.	Kinston, NC
32/33	Pom Sinnock	6-5	Sr.	New Castle, IN
34/35	Jon Speaks	6-2	Sr.	Lexington, KY
40/41	Smedes York	6-4	Jr.	Raleigh, NC
42/43	Les Robinson	6-0	So.	St. Albans, WV
44/45	Ron Gossell	6-10	Jr.	Harvard, IL
50/51	Gary Hale	6-0	So.	Jeffersonville, IN
52/53	Don Greiner	6-3	Sr.	Landisville, PA
54/55	Pete Auskel	6-6	Jr.	East Chicago, IN

COACH: Everett Case
ASSISTANTS: Press Maravich, Lou Pucillo

SOUTH CAROLINA

No.	Name	Hgt.	Yr.	Hometown
20	Ronnie Collins	6-3	Jr.	Winnsboro, SC
21	Jimmy Collins	6-1	Jr.	Dumont, NJ
22	Terry Lucansky	6-0	Jr.	Massillon, OH
23	Rick Grich	6-2	So.	Milford, CT
24	Charles Henderson	6-0	So.	Tarboro, NC
25	Bill Yarbrough	6-3	Jr.	Charleston, SC
33	Joe Laird	5-11	Sr.	Columbia, SC
34	Scotti Ward	6-1	Sr.	Valparaiso, IN
35	Butch Jordan	5-10	So.	Camden, SC
40	Dave Prevoznik	6-6	Sr.	Cleveland, OH
41	Dennis Ostaszewski	6-5	Sr.	Hammond, IN
44	Bob Haney	6-4	Sr.	Lucasville, OH
45	John Gorsage	6-6	So.	Indianapolis, IN

COACH: Chuck Noe
ASSISTANTS: Dwane Morrison

VIRGINIA

No.	Name	Hgt.	Yr.	Hometown
3	Gary Spohn	6-4	Jr.	Elverson, PA
10	Whitey Rockelein	6-4	So.	Ozone Park, NY
13	Gene Flamm	6-6	Sr.	Levittown, NY
20	Jay Lambiotte	5-8	Jr.	Newport News, VA
22	Gene Engel	6-6	Sr.	Cranford, NJ
23	Mickey Haynes	5-11	So.	Martinsville, VA
24	Richard Katstra	6-10	Jr.	Saddle Brook, NJ
25	Bernie Meyer	6-0	So.	Richmond, VA
30	Michael Greenberg	5-11	Jr.	Brooklyn, NY
33	Steven Jarvis	6-4	Sr.	Madison, WV
35	John Eller	6-6	Sr.	Weaverville, NC
40	Chip Conner	6-3	Jr.	Clover, VA
41	Fletcher Arritt	6-0	Jr.	Fayettville, WV
44	Mac Caldwell	6-6	So.	Louisville, KY
55	Ken Goble	6-4	So.	West Van Lear, KY

COACH: Billy McCann
ASSISTANTS: Gene Mehaffey, Chuck Motley

WAKE FOREST

No.	Name	Hgt.	Yr.	Hometown
10/11	Butch Hassell	6-0	Jr.	Beaufort, NC
12/13	Bob Woollard	6-10	Sr.	Bloomfield, NJ
14/15	Ted Zawacki	6-4	Sr.	Linden, NJ
15/14	Jay Martin	6-4	So.	Boonville, NC
20/21	Al Lozier	6-5	So.	Mt. Holly, NJ
22/23	Dave Wiedeman	5-11	Sr.	Delanco, NJ
30/31	Richard Herring	6-5	So.	Winston-Salem, NC
32/33	Danny Loftin	6-2	So.	Troutman, NC
34/35	Billy Smith	6-1	So.	Valdese, NC
40/41	Frank Christie	6-4	Jr.	Marietta, OH
42/43	Richard Carmichael	6-5	Jr.	High Point, NC
44/45	Brad Brooks	6-7	Jr.	Chevy Chase, MD
45/44	Ronny Watts	6-7	So.	Washington, DC
52/53	Al Koehler	6-3	Sr.	Rahway, NJ
54/55	John Anderson	6-0	So.	Waterford, NY

COACH: Bones McKinney
ASSISTANTS: Charlie Bryant, Jackie Murdock

All-America Teams

ASSOCIATED PRESS

FIRST TEAM: *Art Heyman, Duke; Ron Bonham, Cincinnati; Jerry Harkness, Loyola (Ill.); Gary Bradds, Ohio State; Barry Kramer, NYU. **SECOND TEAM:** Bill Bradley, Princeton; Tom Thacker, Cincinnati; Rod Thorn, West Virginia; Cotton Nash, Kentucky; Walt Hazzard, UCLA. **THIRD TEAM:** Bill Green, Colorado State; Eddie Miles, Seattle; Tony Yates, Cincinnati; Jimmy Rayl, Indiana; Nick Werkman, Seton Hall.

UNITED PRESS INTERNATIONAL

FIRST TEAM: *Art Heyman, Duke; Ron Bonham, Cincinnati; Jerry Harkness, Loyola (Ill.); Gary Bradds, Ohio State; Tom Thacker, Cincinnati. **SECOND TEAM:** Barry Kramer, NYU; Rod Thorn, West Virginia; Bill Bradley, Princeton; Cotton Nash, Kentucky; Nate Thurmond, Bowling Green. **THIRD TEAM:** Eddie Miles, Seattle; Nick Werkman, Seton Hall; Bill Green, Colorado State; Dave Stallworth, Wichita State; Walt Hazzard, UCLA.

*Player of the Year

Final Top 20 Polls

AP

1.	Cincinnati	26-2
2.	**Duke**	**27-3**
3.	Loyola (Ill.)	29-2
4.	Arizona State	26-3
5.	Wichita State	19-8
6.	Mississippi St.	22-6
7.	Ohio State	20-4
8.	Illinois	20-6
9.	NYU	18-5
10.	Colorado	19-7

Others receiving votes, listed alphabetically: Auburn, Bowling Green, Bradley, Canisius, Connecticut, Georgia Tech, Indiana, Kansas State, Memphis State, Miami (Fla.), **North Carolina**, Notre Dame, Oklahoma City, Oregon State, Pittsburgh, Providence, St. Joseph's, Seattle, Texas, UCLA, Villanova, **Wake Forest** and West Virginia.

UPI

1.	Cincinnati	26-2
2.	**Duke**	**27-3**
3.	Arizona State	26-3
4.	Loyola (Ill.)	29-2
5.	Illinois	20-6
6.	Wichita State	19-8
7.	Mississippi St.	22-6
8.	Ohio State	20-4
9.	Colorado	19-7
10.	Stanford	16-9
11.	NYU	18-5
12.	Texas	20-7
13.	Providence	24-4
14.	Oregon State	22-9
15.	UCLA	20-9
16.	St. Joseph's	23-5
	West Virginia	23-8
18.	Bowling Green	19-8
19.	Kansas State	16-9
	Seattle	21-6

Loyola (Ill.) beat Cincinnati 60-58 for NCAA title.

'64

Duke's Jeff Mullins

1963-64 Final Standings

Team	Conf.	Overall	Ave.	Opp.
*Duke	13-1	26-5	84.1	69.1
Wake Forest	9-5	16-11	74.1	72.0
Clemson	8-6	13-12	70.2	69.0
South Carolina	7-7	10-14	69.9	73.2
North Carolina	6-8	12-12	77.5	77.5
Maryland	5-9	9-17	70.2	75.5
N.C. State	4-10	8-11	59.3	63.9
Virginia	4-10	8-16	65.5	69.7

*Won ACC Tournament

NCAA—DUKE second in Final Four: beat Villanova 87-73, beat Connecticut 101-54 in East Regional; beat Michigan 91-80, lost to UCLA 98-83 in Final Four.

ACC Tournament

MARCH 5-7, 1964 AT RALEIGH, N.C.

FIRST ROUND: Clemson 81, Maryland 67; Wake Forest 79, Virginia 60; Duke 75, N.C. State 44; North Carolina 80, South Carolina 63. **SEMIFINALS:** Duke 65, North Carolina 49; Wake Forest 86, Clemson 64. **FINAL:** Duke 80, Wake Forest 59.

ALL-TOURNAMENT—FIRST TEAM: Jeff Mullins, Duke; Jay Buckley, Duke; Billy Cunningham, North Carolina; Frank Christie, Wake Forest; Bob Leonard, Wake Forest. **SECOND TEAM:** Hack Tison, Duke; Butch Hassell, Wake Forest; Ronny Watts, Wake Forest; Denny Ferguson, Duke; Nick Milasnovich, Clemson.

All-ACC

FIRST TEAM: *Billy Cunningham, North Carolina (166 votes); *Jeff Mullins, Duke (166); Ronnie Collins, South Carolina (160); Chip Conner, Virginia (129); Frank Christie, Wake Forest (123). **SECOND TEAM:** Jim Brennan, Clemson (108); Hack Tison, Duke (78); Jay Buckley, Duke (62); Butch Hassell, Wake Forest (38); Ronny Watts, Wake Forest (33).

PLAYER OF THE YEAR: Mullins (78); Cunningham (22). **COACH OF THE YEAR:** Vic Bubas, Duke (73); Bones McKinney, Wake Forest (16).

*Unanimous Selection

Scoring, Rebounding Leaders

TOP TEN SCORERS

Player, School	G	FG	FT	TP	Ave.
Cunningham, North Carolina	24	233	157	623	26.0
Mullins, Duke	31	300	150	750	24.2
R. Collins, South Carolina	24	211	147	569	23.7
Lakins, N.C. State	12	97	55	249	20.8
Conner, Virginia	20	142	91	375	18.8
Brennan, Clemson	25	159	139	457	18.3
J. Collins, South Carolina	24	159	71	389	16.2
Christie, Wake Forest	27	178	78	434	16.1
Caldwell, Virginia	24	146	69	361	15.0
Yarbrough, South Carolina	24	122	116	360	15.0

TOP TEN REBOUNDERS

Player, School	G	Rbs.	Ave.
Cunningham, North Carolina	24	379	15.8
Watts, Wake Forest	27	324	12.0
Yarbrough, South Carolina	24	238	9.9
Christie, Wake Forest	27	254	9.4
Buckley, Duke	31	278	9.0
Mahaffey, Clemson	25	223	8.9
Mullins, Duke	31	276	8.9
R. Collins, South Carolina	24	207	8.6
Auskel, N.C. State	19	159	8.3
Caldwell, Virginia	24	193	8.0

Rosters

CLEMSON

No.	Name	Hgt.	Yr.	Hometown
10/11	Nick Milasnovich	6-1	Sr.	Youngstown, OH
12/13	Gary Burnisky	6-6	Sr.	Bridgeville, PA
14/15	Garry Helms	6-4	So.	Pelzer, SC
20/21	Jim Brennan	6-3	Sr.	McKeesport, PA
22/23	Rudy Antoncic	6-4	So.	McKeesport, PA
24/25	Sam Cohn	6-1	So.	Beckley, WV
30/31	Tom Corcoran	6-5	So.	N. Charleston, SC
32/33	Richard Hall	5-11	Jr.	Savannah, GA
34/35	Mike Bohonak	6-2	Sr.	Pittsburgh, PA
40/41	Woody Morgan	6-7	Sr.	Hartsville, SC
42/43	Donnie Seitz	6-5	So.	Morrisonville, IL
44/45	Buddy Benedict	5-7	So.	Duquesne, PA
50/51	Ronnie Cox	6-0	So.	Syracuse, NY
52/53	Manning Privette	6-8	Sr.	Hartsville, SC
54/55	Donnie Mahaffey	6-8	Sr.	LaGrange, GA

COACH: Bobby Roberts
ASSISTANT: Goerge Krajack

DUKE

No.	Name	Hgt.	Yr.	Hometown
12	Frank Harscher	6-3	So.	Lexington, KY
13	Brent Kitching	6-7	Jr.	Sharon Hills, PA
20	Denny Ferguson	6-0	Jr.	Springdale, PA
22	Jay Buckley	6-10	Sr.	Cheverly, MD
23	Ray Cox	6-0	Sr.	Durham, NC
24	Jack Marin	6-6	So.	Farrell, PA
31	Hack Tison	6-10	Jr.	Geneva, IL
32	Jim Liccardo	6-4	So.	West Orange, NJ
33	Steve Vacendak	6-1	So.	Scranton, PA
34	Buzzy Harrison	6-3	Sr.	S. Charleston, WV
35	Phil Allen	6-4	So.	Syracuse, NY
44	Jeff Mullins	6-4	Sr.	Lexington, KY
45	Ted Mann	6-5	Jr.	Durham, NC
52	Terry Murray	6-5	So.	Atlanta, GA
55	Ron Herbster	6-2	Jr.	Chester, PA

COACH: Vic Bubas
ASSISTANTS: Bucky Waters, Chuck Daly

MARYLAND

No.	Name	Hgt.	Yr.	Hometown
10	Bill Franklin	5-10	So.	Mt. Airy, MD
12	Mike DeCosmo	5-10	So.	Camden, NJ
20	Dick Mueller	6-2	So.	Independence, MO
22	Gary Ward	6-5	So.	Washington, DC
25	Terry Truax	6-3	So.	Hancock, MD
30	George Suder	6-2	So.	Aliquippa, PA
33	Neil Brayton	6-4	So.	Youngstown, OH
40	Sam McWilliams	6-1	Jr.	Washington, DC
42	Bob Lewis	6-4	Jr.	Silver Spring, MD
44	Jack Clark	6-4	So.	Beverly, OH
45	Phil Carlson	6-4	Jr.	Tacoma, WA
50	Joe Barton	6-7	Sr.	Beaverdale, PA
54	Scott Ferguson	6-8	Sr.	Hanover, PA
55	Rick Wise	6-8	So.	Wilmington, DE

COACH: Bud Millikan
ASSISTANT: Frank Fellows

NORTH CAROLINA

No.	Name	Hgt.	Yr.	Hometown
11	Ray Hassell	6-0	So.	Beaufort, NC
12	Ray Respess	6-4	Jr.	Pantego, NC
20	John Yokley	6-0	So.	Mt. Airy, NC
22	Mike Cooke	6-2	Sr.	Mt. Airy, NC
30	Pud Hassell	6-3	Jr.	Beaufort, NC
31	Bob Bennett	6-9	So.	Mt. Lebanon, PA
32	Billy Cunningham	6-6	Jr.	Brooklyn, NY
33	Bill Brown	6-3	Jr.	Charlotte, NC
34	Mike Iannarella	5-10	So.	Sharon Hills, PA
34	Earl Johnson	6-5	So.	Raleigh, NC
35	Bill Galantai	6-5	Jr.	Brooklyn, NY
40	Bill Harrison	6-3	So.	Rocky Mount, NC
40	Jim Moore	6-2	So.	Wilmington, NC
41	Terry Ronner	6-6	Jr.	Wilmington, NC
42	Charlie Shaffer	6-3	Sr.	Chapel Hill, NC
43	Art Katz	6-7	Sr.	Williston Park, NY
44	Bryan McSweeney	6-5	Sr.	Hewlett, NY
41	Jim Smithwick	6-4	So.	Morehead City, NC

COACH: Dean Smith
ASSISTANTS: Ken Rosemond, Donnie Walsh

N.C. STATE

No.	Name	Hgt.	Yr.	Hometown
10/11	Tommy Mattocks	6-2	So.	Kinston, NC
12/13	Larry Worsley	6-5	So.	Oak City, NC
14/15	Larry Lakins	6-6	Jr.	Nappanee, IN
20/21	Ron Erb	5-11	Jr.	Lansdale, PA
22/23	Billy Moffitt	5-11	So.	Fayetteville, NC
24/25	Gary Hale	6-0	So.	Jeffersonville, IN
30/31	Hal Blondeau	6-4	So.	Glen Burnie, MD
32/33	Jim Sellers	6-3	So.	Lilesville, NC
40/41	Sam Gealy	6-0	So.	New Castle, PA
42/43	Les Robinson	6-0	Jr.	St. Albans, WV
44/45	Ray Hodgdon	6-4	So.	Arlington, VA
50/51	Phil Taylor	6-9	So.	Akron, OH
52/53	Donald Moore	6-4	So.	Brevard, NC
54/55	Pete Auskel	6-6	Sr.	East Chicago, IN

COACH: Everett Case
ASSISTANTS: Press Maravich, Lou Pucillo

SOUTH CAROLINA

No.	Name	Hgt.	Yr.	Hometown
21	Jimmy Collins	6-1	Sr.	Dumont, NJ
22	Terry Lucansky	6-0	Sr.	Massillon, OH
23	Rick Grich	6-2	Jr.	Milford, CT
24	Jerry White	6-2	So.	Hampton, TN
25	Bill Yarbrough	6-3	Sr.	Charleston, SC
34	Billy Woofter	6-7	So.	Pikeville, KY
35	Ronnie Collins	6-3	Sr.	Winnsboro, NC
40	John Schroeder	6-6	So.	Dundalk, MD
41	Butch Jordan	5-10	Jr.	Camden, SC
44	Jim Fox	6-9	Jr.	Sandy Springs, GA
45	John Gorsage	6-6	Jr.	Indianapolis, IN

COACHES: *Chuck Noe (6-6); Dwane Morrison (4-8)
ASSISTANTS: Dwane Morrison
*Noe retired after 12 games

VIRGINIA

No.	Name	Hgt.	Yr.	Hometown
3	Chuck Rotgin	6-3	Jr.	Charleston, WV
10	Whitey Rockelein	6-4	Jr.	Ozone Park, NY
13	Renny Barnes	6-6	So.	Arlington, VA
20	Jay Lambiotte	5-8	Sr.	Newport News, VA
22	Bob Engel	6-5	So.	Cranford, NJ
23	Gary Spohn	6-3	Sr.	Elverson, PA
24	Richard Katstra	6-10	Sr.	Saddle Brook, NJ
25	Bernie Meyer	6-0	Jr.	Richmond, VA
33	Jerry Sanders	6-4	So.	Louisville, KY
34	Bob Waldruff	6-0	So.	Torrance, CA
35	Ken Goble	6-4	Jr.	West Van Lear, KY
40	Chip Conner	6-3	Sr.	Clover, VA
41	Fletcher Arritt	6-0	Sr.	Fayetteville, WV
42	Mack Wilcox	6-2	So.	Richmond, VA
44	Mac Caldwell	6-6	Jr.	Louisville, KY
55	Thomas Johnson	6-4	Sr.	Virginia Beach, VA

COACH: Bill Gibson
ASSISTANT: Gene Mehaffey

WAKE FOREST

No.	Name	Hgt.	Yr.	Hometown
10/11	Butch Hassell	5-11	Sr.	Beaufort, NC
12/13	Tommy Steele	6-2	So.	New Brockton, AL
14/15	Tommy Byrne	6-3	So.	Wake Forest, NC
15/14	Bob Leonard	6-2	So.	Kingsport, TN
20/21	Al Lozier	6-5	Jr.	Mt. Holly, NJ
22/23	Harry Hutchins	6-0	So.	Trenton, NJ
30/31	Richard Herring	6-5	Jr.	Winston-Salem, NC
32/33	Bill Joyner	5-11	So.	Asheboro, NC
34/35	Billy Smith	6-4	So.	Valdese, NC
40	Frank Christie	6-4	Sr.	Marietta, OH
42/43	Richard Carmichael	6-5	Sr.	High Point, NC
44	Ronny Watts	6-7	Jr.	Washington, DC
45	Brad Brooks	6-7	Sr.	Chevy Chase, MD
52	Bill Nesbit	6-3	So.	Bronxville, NY
53	Dick Myers	5-9	So.	Westfield, NJ
54/55	John Anderson	6-0	Jr.	Waterford, NY

COACH: Bones McKinney
ASSISTANTS: Charlie Bryant, Jackie Murdock

All-America Teams

ASSOCIATED PRESS

FIRST TEAM: *Gary Bradds, Ohio State; Cotton Nash, Kentucky; Walt Hazzard, UCLA; Bill Bradley, Princeton; Dave Stallworth, Wichita State. **SECOND TEAM: Jeff Mullins, Duke**; Cazzie Russell, Michigan; Fred Hetzel, Davidson; Mel Counts, Oregon State; Ron Bonham, Cincinnati. **THIRD TEAM:** Howard Komives, Bowling Green; Paul Silas, Creighton; Bill Buntin, Michigan; Barry Kramer, NYU; Jim Barnes, Texas Western.

UNITED PRESS INTERNATIONAL

FIRST TEAM: *Gary Bradds, Ohio State; Walt Hazzard, UCLA; Cotton Nash, Kentucky; Bill Bradley, Princeton; Dave Stallworth, Wichita State. **SECOND TEAM:** Cazzie Russell, Michigan; **Jeff Mullins, Duke**; Mel Counts, Oregon State; Fred Hetzel, Davidson; Ron Bonham, Cincinnati. **THIRD TEAM:** Howard Komives, Bowling Green; Bill Buntin, Michigan; Paul Silas, Creighton; Jim Barnes, Texas Western; Wally Jones, Villanova.

*Player of the Year

Final Top 20 Polls

AP

1.	UCLA	30-0
2.	Michigan	23-5
3.	**Duke**	**26-5**
4.	Kentucky	21-6
5.	Wichita State	23-6
6.	Oregon State	25-4
7.	Villanova	24-4
8.	Loyola (Ill.)	22-6
9.	DePaul	21-4
10.	Davidson	22-4

Others receiving votes, listed alphabetically: Arizona State, Bradley, Bowling Green, Creighton, Drake, Kansas State, Miami (Fla.), Minnesota, New Mexico, Ohio State, Ohio University, Providence, San Francisco, Seattle, Texas A&M, Texas Western and Vanderbilt.

UPI

1.	UCLA	30-0
2.	Michigan	23-5
3.	Kentucky	21-6
4.	**Duke**	**26-5**
5.	Oregon State	25-4
6.	Wichita State	23-6
7.	Villanova	24-4
8.	Loyola (Ill.)	22-6
9.	Texas Western	25-3
10.	Davidson	22-4
11.	DePaul	21-4
12	Kansas State	22-7
13.	Drake	21-7
	San Francisco	23-5
15.	Utah State	21-8
16.	Ohio State	16-8
	New Mexico	23-6
18.	Texas A&M	18-7
19.	Arizona State	16-11
	Providence	20-6

UCLA beat Duke 98-83 for NCAA title.

ACC BASKETBALL / **REFERENCE**

'65

North Carolina's Billy Cunningham

1964-65 Final Standings

Team	Conf.	Overall	Ave.	Opp.
Duke	11-3	20-5	92.4	77.8
***N.C. State**	10-4	21-5	76.7	68.7
Maryland	10-4	18-8	73.4	68.8
North Carolina	10-4	15-9	79.8	77.6
Wake Forest	6-8	12-15	81.9	84.7
Clemson	4-10	8-15	74.2	75.7
Virginia	3-11	7-18	71.1	80.3
South Carolina	2-12	6-17	66.5	74.0

*Won ACC Tournament

NCAA—N.C. STATE third in East Regional: lost to Princeton 66-48, beat St. Joseph's 103-81.

ACC Tournament

MARCH 4-6, 1965 AT RALEIGH, N.C.

FIRST ROUND: Maryland 61, Clemson 50; N.C. State 106, Virginia 69; Duke 62, South Carolina 60; Wake Forest 92, North Carolina 76. **SEMIFINALS:** Duke 101, Wake Forest 81; N.C. State 76, Maryland 67. **FINAL:** N.C. State 91, Duke 85.

ALL-TOURNAMENT—FIRST TEAM: Bob Leonard, Wake Forest; Larry Worsley, N.C. State; Bob Verga, Duke; Steve Vacendak, Duke; Larry Lakins, N.C. State. **SECOND TEAM:** Tommy Mattocks, N.C. State; Gary Ward, Maryland; Ronny Watts, Wake Forest; Jay McMillen, Maryland; Jack Marin, Duke.

EVERETT CASE AWARD (MVP): Worsley.

All-ACC

FIRST TEAM: Billy Cunningham, North Carolina (170 votes); Larry Lakins, N.C. State (165); Jack Marin, Duke (152); Bob Leonard, Wake Forest (151); Bob Verga, Duke (127). **SECOND TEAM:** Jay McMillen, Maryland (108); Bob Lewis, North Carolina (90); Randy Mahaffey, Clemson (81); Steve Vacendak, Duke (74); Ronny Watts, Wake Forest (38).

PLAYER OF THE YEAR: Cunningham (52); Lakins (16); Leonard (11); Marin, Verga, Vacendak, Larry Worsley, N.C. State, and Gary Ward, Maryland, also received votes. **COACH OF THE YEAR:** Press Maravich, N.C. State (82); Vic Bubas, Duke (9).

Scoring, Rebounding Leaders

TOP TEN SCORERS

Player, School	G	FG	FT	TP	Ave.
Cunningham, North Carolina	24	237	135	609	25.4
Leonard, Wake Forest	27	250	145	645	23.9
Verga, Duke	25	229	76	534	21.4
Lewis, North Carolina	24	191	123	505	21.0
McMillen, Maryland	26	206	100	512	19.7
Watts, Wake Forest	27	175	169	519	19.2
Marin, Duke	25	195	87	477	19.1
Lakins, N.C. State	25	193	90	476	19.0
Connelly, Virginia	25	185	85	455	18.3
Ward, Maryland	26	185	99	469	18.0

TOP TEN REBOUNDERS

Player, School	G	Rbs.	Ave.
Cunningham, North Carolina	24	344	14.3
Fox, South Carolina	23	313	13.6
Watts, Wake Forest	27	352	13.0
Ward, Maryland	26	271	10.4
Marin, Duke	25	257	10.3
Coker, N.C. State	25	250	10.0
Mahaffey, Clemson	23	224	9.7
Tison, Duke	25	221	8.8
Lewis, North Carolina	24	192	8.0
Lakins, N.C. State	25	195	7.8

Rosters

CLEMSON

No.	Name	Hgt.	Yr.	Hometown
10/11	Joe Ayoob	6-0	So.	Pittsburgh, PA
12/13	Jimmy Sutherland	6-5	So.	Clemson, SC
14/15	Garry Helms	6-4	Jr.	Pelzer, SC
20/21	Fred Steiner	6-2	So.	Pittsburgh, PA
22/23	Rudy Antoncic	6-3	Jr.	McKeesport, PA
24/25	Ken Gardner	6-5	So.	Collingswood, NJ
30/31	Tom Corcoran	6-5	So.	N. Charleston, SC
32/33	Richard Hall	6-0	Sr.	Savannah, GA
34/35	Walt Ayers	6-5	So.	Turtle Creek, PA
40/41	Hank Channell	6-5	So.	Warner Robins, GA
42/43	Randy Mahaffey	6-7	So.	La Grange, GA
44/45	Buddy Benedict	5-8	Jr.	Duquesne, PA
50/51	Ronnie Cox	6-0	Jr.	Syracuse, NY
52/53	Donnie Seitz	6-5	Jr.	Morrisonville, IL

COACH: Bobby Roberts
ASSISTANTS: George Krajack

DUKE

No.	Name	Hgt.	Yr.	Hometown
11	Bob Verga	6-0	So.	Sea Girt, NJ
13	Brent Kitching	6-7	Sr.	Sharon Hills, PA
14	Bill Zimmer	6-0	Jr.	Poland, OH
15	Burton Fitts	6-3	Jr.	Winston-Salem, NC
20	Denny Ferguson	6-0	Sr.	Springdale, PA
21	Stuart McKaig	6-1	So.	Charlotte, NC
22	Bob Riedy	6-6	So.	Allentown, PA
23	Elliot McBride	5-11	Sr.	Winston-Salem, NC
24	Jack Marin	6-6	Jr.	Farrell, PA
31	Hack Tison	6-10	Sr.	Geneva, IL
32	Jim Liccardo	6-5	Jr.	West Orange, NJ
33	Steve Vacendak	6-1	Jr.	Scranton, PA
35	Phil Allen	6-4	Jr.	Syracuse, NY
55	Ron Herbster	6-2	Sr.	Chester, PA

COACH: Vic Bubas
ASSISTANTS: Bucky Waters, Chuck Daly

MARYLAND

No.	Name	Hgt.	Yr.	Hometown
10	Bill Franklin	5-10	Jr.	Mt. Airy, MD
12	Mike DeCosmo	5-10	Jr.	Camden, NJ
14	Gary Williams	6-0	So.	Collingswood, NJ
20	Dick Mueller	6-2	Jr.	Independence, MO
22	Gary Ward	6-5	Jr.	Washington, DC
23	Don Brotman	6-3	So.	West Orange, NJ
33	Neil Brayton	6-4	Jr.	Youngstoown, OH
40	Sam McWilliams	6-1	Sr.	Washington, DC
42	Bob Lewis	6-4	Sr.	Silver Spring, MD
44	Jack Clark	6-4	Jr.	Beverly, OH
45	Phil Carlson	6-4	Sr.	Tacoma, WA
50	Joe Harrington	6-5	So.	Phippsburg, ME
53	Paul Hauser	6-7	So.	Cobleskill, NY
54	Jay McMillen	6-7	So.	Mansfield, PA
55	Rick Wise	6-8	Jr.	Wilmington, DE

COACH: Bud Millikan
ASSISTANT: Frank Fellows

NORTH CAROLINA

No.	Name	Hgt.	Yr.	Hometown
11	Ray Hassell	6-0	Jr.	Beaufort, NC
12	Ray Respess	6-4	Sr.	Pantego, NC
13	Ian Morrison	6-2	So.	St. Petersburg, FL
20	John Yokley	6-1	Jr.	Mt. Airy, NC
22	Bob Lewis	6-3	So.	Washington, DC
30	Jim Moore	6-2	So.	Wilmington, NC
31	Bob Bennett	6-6	Jr.	Mt. Lebanon, PA
32	Billy Cunningham	6-6	Sr.	Brooklyn, NY
33	Bill Brown	6-3	Sr.	Charlotte, NC
34	Pud Hassell	6-3	Sr.	Beaufort, NC
35	Jim Pollock	6-4	Jr.	Clinton, NC
40	Donnie Moe	6-2	So.	Brooklyn, NY
41	Jim Smithwick	6-5	Jr.	Morehead City, NC
42	Tom Gauntlett	6-4	So.	Dallas, PA
43	Mike Smith	6-0	Jr.	North Salem, IN
44	Mark Mirken	6-6	So.	Brooklyn, NY

COACH: Dean Smith
ASSISTANT: Ken Rosemond

N.C. STATE

No.	Name	Hgt.	Yr.	Hometown
10/11	Tommy Mattocks	6-2	Jr.	Kinston, NC
12/13	Larry Worsley	6-5	Jr.	Oak City, NC
14/15	Larry Lakins	6-6	Sr.	Nappanee, IN
20/21	Gary Hale	6-0	Jr.	Jeffersonville, IN
22/23	Billy Moffitt	5-11	Jr.	Fayetteville, NC
24/25	Paul Hudson	6-11	So.	Reidsville, NC
30/31	Hal Blondeau	6-4	Jr.	Glen Burnie, MD
32/33	Jerry Moore	6-7	So.	Moline, IL
34/35	Eddie Biedenbach	6-1	So.	Pittsburgh, PA
40/41	Sam Gealy	6-0	So.	New Castle, PA
42/43	Les Robinson	6-0	Sr.	St. Albans, WV
44/45	Ray Hodgdon	6-4	Jr.	Arlington, VA
50/51	Phil Taylor	6-9	Jr.	Akron, OH
52/53	John Sellers	6-8	So.	Lilesville, NC
54/55	Pete Coker	6-5	Jr.	Allentown, PA

COACHES: *Everett Case (1-1), Press Maravich (19-4)
ASSISTANTS: Press Maravich, Charlie Bryant
*Case retired after two games

SOUTH CAROLINA

No.	Name	Hgt.	Yr.	Hometown
14	Jim Finnegan	5-10	Jr.	Rye, NY
15	Al Salvadori	6-9	So.	Beech Bottom, WV
20	John Schroeder	6-6	Jr.	Dundalk, MD
21	Dave Murrell	6-1	Jr.	Florence, SC
22	Dave Walker	6-1	So.	Newport News, VA
25	Jerry Croke	6-1	Jr.	New York, NY
32	Earl Lovelace	5-11	So.	Kingsport, TN
33	John Gorsage	6-6	Sr.	Indianapolis, IN
40	Gary Gregor	6-6	So.	S. Charleston, WV
44	Jim Fox	6-9	Sr.	Sandy Springs, GA
45	Charlie Farrell	6-0	So.	Columbia, SC
45	Bruce Wells	6-8	So.	River Edge, NJ
54	Lyn Burkholder	6-8	So.	Singers Glen, VA

COACH: Frank McGuire
ASSISTANTS: Buck Freeman, Ken Stibler

VIRGINIA

No.	Name	Hgt.	Yr.	Hometown
10	Whitey Rockelein	6-4	Sr.	Ozone Park, NY
10	Bob Davis	6-2	So.	Neptune, NJ
13	Renny Barnes	6-6	Jr.	Arlington, VA
20	Wayne Metzger	6-0	So.	Colonial Heights, VA
22	Bob Engel	6-5	Jr.	Cranford, NJ
23	Jim Connelly	6-3	So.	Williamstown, WV
24	Ted Wafle	6-4	So.	Fredericksburg, VA
25	Bernie Meyer	6-0	Sr.	Richmond, VA
30	Jim Galloway	6-7	So.	Big Stone Gap, VA
33	Jerry Sanders	6-3	Jr.	Louisville, KY
35	Ken Goble	6-3	Sr.	West Van Lear, KY
41	Fred Stant	6-4	So.	Norfolk, VA
42	Mack Wilcox	6-2	Jr.	Richmond, VA
44	Mac Caldwell	6-6	Sr.	Louisville, KY
55	Dale Hilsmier	6-2	So.	Ft. Wayne, IN

COACH: Bill Gibson
ASSISTANT: Gene Mehaffey

WAKE FOREST

No.	Name	Hgt.	Yr.	Hometown
10	Dick Myers	5-9	Jr.	Westfield, NJ
11	Bill Joyner	5-11	Jr.	Asheboro, NC
12	Newton Scott	6-6	So.	Winston-Salem, NC
13	Dennis Moody	6-1	So.	Mt. Airy, NC
14	Clark Pool	6-4	So.	Washington, IL
15	Bob Leonard	6-2	Sr.	Kingsport, TN
20	Al Lozier	6-5	Sr.	Mt. Holly, NJ
22	Jim Altengarten	6-5	So.	Maplewood, NJ
25	Jimmy Snyder	6-6	So.	Lexington, NC
30	Richard Herring	6-5	Sr.	Winston-Salem, NC
35	Billy Smith	6-4	So.	Valdese, NC
40	Jim Boshart	6-5	So.	Huntington Sta., NY
44	Ronny Watts	6-7	Sr.	Washington, DC
45	Sherrill Whitaker	6-7	So.	Hartwell, GA
55	John Anderson	6-0	Sr.	Waterford, NY

COACH: Bones McKinney
ASSISTANTS: Jackie Murdock, Lefty Davis

All-America Teams

ASSOCIATED PRESS

FIRST TEAM: *Bill Bradley, Princeton; Cazzie Russell, Michigan; Rick Barry, Miami (Fla.); Gail Goodrich, UCLA; Fred Hetzel, Davidson; Wayne Estes, Utah State (posthumously). **SECOND TEAM:** Dave Stallworth, Wichita State; Clyde Lee, Vanderbilt; Bill Buntin, Michigan; Dave Schellhase, Purdue; Skip Thoren, Illinois. **THIRD TEAM: Billy Cunningham, North Carolina**; A.W. Davis, Tennessee; Keith Erickson, UCLA; John Austin, Boston College; Jim Walter, Providence.

UNITED PRESS INTERNATIONAL

FIRST TEAM: Cazzie Russell, Michigan; *Bill Bradley, Princeton; Rick Barry, Miami (Fla.); Gail Goodrich, UCLA; Fred Hetzel, Davidson; Wayne Estes, Utah State (posthumously). **SECOND TEAM: Billy Cunningham, North Carolina**; Dave Stallworth, Wichita State; Clyde Lee, Vanderbilt; Bill Buntin, Michigan; Dave Schellhase, Purdue. **THIRD TEAM:** Dick Van Arsdale, Indiana; A.W. Davis, Tennessee; Ollie Johnson, San Francisco; Skip Thoren, Illinois; Keith Erickson, UCLA.

*Player of the Year

Final Top 20 Polls

AP

1.	Michigan	24-4
2.	UCLA	28-2
3.	St. Joseph's	26-3
4.	Providence	24-2
5.	Vanderbilt	24-4
6.	Davidson	24-2
7.	Minnesota	19-5
8.	Villanova	23-5
9.	Brigham Young	21-7
10.	**Duke**	**20-5**

Others receiving votes, listed alphabetically: Connecticut, Dayton, Illinois, Miami (Fla.), Miami (Ohio), New Mexico, NYU, Notre Dame, **N.C. State**, Ohio University, Oklahoma State, Penn State, Princeton, San Francisco, Tennessee and Wichita State.

UPI

1.	Michigan	24-4
2.	UCLA	28-2
3.	St. Joseph's	26-3
4.	Providence	24-2
5.	Vanderbilt	24-4
6.	Brigham Young	21-7
7.	Davidson	24-2
8.	Minnesota	19-5
9.	**Duke**	**20-5**
10.	San Francisco	24-5
11.	Villanova	23-5
12.	**N.C. State**	**21-5**
13.	Oklahoma St.	20-7
14	Wichita State	21-9
15.	Connecticut	23-3
16.	Illinois	18-6
17.	Tennessee	20-5
18.	Indiana	19-5
19.	Miami (Fla.)	22-4
20.	Dayton	22-7

UCLA beat Michigan 91-80 for NCAA title.

ACC BASKETBALL / REFERENCE

'66

Duke's
Steve Vacendak

1965-66 Final Standings

Team	Conf.	Overall	Ave.	Opp.
*Duke	12-2	26-4	82.8	71.6
N.C. State	9-5	18-9	81.3	73.7
Clemson	8-6	15-10	76.9	73.4
North Carolina	8-6	16-11	80.9	74.3
Maryland	7-7	14-11	71.6	68.4
South Carolina	4-10	11-13	64.3	66.8
Virginia	4-10	7-15	73.5	77.7
Wake Forest	4-10	8-18	83.8	93.0

*Won ACC Tournament

NCAA— DUKE third in Final Four: beat St. Joseph's 76-74, beat Syracuse 91-81 in East Regional; lost to Kentucky 83-79, beat Utah 79-77 in Final Four.

ACC Tournament

MARCH 3-5, 1966 AT RALEIGH, N.C.

FIRST ROUND: South Carolina 60, Clemson 52; N.C. State 86, Virginia 77; Duke 103, Wake Forest 73; North Carolina 77, Maryland 70. **SEMIFINALS:** Duke 21, North Carolina 20; N.C. State 75, South Carolina 62. **FINAL:** Duke 71, N.C. State 66.

ALL-TOURNAMENT—FIRST TEAM: Eddie Biedenbach, N.C. State; Steve Vacendak, Duke; Tommy Mattocks, N.C. State; Bob Verga, Duke; Mike Lewis, Duke. **SECOND TEAM:** Skip Harlicka, South Carolina; Larry Miller, North Carolina; Jack Marin, Duke; Bob Riedy, Duke; Bob Lewis, North Carolina.

EVERETT CASE AWARD (MVP): Vacendak.

All-ACC

FIRST TEAM: Bob Lewis, North Carolina (191 votes); Jack Marin, Duke (187); Bob Verga, Duke (161); Eddie Biedenbach, N.C. State (128); Bob Leonard, Wake Forest (128). **SECOND TEAM:** Larry Miller, North Carolina (116); Pete Coker, N.C. State (111); Paul Long, Wake Forest (102); Steve Vacendak, Duke (98); Gary Ward, Maryland (82).

PLAYER OF THE YEAR: Vacendak (51); Marin (29); Lewis (19); Verga, Biedenbach, Ward, Miller, Leonard and Long also received votes.

COACH OF THE YEAR: Vic Bubas, Duke (76); Press Maravich, N.C. State (18); Bobby Roberts, Clemson (13).

Scoring, Rebounding Leaders

TOP TEN SCORERS

Player, School	G	FG	FT	TP	Ave.
Lewis, North Carolina	27	259	222	740	27.4
Long, Wake Forest	26	235	153	623	24.0
Leonard, Wake Forest	26	230	143	603	23.2
Miller, North Carolina	27	219	127	565	20.9
Connelly, Virginia	22	170	110	450	20.5
Helms, Clemson	25	209	62	480	19.2
Marin, Duke	30	221	116	558	18.9
Verga, Duke	28	216	87	519	18.5
Ward, Maryland	25	182	66	430	17.2
Sutherland, Clemson	24	155	91	401	16.7

TOP TEN REBOUNDERS

Player, School	G	Rbs.	Ave.
Lewis, Duke	30	329	11.0
Standard, South Carolina	24	255	10.6
Miller, North Carolina	27	277	10.3
Mahaffey, Clemson	25	256	10.2
Coker, N.C. State	27	268	9.9
Marin, Duke	30	292	9.7
Ward, Maryland	25	241	9.6
Gardner, Clemson	23	201	8.7
Riedy, Duke	29	224	7.7
Harrington, Maryland	15	110	7.3

Rosters

CLEMSON

No.	Name	Hgt.	Yr.	Hometown
10	Fred Steiner	6-2	Jr.	Pittsburgh, PA
12	Jimmy Sutherland	6-5	Jr.	Clemson, SC
15	Garry Helms	6-4	Sr.	Pelzer, SC
21	Dave Demsey	6-4	So.	West Homestead, PA
22	Tom Corcoran	6-5	Jr.	N. Charleston, SC
23	Rudy Antoncic	6-3	Sr.	McKeesport, PA
24	Hank Channell	6-5	Jr.	Warner Robins, GA
25	Denny Danko	6-3	So.	Pittsburgh, PA
32	Joe Ayoob	6-0	Jr.	Pittsburgh, PA
33	Sam Cohn	6-2	Jr.	Beckley, WV
35	Walt Ayers	6-5	Jr.	Turtle Creek, PA
40	Ken Gardner	6-5	Jr.	Collingswood, NJ
42	Randy Mahaffey	6-7	Jr.	La Grange, GA
44	Buddy Benedict	5-8	Sr.	Duquesne, PA
55	Curt Eckard	6-5	So.	Hildebran, NC

COACH: Bobby Roberts
ASSISTANT: Jim Brennan

DUKE

No.	Name	Hgt.	Yr.	Hometown
11	Bob Verga	6-0	Jr.	Sea Girt, NJ
12	Tony Barone	5-8	So.	Chicago, IL
14	Bill Zimmer	6-0	Sr.	Poland, OH
15	Bob Riedy	6-6	Jr.	Allentown, PA
21	Stuart McKaig	6-1	Jr.	Charlotte, NC
22	Ron Wendelin	6-1	So.	Peoria, IL
23	Dick Warren	5-11	So.	Charlotte, NC
24	Jack Marin	6-6	Sr.	Farrell, PA
31	Tim Kolodziej	6-5	So.	Amsterdam, NY
32	Jim Liccardo	6-5	Sr.	West Orange, NJ
33	Steve Vacendak	6-1	Sr.	Scranton, PA
35	Phil Allen	6-4	Sr.	Syracuse, NY
40	Joe Kennedy	6-6	So.	Bowie, MD
42	Mike Lewis	6-7	So.	Missoula, MT
54	Warren Chapman	6-8	So.	Hampton, VA

COACH: Vic Bubas
ASSISTANTS: Chuck Daly, Tom Carmody

MARYLAND

No.	Name	Hgt.	Yr.	Hometown
10	Bill Franklin	5-10	Sr.	Mt. Airy, MD
12	Mike DeCosmo	5-10	Sr.	Camden, NJ
14	Gary Williams	6-0	Jr.	Collingswood, NJ
20	Dick Mueller	6-2	Sr.	Independence, MO
22	Gary Ward	6-5	Sr.	Washington, DC
23	Don Brotman	6-3	Jr.	West Orange, NJ
25	John Avery	5-9	So.	Youngstown, OH
30	Billy Jones	6-1	So.	Towson, MD
33	Neil Brayton	6-4	Sr.	Youngstown, OH
44	Jack Clark	6-4	Sr.	Beverly, OH
45	Dick Drescher	6-4	So.	Cambridge, MD
50	Joe Harrington	6-5	Jr.	Phippsburg, ME
54	Jay McMillen	6-7	Jr.	Mansfield, PA
55	Rick Wise	6-8	Sr.	Wilmington, DE

COACH: Bud Millikan
ASSISTANT: Frank Fellows

NORTH CAROLINA

No.	Name	Hgt.	Yr.	Hometown
11	Ray Hassell	6-0	Sr.	Beaufort, NC
12	Jim Frye	6-5	So.	Homewood, IL
13	Mike Smith	6-0	Sr.	North Salem, IN
20	John Yokley	6-1	Sr.	Mt. Airy, NC
22	Bob Lewis	6-3	Jr.	Washington, DC
30	Greg Campbell	6-0	So.	Bayonne, NJ
31	Bob Bennett	6-8	Sr.	Mt. Lebanon, PA
32	Mark Mirken	6-6	Jr.	Brooklyn, NY
33	Jim Shackelford	6-1	So.	Wilson, NC
34	Jim Moore	6-3	Jr.	Wilmington, NC
35	Ralph Fletcher	6-5	So.	Arlington, VA
40	Donnie Moe	6-2	So.	Brooklyn, NY
41	Jim Smithwick	6-5	Sr.	Morehead City, NC
42	Tom Gauntlett	6-4	Jr.	Dallas, PA
43	Dickson Gribble	6-7	So.	Raleigh, NC
44	Larry Miller	6-3	So.	Catasauqua, PA

COACH: Dean Smith
ASSISTANTS: Larry Brown, John Lotz, Charlie Shaffer

N.C. STATE

No.	Name	Hgt.	Yr.	Hometown
10	Tommy Mattocks	6-2	Sr.	Kinston, NC
12	Larry Worsley	6-5	Sr.	Oak City, NC
14	Merv Gutshall	6-1	So.	Elkins, WV
20	Gary Hale	6-0	Sr.	Jeffersonville, IN
22	Billy Moffitt	5-11	Sr.	Fayetteville, NC
24	Paul Hudson	6-11	So.	Reidsville, NC
30	Hal Blondeau	6-4	Sr.	Glen Burnie, MD
32	Jerry Moore	6-7	Jr.	Moline, IL
34	Eddie Biedenbach	6-1	Jr.	Pittsburgh, PA
40	Sam Gealy	6-0	Jr.	New Castle, PA
44	Ray Hodgdon	6-4	Sr.	Arlington, VA
50	Bill Kretzer	6-7	So.	Springfield, NJ
52	John Sellers	6-8	So.	Lilesville, NC
54	Pete Coker	6-5	Sr.	Allentown, PA

COACH: Press Maravich
ASSISTANT: Charlie Bryant

SOUTH CAROLINA

No.	Name	Hgt.	Yr.	Hometown
13	Larry Womack	6-2	So.	West Columbia, SC
14	Jim Finnegan	5-10	Sr.	Rye, NY
15	Al Salvadori	6-9	Jr.	Beech Bottom, WV
20	John Schroeder	6-6	Sr.	Dundalk, MD
21	Bob Gorgrant	6-2	So.	Binghamton, NY
22	Charlie Farrell	6-0	Jr.	Columbia, SC
23	Frank Standard	6-4	So.	Brooklyn, NY
24	Skip Kickey	6-8	So.	Union City, NJ
31	Skip Harlicka	6-1	So.	Trenton, NJ
32	Earl Lovelace	6-0	Jr.	Kingsport, TN
44	Jack Thompson	6-0	So.	Brooklyn, NY
45	Bruce Wells	6-8	Jr.	River Edge, NJ
54	Lyn Burkholder	6-8	Jr.	Singers Glen, VA
55	John Fairclough	6-3	So.	Hackensack, NJ

COACH: Frank McGuire
ASSISTANTS: Buck Freeman, Donnie Walsh

VIRGINIA

No.	Name	Hgt.	Yr.	Hometown
3	Jeff Crackel	6-2	So.	Arlington, VA
10	Charles Johnson	6-7	So.	Narrows, VA
13	John Naponick	6-10	So.	Irwin, PA
20	John Lettice	5-10	So.	Washington, DC
22	Mike Smith	6-5	So.	Cary, NC
23	Jim Connelly	6-3	Jr.	Williamstown, WV
24	Greer Jackson	6-6	So.	Richmond, VA
25	Dale Hilsmier	6-2	Jr.	Fort Wayne, IN
33	Jerry Sanders	6-3	Sr.	Louisville, KY
35	Buddy Reams	6-4	So.	Richmond, VA
41	Mike Katos	6-5	So.	Lebanon, PA
42	Fred Stant	6-4	Jr.	Norfolk, VA
44	Jackson Mowday	6-1	So.	Wilmington, DE
51	Barry Koval	6-2	So.	Johnstown, PA
55	John Schroeder	6-8	So.	Wilmington, DE

COACH: Bill Gibson
ASSISTANT: Gene Mehaffey

WAKE FOREST

No.	Name	Hgt.	Yr.	Hometown
10	Harry Hutchins	6-0	Sr.	Trenton, NJ
11	Bill Joyner	6-0	Sr.	Asheboro, NC
12	Paul Long	6-2	Jr.	Louisville, KY
13	Dennis Moody	6-1	Jr.	Mt. Airy, NC
14	Clark Pool	6-4	Jr.	Washington, IL
15	Bob Leonard	6-3	Sr.	Kingsport, TN
20	Paul Crinkley	6-4	So.	Newland, NC
21	Roger Mayhew	6-3	So.	Lexington, NC
23	Newton Scott	6-6	Jr.	Winston-Salem, NC
25	Jimmy Snyder	6-6	Jr.	Lexington, NC
30	Bob Wills	6-2	Jr.	Springfield, VA
31	Jim Boshart	6-5	Jr.	Huntington Sta., NY
33	Sherrill Whitaker	6-7	Jr.	Hartwell, GA
34	David Stroupe	6-6	So.	Winston-Salem, NC
35	Larry Cain	6-1	So.	McLean, VA
44	Jimmy Broadway	6-4	So.	Raleigh, NC
55	Bill Owen	6-0	So.	Waynesville, NC

COACH: Jackie Murdock
ASSISTANTS: Billy Packer, Lefty Davis

All-America Teams

ASSOCIATED PRESS

FIRST TEAM: *Cazzie Russell, Michigan; Clyde Lee, Vanderbilt; Dave Schellhase, Purdue; Louie Dampier, Kentucky; Dave Bing, Syracuse. **SECOND TEAM:** Jimmy Walker, Providence; **Jack Marin, Duke; Bob Verga, Duke**; Dick Snyder, Davidson; Matt Goukas, St. Joseph's. **THIRD TEAM:** Walt Wesley, Kansas; Henry Finkel, Dayton; **Bob Lewis, North Carolina**; Thad Jaracz, Kentucky; Pat Riley, Kentucky.

UNITED PRESS INTERNATIONAL

FIRST TEAM: *Cazzie Russell, Michigan; Dave Schellhase, Purdue; Clyde Lee, Vanderbilt; Dave Bing, Syracuse; Jimmy Walker, Providence. **SECOND TEAM:** Louie Dampier, Kentucky; Matt Goukas, St. Joseph's; Walt Wesley, Kansas; Dick Snyder, Davidson; **Bob Verga, Duke. THIRD TEAM:** Pat Riley, Kentucky; Henry Finkel, Dayton; John Austin, Boston College; Lou Hudson, Minnesota; **Jack Marin, Duke.**

*Player of the Year

Final Top 20 Polls

AP			UPI		
1.	Kentucky	27-2	1.	Kentucky	27-2
2.	**Duke**	26-4	**2.**	**Duke**	**26-4**
3.	Texas Western	28-1	3.	Texas Western	28-1
4.	Kansas	23-4	4.	Kansas	23-4
5.	St. Joseph's	24-5	5.	Loyola (Ill.)	22-3
6.	Loyola (Ill.)	22-3	6.	St. Joseph's	24-5
7.	Cincinnati	21-7	7.	Michigan	18-8
8.	Vanderbilt	22-4	8.	Vanderbilt	22-4
9.	Michigan	18-8	9.	Cincinnati	21-7
10.	W. Kentucky	25-3	10.	Providence	22-5
			11.	Nebraska	20-5
			12.	Utah	23-8
			13.	Okla. City	24-4
			14	Houston	23-6
			15.	Oregon State	21-7
			16.	Syracuse	22-6
			17.	Pacific	22-6
			18.	Davidson	21-7
			19.	Brigham Young	20-5
				Dayton	23-6

Others receiving votes, listed alphabetically: Boston College, Bradley, Brigham Young, Colorado State, Davidson, Dayton, Houston, Michigan State, Nebraska, Oklahoma City, Oregon State, Pennsylvania, Rhode Island, San Francisco, SMU, Syracuse, Temple and Utah.

Texas Western beat Kentucky 72-65 for NCAA title.

ACC BASKETBALL / REFERENCE

'67

North Carolina's Larry Miller

1966-67 Final Standings

Team	Conf.	Overall	Ave.	Opp.
*North Carolina	12-2	26-6	82.2	71.2
Duke	9-3	18-9	82.8	76.1
South Carolina	8-4	16-7	73.1	64.6
Clemson	9-5	17-8	74.0	70.3
Maryland	5-9	11-14	65.0	65.1
Wake Forest	5-9	9-18	72.2	77.3
Virginia	4-10	9-17	78.0	82.3
N.C. State	2-12	7-19	64.3	69.2

*Won ACC Tournament

NCAA — NORTH CAROLINA fourth in Final Four: beat Princeton 78-70 (OT), beat Boston College 96-80 in East Regional; lost to Dayton 76-62, lost to Houston 84-62 in Final Four.
NIT — DUKE lost to Southern Illinois 72-63.

ACC Tournament

MARCH 9-11, 1967 AT GREENSBORO, N.C.
FIRST ROUND: South Carolina 57, Maryland 54; Duke 99, Virginia 78; North Carolina 56, N.C. State 53; Wake Forest 63, Clemson 61 (2 OT). **SEMIFINALS:** North Carolina 89, Wake Forest 79; Duke 69, South Carolina 66. **FINAL:** North Carolina 82, Duke 73.
ALL-TOURNAMENT — FIRST TEAM: Larry Miller, North Carolina; Bob Verga, Duke; Al Salvadori, South Carolina; Bob Lewis, North Carolina; Paul Long, Wake Forest. **SECOND TEAM:** Mike Lewis, Duke; Rusty Clark, North Carolina; Jack Thompson, South Carolina; Jerry Montgomery, Wake Forest; Randy Mahaffey, Clemson and Dick Grubar, North Carolina (tie).
EVERETT CASE AWARD (MVP): Miller.

All-ACC

FIRST TEAM: *Bob Verga, Duke (146 votes); Larry Miller, North Carolina (140); Bob Lewis, North Carolina (131); Paul Long, Wake Forest (131); Randy Mahaffey, Clemson (112). **SECOND TEAM:** Jim Connelly, Virginia (87); Mike Lewis, Duke (73); Jim Sutherland, Clemson (71); Jack Thompson, South Carolina (49); Gary Gregor, South Carolina (41).
PLAYER OF THE YEAR: Miller (52); Verga (48). **COACH OF THE YEAR:** Dean Smith, North Carolina (60); Bobby Roberts, Clemson (34).
*Unanimous Selection

Scoring, Rebounding Leaders

TOP TEN SCORERS

Player, School	G	FG	FT	TP	Ave.
Verga, Duke	27	283	139	705	26.1
Long, Wake Forest	27	235	132	602	22.3
Miller, North Carolina	32	278	144	700	21.9
Connelly, Virginia	26	185	151	521	20.0
Sutherland, Clemson	25	183	104	470	18.8
Lewis, North Carolina	32	212	167	591	18.5
Ra. Mahaffey, Clemson	25	155	109	419	16.3
Harlicka, South Carolina	23	150	85	385	16.7
Case, Virginia	26	157	113	427	16.4
McMillen, Maryland	24	146	100	392	16.3

TOP TEN REBOUNDERS

Player, School	G	Rbs.	Ave.
Gregor, South Carolina	23	305	13.3
M. Lewis, Duke	26	320	12.3
Standard, South Carolina	21	237	11.3
Clark, North Carolina	32	330	10.3
Miller, North Carolina	32	299	9.3
Ra. Mahaffey, Clemson	25	225	9.0
Reams, Virginia	26	223	8.6
McMillen, Maryland	24	195	8.1
Ri. Mahaffey, Clemson	25	196	7.8
Moore, N.C. State	23	174	7.6

Rosters

CLEMSON

No.	Name	Hgt.	Yr.	Hometown
10	Dick Thomas	6-3	So.	Warren, OH
12	Jimmy Sutherland	6-5	Sr.	Clemson, SC
14	Jack Swails	6-4	So.	Kingstree, SC
21	Dave Demsey	6-4	So.	W. Homestead, PA
22	Richie Mahaffey	6-7	So.	La Grange, GA
24	Hank Channell	6-5	Sr.	Warner Robins, GA
25	Denny Danko	6-3	So.	Pittsburgh, PA
32	Joe Ayoob	6-0	Sr.	Pittsburgh, PA
33	Trip Jones	6-5	So.	Great Falls, SC
35	Walt Ayers	6-5	Sr.	Turtle Creek, PA
40	Ken Gardner	6-5	Sr.	Collingswood, NJ
42	Randy Mahaffey	6-7	Sr.	La Grange, GA
44	Alan Goldfarb	5-9	So.	Miami Beach, FL
55	Curt Eckard	6-5	So.	Hildebran, NC

COACH: Bobby Roberts
ASSISTANT: Jim Brennan

DUKE

No.	Name	Hgt.	Yr.	Hometown
11	Bob Verga	6-0	Sr.	Sea Girt, NJ
12	Tony Barone	5-8	Jr.	Chicago, IL
15	Bob Riedy	6-6	Jr.	Allentown, PA
20	Dave Golden	6-0	So.	Pekin, IL
21	Stuart McKaig	6-1	Jr.	Charlotte, NC
22	Ron Wendelin	6-1	Jr.	Peoria, IL
23	C. B. Claiborne	6-2	So.	Danville, VA
31	Tim Kolodziej	6-5	Jr.	Amsterdam, NY
32	Jim Liccardo	6-5	Sr.	West Orange, NJ
40	Joe Kennedy	6-6	Jr.	Bowie, MD
42	Mike Lewis	6-7	Jr.	Missoula, MT
52	Steve Vandenberg	6-7	So.	Cresaptown, MD
53	Fred Lind	6-7	So.	Highland Park, IL
54	Warren Chapman	6-8	Jr.	Houston, TX
	Bob Francis			

COACH: Vic Bubas
ASSISTANTS: Chuck Daly, Tom Carmody

MARYLAND

No.	Name	Hgt.	Yr.	Hometown
10	Larry Brown	5-11	So.	Morristown, NJ
12	Mike DeCosmo	5-11	So.	Camden, NJ
14	Gary Williams	6-0	Sr.	Collingswood, NJ
22	Jon MacDonald	6-1	So.	Millinocket, ME
24	Pete Johnson	6-0	So.	Seat Pleasant, MD
25	John Avery	5-9	Jr.	Youngstown, OH
30	Billy Jones	6-1	Jr.	Towson, MD
32	Bob Koepke	6-2	So.	Hyattsville, MD
44	Jack Feeney	6-2	So.	Rye, NY
45	Dennis Veith	6-4	So.	Wheaton, MD
50	Joe Harrington	6-5	Sr.	Phippsburg, ME
53	Terry Truax	6-4	Jr.	Hancock, MD
54	Jay McMillen	6-7	Sr.	Mansfield, PA
55	Dick Drescher	6-4	Jr.	Cambridge, MD

COACH: Bud Millikan
ASSISTANTS: Frank Fellows, Jack Clark, Tom Davis

NORTH CAROLINA

No.	Name	Hgt.	Yr.	Hometown
11	Gerald Tuttle	6-0	So.	London, KY
12	Jim Frye	6-5	Jr.	Homewood, IL
13	Dick Grubar	6-3	So.	Schenectady, NY
22	Bob Lewis	6-3	Sr.	Washington, DC
30	Greg Campbell	6-0	Jr.	Bayonne, NJ
31	Bill Bunting	6-8	So.	New Bern, NC
32	Mark Mirken	6-6	Sr.	Brooklyn, NY
34	Jim Bostick	6-3	So.	Atlanta, GA
35	Ralph Fletcher	6-5	Jr.	Arlington, VA
40	Donnie Moe	6-2	Jr.	Brooklyn, NY
41	Joe Brown	6-5	So.	Valdese, NC
42	Tom Gauntlett	6-4	Sr.	Dallas, PA
43	Rusty Clark	6-10	So.	Fayetteville, NC
44	Larry Miller	6-3	Jr.	Catasauqua, PA

COACH: Dean Smith
ASSISTANTS: Larry Brown, John Lotz

N.C. STATE

No.	Name	Hgt.	Yr.	Hometown
10	Dick Braucher	6-4	So.	Kutztown, PA
12	Bruce Leith	6-6	So.	Havertown, PA
14	Merv Gutshall	6-1	Jr.	Elkins, WV
20	Jack Douglas	6-1	So.	Pittsburgh, PA
22	Nick Trifunovich	5-9	So.	East Chicago, IN
24	Paul Hudson	6-11	Jr.	Reidsville, NC
30	Bill Mavredes	6-4	So.	Richmond, VA
32	Jerry Moore	6-7	Sr.	Moline, IL
34	Eddie Biedenbach	6-1	Sr.	Pittsburgh, PA
40	Sam Gealy	6-0	Sr.	New Castle, PA
42	Bob Lewis	6-6	So.	Marion, NC
44	Joe Serdich	6-4	So.	Fairmont, WV
50	Bill Kretzer	6-7	Jr.	Springfield, NJ
54	Robert McLean	6-7	So.	Morehead City, NC

COACH: Norm Sloan
ASSISTANTS: Charlie Bryant

SOUTH CAROLINA

No.	Name	Hgt.	Yr.	Hometown
13	Larry Womack	6-2	Jr.	West Columbia, SC
15	Al Salvadori	6-9	Sr.	Beech Bottom, WV
21	Bob Gorgrant	6-3	Jr.	Binghampton, NY
22	Tom Farrell	6-4	Jr.	West Keansburg, NJ
23	Frank Standard	6-4	Jr.	Brooklyn, NY
24	Skip Kickey	6-8	Jr.	Union City, NJ
30	Bob Felter	6-7	So.	Westfield, NJ
31	Skip Harlicka	6-1	Jr.	Trenton, NJ
32	Earl Lovelace	6-0	Sr.	Kingsport, TN
40	Gary Gregor	6-7	Jr.	S. Charleston, WV
44	Jack Thompson	6-1	Jr.	Brooklyn, NY
54	Lyn Burkholder	6-8	Sr.	Singers Glen, VA

COACH: Frank McGuire
ASSISTANTS: Donnie Walsh, Buck Freeman

VIRGINIA

No.	Name	Hgt.	Yr.	Hometown
3	Chip Case	6-4	So.	Lockport, NY
13	John Naponick	6-10	Jr.	Irwin, PA
20	John Quinn	5-10	Jr.	Queens Village, NY
22	Mike Smith	6-5	Jr.	Cary, NC
23	Jim Connelly	6-3	Sr.	Williamstown, WV
24	Gary Laws	6-3	So.	Norfolk, VA
25	Sam Harvey	6-2	So.	Louisville, KY
33	Mike Eikenberry	6-6	So.	Peru, IN
35	Buddy Reams	6-4	Jr.	Richmond, VA
41	Mike Katos	6-5	Jr.	Lebanon, PA
42	Fred Stant	6-4	Sr.	Norfolk, VA
44	Norm Carmichael	6-10	Jr.	Washington, DC
51	Barry Koval	6-2	So.	Johnstown, PA
55	John Gidding	6-7	Jr.	Norfolk, VA

COACH: Bill Gibson
ASSISTANT: Gene Mehaffey

WAKE FOREST

No.	Name	Hgt.	Yr.	Hometown
10	Jay Randall	6-2	So.	Kinston, NC
11	Jerry Montgomery	6-0	So.	Charlton Hghts., WV
12	Paul Long	6-2	Sr.	Louisville, KY
13	Mickey Bertram	5-11	So.	Beaufort, NC
20	Paul Crinkley	6-4	Jr.	Newland, NC
23	Newton Scott	6-6	Sr.	Winston-Salem, NC
25	Jimmy Snyder	6-6	Sr.	Lexington, NC
30	Bob Wills	6-2	Sr.	Springfield, VA
31	Jim Boshart	6-5	Sr.	Huntington Sta., NY
33	Sherrill Whitaker	6-7	Sr.	Hartwell, GA
34	David Stroupe	6-6	Jr.	Winston-Salem, NC
44	Jimmy Broadway	6-4	Jr.	Raleigh, NC

COACH: Jack McCloskey
ASSISTANTS: Billy Packer, Neil Johnston

All-America Teams

ASSOCIATED PRESS

FIRST TEAM: *Lew Alcindor, UCLA; Jimmy Walker, Providence; Wes Unseld, Louisville; Clem Haskins, Western Kentucky; Elvin Hayes, Houston. **SECOND TEAM: Bob Verga, Duke**; Ron Widby, Vanderbilt; Bob Lloyd, Rutgers; **Larry Miller, North Carolina**; Louie Dampier, Kentucky. **THIRD TEAM:** Butch Beard, Louisville; Sonny Dove, St. John's; Mel Daniels, New Mexico; Jim Burns, Northwestern; David Lattin, Texas Western.

UNITED PRESS INTERNATIONAL

FIRST TEAM: *Lew Alcindor, UCLA; Jimmy Walker, Providence; Wes Unseld, Louisville; Elvin Hayes, Houston; Bob Lloyd, Rutgers. **SECOND TEAM: Bob Verga, Duke**; Clem Haskins, Western Kentucky; Mel Daniels, New Mexico; Butch Beard, Louisville; Sonny Dove, St. John's. **THIRD TEAM: Larry Miller, North Carolina**; Mal Graham, NYU; Ron Widby, Tennessee; Louie Dampier, Kentucky; Don May, Dayton.
*Player of the Year

Final Top 20 Polls

AP

1.	UCLA	30-0
2.	Louisville	23-5
3.	Kansas	23-4
4.	**North Carolina**	**26-6**
5.	Princeton	25-3
6.	W. Kentucky	23-3
7.	Houston	27-4
8.	Tennessee	21-7
9.	Boston Col.	21-3
10.	Texas Western	22-6

Others receiving votes, listed alphabetically: Dayton, Florida, Gonzaga, Indiana, Marshall, Providence, St. John's, SMU, Syracuse, Toledo, Tulsa, Pacific, Utah State, Vanderbilt, Villanova, Washington State, West Virginia and Wyoming.

UPI

1.	UCLA	30-0
2.	Louisville	23-5
3.	**North Carolina**	**26-6**
4.	Kansas	23-4
5.	Princeton	25-3
6.	Houston	27-4
7.	W. Kentucky	23-3
8.	Texas Western	22-6
9.	Tennessee	21-7
10.	Boston Col.	21-3
11.	Toledo	23-2
12.	St. John's	23-5
13.	Tulsa	19-8
14.	Vanderbilt	21-5
	Utah State	20-6
16.	Pacific	24-4
17.	Providence	21-7
18.	New Mexico	19-8
19.	**Duke**	**18-9**
20.	Florida	21-4

UCLA beat Dayton 79-64 for NCAA title.

ACC BASKETBALL / REFERENCE

'68

North Carolina's Larry Miller

1967-68 Final Standings

Team	Conf.	Overall	Ave.	Opp.
*North Carolina	12-2	28-4	83.8	72.4
Duke	11-3	22-6	79.0	67.5
N.C. State	9-5	16-10	70.8	65.8
South Carolina	9-5	15-7	79.0	69.8
Virginia	5-9	9-16	79.8	86.6
Maryland	4-10	8-16	68.8	73.9
Clemson	3-11	4-20	71.5	82.2
Wake Forest	3-11	5-21	70.7	78.5

*Won ACC Tournament

NCAA—NORTH CAROLINA second in Final Four: beat St. Bonaventure 91-72, beat Davidson 70-66 in East Regional; beat Ohio State 80-66, lost to UCLA 78-55 in Final Four. **NIT**—DUKE beat Oklahoma City 97-81, lost to St. Peter's 100-71.

ACC Tournament
MARCH 7-9, 1968 AT CHARLOTTE, N.C.
FIRST ROUND: N.C. State 63, Maryland 54; Duke 43, Clemson 40; North Carolina 83, Wake Forest 70; South Carolina 101, Virginia 78. **SEMIFINALS:** North Carolina 82, South Carolina 79 (OT); N.C. State 12, Duke 10. **FINAL:** North Carolina 87, N.C. State 50.
ALL-TOURNAMENT—FIRST TEAM: Larry Miller, North Carolina; Gary Gregor, South Carolina; Dick Grubar, North Carolina; Jack Thompson, South Carolina; Skip Harlicka, South Carolina. **SECOND TEAM:** Charlie Scott, North Carolina; Rusty Clark, North Carolina; Eddie Biedenbach, N.C. State; Vann Williford, N.C. State; Mike Lewis, Duke.
EVERETT CASE AWARD (MVP): Miller.

All-ACC
FIRST TEAM: *Mike Lewis, Duke (190 votes); *Larry Miller, North Carolina (190); Charlie Scott, North Carolina (166); Skip Harlicka, South Carolina (159); Eddie Biedenbach, N.C. State (150). **SECOND TEAM:** Butch Zatezalo, Clemson (102); Rusty Clark, North Carolina (94); Gary Gregor, South Carolina (92); Frank Standard, South Carolina (49); Mike Katos, Virginia (37).
PLAYER OF THE YEAR: Miller (76); Lewis (34). **COACH OF THE YEAR:** Dean Smith, North Carolina (47); Vic Bubas, Duke (22); Frank McGuire, South Carolina (22); Norm Sloan, N.C. State (21).
*Unanimous Selection

Scoring, Rebounding Leaders

TOP TEN SCORERS

Player, School	G	FG	FT	TP	Ave.
Zatezalo, Clemson	24	189	174	552	23.0
Miller, North Carolina	32	268	181	717	22.4
Harlicka, South Carolina	22	198	84	480	21.8
Lewis, Duke	28	230	148	608	21.7
Katos, Virginia	25	183	107	463	18.5
Gregor, South Carolina	22	169	55	393	17.9
Kinn, Virginia	25	197	48	442	17.8
Scott, North Carolina	32	234	94	562	17.6
Walker, Wake Forest	26	173	101	447	17.2
Mahaffey, Clemson	24	117	165	399	16.6

TOP TEN REBOUNDERS

Player, School	G	Rbs.	Ave.
Lewis, Duke	28	402	14.4
Gregor, South Carolina	22	269	12.2
Carmichael, Virginia	25	300	12.0
Mahaffey, Clemson	24	276	11.5
Wilkes, Virginia	25	276	11.0
Clark, North Carolina	31	341	11.0
Standard, South Carolina	22	228	10.4
Jones, Clemson	24	230	9.6
Katos, Virginia	25	223	8.9
Drescher, Maryland	24	202	8.4

Rosters

CLEMSON
No.	Name	Hgt.	Yr.	Hometown
10	Dick Thomas	6-3	Jr.	Warren, OH
15	Jack Swails	6-4	Jr.	Kingstree, SC
21	Dave Demsey	6-4	Jr.	W. Homestead, PA
22	Richie Mahaffey	6-7	Sr.	La Grange, GA
23	Mike Faer	6-0	So.	West Mifflin, PA
25	Denny Danko	6-3	Jr.	Pittsburgh, PA
32	Butch Zatezalo	5-11	So.	Aliquippa, PA
33	Trip Jones	6-5	Jr.	Great Falls, SC
44	Alan Goldfarb	5-9	Jr.	Miami Beach, FL
55	Curt Eckard	6-5	Jr.	Hildebran, NC

COACH: Bobby Roberts
ASSISTANT: Jim Brennan

DUKE
No.	Name	Hgt.	Yr.	Hometown
12	Tony Barone	5-8	Sr.	Chicago, IL
20	Dave Golden	6-0	Jr.	Pekin, IL
22	Ron Wendelin	6-1	Sr.	Peoria, IL
23	C.B. Claiborne	6-2	So.	Danville, VA
31	Tim Kolodziej	6-5	Sr.	Amsterdam, NY
33	Doug Jackson	6-5	So.	Overland Park, KS
34	Tim Teer	6-3	So.	Hillsborough, NC
40	Joe Kennedy	6-6	Sr.	Bowie, MD
41	Ray Kuhlmeier	6-2	So.	Aurora, IN
42	Mike Lewis	6-7	Sr.	Missoula, MT
43	John Posen	6-2	So.	Cicero, IL
50	Glen Smiley	6-6	So.	Bozeman, MT
52	Steve Vandenberg	6-7	Jr.	Cresaptown, MD
53	Fred Lind	6-7	Jr.	Highland Park, IL
54	Warren Chapman	6-8	Sr.	Houston, TX

COACH: Vic Bubas
ASSISTANTS: Chuck Daly, Tom Carmody

MARYLAND
No.	Name	Hgt.	Yr.	Hometown
10	Larry Brown	5-11	Jr.	Morristown, NJ
12	Tom Yoho	5-11	Jr.	Pittsburgh, PA
20	John Prebula	6-4	So.	Greenville, PA
22	Jon MacDonald	6-1	Jr.	Millinocket, ME
24	Pete Johnson	6-0	Jr.	Seat Pleasant, MD
25	John Avery	5-9	Sr.	Youngstown, OH
30	Billy Jones	6-1	Sr.	Towson, MD
32	Bill Siebenaler	6-6	So.	Toledo, OH
40	Bill Sullivan	6-4	So.	East Orange, NJ
42	Gene Labonia	6-5	Jr.	Elizabeth, NJ
52	Will Hetzel	6-6	So.	Washington, DC
53	Tom Milroy	6-3	So.	Richwood, WV
54	Rod Horst	6-6	So.	Hagerstown, MD
55	Dick Drescher	6-4	Sr.	Cambridge, MD
53	Homer Warren	6-6	So.	Youngstown, OH

COACH: Frank Fellows
ASSISTANTS: Tom Young, Tom Davis

NORTH CAROLINA
No.	Name	Hgt.	Yr.	Hometown
11	Gerald Tuttle	6-0	Jr.	London, KY
12	Jim Frye	6-5	Sr.	Homewood, IL
13	Dick Grubar	6-3	Jr.	Schenectady, NY
20	Eddie Fogler	5-11	So.	Flushing, NY
22	Jim Delany	5-11	So.	South Orange, NJ
30	Al Armour	6-3	So.	Holland, IL
31	Bill Bunting	6-8	Jr.	New Bern, NC
32	Jim Folds	6-2	So.	Greensboro, NC
33	Charlie Scott	6-4	So.	New York, NY
34	Hall Pollard	6-2	So.	Burlington, NC
35	Ralph Fletcher	6-6	So.	Wakefield, VA
40	Ricky Webb	6-3	So.	Greenville, NC
41	Joe Brown	6-5	Jr.	Valdese, NC
42	Gra Whiteheac	6-4	So.	Scotland Neck, NC
43	Rusty Clark	6-10	Jr.	Fayetteville, NC
44	Larry Miller	6-3	Sr.	Catasauqua, PA

COACH: Dean Smith
ASSISTANTS: John Lotz, Bill Guthridge

N.C. STATE
No.	Name	Hgt.	Yr.	Hometown
10	Dick Braucher	6-4	Jr.	Kutztown, PA
14	Vann Williford	6-6	So.	Fayetteville, NC
20	Jack Douglas	6-1	Jr.	Pittsburgh, PA
22	Nick Trifunovich	5-9	So.	East Chicago, IN
30	Bill Mavredes	6-4	Jr.	Richmond, VA
32	Dale Abernathy	6-3	So.	Hildebran, NC
34	Eddie Biedenbach	6-2	Sr.	Pittsburgh, PA
40	Nelson Isley	6-4	So.	Reidsville, NC
42	Tom Smith	6-4	So.	Albemarle, NC
44	Joe Serdich	6-4	Jr.	Fairmont, WV
50	Bill Kretzer	6-7	Sr.	Springfield, NJ
52	Drago Trifunovich	6-4	So.	East Chicago, IN
54	Robert McLean	6-8	Jr.	Morehead City, NC

COACH: Norm Sloan
ASSISTANTS: Charlie Bryant, Sam Esposito

SOUTH CAROLINA
No.	Name	Hgt.	Yr.	Hometown
15	Clyde Lewellen	6-8	So.	Dayton, OH
21	Bobby Cremins	6-2	So.	The Bronx, NY
22	Tommy Terry	6-2	So.	Columbia, SC
23	Frank Standard	6-4	Sr.	Brooklyn, NY
24	Skip Kickey	6-8	Sr.	Union City, NJ
25	Gene Spencer	6-7	So.	Charleston, SC
30	Bob Felter	6-7	Jr.	Westfield, NJ
31	Skip Harlicka	6-1	Sr.	Trenton, NJ
32	Corky Carnevale	6-3	So.	Norwood, NJ
33	Charlie Vacca	6-3	So.	New York, NY
34	Hank Martin	5-9	So.	Columbia, SC
40	Gary Gregor	6-7	Sr.	S. Charleston, WV
42	Eddie Powell	6-0	So.	The Bronx, NY
44	Jack Thompson	6-5	Sr.	Brooklyn, NY

COACH: Frank McGuire
ASSISTANTS: Buck Freeman, Bill Loving, Donnie Walsh

VIRGINIA
No.	Name	Hgt.	Yr.	Hometown
3	Tony Kinn	6-0	So.	Harrisburg, PA
10	Chip Case	6-4	Jr.	Lockport, NY
13	John Naponick	6-10	Sr.	Irwin, PA
20	John English	6-2	So.	Newport News, VA
22	John Gidding	6-7	Jr.	Norfolk, VA
24	Gary Laws	6-3	Jr.	Norfolk, VA
25	Tom Joyce	6-2	So.	Huntington Sta., NY
33	Mike Eikenberry	6-6	Jr.	Peru, IN
35	Buddy Reams	6-5	Jr.	Richmond, VA
41	Mike Katos	6-5	Sr.	Lebanon, PA
42	Mike Wilkes	6-5	So.	Dallas, PA
44	Norm Carmichael	6-10	Jr.	Washington, DC
51	Barry Koval	6-2	Sr.	Johnstown, PA
55	Bob Cascella	6-4	Sr.	Pittsburgh, PA

COACH: Bill Gibson
ASSISTANT: Chip Connor

WAKE FOREST
No.	Name	Hgt.	Yr.	Hometown
10	Jay Randall	6-2	Jr.	Kinston, NC
11	Jerry Montgomery	6-0	Jr.	Charlton Hghts., WV
12	David Smith	5-10	So.	Raleigh, NC
14	Tommy Lynch	5-11	So.	Barrington, IL
20	Paul Crinkley	6-4	Sr.	Newland, NC
21	Steve Bierly	6-3	So.	Wayne, PA
22	Norwood Todmann	6-3	So.	New York, NY
23	Newton Scott	6-6	Sr.	Winston-Salem, NC
25	Clark Pool	6-3	Sr.	Washington, IL
30	Dan Ackley	6-8	So.	Liverpool, NY
32	Jimmy Broadway	6-4	Sr.	Raleigh, NC
33	Dickie Walker	6-3	So.	Williamsburg, VA
34	David Stroupe	6-6	Sr.	Winston-Salem, NC
35	Larry Habegger	6-7	So.	New Augusta, IN

COACH: Jack McCloskey
ASSISTANTS: Billy Packer, Neil Johnston

All-America Teams
ASSOCIATED PRESS
FIRST TEAM: *Elvin Hayes, Houston; Lew Alcindor, UCLA; Wes Unseld, Louisville; Pete Maravich, LSU; **Larry Miller, North Carolina**. **SECOND TEAM:** Calvin Murphy, Niagara; Bob Lanier, St. Bonaventure; Neal Walk, Florida; Lucius Allen, UCLA; Don May, Dayton. **THIRD TEAM:** Jo Jo White, Kansas; Mike Warren, UCLA; Rick Mount, Purdue; **Mike Lewis, Duke**; Sam Williams, Iowa.

UNITED PRESS INTERNATIONAL
FIRST TEAM: *Elvin Hayes, Houston; Lew Alcindor, UCLA; Wes Unseld, Louisville; Pete Maravich, LSU; Calvin Murphy, Niagara. **SECOND TEAM:** Bob Lanier, St. Bonaventure; Rick Mount, Purdue; **Larry Miller, North Carolina**; Don May, Dayton; Lucius Allen, UCLA. **THIRD TEAM:** Jim McMillan, Columbia; Neal Walk, Florida; Mike Warren, UCLA; **Mike Lewis, Duke**; Jo Jo White, Kansas.
*Player of the Year

Final Top 20 Polls

AP		UPI	
1. Houston	31-2	1. Houston	31-2
2. UCLA	29-1	2. UCLA	29-1
3. St. Bonaventure	23-2	3. St. Bonaventure	23-2
4. **North Carolina**	**28-4**	4. **North Carolina**	**28-4**
5. Kentucky	22-5	5. Kentucky	22-5
6. New Mexico	23-5	6. Columbia	23-5
7. Columbia	23-5	7. New Mexico	23-5
8. Davidson	24-5	8. Louisville	21-7
9. Louisville	21-7	9. Davidson	24-5
10. **Duke**	**22-6**	10. Marquette	23-6
		11. **Duke**	**22-6**
		12. New Mexico St.	23-6
Other receiving votes, listed alphabetically: Army, Dayton, Georgia, Kansas, Kansas State, Marquette, Marshall, New Mexico State, Ohio State, Princeton, Santa Clara, **South Carolina** and Tennessee.		13. Vanderbilt	20-6
		14. Kansas State	19-9
		15. Princeton	20-6
		16. Army	20-5
		17. Santa Clara	22-4
		18. Utah	17-9
		19. Bradley	19-9
		20. Iowa	16-9

UCLA beat North Carolina 78-55 for NCAA title.

ACC BASKETBALL / REFERENCE

'69

South Carolina's John Roche

1968-69 Final Standings

Team	Conf.	Overall	Ave.	Opp.
*North Carolina	12-2	27-5	88.9	75.7
South Carolina	11-3	21-7	70.8	64.5
Wake Forest	8-6	18-9	86.1	79.2
N.C. State	8-6	15-10	71.5	69.3
Duke	8-6	15-13	82.0	79.4
Virginia	5-9	10-15	79.3	83.6
Maryland	2-12	8-18	78.8	84.2
Clemson	2-12	6-19	78.8	85.8

*Won ACC Tournament

NCAA—NORTH CAROLINA fourth in Final Four: beat Duquesne 79-78, beat Davidson 87-85 in East Regional; lost to Purdue 92-65, lost to Drake 104-84 in Final Four.
NIT—SOUTH CAROLINA beat Southern Illinois 82-63, lost to Army 59-45.

ACC Tournament
MARCH 6-8, 1969 AT CHARLOTTE, N.C.
FIRST ROUND: Duke 99, Virginia 86; South Carolina 92, Maryland 71; North Carolina 94, Clemson 70; Wake Forest 81, N.C. State 73. **SEMIFINALS:** North Carolina 80, Wake Forest 72; Duke 68, South Carolina 59. **FINAL:** North Carolina 85, Duke 74.
ALL-TOURNAMENT—FIRST TEAM: Charlie Scott, North Carolina; Charlie Davis, Wake Forest; Dick DeVenzio, Duke; Steve Vandenberg, Duke; John Roche, South Carolina. **SECOND TEAM:** Jerry Montgomery, Wake Forest; Bill Bunting, North Carolina; Dave Golden, Duke; Dick Grubar, North Carolina; Vann Williford, N.C. State.
EVERETT CASE AWARD (MVP): Scott.

All-ACC
FIRST TEAM: *John Roche, South Carolina (176 votes); Charlie Scott, North Carolina (171); Bill Bunting, North Carolina (143); Vann Williford, N.C. State (141); Charlie Davis, Wake Forest (128). **SECOND TEAM:** Butch Zatezalo, Clemson (117); Tom Owens, Maryland (105); Will Hetzel, Maryland (90); Dick Grubar, North Carolina (79); Randy Denton, Duke (67).
PLAYER OF THE YEAR: Roche (56); Scott (39); Zatezalo, Bunting and Williford also received votes. **COACH OF THE YEAR:** Frank McGuire, South Carolina (78); Dean Smith, North Carolina (22).
*Unanimous Selection

Scoring, Rebounding Leaders
TOP TEN SCORERS

Player, School	G	FG	FT	TP	Ave.
Zatezalo, Clemson	25	228	189	645	25.8
Roche, South Carolina	28	239	184	662	23.6
Hetzel, Maryland	26	233	139	605	23.3
Davis, Wake Forest	27	211	194	616	22.8
Scott, North Carolina	32	290	134	714	22.3
Williford, N.C. State	25	204	132	540	21.6
Bunting, North Carolina	32	217	143	577	18.0
Denton, Duke	28	212	62	486	17.4
Owens, South Carolina	28	177	106	460	16.4
Wilkes, Virginia	24	153	71	377	15.7

TOP TEN REBOUNDERS

Player, School	G	Rbs.	Ave.
Owens, South Carolina	28	363	13.0
Denton, Duke	28	358	12.8
Hetzel, Maryland	26	318	12.2
McGregor, Wake Forest	27	323	12.0
Gidding, Virginia	24	268	11.2
Williford, N.C. State	25	250	10.0
Ribock, South Carolina	28	263	9.3
Clark, North Carolina	28	258	9.2
Wilkes, Virginia	24	219	9.1
Horst, Maryland	26	229	8.8

Rosters

CLEMSON
No.	Name	Hgt.	Yr.	Hometown
10	Dick Thomas	6-3	Sr.	Warren, OH
11	Dickie Foster	6-6	So.	Enka, NC
12	John Coakley	6-2	So.	Clemson, SC
14	Dave Thomas	6-1	So.	Warren, OH
15	Jack Swails	6-4	Sr.	Kingtree, SC
20	Ronnie Yates	6-4	Jr.	Anderson, SC
21	Dave Demsey	6-4	Sr.	W. Homestead, PA
22	Richie Mahaffey	6-7	Sr.	La Grange, GA
24	Mike Faer	6-0	Sr.	West Mifflin, PA
31	Paul Holzshu	6-5	So.	Pitcairn, PA
32	Butch Zatezalo	5-11	Jr.	Aliquippa, PA
33	Trip Jones	6-5	Sr.	Great Falls, SC
34	Alan Goldfarb	5-9	Sr.	Miami Beach, FL
44	Pete Weddell	6-6	So.	Goshen, IN
50	Curt Eckard	6-5	Sr.	Hildebran, NC

COACH: Bobby Roberts
ASSISTANTS: Jim Brennan, Art Musselman

DUKE
No.	Name	Hgt.	Yr.	Hometown
20	Dave Golden	6-0	Sr.	Pekin, IL
21	Dick DeVenzio	5-10	So.	Springdale, PA
22	Rick Katherman	6-7	So.	Manchester, MA
23	C. B. Claiborne	6-2	Sr.	Danville, VA
31	Randy Denton	6-10	So.	Raleigh, NC
32	Brad Evans	6-3	So.	Durham, NC
33	Doug Jackson	6-5	Jr.	Overland Park, KS
34	Tim Teer	6-3	Jr.	Hillsborough, NC
40	Steve Litz	6-5	So.	Pittsburgh, PA
41	Ray Kuhlmeier	6-2	Jr.	Aurora, IN
43	John Posen	6-2	Jr.	Cicero, IL
50	Glen Smiley	6-6	Jr.	Bozeman, MT
52	Steve Vandenberg	6-7	Sr.	Cresaptown, MD
53	Fred Lind	6-7	Sr.	Highland Park, IL
54	Warren Chapman	6-8	Sr.	Houston, TX

COACH: Vic Bubas
ASSISTANTS: Chuck Daly, Hubie Brown

MARYLAND
No.	Name	Hgt.	Yr.	Hometown
10	Larry Brown	5-11	Sr.	Morristown, NJ
15	Mickey Wiles	5-11	Jr.	Chillum, MD
20	John Prebula	6-4	Jr.	Greenville, PA
22	Jon MacDonald	6-1	Sr.	Millinocket, ME
24	Pete Johnson	6-5	Sr.	Seat Pleasant, MD
25	Roger Montgomery	6-0	So.	Charlton Hghts., WV
30	Tommy Findreng	6-4	So.	Elkhorn, WI
33	Tom Milroy	6-3	Jr.	Richwood, WV
40	Bill Sullivan	6-4	Jr.	East Orange, NJ
44	Chuck Worthington	6-6	So.	Trenton, NJ
50	Will Hetzel	6-7	Jr.	Washington, DC
53	Homer Warren	6-6	Jr.	Youngstown, OH
54	Rod Horst	6-6	Jr.	Hagerstown, MD
55	Dick Stobaugh	6-7	So.	Burlington,

COACH: Frank Fellows
ASSISTANTS: Tom Young, Tom Davis

NORTH CAROLINA
No.	Name	Hgt.	Yr.	Hometown
11	Gerald Tuttle	5-11	Sr.	London, KY
12	Richard Tuttle	6-0	So.	London, KY
13	Dick Grubar	6-4	Sr.	Schenectady, NY
20	Eddie Fogler	5-11	Jr.	Flushing, NY
22	Jim Delany	5-11	Jr.	South Orange, NJ
30	Dale Gipple	6-0	So.	Burlington, NC
31	Bill Bunting	6-8	Sr.	New Bern, NC
32	Dave Chadwick	6-7	So.	Orlando, FL
33	Charlie Scott	6-5	Jr.	New York, NY
34	Don Eggleston	6-8	So.	Charlotte, NC
35	Lee Dedmon	6-10	So.	Baltimore, MD
40	Ricky Webb	6-4	Sr.	Greenville, NC
41	Joe Brown	6-5	Sr.	Valdese, NC
43	Rusty Clark	6-10	Sr.	Fayetteville, NC

COACH: Dean Smith
ASSISTANTS: John Lotz, Bill Guthridge

All-America Teams
ASSOCIATED PRESS
FIRST TEAM: *Lew Alcindor, UCLA; Pete Maravich, LSU; Spencer Haywood, Detroit; Rick Mount, Purdue; Calvin Murphy, Niagara. **SECOND TEAM:** Charlie Scott, North Carolina; Jo Jo White, Kansas; Mike Maloy, Davidson; Bob Lanier, St. Bonaventure; Dan Issel, Kentucky. **THIRD TEAM:** Neal Walk, Florida; Bobby Smith, Tulsa; Howard Porter, Villanova; Dave Scholz, Illinois; Dave Sorenson, Ohio State.

UNITED PRESS INTERNATIONAL
FIRST TEAM: *Lew Alcindor, UCLA; Pete Maravich, LSU; Rick Mount, Purdue; Spencer Haywood, Detroit; Calvin Murphy, Niagara. **SECOND TEAM:** Charlie Scott, North Carolina; Jo Jo White, Kansas; Bob Lanier, St. Bonaventure; Mike Maloy, Davidson; Bud Ogden, Santa Clara. **THIRD TEAM:** Dan Issel, Kentucky; Neal Walk, Florida; Howard Porter, Villanova; Butch Beard, Louisville; Jim McMillan, Columbia.
*Player of the Year

N.C. STATE
No.	Name	Hgt.	Yr.	Hometown
10	Dick Braucher	6-4	Sr.	Kutztown, PA
14	Vann Williford	6-6	Jr.	Fayetteville, NC
24	Rick Anheuser	6-6	Jr.	Milwaukee, WI
30	Bill Mavredes	6-4	Sr.	Richmond, VA
32	Al Heartley	6-0	So.	Clayton, NC
34	Jim Risinger	6-1	So.	Richmond, IN
40	Nelson Isley	6-4	Sr.	Reidsville, NC
42	Dan Wells	6-6	So.	Windsor, CT
44	Joe Serdich	6-4	Sr.	Fairmont, WV
50	Doug Tilley	6-7	So.	Bethseda, MD
52	Joe Dunning	5-11	So.	Wilmington, DE

COACH: Norm Sloan
ASSISTANTS: Charlie Bryant, Sam Esposito

SOUTH CAROLINA
No.	Name	Hgt.	Yr.	Hometown
10	John Roche	6-2	So.	New York, NY
11	Billy Walsh	6-0	So.	Mamaroneck, NY
21	Bobby Cremins	6-2	Jr.	The Bronx, NY
22	Tommy Terry	6-2	Jr.	Columbia, SC
23	Dennis Powell	6-0	So.	The Bronx, NY
25	Gene Spencer	6-8	Jr.	Charleston, SC
31	Pat Clark	6-1	Sr.	Pittston, PA
32	Corky Carnevale	6-3	Jr.	Norwood, NJ
33	Charlie Vacca	6-3	Jr.	New York, NY
34	Hank Martin	5-9	Jr.	Columbia, SC
40	Tom Owens	6-10	So.	New York, NY
41	John Ribock	6-8	So.	Augusta, GA

COACH: Frank McGuire
ASSISTANTS: Buck Freeman, Bill Loving, Donnie Walsh

VIRGINIA
No.	Name	Hgt.	Yr.	Hometown
3	Tony Kinn	6-0	Jr.	Harrisburg, PA
10	Chip Case	6-4	Sr.	Lockport, NY
13	Kevin Kennelly	5-11	So.	Charlotte, NC
20	John English	6-2	Jr.	Newport News, VA
22	John Gidding	6-7	Jr.	Norfolk, VA
23	Bill Fulton	6-4	So.	Arlington, VA
24	Bill Gerry	6-7	So.	New York, NY
25	Tom Joyce	6-2	Jr.	Huntington Sta., NY
30	John Hill	6-0	So.	Fort Monroe, VA
33	Bill Creason	6-2	So.	Louisville, KY
35	Buddy Reams	6-5	Jr.	Richmond, VA
42	Mike Wilkes	6-5	Jr.	Dallas, PA
44	Norm Carmichael	6-10	Sr.	Washington, DC
51	Bob Galione	6-6	So.	Harrison, NY
55	Joe Morahan	6-4	So.	Lake Ariel, PA

COACH: Bill Gibson
ASSISTANTS: Chip Connor, Dick DiBiaso

WAKE FOREST
No.	Name	Hgt.	Yr.	Hometown
10	Jay Randall	6-2	Sr.	Kinston, NC
11	Jerry Montgomery	6-0	Sr.	Charlton Hghts., WV
12	Charlie Davis	6-1	So.	New York, NY
20	Bo DuBose	6-3	So.	Athens, GA
21	Tommy Lynch	5-11	Sr.	Barrington, IL
22	Norwood Todmann	6-3	Jr.	New York, NY
23	Dan Ackley	6-8	Jr.	Liverpool, NY
30	Bob Rhoads	6-3	So.	Mercer, PA
31	Gilbert McGregor	6-7	So.	Raeford, NC
32	Neil Pastushok	6-4	So.	Roselle Park, NJ
33	Dickie Walker	6-3	Jr.	Williamsburg, VA
34	Larry Habegger	6-7	Jr.	New Augusta, IN

COACH: Jack McCloskey
ASSISTANTS: Billy Packer, Neil Johnston

Final Top 20 Polls

AP
1. UCLA	29-1
2. La Salle	23-1
3. Santa Clara	27-2
4. North Carolina	27-5
5. Davidson	26-3
6. Purdue	23-5
7. Kentucky	23-5
8. St. John's	23-6
9. Duquesne	21-5
10. Villanova	21-5
11. Drake	26-5
12. New Mexico St.	24-5
13. S. Carolina	21-7
14. Marquette	24-5
15. Louisville	21-6
16. Boston Col.	24-4
17. Notre Dame	20-7
18. Colorado	21-7
19. Kansas	20-7
20. Illinois	19-5

UPI
1. UCLA	29-1
2. North Carolina	27-5
3. Davidson	26-3
4. Santa Clara	27-2
5. Kentucky	23-5
6. La Salle	23-1
7. Purdue	23-5
8. St. John's	23-6
9. New Mexico St.	24-5
10. Duquesne	21-5
11. Drake	26-5
12. Colorado	21-7
13. Louisville	21-6
14. Marquette	24-5
15. Villanova	21-5
Boston Col.	24-4
17. Weber State	27-3
Wyoming	19-9
19. Colorado St.	18-7
20. S. Carolina	21-7
Kansas	20-7

UCLA beat Purdue 92-72 for NCAA title.

'70

South Carolina's John Roche

1969-70 Final Standings

Team	Conf.	Overall	Ave.	Opp.
South Carolina	14-0	25-3	74.0	57.4
North Carolina	9-5	18-9	88.9	78.8
*N.C. State	9-5	23-7	83.7	71.7
Duke	8-6	17-9	75.6	72.1
Wake Forest	6-8	14-13	80.6	81.4
Maryland	5-9	13-13	76.1	74.8
Virginia	3-11	10-15	69.8	73.0
Clemson	2-12	7-19	80.3	90.3

*Won ACC Tournament

NCAA — N.C. STATE third in East Regional: lost to St. Bonaventure 80-68, beat Niagara 108-88.
NIT — DUKE lost to Utah 78-75. NORTH CAROLINA lost to Manhattan 95-90.

ACC Tournament

MARCH 5-7, 1970 AT CHARLOTTE, N.C.
FIRST ROUND: South Carolina 34, Clemson 33; Virginia 95, North Carolina 93; N.C. State 67, Maryland 57; Wake Forest 81, Duke 73. **SEMIFINALS:** South Carolina 79, Wake Forest 63; N.C. State 67, Virginia 66. **FINAL:** N.C. State 42, South Carolina 39 (2OT).
ALL-TOURNAMENT — FIRST TEAM: Vann Williford, N.C. State; Charlie Davis, Wake Forest; Tom Owens, Maryland; Chip Case, Virginia; Tom Riker, South Carolina. **SECOND TEAM:** Charlie Scott, North Carolina; John Roche, South Carolina; Bill Gerry, Virginia; Ed Leftwich, N.C. State; Joe Dunning, N.C. State.
EVERETT CASE AWARD (MVP): Williford.

All-ACC

FIRST TEAM: *John Roche, South Carolina (212 votes); *Charlie Scott, North Carolina (212); Vann Williford, N.C. State (208); Charlie Davis, Wake Forest (204); Tom Owens, South Carolina (163). **SECOND TEAM:** Randy Denton, Duke (142); Will Hetzel, Maryland (81); Butch Zatezalo, Clemson (80); Paul Coder, N.C. State (50); Ed Leftwich, N.C. State (44).
PLAYER OF THE YEAR: Roche (51); Scott (47); Williford (16); Davis (4). **COACH OF THE YEAR:** Norm Sloan, N.C. State (57); Frank McGuire, South Carolina (40); Bill Gibson, Virginia (8); Lefty Driesell, Maryland (1); Dean Smith, North Carolina (1); Bucky Waters, Duke (1).
*Unanimous Selection

Scoring, Rebounding Leaders

TOP TEN SCORERS

Player, School	G	FG	FT	TP	Ave.
Scott, North Carolina	27	281	169	731	27.1
Davis, Wake Forest	26	234	196	664	25.5
Williford, N.C. State	30	281	148	710	23.7
Roche, South Carolina	28	222	179	623	22.3
Zatezalo, Clemson	26	213	138	564	21.7
Denton, Duke	26	237	86	560	21.5
Gerry, Virginia	25	153	137	443	17.7
Coder, N.C. State	30	192	119	503	16.8
Case, Virginia	23	150	79	379	16.5
Horst, Maryland	26	183	62	428	16.5

TOP TEN REBOUNDERS

Player, School	G	Rbs.	Ave.
Owens, South Carolina	28	393	14.9
Denton, Duke	26	324	12.5
Gerry, Virginia	25	277	11.1
McGregor, Wake Forest	27	285	10.6
Williford, N.C. State	30	300	10.0
Horst, Maryland	26	258	9.9
Coder, N.C. State	30	293	9.8
McCandlish, Virginia	25	239	9.6
Dedmon, North Carolina	25	235	9.4
Mahaffey, Clemson	16	145	9.1

Rosters

CLEMSON

No.	Name	Hgt.	Yr.	Hometown
11	Dickie Foster	6-6	Jr.	Enka, NC
12	John Coakley	6-2	Jr.	Clemson, SC
14	Dave Thomas	6-1	Jr.	Warren, OH
20	Ronnie Yates	6-4	Sr.	Anderson, SC
22	Richie Mahaffey	6-7	Sr.	La Grange, GA
24	Mike Faer	6-0	Sr.	West Mifflin, PA
25	Greg Latin	6-7	So.	Glassport, PA
31	Paul Holzshu	6-5	Jr.	Pitcairn, PA
32	Butch Zatezalo	5-11	Jr.	Aliquippa, PA
44	Pete Weddell	6-6	Jr.	Goshen, IN
51	Jack Ross	6-5	Jr.	Anderson, SC

COACH: Bobby Roberts
ASSISTANTS: Art Musselman, Jim Brennan

DUKE

No.	Name	Hgt.	Yr.	Hometown
15	Pat Doughty	5-10	So.	Tempe, AZ
20	Larry Saunders	6-9	Jr.	Elmhurst, IL
21	Dick DeVenzio	5-10	Jr.	Springdale, PA
22	Rick Katherman	6-7	Jr.	Manchester, MA
30	Robby West	6-2	So.	South Orange, NJ
31	Randy Denton	6-10	Jr.	Raleigh, NC
32	Brad Evans	6-3	Jr.	Durham, NC
33	Doug Jackson	6-5	Sr.	Overland Park, KS
34	Tim Teer	6-3	Sr.	Hillsborough, NC
35	Stu Yarborough	6-4	So.	Durham, NC
40	Steve Litz	6-5	Jr.	Pittsburgh, PA
41	Ray Kuhlmeier	6-2	Sr.	Aurora, IN
42	Don Blackman	6-6	So.	Brooklyn, NY
43	John Posen	6-2	Sr.	Cicero, IL
50	Glen Smiley	6-6	Sr.	Bozeman, MT

COACH: Bucky Waters
ASSISTANTS: Hubie Brown, Jack Schalow

MARYLAND

No.	Name	Hgt.	Yr.	Hometown
3	Jay Flowers	6-3	So.	Rankin, PA
10	Steve Kebeck	6-1	Jr.	New York, NY
12	Harvey Sanders	6-0	So.	Great Neck, NY
14	Steve Norman	6-1	So.	Parkersburg, WV
15	Mickey Wiles	5-11	Sr.	Chillum, MD
20	John Prebula	6-4	Jr.	Greenville, PA
24	Sparky Still	6-5	So.	Camden, NJ
25	Charlie Blank	6-8	So.	Runnemede, NJ
30	Tommy Findreng	6-4	Jr.	Elkhorn, WI
32	Bill Siebenaler	6-6	So.	Toledo, OH
33	Tom Milroy	6-3	Sr.	Richwood, WV
50	Will Hetzel	6-7	Sr.	Washington, DC
54	Rod Horst	6-6	Sr.	Hagerstown, MD
55	Dick Stobaugh	6-7	Jr.	Burlington, NJ

COACH: Lefty Driesell
ASSISTANTS: George Raveling, Joe Harrington, Jim Maloney

NORTH CAROLINA

No.	Name	Hgt.	Yr.	Hometown
11	Bill Chambers	6-3	So.	Durham, NC
12	Richard Tuttle	6-0	Jr.	London, KY
13	Steve Previs	6-2	So.	Bethel Park, MD
20	Eddie Fogler	5-11	Sr.	Flushing, NY
22	Jim Delany	5-11	Sr.	South Orange, NJ
30	Dale Gipple	6-0	Jr.	Burlington, NC
31	Bill Chamberlain	6-5	So.	New York, NY
32	Dave Chadwick	6-7	Jr.	Orlando, FL
33	Charlie Scott	6-5	Sr.	New York, NY
34	Don Eggleston	6-8	Jr.	Charlotte, NC
35	Lee Dedmon	6-10	Jr.	Baltimore, MD
40	Ricky Webb	6-4	So.	Greenville, NC
41	Mike Earey	6-6	So.	Chapel Hill, NC
42	Kim Huband	6-4	So.	Wilmington, NC
43	Craig Corson	6-9	So.	Contoocook, NH
44	Dennis Wuycik	6-5	So.	Ambridge, PA

COACH: Dean Smith
ASSISTANTS: John Lotz, Bill Guthridge

All-America Teams

ASSOCIATED PRESS

FIRST TEAM: *Pete Maravich, LSU; Dan Issel, Kentucky; Bob Lanier, St. Bonaventure; Rick Mount, Purdue; Calvin Murphy, Niagara. **SECOND TEAM:** **Charlie Scott, North Carolina**; Austin Carr, Notre Dame; Artis Gilmore, Jacksonville; Rudy Tomjanovich, Michigan; **John Roche, South Carolina**. **THIRD TEAM:** Sidney Wicks, UCLA; John Vallely, UCLA; Mike Maloy, Davidson; John Johnson, Iowa; Jim McMillan, Columbia.

UNITED PRESS INTERNATIONAL

FIRST TEAM: *Pete Maravich, LSU; Bob Lanier, St. Bonaventure; Rick Mount, Purdue; Calvin Murphy, Niagara; Dan Issel, Kentucky. **SECOND TEAM:** Austin Carr, Notre Dame; **Charlie Scott, North Carolina**; Artis Gilmore, Jacksonville; **John Roche, South Carolina**; Rudy Tomjanovich, Michigan. **THIRD TEAM:** Rich Yunkus, Georgia Tech; Sidney Wicks, UCLA; John Vallely, UCLA; Mike Maloy, Davidson; John Johnson, Iowa.

*Player of the Year

N.C. STATE

No.	Name	Hgt.	Yr.	Hometown
12	Paul Coder	6-9	So.	Rockville, MD
14	Vann Williford	6-6	Sr.	Fayetteville, NC
24	Rick Anheuser	6-6	Sr.	Milwaukee, WI
30	Ed Leftwich	6-5	So.	Burlington, NJ
32	Al Heartley	6-1	Jr.	Clayton, NC
34	Jim Risinger	6-2	Jr.	Richmond, IN
42	Dan Wells	6-6	Jr.	Windsor, CT
50	Doug Tilley	6-7	Jr.	Bethesda, MD
52	Joe Dunning	5-11	Jr.	Wilmington, DE
54	Renaldo Lovisa	6-8	So.	Homer City, PA

COACH: Norm Sloan
ASSISTANTS: Charlie Bryant, Sam Esposito

SOUTH CAROLINA

No.	Name	Hgt.	Yr.	Hometown
11	John Roche	6-2	Jr.	New York, NY
14	Bob Carver	6-2	So.	Queens, NY
20	Rick Aydlett	6-7	So.	Blacksburg, VA
21	Bobby Cremins	6-2	Sr.	The Bronx, NY
22	Tommy Terry	6-2	Sr.	Columbia, SC
23	Dennis Powell	6-0	Jr.	The Bronx, NY
24	Tom Owens	6-10	Jr.	New York, NY
25	Gene Spencer	6-8	So.	Charleston, SC
31	Billy Grimes	6-5	So.	Staten Island, NY
32	Corky Carnevale	6-3	Sr.	Norwood, NJ
41	John Ribock	6-8	Jr.	Augusta, GA
44	Billy Walsh	6-0	Jr.	Mamaroneck, NY
51	Tom Riker	6-10	So.	Hicksville, NY

COACH: Frank McGuire
ASSISTANTS: Buck Freeman, Donnie Walsh, Bill Loving

VIRGINIA

No.	Name	Hgt.	Yr.	Hometown
3	Tom Bagby	6-2	So.	Roanoke, VA
10	Chip Case	6-3	Sr.	Lockport, NY
20	Tim Rash	6-0	So.	Richmond, VA
23	Frank DeWitt	6-4	So.	Pittsburgh, PA
24	Bill Gerry	6-7	Jr.	New York, NY
25	Tom Joyce	6-2	Sr.	Huntington Sta., NY
30	John Hill	6-0	Jr.	Fort Monroe, VA
35	Scott McCandlish	6-10	So.	Poughkeepsie, NY
41	Kevin Kennelly	5-11	Jr.	Charlotte, NC
42	Mike Slaysman	6-4	Jr.	Hampton, VA
44	Chip Miller	6-0	So.	Lexington, VA
55	Joe Morahan	6-5	Jr.	Lake Ariel, PA

COACH: Bill Gibson
ASSISTANTS: Chip Connor, Dick DiBiaso

WAKE FOREST

No.	Name	Hgt.	Yr.	Hometown
10	Bob Hook	6-4	So.	Louisville, KY
11	John Lewkowicz	6-1	So.	Conshohocken, PA
12	Charlie Davis	6-1	Jr.	New York, NY
21	Tommy Lynch	5-11	Sr.	Barrington, IL
22	Norwood Todmann	6-3	Sr.	New York, NY
23	Dan Ackley	6-8	Sr.	Liverpool, NY
30	Bob Rhoads	6-3	Jr.	Mercer, PA
31	Gilbert McGregor	6-7	Jr.	Raeford, NC
32	Neil Pastushok	6-4	Jr.	Roselle Park, NJ
33	Dickie Walker	6-3	Sr.	Williamsburg, VA
34	Larry Habegger	6-7	Sr.	New Augusta, IN
35	Rich Habegger	6-5	So.	Elkhart, IN

COACH: Jack McCloskey
ASSISTANTS: Billy Packer, Neil Johnston

Final Top 20 Polls

AP

1. Kentucky	26-2
2. UCLA	28-2
3. St. Bonaventure	25-3
4. Jacksonville	27-2
5. New Mexico St.	27-3
6. S. Carolina	25-3
7. Iowa	20-5
8. Marquette	26-3
9. Notre Dame	21-8
10. N.C. State	23-7
11. Florida State	23-3
12. Houston	25-5
13. Pennsylvania	25-2
14. Drake	22-7
15. Davidson	22-5
16. Utah State	22-7
17. Niagara	22-7
18. W. Kentucky	22-3
19. Long Beach St.	24-5
20. Southern Cal	18-8

UPI

1. Kentucky	26-2
2. UCLA	28-2
3. St. Bonaventure	25-3
4. New Mexico St.	27-3
5. Jacksonville	27-2
6. S. Carolina	25-3
7. Iowa	20-5
8. Notre Dame	21-8
9. Drake	22-7
10. Marquette	26-3
11. Houston	25-5
12. N.C. State	23-7
13. Pennsylvania	25-2
14. Florida State	23-3
15. Villanova	22-7
Long Beach St.	24-5
17. W. Kentucky	22-3
Utah State	22-7
Niagara	22-7
20. Cincinnati	21-6
Texas-El Paso	17-8

UCLA beat Jacksonville 80-69 for NCAA title.

'71

Wake Forest's Charlie Davis

1970-71 Final Standings

Team	Conf.	Overall	Ave.	Opp.
North Carolina	11-3	26-6	84.6	71.8
*South Carolina	10-4	23-6	77.9	68.4
Duke	9-5	20-10	79.6	73.7
Wake Forest	7-7	16-10	79.4	74.1
Virginia	6-8	15-11	76.4	74.9
Maryland	5-9	14-12	75.0	73.4
N.C. State	5-9	13-14	76.5	77.5
Clemson	3-11	9-17	58.9	65.9

*Won ACC Tournament

NCAA—SOUTH CAROLINA fourth in East Regional: lost to Pennsylvania 79-64, lost to Fordham 100-90.

NIT—NORTH CAROLINA won championship: beat Massachusetts 90-49, beat Providence 86-79, beat Duke 73-67, beat Georgia Tech 84-66. DUKE finished fourth: beat Dayton 68-60, beat Tennessee 78-64, lost to North Carolina 73-67, lost to St. Bonaventure 92-88 (OT).

ACC Tournament

MARCH 11-13, 1971 AT GREENSBORO, N.C.

FIRST ROUND: North Carolina 76, Clemson 41; South Carolina 71, Maryland 63; N.C. State 68, Duke 61; Virginia 85, Wake Forest 84. **SEMIFINALS:** North Carolina 78, Virginia 68; South Carolina 69, N.C. State 56. **FINAL:** South Carolina 52, North Carolina 51. **ALL-TOURNAMENT—FIRST TEAM:** Barry Parkhill, Virginia; Tom Owens, South Carolina; John Roche, South Carolina; Lee Dedmon, North Carolina; Paul Coder, N.C. State. **SECOND TEAM:** Al Heartley, N.C. State; George Karl, North Carolina; Bill Chamberlain, North Carolina; Tom Riker, South Carolina; Charlie Davis, Wake Forest. **EVERETT CASE AWARD (MVP):** Dedmon and Roche (tie).

All-ACC

FIRST TEAM: *Charlie Davis, Wake Forest (242 votes); John Roche, South Carolina (240); Dennis Wuycik, North Carolina (238); Randy Denton, Duke (233); Tom Owens, South Carolina (176). **SECOND TEAM:** Barry Parkhill, Virginia (125); George Karl, North Carolina (120); Bill Gerry, Virginia (99); Ed Leftwich, N.C. State (74); Jim O'Brien, Maryland (64).
PLAYER OF THE YEAR: Davis (86); Roche (30); Wuycik (4). **COACH OF THE YEAR:** Dean Smith, North Carolina (89); Bill Gibson, Virginia (21).
*Unanimous Selection

Scoring, Rebounding Leaders

TOP TEN SCORERS

Player, School	G	FG	FT	TP	Ave.
Davis, Wake Forest	26	251	188	690	26.5
Roche, South Carolina	29	205	215	625	21.6
Denton, Duke	30	244	124	612	20.4
Wuycik, North Carolina	29	182	169	533	18.4
Leftwich, N.C. State	25	153	103	409	16.4
O'Brien, Maryland	21	104	134	342	16.3
Parkhill, Virginia	26	146	121	413	15.9
White, Maryland	25	157	75	389	15.6
McCandlish, Virginia	26	152	91	395	15.2
Coder, N.C. State	27	156	95	407	15.1

TOP TEN REBOUNDERS

Player, School	G	Rbs.	Ave.
Owens, South Carolina	28	360	12.9
Denton, Duke	30	385	12.8
McCandlish, Virginia	26	258	9.9
McGregor, Wake Forest	26	242	9.3
Gerry, Virginia	26	241	9.3
Yates, Maryland	26	224	8.6
Dedmon, North Carolina	32	273	8.5
Coder, N.C. State	27	227	8.4
Still, Maryland	26	208	8.0
Riker, South Carolina	29	231	8.0

Rosters

CLEMSON

No.	Name	Hgt.	Yr.	Hometown
10	Dave Thomas	6-1	Sr.	Warren, OH
12	John Coakley	6-2	Sr.	Clemson, SC
14	Ron Fenwick	6-3	So.	Rensselaer, IN
20	Bo Hawkins	5-10	Sr.	Louisville, KY
22	Craig Mobley	6-0	So.	Chester, SC
24	Bud Martin	6-1	So.	Wayland, KY
30	Paul Holzshu	6-5	Sr.	Pitcairn, PA
32	Mike Petro	6-2	Sr.	McKeesport, PA
34	Dickie Foster	6-6	Sr.	Enka, NC
40	John Williams	6-11	So.	Dover, DE
42	Dave Angel	6-11	So.	Rock Hill, SC
44	Pete Weddell	6-6	Sr.	Goshen, IN
50	Joe Cooley	6-6	So.	Prestonsburg, KY
52	Jack Ross	6-5	Sr.	Anderson, SC
54	John Webb	6-4	Sr.	Greenville, SC

COACH: Tates Locke
ASSISTANTS: Bill Clendinen, George Hill, Cliff Malpass

DUKE

No.	Name	Hgt.	Yr.	Hometown
12	Richie O'Connor	6-4	So.	Union City, NJ
15	Pat Doughty	5-10	Sr.	Tempe, AZ
20	Larry Saunders	6-9	Sr.	Elmhurst, IL
21	Dick DeVenzio	5-10	Sr.	Springdale, PA
22	Rick Katherman	6-7	Sr.	Manchester, MA
24	Jeff Dawson	6-1	So.	Downers Grove, IL
25	Gary Melchionni	6-2	So.	Woodbury, NJ
30	Robby West	6-2	Jr.	South Orange, NJ
31	Randy Denton	6-10	Sr.	Raleigh, NC
32	Brad Evans	6-3	Sr.	Durham, NC
35	Stu Yarborough	6-4	Jr.	Durham, NC
40	Steve Litz	6-5	Jr.	Pittsburgh, PA
50	Alan Shaw	6-9	So.	Millville, NJ
	Judge Carr	6-2	Jr.	Durham, NC

COACH: Bucky Waters
ASSISTANTS: Hubie Brown, Jack Schalow

MARYLAND

No.	Name	Hgt.	Yr.	Hometown
10	Steve Kebeck	6-1	Sr.	New York, NY
12	Harvey Sanders	6-0	Jr.	Great Neck, NY
13	Howard White	6-1	So.	Hampton, VA
20	Jack Neal	6-8	So.	San Diego, CA
24	Sparky Still	6-7	Jr.	Camden, NJ
25	Barry Yates	6-7	Jr.	Randolph, IA
32	Jay Flowers	6-3	Jr.	Rankin, PA
33	Darrell Brown	6-6	So.	Pittsburgh, PA
35	Bob Bodell	6-4	So.	Frankfort, KY
44	Jim O'Brien	6-7	So.	Falls Church, VA
53	Charlie Blank	6-8	Jr.	Runnemede, NJ
55	Dick Stobaugh	6-7	Sr.	Burlington, NJ

COACH: Lefty Driesell
ASSISTANTS: George Raveling, Joe Harrington, Jim Maloney

NORTH CAROLINA

No.	Name	Hgt.	Yr.	Hometown
11	John Austin	6-2	So.	Charlotte, NC
12	Richard Tuttle	6-0	Jr.	London, KY
13	Steve Previs	6-2	Jr.	Bethel Park, PA
20	Bill Chambers	6-3	Jr.	Durham, NC
22	George Karl	6-1	So.	Penn Hills, PA
30	Dale Gipple	6-1	Sr.	Burlington, NC
31	Bill Chamberlain	6-6	Jr.	New York, NY
32	Dave Chadwick	6-7	Sr.	Orlando, FL
34	Don Eggleston	6-9	Sr.	Charlotte, NC
35	Lee Dedmon	6-10	Sr.	Baltimore, MD
40	Donn Johnston	6-8	So.	Jamestown, NY
41	John Cox	6-1	So.	Sanford, NC
42	Kim Huband	6-4	Jr.	Wilmington, NC
43	Craig Corson	6-9	Jr.	Contoocook, NH
44	Dennis Wuycik	6-5	Jr.	Ambridge, PA

COACH: Dean Smith
ASSISTANTS: John Lotz, Bill Guthridge, Terry Truax

All-America Teams

ASSOCIATED PRESS

FIRST TEAM: Sidney Wicks, UCLA; *Austin Carr, Notre Dame; Artis Gilmore, Jacksonville; Jim McDaniels, Western Kentucky; Dean Meminger, Marquette. **SECOND TEAM:** **John Roche, South Carolina**; Dave Robisch, Kansas; Curtis Rowe, UCLA; Paul Westphal, Southern California; Johnny Neumann, Mississippi. **THIRD TEAM:** George McGinnis, Indiana; Rich Yunkus, Georgia Tech; Howard Porter, Villanova; Fred Brown, Iowa; Cliff Meely, Colorado.

UNITED PRESS INTERNATIONAL

FIRST TEAM: *Austin Carr, Notre Dame; Sidney Wicks, UCLA; Artis Gilmore, Jacksonville; **John Roche, South Carolina**; Dean Meminger, Marquette. **SECOND TEAM:** Jim McDaniels, Western Kentucky; Johnny Neumann, Mississippi; Ken Durrett, La Salle; Howard Porter, Villanova; Curtis Rowe, UCLA. **THIRD TEAM:** George McGinnis, Indiana; Paul Westphal, Southern California; Julius Erving, Massachusetts; Charley Yelverton, Fordam; Dave Robisch, Kansas.
*Player of the Year

N.C. STATE

No.	Name	Hgt.	Yr.	Hometown
12	Paul Coder	6-9	Jr.	Rockville, MD
20	Bill Benson	6-2	So.	Joliet, IL
22	Rick Holdt	6-6	So.	Paramus, NJ
30	Ed Leftwich	6-5	Jr.	Burlington, NJ
32	Al Heartley	6-1	Sr.	Clayton, NC
34	Jim Risinger	6-2	Jr.	Richmond, IN
42	Dan Wells	6-6	So.	Windsor, CT
44	Bob Heuts	6-7	So.	Chicago Heights, IL
50	Doug Tilley	6-7	Sr.	Bethesda, MD
52	Joe Dunning	5-11	Sr.	Wilmington, DE
54	Renaldo Lovisa	6-8	Jr.	Homer City, PA

COACH: Norm Sloan
ASSISTANTS: Eddie Biedenbach, Sam Esposito, Art Musselman

SOUTH CAROLINA

No.	Name	Hgt.	Yr.	Hometown
10	Jimmy Powell	5-11	So.	The Bronx, NY
11	John Roche	6-3	Sr.	New York, NY
14	Bob Carver	6-2	Jr.	Queens, NY
20	Rick Aydlett	6-7	Jr.	Blacksburg, VA
23	Dennis Powell	6-0	So.	The Bronx, NY
24	Tom Owens	6-10	Sr.	New York, NY
31	Billy Grimes	6-5	Jr.	Staten Island, NY
33	Danny Traylor	7-0	So.	Winston-Salem, NC
41	John Ribock	6-8	Sr.	Augusta, GA
43	Kevin Joyce	6-3	So.	Merrick, NY
44	Casey Manning	6-2	So.	Dillion, SC
51	Tom Riker	6-10	Jr.	Hicksville, NY

COACH: Frank McGuire
ASSISTANTS: Buck Freeman, Bill Loving, Donnie Walsh

VIRGINIA

No.	Name	Hgt.	Yr.	Hometown
20	Tim Rash	6-0	Jr.	Richmond, VA
22	Jim Farmer	6-2	So.	Richmond, VA
23	Frank DeWitt	6-4	Jr.	Pittsburgh, PA
24	Bill Gerry	6-7	Sr.	New York, NY
30	John Hill	6-0	Sr.	Fort Monroe, VA
33	Jim Hobgood	6-4	So.	Uniontown, PA
35	Scott McCandlish	6-10	Jr.	Poughkeepsie, NY
40	Barry Parkhill	6-3	So.	State College, PA
41	Kevin Kennelly	5-11	Sr.	Charlotte, NC
42	Mike Wilkes	6-5	Sr.	Dallas, PA
44	Chip Miller	6-1	So.	Lexington, VA
52	Larry Gerry	6-3	So.	Floral Park, NY

COACH: Bill Gibson
ASSISTANTS: Chip Connor, Dick DiBiaso

WAKE FOREST

No.	Name	Hgt.	Yr.	Hometown
10	Bob Hook	6-4	So.	Louisville, KY
12	Charlie Davis	6-1	Sr.	New York, NY
14	John Lewkowicz	6-1	Jr.	Conshohocken, PA
20	Eddie Payne	6-1	So.	Charlotte, NC
21	Joe Neal	6-1	So.	Auburn, NJ
22	Willie Griffin	6-3	So.	Winston-Salem, NC
23	Jeff Stewart	6-7	So.	Mechanicsburg, PA
25	John Orenczak	6-6	So.	Linden, NJ
30	Bob Rhoads	6-3	Sr.	Mercer, PA
31	Gilbert McGregor	6-7	Sr.	Raeford, NC
33	Pat Kelly	6-9	So.	Bountiful, UT
35	Rich Habegger	6-5	Jr.	Elkhart, IN
40	Neil Pastushok	6-4	Sr.	Roselle Park, NJ

COACH: Jack McCloskey
ASSISTANTS: Neil Johnston, Walter Noell

Final Top 20 Polls

AP
1. UCLA 29-1
2. Marquette 28-1
3. Pennsylvania 28-1
4. Kansas 27-3
5. Southern Cal 24-2
6. S. Carolina 23-6
7. W. Kentucky 24-6
8. Kentucky 22-6
9. Fordham 26-3
10. Ohio State 20-6
11. Jacksonville 22-4
12. Notre Dame 20-9
13. North Carolina 26-6
14. Houston 22-7
15. Duquesne 21-4
16. Long Beach St. 23-5
17. Tennessee 21-7
18. Villanova 23-6
19. Drake 21-8
20. Brigham Young 18-11

UPI
1. UCLA 29-1
2. Marquette 28-1
3. Pennsylvania 28-1
4. Kansas 27-3
5. Southern Cal 24-2
6. S. Carolina 23-6
7. W. Kentucky 24-6
8. Kentucky 22-6
9. Fordham 26-3
10. Ohio State 20-6
11. Jacksonville 22-4
   Brigham Young 18-11
13. North Carolina 26-6
14. Notre Dame 20-9
   Long Beach St. 23-5
16. Drake 21-8
17. Villanova 23-6
18. Duquesne 21-4
   Houston 22-7
20. Weber State 21-6

UCLA beat Villanova 68-62 for NCAA title.

295

'72

Virginia's Barry Parkhill

1971-72 Final Standings

Team	Conf.	Overall	Ave.	Opp.
*North Carolina	9-3	26-5	89.1	71.4
Maryland	8-4	27-5	76.4	65.8
Virginia	8-4	21-7	81.8	70.7
Duke	6-6	14-12	68.5	68.2
N.C. State	6-6	16-10	78.5	72.3
Wake Forest	3-9	8-18	69.2	71.0
Clemson	2-10	10-16	63.4	66.1

*Won ACC Tournament

NCAA — NORTH CAROLINA third in Final Four: beat South Carolina 92-69, beat Pennsylvania 73-59 in East Regional; lost to Florida State 79-75, beat Louisville 105-91 in Final Four.
NIT — MARYLAND won championship: beat St. Joseph's 67-55, beat Syracuse 71-65, beat Jacksonville 91-77, beat Niagara 100-69. VIRGINIA lost to Lafayette 72-71.

ACC Tournament

MARCH 9-11, 1972 AT GREENSBORO, N.C.
FIRST ROUND: North Carolina, bye; Maryland 54, Clemson 52; Virginia 74, Wake Forest 65; Duke 73, N.C. State 60. **SEMIFINALS:** North Carolina 63, Duke 48; Maryland 62, Virginia 57. **FINAL:** North Carolina 73, Maryland 64.
ALL-TOURNAMENT — FIRST TEAM: Barry Parkhill, Virginia; Dennis Wuycik, North Carolina; Bob McAdoo, North Carolina; George Karl, North Carolina; Tom McMillen, Maryland. **SECOND TEAM:** Jim O'Brien, Maryland; Scott McCandlish, Virginia; Gary Melchionni, Duke; Len Elmore, Maryland; Steve Previs, North Carolina.
EVERETT CASE AWARD (MVP): McAdoo.

All-ACC

FIRST TEAM: *Barry Parkhill, Virginia (214 votes); Bob McAdoo, North Carolina (209); Tom McMillen, Maryland (198); Dennis Wuycik, North Carolina (189); Tom Burleson, N.C. State (178). **SECOND TEAM:** Bill Chamberlain, North Carolina (112); Gary Melchionni, Duke (89); Alan Shaw, Duke (88); George Karl, North Carolina (82); Len Elmore, Maryland (69).
PLAYER OF THE YEAR: Parkhill (80); Wuycik (12); McAdoo (10); McMillen, Burleson and Chamberlain also received votes. **COACH OF THE YEAR:** Bill Gibson, Virginia (70); Dean Smith, North Carolina (21); Bucky Waters, Duke (15).
*Unanimous Selection

Scoring, Rebounding Leaders

TOP TEN SCORERS

Player, School	G	FG	FT	TP	Ave.
Parkhill, Virginia	28	239	127	605	21.6
Burleson, N.C. State	26	214	126	554	21.3
McMillen, Maryland	32	235	197	667	20.8
McAdoo, North Carolina	31	243	118	604	19.5
Wuycik, North Carolina	31	189	181	559	18.0
Griffin, Wake Forest	26	178	58	414	15.9
Redding, Duke	26	124	137	385	14.8
Cafferky, N.C. State	26	155	63	373	14.3
Angel, Clemson	26	116	129	361	13.9
Jackson, Wake Forest	26	159	30	348	13.4

TOP TEN REBOUNDERS

Player, School	G	Rbs.	Ave.
Burleson, N.C. State	26	365	14.0
Shaw, Duke	26	308	11.8
Elmore, Maryland	32	351	11.0
McAdoo, North Carolina	31	312	10.1
Angel, Clemson	26	253	9.7
McMillen, Maryland	32	306	9.6
McCandlish, Virginia	28	264	9.4
Habegger, Wake Forest	26	203	7.8
Browning, Clemson	26	189	7.3
Jackson, Wake Forest	26	172	6.6

Rosters

CLEMSON

No.	Name	Hgt.	Yr.	Hometown
10	Terrell Suit	6-0	So.	Anderson, SC
12	Jive Brown	6-2	Jr.	Eastover, SC
14	Danny Miller	5-11	Jr.	Spring Lake, NJ
20	Bo Hawkins	5-10	Sr.	Louisville, KY
22	Craig Mobley	6-0	Jr.	Chester, SC
24	Bud Martin	6-1	Jr.	Wayland, KY
34	Mike Browning	6-7	So.	Gahanna, OH
42	Dave Angel	6-11	Jr.	Rock Hill, SC
44	Mel Francisco	6-7	Jr.	Brentwood, MD
50	Joe Cooley	6-6	Jr.	Prestonsburg, KY
52	Dennis Odle	6-5	So.	Newark, OH
54	John Williams	6-11	Jr.	Dover, DE

COACH: Tates Locke
ASSISTANTS: Bill Clendinen, George Hill, Cliff Malpass

DUKE

No.	Name	Hgt.	Yr.	Hometown
11	Zeno Edwards	6-1	So.	Washington, DC
12	Richie O'Conncr	6-4	Jr.	Union City, NJ
15	Pat Doughty	5-10	Sr.	Tempe, AZ
21	Jeff Burdette	5-11	So.	Buena Park, CA
25	Gary Melchionni	6-2	Jr.	Woodbury, NJ
30	Robby West	6-2	Sr.	South Orange, NJ
32	Ron Righter	6-7	So.	Chalfont, PA
35	Stu Yarborough	6-4	Sr.	Durham, NC
50	Alan Shaw	6-9	Jr.	Millville, NJ
51	Dave Elmer	6-9	So.	Fort Wayne, IN
53	Chris Redding	6-8	So.	Bethesda, MD

COACH: Bucky Waters
ASSISTANTS: Hubie Brown, Jim Lewis, Neill McGeachy

MARYLAND

No.	Name	Hgt.	Yr.	Hometown
5	Mark Cartwright	6-11	So.	Morton Grove, IL
10	Rich Porac	6-0	So.	Monroeville, PA
12	Stan Swetnam	6-3	So.	Baltimore, MD
13	Howard White	6-1	Jr.	Hampton, VA
20	Jack Neal	6-8	Jr.	San Diego, CA
22	Jap Trimble	6-3	So.	New York, NY
24	Sparky Still	6-7	Sr.	Camden, NJ
33	Darrell Brown	6-6	Jr.	Pittsburgh, PA
35	Bob Bodell	6-4	Jr.	Frankfort, KY
41	Len Elmore	6-9	So.	Springfield Grdn., NY
44	Jim O'Brien	6-7	Jr.	Falls Church, VA
53	Charlie Blank	6-8	Sr.	Runnemede, NJ
54	Tom McMillen	6-11	So.	Mansfield, PA

COACH: Lefty Driesell
ASSISTANTS: George Raveling, Joe Harrington, Jim Maloney

NORTH CAROLINA

No.	Name	Hgt.	Yr.	Hometown
11	John Austin	6-2	Jr.	Charlotte, NC
12	Ray Hite	5-10	So.	Hyattsville, MD
13	Steve Previs	6-3	Sr.	Bethel Park, PA
20	Bill Chambers	6-4	Jr.	Durham, NC
22	George Karl	6-2	Jr.	Penn Hills, PA
30	John O'Donnell	6-6	So.	New York, NY
31	Bill Chamberlain	6-6	Sr.	New York, NY
32	Darrell Elston	6-3	So.	Tipton, IN
33	Roger Jamison	5-11	Jr.	Greensboro, NC
33	Alan Mayfield	6-2	So.	Charlotte, NC
34	Bobby Jones	6-8	So.	Charlotte, NC
35	Bob McAdoo	6-9	Jr.	Greensboro, NC
40	Donn Johnston	6-8	Jr.	Jamestown, NY
41	John Cox	6-1	Jr.	Sanford, NC
42	Kim Huband	6-5	Sr.	Wilmington, NC
43	Craig Corson	6-10	Jr.	Contoocook, NH
44	Dennis Wuycik	6-6	Sr.	Ambridge, PA

COACH: Dean Smith
ASSISTANTS: John Lotz, Bill Guthridge, Eddie Fogler

All-America Teams

ASSOCIATED PRESS

FIRST TEAM: *Bill Walton, UCLA; Dwight Lamar, SW Louisiana; Ec Ratleff, Long Beach State; Jim Chones, Marquette; Tom Riker, South Carolina. **SECOND TEAM: Barry Parkhill, Virginia;** Dwight Davis, Houston; J m Price, Louisville; Henry Bibby, UCLA; **Bob McAdoo, North Carolina. THIRD TEAM:** Richie Fuqua, Oral Roberts; Brian Taylor, Princeton; **Tom McMillen, Maryland;** Bud Stallworth, Kansas; Will Robinson, West Virginia.

UNITED PRESS INTERNATIONAL

FIRST TEAM: *Bill Walton, UCLA; Dwight Lamar, SW Louisiana; Jim Chones, Marquette; Ed Ratleff, Long Beach State; Henry Bibby, UCLA. **SECOND TEAM:** Tom Riker, South Carolina; **Barry Parkhill, Virginia;** Allan Ho nyak, Ohio State; **Bob McAdoo, North Carolina;** Jim Price, Louisville. **THIRD TEAM:** Henry Wilmore, Michigan; **Tom McMillen, Maryland;** Kresimir Cosic, Brigham Young; Paul Westphal, Southern California; Brian Taylor, Princeton.
*Player of the Year

N.C. STATE

No.	Name	Hgt.	Yr.	Hometown
10	Carl Lile	5-10	So.	Indianapolis, IN
12	Paul Coder	6-9	Sr.	Rockville, MD
14	Billy Mitchell	6-0	So.	Greensboro, NC
20	Steve Smoral	6-3	So.	Danville, VA
22	Rick Holdt	6-6	Jr.	Paramus, NJ
24	Tom Burleson	7-4	So.	Newland, NC
30	Kim Williamson	6-1	So.	Clinton, NC
32	Joe Cafferky	6-2	Jr.	Haverford, PA
40	Danny Gatewood	6-1	Jr.	Raleigh, NC
44	Bob Heuts	6-7	So.	Chicago Heights, IL
50	Steve Graham	6-6	So.	Chevy Chase, MD
52	Steve Nuce	6-8	So.	Rockville, MD
54	Renaldo Lovisa	6-8	Sr.	Homer City, PA

COACH: Norm Sloan
ASSISTANTS: Eddie Biedenbach, Sam Esposito, Art Musselman

VIRGINIA

No.	Name	Hgt.	Yr.	Hometown
10	Al Drummond	6-2	So.	Waverly, NY
11	Steve Boettner	6-8	So.	Winchester, VA
20	Tim Rash	6-0	Sr.	Richmond, VA
21	Larry Gerry	6-3	Jr.	Floral Park, NY
22	Jim Farmer	6-2	Jr.	Richmond, VA
23	Frank DeWitt	6-5	Sr.	Pittsburgh, PA
24	Bob McKeag	6-5	So.	Erie, PA
25	Bob McCurdy	6-7	So.	Deer Park, NY
30	Steve Morris	5-11	So.	Alexandria, VA
33	Jim Hobgood	6-4	Jr.	Uniontown, PA
35	Scott McCandlish	6-10	Sr.	Poughkeepsie, NY
40	Barry Parkhill	6-4	Jr.	State College, PA
42	Keith Suddith	6-0	So.	Virginia Beach, PA
44	Chip Miller	6-1	Sr.	Lexington, VA
55	Lanny Stahurski	6-10	So.	Swissvale, PA

COACH: Bill Gibson
ASSISTANTS: Chip Connor, Terry Truax

WAKE FOREST

No.	Name	Hgt.	Yr.	Hometown
3	Sam Jackson	6-6	Jr.	Oakland, CA
10	Bob Hook	6-5	Jr.	Louisville, KY
13	Bobby Dwyer	6-1	So.	Silver Spring, MD
14	John Lewkowicz	6-1	Sr.	Conshohocken, PA
20	Eddie Payne	6-1	Jr.	Charlotte, NC
21	Morris Catlett	6-1	So.	Youngsville, NC
22	Willie Griffin	6-3	Jr.	Winston-Salem, NC
25	John Orenczak	6-6	Jr.	Linden, NJ
35	Rich Habegger	6-6	Sr.	Elkhart, IN
41	Michael Dean	6-9	Jr.	Cincinnati, OH
42	Jerry Campbell	6-3	So.	Belmont, NC
44	Jeff Stewart	6-7	Jr.	Mechanicsburg, PA
45	Pat Kelly	6-9	Jr.	Bountiful, UT

COACH: Jack McCloskey
ASSISTANTS: Neil Johnston, Walter Noell

Final Top 20 Polls

AP

1. UCLA	30-0
2. North Carolina	26-5
3. Pennsylvania	25-3
4. Louisville	26-5
5. Long Beach St.	25-4
6. S. Carolina	24-5
7. Marquette	25-4
8. SW Louisiana	25-4
9. Brigham Young	21-5
10. Florida State	27-6
11. Minnesota	18-7
12. Marshall	23-4
13. Memphis St.	21-7
14. Maryland	27-5
15. Villanova	20-6
16. Oral Roberts	26-2
17. Indiana	17-8
18. Kentucky	21-7
19. Ohio State	18-6
20. Virginia	21-7

UPI

1. UCLA	30-0
2. North Carolina	26-5
3. Pennsylvania	25-3
4. Louisville	26-5
5. S. Carolina	24-5
6. Long Beach St.	25-4
7. Marquette	25-4
8. SW Louisiana	25-4
9. Brigham Young	21-5
10. Florida State	27-6
11. Maryland	27-5
12. Minnesota	18-7
13. Memphis St.	21-7
14. Kentucky	21-7
15. Villanova	20-6
16. Kansas State	19-9
17. Texas-El Paso	20-7
18. Marshall	23-4
19. Missouri	21-6
Weber State	18-10

UCLA beat Florida State 81-76 for NCAA title.

'73

N.C. State's David Thompson

1972-73 Final Standings

Team	Conf.	Overall	Ave.	Opp.
*N.C. State	12-0	27-0	92.9	71.1
North Carolina	8-4	25-8	84.7	72.8
Maryland	7-5	23-7	87.1	74.2
Duke	4-8	12-14	78.1	76.9
Virginia	4-8	13-12	74.8	71.2
Clemson	4-8	12-14	69.8	69.4
Wake Forest	3-9	12-15	72.3	77.4

*Won ACC Tournament

NCAA—MARYLAND second in East Regional: beat Syracuse 91-75, lost to Providence 103-89.

NIT—NORTH CAROLINA third: beat Oral Roberts 82-65, beat Massachusetts 73-63, lost to Notre Dame 78-71, beat Alabama 88-69.

ACC Tournament

MARCH 8-10, 1973 AT GREENSBORO, N.C.
FIRST ROUND: N.C. State, bye; Wake Forest 54, North Carolina 52 (OT); Maryland 77, Clemson 61; Virginia 59, Duke 55. **SEMIFINALS:** N.C. State 63, Virginia 51; Maryland 73, Wake Forest 65. **FINAL:** N.C. State 76, Maryland 74.
ALL-TOURNAMENT—FIRST TEAM: Tom Burleson, N.C. State; David Thompson, N.C. State; Tom McMillen, Maryland; John Lucas, Maryland; Eddie Payne, Wake Forest. **SECOND TEAM:** Bobby Jones, North Carolina; Jim O'Brien, Maryland; Gus Gerard, Virginia; Barry Parkhill, Virginia; Tony Byers, Wake Forest.
EVERETT CASE AWARD (MVP): Burleson.

All-ACC

FIRST TEAM: *David Thompson, N.C. State (248 votes); Tom Burleson, N.C. State (238); George Karl, North Carolina (232); Tom McMillen, Maryland (212); Gary Melchionni, Duke (176). **SECOND TEAM:** Bobby Jones, North Carolina (163); Barry Parkhill, Virginia (159); Len Elmore, Maryland (84); Chris Redding, Duke (67); Tony Byers, Wake Forest (56).
PLAYER OF THE YEAR: Thompson (116); Karl (4); Parkhill (1); Burleson (1); McMillen (1). **COACH OF THE YEAR:** Norm Sloan, N.C. State (95); Dean Smith, North Carolina (22).
*Unanimous Selection

Scoring, Rebounding Leaders

TOP TEN SCORERS

Player, School	G	FG	FT	TP	Ave.
Thompson, N.C. State	27	267	132	666	24.7
Byers, Wake Forest	27	240	106	586	21.7
McMillen, Maryland	29	250	116	616	21.2
Burleson, N.C. State	27	199	84	482	17.9
Karl, North Carolina	33	219	124	562	17.0
Redding, Duke	26	158	124	440	16.9
Parkhill, Virginia	25	164	91	419	16.8
O'Brien, Maryland	30	203	92	498	16.6
Melchionni, Duke	26	165	82	412	15.8
Payne, Wake Forest	27	174	70	418	15.5

TOP TEN REBOUNDERS

Player, School	G	Rbs.	Ave.
Burleson, N.C. State	27	324	12.0
Elmore, Maryland	26	290	11.2
Jones, North Carolina	33	348	10.5
McMillen, Maryland	29	284	9.8
Fleischer, Duke	26	221	8.5
Gerard, Virginia	25	206	8.2
Thompson, N.C. State	27	220	8.1
Shaw, Duke	26	197	7.6
Parrish, Wake Forest	27	203	7.5
Foye, Wake Forest	27	191	7.1

Rosters

CLEMSON

No.	Name	Hgt.	Yr.	Hometown
3	Doug Lowe	5-8	So.	Spartanburg, SC
4	Ron DiPasquale	6-1	So.	North Bergen, NJ
5	Van Gregg	6-2	So.	Columbus, OH
10	Terrell Suit	6-0	Jr.	Anderson, SC
12	Jive Brown	6-1	Sr.	Eastover, SC
14	Danny Miller	5-11	Sr.	Spring Lake, NJ
20	Archie McIntosh	6-2	So.	Marion, NC
22	Ricky Hunt	6-6	So.	Hyattsville, MD
24	Bud Martin	6-1	Sr.	Wayland, KY
30	Tim Capehart	6-0	Fr.	Columbus, OH
32	Bruce Harman	6-0	Fr.	Pittsburgh, PA
33	Jeff Reisinger	6-6	Jr.	Kingston, OH
34	Mike Browning	6-7	Jr.	Gahanna, OH
41	Marty Patterson	6-8	So.	Hendersonville, NC
42	Dave Angel	6-11	Fr.	Rock Hill, SC
44	Scott Conant	6-9	Fr.	Sunbury, OH
45	Wayne Croft	6-8	So.	Bamberg, SC
54	Charlie Rogers	6-8	Fr.	Lindenhurst, NY

COACH: Tates Locke
ASSISTANTS: Bill Clendinen, George Hill, Cliff Malpass, Ray Loucks

DUKE

No.	Name	Hgt.	Yr.	Hometown
14	Willie Hodge	6-9	Fr.	San Antonio, TX
20	Dave O'Connell	6-4	Fr.	Cincinnati, OH
21	Jeff Burdette	5-11	Jr.	Buena Park, CA
22	Paul Fox	6-2	Fr.	Radnor, PA
23	Bill Suk	6-5	So.	Midlothian, IL
24	Kevin Billerman	6-2	So.	Bricktown, NJ
25	Gary Melchionni	6-3	Sr.	Woodbury, NJ
34	Bob Cook	6-6	Fr.	Glen Rock, NJ
40	Neil Chinault	6-5	So.	Peterstown, WV
42	Bob Fleischer	6-8	So.	Youngstown, OH
43	Terry Chili	6-9	Fr.	Jamestown, NY
44	Pete Kramer	6-4	So.	Camp Hill, PA
50	Alan Shaw	6-10	Sr.	Millville, NJ
53	Chris Redding	6-8	Jr.	Bethesda, MD

COACH: Bucky Waters
ASSISTANTS: Neill McGeachy, Jim Lewis, Tony Barone

MARYLAND

No.	Name	Hgt.	Yr.	Hometown
10	Rich Porac	6-0	Jr.	Monroeville, PA
13	Howard White	6-1	Sr.	Hampton, VA
14	Don White	6-4	So.	Pittsburgh, PA
15	John Lucas	6-3	Fr.	Durham, NC
20	Jack Neal	6-8	Sr.	San Diego, CA
21	Bill Hahn	5-11	So.	Mishawaka, IN
22	Jap Trimble	6-3	Jr.	New York, NY
23	Varick Cutler	6-7	So.	N. Tonawanda, NY
24	Maurice Howard	6-3	Fr.	Philadelphia, PA
33	Darrell Brown	6-6	Sr.	Pittsburgh, PA
35	Bob Bodell	6-4	Sr.	Frankfort, KY
41	Len Elmore	6-9	Jr.	Springfield Grdn., NY
42	Owen Brown	6-8	So.	La Grange, IL
43	Tom McMillen	6-11	Jr.	Mansfield, PA
44	Jim O'Brien	6-7	Sr.	Falls Church, VA
45	Tom Roy	6-9	So.	South Windsor, CT

COACH: Lefty Driesell
ASSISTANTS: Jim Maloney, Joe Harrington, Tim Autry

NORTH CAROLINA

No.	Name	Hgt.	Yr.	Hometown
12	Ray Hite	6-0	Jr.	Hyatttsville, MD
13	Brad Hoffman	5-10	So.	Columbus, OH
14	Dave Hanners	6-0	Fr.	Columbus, OH
20	Ray Harrison	6-2	So.	Greensboro, NC
21	Mitch Kupchak	6-9	Fr.	Brentwood, NY
22	George Karl	6-3	Sr.	Penn Hills, PA
23	Jimmy Guill	6-3	Fr.	Winston-Salem, NC
30	John O'Donnell	6-5	Jr.	New York, NY
31	Mickey Bell	6-5	So.	Goldsboro, NC
32	Darrell Elston	6-4	Jr.	Tipton, IN
34	Bobby Jones	6-9	Jr.	Charlotte, NC
35	Charles Waddell	6-6	Jr.	Southern Pines, NC
40	Donn Johnston	6-8	Sr.	Jamestown, NY
42	Bill Chambers	6-4	Fr.	Greensboro, NC
43	Ed Stahl	6-10	Jr.	Columbus, OH
44	Donald Washington	6-7	So.	Washington, DC

COACH: Dean Smith
ASSISTANTS: John Lotz, Bill Guthridge, Eddie Fogler

N.C. STATE

No.	Name	Hgt.	Yr.	Hometown
12	Steve Smith	6-10	Fr.	East McDowell, KY
14	Greg Hawkins	6-5	Jr.	Huntington, WV
20	Steve Smoral	6-3	Sr.	Danville, VA
22	Rick Holdt	6-6	Sr.	Paramus, NY
24	Tom Burleson	7-4	Jr.	Newland, NC
25	Monte Towe	5-7	So.	Converse, IN
30	David Thompson	6-4	So.	Shelby, NC
32	Joe Cafferky	6-1	Sr.	Havertown, PA
34	Craig Kuszmaul	6-5	So.	Warren, OH
40	Mark Moeller	6-3	So.	Canfield, OH
42	Tim Stoddard	6-7	So.	Hammond, IN
44	Jerry Hunt	6-5	Fr.	Shelby, NC
50	Leo Campbell	6-6	So.	Gary, IN
52	Steve Nuce	6-8	Jr.	Rockville, MD
54	Mike Dempsey	6-6	So.	Greensboro, NC

COACH: Norm Sloan
ASSISTANTS: Eddie Biedenbach, Sam Esposito, Art Musselman

VIRGINIA

No.	Name	Hgt.	Yr.	Hometown
10	Al Drummond	6-2	Jr.	Waverly, NY
20	Andy Boninti	6-3	So.	New York, NY
21	Larry Gerry	6-3	Sr.	Floral Park, NY
22	Gus Gerard	6-7	So.	Uniontown, PA
24	Bob McKeag	6-5	Jr.	Erie, PA
30	Steve Morris	5-11	Jr.	Alexandria, VA
32	Bob Sefcik	6-2	Jr.	Rochelle Park, NJ
33	Jim Hobgood	6-4	Sr.	Uniontown, PA
35	Brian Tully	6-1	So.	Merrick, NY
40	Barry Parkhill	6-4	Sr.	State College, PA
41	Wally Walker	6-6	Fr.	Millersville, PA
42	Dan Bonner	6-7	So.	Pittsburgh, PA
44	Spencer Graham	6-8	So.	Bethesda, MD
55	Lanny Stahurski	6-10	Jr.	Swissvale, PA

COACH: Bill Gibson
ASSISTANTS: Chip Connor, Mike Schuler

WAKE FOREST

No.	Name	Hgt.	Yr.	Hometown
10	Tony Byers	6-2	Jr.	Bessemer City, NC
13	Bobby Dwyer	6-1	Jr.	Silver Spring, MD
14	Phil Perry	6-3	So.	Frankfort, KY
20	Eddie Payne	6-1	Sr.	Charlotte, NC
22	Willie Griffin	6-3	So.	Winston-Salem, NC
30	Bob Hook	6-5	Sr.	Louisville, KY
32	Sam Jackson	6-6	Sr.	Oakland, CA
33	Randy Adams	6-8	So.	Beacon, NY
34	Mike Parrish	6-6	So.	Canton, NC
40	Danny Moses	6-11	Fr.	Williamston, WV
41	John Orenczak	6-6	Sr.	Linden, NJ
44	J.J. Grant	6-8	Jr.	Castle Dale, UT
45	Pat Kelly	6-9	Sr.	Bountiful, UT
52	Tim Stare	6-9	So.	Palos Verdes, CA
53	Lee Foye	6-6	Fr.	Wilmington, NC

COACH: Carl Tacy
ASSISTANTS: Walter Noell, Larry Williams

All-America Teams

ASSOCIATED PRESS

FIRST TEAM: *Bill Walton, UCLA; Ed Ratleff, Long Beach State; **David Thompson, N.C. State**; Ernie DiGregorio, Providence; Kermit Washington, American. **SECOND TEAM:** Doug Collins, Illinois State; Keith Wilkes, UCLA; Dwight Lamar, SW Louisiana; Jim Brewer, Minnesota; Kevin Joyce, South Carolina. **THIRD TEAM:** Bill Schaeffer, St. John's; Mike Bantom, St. Joseph's; John Brown, Missouri; **Tom McMillen, Maryland**; Richie Fuqua, Oral Roberts.

UNITED PRESS INTERNATIONAL

FIRST TEAM: *Bill Walton, UCLA; Ed Ratleff, Long Beach State; **David Thompson, N.C. State**; Doug Collins, Illinois State; Dwight Lamar, SW Louisiana. **SECOND TEAM:** Keith Wilkes, UCLA; **Tom McMillen, Maryland**; Kevin Joyce, South Carolina; Ernie DiGregorio, Providence; Jim Brewer, Minnesota. **THIRD TEAM:** Allan Hornyak, Ohio State; **Tom Burleson, N.C. State**; Ron Behagen, Minnesota; Bill Schaeffer, St. John's; Marvin Barnes, Providence.
*Player of the Year

Final Top 20 Polls

AP		UPI	
1. UCLA	30-0	1. UCLA	30-0
2. N.C. State	27-0	2. N.C. State	27-0
3. Long Beach St.	26-3	3. Long Beach St.	26-3
4. Providence	27-4	4. Marquette	25-4
5. Marquette	25-4	5. Providence	27-4
6. Indiana	22-6	6. Indiana	22-6
7. SW Louisiana	24-5	7. SW Louisiana	24-5
8. Maryland	23-7	Kansas State	23-5
9. Kansas State	23-5	9. Minnesota	21-5
10. Minnesota	21-5	10. Maryland	23-7
11. North Carolina	25-8	11. Memphis St.	24-6
12. Memphis St.	24-6	12. North Carolina	25-8
13. Houston	23-3	13. Arizona State	19-9
14. Syracuse	24-5	14. Syracuse	24-5
15. Missouri	21-6	15. Kentucky	20-8
16. Arizona State	19-9	16. S. Carolina	22-7
17. Kentucky	20-8	17. Missouri	21-6
18. Pennsylvania	21-7	18. Weber State	20-7
19. Austin Peay	22-7	Houston	23-3
20. San Francisco	23-5	20. Pennsylvania	21-7

UCLA beat Memphis St. 87-66 for NCAA title.

'74

N.C. State's David Thompson

1973-74 Final Standings

Team	Conf.	Overall	Ave.	Opp.
*N.C. State	12-0	30-1	91.4	74.7
Maryland	9-3	23-5	85.7	69.0
North Carolina	9-3	22-6	87.0	75.3
Virginia	4-8	11-16	77.3	80.0
Clemson	3-9	14-12	68.3	69.3
Wake Forest	3-9	13-13	76.2	74.1
Duke	2-10	10-16	75.3	77.6

*Won ACC Tournament

NCAA — N.C. STATE won NCAA title: beat Providence 92-78, beat Pittsburgh 100-72 in East Regional; beat UCLA 80-77 (2OT), beat Marquette 76-64 in Final Four.
NIT — NORTH CAROLINA lost to Purdue 82-71.

ACC Tournament

MARCH 7-9, 1974 AT GREENSBORO, N.C.

FIRST ROUND: N.C. State, bye; Maryland 85, Duke 66; North Carolina 76, Wake Forest 62; Virginia 68, Clemson 63. **SEMIFINALS:** N.C. State 87, Virginia 66; Maryland 105, North Carolina 85. **FINALS:** N.C. State 103, Maryland 100 (OT).
ALL-TOURNAMENT — FIRST TEAM: David Thompson, N.C. State; Tom Burleson, N.C. State; Tom McMillen, Maryland; John Lucas, Maryland; Maurice Howard, Maryland. **SECOND TEAM:** Len Elmore, Maryland; Owen Brown, Maryland; Gus Gerard, Virginia; Monte Towe, N.C. State; Billy Langloh, Virginia.
EVERETT CASE AWARD (MVP): Burleson.

All-ACC

FIRST TEAM: *David Thompson, N.C. State (274 votes); Monte Towe, N.C. State (251); John Lucas, Maryland (242); Bobby Jones, North Carolina (209); Len Elmore, Maryland (195). **SECOND TEAM:** Tom Burleson, N.C. State (163); Tom McMillen, Maryland (160); Darrell Elston, North Carolina (151); Gus Gerard, Virginia (128); Tony Byers, Wake Forest (71).
PLAYER OF THE YEAR: Thompson (139); Jones (2); Towe (1).
COACH OF THE YEAR: Norm Sloan, N.C. State (121); Carl Tacy, Wake Forest (7); Lefty Driesell, Maryland; Dean Smith, North Carolina; and Tates Locke, Clemson; also received votes.
*Unanimous Selection

Scoring, Rebounding Leaders

TOP TEN SCORERS

Player, School	G	FG	FT	TP	Ave.
Thompson, N.C. State	31	325	155	805	26.0
Gerard, Virginia	27	227	108	562	20.8
Lucas, Maryland	28	253	58	564	20.1
McMillen, Maryland	27	214	96	524	19.4
Burleson, N.C. State	31	228	106	562	18.1
Byers, Wake Forest	26	192	84	468	18.0
Walker, Virginia	26	199	58	456	17.5
Jones, North Carolina	28	189	74	452	16.1
Fleischer, Duke	26	163	81	407	15.7
Elston, North Carolina	28	173	81	427	15.3

TOP TEN REBOUNDERS

Player, School	G	Rbs.	Ave.
Elmore, Maryland	28	412	14.7
Fleischer, Duke	26	323	12.4
Burleson, N.C. State	31	377	12.2
Rollins, Clemson	26	316	12.2
Gerard, Virginia	27	275	10.2
McMillen, Maryland	27	269	10.0
Jones, North Carolina	28	274	9.8
Stamp, Wake Forest	26	225	8.6
Croft, Clemson	25	201	8.0
Thompson, N.C. State	31	245	7.9

Rosters

CLEMSON

No.	Name	Hgt.	Yr.	Hometown
3	Donald Boop	6-3	Fr.	Orville, OH
4	John Franken	6-2	Fr.	Colonia, NJ
5	Van Gregg	6-2	Jr.	Columbus, OH
10	Terrell Suit	6-0	Sr.	Anderson, SC
11	Bruce Harman	6-0	So.	Pittsburgh, PA
12	Kenny Davis	5-11	So.	Columbia, SC
15	Jo Jo Bethea	6-1	Jr.	Newport News, VA
21	Tim Capehart	6-0	So.	Columbus, OH
22	David Brown	6-8	Fr.	York, PA
30	Wayne Rollins	7-1	Fr.	Cordele, GA
33	Jeff Reisinger	6-6	Sr.	Kingston, OH
34	Andy Butchko	6-6	Fr.	Sharon, PA
41	Marty Patterson	6-8	Jr.	Hendersonville, NC
44	Charlie Rogers	6-9	So.	Lindenhurst, NY
45	Wayne Croft	6-9	Jr.	Bamberg, SC
55	Scott Conant	6-9	So.	Sunbury, OH

COACH: Tates Locke
ASSISTANTS: Bill Clendinen, Cliff Malpass, Anthony Brown, Charlie Harrison

DUKE

No.	Name	Hgt.	Yr.	Hometown
11	Edgar Burch	6-3	Fr.	Pontiac, MI
12	Tate Armstrong	6-2	Fr.	Houston, TX
14	Willie Hodge	6-9	So.	San Antonio, TX
20	Dave O'Connell	6-4	So.	Cincinnati, OH
21	Jeff Burdette	5-11	Fr.	Buena Park, CA
22	Paul Fox	6-2	So.	Radnor, PA
23	Bill Suk	6-5	Jr.	Midlothian, IL
24	Kevin Billerman	6-2	Jr.	Bricktown, NJ
25	Mark Crow	6-7	Fr.	Richmond, VA
30	William Hannon	5-11	So.	Belmont, NC
33	Randy Abernethy	6-2	Fr.	Hildebran, NC
34	Bob Cook	6-6	So.	Glen Rock, NJ
35	Phil McLeod	6-5	Sr.	St. Petersburg, FL
40	Neil Chinault	6-5	Jr.	Peterstown, WV
42	Bob Fleischer	6-8	Jr.	Youngstown, OH
43	Pete Chili	6-9	So.	Jamestown, NY
44	Pete Kramer	6-4	Jr.	Camp Hill, PA
53	Chris Redding	6-10	Sr.	Bethesda, MD

COACH: Neill McGeachy
ASSISTANTS: Jim Lewis, Tony Barone

MARYLAND

No.	Name	Hgt.	Yr.	Hometown
5	John Boyle	6-7	So.	Hyattsville, MD
10	Rich Porac	6-0	Sr.	Monroeville, PA
13	Stan Swetnam	6-3	Jr.	Baltimore, MD
15	John Lucas	6-4	So.	Durham, NC
21	Bill Hahn	5-11	Sr.	Mishawaka, IN
22	Jap Trimble	6-3	Sr.	New York, NY
24	Maurice Howard	6-3	So.	Philadelphia, PA
32	Wilson Washington	6-8	Fr.	Norfolk, VA
41	Len Elmore	6-9	Sr.	Springfield Grdn., NY
42	Owen Brown	6-8	Jr.	La Grange, IL
45	Tom Roy	6-9	Jr.	South Windsor, CT
54	Tom McMillen	6-11	Sr.	Mansfield, PA

COACH: Lefty Driesell
ASSISTANTS: Dave Pritchett, Joe Harrington, Howard White

NORTH CAROLINA

No.	Name	Hgt.	Yr.	Hometown
11	Tony Shaver	5-11	So.	High Point, NC
12	Ray Hite	6-0	Jr.	Hyattsville, MD
13	Brad Hoffman	5-10	Jr.	Columbus, OH
14	Dave Hanners	6-0	So.	Columbus, OH
15	John Kuester	6-2	Fr.	Richmond, VA
20	Ray Harrison	6-2	Jr.	Greensboro, NC
21	Mitch Kupchak	6-9	So.	Brentwood, NY
23	Jimmy Guill	6-3	So.	Winston-Salem, NC
24	Walter Davis	6-5	Fr.	Pineville, NC
25	James Smith	6-6	Fr.	Lantana, FL
30	John O'Donnell	6-6	Sr.	New York, NY
31	Mickey Bell	6-5	Jr.	Goldsboro, NC
32	Darrell Elston	6-4	Sr.	Tipton, IN
34	Bobby Jones	6-9	Sr.	Charlotte, NC
35	Charles Waddell	6-6	Jr.	Southern Pines, NC
40	Bruce Buckley	6-8	Fr.	Bladensburg, MD
41	Jeff Crompton	6-11	Fr.	Burlington, NC
42	Bill Chambers	6-5	So.	Greensboro, NC
43	Ed Stahl	6-10	Sr.	Columbus, OH
45	Tommy LaGarde	6-10	Fr.	Detroit, MI

COACH: Dean Smith
ASSISTANTS: Bill Guthridge, Eddie Fogler, Kim Huband

All-America Teams

ASSOCIATED PRESS
FIRST TEAM: Bill Walton, UCLA; Keith Wilkes, UCLA; *David Thompson, N.C. State; John Shumate, Notre Dame; Marvin Barnes, Providence; **SECOND TEAM:** John Lucas, Maryland; Larry Fogle, Canisius; **Bobby Jones, North Carolina; Len Elmore, Maryland;** Bill Knight, Pittsburgh. **THIRD TEAM:** Dennis DuVal, Syracuse; **Tom McMillen, Maryland;** Tom Henderson, Hawaii; **Tom Burleson, N.C. State;** Campy Russell, Michigan.

UNITED PRESS INTERNATIONAL
FIRST TEAM: *Bill Walton, UCLA; **David Thompson, N.C. State**; John Shumate, Notre Dame; Keith Wilkes, UCLA; Marvin Barnes, Providence; **SECOND TEAM:** **Tom McMillen, Maryland;** Larry Fogle, Canisius; **Bobby Jones, North Carolina; Len Elmore, Maryland; Tom Burleson, N.C. State.** **THIRD TEAM:** Kevin Stacom, Providence; Campy Russell, Michigan; James Williams, Austin Peay; Bill Knight, Pittsburgh; Gary Brokaw, Notre Dame.
*Player of the Year

N.C. STATE

No.	Name	Hgt.	Yr.	Hometown
10	Morris Rivers	6-1	Jr.	Brooklyn, NY
12	Jerry Hunt	6-5	So.	Shelby, NC
12	Steve Smith	6-10	So.	East McDowell, KY
14	Greg Hawkins	6-5	So.	Huntington, WV
22	Dwight Johnson	6-0	So.	Raleigh, NC
24	Tom Burleson	7-4	Sr.	Newland, NC
25	Monte Towe	5-7	Jr.	Converse, IN
30	Phil Spence	6-8	So.	Raleigh, NC
32	Bruce Dayhuff	6-2	Fr.	Walkerton, IN
34	Craig Kuszmaul	6-5	Jr.	Warren, OH
35	Bill Lake	6-11	Fr.	Carmel, IN
40	Mark Moeller	6-3	Jr.	Canfield, OH
42	Tim Stoddard	6-7	Jr.	Hammond, IN
44	David Thompson	6-4	Jr.	Shelby, NC
50	Mike Buurma	6-10	Fr.	Willard, OH
52	Steve Nuce	6-5	Sr.	Rockville, MD
54	Ken Gehring	6-9	Fr.	Akron, OH

COACH: Norm Sloan
ASSISTANTS: Eddie Biedenbach, Sam Esposito, Art Musselman

VIRGINIA

No.	Name	Hgt.	Yr.	Hometown
10	Al Drummond	6-2	Sr.	Waverly, NY
20	Andy Boniniti	6-3	Jr.	New York, NY
21	Billy Langloh	6-2	Fr.	Laurel, MD
22	Gus Gerard	6-7	Jr.	Uniontown, PA
23	Mark Newlen	6-4	Fr.	Staunton, VA
24	Bob McKeag	6-5	Sr.	Erie, PA
25	Ray Morningstar	6-9	Fr.	Depew, NY
30	Steve Morris	5-11	Sr.	Alexandria, VA
32	Bob Sefcik	6-2	So.	Rochelle Park, NY
35	Brian Tully	6-1	Jr.	Merrick, NY
41	Wally Walker	6-6	So.	Millersville, PA
43	Dan Bonner	6-7	Jr.	Pittsburgh, PA
44	Spencer Graham	6-8	Jr.	Bethesda, MD
50	Ed Schetlick	6-8	Fr.	Newark, NJ
55	Lanny Stahurski	6-10	Sr.	Swissvale, PA

COACH: Bill Gibson
ASSISTANTS: Chip Connor, Mike Schuler

WAKE FOREST

No.	Name	Hgt.	Yr.	Hometown
10	Tony Byers	6-2	Sr.	Bessemer City, NC
13	Bobby Dwyer	6-1	Sr.	Silver Spring, MD
14	Phil Perry	6-3	Jr.	Frankfort, KY
15	Skip Brown	6-0	Fr.	Kingsport, TN
20	Charlie Ryan	6-0	Fr.	Philadelphia, PA
25	Jerry Schellenberg	6-6	Fr.	Floyds Knobs, IN
30	Dan Moody	6-5	Jr.	Blountville, TN
33	Henry Hicks	6-5	So.	Erwin, NC
34	Mike Parrish	6-6	Jr.	Canton, NC
40	Haley Hall	6-7	Jr.	Pink Hill, NC
41	Lee Foye	6-6	So.	Wilmington, NC
44	Don Mulnix	6-8	Fr.	Northglenn, CO
45	Cal Stamp	6-8	Jr.	East Moline, IL
52	Tim Stare	6-9	Jr.	Palos Verdes, CA
53	Al Myatt	6-8	So.	Raleigh, NC

COACH: Carl Tacy
ASSISTANTS: Bobby Watson, Larry Williams

Final Top 20 Polls

AP

1.	N.C. State	30-1
2.	UCLA	26-4
3.	Marquette	26-5
4.	Maryland	23-5
5.	Notre Dame	26-3
6.	Michigan	22-5
7.	Kansas	23-7
8.	Providence	28-4
9.	Indiana	23-5
10.	Long Beach St.	24-2
11.	Purdue	22-8
12.	North Carolina	22-6
13.	Vanderbilt	23-5
14.	Alabama	22-4
15.	Utah	22-8
16.	Pittsburgh	25-4
17.	Southern Cal	24-5
18.	Oral Roberts	23-6
19.	South Carolina	22-5
20.	Dayton	20-9

UPI

1.	N.C. State	30-1
2.	UCLA	26-4
3.	Notre Dame	26-3
4.	Maryland	23-5
5.	Marquette	26-5
6.	Providence	28-4
7.	Vanderbilt	23-5
8.	North Carolina	22-6
9.	Indiana	23-5
10.	Kansas	23-7
11.	Long Beach St.	24-2
12.	Michigan	22-5
13.	Southern Cal	24-5
14.	Pittsburgh	25-4
15.	Louisville	21-7
16.	South Carolina	22-5
17.	Creighton	23-7
18.	New Mexico	22-7
19.	Alabama	22-4
20.	Dayton	20-9

N.C. State beat Marquette 76-64 for NCAA title.

'75

N.C. State's David Thompson

1974-75 Final Standings

Team	Conf.	Overall	Ave.	Opp.
Maryland	10-2	24-5	89.9	74.6
*North Carolina	8-4	23-8	84.6	78.0
Clemson	8-4	17-11	80.3	72.1
N.C. State	8-4	22-6	92.7	77.9
Virginia	4-8	12-13	68.4	70.0
Duke	2-10	13-13	82.9	81.5
Wake Forest	2-10	13-13	80.6	79.1

*Won ACC Tournament

NCAA — MARYLAND second in Midwest Regional: beat Creighton 83-79, beat Notre Dame 83-71, lost to Louisville 96-82. NORTH CAROLINA third in East Regional: beat New Mexico State 93-69, lost to Syracuse 78-76, beat Boston College 110-90.
NIT — CLEMSON lost to Providence 91-86.

ACC Tournament
MARCH 6-8, 1975 AT GREENSBORO, N.C.
FIRST ROUND: Maryland, bye; North Carolina 101, Wake Forest 100 (OT); Clemson 78, Duke 76; N.C. State 91, Virginia 85. **SEMIFINALS:** N.C. State 87, Maryland 85; North Carolina 76, Clemson 71 (OT). **FINAL:** North Carolina 70, N.C. State 66.
ALL-TOURNAMENT – FIRST TEAM: David Thompson, N.C. State; Mitch Kupchak, North Carolina; Kenny Carr, N.C. State; Phil Ford, North Carolina; Skip Wise, Clemson. **SECOND TEAM:** John Lucas, Maryland; Wally Walker, Virginia; Walter Davis, North Carolina; Skip Brown, Wake Forest; Monte Towe, N.C. State.
EVERETT CASE AWARD (MVP): Ford

All-ACC
FIRST TEAM: *David Thompson, N.C. State (296 votes); Skip Brown, Wake Forest (259); Mitch Kupchak, North Carolina (252); John Lucas, Maryland (215); Skip Wise, Clemson (191). **SECOND TEAM:** Wayne Rollins, Clemson (189); Brad Davis, Maryland (159); Bob Fleischer, Duke (150); Mo Howard, Maryland (95); Owen Brown, Maryland (61).
PLAYER OF THE YEAR: *Thompson (voting totals not available).
COACH OF THE YEAR: Lefty Driesell, Maryland (66 votes); Tates Locke, Clemson (59).
*Unanimous Selection

Scoring, Rebounding Leaders

TOP TEN SCORERS

Player, School	G	FG	FT	TP	Ave.
Thompson, N.C. State	28	347	144	838	29.9
Brown, Wake Forest	26	250	89	589	22.7
Lucas, Maryland	24	186	97	469	19.5
Kupchak, North Carolina	31	239	97	575	18.5
Wise, Clemson	25	188	86	462	18.5
Fleischer, Duke	26	178	91	447	17.2
Walker, Virginia	25	179	55	413	16.5
Ford, North Carolina	31	191	126	508	16.4
Davis, North Carolina	31	200	98	498	16.1
Kramer, Duke	26	164	65	393	15.1

TOP TEN REBOUNDERS

Player, School	G	Rbs.	Ave.
Rollins, Clemson	28	328	11.7
Roy, Maryland	29	321	11.1
Kupchak, North Carolina	31	334	10.8
Fleischer, Duke	26	273	10.5
Spence, N.C. State	28	281	10.0
Thompson, N.C. State	28	229	8.2
Iavaroni, Virginia	25	198	7.9
Brown, Maryland	29	226	7.8
Griffin, Wake Forest	25	190	7.6
Sheppard, Maryland	29	217	7.5

Rosters

CLEMSON

No.	Name	Hgt.	Yr.	Hometown
3	Stan Rome	6-5	Fr.	Valdosta, GA
4	John Franken	6-2	So.	Colonia, NJ
5	Van Gregg	6-2	Sr.	Columbus, OH
10	Billy Noland	6-4	Fr.	Waynesville, NC
11	Bruce Harman	6-0	Jr.	Pittsburgh, PA
12	Donnie Joy	6-3	Fr.	Baltimore, MD
15	Jo Jo Bethea	6-1	Sr.	Newport News, VA
21	Colon Abraham	6-6	Sr.	Darlington, SC
22	David Brown	6-8	So.	York, PA
23	Terry Gettys	6-5	Fr.	Darlington, SC
30	Wayne Rollins	7-1	Sr.	Cordele, GA
32	Jimmy Howell	6-6	Fr.	Williston, SC
34	Andy Butchko	6-6	So.	Sharon, PA
41	Marty Patterson	6-8	Sr.	Hendersonville, NC
43	Charlie Rogers	6-9	Jr.	Lindenhurst, NY
44	Skip Wise	6-4	Fr.	Baltimore, MD
45	Wayne Croft	6-9	Sr.	Bamberg, SC
55	Scott Conant	6-9	Jr.	Sunbury, OH

COACH: Tates Locke
ASSISTANTS: Bill Clendinen, Charlie Harrison, Tommy Gaither

DUKE

No.	Name	Hgt.	Yr.	Hometown
11	Rick Gomez	6-3	Fr.	Roselle, NJ
12	Tate Armstrong	6-2	So.	Houston, TX
14	Willie Hodge	6-9	Jr.	San Antonio, TX
15	Bruce Bell	6-0	Fr.	Lexington, KY
20	Dave O'Connell	6-4	Jr.	Cincinnati, OH
21	Ken Young	5-10	Fr.	East Orange, NJ
22	Paul Fox	6-2	Jr.	Radnor, PA
23	Bill Suk	6-5	Sr.	Midlothian, IL
24	Kevin Billerman	6-2	Sr.	Bricktown, NJ
25	Mark Crow	6-7	So.	Richmond, VA
42	Bob Fleischer	6-8	Sr.	Youngstown, OH
43	Terry Chili	6-10	Jr.	Jamestown, NY
44	Pete Kramer	6-4	Sr.	Camp Hill, PA
53	George Moses	6-5	Jr.	New York, NY

COACH: Bill Foster
ASSISTANTS: Lou Goetz, Jim Lewis, Bob Wenzel

MARYLAND

No.	Name	Hgt.	Yr.	Hometown
5	John Boyle	6-7	Jr.	Hyattsville, MD
10	Steve Sheppard	6-6	So.	New York, NY
12	Mike Brashears	6-1	Fr.	Hagerstown, MD
13	James Jones	6-4	Jr.	Seat Pleasant, MD
15	John Lucas	6-4	Jr.	Durham, NC
20	John Newsome	6-6	Fr.	Norfolk, VA
21	Bill Hahn	5-11	Fr.	Mishawaka, IN
22	Mike Cherry	6-5	Fr.	Elm City, NC
24	Maurice Howard	6-3	Jr.	Philadelphia, PA
30	Brad Davis	6-3	Fr.	Monaca, PA
42	Owen Brown	6-8	Sr.	La Grange, IL
44	Chris Patton	6-9	Fr.	Bessemer, AL
45	Tom Roy	6-9	Sr.	South Windsor, CT

COACH: Lefty Driesell
ASSISTANTS: Dave Pritchett, Howard White, Joe Harrington

NORTH CAROLINA

No.	Name	Hgt.	Yr.	Hometown
12	Phil Ford	6-2	Fr.	Rocky Mount, NC
13	Brad Hoffman	5-10	Sr.	Columbus, OH
14	Dave Hanners	6-0	Jr.	Columbus, OH
15	John Kuester	6-2	So.	Richmond, VA
21	Mitch Kupchak	6-9	Jr.	Brentwood, NY
24	Walter Davis	6-5	So.	Pineville, NC
31	Mickey Bell	6-5	Sr.	Goldsboro, NC
32	Tom Zaligiris	6-5	Fr.	Livonia, MI
35	Charles Waddell	6-6	Sr.	Southern Pines, NC
40	Bruce Buckley	6-8	So.	Bladensburg, MD
42	Bill Chambers	6-5	Jr.	Greensboro, NC
43	Ed Stahl	6-10	Sr.	Columbus, OH
45	Tommy LaGarde	6-10	So.	Detroit, MI
30	Woody Coley	6-6	So.	Lumberton, NC
44	Eric Harry	6-6	So.	Durham, NC

COACH: Dean Smith
ASSISTANTS: Bill Guthridge, Eddie Fogler

All-America Teams

ASSOCIATED PRESS
FIRST TEAM: *David Thompson, N.C. State; Adrian Dantley, Notre Dame; David Meyers, UCLA; Ticky Burden, Utah; Scott May, Indiana. **SECOND TEAM:** John Lucas, Maryland; Rudy Hackett, Syracuse; Gus Williams, Southern California; Leon Douglas, Alabama; Kevin Grevey, Kentucky. **THIRD TEAM:** Clyde Mayes, Furman; Phil Sellers, Rutgers; Bob McCurdy, Richmond; Lionel Hollins, Arizona State; Ron Lee, Oregon.

UNITED PRESS INTERNATIONAL
FIRST TEAM: *David Thompson, N.C. State; Adrian Dantley, Notre Dame; David Meyers, UCLA; John Lucas, Maryland; Scott May, Indiana. **SECOND TEAM:** Kevin Grevey, Kentucky; Quinn Buckner, Indiana; Ticky Burden, Utah; Ron Lee, Oregon; Bernard King, Tennessee. **THIRD TEAM:** Leon Douglas, Alabama; Gus Williams, Southern California; Rich Kelley, Stanford; Steve Green, Indiana; Junior Bridgeman, Louisville.
*Player of the Year

N.C. STATE

No.	Name	Hgt.	Yr.	Hometown
10	Morris Rivers	6-1	Sr.	Brooklyn, NY
14	Bruce Dayhuff	6-2	So.	Walkerton, IN
20	Jerry Hunt	6-5	Jr.	Shelby, NC
20	Craig Davis	5-8	Fr.	Rockville, MD
22	Dwight Johnson	6-0	Jr.	Raleigh, NC
25	Monte Towe	5-7	Sr.	Converse, IN
30	Phil Spence	6-8	Jr.	Raleigh, NC
32	Kenny Carr	6-8	Fr.	Hyattsville, MD
33	Robert Jackson	6-2	Fr.	East Chicago, IN
34	Craig Kuszmaul	6-5	Sr.	Warren, OH
35	Bill Lake	6-11	Sr.	Carmel, IN
40	Mark Moeller	6-3	Sr.	Canfield, OH
42	Tim Stoddard	6-7	Sr.	Hammond, IN
44	David Thompson	6-4	Sr.	Shelby, NC
50	Mike Buurma	6-10	So.	Williard, OH

COACH: Norm Sloan
ASSISTANTS: Eddie Biedenbach, Sam Esposito, Wilbert Johnson

VIRGINIA

No.	Name	Hgt.	Yr.	Hometown
10	Lamont Carr	6-7	Jr.	Chicago, IL
20	Andy Boninti	6-3	Sr.	New York, NY
21	Billy Langloh	6-3	So.	Laurel, MD
23	Mark Newlen	6-4	So.	Staunton, VA
24	Dave Koesters	6-2	Fr.	Springfield, VA
25	Ray Morningstar	6-9	So.	Depew, NY
30	Tom Briscoe	6-0	Fr.	Lakewood, NJ
32	Bob Sefcik	6-2	Jr.	Rochelle Park, NJ
35	Brian Tully	6-1	Sr.	Merrick, NY
41	Wally Walker	6-7	Jr.	Millersville, PA
43	Dan Bonner	6-7	Sr.	Pittsburgh, PA
44	Marc Iavaroni	6-8	Fr.	Plainview, NY
50	Ed Schetlick	6-9	So.	Newark, NJ

COACH: Terry Holland
ASSISTANTS: Bill Cofield, Mike Schuler

WAKE FOREST

No.	Name	Hgt.	Yr.	Hometown
14	Phil Perry	6-3	Sr.	Frankfort, KY
15	Skip Brown	6-0	So.	Kingsport, TN
25	Jerry Schellenberg	6-6	So.	Floyds Knobs, IN
30	Dan Moody	6-5	Sr.	Kingsport, TN
32	Rod Griffin	6-6	Fr.	Fairmont, NC
33	Henry Hicks	6-5	Jr.	Erwin, NC
34	Mike Parrish	6-7	Sr.	Canton, NC
40	Haley Hall	6-7	Sr.	Pink Hill, NC
41	Lee Foye	6-6	Jr.	Wilmington, NC
42	Daryl Peterson	6-8	Jr.	Philadelphia, PA
43	Charlie Floyd	6-7	Fr.	Philadelphia, PA
44	Don Mulnix	6-8	So.	Northglenn, CO
45	Cal Stamp	6-8	Sr.	East Moline, IL
53	Al Myatt	6-8	Jr.	Raleigh, NC

COACH: Carl Tacy
ASSISTANTS: Larry Williams, Neil McGeachy, Stafford Stephenson

Final Top 20 Polls

AP

1.	UCLA	28-3
2.	Kentucky	26-5
3.	Indiana	31-1
4.	Louisville	28-3
5.	Maryland	24-5
6.	Syracuse	23-9
7.	N.C. State	22-6
8.	Arizona State	25-4
9.	North Carolina	23-8
10.	Alabama	22-5
11.	Marquette	23-4
12.	Princeton	22-8
13.	Cincinnati	23-6
14.	Notre Dame	19-10
15.	Kansas State	20-9
16.	Drake	19-10
17.	Nevada-L.V.	24-5
18.	Oregon State	19-12
19.	Michigan	19-8
20.	Pennsylvania	23-5

UPI

1.	Indiana	31-1
2.	UCLA	28-3
3.	Louisville	28-3
4.	Kentucky	26-5
5.	Maryland	24-5
6.	Marquette	23-4
7.	Arizona State	25-4
8.	Alabama	22-5
9.	N.C. State	22-6
10.	North Carolina	23-8
11.	Pennsylvania	23-5
12.	Southern Cal	18-8
13.	Utah State	21-6
14.	Nevada-L.V.	24-5
	Notre Dame	19-10
16.	Creighton	20-7
17.	Arizona	22-7
18.	New Mexico St.	20-7
19.	Clemson	17-11
20.	Texas-El Paso	20-6

UCLA beat Kentucky 92-85 for NCAA title.

ACC BASKETBALL / REFERENCE

'76

North Carolina's Mitch Kupchak

1975-76 Final Standings

Team	Conf.	Overall	Ave.	Opp.
North Carolina	11-1	25-4	85.1	74.3
Maryland	7-5	22-6	88.2	74.3
N.C. State	7-5	21-9	87.4	81.4
Clemson	5-7	18-10	83.4	75.1
Wake Forest	5-7	17-10	87.8	82.6
*Virginia	4-8	18-12	76.5	70.7
Duke	3-9	13-14	88.3	85.0

*Won ACC Tournament

NCAA—VIRGINIA lost in first round of East Regional to De-Paul 69-60. NORTH CAROLINA lost in first round of Mideast Regional to Alabama 79-64.
NIT—N.C. STATE third: beat Holy Cross 78-68, lost to UNC-Charlotte 80-79, beat Providence 74-69.

ACC Tournament
MARCH 4-6, 1976 AT LANDOVER, MD.
FIRST ROUND: North Carolina, bye; Maryland 80, Duke 78 (OT); Virginia 75, N.C. State 63; Clemson 76, Wake Forest 63. **SEMIFINALS:** North Carolina 82, Clemson 74; Virginia 73, Maryland 65. **FINAL:** Virginia 67, North Carolina 62.
ALL-TOURNAMENT—FIRST TEAM: Wally Walker, Virginia; Billy Langloh, Virginia; Mitch Kupchak, North Carolina; Phil Ford, North Carolina; Marc Iavaroni, Virginia, and Tate Armstrong, Duke (tie). **SECOND TEAM:** Maurice Howard, Maryland; Steve Sheppard, Maryland; Bobby Stokes, Virginia; Stan Rome, Clemson; Walter Davis, North Carolina.
EVERETT CASE AWARD (MVP): Walker.

All-ACC
FIRST TEAM: Mitch Kupchak, North Carolina (310 votes); Kenny Carr, N.C. State (310); Phil Ford, North Carolina (306); John Lucas, Maryland (282); Tate Armstrong, Duke (237). **SECOND TEAM:** Wally Walker, Virginia (208); Skip Brown, Wake Forest (176); Walter Davis, North Carolina (125); Wayne Rollins, Clemson (79); Rod Griffin, Wake Forest (79).
PLAYER OF THE YEAR: Kupchak (74); Carr (50); Ford (21); Walker, Lucas and Armstrong also received votes. **COACH OF THE YEAR:** Dean Smith, North Carolina (102); Norm Sloan, N.C. State (19); Bill Foster, Clemson (17).

Scoring, Rebounding Leaders
TOP TEN SCORERS

Player, School	G	FG	FT	TP	Ave.
Carr, N.C. State	30	322	154	798	26.6
Armstrong, Duke	27	265	124	654	24.2
Walker, Virginia	30	262	140	664	22.1
Brown, Wake Forest	26	223	97	543	20.9
Lucas, Maryland	28	233	91	557	19.9
Ford, North Carolina	29	206	128	540	18.6
Griffin, Wake Forest	27	190	102	482	17.6
Sheppard, Maryland	28	203	88	494	17.6
Kupchak, North Carolina	28	190	112	492	17.6
Hodge, Duke	27	189	78	456	16.9

TOP TEN REBOUNDERS

Player, School	G	Rbs.	Ave.
Kupchak, North Carolina	28	316	11.3
Rollins, Clemson	28	308	11.0
Carr, N.C. State	30	310	10.3
Gibson, Maryland	16	157	9.8
Moses, Duke	27	262	9.7
Spence, N.C. State	30	273	9.1
Griffin, Wake Forest	27	242	9.0
Boston, Maryland	28	249	8.9
Sheppard, Maryland	28	246	8.8
Hodge, Duke	27	210	7.8

Rosters

CLEMSON
No.	Name	Hgt.	Yr.	Hometown
3	Stan Rome	6-5	So.	Valdosta, GA
4	John Franken	6-2	Jr.	Colonia, NJ
10	Lee Anderson	6-0	Fr.	Mayesville, SC
11	Bruce Harmar	6-0	Sr.	Pittsburgh, PA
12	Derrick Johnson	6-2	Fr.	Indianapolis, IN
15	Greg Coles	6-3	Fr.	East Elmhurst, NY
20	Alan Hoover	6-4	So.	Matthews, NC
21	Colon Abraham	6-6	So.	Darlington, SC
22	David Brown	6-8	Jr.	York, PA
25	Marvin Dickerson	6-7	Fr.	Charleston, SC
30	Wayne Rollins	7-1	Jr.	Cordele, GA
32	Jimmy Howell	6-6	So.	Williston, SC
34	Andy Butchko	6-6	Jr.	Sharon, PA
43	Charlie Rogers	6-9	Jr.	Lindenhurst, NY

COACH: Bill Foster
ASSISTANTS: Joe Kingery, Dwight Rainey, Eddie Payne

DUKE
No.	Name	Hgt.	Yr.	Hometown
11	Rick Gomez	6-3	So.	Roselle, NJ
12	Tate Armstrong	6-2	Jr.	Houston, TX
14	Willie Hodge	6-9	Sr.	San Antonio, TX
15	Bruce Bell	6-0	Sr.	Lexington, KY
20	Dave O'Connell	6-4	Sr.	Cincinnati, OH
21	Ken Young	5-10	So.	East Orange, NJ
22	Paul Fox	6-2	Sr.	Radnor, PA
23	Steve Gray	6-2	Fr.	Woodland Hills, CA
24	Harold Morrison	6-7	Fr.	West Orange, NJ
25	Mark Crow	6-7	Jr.	Richmond, VA
34	Jim Spanarkel	6-5	Fr.	Jersey City, NJ
35	Cameron Hal	6-9	Fr.	Dundas, Canada
43	Terry Chili	6-10	Fr.	Jamestown, NY
44	Scott Goetsch	6-9	Fr.	Chatsworth, CA
53	George Moses	6-5	Sr.	New York, NY

COACH: Bill Foster
ASSISTANTS: Lou Goetz, Jim Lewis, Bob Wenzel

MARYLAND
No.	Name	Hgt.	Yr.	Hometown
5	John Boyle	6-7	Sr.	Hyattsville, MD
10	Steve Sheppard	6-6	Jr.	New York, NY
20	John Newsome	6-6	So.	Norfolk, VA
21	Eric Shrader	5-10	Fr.	Malvern, PA
15	John Lucas	6-4	Sr.	Durham, NC
24	Maurice Howard	6-3	Sr.	Philadelphia, PA
25	James Tillman	6-4	Fr.	Washington, DC
30	Brad Davis	6-3	So.	Monaca, PA
32	Larry Gibson	6-10	Fr.	Baltimore, MD
42	Pat Hand	6-4	Fr.	Newport News, VA
43	Lawrence Boston	6-8	So.	Cleveland, OH
44	Chris Patton	6-9	So.	Bessemer, AL
45	Brian Magid	6-2	Fr.	Silver Spring, MD

COACH: Lefty Driesell
ASSISTANTS: Dave Pritchett, Howard White, Joe Harrington

NORTH CAROLINA
No.	Name	Hgt.	Yr.	Hometown
11	Keith Valentine	6-0	Fr.	Richmond, VA
12	Phil Ford	6-2	So.	Rocky Mount, NC
14	Dave Hanners	6-0	Sr.	Columbus, OH
15	John Kuester	6-2	Jr.	Richmond, VA
21	Mitch Kupchak	6-10	Sr.	Brentwood, NY
22	Dudley Bradley	6-5	Fr.	Edgewood, MD
23	Ged Doughton	6-0	Fr.	Winston-Salem, NC
24	Walter Davis	6-5	Jr.	Pineville, NC
25	Randy Wiel	6-4	Fr.	Curacao, Neth. Ant.
30	Woody Coley	6-6	Jr.	Lumberton, NC
31	Loren Lutz	6-4	Fr.	Alamosa, CO
32	Tom Zaliagiris	6-5	So.	Livonia, MI
40	Bruce Buckley	6-8	Sr.	Bladensburg, MD
41	Jeff Crompton	6-11	So.	Burlington, NC
42	Bill Chambers	6-6	Sr.	Greensboro, NC
44	Eric Harry	6-6	Jr.	Durham, NC
45	Tommy LaGarde	6-10	Jr.	Detroit, MI

COACH: Dean Smith
ASSISTANTS: Bill Guthridge, Eddie Fogler

All-America Teams
ASSOCIATED PRESS
FIRST TEAM: Adrian Dantley, Notre Dame; *Scott May, Indiana; Kent Benson, Indiana; **John Lucas, Maryland**; Phil Sellers, Rutgers. **SECOND TEAM:** Richard Washington; UCLA; **Mitch Kupchak, North Carolina**; **Phil Ford, North Carolina**; Ron Lee, Oregon; Robert Parish, Centenary. **THIRD TEAM:** Bernard King, Tennessee; Earl Tatum, Marquette; Leon Douglas, Alabama; **Kenny Carr, N.C. State**; Terry Furlow, Michigan State.

UNITED PRESS INTERNATIONAL
FIRST TEAM: *Scott May, Indiana; Adrian Dantley, Notre Dame; **John Lucas, Maryland**; Richard Washington, UCLA; Kent Benson, Indiana. **SECOND TEAM:** Phil Sellers, Rutgers; **Phil Ford, North Carolina**; Bernard King, Tennessee; **Mitch Kupchak, North Carolina**; Earl Tatum, Marquette. **THIRD TEAM:** Ernie Grunfeld, Tennessee; Leon Douglas, Alabama; Terry Furlow, Michigan State; **Kenny Carr, N.C. State**; Ron Lee, Oregon.
*Player of the Year

N.C. STATE
No.	Name	Hgt.	Yr.	Hometown
10	Al Green	6-1	So.	New York, NY
14	Sotella Long	6-0	Fr.	Kinston, NC
20	Craig Davis	5-8	So.	Rockville, MD
22	Darnell Adell	6-2	Sr.	East Chicago, IL
24	Eric Agardy	6-9	Fr.	Plymouth, MI
25	Gary Stokan	5-11	So.	Pittsburgh, PA
30	Phil Spence	6-8	Sr.	Raleigh, NC
32	Kenny Carr	6-8	So.	Hyattsville, MD
33	Robert Jackson	6-2	So.	East Chicago, IN
34	Dirk Ewing	6-3	Fr.	Raleigh, NC
42	Steve Walker	6-5	Fr.	Lebanon, IN
50	Mike Buurma	6-10	Jr.	Williard, OH
54	Glenn Sudhop	7-1	Fr.	South Bend, IN

COACH: Norm Sloan
ASSISTANTS: Eddie Biedenbach, Sam Esposito, Wilbert Johnson

VIRGINIA
No.	Name	Hgt.	Yr.	Hometown
10	Lamont Carr	6-7	Sr.	Chicago, IL
20	Bobby Stokes	5-11	Fr.	King William, VA
21	Billy Langloh	6-3	Jr.	Laurel, MD
23	Mark Newlen	6-4	Jr.	Staunton, VA
24	Dave Koesters	6-2	So.	Springfield, VA
25	Ray Morningstar	6-9	Jr.	Depew, NY
30	Tom Briscoe	6-0	So.	Lakewood, NJ
31	Otis Fulton	6-10	Fr.	Richmond, VA
32	Bob Sefcik	6-2	Sr.	Rochelle Park, NY
41	Wally Walker	6-7	Sr.	Millersville, PA
42	Kevin Moore	6-6	Fr.	Detroit, MI
44	Marc Iavaroni	6-9	So.	Plainview, NY
50	Ed Schetlick	6-9	Jr.	Newark, NJ
55	Steve Castellan	6-9	Fr.	Cheverly, MD

COACH: Terry Holland
ASSISTANTS: Bill Cofield, Mike Schuler

WAKE FOREST
No.	Name	Hgt.	Yr.	Hometown
11	Mark Dale	5-8	Fr.	Kinston, NC
15	Skip Brown	6-0	Jr.	Kingsport, TN
25	Jerry Schellenberg	6-6	Jr.	Floyds Knobs, IN
30	Maurice Davis	6-6	Jr.	Baltimore, MD
32	Rod Griffin	6-6	So.	Fairmont, NC
33	Henry Hicks	6-5	Sr.	Erwin, NC
34	Steve Young	6-5	Sr.	Gaithersburg, MD
41	Lee Foye	6-6	Sr.	Wilmington, NC
42	Daryl Peterson	6-8	Sr.	Philadelphia, PA
43	Charlie Floyd	6-7	So.	Philadelphia, PA
44	Mike Palma	6-5	Fr.	Merrick, NY
52	Larry Harrison	6-11	Fr.	Baltimore, MD
53	Al Myatt	6-8	Sr.	Raleigh, NC
54	Don Mulnix	6-8	Jr.	Northglenn, CO

COACH: Carl Tacy
ASSISTANTS: Larry Williams, Neil McGeachy, Mike Parrish

Final Top 20 Polls

AP
1. Indiana	32-0
2. Marquette	27-2
3. Nevada-L.V.	29-2
4. Rutgers	31-2
5. UCLA	28-4
6. Alabama	23-5
7. Notre Dame	23-6
8. North Carolina	25-4
9. Michigan	25-7
10. W. Michigan	25-3
11. Maryland	22-6
12. Cincinnati	25-6
13. Tennessee	21-6
14. Missouri	26-5
15. Arizona	24-9
16. Texas Tech	25-6
17. DePaul	20-9
18. Virginia	18-12
19. Centenary	22-5
20. Pepperdine	22-6

UPI
1. Indiana	32-0
2. Marquette	27-2
3. Rutgers	31-2
4. Nevada-L.V.	29-2
5. UCLA	28-4
6. North Carolina	25-4
7. Alabama	23-5
8. Notre Dame	23-6
9. Michigan	25-7
10. Washington	23-5
11. Missouri	26-5
12. Arizona	24-9
13. Maryland	22-6
14. Tennessee	21-6
15. Virginia	18-12
16. Cincinnati	25-6
	Florida State	22-5
18. St. John's	23-6
19. W. Michigan	25-3
	Princeton	22-5

Indiana beat Michigan 86-68 for NCAA title.

'77

Wake Forest's Rod Griffin

1976-77 Final Standings

Team	Conf.	Overall	Ave.	Opp.
*North Carolina	9-3	28-5	83.6	72.6
Clemson	8-4	22-6	86.6	68.9
Wake Forest	8-4	22-8	81.9	76.2
Maryland	7-5	19-8	78.3	74.1
N.C. State	6-6	17-11	78.9	70.8
Duke	2-10	14-13	76.4	72.9
Virginia	2-10	12-17	65.6	67.3

*Won ACC Tournament

NCAA—NORTH CAROLINA second in Final Four: beat Purdue 69-66, beat Notre Dame 79-77, beat Kentucky 79-72 in East Regional; beat Nevada-Las Vegas 84-83, lost to Marquette 67-59 in Final Four. WAKE FOREST second in Midwest Regional: beat Arkansas 86-80, beat Southern Illinois 86-81, lost to Marquette 82-68.

ACC Tournament

MARCH 3-5, 1977 AT GREENSBORO, N.C.

FIRST ROUND: North Carolina, bye; Virginia 59, Wake Forest 57; Clemson 82, Duke 74; N.C. State 82, Maryland 72. **SEMIFINALS:** North Carolina 70, N.C. State 56; Virginia 72, Clemson 60. **FINAL:** North Carolina 75, Virginia 69.

ALL-TOURNAMENT—FIRST TEAM: Phil Ford, North Carolina; Mike O'Koren, North Carolina; Bob Stokes, Virginia; Marc Iavaroni, Virginia; John Kuester, North Carolina; Kenny Carr, N.C. State. **SECOND TEAM:** Steve Castellan, Virginia; Billy Langloh, Virginia; Walter Davis, North Carolina; Jim Spanarkel, Duke; Mike Gminski, Duke.

EVERETT CASE AWARD (MVP): Kuester.

All-ACC

FIRST TEAM: Rod Griffin, Wake Forest (265 votes); Phil Ford, North Carolina (264); Skip Brown, Wake Forest (218); Kenny Carr, N.C. State (217); Walter Davis, North Carolina (203). **SECOND TEAM:** Wayne Rollins, Clemson (200); Jim Spanarkel, Duke (186); Brad Davis, Maryland (94); Tommy LaGarde, North Carolina (60); Stan Rome, Clemson (55).

PLAYER OF THE YEAR: Griffin (89); Ford (31); Brown, Rollins, Carr and Davis also received votes. **COACH OF THE YEAR:** Dean Smith, North Carolina (47); Carl Tacy, Wake Forest (33); Bill Foster, Clemson (16); Terry Holland, Virginia; Bill Foster, Duke; and Norm Sloan, N.C. State; also received votes. **ROOKIE OF THE YEAR:** Mike Gminski, Duke (58); Hawkeye Whitney, N.C. State (58); Mike O'Koren, North Carolina (9); Chubby Wells, Clemson; Clyde Austin, N.C. State; Frank Johnson, Wake Forest; and Jo Jo Hunter, Maryland, also received votes.

Scoring, Rebounding Leaders

TOP TEN SCORERS

Player, School	G	FG	FT	TP	Ave.
Carr, N.C. State	28	230	128	588	21.0
Griffin, Wake Forest	26	198	136	532	20.5
Spanarkel, Duke	27	172	175	519	19.2
Ford, North Carolina	33	230	157	617	18.7
Brown, Wake Forest	30	223	112	558	18.6
Sheppard, Maryland	19	122	65	309	16.2
Davis, North Carolina	32	203	91	497	15.5
Gminski, Duke	27	175	64	414	15.3
Rome, Clemson	28	174	79	427	15.3
LaGarde, North Carolina	20	108	86	302	15.1

TOP TEN REBOUNDERS

Player, School	G	Rbs.	Ave.
Rollins, Clemson	28	359	12.8
Gminski, Duke	27	289	10.7
Carr, N.C. State	28	278	9.9
Griffin, Wake Forest	26	224	8.6
Gibson, Maryland	27	228	8.4
Castellan, Virginia	29	219	7.6
LaGarde, North Carolina	20	147	7.4
Harrison, Wake Forest	30	216	7.2
Boston, Maryland	26	174	6.6
O'Koren, North Carolina	33	217	6.6

Rosters

CLEMSON

No.	Name	Hgt.	Yr.	Hometown
3	Stan Rome	6-5	Jr.	Valdosta, GA
4	John Franken	6-2	Sr.	Colonia, NJ
5	Randy Gray	6-3	So.	Indianapolis, IN
10	Bobby Conrad	6-1	Fr.	Glen Ellyn, IL
11	Lee Anderson	6-0	So.	Mayesville, SC
12	Derrick Johnson	6-2	So.	Indianapolis, IN
14	David Poole	6-2	So.	Columbia, SC
15	Greg Coles	6-3	So.	East Elmhurst, NY
20	Alan Hoover	6-4	Jr.	Matthews, NC
21	Colon Abraham	6-7	So.	Darlington, SC
22	David Brown	6-8	Sr.	York, PA
25	Marvin Dickerson	6-7	So.	Charleston, SC
30	Wayne Rollins	7-1	Sr.	Cordele, GA
32	Chubby Wells	6-6	So.	Philadelphia, PA
41	Jimmy Howell	6-6	Jr.	Williston, SC

COACH: Bill Foster
ASSISTANTS: Joe Kingery, Dwight Rainey, Eddie Payne, Bruce Harman

DUKE

No.	Name	Hgt.	Yr.	Hometown
12	Tate Armstrong	6-3	Sr.	Houston, TX
15	Bruce Bell	6-0	Jr.	Lexington, KY
20	Rick Mainwaring	6-3	Jr.	Center Valley, PA
23	Steve Gray	6-2	So.	Woodland Hills, CA
24	Harold Morrison	6-7	So.	West Orange, NJ
25	Mark Crow	6-7	So.	Richmond, VA
30	Rob Hardy	6-3	So.	Columbus, OH
34	Jim Spanarkel	6-5	So.	Jersey City, NJ
40	Geoff Northrop	6-6	Jr.	La Jolla, CA
35	Cameron Hall	6-9	Fr.	Dundas, Canada
44	Scott Goetsch	6-9	So.	Chatsworth, CA
53	Mike Gminski	6-11	Fr.	Monroe, CT

COACH: Bill Foster
ASSISTANTS: Lou Goetz, Ray Jones, Bob Wenzel

MARYLAND

No.	Name	Hgt.	Yr.	Hometown
10	Steve Sheppard	6-6	Sr.	New York, NY
11	Bill Bryant	6-6	Fr.	Washington, DC
12	Mark Crawford	6-3	Fr.	Newport News, VA
14	Mike Davis	6-10	Jr.	Jacksonville, FL
21	Eric Shrader	5-9	So.	Malvern, PA
22	James Tillman	6-4	So.	Washington, DC
23	David Henderson	6-9	Fr.	Roanoke, VA
30	Brad Davis	6-3	Jr.	Monaca, PA
32	Larry Gibson	6-10	So.	Baltimore, MD
35	Jo Jo Hunter	6-3	Fr.	Washington, DC
43	Lawrence Boston	6-8	Jr.	Cleveland, OH
45	Brian Magid	6-2	So.	Silver Spring, MD
50	John Bilney	6-8	Fr.	Woodcliff Lake, NJ

COACH: Lefty Driesell
ASSISTANTS: Howard White, Joe Harrington, Wil Jones

NORTH CAROLINA

No.	Name	Hgt.	Yr.	Hometown
12	Phil Ford	6-2	Jr.	Rocky Mount, NC
15	John Kuester	6-2	Sr.	Richmond, VA
20	Dave Colescott	6-1	Fr.	Marion, IN
22	Dudley Bradley	6-5	So.	Edgewood, MD
23	Ged Doughton	6-0	So.	Winston-Salem, NC
24	Walter Davis	6-5	Sr.	Pineville, NC
25	Randy Wiel	6-4	So.	Curacao, Neth. Ant.
30	Woody Coley	6-6	Sr.	Lumberton, NC
31	Mike O'Koren	6-6	Fr.	Jersey City, NJ
32	Tom Zaliagiris	6-5	Jr.	Livonia, MI
40	Bruce Buckley	6-8	Sr.	Bladensburg, MD
42	Jeff Wolf	6-10	Fr.	Kohler, WI
43	John Virgil	6-4	Fr.	Elm City, NC
45	Tommy LaGarde	6-10	Sr.	Detroit, MI
50	Rich Yonakor	6-9	Fr.	Euclid, OH
54	Steve Krafcsin	6-9	Fr.	Chicago Ridge, IL

COACH: Dean Smith
ASSISTANTS: Bill Guthridge, Eddie Fogler

All-America Teams

ASSOCIATED PRESS

FIRST TEAM: *Marques Johnson, UCLA; Rickey Green, Michigan; **Phil Ford, North Carolina**; Kent Benson, Indiana; Bernard King, Tennessee. **SECOND TEAM:** Ernie Grunfeld, Tennessee; Bill Cartwright, San Francisco; Otis Birdsong, Houston; Mychal Thompson, Minnesota; Butch Lee, Marquette. **THIRD TEAM: Rod Griffin, Wake Forest; Wayne Rollins, Clemson**; Phil Hubbard, Michigan; Bo Ellis, Marquette; Freeman Williams, Portland State.

UNITED PRESS INTERNATIONAL

FIRST TEAM: *Marques Johnson, UCLA; Rickey Green, Michigan; Kent Benson, Indiana; Bernard King, Tennessee; Otis Birdsong, Houston. **SECOND TEAM:** Ernie Grunfeld, Tennessee; **Phil Ford, North Carolina**; Butch Lee, Marquette; Mychal Thompson, Minnesota; Bill Cartwright, San Francisco. **THIRD TEAM:** Freeman Williams, Portland State; Larry Bird, Indiana State; **Rod Griffin, Wake Forest**; Cedric Maxwell, UNC-Charlotte; **Kenny Carr, N.C. State**.

*Player of the Year

N.C. STATE

No.	Name	Hgt.	Yr.	Hometown
3	Clyde Austin	6-2	Fr.	Richmond, VA
10	Al Green	6-2	Jr.	New York, NY
12	Fred Sherrill	6-6	Fr.	Durham, NC
14	Brian Walker	6-2	Fr.	Lebanon, IN
20	Craig Davis	5-8	Jr.	Rockville, MD
24	Tony Warren	6-6	So.	Raleigh, NC
25	Gary Stokan	6-0	Jr.	Pittsburgh, PA
32	Kenny Carr	6-8	Jr.	Washington, DC
34	Dirk Ewing	6-4	So.	Raleigh, NC
42	Steve Walker	6-5	So.	Lebanon, IN
43	Hawkeye Whitney	6-5	Fr.	Washington, DC
54	Glenn Sudhop	7-2	So.	South Bend, IN

COACH: Norm Sloan
ASSISTANTS: Eddie Biedenbach, Sam Esposito, Wilbert Johnson

VIRGINIA

No.	Name	Hgt.	Yr.	Hometown
5	William Napper	6-2	Jr.	Arlington, VA
11	Garland Jefferson	6-3	Fr.	Covington, VA
20	Bobby Stokes	5-10	So.	King William, VA
21	Billy Langloh	6-3	Sr.	Laurel, MD
23	Mark Newlen	6-4	Sr.	Staunton, VA
24	Dave Koesters	6-2	Jr.	Springfield, VA
30	Tom Briscoe	6-0	Jr.	Lakewood, NJ
31	Otis Fulton	6-10	So.	Richmond, VA
32	Joe Perry	6-7	Fr.	Raleigh, NC
35	Mike Owens	6-6	Fr.	Kensington, MD
44	Marc Iavaroni	6-9	Jr.	Plainview, NY
50	Ed Schetlick	6-9	Jr.	Newark, NJ
55	Steve Castellan	6-9	So.	Cheverly, MD

COACH: Terry Holland
ASSISTANTS: Craig Littlepage, Mike Schuler

WAKE FOREST

No.	Name	Hgt.	Yr.	Hometown
11	Mark Dale	5-8	So.	Kinston, NC
14	Frank Johnson	6-2	Fr.	Weirsdale, FL
15	Skip Brown	6-1	Sr.	Kingsport, TN
20	David Morris	6-3	So.	Winston-Salem, NC
25	Jerry Schellenberg	6-5	Sr.	Floyds Knobs, IN
30	Maurice Davis	6-6	So.	Baltimore, MD
32	Rod Griffin	6-6	Jr.	Fairmont, NC
33	Leroy McDonald	6-5	Jr.	New York, NY
34	Steve Young	6-5	Jr.	Gaithersburg, MD
40	John Hendler	6-7	Fr.	River Grove, IL
44	Mike Palma	6-5	So.	Merrick, NY
52	Larry Harrison	6-11	So.	Baltimore, MD
54	Don Mulnix	6-8	Sr.	Northglenn, CO

COACH: Carl Tacy
ASSISTANTS: Ed Hall, Dave Odom, Mike Parrish

Final Top 20 Polls

AP

1. Michigan	26-4
2. UCLA	24-5
3. Kentucky	26-4
4. Nevada-L.V.	29-3
5. **North Carolina**	**28-5**
6. Syracuse	26-4
7. Marquette	25-7
8. San Francisco	29-2
9. **Wake Forest**	**22-8**
10. Notre Dame	22-7
11. Alabama	25-6
12. Detroit	25-4
13. Minnesota	24-3
14. Utah	22-7
15. Tennessee	22-6
16. Kansas State	23-9
17. UNC-Char.	28-5
18. Arkansas	26-2
19. Louisville	21-7
20. Va. Military	26-4

UPI

1. Michigan	26-4
2. San Francisco	29-2
3. **North Carolina**	**28-5**
4. UCLA	24-5
5. Kentucky	26-4
6. Nevada-L.V.	29-3
7. Arkansas	26-2
8. Tennessee	22-6
9. Syracuse	26-4
10. Utah	22-7
11. Kansas State	23-9
12. Cincinnati	25-5
13. Louisville	21-7
14. Marquette	25-7
15. Providence	24-5
16. Indiana State	25-3
17. Minnesota	24-3
18. Alabama	25-6
19. Detroit	25-4
20. Purdue	19-9

Marquette beat North Carolina 67-59 for NCAA title.

'78

North Carolina's Phil Ford

1977-78 Final Standings

Team	Conf.	Overall	Ave.	Opp.
North Carolina	9-3	23-8	81.1	70.7
*Duke	8-4	27-7	85.6	74.4
N.C. State	7-5	21-10	82.4	75.2
Virginia	6-6	20-8	71.9	66.9
Wake Forest	6-6	19-10	83.2	76.4
Maryland	3-9	15-13	82.1	79.5
Clemson	3-9	15-12	82.6	73.7

*Won ACC Tournament

NCAA — DUKE second in Final Four: beat Rhode Island 63-62, beat Pennsylvania 84-80, beat Villanova 90-72 in East Regional; beat Notre Dame 90-86, lost to Kentucky 94-88 in Final Four. NORTH CAROLINA lost in first round of West Regional to San Francisco 68-64.

NIT — N.C. STATE second: beat South Carolina 82-70, beat Detroit 84-77, beat Georgetown 86-85 (OT), lost to Texas 101-93. VIRGINIA lost to Georgetown 70-68 (OT).

ACC Tournament
MARCH 1-4, 1978 AT GREENSBORO, N.C.

FIRST ROUND: North Carolina, bye; Duke 83, Clemson 72; Maryland 109, N.C. State 108 (3 OT); Wake Forest 72, Virginia 61. **SEMI-FINALS:** Duke 81, Maryland 69; Wake Forest 82, North Carolina 77. **FINAL:** Duke 85, Wake Forest 77.

ALL-TOURNAMENT—FIRST TEAM: Mike Gminski, Duke; Leroy McDonald, Wake Forest; Rod Griffin, Wake Forest; Jim Spanarkel, Duke; Gene Banks, Duke. **SECOND TEAM:** Phil Ford, North Carolina; Frank Johnson, Wake Forest; Kenny Dennard, Duke; Lawrence Boston, Maryland; Larry Gibson, Maryland.
EVERETT CASE AWARD (MVP): Spanarkel.

All-ACC

FIRST TEAM: *Phil Ford, North Carolina (258 votes); *Rod Griffin, Wake Forest (258); Mike Gminski, Duke (256); Jim Spanarkel, Duke (253); Mike O'Koren, North Carolina (246). **SECOND TEAM:** Gene Banks, Duke (120); Jeff Lamp, Virginia (99); Frank Johnson, Wake Forest (97); Hawkeye Whitney, N.C. State (71); Clyde Austin, N.C. State (60).
PLAYER OF THE YEAR: Ford (86); Griffin (33). **COACH OF THE YEAR:** Bill Foster, Duke (82); Dean Smith, North Carolina (20); Norm Sloan, N.C. State (18). **ROOKIE OF THE YEAR:** Banks (115); Lamp (10).
*Unanimous Selection

Scoring, Rebounding Leaders

TOP TEN SCORERS

Player, School	G	FG	FT	TP	Ave.
Griffin, Wake Forest	29	243	137	623	21.5
Ford, North Carolina	30	238	149	625	20.8
Spanarkel, Duke	34	244	220	708	20.8
Gminski, Duke	32	246	148	640	20.0
O'Koren, North Carolina	27	173	122	468	17.3
Lamp, Virginia	28	156	173	485	17.3
Banks, Duke	34	238	105	581	17.1
Johnson, Wake Forest	29	193	84	470	16.2
Boston, Maryland	28	182	59	423	15.5
Whitney, N.C. State	31	193	87	473	15.3

TOP TEN REBOUNDERS

Player, School	G	Rbs.	Ave.
Griffin, Wake Forest	29	291	10.0
Gminski, Duke	32	319	10.0
Gibson, Maryland	28	253	9.0
Banks, Duke	34	292	8.6
Castellan, Virginia	28	221	7.9
Harrison, Wake Forest	29	221	7.6
Boston, Maryland	28	206	7.4
Campbell, Clemson	27	195	7.2
King, Maryland	28	187	6.7
O'Koren, North Carolina	27	180	6.7

Rosters

CLEMSON

No.	Name	Hgt.	Yr.	Hometown
3	Stan Rome	6-5	Sr.	Valdosta, GA
5	Bob Fuzy	6-2	So.	Warrenville, IL
10	Bobby Conrad	6-2	So.	Glen Ellyn, IL
11	Lee Anderson	6-0	Fr.	Mayesville, SC
12	Derrick Johnson	6-2	Jr.	Indianapolis, IN
14	David Poole	6-3	Jr.	Columbia, SC
15	Greg Coles	6-3	Jr.	East Elmhurst, NY
20	Alan Hoover	6-4	Sr.	Matthews, NC
21	Colon Abraham	6-7	Sr.	Darlington, SC
22	Larry Nance	6-8	Fr.	Anderson, SC
23	John Campbell	6-9	So.	Blenheim, SC
24	Billy Williams	6-3	So.	Raleigh, NC
25	Marvin Dickerson	6-7	Jr.	Charleston, SC
31	Sam Hunter	6-1	So.	Sumter, SC
31	Randy Gray	6-2	So.	Chicago, IL
32	Chubby Wells	6-6	Jr.	Philadelphia, PA
41	Jimmy Howell	6-7	So.	Williston, SC
44	Stewart Zane	6-10	Jr.	Chattanooga, TN
	Mike McGrady	6-5	So.	Greenville, SC

COACH: Bill Foster
ASSISTANTS: Joe Kingery, Dwight Rainey, Eddie Payne, Cliff Bryant

DUKE

No.	Name	Hgt.	Yr.	Hometown
14	Rob Hardy	6-3	Jr.	Columbus, OH
15	Bruce Bell	6-0	Sr.	Lexington, KY
20	Gene Banks	6-7	Fr.	Philadelphia, PA
21	Bob Bender	6-2	So.	Crown Point, IN
22	John Harrell	6-0	So.	Durham, NC
23	Steve Gray	6-2	Jr.	Woodland Hills, CA
24	Harold Morrison	6-7	Jr.	West Orange, NJ
30	Jim Suddath	6-6	Fr.	East Point, GA
33	Kenny Dennard	6-7	Fr.	King, NC
34	Jim Spanarkel	6-5	Jr.	Jersey City, NJ
35	Cameron Hall	6-9	So.	Dundas, Canada
43	Mike Gminski	6-11	So.	Monroe, CT
44	Scott Goetsch	6-9	Jr.	Chatsworth, CA

COACH: Bill Foster
ASSISTANTS: Lou Goetz, Ray Jones, Bob Wenzel

MARYLAND

No.	Name	Hgt.	Yr.	Hometown
10	Greg Manning	6-1	Fr.	Steelton, PA
11	Bill Bryant	6-4	So.	Washington, DC
12	Bob Hart	6-3	So.	Laurel, MD
14	Mike Davis	6-8	Sr.	Jacksonville, FL
20	Kim Camp	6-4	So.	Little Rock, AR
21	Eric Shrader	5-9	Jr.	Malvern, PA
22	Bruce Peterson	6-6	So.	Levittown, NY
23	David Henderson	6-9	So.	Roanoke, VA
27	Ernest Graham	6-7	Fr.	Baltimore, MD
32	Larry Gibson	6-10	Jr.	Baltimore, MD
35	Jo Jo Hunter	6-3	So.	Washington, DC
43	Lawrence Boston	6-8	Sr.	Cleveland, OH
50	John Bilney	6-8	So.	Woodcliff Lake, NJ
55	Albert King	6-6	Fr.	Brooklyn, NY

COACH: Lefty Driesell
ASSISTANTS: Joe Harrington, Wil Jones, Bill Turner

NORTH CAROLINA

No.	Name	Hgt.	Yr.	Hometown
11	Mike Pepper	6-2	Fr.	Vienna, VA
12	Phil Ford	6-2	Sr.	Rocky Mount, NY
20	Dave Colescott	6-1	So.	Marion, IN
22	Dudley Bradley	6-5	Jr.	Edgewood, MD
23	Ged Doughton	6-0	Jr.	Winston-Salem, NC
25	Randy Wiel	6-4	Jr.	Curacao, Neth. Ant.
30	Al Wood	6-6	Fr.	Gray, GA
31	Mike O'Koren	6-7	So.	Jersey City, NJ
32	Tom Zaliagiris	6-6	Sr.	Livonia, MI
34	Pete Budko	6-8	Fr.	Lutherville, MD
41	Jeff Crompton	6-11	Sr.	Burlington, NC
42	Jeff Wolf	6-10	So.	Kohler, WI
43	John Virgil	6-5	So.	Elm City, NC
50	Rich Yonakor	6-9	So.	Euclid, OH

COACH: Dean Smith
ASSISTANTS: Bill Guthridge, Eddie Fogler

N.C. STATE

No.	Name	Hgt.	Yr.	Hometown
3	Clyde Austin	6-2	So.	Richmond, VA
20	Craig Davis	5-8	Sr.	Rockville, MD
21	Keith Almond	6-2	Fr.	Albermarle, NC
22	Pete Keefer	6-2	Fr.	Baltimore, MD
24	Tony Warren	6-6	Jr.	Raleigh, NC
25	Kenny Matthews	6-3	Fr.	Washington, DC
33	Art Jones	6-7	Fr.	Hampton, VA
40	Ken Montgomery	6-5	Fr.	Indianapolis, IN
41	Tiny Pinder	6-7	Jr.	Miami, FL
42	Craig Watts	6-11	Fr.	South Easton, MA
43	Hawkeye Whitney	6-5	So.	Washington, DC
45	Donnie Perkins	6-3	Fr.	Bethel, NC
50	Joe Stiltner	6-8	Fr.	Bland, VA
54	Glenn Sudhop	7-2	Jr.	South Bend, IN
55	Chuck Nevitt	7-0	Fr.	Marietta, GA

COACH: Norm Sloan
ASSISTANTS: Eddie Biedenbach, Sam Esposito, Wilbert Johnson

VIRGINIA

No.	Name	Hgt.	Yr.	Hometown
5	William Napper	6-2	Sr.	Arlington, VA
10	Tommy Hicks	6-2	Jr.	Huntington, NY
11	Garland Jefferson	6-3	So.	Covington, VA
20	Bobby Stokes	5-10	Jr.	King William, VA
23	Jeff Klein	6-5	Fr.	Stow, OH
24	David Koesters	6-2	Sr.	Springfield, VA
25	Lee Raker	6-5	Fr.	Louisville, KY
30	Tom Briscoe	6-0	Sr.	Lakewood, NJ
33	Jeff Lamp	6-5	Fr.	Louisville, KY
44	Marc Iavaroni	6-9	Sr.	Plainview, NY
45	Mike Owens	6-6	So.	Kensington, MD
50	Ed Schetlick	6-9	Sr.	Newark, NJ
55	Steve Castellan	6-9	Jr.	Cheverly, MD

COACH: Terry Holland
ASSISTANTS: Craig Littlepage, Richard Schmidt

WAKE FOREST

No.	Name	Hgt.	Yr.	Hometown
10	Ed Thurman	6-1	Fr.	Lynn, MA
11	Mark Dale	5-8	Jr.	Kinston, NC
14	Frank Johnson	6-2	So.	Weirsdale, FL
20	David Morris	6-3	So.	Winston-Salem, NC
22	Fran McCaffery	6-4	Fr.	Philadelphia, PA
31	Justin Ellis	6-10	Fr.	Washington, DC
32	Rod Griffin	6-6	Sr.	Fairmont, NC
33	Leroy McDonald	6-5	Sr.	New York, NY
40	John Hendler	6-7	So.	River Grove, IL
41	Will Singleton	6-6	Fr.	Sumter, SC
44	Mike Palma	6-5	Jr.	Merrick, NY
52	Larry Harrison	6-11	Jr.	Baltimore, MD

COACH: Carl Tacy
ASSISTANTS: Ed Hall, Dave Odom, Bob Burton

All-America Teams

ASSOCIATED PRESS

FIRST TEAM: *Butch Lee, Marquette; **Phil Ford, North Carolina**; Mychal Thompson, Minnesota; Larry Bird, Indiana State; David Greenwood, UCLA. **SECOND TEAM:** Jack Givens, Kentucky; Freeman Williams, Portland State; Ron Brewer, Arkansas; Dave Corzine, DePaul; Reggie King, Alabama. **THIRD TEAM:** Sidney Moncrief, Arkansas; **Rod Griffin, Wake Forest**; Rick Robey, Kentucky; Magic Johnson, Michigan State; Mike Evans, Kansas State.

UNITED PRESS INTERNATIONAL

FIRST TEAM: *Butch Lee, Marquette; **Phil Ford, North Carolina**; Mychal Thompson, Minnesota; Larry Bird, Indiana State; David Greenwood, UCLA. **SECOND TEAM:** Freeman Williams, Portland State; Sidney Moncrief, Arkansas; Rick Robey, Kentucky; Jack Givens, Kentucky; James Bailey, Rutgers. **THIRD TEAM:** Roger Phegley, Bradley; Kyle Macy, Kentucky; Dave Corzine, DePaul; **Rod Griffin, Wake Forest**; Magic Johnson, Michigan State.

*Player of the Year

Final Top 20 Polls

AP

1. Kentucky	30-2
2. UCLA	25-3
3. DePaul	27-3
4. Michigan St.	25-5
5. Arkansas	32-4
6. Notre Dame	23-8
7. Duke	27-7
8. Marquette	24-4
9. Louisville	23-7
10. Kansas	24-5
11. San Francisco	23-6
12. New Mexico	24-4
13. Indiana	21-8
14. Utah	23-6
15. Florida State	23-6
16. **North Carolina**	**23-8**
17. Texas	26-5
18. Detroit	25-4
19. Miami (Ohio)	19-9
20. Pennsylvania	20-8

UPI

1. Kentucky	30-2
2. UCLA	25-3
3. Marquette	24-4
4. New Mexico	24-4
5. Michigan St.	25-5
6. Arkansas	32-4
7. DePaul	27-3
8. Kansas	24-5
9. **Duke**	**27-7**
10. **North Carolina**	**23-8**
11. Notre Dame	23-8
12. Florida State	23-6
13. San Francisco	23-6
14. Louisville	23-7
15. Indiana	21-8
16. Houston	25-8
17. Utah State	21-7
18. Utah	23-6
19. Texas	26-5
20. Georgetown	23-8

Kentucky beat Duke 94-88 for NCAA title.

'79

Duke's Mike Gminski

1978-79 Final Standings

Team	Conf.	Overall	Ave.	Opp.
Duke	9-3	22-8	71.9	65.5
*North Carolina	9-3	23-6	76.5	65.4
Virginia	7-5	19-10	76.3	69.7
Maryland	6-6	19-11	77.9	74.7
Clemson	5-7	19-10	72.0	65.6
N.C. State	3-9	18-12	78.5	70.0
Wake Forest	3-9	12-15	72.4	73.4

*Won ACC Tournament

NCAA — NORTH CAROLINA lost in first round of East Regional to Pennsylvania 72-71. DUKE lost in first round of East Regional to St. John's 80-78.

NIT — CLEMSON beat Kentucky 68-67 (OT), lost to Old Dominion 71-69 (2OT). VIRGINIA beat Northeastern Louisiana 79-78, lost to Alabama 90-88. MARYLAND beat Rhode Island 67-65 (3OT), lost to Ohio State 79-72.

ACC Tournament
MARCH 1-3, 1979 AT GREENSBORO, N.C.

FIRST ROUND: North Carolina, bye; Duke 58, Wake Forest 56; N.C. State 82, Virginia 78; Maryland 75, Clemson 67. **SEMIFINALS:** North Carolina 102, Maryland 79; Duke 62, N.C. State 59. **FINAL:** North Carolina 71, Duke 63.

ALL-TOURNAMENT — FIRST TEAM: Jim Spanarkel, Duke; Mike O'Koren, North Carolina; Dudley Bradley, North Carolina; Dave Colescott, North Carolina; Mike Gminski, Duke. **SECOND TEAM:** Hawkeye Whitney, N.C. State; Al Wood, North Carolina; Larry Gibson, Maryland; Jeff Lamp, Virginia; Clyde Austin, N.C. State.

EVERETT CASE AWARD (MVP): Bradley.

All-ACC

FIRST TEAM: *Mike Gminski, Duke (222 votes); Jeff Lamp, Virginia (214); Jim Spanarkel, Duke (194); Hawkeye Whitney, N.C. State (177); Al Wood, North Carolina (170). **SECOND TEAM:** Mike O'Koren, North Carolina (168); Gene Banks, Duke (110); Lee Raker, Virginia (83); Frank Johnson, Wake Forest (76); Larry Gibson, Maryland (44).

PLAYER OF THE YEAR: Gminski (70); Lamp (16); Spanarkel; Dudley Bradley, North Carolina; O'Koren; Wood; Whitney; and Bobby Conrad, Clemson; also received votes. **COACH OF THE YEAR:** *Dean Smith, North Carolina (85). **ROOKIE OF THE YEAR:** Buck Williams, Maryland (81); Alvis Rogers, Wake Forest (12); Jeff Jones, Virginia (6); Guy Morgan, Wake Forest (6).

*Unanimous Selection

Scoring, Rebounding Leaders

TOP TEN SCORERS

Player, School	G	FG	FT	TP	Ave.
Lamp, Virginia	28	230	181	641	22.9
Gminski, Duke	30	218	129	565	18.8
Whitney, N.C. State	30	238	84	560	18.7
Wood, North Carolina	29	210	95	515	17.8
Graham, Maryland	30	222	55	499	16.6
Raker, Virginia	25	164	85	413	16.5
Johnson, Wake Forest	27	169	96	434	16.1
Spanarkel, Duke	30	188	102	478	15.9
King, Maryland	28	191	62	444	15.9
O'Koren, North Carolina	28	135	144	414	14.8

TOP TEN REBOUNDERS

Player, School	G	Rbs.	Ave.
Williams, Maryland	30	323	10.8
Gminski, Duke	30	275	9.2
Gibson, Maryland	30	257	8.6
Banks, Duke	30	255	8.5
Nance, Clemson	29	210	7.2
O'Koren, North Carolina	28	202	7.2
Castellan, Virginia	29	207	7.1
Morgan, Wake Forest	27	171	6.3
Rogers, Wake Forest	26	160	6.2
Whitney, N.C. State	30	184	6.1

Rosters

CLEMSON

No.	Name	Hgt.	Yr.	Hometown
5	Bob Fuzy	6-2	Jr.	Warrenville, IL
10	Bobby Conrad	6-2	Sr.	Glen Ellyn, IL
12	Derrick Johnson	6-2	Sr.	Indianapolis, IN
13	Dan Mayfield	6-1	Fr.	Toccoa, GA
14	David Poole	6-3	Sr.	Columbia, SC
15	Greg Coles	6-3	Sr.	East Elmhurst, NY
20	Keith Whitt	6-6	Fr.	Hanover, MA
22	Larry Nance	6-9	So.	Anderson, SC
23	John Campbell	6-9	Jr.	Blenheim, SC
24	Billy Williams	6-3	Jr.	Raleigh, NC
25	Marvin Dickerson	6-7	Sr.	Charleston, SC
31	Horace Wyatt	6-10	Fr.	Hartsville, SC
32	Chubby Wells	6-6	Sr.	Philadelphia, PA
40	Marvin Key	6-2	Fr.	Dunwoody, GA
42	Keith Walker	6-5	So.	Statesville, NC
44	Stewart Zane	6-10	Jr.	Chattanooga, TN
54	Bill Ross	6-10	Fr.	Lake Placid, FL

COACH: Bill Foster
ASSISTANTS: Joe Kingery, Dwight Rainey, Clint Bryant, Bob Strunk

DUKE

No.	Name	Hgt.	Yr.	Hometown
12	Vince Taylor	6-5	Fr.	Lexington, KY
14	Rob Hardy	6-3	Sr.	Columbus, OH
20	Gene Banks	6-7	So.	Philadelphia, PA
21	Bob Bender	6-2	Jr.	Crown Point, IN
22	John Harrell	6-0	Jr.	Durham, NC
23	Steve Gray	6-2	Sr.	Woodland Hills, CA
24	Harold Morrison	6-7	Sr.	West Orange, NJ
30	Jim Suddath	6-6	So.	East Point, GA
33	Kenny Dennard	6-7	So.	King, NC
34	Jim Spanarkel	6-5	Sr.	Jersey City, NJ
43	Mike Gminski	6-11	Jr.	Monroe, CT
44	Scott Goetsch	6-9	Jr.	Chatsworth, CA

COACH: Bill Foster
ASSISTANTS: Bob Wenzel, Terry Chili, Steve Steinwedel

MARYLAND

No.	Name	Hgt.	Yr.	Hometown
5	Eric Shrader	5-9	Sr.	Malvern, PA
10	Greg Manning	6-1	So.	Steelton, PA
11	Bill Bryant	6-4	Jr.	Washington, DC
12	Bob Hart	6-3	Jr.	Laurel, MD
15	Reggie Jackson	6-4	Fr.	Philadelphia, PA
21	Dutch Morley	6-2	Fr.	Hyattsville, MD
23	David Henderson	6-9	Jr.	Roanoke, VA
25	Ernest Graham	6-7	So.	Baltimore, MD
32	Larry Gibson	6-10	Sr.	Baltimore, MD
50	John Bilney	6-8	Fr.	Woodcliff Lake, NJ
52	Buck Williams	6-8	Fr.	Rocky Mount, NC
54	Taylor Baldwin	6-10	Fr.	Greenwich, CT
55	Albert King	6-6	So.	Brooklyn, NY

COACH: Lefty Driesell
ASSISTANTS: Joe Harrington, Wil Jones, Bill Turner

NORTH CAROLINA

No.	Name	Hgt.	Yr.	Hometown
11	Mike Pepper	6-3	So.	Vienna, VA
20	Dave Colescott	6-1	Jr.	Marion, IN
21	Jimmy Black	6-2	Fr.	The Bronx, NY
22	Dudley Bradley	6-6	Sr.	Edgewood, MD
23	Ged Doughton	6-1	Sr.	Winston-Salem, NC
25	Randy Wiel	6-4	Sr.	Curacao, Neth. Ant.
30	Al Wood	6-6	So.	Gray, GA
31	Mike O'Koren	6-7	Jr.	Jersey City, NJ
32	Eric Kenny	6-6	So.	Asheville, NC
34	Pete Budko	6-8	So.	Lutherville, MD
42	Jeff Wolf	6-11	Jr.	Kohler, WI
43	John Virgil	6-5	Jr.	Elm City, NC
45	Chris Brust	6-9	Fr.	Babylon, NY
50	Rich Yonakor	6-9	Jr.	Euclid, OH

COACH: Dean Smith
ASSISTANTS: Bill Guthridge, Eddie Fogler, Roy Williams

N.C. STATE

No.	Name	Hgt.	Yr.	Hometown
3	Clyde Austin	6-3	Jr.	Richmond, VA
5	Pete Keller	5-10	Fr.	Richmond, IN
12	Emmett Lay	6-4	Fr.	Tabor City, NC
24	Tony Warren	6-6	Sr.	Raleigh, NC
25	Steve Wolf	6-3	Fr.	Fort Mitchell, KY
33	Art Jones	6-7	So.	Hampton, VA
34	Kenny Matthews	6-3	So.	Washington, DC
40	Scott Parzych	6-7	Jr.	Lockport, IL
41	Tiny Pinder	6-7	Sr.	Miami, FL
42	Craig Watts	6-11	So.	South Easton, MA
43	Hawkeye Whitney	6-5	Jr.	Washington, DC
45	Donnie Perkins	6-3	So.	Bethel, NC
54	Glenn Sudhop	7-2	Sr.	South Bend, IN
55	Chuck Nevitt	7-3	Fr.	Marietta, GA

COACH: Norm Sloan
ASSISTANTS: Marty Fletcher, Monte Towe, Gary Stokan

VIRGINIA

No.	Name	Hgt.	Yr.	Hometown
3	Jeff Lamp	6-5	So.	Louisville, KY
10	Tommy Hicks	6-2	Sr.	Huntington, NY
11	Garland Jefferson	6-3	Jr.	Covington, VA
12	Dean Carpenter	6-9	Jr.	New Orleans, LA
20	Bobby Stokes	5-10	Sr.	King William, VA
23	Jeff Klein	6-5	So.	Stow, OH
24	Jeff Jones	6-3	Fr.	Owensboro, KY
25	Lee Raker	6-5	So.	Louisville, KY
31	Otis Fulton	6-10	Jr.	Richmond, VA
42	Peter MacBeth	6-9	Fr.	Marietta, GA
44	Terry Gates	6-8	So.	Louisville, KY
45	Mike Owens	6-6	Jr.	Kensington, MD
55	Steve Castellan	6-9	Sr.	Cheverly, MD

COACH: Terry Holland
ASSISTANTS: Craig Littlepage, Richard Schmidt

WAKE FOREST

No.	Name	Hgt.	Yr.	Hometown
5	Ed Thurman	6-1	So.	Lynn, MA
11	Mark Dale	5-8	Fr.	Kinston, NC
14	Frank Johnson	6-2	Jr.	Weirsdale, FL
20	David Morris	6-3	Jr.	Winston-Salem, NC
23	Benny McKaig	6-4	Jr.	Raleigh, NC
30	Alvis Rogers	6-6	Fr.	Washington, NC
31	Justin Ellis	6-10	So.	Washington, DC
35	Guy Morgan	6-8	Fr.	Virginia Beach, VA
40	John Hendler	6-7	Jr.	River Grove, IL
41	Will Singleton	6-6	So.	Sumter, SC
44	Mike Helms	6-3	Fr.	Bassett, VA
52	Larry Harrison	6-11	Sr.	Baltimore, MD
54	Jim Johnstone	6-11	Fr.	Youngstown, NY

COACH: Carl Tacy
ASSISTANTS: Ed Hall, Dave Odom, Mark Sandy

All-America Teams

ASSOCIATED PRESS

FIRST TEAM: *Larry Bird, Indiana State; Bill Cartwright, San Francisco; David Greenwood, UCLA; Sidney Moncrief, Arkansas; Magic Johnson, Michigan State. **SECOND TEAM:** Mike Gminski, Duke; Reggie King, Alabama; Calvin Natt, Northeast Louisiana; Vinnie Johnson, Baylor; Ronnie Lester, Iowa. **THIRD TEAM:** Joe Barry Carroll, Purdue; Greg Kelser, Michigan State; Kelly Tripucka, Notre Dame; Sly Williams, Rhode Island; Roy Hamilton, UCLA.

UNITED PRESS INTERNATIONAL

FIRST TEAM: *Larry Bird, Indiana State; David Greenwood, UCLA; Mike Gminski, Duke; Magic Johnson, Michigan State; Jim Spanarkel, Duke. **SECOND TEAM:** Kelly Tripucka, Notre Dame; Mike O'Koren, North Carolina; Bill Cartwright, San Francisco; Sidney Moncrief, Arkansas; Darrell Griffith, Louisville. **THIRD TEAM:** Gene Banks, Duke; Sly Williams, Rhode Island; James Bailey, Rutgers; Kelvin Ransey, Ohio State; Ronnie Lester, Iowa.

*Player of the Year

Final Top 20 Polls

AP

1.	Indiana State	33-1
2.	UCLA	25-5
3.	Michigan St.	26-6
4.	Notre Dame	24-6
5.	Arkansas	25-5
6.	DePaul	26-6
7.	LSU	23-6
8.	Syracuse	26-4
9.	North Carolina	23-6
10.	Marquette	22-7
11.	Duke	22-8
12.	San Francisco	22-7
13.	Louisville	24-8
14.	Pennsylvania	25-7
15.	Purdue	27-8
16.	Oklahoma	20-11
17.	St. John's	21-11
18.	Rutgers	22-9
19.	Toledo	21-8
20.	Iowa	20-8

UPI

1.	Indiana State	33-1
2.	UCLA	25-5
3.	North Carolina	23-6
4.	Michigan St.	26-6
5.	Notre Dame	24-6
6.	Arkansas	25-5
7.	Duke	22-8
8.	DePaul	26-6
9.	LSU	23-6
10.	Syracuse	26-4
11.	Iowa	20-8
12.	Georgetown	24-5
13.	Marquette	22-7
14.	Purdue	27-8
15.	Texas	21-8
16.	Temple	25-4
17.	San Francisco	22-7
18.	Tennessee	21-12
19.	Louisville	24-8
20.	Detroit	22-6

Michigan St. beat Indiana St. 75-64 for NCAA title.

ACC BASKETBALL / REFERENCE

'80

Maryland's Albert King

1979-80 Final Standings

Team	Conf.	Overall	Ave.	Opp.
Maryland	11-3	24-7	80.0	71.8
North Carolina	9-5	21-8	73.2	68.0
N.C. State	9-5	20-8	69.5	61.4
Clemson	8-6	23-9	80.0	70.2
*Duke	7-7	24-9	73.3	68.3
Virginia	7-7	24-10	71.1	63.7
Wake Forest	4-10	13-14	70.4	67.6
Georgia Tech	1-13	8-18	57.0	59.9

*Won ACC Tournament

NCAA—DUKE second in Mideast Regional: beat Pennsylvania 52-42, beat Kentucky 55-54, lost to Purdue 68-60. CLEMSON second in West Regional: beat Utah State 76-73, beat Brigham Young 71-66, beat Lamar 74-66, lost to UCLA 85-74. MARYLAND lost in second round of East Regional: beat Tennessee 86-75, lost to Georgetown 74-68. NORTH CAROLINA lost in first round of Midwest Regional to Texas A&M 78-61 (2OT). N.C. STATE lost in first round of East Regional to Iowa 77-64.
NIT—VIRGINIA won championship: beat Lafayette 67-56, beat Boston College 57-55, beat Michigan 78-69, beat Nevada-Las Vegas 90-71, beat Minnesota 58-55.

ACC Tournament

FEBRUARY 28-MARCH 1, 1980 AT GREENSBORO, N.C.

FIRST ROUND: North Carolina 75, Wake Forest 62; Maryland 51, Georgia Tech 49 (OT); Duke 68, N.C. State 62; Clemson 57, Virginia 49. **SEMIFINALS:** Maryland 91, Clemson 85; Duke 75, North Carolina 61. **FINAL:** Duke 73, Maryland 72.

ALL-TOURNAMENT—FIRST TEAM: Albert King, Maryland; Gene Banks, Duke; Mike Gminski, Duke; Al Wood, North Carolina; Greg Manning, Maryland. **SECOND TEAM:** Vince Taylor, Duke; Billy Williams, Clemson; Brook Steppe, Georgia Tech; Buck Williams, Maryland; Ernest Graham, Maryland.

EVERETT CASE AWARD (MVP): King.

All-ACC

FIRST TEAM: Hawkeye Whitney, N.C. State (270 votes); Albert King, Maryland (265); Mike Gminski, Duke (253); Mike O'Koren, North Carolina (186); Billy Williams, Clemson (186). **SECOND TEAM:** Jeff Lamp, Virginia (167); Gene Banks, Duke (142); Buck Williams, Maryland (130); Greg Manning, Maryland (127); Al Wood, North Carolina (121).

PLAYER OF THE YEAR: King (71); Whitney (26); Gminski, Manning, O'Koren, Lamp and Buck Williams also received votes. **COACH OF THE YEAR:** Lefty Driesell, Maryland (89); Norm Sloan, N.C. State (9). **ROOKIE OF THE YEAR:** Ralph Sampson, Virginia (88); Sidney Lowe, N.C. State (16).

Scoring, Rebounding Leaders

TOP TEN SCORERS

Player, School	G	FG	FT	TP	Ave.
King, Maryland	31	275	124	674	21.7
Gminski, Duke	33	262	180	704	21.3
Wood, North Carolina	29	216	118	550	19.0
Steppe, Georgia Tech	26	135	111	491	18.9
Whitney, N.C. State	28	207	107	521	18.6
Williams, Clemson	32	229	104	562	17.6
Lamp, Virginia	34	232	127	591	17.4
Banks, Duke	33	212	146	570	17.3
Horton, Georgia Tech	26	104	170	446	17.2
Manning, Maryland	30	196	79	471	15.7

TOP TEN REBOUNDERS

Player, School	G	Rbs.	Ave.
Sampson, Virginia	34	381	11.2
Gminski, Duke	33	359	10.9
Williams, Maryland	24	242	10.1
Nance, Clemson	32	259	8.1
Banks, Duke	33	254	7.7
O'Koren, North Carolina	29	216	7.4
Graham, Maryland	31	230	7.4
Morgan, Wake Forest	27	197	7.3
King, Maryland	31	207	6.7
Rogers, Wake Forest	26	172	6.6

Rosters

CLEMSON

No.	Name	Hgt.	Yr.	Hometown
5	Bob Fuzy	6-2	Sr.	Warrenville, IL
10	Bobby Conrad	6-2	Sr.	Glen Ellyn, IL
11	Chris Dodds	6-1	So.	State College, PA
12	Scott Wilkes	6-3	Fr.	Deland, FL
13	Dan Mayfield	6-1	So.	Toccoa, GA
20	Keith Whitt	6-5	Fr.	Hanover, MA
21	Mitchell Wiggins	6-4	So.	Grifton, NC
22	Larry Nance	6-10	Jr.	Anderson, SC
23	John Campbell	6-10	Sr.	Blenheim, SC
24	Billy Williams	6-3	Sr.	Raleigh, NC
25	Rick McKinstry	6-5	Fr.	Indianapolis, IN
31	Horace Wyatt	6-10	So.	Hartsville, SC
40	Marvin Key	6-2	So.	Dunwoody, GA
42	Keith Walker	6-5	Jr.	Statesville, NC
43	Don Witherspoon	6-9	Fr.	Lexington, KY
44	Fred Gilliam	6-8	Fr.	Pelzer, SC
54	Bill Ross	6-10	So.	Lake Placid, FL

COACH: Bill Foster
ASSISTANTS: Joe Kingery, Dwight Rainey, Clint Bryant, Bob Strunk

DUKE

No.	Name	Hgt.	Yr.	Hometown
11	Jim Corrigan	5-11	Sr.	Winston-Salem, NC
12	Vince Taylor	6-5	So.	Lexington, KY
14	Chip Engelland	6-4	Fr.	Pac. Palisades, CA
20	Gene Banks	6-7	Jr.	Philadelphia, PA
21	Bob Bender	6-2	Sr.	Crown Point, IN
22	Tom Emma	6-2	Fr.	Manhasset, NY
23	Larry Linney	6-4	Jr.	Asheville, NC
30	Jim Suddath	6-6	Jr.	East Point, GA
31	Mike Tissaw	6-8	Fr.	Fairfax, VA
33	Kenny Dennard	6-8	Jr.	King, NC
41	Allen Williams	6-8	Fr.	Princeton, WV
43	Mike Gminski	6-11	Sr.	Monroe, CT

COACH: Bill Foster
ASSISTANTS: Bob Wenzel, Steve Steinwedel, Terry Chili

GEORGIA TECH

No.	Name	Hgt.	Yr.	Hometown
11	Toby Nidiffer	5-10	Sr.	Marietta, GA
14	Brook Steppe	6-4	Jr.	Atlanta, GA
15	Steve Peck	6-5	Fr.	Jefferson City, TN
21	Fred Hall	6-5	So.	Atlanta, GA
22	Kerry O'Brien	6-1	Sr.	Louisville, KY
23	George Thomas	6-3	Fr.	Cocoa, FL
24	John Williams	6-2	Fr.	Piedmont, SC
33	Steve Shaw	6-9	Fr.	Cartersville, GA
34	Lenny Horton	6-7	Sr.	Union, NJ
42	Rob Noyes	6-7	Sr.	Marion, NC
43	Steve Neal	6-11	So.	Tampa, FL
45	John Mann	6-4	Sr.	Normal, IL
52	Dave Cole	6-10	So.	Latham, NY

COACH: Dwane Morrison
ASSISTANTS: Jay Nidiffer, Benny Dees

MARYLAND

No.	Name	Hgt.	Yr.	Hometown
10	Greg Manning	6-1	Jr.	Steelton, PA
15	Reggie Jackson	6-4	So.	Philadelphia, PA
21	Dutch Morley	6-2	So.	Hyattsville, MD
22	Mark Fothergill	6-9	Fr.	Somerset, KY
23	David Henderson	6-9	Sr.	Roanoke, VA
25	Ernest Graham	6-7	Jr.	Baltimore, MD
41	Jon Robinson	6-4	Fr.	Gastonia, NC
42	Herman Veal	6-6	Fr.	Jackson, MS
50	John Bilney	6-8	Sr.	Woodcliff Lake, NJ
52	Buck Williams	6-8	So.	Rocky Mount, NC
54	Taylor Baldwin	6-10	So.	Greenwich, CT
55	Albert King	6-6	Jr.	Brooklyn, NY

COACH: Lefty Driesell
ASSISTANTS: Tom Abatemarco, John Kochan, Sherman Dilliard

NORTH CAROLINA

No.	Name	Hgt.	Yr.	Hometown
11	Mike Pepper	6-3	Jr.	Vienna, VA
20	Dave Colescott	6-2	Sr.	Marion, IN
21	Jimmy Black	6-2	So.	The Bronx, NY
24	Jim Braddock	6-1	Fr.	Chattanooga, TN
30	Al Wood	6-6	Jr.	Gray, GA
31	Mike O'Koren	6-8	Sr.	Jersey City, NJ
32	Eric Kenny	6-6	Jr.	Asheville, NC
34	Pete Budko	6-8	Jr.	Lutherville, MD
42	Jeff Wolf	6-11	Sr.	Kohler, WI
43	John Virgil	6-6	Sr.	Elm City, NC
45	Chris Brust	6-9	So.	Babylon, NY
50	Rich Yonakor	6-10	Sr.	Euclid, OH
52	James Worthy	6-8	Fr.	Gastonia, NC

COACH: Dean Smith
ASSISTANTS: Bill Guthridge, Eddie Fogler, Roy Williams

N.C. STATE

No.	Name	Hgt.	Yr.	Hometown
3	Clyde Austin	6-3	Sr.	Richmond, VA
4	Dereck Whittenburg	6-1	Fr.	Washington, DC
10	Max Perry	6-1	So.	Hanover, IN
12	Emmett Lay	6-4	So.	Tabor City, NC
14	Phil Weber	6-2	Fr.	Northport, NY
33	Art Jones	6-7	Jr.	Hampton, VA
34	Kenny Matthews	6-4	Jr.	Washington, DC
35	Sidney Lowe	6-0	Fr.	Washington, DC
40	Scott Parzych	6-7	So.	Lockport, IL
41	Thurl Bailey	6-11	Fr.	Seat Pleasant, MD
42	Craig Watts	6-11	Jr.	South Easton, MA
43	Hawkeye Whitney	6-5	Sr.	Washington, DC
45	Donnie Perkins	6-3	Jr.	Bethel, NC
52	Chuck Nevitt	7-4	So.	Marietta, GA

COACH: Norm Sloan
ASSISTANTS: Marty Fletcher, Monte Towe, Gary Stokan

VIRGINIA

No.	Name	Hgt.	Yr.	Hometown
3	Jeff Lamp	6-6	Jr.	Louisville, KY
10	Craig Robinson	6-8	Fr.	Montclair, NJ
11	Garland Jefferson	6-3	Sr.	Covington, VA
12	Dean Carpenter	6-9	So.	New Orleans, LA
21	Darren Cross	6-4	Fr.	Queens, NY
23	Jeff Klein	6-5	Jr.	Akron, OH
24	Jeff Jones	6-3	So.	Owensboro, KY
25	Lee Raker	6-5	Jr.	Louisville, KY
31	Otis Fulton	6-10	Sr.	Richmond, VA
32	Doug Newburg	6-2	Fr.	McLean, VA
42	Peter MacBeth	6-9	So.	Marietta, GA
44	Terry Gates	6-8	Jr.	Louisville, KY
45	Mike Owens	6-6	Sr.	Kensington, MD
50	Ralph Sampson	7-4	Fr.	Harrisonburg, VA
55	Lewis Lattimore	6-9	Jr.	Dayton, OH

COACH: Terry Holland
ASSISTANTS: Craig Littlepage, Jim Larranaga

WAKE FOREST

No.	Name	Hgt.	Yr.	Hometown
14	Frank Johnson	6-2	Sr.	Weirsdale, FL
20	David Morris	6-3	Sr.	Winston-Salem, NC
23	Benny McKaig	6-4	Sr.	Raleigh, NC
30	Alvis Rogers	6-6	So.	Washington, NC
31	Kenny Vaughns	6-2	Fr.	Ocala, FL
33	Matt Knowles	6-5	Fr.	Elizabethtown, KY
34	Brad Williamson	5-9	Fr.	Richmond, VA
35	Guy Morgan	6-8	So.	Virginia Beach, VA
40	John Hendler	6-7	Sr.	River Grove, IL
41	Will Singleton	6-6	Jr.	Sumter, SC
42	Chuck Dahms	6-9	Jr.	River Forest, IL
44	Mike Helms	6-4	So.	Bassett, VA
54	Jim Johnstone	6-11	So.	Youngstown, NY

COACH: Carl Tacy
ASSISTANTS: Ed Hall, Ernie Nestor, Rich Knarr

All-America Teams

ASSOCIATED PRESS

FIRST TEAM: *Mark Aguirre, DePaul; Joe Barry Carroll, Purdue; **Albert King, Maryland**; Darrell Griffith, Louisville; Kyle Macy, Kentucky. **SECOND TEAM: Mike Gminski, Duke**; Don Collins, Washington State; Michael Brooks, La Salle; Reggie Carter, St. John's; Ray Blume, Oregon State. **THIRD TEAM:** Herb Williams, Ohio State; John Stroud, Mississippi; Lewis Lloyd, Drake; Rolando Blackman, Kansas State; Sam Worthen, Marquette.

UNITED PRESS INTERNATIONAL

FIRST TEAM: *Mark Aguirre, DePaul; Kyle Macy, Kentucky; Darrell Griffith, Louisville; Joe Barry Carroll, Purdue; Michael Brooks, LaSalle. **SECOND TEAM: Mike Gminski, Duke; Albert King, Maryland; Mike O'Koren, North Carolina**; Kelvin Ransey, Ohio State; Reggie Carter, St. John's. **THIRD TEAM:** Sam Worthen, Marquette; **Jeff Lamp, Virginia**; Roosevelt Bouie, Syracuse; Lewis Lloyd, Drake; Kelly Tripucka, Notre Dame.

*Player of the Year

Final Top 20 Polls

AP		UPI	
1. DePaul	26-2	1. DePaul	26-2
2. Louisville	33-3	2. LSU	26-6
3. LSU	26-6	3. Kentucky	29-6
4. Kentucky	29-6	4. Louisville	33-3
5. Oregon State	26-4	5. Oregon State	26-4
6. Syracuse	26-4	6. Syracuse	26-4
7. Indiana	21-8	7. Indiana	21-8
8. Maryland	**24-7**	**8. Maryland**	**24-7**
9. Notre Dame	22-6	9. Ohio State	21-8
10. Ohio State	21-8	10. Georgetown	26-6
11. Georgetown	26-6	11. Notre Dame	22-6
12. Brigham Young	24-5	12. Brigham Young	24-5
13. St. John's	24-5	13. St. John's	24-5
14. Duke	**24-9**	14. Missouri	25-6
15. North Carolina	**21-8**	**15. North Carolina**	**21-8**
16. Missouri	25-6	**16. Duke**	**24-9**
17. Weber State	26-3	17. Weber State	26-3
18. Arizona State	22-7	18. Texas A&M	28-6
19. Iona	29-5	19. Arizona State	22-7
20. Purdue	23-10	20. Kansas State	22-9

Louisville beat UCLA 59-54 for NCAA title.

'81

Virginia's
Ralph Sampson

1980-81 Final Standings

Team	Conf.	Overall	Ave.	Opp.
Virginia	13-1	29-4	73.3	60.6
*North Carolina	10-4	29-8	71.9	63.4
Wake Forest	9-5	22-7	77.3	65.1
Maryland	8-6	21-10	75.9	69.8
Clemson	6-8	20-11	75.5	66.8
Duke	6-8	17-13	69.9	66.9
N.C. State	4-10	14-13	66.2	63.1
Georgia Tech	0-14	4-23	55.7	71.5

*Won ACC Tournament

NCAA—NORTH CAROLINA second in Final Four: beat Pittsburgh 74-57, beat Utah 61-56, beat Kansas State 81-68 in West Regional; beat Virginia 78-65, lost to Indiana 63-50 in Final Four. VIRGINIA third in Final Four: beat Villanova 54-50, beat Tennessee 62-48, beat Brigham Young 74-60 in East Regional; lost to North Carolina 78-65, beat LSU 78-74 in Final Four. MARYLAND lost in second round of Mideast Regional: beat UT-Chattanooga 81-69, lost to Indiana 99-64. WAKE FOREST lost in second round of Mideast Regional to Boston College 67-64.

NIT—DUKE beat North Carolina A&T 79-69, beat Alabama 75-70, lost to Purdue 81-69. CLEMSON lost to Temple 90-82.

ACC Tournament

MARCH 5-7, 1981 AT LANDOVER, MD.

FIRST ROUND: Wake Forest 80, Clemson 71; Virginia 76, Georgia Tech 47; North Carolina 69, N.C. State 54; Maryland 56, Duke 53. **SEMIFINALS:** Maryland 85, Virginia 62; North Carolina 58, Wake Forest 57. **FINAL:** North Carolina 61, Maryland 60.

ALL-TOURNAMENT—FIRST TEAM: Sam Perkins, North Carolina; Frank Johnson, Wake Forest; Albert King, Maryland; James Worthy, North Carolina; Buck Williams, Maryland. **SECOND TEAM:** Ernest Graham, Maryland; Jeff Lamp, Virginia; Al Wood, North Carolina; Larry Nance, Clemson; Jimmy Black, North Carolina.

EVERETT CASE AWARD (MVP): Perkins.

All-ACC

FIRST TEAM: Ralph Sampson, Virginia (239 votes); Al Wood, North Carolina (236); Jeff Lamp, Virginia (223); Frank Johnson, Wake Forest (218); Gene Banks, Duke (184). **SECOND TEAM:** Buck Williams, Maryland (161); Albert King, Maryland (147); James Worthy, North Carolina (105); Larry Nance, Clemson (56); Sidney Lowe, N.C. State (53).

PLAYER OF THE YEAR: Sampson (79); Lamp, Banks, Wood, Johnson and Williams also received votes. **COACH OF THE YEAR:** Terry Holland, Virginia (32); Carl Tacy, Wake Forest (28); Dean Smith, North Carolina (26). **ROOKIE OF THE YEAR:** Sam Perkins, North Carolina (85); Othell Wilson, Virginia; Vincent Hamilton, Clemson; and Clark Bynum, Clemson; also received votes.

Scoring, Rebounding Leaders

TOP TEN SCORERS

Player, School	G	FG	FT	TP	Ave.
Banks, Duke	27	202	95	499	18.5
Lamp, Virginia	33	223	154	600	18.2
Wood, North Carolina	37	274	121	669	18.1
King, Maryland	31	232	95	559	18.0
Sampson, Virginia	33	230	125	585	17.7
Johnson, Wake Forest	29	187	95	469	16.2
Nance, Clemson	31	207	80	494	15.9
Williams, Maryland	31	183	116	482	15.6
Perkins, North Carolina	37	199	152	550	14.9
Taylor, Duke	30	169	104	442	14.7

TOP TEN REBOUNDERS

Player, School	G	Rbs.	Ave.
Williams, Maryland	31	363	11.7
Sampson, Virginia	33	378	11.5
Worthy, North Carolina	36	301	8.4
Perkins, North Carolina	37	289	7.8
Nance, Clemson	31	237	7.6
Dennard, Duke	30	206	6.9
Banks, Duke	27	184	6.8
Goza, Georgia Tech	27	177	6.6
Wood, North Carolina	37	233	6.3
Bailey, N.C. State	27	165	6.1

Rosters

CLEMSON

No.	Name	Hgt.	Yr.	Hometown
10	Mike Eppley	6-1	Fr.	Charlotte, NC
11	Chris Dodds	6-1	Jr.	State College, PA
12	Jeff White	5-11	Fr.	Gastonia, NC
15	Vincent Hamilton	6-4	Fr.	Rutherfordton, NC
20	Marc Campbell	6-2	Fr.	Elizabethton, TN
21	Mitchell Wiggins	6-4	Jr.	Grifton, NC
22	Larry Nance	6-10	Sr.	Anderson, SC
23	Raymond Jones	6-8	Fr.	Union, SC
24	Clark Bynum	6-7	Fr.	Sumter, SC
31	Horace Wyatt	6-10	Jr.	Hartsville, SC
32	Murray Jarman	6-6	So.	Delray Beach, FL
40	Marvin Key	6-2	Jr.	Dunwoody, GA
42	Keith Walker	6-5	Sr.	Statesville, NC
43	Don Witherspoon	6-9	So.	Lexington, KY
44	Fred Gilliam	6-8	So.	Pelzer, SC
54	Bill Ross	6-10	Jr.	Lake Placid, FL

COACH: Bill Foster
ASSISTANTS: Dwight Rainey, Clint Bryant, Jerry Faulkner, Bob Strunk

DUKE

No.	Name	Hgt.	Yr.	Hometown
11	Doug McNeely	6-5	Fr.	El Paso, TX
12	Vince Taylor	6-5	Jr.	Lexington, KY
14	Chip Engelland	6-4	So.	Pac. Palisades, CA
20	Gene Banks	6-7	Sr.	Philadelphia, PA
21	Gordon Whitted	6-2	Fr.	Winston-Salem, NC
22	Tom Emma	6-2	So.	Manhasset, NY
23	Larry Linney	6-4	Sr.	Asheville, NC
30	Jim Suddath	6-6	Sr.	East Point, GA
31	Mike Tissaw	6-8	So.	Fairfax, VA
33	Kenny Dennard	6-8	Sr.	King, NC
42	Jon Weingart	6-5	So.	Bath, OH
44	Mac Dyke	6-7	So.	Redlands, CA
55	Allen Williams	6-8	So.	Princeton, WV

COACH: Mike Krzyzewski
ASSISTANTS: Bobby Dwyer, Tom Rogers, Chuck Swenson, Rick Johnson

GEORGIA TECH

No.	Name	Hgt.	Yr.	Hometown
11	Bill Patterson	6-3	Jr.	Harrisonburg, PA
15	George Thomas	6-3	So.	Cocoa, FL
24	David New	6-5	Fr.	Valdosta, GA
32	Dave Kowalski	6-7	Fr.	South Bend, IN
33	Steve Shaw	6-9	So.	Cartersville, GA
34	Fred Hall	6-5	Jr.	Atlanta, GA
42	Henry Lee	6-4	Jr.	Salisbury, NC
43	Greg Wilson	6-8	Fr.	Grand Ridge, FL
44	Stu Lyon	6-4	Jr.	Pittsburgh, PA
52	Dave Cole	6-10	So.	Latham, NY
53	Steve Neal	7-0	Jr.	Tampa, FL
54	Lee Goza	6-9	Jr.	Atlanta, GA

COACH: Dwane Morrison
ASSISTANTS: Jay Nidiffer

MARYLAND

No.	Name	Hgt.	Yr.	Hometown
10	Greg Manning	6-1	Sr.	Steelton, PA
14	Steve Rivers	6-3	Fr.	Brockville, NY
15	Reggie Jackson	6-4	Jr.	Philadelphia, PA
21	Dutch Morley	6-2	Jr.	Hyattsville, MD
22	Mark Fothergill	6-9	So.	Somerset, KY
25	Ernest Graham	6-7	Sr.	Baltimore, MD
32	Charles Pittman	6-8	Jr.	Rocky Mount, NC
33	Pete Holbert	6-6	Fr.	Fairfax, VA
41	Jon Robinson	6-4	So.	Gastonia, NC
42	Herman Veal	6-6	Fr.	Jackson, MI
52	Buck Williams	6-8	Jr.	Rocky Mount, NC
54	Taylor Baldwin	6-10	Jr.	Greenwich, CT
55	Albert King	6-6	Sr.	Brooklyn, NY

COACH: Lefty Driesell
ASSISTANTS: Tom Abatemarco, John Kochan, Sherman Dilliard

NORTH CAROLINA

No.	Name	Hgt.	Yr.	Hometown
11	Mike Pepper	6-3	Sr.	Vienna, VA
21	Jimmy Black	6-2	Jr.	The Bronx, NY
24	Jim Braddock	6-1	So.	Chattanooga, TN
30	Al Wood	6-6	Sr.	Gray, GA
32	Eric Kenny	6-6	Sr.	Asheville, NC
33	Dean Shaffer	6-3	Fr.	Durham, NC
34	Pete Budko	6-9	Sr.	Lutherville, MD
41	Sam Perkins	6-9	Fr.	Latham, NY
43	Jeb Barlow	6-7	Jr.	Fuquay-Varina, NC
44	Matt Doherty	6-7	Fr.	East Meadow, NY
45	Chris Brust	6-9	Jr.	Babylon, NY
50	Cecil Exum	6-6	Fr.	Dudley, NC
51	Timo Makkonen	6-11	Fr.	Lahti, Finland
52	James Worthy	6-8	So.	Gastonia, NC

COACH: Dean Smith
ASSISTANTS: Bill Guthridge, Eddie Fogler, Roy Williams

N.C. STATE

No.	Name	Hgt.	Yr.	Hometown
10	Max Perry	6-1	Jr.	Hanover, IN
12	Emmett Lay	6-4	Jr.	Tabor City, NC
14	Phil Weber	6-2	So.	Northport, NY
25	Dereck Whittenburg	6-1	So.	Washington, DC
30	Harold Thompson	6-5	Fr.	Raeford, NC
33	Art Jones	6-7	Sr.	Hampton, VA
34	Kenny Matthews	6-4	Sr.	Washington, DC
35	Sidney Lowe	6-0	So.	Washington, DC
40	Scott Parzych	6-7	Jr.	Lockport, IL
41	Thurl Bailey	6-11	So.	Seat Pleasant, MD
42	Craig Watts	7-0	Sr.	South Easton, MA
52	Chuck Nevitt	7-5	Jr.	Marietta, GA

COACH: Jim Valvano
ASSISTANTS: Ray Martin, Marty Fletcher, Benny McKaig

VIRGINIA

No.	Name	Hgt.	Yr.	Hometown
3	Jeff Lamp	6-6	Sr.	Louisville, KY
5	Louis Collins	6-5	Sr.	Highland Sprgs., VA
10	Craig Robinson	6-8	So.	Montclair, NJ
11	Othell Wilson	6-0	Fr.	Woodbridge, VA
12	Dean Carpenter	6-9	Jr.	New Orleans, LA
14	Ricky Stokes	5-10	Fr.	Richmond, VA
21	Darren Cross	6-4	So.	Queens, NY
23	Jeff Klein	6-5	Sr.	Akron, OH
24	Jeff Jones	6-4	Jr.	Owensboro. KY
25	Lee Raker	6-5	Sr.	Louisville, KY
32	Doug Newburg	6-2	So.	McLean, VA
42	Peter MacBeth	6-9	So.	Marietta, GA
44	Terry Gates	6-8	Sr.	Louisville, KY
50	Ralph Sampson	7-4	So.	Harrisonburg, VA
55	Lewis Lattimore	6-9	Sr.	Dayton, OH

COACH: Terry Holland
ASSISTANTS: Craig Littlepage, Jim Larranaga

WAKE FOREST

No.	Name	Hgt.	Yr.	Hometown
10	Scott Davis	6-2	Fr.	Monaca, PA
14	Frank Johnson	6-2	Sr.	Weirsdale, FL
20	Danny Young	6-3	Fr.	Raleigh, NC
25	Stewart Wallace	6-4	Fr.	Richmond, VA
30	Alvis Rogers	6-7	Jr.	Washington, NC
31	Kenny Vaughns	6-2	So.	Ocala, FL
35	Guy Morgan	6-8	Jr.	Virginia Beach, VA
40	Glenn Mayers	6-3	Fr.	Cambria Hghts., NY
41	Will Singleton	6-6	Sr.	Sumter, NC
42	Chuck Dahms	6-9	Sr.	River Forest, IL
44	Mike Helms	6-4	Jr.	Bassett, VA
54	Jim Johnstone	6-11	Jr.	Youngstown, NY
55	Anthony Teachey	6-9	Fr.	Goldsboro, NC

COACH: Carl Tacy
ASSISTANTS: Ernie Nestor, Mark Freidinger, Rich Knarr

All-America Teams

ASSOCIATED PRESS

FIRST TEAM: Mark Aguirre, DePaul; Kevin Magee, California-Irvine; ***Ralph Sampson, Virginia**; Danny Ainge, Brigham Young; Isiah Thomas, Indiana. **SECOND TEAM: Al Wood, North Carolina**; Danny Vranes, Utah; Steve Johnson, Oregon State; Eric Floyd, Georgetown; Darnell Valentine, Kansas. **THIRD TEAM:** Lewis Lloyd, Drake; Jay Vincent, Michigan State; Sam Bowie, Kentucky; **Jeff Lamp, Virginia**; Rob Williams, Houston.

UNITED PRESS INTERNATIONAL

FIRST TEAM: Isiah Thomas, Indiana; Danny Ainge, Brigham Young; ***Ralph Sampson, Virginia**; Mark Aguirre, DePaul; Kelly Tripucka, Notre Dame. **SECOND TEAM: Jeff Lamp, Virginia**; Rod Foster, UCLA; Steve Johnson, Oregon State; Durand Macklin, LSU; **Albert King, Maryland. THIRD TEAM:** Ray Blume, Oregon State; Clyde Bradshaw, DePaul; Sam Bowie, Kentucky; Danny Vranes, Utah; Lewis Lloyd, Drake.

*Player of the Year

Final Top 20 Polls

AP		UPI	
1. DePaul	27-2	1. DePaul	27-2
2. Oregon State	26-2	2. Oregon State	26-2
3. Arizona State	24-4	**3. Virginia**	**29-4**
4. LSU	31-5	4. LSU	31-5
5. Virginia	**29-4**	5. Arizona State	24-4
6. North Carolina	**29-8**	**6. North Carolina**	**29-8**
7. Notre Dame	23-6	7. Indiana	26-9
8. Kentucky	22-6	8. Kentucky	22-6
9. Indiana	26-9	9. Notre Dame	23-6
10. UCLA	20-7	10. Utah	25-5
11. Wake Forest	**22-7**	11. UCLA	20-7
12. Louisville	21-9	12. Iowa	21-7
13. Iowa	21-7	13. Louisville	21-9
14. Utah	25-5	**14. Wake Forest**	**22-7**
15. Tennessee	21-8	15. Tennessee	21-8
16. Brigham Young	25-7	16. Wyoming	24-6
17. Wyoming	24-6	17. Brigham Young	25-7
18. Maryland	**21-10**	18. Illinois	21-8
19. Illinois	21-8	19. Kansas	24-8
20. Arkansas	24-8	**20. Maryland**	**21-10**

Indiana beat North Carolina 63-50 for NCAA title.

'82

Virginia's Ralph Sampson

1981-82 Final Standings

Team	Conf.	Overall	Ave.	Opp.
*North Carolina	12-2	32-2	66.7	55.4
Virginia	12-2	30-4	70.7	57.2
Wake Forest	9-5	21-9	67.8	58.2
N.C. State	7-7	22-10	57.5	49.1
Maryland	5-9	16-13	61.3	58.8
Clemson	4-10	14-14	69.9	65.2
Duke	4-10	10-17	64.0	70.0
Georgia Tech	3-11	10-16	59.4	60.7

*Won ACC Tournament

NCAA—NORTH CAROLINA won NCAA title: beat James Madison 52-50, beat Alabama 74-69, beat Villanova 70-60 in East Regional; beat Houston 68-63, beat Georgetown 63-62 in Final Four. VIRGINIA lost in semifinals of Mideast Regional: beat Tennessee 54-51, lost to Alabama-Birmingham 68-66. WAKE FOREST lost in second round of East Regional: beat Old Dominion 74-57, lost to Memphis State 56-55. N.C. STATE lost in first round of Mideast Regional to Tennessee-Chattanooga 58-51.

NIT—MARYLAND beat Richmond 66-50, lost to Georgia 83-69. CLEMSON lost to Mississippi 53-49.

ACC Tournament

MARCH 5-7, 1982 AT GREENSBORO, N.C.

FIRST ROUND: North Carolina 55, Georgia Tech 39; N.C. State 40, Maryland 28; Virginia 56, Clemson 54; Wake Forest 88, Duke 53. **SEMIFINALS:** North Carolina 58, N.C. State 46; Virginia 51, Wake Forest 49 (OT). **FINAL:** North Carolina 47, Virginia 45.

ALL-TOURNAMENT—FIRST TEAM: James Worthy, North Carolina; Ralph Sampson, Virginia; Michael Jordan, North Carolina; Sam Perkins, North Carolina; Mike Helms, Wake Forest. **SECOND TEAM:** Vincent Hamilton, Clemson; Ricky Stokes, Virginia; Jim Johnstone, Wake Forest; Dereck Whittenburg, N.C. State; Matt Doherty, North Carolina.

EVERETT CASE AWARD (MVP): Worthy.

All-ACC

FIRST TEAM: *Ralph Sampson, Virginia (232 votes); James Worthy, North Carolina (231); Sam Perkins, North Carolina (216); Vince Taylor, Duke (207); Othell Wilson, Virginia (169). **SECOND TEAM:** Brook Steppe, Georgia Tech (142); Thurl Bailey, N.C. State (91); Vince Hamilton, Clemson (80); Dereck Whittenburg, N.C. State (78); Jim Johnstone, Wake Forest (62).

PLAYER OF THE YEAR: Sampson (69); Worthy (33). **COACH OF THE YEAR:** Terry Holland, Virginia (49); Dean Smith, North Carolina (24); Jim Valvano, N.C. State (14); Lefty Driesell, Maryland (11). **ROOKIE OF THE YEAR:** Michael Jordan, North Carolina (78); Adrian Branch, Maryland (24).

*Unanimous Selection

Scoring, Rebounding Leaders

TOP TEN SCORERS

Player, School	G	FG	FT	TP	Ave.
Taylor, Duke	27	217	115	549	20.3
Steppe, Georgia Tech	25	175	95	445	17.8
Sampson, Virginia	32	198	110	506	15.8
Worthy, North Carolina	34	203	126	532	15.6
Branch, Maryland	29	164	114	442	15.2
Engelland, Duke	27	167	77	411	15.2
Hamilton, Clemson	28	181	58	420	15.0
Perkins, North Carolina	32	174	109	457	14.3
Bailey, N.C. State	32	171	96	438	13.7
Jordan, North Carolina	34	191	78	460	13.5

TOP TEN REBOUNDERS

Player, School	G	Rbs.	Ave.
Sampson, Virginia	32	366	11.4
Perkins, North Carolina	32	250	7.8
Veal, Maryland	29	213	7.3
Pittman, Maryland	24	174	7.3
Bailey, N.C. State	32	216	6.8
Wyatt, Clemson	28	187	6.7
Worthy, North Carolina	34	215	6.3
Teachey, Wake Forest	30	182	6.1
Morgan, Wake Forest	30	169	5.6
Steppe, Georgia Tech	25	136	5.4

Rosters

CLEMSON

No.	Name	Hgt.	Yr.	Hometown
10	Mike Eppley	6-1	So.	Charlotte, NC
11	Chris Dodds	6-1	Sr.	State College, PA
12	Jeff White	5-11	So.	Gastonia, NC
14	Milan Belich	6-1	Fr.	Solon, OH
15	Vincent Hamilton	6-4	So.	Rutherfordton, NC
20	Marc Campbell	6-2	So.	Elizabethton, TN
23	Raymond Jones	6-8	So.	Union, SC
24	Clarke Bynum	6-7	So.	Sumter, SC
25	Murray Jarman	6-6	Jr.	Delray Beach, FL
31	Horace Wyatt	6-10	Sr.	Hartsville, SC
32	Joe Ward	6-5	Fr.	Griffin, GA
40	Marvin Key	6-2	Sr.	Dunwoody, GA
42	David Shaffer	6-7	Fr.	Durham, NC
43	Don Witherspoon	6-9	Jr.	Lexington, KY
44	Fred Gilliam	6-8	Jr.	Pelzer, SC
54	Bill Ross	6-10	Sr.	Lake Placid, FL

COACH: Bill Foster
ASSISTANTS: Dwight Rainey, Clint Bryant, Jerry Faulkner, Bob Strunk

DUKE

No.	Name	Hgt.	Yr.	Hometown
11	Doug McNeely	6-5	So.	El Paso, TX
12	Vince Taylor	6-5	Sr.	Lexington, KY
14	Chip Engelland	6-4	Jr.	Pac. Palisades, CA
22	Tom Emma	6-2	Jr.	Manhasset, NY
23	Richard Ford	5-10	So.	Durham, NC
25	Greg Wendt	6-6	Fr.	Livonia, MI
31	Mike Tissaw	6-8	Jr.	Fairfax, VA
33	Jay Bryan	6-8	Fr.	Lakewood, CO
42	Ned Franke	6-5	Jr.	Pinehurst, NC
44	Todd Anderson	6-9	Fr.	Golden Valley, MN
45	Dan Meagher	6-7	Fr.	St. Catharines, ONT
55	Allen Williams	6-8	Jr.	Princeton, WV

COACH: Mike Krzyzewski
ASSISTANTS: Bobby Dwyer, Tom Rogers, Chuck Swenson, Rick Johnson

GEORGIA TECH

No.	Name	Hgt.	Yr.	Hometown
14	Brook Steppe	6-5	Sr.	Atlanta, GA
15	George Thomas	6-3	Jr.	Cocoa, FL
20	Brian Howard	5-10	Fr.	Rockville, MD
22	Scott Gardner	6-4	Fr.	Greenville, NC
30	Anthony Byrd	6-2	So.	Apex, NC
33	Steve Shaw	6-9	Jr.	Cartersville, GA
35	Maurice Bradford	6-5	Jr.	Cincinnati, OH
43	Greg Wilson	6-9	So.	Grand Ridge, FL
44	Stu Lyon	6-4	Sr.	Pittsburgh, PA
52	Dave Cole	6-10	Jr.	Latham, NY
53	Steve Neal	7-0	Sr.	Tampa, FL
54	Lee Goza	6-9	Sr.	Atlanta, GA

COACH: Bobby Cremins
ASSISTANTS: George Felton, Ben Jobe, Jimmy Hebron

MARYLAND

No.	Name	Hgt.	Yr.	Hometown
11	Chuck Driesell	6-2	Fr.	Silver Spring, MD
14	Steve Rivers	6-3	So.	Brockville, NY
15	Reggie Jackson	6-4	Sr.	Philadelphia, PA
20	Jeff Adkins	6-5	Fr.	Martinsville, VA
21	Dutch Morley	6-2	Sr.	Hyattsville, MD
22	Mark Fothergill	6-9	So.	Somerset, KY
24	Adrian Branch	6-8	Fr.	Largo, MD
32	Charles Pittman	6-8	Sr.	Rocky Mount, NC
33	Pete Holbert	6-6	So.	Fairfax, VA
41	Jon Robinson	6-4	Jr.	Gastonia, NC
42	Herman Veal	6-6	So.	Jackson, MS
54	Taylor Baldwin	6-11	Sr.	Greenwich, CT

COACH: Lefty Driesell
ASSISTANTS: John Kochan, Sherman Dilliard, Mel Cartwright

All-America Teams

ASSOCIATED PRESS

FIRST TEAM: ***Ralph Sampson, Virginia**; Terry Cummings, DePaul; Kevin Magee, California-Irvine; Eric Floyd, Georgetown; Quintin Dailey, San Francisco. **SECOND TEAM:** Keith Lee, Memphis State; Dale Ellis, Tennessee; **James Worthy, North Carolina**; Lester Conner, Oregon State; Terry Teagle, Baylor. **THIRD TEAM:** Dominique Wilkins, Georgia; Ricky Frazier, Missouri; Paul Pressey, Tulsa; Ricky Pierce, Rice; Dan Callandrillo, Seton Hall.

UNITED PRESS INTERNATIONAL

FIRST TEAM: *Ralph Sampson, Virginia; Eric Floyd, Georgetown; Quintin Dailey, San Francisco; **James Worthy, North Carolina**; Terry Cummings, DePaul. **SECOND TEAM:** John Paxson, Notre Dame; Paul Pressey, Tulsa; **Sam Perkins, North Carolina**; Kevin Magee, California-Irvine; Dominique Wilkins, Georgia. **THIRD TEAM:** Dan Callandrillo, Seton Hall; Lester Conner, Oregon State; Mark McNamara, California; Ricky Frazier, Missouri; Ted Kitchel, Indiana.

*Player of the Year

NORTH CAROLINA

No.	Name	Hgt.	Yr.	Hometown
4	Lynwood Robinson	6-1	Fr.	Mt. Olive, NC
21	Jimmy Black	6-3	Sr.	The Bronx, NY
22	Buzz Peterson	6-3	Fr.	Asheville, NC
23	Michael Jordan	6-4	Fr.	Wilmington, NC
24	Jim Braddock	6-2	Jr.	Chattanooga, TN
32	John Brownlee	6-10	Fr.	Fort Worth, TX
33	Dean Shaffer	6-4	So.	Durham, NC
41	Sam Perkins	6-9	So.	Latham, NY
43	Jeb Barlow	6-7	Sr.	Fuquay-Varina, NC
44	Matt Doherty	6-7	So.	East Meadow, NY
45	Chris Brust	6-9	Sr.	Babylon, NY
50	Cecil Exum	6-6	So.	Dudley, NC
51	Timo Makkonen	6-11	So.	Lahti, Finland
52	James Worthy	6-9	Jr.	Gastonia, NC
54	Warren Martin	6-11	Fr.	Axton, VA

COACH: Dean Smith
ASSISTANTS: Bill Guthridge, Eddie Fogler, Roy Williams

N.C. STATE

No.	Name	Hgt.	Yr.	Hometown
10	Max Perry	6-1	Sr.	Hanover, IN
12	Emmett Lay	6-4	Sr.	Tabor City, NC
14	Phil Weber	6-2	Jr.	Northport, NY
15	Walter Proctor	6-8	Fr.	Southampton, NY
24	Terry Gannon	6-0	Fr.	Joliet, IL
25	Dereck Whittenburg	6-1	Jr.	Washington, DC
30	Harold Thompson	6-5	So.	Raeford, NC
34	Quinton Leonard	6-8	Jr.	Louisburg, NC
35	Sidney Lowe	6-0	Jr.	Washington, DC
40	Scott Parzych	6-7	Sr.	Lockport, IL
41	Thurl Bailey	6-11	Jr.	Seat Pleasant, MD
42	Mike Warren	6-7	Fr.	Raleigh, NC
43	Lorenzo Charles	6-7	Fr.	Brooklyn, NY
45	Cozell McQueen	6-11	Fr.	Bennettsville, SC
52	Chuck Nevitt	7-5	Sr.	Marietta, GA

COACH: Jim Valvano
ASSISTANTS: Ray Martin, Marty Fletcher, Benny McKaig

VIRGINIA

No.	Name	Hgt.	Yr.	Hometown
4	Jim Miller	6-8	Fr.	Princeton, WV
10	Craig Robinson	6-8	Jr.	Montclair, NJ
11	Othell Wilson	6-0	So.	Woodbridge, VA
12	Dean Carpenter	6-9	Sr.	New Orleans, LA
14	Ricky Stokes	5-10	So.	Richmond, VA
21	Jim Runcie	6-1	Fr.	Hyde Park, NY
24	Jeff Jones	6-4	Sr.	Owensboro, KY
30	Kenton Edelin	6-7	So.	Alexandria, VA
32	Doug Newburg	6-2	Jr.	McLean, VA
33	Kenny Johnson	6-0	Fr.	Baltimore, MD
42	Peter MacBeth	6-9	Jr.	Marietta, GA
45	Tim Mullen	6-5	Fr.	Ridgewood, NJ
51	Dan Merrifield	6-6	Fr.	Linwood, NJ
55	Ralph Sampson	7-4	Jr.	Harrisonburg, VA

COACH: Terry Holland
ASSISTANTS: Craig Littlepage, Jim Larranaga

WAKE FOREST

No.	Name	Hgt.	Yr.	Hometown
3	John Toms	6-6	So.	Shelby, NC
10	Scott Davis	6-2	So.	Monaca, PA
15	Delaney Rudd	6-2	Fr.	Hollister, NC
20	Danny Young	6-3	So.	Raleigh, NC
22	Chuck Kepley	6-4	Fr.	Roanoke, VA
25	Stewart Wallace	6-4	So.	Richmond, VA
30	Alvis Rogers	6-7	Sr.	Washington, NC
33	Sylvester Charles	6-8	Fr.	St. Thomas, V.I.
34	Lee Garber	6-5	Fr.	Kingsport, TN
35	Guy Morgan	6-8	Sr.	Virginia Beach, VA
44	Mike Helms	6-4	Sr.	Bassett, VA
54	Jim Johnstone	6-11	Sr.	Youngstown, NY
55	Anthony Teachey	6-9	So.	Goldsboro, NC

COACH: Carl Tacy
ASSISTANTS: Ernie Nestor, Mark Freidinger, Herb Cline

Final Top 20 Polls

AP		UPI	
1. North Carolina	**32-2**	**1. North Carolina**	**32-2**
2. DePaul	26-2	2. DePaul	26-2
3. Virginia	**30-4**	**3. Virginia**	**30-4**
4. Oregon State	25-5	4. Oregon State	25-5
5. Missouri	27-4	5. Missouri	27-4
6. Georgetown	30-7	6. Minnesota	23-6
7. Minnesota	23-6	7. Georgetown	30-7
8. Idaho	27-3	8. Idaho	27-3
9. Memphis St.	24-5	9. Memphis St.	24-5
10. Tulsa	24-6	10. Fresno State	27-3
11. Fresno State	27-3	11. Tulsa	24-6
12. Arkansas	23-6	12. Alabama	24-7
13. Alabama	24-7	13. Arkansas	23-6
14. West Virginia	27-4	14. Kentucky	22-8
15. Kentucky	22-8	15. Wyoming	23-7
16. Iowa	21-8	16. Iowa	21-8
17. Ala.-Birming.	25-6	17. West Virginia	27-4
18. Wake Forest	**21-9**	18. Kansas State	23-8
19. UCLA	21-6	**19. Wake Forest**	**21-9**
20. Louisville	23-10	20. Louisville	23-10

North Carolina beat Georgetown 63-62 for NCAA title.

'83

Virginia's Ralph Sampson

1982-83 Final Standings

Team	Conf.	Overall	Ave.	Opp.
North Carolina	12-2	28-8	80.7	68.6
Virginia	12-2	29-5	83.6	68.9
Maryland	8-6	20-10	74.1	71.4
*N.C. State	8-6	26-10	74.2	67.6
Wake Forest	7-7	20-12	79.3	74.0
Georgia Tech	4-10	13-15	71.8	73.2
Duke	3-11	11-17	80.2	83.7
Clemson	2-12	11-20	75.6	78.0

*Won ACC Tournament

NCAA—N.C. STATE won NCAA title: beat Pepperdine 69-67 (2OT), beat Nevada-Las Vegas 71-70, beat Utah 75-56, beat Virginia 63-62 in West Regional; beat Georgia 67-60, beat Houston 54-52 in Final Four. NORTH CAROLINA second in East Regional: beat James Madison 68-49, beat Ohio State 64-51, lost to Georgia 82-77. VIRGINIA second in West Regional: beat Washington State 54-49, beat Boston College 95-92, lost to N.C. State 63-62. MARYLAND lost in second round of Midwest Regional: beat Tennessee-Chattanooga 52-51, lost to Houston 60-50.

NIT—WAKE FOREST tied for third: beat Murray State 87-80, beat Vanderbilt 75-68, beat South Carolina 78-61, lost to Fresno State 86-62. (No third place game played.)

ACC Tournament

MARCH 11-13, 1983 AT ATLANTA, GA.

FIRST ROUND: North Carolina 105, Clemson 79; N.C. State 71, Wake Forest 70; Virginia 109, Duke 66; Georgia Tech 64, Maryland 58 (OT). **SEMIFINALS:** N.C. State 91, North Carolina 84 (OT); Virginia 96, Georgia Tech 67. **FINAL:** N.C. State 81, Virginia 78.

ALL-TOURNAMENT—FIRST TEAM: Thurl Bailey, N.C. State; Ralph Sampson, Virginia; Sidney Lowe, N.C. State; Othell Wilson, Virginia; Dereck Whittenburg, N.C. State. **SECOND TEAM:** Mark Price, Georgia Tech; Michael Jordan, North Carolina; Matt Doherty, North Carolina; Lorenzo Charles, N.C. State; Sam Perkins, North Carolina.

EVERETT CASE AWARD (MVP): Lowe.

All-ACC

FIRST TEAM: *Ralph Sampson, Virginia (284); *Michael Jordan, North Carolina (284); Sam Perkins, North Carolina (282); Thurl Bailey, N.C. State (191); Sidney Lowe, N.C. State (166). **SECOND TEAM:** Othell Wilson, Virginia (162); Ben Coleman, Maryland (158); Adrian Branch, Maryland (157); Mark Price, Georgia Tech (149); Johnny Dawkins, Duke (117).

PLAYER OF THE YEAR: Sampson (75); Jordan (61); Perkins (2).

COACH OF THE YEAR: Bobby Cremins, Georgia Tech (61); Dean Smith, North Carolina (25); Lefty Driesell, Maryland (24); Jim Valvano, N.C. State (21); Terry Holland, Virginia (6); Bill Foster, Clemson (1).

ROOKIE OF THE YEAR: Price (83 votes); Dawkins (53); Ernie Myers, N.C. State (1).

*Unanimous Selection

Scoring, Rebounding Leaders

TOP TEN SCORERS

Player, School	G	FG	FT	TP	Ave.
Price, Georgia Tech	28	201	93	568	20.3
Jordan, North Carolina	36	282	123	721	20.0
Sampson, Virginia	33	250	126	629	19.1
Branch, Maryland	29	197	118	541	18.7
Dawkins, Duke	28	207	73	506	18.1
Whittenburg, N.C. State	22	141	64	385	17.5
Perkins, North Carolina	35	218	145	593	16.9
Bailey, N.C. State	36	250	91	601	16.7
Coleman, Maryland	30	182	90	454	15.1
Wilson, Virginia	34	178	107	492	14.5

TOP TEN REBOUNDERS

Player, School	G	Rbs.	Ave.
Sampson, Virginia	33	386	11.7
Perkins, North Carolina	35	330	9.4
Teachey, Wake Forest	32	272	8.5
Coleman, Maryland	30	242	8.1
Bailey, N.C. State	36	276	7.7
Jones, Clemson	31	219	7.1
Veal, Maryland	26	179	6.9
Alarie, Duke	28	181	6.5
Robinson, Virginia	33	199	6.0
Charles, N.C. State	36	215	6.0

Rosters

CLEMSON

No.	Name	Hgt.	Yr.	Hometown
3	Chris Michael	6-5	Fr.	Rutherfordton, NC
10	Mike Eppley	6-2	Jr.	Charlotte, NC
11	Warren Wallace	6-2	Fr.	Charlotte, NC
14	Milan Belich	6-1	So.	Solon, OH
15	Vincent Hamilton	6-4	Jr.	Rutherfordton, NC
20	Marc Campbell	6-2	Jr.	Elizabethton, TN
21	Glen McCants	6-9	Fr.	Columbia, SC
23	Raymond Jones	6-8	So.	Union, SC
24	Clarke Bynum	6-7	Jr.	Sumter, SC
25	Murray Jarman	6-6	Jr.	Delray Beach, FL
33	Kenny Richardson	6-4	Fr.	Sumter, SC
34	David Shaffer	6-7	So.	Durham, NC
42	Anthony Jenkins	6-7	Fr.	Spartanburg, SC
44	Fred Gilliam	6-8	Sr.	Pelzer, SC
55	Ed Bleynat	6-10	Fr.	Valdese, NC

COACH: Bill Foster
ASSISTANTS: Dwight Rainey, Clint Bryant, Jerry Faulkner, Bob Strunk

DUKE

No.	Name	Hgt.	Yr.	Hometown
11	Doug McNeely	6-5	Jr.	El Paso, TX
12	David Henderson	6-5	Fr.	Drewry, NC
14	Chip Engelland	6-4	Sr.	Pac. Palisades, CA
21	Jay Bilas	6-8	Fr.	Rolling Hills, CA
22	Tom Emma	6-2	Sr.	Manhasset, NY
23	Richard Ford	5-10	Jr.	Durham, NC
24	Johnny Dawkins	6-2	Fr.	Washington, DC
25	Greg Wendt	6-6	So.	Livonia, MI
31	Mike Tissaw	6-8	Sr.	Fairfax, VA
32	Mark Alarie	6-8	Fr.	Scottsdale, AZ
33	Jay Bryan	6-8	So.	Lakewood, CO
34	Bill Jackman	6-8	Fr.	Grant, NE
40	Weldon Williams	6-6	Fr.	Park Forest, IL
44	Todd Anderson	6-9	So.	Golden Valley, MN
45	Dan Meagher	6-7	So.	St. Catharines, ONT

COACH: Mike Krzyzewski
ASSISTANTS: Bobby Dwyer, Tom Rogers, Chuck Swenson, Rick Johnson

GEORGIA TECH

No.	Name	Hgt.	Yr.	Hometown
12	David Mills	5-8	Sr.	Cleveland, OH
15	George Thomas	6-3	Sr.	Cocoa, FL
20	Scott Gardner	6-4	So.	Greenville, NC
22	John Salley	6-9	Fr.	Brooklyn, NY
25	Mark Price	6-0	Fr.	Enid, OK
30	Anthony Byrd	6-2	Jr.	Apex, NC
33	Danny Pearson	6-5	Fr.	Columbia, SC
34	Jack Mansell	6-7	Sr.	Sharon, PA
35	Maurice Bradford	6-5	Sr.	Cincinnati, OH
43	Greg Wilson	6-9	Jr.	Grand Ridge, FL
44	Tim Harvey	6-10	Fr.	Plainfield, NJ
54	Yvon Joseph	6-10	Jr.	Cap-Haitian, Haiti

COACH: Bobby Cremins
ASSISTANTS: George Felton, Perry Clark, Jimmy Hebron

MARYLAND

No.	Name	Hgt.	Yr.	Hometown
10	Jeff Adkins	6-5	So.	Martinsville, VA
11	Chuck Driesell	6-2	So.	Silver Spring, MD
12	Jeff Baxter	6-1	Fr.	Washington, DC
14	Steve Rivers	6-3	Jr.	Brookville, NY
20	Ed Farmer	6-8	Fr.	Wilson, NC
22	Mark Fothergill	6-9	Jr.	Somerset, KY
24	Adrian Branch	6-8	So.	Largo, MD
31	Bryan Palmer	6-10	Fr.	Glen Rock, PA
33	Pete Holbert	6-6	Jr.	Fairfax, VA
34	Len Bias	6-8	Fr.	Landover, MD
42	Herman Veal	6-6	Jr.	Jackson, MS
52	Greg Stevens	7-2	Fr.	Stow, OH
54	Ben Coleman	6-9	Jr.	Minneapolis, MN

COACH: Lefty Driesell
ASSISTANTS: John Kochan, Sherman Dilliard, Mel Cartwright

NORTH CAROLINA

No.	Name	Hgt.	Yr.	Hometown
4	Lynwood Robinson	6-1	So.	Mt. Olive, NC
22	Buzz Peterson	6-3	So.	Asheville, NC
23	Michael Jordan	6-5	So.	Wilmington, NC
24	Jim Braddock	6-2	Sr.	Chattanooga, TN
25	Steve Hale	6-3	Fr.	Jenks, OK
32	John Brownlee	6-10	So.	Fort Worth, TX
41	Sam Perkins	6-9	Jr.	Latham, NY
42	Brad Daughtery	6-11	Fr.	Black Mountain, NC
43	Curtis Hunter	6-4	Fr.	Durham, NC
44	Matt Doherty	6-8	Jr.	East Meadow, NY
50	Cecil Exum	6-6	Jr.	Dudley, NC
51	Timo Makkonen	6-11	Jr.	Lahti, Finland
54	Warren Martin	6-11	So.	Axton, VA

COACH: Dean Smith
ASSISTANTS: Bill Guthridge, Eddie Fogler, Roy Williams

N.C. STATE

No.	Name	Hgt.	Yr.	Hometown
10	Tommy DiNardo	6-5	Jr.	Jamesville, NC
12	George McClain	6-0	Fr.	Rocky Mount, NC
15	Walter Proctor	6-8	So.	Southhampton, NY
24	Terry Gannon	6-0	So.	Joliet, IL
25	Dereck Whittenburg	6-1	Sr.	Washington, DC
30	Harold Thompson	6-5	Jr.	Raeford, NC
31	Ernie Myers	6-4	Fr.	New York, NY
33	Alvin Battle	6-7	Jr.	Rocky Mount, NC
34	Quinton Leonard	6-8	Sr.	Louisburg, NC
35	Sidney Lowe	6-0	Sr.	Washington, DC
40	Walt Densmore	6-6	Fr.	Tuscaloosa, AL
41	Thurl Bailey	6-11	Sr.	Seat Pleasant, MD
42	Mike Warren	6-7	So.	Raleigh, NC
43	Lorenzo Charles	6-7	So.	Brooklyn, NY
45	Cozell McQueen	6-11	So.	Bennettsville, SC

COACH: Jim Valvano
ASSISTANTS: Ray Martin, Tom Abatemarco, Ed McLean

VIRGINIA

No.	Name	Hgt.	Yr.	Hometown
4	Jim Miller	6-8	So.	Princeton, WV
10	Craig Robinson	6-8	Sr.	Montclair, NJ
11	Othell Wilson	6-0	Jr.	Woodbridge, VA
14	Ricky Stokes	5-10	Jr.	Richmond, VA
30	Kenton Edelin	6-7	Jr.	Alexandria, VA
32	Doug Newburg	6-2	Sr.	McLean, VA
33	Kenny Johnson	6-0	So.	Baltimore, MD
34	Rick Carlisle	6-5	Jr.	Ogdensburg, NY
42	Wingo Smith	6-9	Jr.	Indialantic, FL
44	Kenny Lambiotte	6-4	Fr.	Woodstock, VA
45	Tim Mullen	6-5	So.	Ridgewood, NJ
51	Dan Merrifield	6-6	So.	Linwood, NJ
55	Ralph Sampson	7-4	Sr.	Harrisonburg, VA

COACH: Terry Holland
ASSISTANTS: Jim Larranaga, Dave Odom

WAKE FOREST

No.	Name	Hgt.	Yr.	Hometown
3	John Toms	6-6	Jr.	Shelby, NC
10	Scott Davis	6-2	Jr.	Monaca, PA
11	Steve Warden	6-5	Fr.	Lewisville, NC
15	Delaney Rudd	6-2	So.	Hollister, NC
20	Danny Young	6-3	Jr.	Raleigh, NC
21	Kenny Green	6-6	Fr.	Eustis, FL
22	Chuck Kepley	6-4	So.	Roanoke, VA
25	Stewart Wallace	6-4	Jr.	Richmond, VA
30	Alvis Rogers	6-7	Sr.	Washington, DC
33	Sylvester Charles	6-8	So.	St. Thomas, V.I.
34	Lee Garber	6-5	So.	Kingsport, TN
44	Tony Karasek	6-9	Fr.	East Moline, IL
55	Anthony Teachey	6-9	Jr.	Goldsboro, NC

COACH: Carl Tacy
ASSISTANTS: Ernie Nestor, Mark Freidinger, Herb Krusen

All-America Teams

ASSOCIATED PRESS

FIRST TEAM: *Ralph Sampson, Virginia; Michael Jordan, North Carolina; Dale Ellis, Tennessee; Patrick Ewing, Georgetown; Wayman Tisdale, Oklahoma. **SECOND TEAM:** Steve Stipanovich, Missouri; Darrell Walker, Arkansas; Derek Harper, Illinois; Clyde Drexler, Houston; Keith Lee, Memphis State. **THIRD TEAM:** Antoine Carr, Wichita State; John Pinone, Villanova; **Sam Perkins, North Carolina**; Ennis Whatley, Alabama; Kenny Fields, UCLA.

UNITED PRESS INTERNATIONAL

FIRST TEAM: *Ralph Sampson, Virginia; Michael Jordan, North Carolina; Sam Perkins, North Carolina; Keith Lee, Memphis State; John Paxson, Notre Dame. **SECOND TEAM:** Jon Sundvold, Missouri; Darrell Walker, Arkansas; Patrick Ewing, Georgetown; Dale Ellis, Tennessee; Wayman Tisdale, Oklahoma. **THIRD TEAM:** Ennis Whatley, Alabama; Chris Mullin, St. John's; John Pinone, Villanova; Sidney Green, Nevada-Las Vegas; Clyde Drexler, Houston.

*Player of the Year

Final Top 20 Polls

AP		UPI	
1. Houston	31-3	1. Houston	31-3
2. Louisville	32-4	2. Louisville	32-4
3. St. John's	28-5	3. St. John's	28-5
4. Virginia	**29-5**	**4. Virginia**	**29-5**
5. Indiana	24-6	5. Indiana	24-6
6. Nevada-L.V.	28-3	6. Nevada-L.V.	28-3
7. UCLA	23-6	7. UCLA	23-6
8. North Carolina	**28-8**	**8. North Carolina**	**28-8**
9. Arkansas	26-4	9. Arkansas	26-4
10. Missouri	26-8	10. Kentucky	23-8
11. Boston Col.	25-7	11. Villanova	24-8
12. Kentucky	23-8	12. Missouri	26-8
13. Villanova	24-8	13. Boston Col.	25-7
14. Wichita State	24-3	**14. N.C. State**	**26-10**
15. Tenn.-Chat.	26-4	15. Georgia	24-10
16. N.C. State	**26-10**	16. Tenn.-Chat.	26-4
17. Memphis St.	23-8	17. Memphis St.	23-8
18. Georgia	24-10	18. Illinois State	24-7
19. Oklahoma St.	24-7	19. Oklahoma St.	24-7
20. Georgetown	22-10	20 Georgetown	22-10

N.C. State beat Houston 54-52 for NCAA title.

'84

North Carolina's Michael Jordan

1983-84 Final Standings

Team	Conf.	Overall	Ave.	Opp.
North Carolina	14-0	28-3	80.1	64.8
*Maryland	9-5	24-8	74.7	67.2
Duke	7-7	24-10	77.2	72.3
Wake Forest	7-7	23-9	74.6	66.8
Georgia Tech	6-8	18-11	69.8	64.5
Virginia	6-8	21-12	66.6	61.5
N.C. State	4-10	19-14	70.6	67.1
Clemson	3-11	14-14	74.5	68.1

*Won ACC Tournament

NCAA—VIRGINIA tied for third in Final Four: beat Iona 58-57, beat Arkansas 53-51 (OT), beat Syracuse 63-55, beat Indiana 50-48 in East Regional; lost to Houston 49-47 (OT) in Final Four. WAKE FOREST second in Midwest Regional: beat Kansas 69-59, beat DePaul 73-71 (OT), lost to Houston 68-63. NORTH CAROLINA lost in East Regional semifinals: beat Temple 77-66, lost to Indiana 72-68. MARYLAND lost in Mideast Regional semifinals: beat West Virginia 102-77, lost to Illinois 72-70. DUKE lost in second round of West Regional to Washington 80-78.

NIT—GEORGIA TECH lost to Virginia Tech 77-74. N.C. STATE lost to Florida State 74-71 (OT).

ACC Tournament

MARCH 9-11, 1984 AT GREENSBORO, N.C.

FIRST ROUND: North Carolina 78, Clemson 66; Duke 67, Georgia Tech 63 (OT); Maryland 69, N.C. State 63; Wake Forest 63, Virginia 51. **SEMIFINALS:** Duke 77, North Carolina 75; Maryland 66, Wake Forest 64. **FINAL:** Maryland 74, Duke 62.

All-TOURNAMENT—FIRST TEAM: Len Bias, Maryland; Mark Alarie, Duke; Johnny Dawkins, Duke; Matt Doherty, North Carolina; Ben Coleman, Maryland. **SECOND TEAM:** Adrian Branch, Maryland; Michael Jordan, North Carolina; Murray Jarman, Clemson; Anthony Teachey, Wake Forest; Mark Price, Georgia Tech.

EVERETT CASE AWARD (MVP): Bias.

All-ACC

FIRST TEAM: *Sam Perkins, North Carolina (256); *Michael Jordan, North Carolina (256); Lorenzo Charles, N.C. State(239); Mark Alarie, Duke (185); Mark Price, Georgia Tech (177). **SECOND TEAM:** Ben Coleman, Maryland (167); Johnny Dawkins, Duke (157); Anthony Teachey, Wake Forest (139); Othell Wilson, Virginia (130); Kenny Green, Wake Forest (85).

PLAYER OF THE YEAR: Jordan (113); Perkins (15); Charles (2). **COACH OF THE YEAR:** Mike Krzyzewski, Duke (73); Dean Smith, North Carolina (34); Bobby Cremins, Georgia Tech (17); Lefty Driesell, Maryland (6). **ROOKIE OF THE YEAR:** Bruce Dalrymple, Georgia Tech (74); Kenny Smith, North Carolina (29); Tommy Amaker, Duke (20); Olden Polynice, Virginia (5).

*Unanimous Selection

Scoring, Rebounding Leaders

TOP TEN SCORERS

Player, School	G	FG	FT	TP	Ave.
Jordan, North Carolina	31	247	113	607	19.6
Dawkins, Duke	34	263	133	659	19.4
Charles, N.C. State	33	222	151	595	18.0
Green, Wake Forest	31	229	94	552	17.8
Perkins, North Carolina	31	195	155	545	17.6
Alarie, Duke	34	230	134	594	17.5
Price, Georgia Tech	29	191	70	452	15.6
Coleman, Maryland	32	194	103	491	15.3
Bias, Maryland	32	211	66	488	15.3
Jarman, Clemson	27	157	90	404	15.0

TOP TEN REBOUNDERS

Player, School	G	Rbs.	Ave.
Teachey, Wake Forest	32	321	10.0
Perkins, North Carolina	31	298	9.6
McQueen, N.C. State	33	297	9.0
Coleman, Maryland	32	269	8.4
Charles, N.C. State	33	275	8.3
Alarie, Duke	34	245	7.2
Joseph, Georgia Tech	29	208	7.2
Pierre, N.C. State	33	230	7.0
Dalrymple, Georgia Tech	29	201	6.9
Green, Wake Forest	31	211	6.8

Rosters

CLEMSON

No.	Name	Hgt.	Yr.	Hometown
3	Chris Michael	6-5	So.	Rutherfordton, NC
10	Mike Eppley	6-2	Sr.	Charlotte, NC
11	Warren Wallace	6-2	So.	Charlotte, NC
15	Vincent Hamilton	6-4	Jr.	Rutherfordton, NC
20	Marc Campbell	6-2	Sr.	Elizabethton, TN
21	Glen McCants	6-9	So.	Columbia, SC
23	Raymond Jones	6-8	Jr.	Union, SC
24	Clarke Bynum	6-7	Sr.	Sumter, SC
25	Murray Jarman	6-6	Sr.	Delray Beach, FL
33	Glenn Corbit	6-6	Jr.	Orangeburg, SC
34	David Shaffer	6-7	Jr.	Durham, NC
42	Anthony Jenkins	6-7	So.	Spartanburg, SC
44	Harvey Grant	6-8	Fr.	Sparta, GA
54	Horace Grant	6-8	Fr.	Sparta, GA
55	Ed Bleynat	6-10	Fr.	Valdese, NC

COACH: Bill Foster
ASSISTANTS: Dave Campbell, Clint Bryant, Jerry Faulkner, Mike Williams, Jimmy Gaffney

DUKE

No.	Name	Hgt.	Yr.	Hometown
4	Tommy Amaker	6-0	Fr.	Falls Church, VA
11	Doug McNeely	6-5	Sr.	El Paso, TX
12	David Henderson	6-5	So.	Drewry, NC
14	Vince Crump	6-6	So.	Durham, NC
21	Jay Bilas	6-8	So.	Rolling Hills, CA
23	Richard Ford	5-10	Sr.	Durham, NC
24	Johnny Dawkins	6-2	So.	Washington, DC
32	Mark Alarie	6-8	So.	Scottsdale, AZ
33	Jay Bryan	6-8	Jr.	Lakewood, CO
40	Weldon Williams	6-6	So.	Park Forest, IL
44	Todd Anderson	6-9	Jr.	Golden Valley, MN
45	Dan Meagher	6-7	Jr.	St. Catherines, ONT
51	Martin Nessley	7-2	Fr.	Whitehall, OH

COACH: Mike Krzyzewski
ASSISTANTS: Chuck Swenson, Bob Bender, Pete Gaudet, Tom Rogers

GEORGIA TECH

No.	Name	Hgt.	Yr.	Hometown
10	Craig Neal	6-4	Fr.	Washington, IN
20	Scott Gardner	6-4	Jr.	Greenville, SC
22	John Salley	6-9	So.	Brooklyn, NY
24	Scott Petway	6-6	Jr.	Chicago, IL
25	Mark Price	6-0	So.	Enid, OK
30	Anthony Byrd	6-2	Sr.	Apex, NC
34	Jack Mansell	6-7	So.	Sharon, PA
42	Ron Williams	6-0	Fr.	Columbia, SC
43	Greg Wilson	6-8	Sr.	Grand Ridge, FL
44	Tim Harvey	6-10	So.	Plainfield, NJ
45	Bruce Dalrymple	6-4	Fr.	New York, NY
54	Yvon Joseph	6-11	Jr.	Cap-Haitian, Haiti

COACH: Bobby Cremins
ASSISTANTS: George Felton, Perry Clark, Jimmy Hebron

MARYLAND

No.	Name	Hgt.	Yr.	Hometown
3	Keith Gatlin	6-5	Fr.	Grimesland, NC
10	Jeff Adkins	6-5	Jr.	Martinsville, VA
11	Chuck Driesell	6-2	Jr.	Silver Spring, MD
12	Jeff Baxter	6-1	So.	Washington, DC
14	Steve Rivers	6-3	Sr.	Brookville, NY
20	Ed Farmer	6-8	So.	Wilson, NC
22	Mark Fothergill	6-9	Sr.	Somerset, KY
24	Adrian Branch	6-8	Jr.	Largo, MD
31	Bryan Palmer	6-10	So.	Glen Rock, PA
32	Terry Long	6-8	Fr.	Richmond, VA
33	Pete Holbert	6-6	Sr.	Fairfax, VA
34	Len Bias	6-8	So.	Landover, MD
42	Herman Veal	6-6	Sr.	Jackson, MS
54	Ben Coleman	6-9	Sr.	Minneapolis, MN

COACH: Lefty Driesell
ASSISTANTS: Sherman Dilliard, Mel Cartwright, Ron Bradley

NORTH CAROLINA

No.	Name	Hgt.	Yr.	Hometown
20	Cliff Morris	6-3	Jr.	Durham, NC
22	Buzz Peterson	6-4	Jr.	Asheville, NC
23	Michael Jordan	6-5	Jr.	Wilmington, NC
24	Joe Wolf	6-10	Fr.	Kohler, WI
25	Steve Hale	6-3	So.	Jenks, OK
30	Kenny Smith	6-3	Fr.	Queens, NY
35	Dave Popson	6-9	Fr.	Ashley, PA
41	Sam Perkins	6-10	Sr.	Latham, NY
42	Brad Daughtery	6-11	So.	Black Mountain, NC
43	Curtis Hunter	6-5	So.	Durham, NC
44	Matt Doherty	6-8	Sr.	East Meadow, NY
50	Cecil Exum	6-7	Sr.	Dudley, NC
51	Timo Makkonen	6-11	Jr.	Lahti, Finland
54	Warren Martin	6-11	Jr.	Axton, VA

COACH: Dean Smith
ASSISTANTS: Bill Guthridge, Eddie Fogler, Roy Williams

N.C. STATE

No.	Name	Hgt.	Yr.	Hometown
10	Tommy DiNardo	6-5	Sr.	Jamesville, NC
12	George McClain	6-0	So.	Rocky Mount, NC
14	Phil Weber	6-2	Sr.	Northport, NY
15	Walter Proctor	6-8	Jr.	Southampton, NY
22	Spud Webb	5-6	Jr.	Dallas, TX
24	Terry Gannon	6-0	Jr.	Joliet, IL
30	Harold Thompson	6-5	Sr.	Raeford, NC
31	Ernie Myers	6-4	So.	New York, NY
32	Russell Pierre	6-7	Fr.	North Babylon, NY
33	Alvin Battle	6-7	Sr.	Rocky Mount, NC
34	Rodney Butts	6-7	Fr.	College Park, GA
35	Bennie Bolton	6-7	Fr.	Washington, DC
40	Walt Densmore	6-6	So.	Tuscaloosa, AL
42	Mike Warren	6-7	Jr.	Raleigh, NC
43	Lorenzo Charles	6-7	Jr.	Brooklyn, NY
45	Cozell McQueen	6-11	Jr.	Bennettsville, SC
50	Terry Shackleford	6-10	Fr.	Denton, NC

COACH: Jim Valvano
ASSISTANTS: Tom Abatemarco, Ray Martin, Ed McLean, Dick Stewart

VIRGINIA

No.	Name	Hgt.	Yr.	Hometown
4	Jim Miller	6-8	Fr.	Princeton, WV
11	Othell Wilson	6-0	Sr.	Woodbridge, VA
12	Anthony Solomon	5-10	Fr.	Newport News, VA
15	Ricky Stokes	5-10	Sr.	Richmond, VA
22	Tom Sheehey	6-8	Fr.	Rochester, NY
24	Olden Polynice	6-10	Fr.	New York, NY
30	Kenton Edelin	6-7	Sr.	Alexandria, VA
33	Kenny Johnson	6-0	Jr.	Baltimore, MD
34	Rick Carlisle	6-5	Sr.	Ogdensburg, NY
42	Wingo Smith	6-9	Sr.	Indialantic, FL
44	Kenny Lambiotte	6-4	So.	Woodstock, VA
45	Tim Mullen	6-5	Jr.	Ridgewood, NJ
51	Dan Merrifield	6-6	Jr.	Linwood, NJ

COACH: Terry Holland
ASSISTANTS: Jim Larranaga, Dave Odom

WAKE FOREST

No.	Name	Hgt.	Yr.	Hometown
3	John Toms	6-6	Sr.	Shelby, NC
10	Scott Davis	6-2	Sr.	Monaca, PA
14	Tyrone Bogues	5-3	Fr.	Baltimore, MD
15	Delaney Rudd	6-2	Jr.	Hollister, NC
20	Danny Young	6-3	Sr.	Raleigh, NC
21	Kenny Green	6-6	So.	Eustis, FL
22	Chuck Kepley	6-4	Jr.	Roanoke, VA
34	Lee Garber	6-5	Jr.	Kingsport, TN
42	Mark Cline	6-7	Fr.	S. Williamson, KY
43	Todd May	6-8	Fr.	Virgie, KY
44	Tony Karasek	6-9	So.	East Moline, IL
52	Mike Hillman	6-9	Fr.	Aitkan, MN
53	Craig Wessel	7-0	Fr.	Elkhorn, WI
55	Anthony Teachey	6-9	Sr.	Goldsboro, NC

COACH: Carl Tacy
ASSISTANTS: Ernie Nestor, Mark Freidinger, Herb Krusen

All-America Teams

ASSOCIATED PRESS

FIRST TEAM: *Michael Jordan, North Carolina; Sam Perkins, North Carolina; Wayman Tisdale, Oklahoma; Patrick Ewing, Georgetown; Akeem Olajuwon, Houston. **SECOND TEAM:** Devin Durrant, Brigham Young; Michael Cage, San Diego State; Sam Bowie, Kentucky; Chris Mullin, St. John's; Leon Wood, Cal. State-Fullerton. **THIRD TEAM: Lorenzo Charles, N.C. State**; Keith Lee, Memphis State; Melvin Turpin, Kentucky; Michael Young, Houston; Alvin Robertson, Arkansas.

UNITED PRESS INTERNATIONAL

FIRST TEAM: *Michael Jordan, North Carolina; Sam Perkins, North Carolina; Chris Mullin, St. John's; Wayman Tisdale, Oklahoma; Patrick Ewing, Georgetown. **SECOND TEAM:** Leon Wood, Cal. State-Fullerton; Alvin Robertson, Arkansas; Akeem Olajuwon, Houston; Keith Lee, Memphis State; Michael Cage, San Diego State. **THIRD TEAM:** Bruce Douglas, Illinois; **Mark Price, Georgia Tech**; Melvin Turpin, Kentucky; Devin Durrant, Brigham Young; Michael Young, Houston.

*Player of the Year

Final Top 20 Polls

AP		UPI	
1. North Carolina	**28-3**	**1. North Carolina**	**28-3**
2. Georgetown	34-3	2. Georgetown	34-3
3. Kentucky	29-5	3. Kentucky	29-5
4. DePaul	27-3	4. DePaul	27-3
5. Houston	32-5	5. Houston	32-5
6. Illinois	26-5	6. Illinois	26-5
7. Oklahoma	29-5	7. Arkansas	25-7
8. Arkansas	25-7	8. Oklahoma	29-5
9. Texas-El Paso	27-4	9. Texas-El Paso	27-4
10. Purdue	22-7	**10. Maryland**	**24-8**
11. Maryland	**24-8**	11. Purdue	22-7
12. Tulsa	27-4	12. Tulsa	27-4
13. Nevada-L.V.	29-6	13. Nevada-L.V.	29-6
14. Duke	**24-10**	**14. Duke**	**24-10**
15. Washington	24-7	15. Washington	24-7
16. Memphis St.	26-7	16. Memphis St.	26-7
17. Oregon State	22-7	Syracuse	23-9
18. Syracuse	23-9	18. Indiana	22-9
19. Wake Forest	**22-9**	19. Auburn	20-11
20. Temple	26-5	20. Oregon State	22-7

Georgetown beat Houston 84-75 for NCAA title.

'85

Maryland's Len Bias

1984-85 Final Standings

Team	Overall	Total	Ave.	Opp.
*Georgia Tech	9-5	27-8	69.9	60.9
North Carolina	9-5	27-9	73.5	66.0
N.C. State	9-5	23-10	73.3	65.0
Duke	8-6	23-8	78.9	67.9
Maryland	8-6	25-12	70.3	65.0
Clemson	5-9	16-13	75.0	71.0
Wake Forest	5-9	15-14	73.1	68.7
Virginia	3-11	17-16	61.2	59.6

*Won ACC Tournament

NCAA—GEORGIA TECH second in East Regional: beat Mercer 65-58, beat Syracuse 70-53, beat Illinois 61-53, lost to Georgetown 60-54. NORTH CAROLINA second in Southeast Regional: beat Middle Tennessee State 76-57, beat Notre Dame 60-58, beat Auburn 62-56, lost to Villanova 56-44. N.C. STATE second in West Regional: beat Nevada-Reno 65-56, beat Texas-El Paso 86-73, beat Alabama 61-55, lost to St. John's 69-60. MARYLAND lost in Southeast Regional semifinals: beat Miami (Ohio) 69-68 (OT), beat Navy 64-59, lost to Villanova 46-43. DUKE lost in second round of Midwest Regional: beat Pepperdine 75-62, lost to Boston College 74-73.
NIT—VIRGINIA beat West Virginia 56-55, beat St. Joseph's 68-61, lost to Tennessee 61-54. CLEMSON lost to Tennessee-Chattanooga 67-65. WAKE FOREST lost to South Florida 77-66.

ACC Tournament

MARCH 8-10, 1985 AT ATLANTA, GA.

FIRST ROUND: Georgia Tech 55, Virginia 48; Duke 86, Maryland 73; North Carolina 72, Wake Forest 61 (OT); N.C. State 70, Clemson 63. **SEMIFINALS:** Georgia Tech 75, Duke 64; North Carolina 57, N.C. State 51. **FINAL:** Georgia Tech 57, North Carolina 54.

ALL-TOURNAMENT—FIRST TEAM: Mark Price, Georgia Tech; Brad Daugherty, North Carolina; Bruce Dalrymple, Georgia Tech; Kenny Smith, North Carolina; Johnny Dawkins, Duke. **SECOND TEAM:** John Salley, Georgia Tech; Spud Webb, N.C. State; Jay Bilas, Duke; Delaney Rudd, Wake Forest; Yvon Joseph, Georgia Tech.

EVERETT CASE AWARD (MVP): Price

All-ACC

FIRST TEAM: Lorenzo Charles, N.C. State (246 votes); Len Bias, Maryland, Maryland (246); Mark Price, Georgia Tech (223); Johnny Dawkins, Duke (199); Brad Daughtery, North Carolina (194). **SECOND TEAM:** Kenny Green, Wake Forest (155); Mark Alarie, Duke (138); John Salley, Georgia Tech (127); Adrian Branch, Maryland (85); Kenny Smith, North Carolina (67).

PLAYER OF THE YEAR: Bias (54); Charles (35); Price (28); Daughtery (4); Dawkins (2); Green (2); Salley (1); Branch (1). **COACH OF THE YEAR:** Bobby Cremins, Georgia Tech (43); Dean Smith, North Carolina (35); Jim Valvano, N.C. State (21); Mike Krzyzewski, Duke (20); Cliff Ellis, Clemson (20); Carl Tacy, Wake Forest (3); Lefty Driesell, Maryland (2). **ROOKIE OF THE YEAR:** Duane Ferrell, Georgia Tech (78); Mel Kennedy, Virginia (20); Derrick Lewis, Maryland (13); Charlie Thomas, Wake Forest (6); Grayson Marshall, Clemson (4); Kevin Strickland, Duke (1).

Scoring, Rebounding Leaders

TOP TEN SCORERS

Player, School	G	FG	FT	TP	Ave.
Bias, Maryland	37	274	153	701	18.9
Dawkins, Maryland	31	225	132	582	18.8
Branch, Maryland	37	270	131	671	18.1
Charles, N.C. State	33	236	125	597	18.1
Daughtery, North Carolina	36	238	147	623	17.3
Green, Wake Forest	28	203	69	475	17.0
Price, Georgia Tech	35	223	137	583	16.7
Rudd, Wake Forest	29	210	63	483	16.7
Alarie, Duke	31	206	80	492	15.9
Hamilton, Clemson	29	188	61	437	15.1

TOP TEN REBOUNDERS

Player, School	G	Rbs.	Ave.
Daughtery, North Carolina	36	349	9.7
Green, Wake Forest	28	233	8.3
Polynice, Virginia	32	243	7.6
Salley, Georgia Tech	35	250	7.1
Hamilton, Clemson	29	200	6.9
McQueen, N.C. State	33	227	6.9
Bias, Maryland	37	251	6.8
Grant, Clemson	29	195	6.7
Joseph, Georgia Tech	34	224	6.6
Lewis, Maryland	37	241	6.5

Rosters

CLEMSON

No.	Name	Hgt.	Yr.	Hometown
3	Chris Michael	6-5	Jr.	Rutherfordton, NC
10	Grayson Marshall	6-2	Fr.	Temple Hills, MD
11	Warren Wallace	6-2	Jr.	Charlotte, NC
15	Vincent Hamilton	6-4	Sr.	Rutherfordton, NC
20	Harlan Graham	6-4	Fr.	Decatur, GA
21	Glen McCants	6-9	Jr.	Columbia, SC
22	Anthony Blackman	6-3	Fr.	Buffalo, NY
23	Raymond Jones	6-8	Sr.	Union, SC
33	Glenn Corbit	6-6	Jr.	Orangeburg, SC
35	Edward Bynum	6-5	Sr.	Sumter, SC
43	Anthony Jenkins	6-7	Jr.	Spartanburg, SC
44	Harvey Grant	6-9	Fr.	Sparta, GA
54	Horace Grant	6-9	So.	Sparta, GA
55	Ed Bleynat	6-10	So.	Valdese, NC

COACH: Cliff Ellis
ASSISTANTS: Rudy Washington, Bobby Lutz, Don Hogan, Eugene Harris

DUKE

No.	Name	Hgt.	Yr.	Hometown
4	Tommy Amaker	6-0	So.	Falls Church, VA
12	David Henderson	6-5	Jr.	Drewry, NC
21	Jay Bilas	6-8	Jr.	Rolling Hills, CA
24	Johnny Dawkins	6-2	Jr.	Washington, DC
31	Kevin Strickland	6-5	Fr.	Mount Airy, NC
32	Mark Alarie	6-9	Jr.	Scottsdale, AZ
33	Jay Bryan	6-7	Sr.	Lakewood, CO
40	Weldon Williams	6-6	Jr.	Park Forest, IL
44	Todd Anderson	6-9	Sr.	Golden Valley, MN
45	Dan Meagher	6-7	Sr.	St. Catharines, ONT
51	Martin Nessley	7-2	So.	Whitehall, OH
55	Billy King	6-6	Fr.	Sterling, VA

COACH: Mike Krzyzewski
ASSISTANTS: Chuck Swenson, Bob Bender, Pete Gaudet, Tom Rogers

GEORGIA TECH

No.	Name	Hgt.	Yr.	Hometown
10	Craig Neal	6-4	So.	Washington, IN
22	John Salley	7-0	Jr.	Brooklyn, NY
23	Bud Adams	6-7	Fr.	Atlanta, GA
24	Scott Petway	6-6	Sr.	Chicago, IL
25	Mark Price	6-0	Jr.	Enid, OK
31	Willie Reese	6-9	Fr.	Atlanta, GA
32	John Martinson	6-0	Fr.	Rockaway, NY
33	Duane Ferrell	6-6	Fr.	Towson, MD
34	Jack Mansell	6-8	Jr.	Sharon, PA
42	Ron Williams	6-0	So.	Columbia, SC
44	Antoine Ford	7-0	Fr.	The Bronx, NY
45	Bruce Dalrymple	6-4	So.	New York, NY
54	Yvon Joseph	6-11	Sr.	Cap-Haitian, Haiti

COACH: Bobby Cremins
ASSISTANTS: George Felton, Perry Clark, Jimmy Hebron

MARYLAND

No.	Name	Hgt.	Yr.	Hometown
3	Keith Gatlin	6-5	So.	Grimesland, NC
10	Jeff Adkins	6-5	Sr.	Martinsville, VA
11	Chuck Driesell	6-2	Sr.	Silver Spring, MD
12	Jeff Baxter	6-1	Jr.	Washington, DC
22	Wally Lancaster	6-4	Fr.	Lanham, MD
24	Adrian Branch	6-8	Sr.	Largo, MD
31	Bryan Palmer	6-10	So.	Glen Rock, PA
32	Terry Long	6-8	So.	Richmond, VA
33	Derrick Lewis	6-7	Fr.	Temple Hills, MD
34	Len Bias	6-8	Jr.	Landover, MD
41	Tom Jones	6-6	Jr.	Oak Hill, WV
50	Ed Woods	6-9	Fr.	Rockville, MD

COACH: Lefty Driesell
ASSISTANTS: Ron Bradley, Mel Cartwright, Sherman Dillard

NORTH CAROLINA

No.	Name	Hgt.	Yr.	Hometown
4	James Daye	5-11	Jr.	Burlington, NC
20	Cliff Morris	6-3	Sr.	Durham, NC
22	Buzz Peterson	6-5	Sr.	Asheville, NC
24	Joe Wolf	6-10	So.	Kohler, WI
25	Steve Hale	6-3	Jr.	Jenks, OK
30	Kenny Smith	6-3	So.	Queens, NY
31	Matt Brust	6-4	Fr.	Babylon, NY
33	Ranzino Smith	6-1	Fr.	Chapel Hill, NC
35	Dave Popson	6-10	So.	Ashley, PA
40	Gary Roper	6-7	Sr.	Andrews, NC
42	Brad Daughtery	6-11	Jr.	Black Mountain, NC
43	Curtis Hunter	6-5	So.	Durham, NC
51	Timo Makkonen	6-11	Sr.	Lahti, Finland
54	Warren Martin	6-11	Jr.	Axton, VA

COACH: Dean Smith
ASSISTANTS: Bill Guthridge, Eddie Fogler, Roy Williams

N.C. STATE

No.	Name	Hgt.	Yr.	Hometown
4	Spud Webb	5-7	Sr.	Dallas, TX
10	Nate McMillan	6-5	Jr.	Raleigh, NC
12	George McClain	6-0	Jr.	Rocky Mount, NC
14	Vinny Del Negro	6-3	Fr.	Springfield, MA
23	Bennie Bolton	6-7	So.	Washington, DC
24	Terry Gannon	6-1	Sr.	Joliet, IL
31	Ernie Myers	6-5	Jr.	New York, NY
32	Russell Pierre	6-8	So.	North Babylon, NY
35	Quentin Jackson	6-0	Fr.	Annapolis, MD
41	John Thompson	6-7	Fr.	Lawrenceville, VA
42	Mike Warren	6-7	Sr.	Raleigh, NC
43	Lorenzo Charles	6-7	Sr.	Brooklyn, NY
45	Cozell McQueen	6-11	Sr.	Bennettsville, SC
50	Chris Washburn	6-11	Fr.	Hickory, NC

COACH: Jim Valvano
ASSISTANTS: Tom Abatemarco, Ray Martin, Ed McLean, Dick Stewart

VIRGINIA

No.	Name	Hgt.	Yr.	Hometown
4	Jim Miller	6-8	Sr.	Princeton, WV
5	Tom Calloway	6-0	So.	Charlottesville, NC
10	John Johnson	5-11	Fr.	Brooklyn, NY
12	Anthony Solomon	5-10	So.	Newport News, VA
20	Darrick Simms	6-3	Fr.	Alexandria, VA
21	Mel Kennedy	6-5	Fr.	Long Island City, NY
22	Tom Sheehey	6-9	So.	Rochester, NY
24	Olden Polynice	6-11	So.	New York, NY
33	Kenny Johnson	6-0	Sr.	Baltimore, MD
45	Tim Mullen	6-5	Sr.	Ridgewood, NJ
51	Dan Merrifield	6-6	Sr.	Linwood, NJ
52	John Dyslin	6-11	Fr.	Knoxville, TN
54	Tim Martin	6-11	Fr.	Ridgeway, VA

COACH: Terry Holland
ASSISTANTS: Jim Larranaga, Dave Odom

WAKE FOREST

No.	Name	Hgt.	Yr.	Hometown
5	Billy Robinson	6-0	So.	Washington, DC
10	Duane Owens	5-11	Jr.	Syracuse, NY
10	Jeff McGill	6-2	Fr.	Charlotte, NC
14	Tyrone Bogues	5-3	So.	Baltimore, MD
15	Delaney Rudd	6-2	Sr.	Hollister, NC
21	Kenny Green	6-6	Jr.	Eustis, FL
22	Chuck Kepley	6-4	Sr.	Roanoke, VA
23	Hartmut Ortmann	6-8	Fr.	Bremerhaven, W. Ger.
31	Dennis Calvert	6-5	Jr.	Memphis, TN
34	Lee Garber	6-5	Sr.	Kingsport, TN
42	Mark Cline	6-7	So.	S. Williamson, KY
43	Todd May	6-8	So.	Virgie, KY
44	Charlie Thomas	6-7	Fr.	Sandy Springs, MD
53	Craig Wessel	7-0	So.	Elkhorn, WI

COACH: Carl Tacy
ASSISTANTS: Ernie Nestor, Mark Freidinger, Herb Krusen

All-America Teams

ASSOCIATED PRESS

FIRST TEAM: *Patrick Ewing, Georgetown; Wayman Tisdale, Oklahoma; Chris Mullin, St. John's; Keith Lee, Memphis State; Xavier McDaniel, Wichita State. **SECOND TEAM: Len Bias, Maryland; Johnny Dawkins, Duke;** Jon Koncak, Southern Methodist; **Mark Price, Georgia Tech;** Kenny Walker, Kentucky. **THIRD TEAM:** A.C. Green, Oregon State; Alfredrick Hughes, Loyola (Ill.); Roy Tarpley, Michigan State; Sam Vincent, Michigan State; Dwayne Washington, Syracuse.

UNITED PRESS INTERNATIONAL

FIRST TEAM: *Chris Mullin, St. John's; **Johnny Dawkins, Duke;** Patrick Ewing, Georgetown; Wayman Tisdale, Oklahoma; Keith Lee, Memphis State. **SECOND TEAM:** Dwayne Washington, Syracuse; Steve Harris, Tulsa; Jon Koncak, Southern Methodist; Xavier McDaniel, Wichita State; Kenny Walker, Kentucky. **THIRD TEAM: Mark Price, Georgia Tech;** Sam Vincent, Michigan State; Roy Tarpley, Michigan; Alfredrick Hughes, Loyola (Ill.); A.C. Green, Oregon State.

*Player of the Year

Final Top 20 Polls

AP			UPI		
1.	Georgetown	35-3	1.	Georgetown	35-3
2.	Michigan	26-4	2.	Michigan	26-4
3.	St. John's	31-4	3.	St. John's	31-4
4.	Oklahoma	31-6	4.	Memphis St.	31-3
5.	Memphis St.	31-3	5.	Oklahoma	31-6
6.	**Georgia Tech**	**27-8**	**6.**	**Georgia Tech**	**27-8**
7.	**North Carolina**	**27-9**	**7.**	**North Carolina**	**27-9**
8.	Louisiana Tech	29-3	8.	Louisiana Tech	29-3
9.	Nevada-L.V.	28-4	9.	Nevada-L.V.	28-4
10.	**Duke**	**23-8**	10.	Illinois	26-9
11.	Va. Common.	26-6	11.	Va. Common.	26-6
12.	Illinois	26-9	**12.**	**Duke**	**23-8**
13.	Kansas	26-8	13.	Kansas	26-8
14.	Loyola (Ill.)	27-6	14.	Tulsa	23-8
15.	Syracuse	22-9	15.	Syracuse	22-9
16.	**N.C. State**	**23-10**	16.	Texas Tech	23-8
17.	Texas Tech	23-8	17.	Loyola (Ill.)	27-6
18.	Tulsa	23-8	**18.**	**N.C. State**	**23-10**
19.	Georgia	22-9	19.	LSU	19-10
20.	LSU	19-10	20.	Michigan St.	19-10

Villanova beat Georgetown 66-64 for NCAA title.

'86

Maryland's Len Bias

1985-86 Final Standings

Team	Conf.	Overall	Ave.	Opp.
*Duke	12-2	37-3	79.9	67.2
Georgia Tech	11-3	27-7	75.1	63.5
North Carolina	10-4	28-6	86.6	69.0
N.C. State	7-7	21-13	70.6	63.2
Virginia	7-7	19-11	70.4	64.9
Maryland	6-8	19-14	70.4	65.6
Clemson	3-11	19-15	74.9	67.5
Wake Forest	0-14	8-21	59.8	67.3

*Won ACC Tournament

NCAA— DUKE second in Final Four: beat Mississippi Valley State 85-78, beat Old Dominion 89-61, beat DePaul 74-67, beat Navy 71-50 in East Regional; beat Kansas 71-67, lost to Louisville 72-69 in Final Four. N.C. STATE lost in Midwest Regional final: beat Iowa 66-64, beat Arkansas-Little Rock 80-66 (2OT), beat Iowa State 70-66, lost to Kansas 75-67. GEORGIA TECH lost in Southeast Regional semifinals: beat Marist 68-53, beat Villanova 66-61, lost to LSU 70-64. NORTH CAROLINA lost in West Regional semifinals: beat Utah 84-72, beat Alabama-Birmingham 77-59, lost to Louisville 94-79. MARYLAND lost in second round of West Regional: beat Pepperdine 69-64, lost to Nevada-Las Vegas 70-64. VIRGINIA lost in first round of East Regional to DePaul 72-68.

NIT— CLEMSON beat Middle Tennessee State 99-81, beat Georgia 77-65, lost to Wyoming 62-57.

ACC Tournament

MARCH 7-9, 1986 AT GREENSBORO, N.C.

FIRST ROUND: Duke 68, Wake Forest 60; Virginia 64, N.C. State 62; Georgia Tech 79, Clemson 61; Maryland 85, North Carolina 75. **SEMIFINALS:** Duke 75, Virginia 70; Georgia Tech 64, Maryland 62. **FINAL:** Duke 68, Georgia Tech 67.

ALL-TOURNAMENT—FIRST TEAM: Johnny Dawkins, Duke; Duane Ferrell, Georgia Tech; Len Bias, Maryland; Mark Alarie, Duke; David Henderson, Duke. **SECOND TEAM:** John Salley, Georgia Tech; Mark Price, Georgia Tech; Tom Hammonds, Georgia Tech; Tom Sheehey, Virginia; Olden Polynice, Virginia.

EVERETT CASE AWARD (MVP): Dawkins.

All-ACC

FIRST TEAM: *Len Bias, Maryland (250 votes); Brad Daugherty, North Carolina (249); Johnny Dawkins, Duke (243); Mark Price, Georgia Tech (236); Mark Alarie, Duke (201). **SECOND TEAM:** Olden Polynice, Virginia (134); Chris Washburn, N.C. State (111); Kenny Smith, North Carolina (82); Steve Hale, North Carolina (75); John Salley, Georgia Tech (64).

PLAYER OF THE YEAR: Bias (81); Dawkins (40); Daugherty (5); Price (5); Alarie (1); David Henderson, Duke (1). **COACH OF THE YEAR:** Mike Krzyzewski, Duke (80); Terry Holland, Virginia (31); Jim Valvano, N.C. State (11); Dean Smith, North Carolina (6); Bobby Cremins, Georgia Tech (3); Lefty Driesell, Maryland (1); Cliff Ellis, Clemson (1). **ROOKIE OF THE YEAR:** Tom Hammonds, Georgia Tech (120); Jeff Lebo, North Carolina (8); Danny Ferry, Duke (2); Richard Morgan, Virginia (2); Rod Watson, Wake Forest (1).

*Unanimous Selection

Scoring, Rebounding Leaders

TOP TEN SCORERS

Player, School	G	FG	FT	TP	Ave.
Bias, Maryland	32	267	209	743	23.2
Dawkins, Duke	40	331	147	809	20.2
Daughtery, North Carolina	34	284	119	687	20.2
Washburn, N.C. State	34	241	117	599	17.6
Alarie, Duke	40	262	162	686	17.2
Price, Georgia Tech	34	233	124	590	17.4
Grant, Clemson	34	208	140	556	16.4
Polynice, Virginia	30	183	116	482	16.1
Henderson, Duke	39	217	119	553	14.2
Salley, Georgia Tech	34	172	101	445	13.1

TOP TEN REBOUNDERS

Player, School	G	Rbs.	Ave.
Grant, Clemson	34	357	10.5
Daughtery, North Carolina	34	306	9.0
Polynice, Virginia	30	240	8.0
Bias, Maryland	32	224	7.0
Washburn, N.C. State	34	229	6.7
Lewis, Maryland	33	222	6.7
Salley, Georgia Tech	34	228	6.7
Wolf, North Carolina	34	224	6.6
Hammonds, Georgia Tech	34	219	6.4
Alarie, Duke	40	249	6.2

Rosters

CLEMSON

No.	Name	Hgt.	Yr.	Hometown
3	Chris Michael	6-5	Sr.	Rutherfordton, NC
4	Michael Tait	6-2	So.	Compton, CA
10	Grayson Marshall	6-2	So.	Temple Hills, MD
12	Chris Couch	6-3	Jr.	Greenville, SC
14	Larry Middleton	6-3	Jr.	Los Angles, CA
20	Michael Best	6-4	Fr.	Washington, DC
21	Glen McCants	6-9	Sr.	Columbia, SC
23	Jerry Pryor	6-8	Fr.	Brooklet, GA
24	Jeff Holstein	6-6	Jr.	Orangeburg, SC
32	Kimble McHone	5-11	Fr.	Cleveland, OH
33	Glenn Corbit	6-6	Sr.	Orangeburg, SC
35	Robert Stone	6-9	Fr.	Augusta, GA
40	John Hall	6-10	Fr.	Mobile, AL
42	Anthony Jenkins	6-7	Jr.	Spartanburg, SC
54	Horace Grant	6-9	Jr.	Sparta, GA

COACH: Cliff Ellis
ASSISTANTS: Len Gordy, Don Hogan, Eugene Harris, Bobby Lutz, Maury Hanks

DUKE

No.	Name	Hgt.	Yr.	Hometown
4	Tommy Amaker	6-0	Jr.	Falls Church, VA
12	David Henderson	6-5	Sr.	Drewry, NC
14	Quin Snyder	6-2	Fr.	Mercer Island, WA
21	Jay Bilas	6-8	Sr.	Rolling Hills, CA
24	Johnny Dawkins	6-2	Sr.	Washington, DC
31	Kevin Strickland	6-5	So.	Mount Airy, NC
32	Mark Alarie	6-8	Sr.	Scottsdale, AZ
33	John Smith	6-7	Fr.	Ft. Washington, MD
35	Danny Ferry	6-10	Fr.	Bowie, MD
40	Weldon Williams	6-6	Sr.	Park Forest, IL
42	George Burgin	7-0	Fr.	Fairfax, VA
51	Martin Nessley	7-2	Jr.	Whitehall, OH
55	Billy King	6-6	So.	Sterling, VA

COACH: Mike Krzyzewski
ASSISTANTS: Chuck Swenson, Bob Bender, Pete Gaudet, Tom Rogers

GEORGIA TECH

No.	Name	Hgt.	Yr.	Hometown
10	Craig Neal	6-4	So.	Washington, IN
12	Michael Carr	6-3	Fr.	Irwinton, GA
20	Tom Hammonds	6-8	Fr.	Crestview, FL
22	John Salley	7-0	Sr.	Brooklyn, NY
25	Mark Price	6-0	Sr.	Enid, OK
31	Willie Reese	6-9	Fr.	Atlanta, GA
32	John Martinson	6-0	So.	Rockaway, NY
33	Duane Ferrell	6-6	So.	Towson, MD
34	Jack Mansel	6-8	So.	Sharon, PA
42	Anthony Sherrod	6-6	Fr.	Millen, GA
44	Antoine Ford	7-0	So.	The Bronx, NY
45	Bruce Dalrymple	6-4	Jr.	New York, NY

COACH: Bobby Cremins
ASSISTANTS: George Felton, Perry Clark, Jimmy Hebron

MARYLAND

No.	Name	Hgt.	Yr.	Hometown
3	Keith Gatlin	6-5	Jr.	Grimesland, NC
12	Jeff Baxter	6-1	Sr.	Washington, DC
21	John Johnson	6-4	Fr.	Knoxville, TN
22	Greg Nared	6-4	Fr.	Wilmington, OH
23	Dave Dickerson	6-7	Fr.	Denmark, SC
25	Tony Massenburg	6-8	Fr.	Sussex, VA
31	Bryan Palmer	6-10	Jr.	Glen Rock, PA
32	Terry Long	6-8	Jr.	Glen Allen, VA
33	Derrick Lewis	6-7	So.	Temple Hills, MD
34	Len Bias	6-8	Sr.	Landover, MD
40	David Gregg	6-9	Fr.	Hyattsville, MD
41	Tom Jones	6-6	Sr.	Oak Hill, WV
50	Phil Nevin	6-11	Fr.	Vandergrift, PA

COACH: Lefty Driesell
ASSISTANTS: Ron Bradley, Oliver Purnell, Bart Bellairs

NORTH CAROLINA

No.	Name	Hgt.	Yr.	Hometown
4	James Daye	5-11	Sr.	Burlington, NC
14	Jeff Lebo	6-2	Fr.	Carlisle, PA
20	Steve Bucknall	6-6	Fr.	London, England
21	Michael Norwood	6-2	Jr.	Henderson, NC
22	Kevin Madden	6-5	Fr.	Staunton, VA
24	Joe Wolf	6-10	Jr.	Kohler, WI
25	Steve Hale	6-3	Sr.	Jenks, OK
30	Kenny Smith	6-3	Jr.	Queens, NY
33	Ranzino Smith	6-1	So.	Chapel Hill, NC
35	Dave Popson	6-10	Jr.	Ashley, PA
42	Brad Daughtery	6-11	Sr.	Black Mountain, NC
43	Curtis Hunter	6-5	Jr.	Durham, NC
45	Marty Hensley	6-10	Fr.	Marion, NC
54	Warren Martin	6-11	Sr.	Axton, VA

COACH: Dean Smith
ASSISTANTS: Bill Guthridge, Eddie Fogler, Roy Williams

N.C. STATE

No.	Name	Hgt.	Yr.	Hometown
10	Nate McMillan	6-5	Sr.	Raleigh, NC
11	Kelsey Weems	6-1	Fr.	Atlanta, GA
13	Panagiotis Fasoulas	7-0	Sr.	Thessaloniki, Greece
14	Vinny Del Negro	6-4	So.	Springfield, MA
23	Bennie Bolton	6-7	Jr.	Washington, DC
30	Kenny Poston	6-7	Fr.	Cherryville, NC
31	Ernie Myers	6-5	Sr.	New York, NY
33	Charles Shackleford	6-9	Fr.	Kinston, NC
34	Walker Lambiotte	6-7	Fr.	Woodstock, VA
35	Quentin Jackson	6-0	So.	Annapolis, MD
40	Teviin Binns	6-10	Jr.	The Bronx, NY
41	John Thompson	6-7	So.	Lawrenceville, VA
50	Chris Washburn	6-11	So.	Hickory, NC
52	Chucky Brown	6-8	Fr.	Leland, NC

COACH: Jim Valvano
ASSISTANTS: Tom Abatemarco, Ray Martin, Ed McLean, Terry Gannon, Dereck Whittenburg

VIRGINIA

No.	Name	Hgt.	Yr.	Hometown
5	Tom Calloway	6-0	Jr.	Charlottesville, VA
10	John Johnson	6-0	So.	Brooklyn, NY
11	Richard Morgan	6-3	Fr.	Salem, VA
12	Anthony Solomon	5-10	Jr.	Newport News, VA
14	Bill Batts	6-8	Fr.	South Euclid, OH
20	Darrick Simms	6-3	So.	Alexandria, VA
21	Mel Kennedy	6-5	So.	Long Island City, NY
22	Tom Sheehey	6-9	Jr.	Rochester, NY
24	Olden Polynice	6-11	Jr.	New York, NY
32	Lance Blanks	6-4	Fr.	The Woodlands, TX
42	Andrew Kennedy	6-7	Jr.	Kingston, Jamaica
44	Jeff Daniel	6-9	Fr.	Indianapolis, IN
52	John Dyslin	6-11	So.	Knoxville, TN
54	Tim Martin	6-11	So.	Ridgeway, VA

COACH: Terry Holland
ASSISTANTS: Jim Larranaga, Dave Odom

WAKE FOREST

No.	Name	Hgt.	Yr.	Hometown
4	Clay Dade	5-10	Fr.	Silver Spring, MD
5	Billy Robinson	6-0	Jr.	Washington, DC
10	Cal Boyd	6-1	Fr.	Smyrna, GA
14	Tyrone Bogues	5-3	Jr.	Baltimore, MD
20	Rod Watson	6-2	Fr.	Memphis, TN
21	Arthur Larkins	6-4	Fr.	Sarasota, FL
22	Drew Boggs	6-6	Jr.	Monroe, NC
23	Marco Pickett	6-3	Jr.	Raeford, NC
31	Dennis Calvert	6-5	Sr.	Memphis, TN
34	Duane Owens	5-11	Sr.	Syracuse, NY
42	Mark Cline	6-7	Jr.	Williamson, WV
44	Charlie Thomas	6-7	So.	Sandy Springs, MD
45	Paul Deibert	6-9	Fr.	Johnstown, PA
55	Mike Scott	6-11	Fr.	Greenup, KY
55	Alan Dickens	6-8	Jr.	Greenville, NC

COACH: Bob Staak
ASSISTANTS: Jerry Wainwright, Dennis Wolff, Tom McConnell

All-America Teams

ASSOCIATED PRESS

FIRST TEAM: Len Bias, Maryland; Kenny Walker, Kentucky; *Walter Berry, St. John's; Steve Alford, Indiana; **Johnny Dawkins, Duke. SECOND TEAM:** Dell Curry, Virginia Tech; **Brad Daugherty, North Carolina**; Danny Manning, Kansas; Ron Harper, Miami (Ohio) Scott Skiles, Michigan State. **THIRD TEAM:** William Bedford, Memphis State; **Mark Price, Georgia Tech**, David Robinson, Navy; Roy Tarpley, Michigan; Dwayne Washington, Syracuse.

UNITED PRESS INTERNATIONAL

FIRST TEAM: Johnny Dawkins, Duke; *Walter Berry, St. John's; Kenny Walker, Kentucky; **Len Bias, Maryland**; Scott Skiles, Michigan State. **SECOND TEAM:** Dwayne Washington, Syracuse; Steve Alford, Indiana; **Brad Daugherty, North Carolina**; Danny Manning, Kansas; Ron Harper, Miami (Ohio). **THIRD TEAM:** Dell Curry, Virginia Tech; **Mark Price, Georgia Tech**; David Robinson, Navy; **Mark Alarie, Duke**; Reggie Miller, UCLA.

*Player of the Year

Final Top 20 Polls

AP		UPI	
1. **Duke**	**37-3**	1. **Duke**	**37-3**
2. Kansas	35-4	2. Kansas	35-4
3. Kentucky	32-4	3. St. John's	31-5
4. St. John's	31-5	4. Kentucky	32-4
5. Michigan	28-5	5. Michigan	28-5
6. **Georgia Tech**	**27-7**	6. **Georgia Tech**	**27-7**
7. Louisville	32-7	7. Louisville	32-7
8. **North Carolina**	**28-6**	8. **North Carolina**	**28-6**
9. Syracuse	26-6	9. Syracuse	26-6
10. Notre Dame	23-6	10. Nevada-L.V.	33-5
11. Nevada-L.V.	33-5	11. Notre Dame	23-6
12. Memphis St.	28-6	12. Memphis St.	28-6
13. Georgetown	24-8	13. Bradley	32-3
14. Bradley	32-3	14. Indiana	21-8
15. Oklahoma	26-9	15. Georgetown	24-8
16. Indiana	21-8	16. Texas-El Paso	27-6
17. Navy	30-5	17. Oklahoma	26-9
18. Michigan St.	23-8	18. Michigan St.	23-8
19. Illinois	22-10	19. Alabama	24-9
20. Texas-El Paso	27-6	20. Illinois	22-10

Louisville beat Duke 72-69 for NCAA title.

'87

Clemson's Horace Grant

1986-87 Final Standings

Team	Conf.	Overall	Ave.	Opp.
North Carolina	14-0	32-4	91.3	74.9
Clemson	10-4	25-6	86.1	71.5
Duke	9-5	24-9	77.2	67.3
Virginia	8-6	21-10	74.2	68.4
Georgia Tech	7-7	16-13	70.7	68.5
***N.C. State**	6-8	20-15	77.5	74.8
Wake Forest	2-12	14-15	68.9	68.1
Maryland	0-14	9-17	71.7	73.3

*Won ACC Tournament

NCAA—NORTH CAROLINA second in East Regional: beat Pennsylvania 113-82, beat Michigan 109-97, beat Notre Dame 74-68, lost to Syracuse 79-75. DUKE lost in semifinals of Midwest Regional: beat Texas A&M 58-51, beat Xavier 65-60, lost to Indiana 88-82. CLEMSON lost in first round of Southeast Regional to Southwest Missouri State 65-60. GEORGIA TECH lost in first round of Midwest Regional to LSU 85-79. N.C. STATE lost in first round of East Regional to Florida 82-70. VIRGINIA lost in first round of West Regional to Wyoming 64-60.

ACC Tournament

MARCH 6-8, 1987 AT LANDOVER, MD.

FIRST ROUND: North Carolina 82, Maryland 63; Virginia 55, Georgia Tech 54; Wake Forest 69, Clemson 62; N.C. State 71, Duke 64 (OT). **SEMIFINALS:** North Carolina 84, Virginia 82 (2 OT); N.C. State 77, Wake Forest 73 (2 OT). **FINAL:** N.C. State 68, North Carolina 67.

ALL-TOURNAMENT—FIRST TEAM: Vinny Del Negro, N.C. State; Andrew Kennedy, Virginia; Tyrone Bogues, Wake Forest; Jeff Lebo, North Carolina; Joe Wolf, North Carolina. **SECOND TEAM:** Bennie Bolton, N.C. State; Chucky Brown, N.C. State; Charles Shackleford, N.C. State; J.R. Reid, North Carolina; Kenny Smith, North Carolina.

EVERETT CASE AWARD (MVP): Del Negro.

All-ACC

FIRST TEAM: Horace Grant, Clemson (245 votes); Kenny Smith, North Carolina (242); Joe Wolf, North Carolina (184); Derrick Lewis, Maryland (182); Tyrone Bogues, Wake Forest (160). **SECOND TEAM:** J.R. Reid, North Carolina (159); Danny Ferry, Duke (129); Andrew Kennedy, Virginia (117); Tommy Amaker, Duke (115); Duane Ferrell, Georgia Tech (89).

PLAYER OF THE YEAR: Grant (102); Smith (27); Lewis (7); Bogues (2); Wolf (2). **COACH OF THE YEAR:** Cliff Ellis, Clemson (64); Mike Krzyzewski, Duke (44); Dean Smith, North Carolina (27); Terry Holland, Virginia (2); Bob Staak, Wake Forest (2); Bob Wade, Maryland (1). **ROOKIE OF THE YEAR:** Reid (135); Sam Ivy, Wake Forest (5).

Scoring, Rebounding Leaders

TOP TEN SCORERS

Player, School	G	FG	FT	TP	Ave.
Grant, Clemson	31	256	138	651	21.0
Lewis, Maryland	26	195	119	510	19.6
Ferrell, Georgia Tech	29	201	112	520	17.9
K. Smith, North Carolina	34	208	71	574	16.9
A. Kennedy, Virginia	31	191	130	512	16.5
Hammonds, Georgia Tech	29	206	59	471	16.2
Wolf, North Carolina	34	212	69	516	15.2
Bolton, N.C. State	35	148	159	524	15.0
Bogues, Wake Forest	29	159	75	428	14.8
Reid, North Carolina	36	198	132	528	14.7

TOP TEN REBOUNDERS

Player, School	G	Rbs.	Ave.
Grant, Clemson	31	299	9.6
Lewis, Maryland	26	248	9.5
Ferry, Duke	33	256	7.8
Shackleford, N.C. State	34	260	7.6
A. Kennedy, Virginia	31	232	7.5
Reid, North Carolina	36	268	7.4
Hammonds, Georgia Tech	29	208	7.2
Wolf, North Carolina	34	240	7.1
Sheehey, Virginia	31	192	6.2
Ivy, Wake Forest	29	178	6.1

Rosters

CLEMSON

No.	Name	Hgt.	Yr.	Hometown
4	Michael Tait	6-2	Sr.	Compton, CA
10	Grayson Marshall	6-2	Jr.	Temple Hills, MD
12	Chris Couch	6-3	Sr.	Greenville, SC
14	Larry Middleton	6-3	Sr.	Los Angeles, CA
20	Michael Best	6-4	So.	Washington, DC
23	Jerry Pryor	6-7	So.	Brooklet, GA
24	Jeff Holstein	6-6	Sr.	Orangeburg, SC
25	Ricky Jones	6-7	Fr.	Pendleton, SC
33	Tim Kincaid	6-3	Fr.	Spindale, NC
35	Michael Brown	6-4	Jr.	Baltimore, MD
41	Elden Campbell	6-10	Fr.	Inglewood, CA
42	Anthony Jenkins	6-7	Sr.	Spartanburg, SC
54	Horace Grant	6-10	Sr.	Sparta, GA

COACH: Cliff Ellis
ASSISTANTS: Eugene Harris, Len Gordy, Don Hogan, Maury Hanks, Bobby Skelton

DUKE

No.	Name	Hgt.	Yr.	Hometown
4	Tommy Amaker	6-0	Sr.	Falls Church, VA
14	Quin Snyder	6-2	So.	Mercer Island, WA
21	Robert Brickey	6-5	Fr.	Fayetteville, NC
22	Andy Berndt	6-6	So.	Chatham, NJ
30	Alaa Abdelnaby	6-10	Fr.	Bloomfield, NJ
31	Kevin Strickland	6-5	Jr.	Mount Airy, NC
33	John Smith	6-7	So.	Ft. Washington, MD
34	Dave Colonna	6-5	So.	High Point, NC
35	Danny Ferry	6-10	So.	Bowie, MD
41	Jon Goodman	5-9	Fr.	Pocatello, ID
42	George Burgin	7-0	Fr.	Fairfax, VA
44	Phil Henderson	6-4	Fr.	University Park, IL
50	Rey Essex	6-6	So.	Atlanta, GA
51	Martin Nessley	7-2	Sr.	Whitehall, OH
55	Billy King	6-6	Jr.	Sterling, VA

COACH: Mike Krzyzewski
ASSISTANTS: Pete Gaudet, Chuck Swenson, Bob Bender, Tom Rogers

GEORGIA TECH

No.	Name	Hgt.	Yr.	Hometown
10	Craig Neal	6-5	Jr.	Washington, IN
13	Brian Oliver	6-4	Fr.	Smyrna, GA
20	Tom Hammonds	6-8	So.	Crestview, FL
23	Michael Christian	6-3	Fr.	Denver, CO
24	James Munlyn	6-11	Fr.	Aiken, SC
31	Willie Reese	6-9	So.	Atlanta, GA
32	John Martinson	6-1	Jr.	Rockaway, NY
33	Duane Ferrell	6-6	Jr.	Towson, MD
42	Anthony Sherrod	6-6	So.	Millen, GA
44	Antoine Ford	7-0	Jr.	The Bronx, NY
45	Bruce Dalrymple	6-4	Sr.	New York, NY

COACH: Bobby Cremins
ASSISTANTS: Perry Clark, Jimmy Hebron, Kevin Cantwell

MARYLAND

No.	Name	Hgt.	Yr.	Hometown
4	Ivan Powell	6-4	So.	Waterbury, CT
5	Mitch Kasoff	6-1	Fr.	Pikesville, MD
10	Mark Karver	6-7	Fr.	Bethesda, MD
11	Teyon McCoy	6-1	Fr.	Hammond, IN
13	Pat Holland	6-8	Fr.	University Park, MD
20	Tom Worstell	6-2	Jr.	Manassas, VA
21	John Johnson	6-4	So.	Knoxville, TN
22	Greg Nared	6-4	So.	Wilmington, OH
23	Dave Dickerson	6-6	So.	Denmark, SC
33	Derrick Lewis	6-7	Jr.	Temple Hills, MD
44	Steve Hood	6-6	Fr.	Hyattsville, MD
45	Andre Reyes	6-11	Fr.	Manning, SC
50	Phil Nevin	6-11	Fr.	Vandergrift, PA

COACH: Bob Wade
ASSISTANTS: Ron Bradley, Oliver Purnell, Jeff Adkins

NORTH CAROLINA

No.	Name	Hgt.	Yr.	Hometown
3	Jeff Denny	6-4	Fr.	Rural Hall, NC
11	Rodney Hyatt	5-8	Fr.	Wadesboro, NC
14	Jeff Lebo	6-2	So.	Carlisle, PA
20	Steve Bucknall	6-6	So.	London, England
21	Michael Norwood	6-2	Sr.	Henderson, NC
24	Joe Wolf	6-10	Sr.	Kohler, WI
30	Kenny Smith	6-3	Sr.	Queens, NY
32	Pete Chilcutt	6-8	Fr.	Eutaw, AL
33	Ranzino Smith	6-1	Jr.	Chapel Hill, NC
34	J.R. Reid	6-9	Fr.	Virginia Beach, VA
35	Dave Popson	6-10	Sr.	Ashley, PA
42	Scott Williams	6-10	Fr.	Hacienda Hgts., CA
43	Curtis Hunter	6-5	Sr.	Durham, NC
45	Marty Hensley	6-10	Fr.	Marion, NC

COACH: Dean Smith
ASSISTANTS: Bill Guthridge, Roy Williams, Randy Wiel, Dick Harp

N.C. STATE

No.	Name	Hgt.	Yr.	Hometown
4	Kenny Drummond	5-10	Jr.	Peoria, IL
11	Kelsey Weems	6-1	So.	Atlanta, GA
14	Vinny Del Negro	6-5	Jr.	Springfield, MA
21	Andy Kennedy	6-7	Fr.	Louisville, MS
22	Brian Howard	6-7	Fr.	Winston-Salem, NC
23	Bennie Bolton	6-7	Sr.	Washington, DC
30	Kenny Poston	6-6	So.	Cherryville, NC
32	Avie Lester	6-9	Fr.	Roxboro, NC
33	Charles Shackleford	6-10	So.	Kinston, NC
34	Walker Lambiotte	6-7	So.	Woodstock, VA
35	Quentin Jackson	6-0	Jr.	Annapolis, MD
40	Teviin Binns	6-10	Sr.	The Bronx, NY
41	Mike Giomi	6-9	Sr.	Newark, OH
52	Chucky Brown	6-8	So.	Leland, NC

COACH: Jim Valvano
ASSISTANTS: Ray Martin, Ed McLean, Dick Steward

VIRGINIA

No.	Name	Hgt.	Yr.	Hometown
4	Rob Metcalf	6-6	Fr.	Port Edwards, WI
5	Tom Calloway	6-0	Sr.	Charlottesville, VA
10	John Johnson	6-0	Jr.	Brooklyn, NY
11	Richard Morgan	6-3	So.	Salem, VA
12	Anthony Solomon	5-10	Sr.	Newport News, VA
20	Darrick Simms	6-3	Jr.	Alexandria, VA
21	Mel Kennedy	6-5	Jr.	Long Island City, NY
22	Tom Sheehey	6-9	Sr.	Rochester, NY
31	Mark Cooke	6-5	Fr.	Martinsville, VA
32	Lance Blanks	6-4	So.	The Woodlands, TX
34	Bill Batts	6-8	Fr.	South Euclid, OH
42	Andrew Kennedy	6-7	Sr.	Kingston, Jamaica
44	Jeff Daniel	6-9	So.	Indianapolis, IN
52	John Dyslin	6-11	Jr.	Knoxville, TN
54	Tim Martin	6-11	So.	Ridgeway, VA

COACH: Terry Holland
ASSISTANTS: Dave Odom, Jeff Jones

WAKE FOREST

No.	Name	Hgt.	Yr.	Hometown
3	Greg Keith	6-11	Fr.	Norwich, CT
5	Mitch Cullen	6-3	So.	Barrington, RI
10	Cal Boyd	6-1	So.	Smyrna, GA
14	Tyrone Bogues	5-3	Sr.	Baltimore, MD
20	Rod Watson	6-2	So.	Memphis, TN
21	Authur Larkins	6-4	So.	Sarasota, FL
22	Tony Black	6-4	Fr.	Florence, SC
23	Antonio Johnson	6-4	Fr.	Southern Pines, NC
33	Ralph Kitley	6-10	Fr.	Spencer, NC
40	Sam Ivy	6-7	Fr.	St. Louis, MO
42	Mark Cline	6-7	Sr.	Williamson, WV
55	Alan Dickens	6-8	Sr.	Greenville, NC

COACH: Bob Staak
ASSISTANTS: Jerry Wainwright, Dennis Wolfe, Jeff Capel

All-America Teams

ASSOCIATED PRESS

FIRST TEAM: *David Robinson, Navy; Danny Manning, Kansas; Reggie Williams, Georgetown; **Kenny Smith, North Carolina**; Steve Alford, Indiana. **SECOND TEAM: Horace Grant, Clemson**; Armon Gilliam, Nevada-Las Vegas; Dennis Hopson, Ohio State; Mark Jackson, St. John's; Ken Norman, Illinois. **THIRD TEAM:** Derrick Chievous, Missouri; Dallas Comegys, DePaul; Jerome Lane, Pittsburgh; Derrick McKey, Alabama; Tony White, Tennessee.

UNITED PRESS INTERNATIONAL

FIRST TEAM: *David Robinson, Navy; **Kenny Smith, North Carolina**; Steve Alford, Indiana; Reggie Williams, Georgetown; Danny Manning, Kansas. **SECOND TEAM:** Derrick Chievous, Missouri; Armon Gilliam, Nevada-Las Vegas; Dennis Hopson, Ohio State; Mark Jackson, St. John's; Derrick McKey, Alabama. **THIRD TEAM:** Nate Blackwell, Temple; Dallas Comegys, DePaul; **Horace Grant, Clemson**; Jerome Lane, Pittsburgh; Tony White, Tennessee.

*Player of the Year

Final Top 20 Polls

AP		UPI	
1. Nevada-L.V.	37-2	1. Nevada-L.V.	37-2
2. North Carolina	**32-4**	2. Indiana	30-4
3. Indiana	30-4	**3. North Carolina**	**32-4**
4. Georgetown	29-5	4. Georgetown	29-5
5. DePaul	28-3	5. DePaul	28-3
6. Iowa	30-5	6. Purdue	25-5
7. Purdue	25-5	7. Iowa	30-5
8. Temple	32-4	8. Temple	32-4
9. Alabama	28-5	9. Alabama	28-5
10. Syracuse	31-7	10. Syracuse	31-7
11. Illinois	23-8	11. Illinois	23-8
12. Pittsburgh	25-8	12. Pittsburgh	25-8
13. Clemson	**25-6**	13. UCLA	25-7
14. Missouri	24-10	14. Missouri	24-10
15. UCLA	25-7	**15. Clemson**	**25-6**
16. New Orleans	26-4	16. Texas Christian	24-7
17. Duke	**24-9**	17. Wyoming	24-10
18. Notre Dame	24-8	18. Notre Dame	24-8
19. Texas Christian	24-7	19 New Orleans	26-4
20. Kansas	25-11	Oklahoma	24-10
		Texas-El Paso	25-7

Indiana beat Syracuse 74-73 for NCAA title

'88

Duke's Danny Ferry

1987-88 Final Standings

Team	Conf.	Overall	Ave.	Opp.
North Carolina	11-3	27-7	78.9	70.1
N.C. State	10-4	24-8	77.1	73.1
*Duke	9-5	28-7	83.8	68.8
Georgia Tech	8-6	22-10	81.0	78.8
Maryland	6-8	18-13	74.9	76.3
Virginia	5-9	13-18	65.6	70.2
Clemson	4-10	14-15	68.7	79.2
Wake Forest	3-11	10-18	70.6	79.9

*Won ACC Tournament

NCAA— DUKE tied for third in Final Four: Beat Boston U. 85-69, beat SMU 94-79, beat Rhode Island 73-72, beat Temple 63-53 in East Regional; lost to Kansas 66-59 in Final Four. NORTH CAROLINA lost in West Regional final: beat North Texas St. 83-65, beat Loyola (Cal.) 123-97, beat Michigan 78-69, lost to Arizona 70-52. GEORGIA TECH lost in second round of East Regional: beat Iowa State 90-78, lost to Richmond 59-55. MARYLAND lost in second round of Southeast Regional: beat Cal-Santa Barbara 92-82, lost to Kentucky 90-81. N.C. STATE lost in first round of Midwest Regional to Murray State 78-75.

NIT— CLEMSON lost to Southern Mississippi 74-69.

ACC Tournament

MARCH 11-13, 1988 AT GREENSBORO, N.C.

FIRST ROUND: North Carolina 83, Wake Forest 62; N.C. State 79, Clemson 72; Duke 60, Virginia 48; Maryland 84, Georgia Tech 67. **SEMIFINALS:** North Carolina 74, Maryland 64; Duke 73, N.C. State 71. **FINAL:** Duke 65, North Carolina 61.

ALL-TOURNAMENT—FIRST TEAM: Danny Ferry, Duke; J.R. Reid, North Carolina; Robert Brickey, Duke; Scott Williams, North Carolina; Charles Shackleford, N.C. State. **SECOND TEAM:** Jeff Lebo, North Carolina; Quin Snyder, Duke; Keith Gatlin, Maryland; Vinny Del Negro, N.C. State; Rodney Monroe, N.C. State.

EVERETT CASE AWARD (MVP): Ferry.

All-ACC

FIRST TEAM: *Danny Ferry, Duke (239 votes); *J.R. Reid, North Carolina (239); Tom Hammonds, Georgia Tech (221); Vinny Del Negro, N.C. State (175); Charles Shackleford, N.C. State (170). **SECOND TEAM:** Duane Ferrell, Georgia Tech (162); Jeff Lebo, North Carolina (123); Sam Ivy, Wake Forest (102); Mel Kennedy, Virginia (82); Derrick Lewis, Maryland (69).

PLAYER OF THE YEAR: Ferry (90); Reid (25); Hammonds (8); Ferrell (2). **COACH OF THE YEAR:** Dean Smith, North Carolina (39), Jim Valvano, N.C. State (38); Bobby Cremins, Georgia Tech (15); Bob Wade, Maryland (14); Mike Krzyzewski, Duke (7), Bob Staak, Wake Forest (7). **ROOKIE OF THE YEAR:** Dennis Scott, Georgia Tech (103); Chris Corchiani, N.C. State (14); Brian Williams, Maryland (8).

*Unanimous Selection

Scoring, Rebounding Leaders

TOP TEN SCORERS

Player, School	G	FG	FT	TP	Ave.
Ferry, Duke	35	247	135	667	19.1
Hammonds, Georgia Tech	30	229	109	567	18.9
Campbell, Clemson	28	217	91	525	18.8
Ivy, Wake Forest	28	213	95	521	18.6
Ferrell, Georgia Tech	32	230	131	595	18.6
Reid, North Carolina	33	222	151	595	18.0
Shackleford, N.C. State	31	224	68	516	16.6
Brown, N.C. State	32	226	77	530	16.6
Strickland, Duke	35	213	84	565	16.1
Del Negro, N.C. State	32	187	104	509	15.9

TOP TEN REBOUNDERS

Player, School	G	Rbs.	Ave.
Shackleford, N.C. State	31	297	9.6
Reid, North Carolina	33	293	8.9
Davis, Clemson	29	223	7.7
Lewis, Maryland	31	237	7.6
Ivy, Wake Forest	28	213	7.6
Ferry, Duke	35	266	7.6
Campbell, Clemson	28	207	7.4
Hammonds, Georgia Tech	30	216	7.2
Ferrell, Georgia Tech	32	211	6.6
Williams, North Carolina	34	217	6.4

Rosters

CLEMSON

No.	Name	Hgt.	Yr.	Hometown
10	Grayson Marshall	6-2	Sr.	Temple Hills, MD
11	Jeff Jenrette	6-2	Sr.	Blacksburg, VA
12	Chris Boozer	6-3	Fr.	Brevard, NC
14	Donnell Bruce	6-5	Fr.	Branchville, SC
15	Chri Duncan	6-5	So.	Jonesboro, GA
22	Sean Tyson	6-7	So.	Baltimore, MD
23	Jerry Pryor	6-7	Jr.	Brooklet, GA
24	Gary Cooper	6-4	So.	Ambridge, PA
25	Ricky Jones	6-7	Fr.	Pendelton, SC
33	Tim Kincaid	6-3	So.	Spindale, NC
34	Dale Davis	6-9	Fr.	Toccoa, GA
41	Elden Campbell	6-1	So	Inglewood, CA
44	Colby Brown	6-8	Fr.	Baconton, GA
55	Rod Mitchell	6-9	So.	Patrick, SC

COACH: Cliff Ellis

ASSISTANTS: Len Gordy, Bobby Skelton, Eugene Harris, Tom Kaiser

NORTH CAROLINA

No.	Name	Hgt.	Yr.	Hometown
3	Jeff Denny	6-3	So.	Rural Hall, NC
11	Rodney Hyatt	5-8	So.	Wadesboro, NC
14	Jeff Lebo	6-3	Jr.	Carlisle, PA
20	Steve Bucknall	6-6	Jr.	London, England
21	King Rice	6-0	Fr.	Binghamton, NY
22	Kevin Madden	6-5	So.	Staunton, VA
24	Doug Elstun	6-3	Fr.	Overland Park, KS
31	David May	6-6	Jr.	Greensboro, NC
32	Pete Chilcutt	6-9	Jr.	Eutaw, AL
33	Ranzino Smith	6-1	Sr.	Chapel Hill, NC
34	J.R. Reid	6-9	So.	Virginia Beach, VA
35	Joe Jenkins	6-5	Sr.	Elizabeth City, NC
42	Scott Williams	6-10	So.	Hacienda Hgts., CA
44	Rick Fox	6-7	Fr.	Nassau, Bahamas

COACH: Dean Smith

ASSISTANTS: Dick Harp, Randy Wiel, Bill Guthridge, Roy Williams

DUKE

No.	Name	Hgt.	Yr.	Hometown
13	Joe Cook	6-2	Fr.	Lincoln, IL
14	Quin Snyder	6-3	Jr.	Mercer Island, WA
21	Robert Brickey	6-5	So.	Fayetteville, NC
22	Greg Koubek	6-6	Fr.	Clifton Park, NJ
30	Alaa Abdelnaby	6-10	So.	Bloomfield, NJ
31	Kevin Strickland	6-5	Sr.	Mount Airy, NC
33	John Smith	6-7	Jr.	Ft. Washington, MD
35	Danny Ferry	6-10	Jr.	Bowie, MD
42	George Burgin	7-0	So.	Fairfax, VA
44	Phil Henderson	6-4	So.	University Park, IL
45	Clay Buckley	6-10	Fr.	Wayne, PA
55	Billy King	6-6	Sr.	Sterling, VA

COACH: Mike Krzyzewski

ASSISTANTS: Mike Brey, Bob Bender, Pete Gaudet, Scott Easton

N.C. STATE

No.	Name	Hgt.	Yr.	Hometown
11	Kelsey Weems	6-1	Jr.	Atlanta, GA
12	Chris Corchiani	6-0	Fr.	Miami, FL
14	Vinny Del Negro	6-5	Sr.	Springfield, MA
21	Rodney Monroe	6-3	Fr.	Hagerstown, MD
22	Brian Howard	6-7	So.	Winston-Salem, NC
23	Sean Green	6-6	Fr.	Long Island City, NY
30	Kenny Poston	6-6	Jr.	Cherryville, NC
32	Avie Lester	6-9	So.	Roxboro, NC
33	Charles Shackleford	6-10	Jr.	Kinston, NC
35	Quentin Jackson	6-0	Sr.	Annapolis, MD
52	Chucky Brown	6-8	Jr.	Leland, NC
54	Brian D'Amico	6-10	So.	Reading, PA

COACH: Jim Valvano

ASSISTANTS: Dick Stewart, Ray Martin

GEORGIA TECH

No.	Name	Hgt.	Yr.	Hometown
4	Dennis Scott	6-7	Fr.	Oakton, VA
10	Craig Neal	6-5	Sr.	Washington, IN
13	Brian Oliver	6-4	So.	Smyrna, GA
14	David Boisvert	6-2	Sr.	Orlando, FL
20	Tom Hammonds	6-9	Jr.	Crestview, FL
23	Michael Christian	6-3	Fr.	Denver, CO
24	James Munlyn	6-11	So.	Aiken, SC
31	Willie Reese	6-9	Jr.	Atlanta, GA
32	John Martinson	6-1	Sr.	Rockaway, NY
33	Duane Ferrell	6-7	Sr.	Towson, MD
34	David Whitmore	6-5	Fr.	Los Angeles, CA
42	Anthony Sherrod	6-7	Jr.	Millen, GA

COACH: Bobby Cremins

ASSISTANTS: Kevin Cantwell, Perry Clark, Jimmy Hebron

VIRGINIA

No.	Name	Hgt.	Yr.	Hometown
13	Ron Price	5-8	So.	Spencer, VA
10	John Johnson	6-0	Sr.	Brooklyn, NY
11	Richard Morgan	6-3	Jr.	Salem, VA
12	Kenny Turner	6-6	Fr.	Indianapolis, IN
20	Darrick Simms	6-3	Sr.	Alexandria, VA
21	Mel Kennedy	6-5	Jr.	Long Island City, NY
22	John Crotty	6-1	Fr.	Spring Lake, NJ
24	Dirk Katstra	6-5	Fr.	Stilwell, KS
30	Matt Blundin	6-6	Fr.	Milmont Park, PA
31	Mark Cooke	6-4	So.	Martinsville, VA
34	Bill Batts	6-8	So.	South Euclid, OH
42	Brent Bair	6-10	Jr.	Ankeny, IA
44	Jeff Daniel	6-9	So.	Indianapolis, IN
54	Tim Martin	6-11	Jr.	Ridgeway, VA

COACH: Terry Holland

ASSISTANTS: Jeff Jones, Dave Odom

MARYLAND

No.	Name	Hgt.	Yr.	Hometown
3	Keith Gatlin	6-5	Sr.	Grimesland, NC
5	Mitch Kasoff	6-1	So.	Pikesville, MD
10	Mark Karver	6-7	So.	Bethesda, MD
11	Teyon McCoy	6-1	So.	Hammond, IN
12	Rudy Archer	6-1	Jr.	Baltimore, MD
21	John Johnson	6-4	Jr.	Knoxville, TN
22	Greg Nared	6-4	Jr.	Wilmington, OH
23	Dave Dickerson	6-6	Jr.	Denmark, SC
24	Brian Williams	6-10	Fr.	Santa Monica, CA
25	Tony Massenburg	6-8	So.	Sussex, VA
30	Rodney Walker	6-9	Jr.	Baltimore, MD
33	Derrick Lewis	6-7	Sr.	Temple Hills, MD
43	Cedric Lewis	6-9	Fr.	Temple Hills, MD
44	Steve Hood	6-6	So.	Hyattsville, MD

COACH: Bob Wade

ASSISTANTS: Ron Bradley, Oliver Purnell, Jeff Adkins

WAKE FOREST

No.	Name	Hgt.	Yr.	Hometown
4	Greg Keith	6-11	So.	Norwich, CT
4	Kyle White	6-0	Sr.	Silver Spring, MD
5	Daric Keys	6-6	Fr.	Marion, IN
10	Cal Boyd	6-1	Jr.	Smyrna, GA
11	Mitch Cullen	6-3	Jr.	Barrington, RI
13	Steve Ray	5-11	Fr.	Burnsville, NC
21	Robert Siler	6-3	Fr.	Siler City, NC
22	Tony Black	6-4	So.	Florence, SC
23	Antonio Johnson	6-4	So.	Southern Pines, NC
25	David Carlyle	6-8	So.	Winston-Salem, NC
30	Tom Wise	6-9	Fr.	Winchester, VA
33	Ralph Kitley	6-10	So.	Spencer, NC
34	Todd Sanders	6-6	Fr.	Pittsboro, WV
40	Sam Ivy	6-7	So.	St. Louis, MO
55	Alan Dickens	6-8	Sr.	Greenville, NC

COACH: Bob Staak

ASSISTANTS: Jerry Wainwright, Dennis Wolff, Jeff Capel

All-America Teams

ASSOCIATED PRESS

FIRST TEAM: Sean Elliot, Arizona; Gary Grant, Michigan; *Hersey Hawkins, Bradley; Danny Manning, Kansas; **J.R. Reid, North Carolina**. **SECOND TEAM: Danny Ferry, Duke**; Jeff Grayer, Iowa State; Steve Kerr, Arizona; Jerome Lane; Pittsburgh; Mark Macon, Temple. **THIRD TEAM:** Fennis Dembo, Wyoming; Sherman Douglas, Syracuse; Byron Larkin, Xavier (Ohio); Will Perdue, Vanderbilt; Michael Smith, Brigham Young.

UNITED PRESS INTERNATIONAL

FIRST TEAM: Danny Ferry, Duke; *Hersey Hawkins, Bradley; Gary Grant, Michigan; Sean Elliot, Arizona; Danny Manning, Kansas. **SECOND TEAM:** Sherman Douglas, Syracuse; Byron Larkin, Xavier (Ohio); **J.R. Reid, North Carolina**; Mitch Richmond, Kansas State; Michael Smith, Brigham Young. **THIRD TEAM:** Harvey Grant, Oklahoma; Jeff Grayer, Iowa State; Rony Seikaly, Syracuse; Lionel Simmons, La Salle; Rodney Strickalnd, DePaul.

*Player of the Year

Final Top 20 Polls

AP			UPI		
1.	Temple	32-2	1.	Temple	32-2
2.	Arizona	35-3	2.	Arizona	35-3
3.	Purdue	29-4	3.	Purdue	29-4
4.	Oklahoma	35-4	4.	Oklahoma	35-4
5.	**Duke**	**27-8**	**5.**	**Duke**	**27-8**
6.	Kentucky	27-6	6.	Kentucky	27-6
7.	**North Carolina**	**27-7**	7.	Pittsburgh	24-7
8.	Pittsburgh	24-7	**8.**	**North Carolina**	**27-7**
9.	Syracuse	26-9	9.	Syracuse	26-9
10.	Michigan	26-8	10.	Michigan	26-8
11.	Bradley	26-5	11.	Nevada-L.V.	28-6
12.	Nevada-L.V.	28-6	12.	Bradley	26-5
13.	Wyoming	26-6	**13.**	**N.C. State**	**24-8**
14.	**N.C. State**	**24-8**	14.	Wyoming	26-6
15.	Loyola (Cal.)	28-4	15.	Illinois	23-10
16.	Illinois	22-10	16.	Loyola (Cal.)	28-4
17.	Iowa	24-10	17.	Brigham Young	26-6
18.	Xavier (Ohio)	26-4	18.	Iowa	24-10
19.	Brigham Young	26-6	19.	Indiana	19-10
20.	Kansas State	25-9	20.	Kansas State	25-9

Kansas beat Oklahoma 83-79 for NCAA title.

Key play in '88 ACC final: UNC's King Rice misses last-minute layup as Duke's Quin Snyder defends.

INDEX

Photos indicated in parentheses.

A

Abdelnaby, Alaa 260.
Abdul-Jabbar, Kareem (see also Alcindor, Lew) 159.
Abraham, Colon 179.
Adams, Bud 257.
Adams, George 204.
Adkins, Jeff 224.
Adrian, Bryan 156.
Agee, Joe 160.
Alarie, Mark 243, 248, (249), 261.
Albeck, Stan 29.
Alcindor, Lew (see also Abdul-Jabbar, Kareem) 105, 115, 120, (125), 126, 133, 140, 153, 165, 206, 218, 226, 230, 244, 269.
Ali, Muhammad 194.
Allen, Phog 267.
Almond, Otis 161.
Amaker, Tommy 248.
Anderson, Butter 66-70, 78.
Anheuser, Rick 156.
Armstrong, Tate 178, 187, 191.
Arnelle, Jesse 108.
Arnold, Frank 227.
Atkins, Harold 78.
Atkins, John 161.
Attner, Paul 144, 204.
Auerbach, Red 26.
Austin, Clyde 196, 200, (200), (217), 218.
Austin, John 108.
Autry, Gene 237.
Aycock, William 62, 80, 87.
Aydlett, Rick 160.

B

Bailey, Thurl 231, 233-235.
Baker, John 20.
Baker, Lenox 131-132.
Balentine, Charles 236.
Ballenger, Bill 110-111.
Banks, Ernie 157.
Banks, Gene 42, 191-196, (195), 198-199, 219, 222, 271.
Banks, Roger 159.
Banks, Venesse 195.
Barakat, Fred 238, 275.
Barnes, Marvin 207.
Barone, Tony 115.
Barry, Rick 94.
Barry, Sam 66.
Barshak, Lou 80.
Bartels, Eddie 66, 134.
Bass, Marvin 114.
Bateman, Larry (58).
Baucom, Ladd 142.
Baxter, Jeff 243.
Baylor, Elgin 38-39, 108, 202.
Beard, Ralph 38.
Beck, Ernie 29.
Bell, Bruce 192.
Bello, Lou 28, 33, 52, 70, 275, (275).
Belmont, Joe 28-29, (29), 33, 57.
Bender, Bob 191-192, 199.
Bennett, Bob 112.
Bennett, Willett 78.
Bias, James 250-251.
Bias, Len 238, 243, 250-251, (250), 257.
Bias, Lonise 250.
Biedenbach, Eddie 102, 111, 148, 152, 170, 205.
Bilas, Jay 243, 248-249, (249), 261.
Bing, Dave 108, 112.
Blab, Uwe 261.
Black, Jimmy 221, 224-225, 228, (228), 230, 266.
Blackburn, John 170.
Bodell, Bob 161, 171, 206.
Bogues, Elaine 253.
Bogues, Tyrone 241, 252-253, (253).
Boozer, Bob 108.
Bortko, Walter 78.
Bostian, Carey 42.
Boston, Lawrence 187.
Bowie, Sam 221.
Boyd, Bob 217.
Boylan, Jim 190.
Braddock, Jimmy 220, 230.
Bradley, Bill 93-94, 103.
Bradley, Dudley (168), 188, 200, (200), (246), 264.
Bradley, Hal 31-32, 36, 40, 42, 44, (58), 87, 93, 131, 213.
Bradley, Tom 194.
Bradley, Warren 94.
Branch, Adrian 224, 238.
Braucher, Dick 124.
Brayton, Neil (89).
Brennan, Jim 92.
Brennan, Pete 21, 23, 27, 40, 43-44, 46-47, 55.
Brenner, David 220.
Breuer, Randy 218.
Brickey, Robert 210, 260, (262).
Bridgeman, Junior 149.
Broadway, Olin 21, 24, (54), 55.
Brogden, Blackwell 84.
Broughton, J. Melville 32.
Brown, Chucky 256.
Brown, Darrell 171.
Brown, Fred (229), 230, 266, 272.
Brown, Hubie 127, 133, 152.
Brown, Jim 84.
Brown, Joe 126, (128).
Brown, Larry 84, 86-89, 96, 126, 208, 264, (264), 268.
Brown, Lou 62, 76, 80, 88.
Brown, Michael 253.
Brown, Owen 149-150, 152-154, 171, 173, 179, 206.
Brown, Skip 178-179, (184).
Bryant, Charlie 56.
Bubas, Tootie 135, 137.
Bubas, Vic 21, 32-33, 43, 55, 58, 68-69, 71, 78, 82-86, 89, 93-94, 96-98, 100, 102, 104, 109-110, 112-113, 115, 118, 120-121, 124, 126-137, (129), (130), (131), (132), (133), (134), (137), 178, 241, 269.
Buckley, Bruce 93, 182, (189), 190, 271.
Buckley, Clay 93.
Buckley, Danny 162.
Buckley, Jay (93), 96-98, 136.
Bucknall, Steve 210, 260.
Budd, Dave 32, (54), 60, 62, (62), 77, 82-83, 108.
Bunch, Herman 148.
Bunge, Al 49.
Bunting, Bill 115, 118, 124, (125), 126, (128), 269.
Burleson, Tom (147), 148-150, (151), 152-155, 158-159, (159), 170-175, (175), (176), 178, 191, 202, 205-206, 208.
Burton, Ed 104.
Butters, Tom 198, 219.
Byers, Walter 42.
Byrd, Don 108.

C

Cafferky, Joe 171, 174, 205.
Caldwell, John 102, 205.
Callahan, Mike 77.
Cameron, Eddie 114, 118, 131, (132), 137, 166, 213-214.
Campbell, Marc 231.
Cann, Howard 64.
Carlisle, Rick 230, 240.
Carmichael, Billy 25, 31, 213.
Carmichael, Norm 126.
Carmody, Tom 133.
Carr, Kenny 178-179, 187.
Carr, M.L. 241.
Carr, Wendell 24, 212.
Carroll, Joe Barry 219.
Cartier, Warren 66.
Cartwright, Mark 165.
Carver, Bobby 160.
Case, Everett 23, 26-28, 30-33, (30), 36-37, (37), 40-44, 47-48, (50), 52, 56-57, 60, 64, 65-72, (65), (67), (68), (71), (72), 76-78, 80-83, 87, 92-93, 96, 98, 101-103, 108, 110, 123, 127, 130-131, 134-137, 149, 155, 212-214, 241.
Casey, Willis 68, 215, 219.
Catino, Ed 52.
Catlett, Gale 193.
Cavaretta, Phil 134.
Chalmers, Lester 76.
Chamberlain, Bill 164, 166, (167), 170.
Chamberlain, Wilt 25, 29, 38-39, 42-44, (45), 46, 89, 108, 114, 123, 194, 214.
Chaney, Don 99.
Chaney, John 253.
Chapman, Warren 115.
Chappell, Len 77, 87-89, (88), 92-93.
Charles, Lorenzo (232), 233-236, 250.
Chesley, C.D. 25, 171, 191, (211), 213-216.
Chesley, Ruth 214.
Christie, Frank 89, 94.
Church, Kenny 159.
Claiborne, C.B. 109, 115.
Clark, Ken 78.
Clark, Rusty 115, 118, (120), 121, 124, 126, (128), 269.
Clarkson, Rich 269.
Clogston, Roy 214.
Clonts, Forrest 62.
Coker, Pete 110.
Cole, Nat King 123.
Como, Perry 37.
Conley, Gene 160.
Conley, George 115.
Conley, Larry 112-113.
Conner, Chip 94-95.
Cook, Doug 126.
Corcoran, Frank 37.
Corrigan, Gene 216, (263).
Cousy, Bob 26, 63, 66, 119.
Cowens, Dave 159.
Cremins, Bobby (106), 121, 126-127, 155-156, 160, 162-163, 217, 221, 224, 231, 241-245, (245), 252, 256, 260.
Crinkley, Paul 110.
Crook, Herbert 249.
Crosby, Bill 86.
Crossman, Herb 228.
Crow, Mark 96.
Crowder, Max 192.
Crum, Bunk 38.
Crum, Frankie Gene 38.
Cullin, Mitch 257.
Cunningham, Billy 91, 94, 102, (103), 114, 121, 123, 268.
Cunningham, Bob 21, 23, 24, 40, 43-44, 46, 54-55, 103, 225.
Cunningham, Jim 86.
Curran, Jack 228.
Curran, Joe 40.
Currie, Bill 120, 124.
Curtis, Tommy 176.

D

D'Emilio, Rudy 28.
Dalrymple, Bruce 243, 245.
Daly, Chuck 109, 127, 133, 135-136.
Dampier, Louie 113.
Darden, Colgate 52.
Daugherty, Brad 236, 243, 251, 272.
Davidson, John 267.
Davis, Brad 178-179, 271.
Davis, Charlie 109, 157, (157), 163, 166.
Davis, Charlie Sr. 157.
Davis, Lefty 18, 25, (48).
Davis, Mike 187.
Davis, Walter 173, (173), 175, 179-180, (181), 182, 187-190, (190), 207, 271.
Dawkins, Johnny 241, 243, 248, 251, 261.
Dedmon, Lee 126, 128, 164.
Del Negro, Vinny 256-257.
Dennard, Kenny 191-192, 194, 196, 198-199, 219, 222.
DeVenzio, Chuck 166.
DeVenzio, Dick 42, 160, 163, 166, (169).
DeWitt, Frank 95.
Dial, Larry 77.
Dickey, Dick 66, 71, 152.
Dickman, Lou 37, 71.
DiGregorio, Ernie 172.
DiMaggio, Joe 27.
DiNardo, Phil Sr. 36, 37, (72).
DiStefano, Bob 80.
Doherty, Marty 52.

314

Doherty, Matt 221-222, 224-225, 228, (228), 230, 236.
Douglas, Leon 187.
Dow, Mike 187.
Dreiling, Greg 249.
Drew, John 241.
Driesell, Chuck 187, 221.
Driesell, Lefty 93, 97, 99, (105), (107), 120-121, 123, 126, 128, 140-144, (141), 146, 148-150, 152-156, (154), 160-161, 165-166, 170-171, (171), 173, 175, 178-179, 182, 186-187, 191, 196-197, 206-207, (211), 215, 235, 238, (240), 241, 243, 250-252, (254), 257, 273.
Drummond, Al 109.
Dull, Dick 250-251.
Dunning, Joe 156.
Durham, Woody 214.
Dwyer, Cliff 33, (34), (50), 52, (64).
Dyslin, John 257.

E

Eckman, Charlie 86, 115, 275.
Edelin, Kenton 240.
Eisenstein, Lou 82.
Ellis, Bo (189), 190, 271.
Ellis, Boo 104.
Ellis, Cliff 239, 241, 252, 260.
Ellison, Pervis 249.
Elmore, Len 146, 146, 148-150, (151), 152-155, 165, 171-173, 196, 207.
Elstun, Gene 46.
Englehardt, Dan 78.
Enright, Rex 213.
Erickson, Chuck 23, 213.
Erving, Julius 205.
Eskridge, Jack 46.
Esposito, Sal 140.
Esposito, Sam 149.
Estis, Harold 78.
Ewing, Joan 266-267.
Ewing, Patrick 226, 228, 230.

F

Fadum, Ralph 114.
Fannin, Benny 38-39.
Ferguson, Denny 96-97, 100.
Ferrell, Duane 243, 245, 257.
Ferry, Danny 42, 210, 237, 248, 260, (262), 263.
Finkel, Henry 99.
Fisher, H.A. 66.
Fleishman, Joel 18, 25.
Fleming, Bill 28.
Flowers, Jay 160.
Floyd, Sleepy 228, 230.
Fogle, Larry 153.
Fogler, Eddie 126, 269, 271.
Ford, Antoine 257.
Ford, Phil 178-179, (180), 182-183, (183), 186-188, 190, 192, 220, 222, 228, 271.
Forte, Charlie 62.
Forte, Joe 212, 275.
Foster, Bill [C] 184-185, (186), 238-239, (254).
Foster, Bill [D] 175, 178, 183, (186), 187, 191-196, 199, 217-219, (254), 272.
Fox, Phil 36, 55, 70.
Foye, Lee 171-172, 196.
Francis, Bob 115.
Francis, Skeeter 214.

Franklin, Alvin 235.
Frantz, Robert 77.
Frazier, Walt 119.
Free, Lloyd 241.
Freeman, Buck 20, 22, 46, 123.
Friday, William 83.
Frye, John 83.

G

Galantai, Billy 87.
Gallagher, Betty 74, 77-78.
Gallagher, Craig 79.
Gallagher, Don 74-82, (75), (81), 88.
Gallagher, Frank 71.
Gannon, Terry 231, 233-235.
Garfinkel, Howard 43.
Gatlin, Keith 250.
Gibbon, Joe 38-39.
Gibson, Bill [V] 94-95, (95), 101, 115, 127, 140-144, (141), 161, 165, 175, 180.
Gibson, Bill [WF] 25, 62.
Gibson, Larry 187, 199.
Gilley, Jim 21, 22, (22), 24, 54.
Gilmore, Artis 166, 204, 241.
Givens, Jack 198.
Glenn, John 103.
Glover, Jerry 226.
Gminski, Mike 191-196, (193), 198-200, (198), 219, 243, 271.
Goetsch, Scott 192.
Gola, Tom 29, 31, 41.
Goldberg, Dave 76-80.
Golden, Dave 115, 124.
Goldenberg, Joe 194.
Gossage, Goose 272.
Gotkin, Davey 27, 31, 52, 78.
Gotkin, Harry 27, 40, 43, 86.
Gotkin, Hy 26-27.
Graham, Ernest 199, 219.
Graham, Gary 253.
Grant, Harvey 239.
Grant, Horace 239, (239), 252.
Greason, Murray 18, 20, 23, 37, 40, 47, 59, 61, 116, 135.
Green, Al 184.
Green, Johnny 46, 61, 108.
Green, Kenny 248.
Green, Ron 202.
Green, Sidney 233.
Green, Sihugo 26.
Greene, Joe 74, 76-80.
Gregor, Gary 121.
Griffin, Rod 178, 187.
Groat, Dick 28-29, 96, 108.
Groll, Stan 43.
Grosso, Mike 114-115, (114), 118, 123.
Groza, Alex 38.
Grubar, Dick 104, 115, 118, 124, 126, 128, (128), 269.
Guthridge, Bill 140, 220, 228, 273.

H

Hacken, Joseph 80.
Hafer, Cliff 36-37, (72).
Hagan, Cliff 38, 41.
Hahn, Billy 153-154.
Hahn, Bob 66.
Haig, Bill (42).
Hale, Steve 236, 242-243, 245, (246), 272.
Hallman, Joe 66.
Hambrick, Walt (33), 38-39, 42.
Hammonds, Tom 245.
Hancock, Mike 230.

Hanners, Dave 179.
Harlicka, Skip 121.
Harp, Dick 46.
Harrell, John 192, 196, 199.
Harrington, Joe 140-142, 144, 186, 197.
Harris, Bobby Joe 44, (58).
Harrison, Buzzy 94, 96-98, 136.
Harrison, Charlie 235.
Harrison, Ray 205.
Harrison, Wilbert 100.
Hart, Alley 87-88.
Harville, Charlie 214.
Hassell, Butch (101).
Hassell, John (101).
Hassell, Pud (101).
Hassell, Ray (101).
Hathaway, Bill 43.
Havlicek, John 92-93.
Hawkins, Greg 171.
Hayes, Elvin 89, 99, 105, 119, 230.
Haywood, Spencer 29.
Heartley, Al 109, 156.
Hebron, Jimmy (217).
Hedberg, John 161.
Heinsohn, Tom 149.
Helms, Herman 161.
Helms, Jesse 273.
Hemric, Dickie 30, 33, 40-41, (41), 212.
Henderson, David 243, 248, 261.
Herbert, Dick 24.
Hernjak, Jim 149, 161, 193, 275.
Herring, Pop 220.
Herring, Richard 100.
Hetzel, Fred 93.
Hetzel, Will 156.
Heyman, Art 33, 42, 61, 83-86, (85), (87), 89, 94, 96-97, (96), 114, 131, 136.
Hightower, Wayne 29.
Hikel, Fred 179.
Hill, Daryl 108.
Hinckley, John 223.
Hoffman, Brad 179.
Hoffman, Dick 55.
Hoffman, Richard 77.
Hogan, Frank 80.
Holdt, Rick 171, 174, 205.
Holland, Terry 121, 156, 178, 180-181, 186, 193, 200, 218, 222, 224, 226-227, 240-241, 250, 252, 272.
Holmes, Irwin 108.
Holton, Linwood 165.
Honzo, Steve 156.
Hooks, Gene 199, 224, 248.
Hopper, Tom (72).
Horner, Jack 28.
Horton, Lenny 218.
Housman, Paul 275.
Howard, Frank 23, 59, 90.
Howard, Harkness 78.
Howard, Mo 148, 150, 152-154, 171, 173, 179, 207, 271.
Howell, Jim 186.
Howerton, Carr 54.
Huband, Kim 166.
Hudock, Jim 86.
Hudson, Lou 108.
Hull, Bill 87-89, (120).
Hundley, Hot Rod 29.
Hunt, Jim 80, 273.
Hunter, Curtis 242.
Hurt, Howard 83.

I

Iavaroni, Marc 178, 189, 193, 272.
Iba, Henry 52-53.

J

Jackman, Bill 248, 261.
Jackson, Sonny 108.
James, Bob (163), 193, 205, 216, (263).
James, Carl 131.
James, Keith 253.
Janicki, Bernie 28.
Jefferson, Thomas 226.
Johnson, Earvin "Magic" 200, 221.
Johnson, Frank [SC] 33, 39-40, 42.
Johnson, Frank [WF] (184).
Johnson, John [M] 243.
Johnson, John [V] 257.
Johnson, Pete 98-99, 108.
Johnson, Ronnie 77.
Johnstone, Jim 224.
Jones, Billy 98-99, (99), 108-109.
Jones, Blanche 72.
Jones, Bobby 166, 170, 173, 175, 202, 207.
Jones, Jeff 222.
Jordan, James 220.
Jordan, Johnny 89.
Jordan, Michael 42, 208, 220-221, (221), 224, 228, (228), 230, (234), 236, 241, 250, 266, 272.
Joseph, Yvon (242), 245.
Joyce, Kevin 160, 163-164.

K

Karl, George 152, 164, 166, (169), 170, 197, 250.
Katkaveck, Leo 66, 134.
Kauffman, Frank 166.
Kearns, Tommy 21, 22, (22), 23, 24, 40, 43-44, 46, 162, 225.
Keech, Larry 202.
Kehoe, Jim 154, 161.
Keller, Bill 128.
Kennedy, Bud 89.
Kennedy, Joe 115.
Kennedy, Mel 257.
Kenney, Bill 244.
Kessler, Bob 33.
King, Albert 219, (219).
King, Billy 243, (247), 248, 260, 263-264, (263).
King, Maurice 46.
Kirkpatrick, Curry 143, 149.
Kistler, Doug 83, (83).
Kitching, Brent 98.
Klores, Dan 40.
Knight, Bob 92, 99, 129, 136, 205, 219, 256, 260-261.
Knight, Douglas 137.
Knight, Footsie 82.
Kolodziej, Tim 115.
Krafcisin, Steve 188-189.
Kramer, Pete 175.
Kratzer, John 193.
Krause, Dieter 86.
Kretzer, Bill (121), 124, (168-9).
Kroll, Jerry 128.
Krzyzewski, Mike 187, 195, (218), 219, 222, 231, 237-238, 241, 243, 246, 248-249, 251-252, 256, 260-261, (261), 264, 272.
Kuester, John 175, 182, 188, (188-189), 190, (190), 271-272.
Kupchak, Mitch 173, (175), 179, (181), 182, 186-187, 196, 207.

315

L

LaGarde, Tom 173, 182, 187-190, 271.
Lakins, Larry (86), 103, 110.
Lamp, Jeff 222, 226.
Lanier, Bob 104, 124, 158.
Larese, York 83, 86, 118.
Larranaga, Jim 233.
Laughlin, Dwight 43.
Lebo, Jeff 210, 212, 247, 256, 260.
Lee, Greg 176.
Lee, Jimmy 180.
Leftwich, Ed 156, (158), 244.
Lekometros, Steve 77-80.
Lemons, Abe 124.
Leonard, Bob 110.
Lewis, Bob 102, 110, 115, 118, (118), 120, 126, 269.
Lewis, Derrick 251, 257.
Lewis, Guy 235.
Lewis, Mike 109-110, 112-113, 115, (120), 121, 124, 130, (130), 136.
Lewis, Reggie 253.
Lewkowicz, John 156.
Liccardo, Jim 115.
Lienhard, Bill 267.
Lind, Fred 115, 121, 124.
Lipper, Bob 202.
Litchfield, Alfred 82.
Litchfield, Terry 76, (79), 80, 82, 88.
Litwack, Harry 194.
Locke, Tates 162, 164, 179, 184-185.
Loeffler, Ken 36.
Logan, Henry 241.
Lombardi, Vince 137.
Long, Paul (97).
Lotz, Danny 40, 49.
Lowe, Bernard 66.
Lowe, Sidney 233-234.
Lucas, Jerry 92-93.
Lucas, John 146, 148-150, 152-154, (153), 171, 173, 179-180, 186-187, 196-197, (197), 207, 271.
Lucas, John Sr. 197.
Lyon, Bill 155.

M

Macauley, Ed 135.
MacGillivray, Bob 55.
Macon, Mark (247), (263), 264.
Macy, Kyle 219.
Madden, Kevin 263.
Magid, Brian (178).
Maglio, John 33, 36-37, (36), 60.
Mahaffey, Donnie 90-91, (91).
Mahaffey, H.T. 90.
Mahaffey, Randy 32, 90-91, (91).
Mahaffey, Richie 90-91, (91).
Mahaffey, Tommy (55), 90-91, (91), 110.
Makkonen, Timo (222).
Male, Bus 62-63, (63).
Malone, Moses 42, 179, 217.
Manning, Casey 109.
Manning, Danny 249, 264.
Manning, Ed 264.
Manton, Jack 187.
Maravich, Press 20, (20), 72, 83, 86, 89-90, 92-93, 101-103, 110-111, (111), 205.
Maravich, Pete 105, 109, 111, 126.
Marin, Jack 97-98, 109-110, 112-113, (113), 136.
Mark, Joe 226.
Marshall, Catherine 268.

Marshall, Grayson 253, 257.
Martin, Tim 257.
Marvel, Russ (55).
Massey, Lew 190.
Matheson, Bob 115.
Matthews, Bill 97.
Maxwell, Cedric 186, 220, 239.
May, Don 119.
Maye, Paul 38.
Mayer, Ronnie 28, 29, 54.
McAdoo, Bob 166, (167), 170, 271-272.
McCabe, Gerry 31, 52.
McCandlish, Scott 95.
McCloskey, Jack (97), 157, 166.
McComas, Jack 66.
McCoy, Bobby 38-39.
McCoy, Mike 94.
McCoy, Tommy 89.
McCue, Frank 141.
McDuffie, Frank 121.
McDuffie, Sammie 121.
McFadden, Banks 59.
McGeachy, Neill 175.
McGinnis, George 194.
McGregor, Gil 157.
McGuire, Al 176, 183, 190, 253, 272.
McGuire, Frank 18, 20-25, (25), 27-28, 30-33, (31), 40-44, (44), 46-49, (47), 52, 54-55, 58-59, 60, 62, 64, 70-71, 76, 82-84, 86, 89, 101, 108-110, 114-115, 118, 121-123, (122), 126, 155-156, 158, 160-163, (164), 165, 170, 187, 191, 213-214, 225, 228, 244-245, 246, (254), 267-269, (270).
McGuire, Frankie 123.
McHale, Kevin 218.
McKaig, Stuart 115.
McKinney, Bones (19), 20-26, 33, 40-41, 54, 61-62, (61), 77, 82, 86-88, (88), 92-93, 97, 100-101, 103, 116-117, (117), 126, 135, (211), 212, 214, 236.
McKinney, Edna 117.
McLellan, Bill 216.
McLendon, John 29.
McMillan, Nate 248, 252.
McMillen, Jay 102, 115, 140-141, 143-144.
McMillen, Jim 140, 142-144.
McMillen, Margaret 140-144.
McMillen, Paul 141.
McMillen, Shela 140.
McMillen, Tom 42, 95, 138-144, (138), (139), (141), (142), (144), 148-150, 152-155, (153), 165, 170-171, (172), 173, 202, 207.
McNair, Robert 162.
McNeil, Charles 49.
McQueen, Cozell 233-235.
Melchionni, Gary 96.
Mengelt, John 152.
Merrifield, Dan 240.
Meyer, Ray 238.
Meyers, Dave 173, 176.
Mihalik, Red 82.
Mikan, George 135.
Miller, Bill (63).
Miller, Chip 95.
Miller, Jim 225, 240, 261.
Miller, Larry 42, 104-105, (105), 114-115, 118-121, (118), 124, (124), 126, 136, 269, 272.
Miller, Rich 141-142.
Millikan, Bud 28, 33, 40, 42, 47-49, (49), 52-53, (53), 58, 62, 82, 98-99, 102, 108-109.
Mills, Jim 21, 24, 86, 212, 275.

Mills, Joe 21, 86, 115, 275.
Millsaps, Bill 144.
Mincer, Bobby 227.
Mobley, Craig 109.
Moe, Doug 61-62, 80, 83-84, 86, 118, 140, (246).
Moeller, Mark 148, 171-172, 202, 204-208.
Moffitt, Billy 103.
Molinas, Jack 80.
Molodet, Vic 36-37, (36), 40, 71.
Moncrief, Sidney 247.
Monroe, Earl 241.
Montgomery, Jerry 104.
Moreau, John 186.
Moreland, Jackie 23, 36, 42-43, (42), 71, 78, 102.
Morgan, Junior 28.
Morrison, Dwane (96), 218, 224, (231), 241.
Morrison, Harold 192.
Moser, Lou 275.
Moser, Mike 275.
Mount, Rick 128, 140.
Muehlbauer, Anton 76, (79), 80-82, 88.
Mullen, Jack 83.
Mullen, Tim 233-234, 240.
Mullin, Chris 242, 261.
Mullins, Jeff 94, 96-98, 100, (100), 136, 214.
Murdock, Jackie 18, (22), 23-24, 52, 97, (107), 110.
Murnick, Elliott 268.
Murray, Bill 55, 58.
Myers, Ernie 234.

N

Naismith, James 272.
Namath, Joe 104, 237.
Nance, Larry 219, 239.
Neal, Craig 243.
Neal, Curly 217.
Neal, Jack 160.
Negley, Pete 66.
Nelson, Lindsey 213-214.
Nessley, Martin (238).
Nestor, Ernie 253.
Neve, Norvall 161.
Nevitt, Chuck 234, (238).
Nichols, Hank 149, 152, 275, (275).
Nicklaus, Jack 269.
Niewierowski, Stan 76, 79-80, (79), (81), 88.
Nixon, Richard 140, 191, 202.
Noe, Chuck 120.
Nucatola, John 21-22.
Nuce, Steve 171.

O

O'Brien, Bob 33.
O'Brien, Jim 161, 171, 191, 206.
O'Koren, Mike 183, 188, (188-9), 190, (190), 200, 220, 271, 273.
Odom, Dickie 62.
Olajuwon, Akeem 221, 235.
Oliver, Pat 22.
Owen, Roy 115.
Owens, Tom 127, 155, 158, 160, 162, 164, (164).

P

Packer, Billy 61, (61), 77, 81, 87-89, 93, 116, (211), 214, (228).

Packer, Tony 87.
Padecky, Bob 204.
Parker, Ace 87, 131.
Parkhill, Barry 95, 159, 161, 165, (166), 181, 226.
Parrish, Robert 187.
Patrick, Mike (211).
Patterson, Choppy (108).
Peeler, Ed 204-205.
Perkins, Martha 228.
Perkins, Sam 221-224, 228, (228), 230, 236, 272.
Perry, Phil 172.
Peterson, Buzz 236, (246).
Petrie, Geoff 166.
Petty, Otto 170.
Pinder, Tiny 191, (217).
Pitt, Malcolm 49.
Polynice, Olden 240-241.
Pond, Nick 33, 36-37, 57, (72), 78.
Pons, Richard 77-78.
Popson, Dave 236.
Porac, Rich 165.
Porter, Russ 39.
Poteet, Yogi 96.
Potts, Russ 144.
Powell, Jimmy 160.
Preston, Woody 39.
Previs, Steve 163, 166, (167), 170.
Price, Mark 178, 242-245, (245).
Pritchett, Dave 148, 153.
Pritchett, Newton 72.
Pucillo, Lou 61, 64, 68-69, 71, 135.

Q

Quigg, Joe 18, 21, 23, 25, 40, 43-44, (44), 46, 49, 54, 225.
Quiggle, Jack 46.

R

Radovich, Tony 43.
Rainey, Dwight 239.
Raker, Lee 222.
Ramsay, Jack 112.
Ramsey, Frank 38.
Ranzino, Sammy 59, 71, 135.
Rash, Tim 95.
Raveling, George 197, 236.
Ray, Dee 212, (212-213), 215-216.
Ray, Rick 212, (212-213), 215-216.
Reagan, Ronald 215, 223, 237.
Reese, Willie 257.
Reeve, Ray 22, 213.
Reid, J.R. 42, 212, 260, (262).
Rencher, Bernard 200.
Reynolds, William Neal 32.
Rhea, Betty Clara 42.
Ribock, John 126-127, 155, 158, 160-162, 164, (164).
Rice, King 210, (313).
Richardson, Sol 39.
Richmond, Chris 108.
Richter, John 60-61, (64), 69, 71.
Rickey, Branch 108.
Riedy, Bob 109-110, 112, 115.
Riker, Tom 155, 160-161.
Riley, Pat 113.
Rivers, David 247.
Rivers, Moe 148-150, 154, 174, 176, 191, 206.
Rivers, Steve 238.
Roberts, Bobby 91, 101, 214.
Robertson, Oscar (54), 58, 60-61, 76, 84, 108, 205.
Robey, Rick 190, 272.
Robinson, Craig 222, 224.

Robinson, David 249.
Robinson, Jackie 98, 108.
Robinson, Smokey 121.
Robinson, Wilma 184.
Roche, John 57, 109, 127-128, 155-158, (158), 160-164, (163), 179, 191.
Rodgers, Guy 29, 108.
Rohloff, Ken 81.
Rollins, Tree 174, 178, 184-185 (185).
Rome, Stan 178.
Rose, Lee 186, 235-236.
Rose, Pete 111.
Rosemond, Ken 18, 21, 25, 93.
Rosenbluth, Helen 27.
Rosenbluth, Lennie 18, 20-27, (20), (26), (34), 40, 43-44, (45), 46, (50), 55, 71, 84, 93, 123, 162, 179, 192, 212, 225.
Rotella, Bob 240.
Roy, Tom 149-150, 152-153, 171, 179, 207.
Rudd, Delaney 238.
Rupp, Adolph 38, 53, 63-64, 70, 78, 86, 93, 104, 121, 175.
Russell, Bill 37, 57.
Russell, Cazzie 100.
Russell, Honey 52.
Ryder, Mitch 191.

S

Salley, John (242), 245.
Salvadori, Al 118.
Salz, Harvey 43, 64.
Sampson, Ralph 42, 62, 179, 217-218, 222-227, (225), (227), 230-234, 240.
Sandbower, John 33, 52.
Sanders, Satch 83.
Sanders, Twiggy (217).
Sanford, Terry 83, 137.
Scarborough, Dave 28.
Schalow, Jack 166.
Schaus, Fred 202.
Scheffel, Ronnie 36.
Schellenberg, Jerry 179, 187.
Schetlick, Ed 187.
Schmidt, Fred 96.
Schwarzenegger, Arnold 248.
Scott, Charlie 109, 120-121, 124, (127), 128, 143-144, 170, 202, 204, 221, 269.
Scott, Dennis 257.
Scott, Lester 32.
Scott, Tom 79.
Sebo, Steve 95, 127, 142.
Seitz, Bob 37, (64), (72).
Selvy, Frank 40.
Seymour, Robert 268.
Shabel, Fred 100, 133.
Shaffer, Lee 62, 64, 82.
Sharman, Bill 26, 63.
Shavlik, Ronnie 27, 32, 36-37, (37), 40, 42, 56-57, (56), 60, (64), 71, (72), 179, 213.
Sheehey, Tom 240.
Sheppard, Steve 179, 187.
Shirley, Dallas 52.
Shue, Gene 30, 275.
Siegal, Michael 80.
Silva, John 236.
Simms, Darrick 257.
Simpson, Jim 214.
Sinatra, Frank 123.
Slaughter, Jim 69.
Slaughter, John 250-251.
Slingland, Frank 214.
Sloan, Norm 39, 66, 115, (121), 124, 148-150, 152, 154-156, (154), 158, 166, 170-171, 174, 176, 187, 191, 199, 204-205, (207), 215, 217-218, (218), 236, (254), 256.
Smith, Alfred 266.
Smith, Anne 273.
Smith, Dean 48, 89, 93, 98, 102, 104, 108, 112, 115, 118-120, (119), 123-124, 126-128, 136, 138, (139), 140-144, (141), 152, 156-157, 161, 163-166, 170, 172, 175, 182-184, 187, 189-191, 193, 197, 199-200, 205, 210, 218, 220-222, (221), 224-225, 228, 230, 236-238, 241-242, 246, 252, (255), 256, 260-261, 264-273 (265), (266-267), (270), (271), (273).
Smith, John 260.
Smith, Kenny 183, 236, 251-252, 256, (256).
Smith, Ranzino 257.
Smith, Sam 39.
Smith, Vesta 266.
Snead, J.C. 231.
Snead, Norman (120).
Snow, Harold 66.
Snyder, Quin 210, 212, 260, 263.
Spanarkel, Jim 191-193, 196, 198-200, (198), 271.
Speaks, Jon 81.
Spear, Bob 267.
Speight, Bob 71.
Spence, Phil 150, 152-154, 175-176, 202, 204, 206-207.
Staak, Bob 248, 252, 257, (257).
Stacom, Kevin 172.
Stahl, Ed 174-175.
Standard, Frank 109, 121.
Stanley, Ray 80.
Starr, Keith 175.
Staubach, Roger 269.
Steele, Jerry 88.
Steinbrenner, George 123.
Steinwedel, Steve 195.
Stepanovich, George 78.
Steppe, Brook 218, 224.
Stevens, Laura 72.
Stewart, Harry 71.
Stine, Charles 66.
Stobaugh, Dick 161.
Stoddard, Tim 149-150, 152, 171, 174, 205.
Stokes, Ricky 224, 240.
Stone, Rock (255).
Stout, Ralph 275.
Strickland, Kevin 210, 237, 260.
Strong, Guy 97.
Stubbs, Dale 115.
Suddath, Jim 192.
Sullivan, Claude 38.
Suttle, Dane 233.
Sweeney, Robert 131.
Swetnam, Stan 165.
Sykes, Paul 116.

T

Tacy, Carl 178-179, 187, 199, 241, 248, (248), 252, 257.
Tatum, Jim 52, 58, 89.
Taylor, Chuck 24, 66.
Taylor, Vince 200.
Terrill, Lee 68-72, 78, 134.
Thacker, Jim (211), 214.
Thomas, Charlie 242.
Thomas, Gorman 39.
Thomas, Isiah 223.
Thomas, Jim 223.
Thompson, David 42, 57, 85, 96, 148-150, (151), 152-154, (152), 159, 166, 170-172, (172), 174-176, (177), 179, 199, 201-208 (201), (203), (204), (206), (207), (208), 215, 230, 271.
Thompson, Ida 204.
Thompson, Jack 121.
Thompson, John 228, 268.
Thompson, Vellie 204.
Thorn, Rod 85, 131.
Thurman, Nate 85.
Tisdale, Wayman 245.
Tison, Hack 91, 94, 96-98, 136.
Todmann, Norwood 109, 157.
Tolbert, Ray 223.
Toone, Bernard 190.
Towe, Monte 148-150, 152-155, (153), 159, 170, 174-176, (177), 202-205, 207-208, 215, 252.
Trgovich, Pete 149.
Tribble, Harold 117.
Trifunovich, Nick 115.
Trimble, Jap 149, 165.
Tucker, Bill 54-55.
Tucker, Jim 41.
Turner, Landon 223.
Tuttle, Gerald 126, 128, (128).
Tyler, Dick 52.
Tynberg, Mike 43.

U

Unitas, Johnny 111.
Unseld, Wes 105.

V

Vacendak, Steve 97-98, 109, (113), 136, 275.
Valenti, Paul 104.
Valvano, Jim 187, (218), 219, 222, 228, 231, (232), 234-237, (237), 241, 248, 250, 252, 257, 261, 273.
Valvano, Pam 236-237.
van Breda Kolff, Butch 84.
Vandenberg, Steve 115, 124, 127.
Vayda, Jerry 59.
Veal, Herman 238.
Veeck, Bill 132.
Verga, Bob 109-110, 112-113, (112), 115, 118, (130), 136, 195.
Vincent, Jay 200.
Virgil, John 188.
Vogel, Jerry 80.
Von Glahn, J.L. 66.

W

Waddell, Charles 269.
Wade, Bob 98, 109, 251-253, 257, (257).
Wagman, Aaron 80.
Walker, Herschel 187.
Walker, Paul 80.
Walker, Wally 171, 180-181, (181), 186-187, 196, 226.
Wallace, Grady 20, 22, 28, 33, 38-40, (39), 42, 44, 164.
Walsh, Billy 126-127, 155, 162.
Walsh, Donnie 84, 86-87, 115, 268.
Walton, Bill 159, 174, 176-177, (177), 198, 206.
Ward, Gary 102.
Warren, Bob 66.
Warren, Tony 191.
Washburn, Chris 241, 256-257.
Washington, Kenny 100.
Waters, Bucky (72), 80, 94, (106), 109-110, 131-133, 135-136, (137), 156, 166, 170, 175, 202, 247.
Weaver, Jim 23, 42, 48, 52, 54-55, 62, 82, 86-87, 115, 142, 161, 212, (263).
Webb, Paul 219.
Weedon, Frank 72.
Weinhauer, Bob 196.
Weltlich, Bob 219.
Wendelin, Ron 115.
Wendt, Greg 96.
Wennington, Bill 261.
Wenzel, Bob 219.
West, Jerry 202, 223.
West, Robbie 166.
West, Tom 104.
Whicker, Mark 273.
White, Curly 110.
White, Howard 160, 166.
Whittenburg, Dereck 231, 233-235, (233).
Wiedeman, Dave 89.
Wiggins, Ernie 18, 21, 23, 24.
Wiggins, Winston 62.
Wilkes, Keith 174, 206.
Wilkins, Dominique 250.
Wilkinson, Buzz 30, 62-63, (63), 179, 226.
Williams, Buck 219.
Williams, Don 206.
Williams, Duck 196.
Williams, Gary 248.
Williams, Jack [NC] 104, 142.
Williams, Jack [WF] 21, (22), 23-24.
Williams, Rob 228.
Williams, Rodney 261.
Williams, Scott 210.
Williams, Weldon 248, 261.
Williford, Vann 124, 156, 158.
Wilson, Othell 222, 224, 234, 240.
Wingate, David 253.
Winters, Jonathan 53.
Wirtz, Lenny 275, (275).
Wise, Skip (174), 178-179, 253.
Wolf, Jeff 188-189.
Wolf, Joe 236, 243.
Wood, Al 200, 222-223, (223).
Wooden, John 109, 130, 133, 176, 217.
Woollard, Bob 88-89, 93.
Wootten, Morgan 219.
Worsley, Larry 72, 103, 110.
Worthy, James 219-222, 224, (225), 228, (228), (229), 230, (230), 241, 272.
Wuycik, Dennis 166, (167), 170.
Wyatt, Horace 224.

Y

Yarborough, Bill 59, (59).
Yarborough, Stu 136.
Yates, Barry 165.
Yeager, Herman 66.
Yepremian, Garo 202.
Yokley, Johnny 112.
Yonakor, Rich 188-189, 200.
Young, Bob (34), 43, 46.
Young, Danny 253.
Young, Ken 178.
Youngkin, Carroll 82-83.
Yunkus, Rich 152.

Z

Zaliagiris, Tom 188.
Zatezalo, Butch 202.
Zollner, Fred 275.

PHOTOGRAPHS

Introduction

Full Title: Hugh Morton; **Table of Contents:** P. 6 (L) N.C. State University, (R) Duke Sports Information; P. 7 (L) Manny Millan/Sports Illustrated, (R) Bob Donnan; P. 9 Bob Donnan; P. 10-11 Bob Donnan (5); P. 12-13 John Zimmerman/Sports Illustrated; P. 14-15 Bob Donnan.

The '50s

P. 19 The News and Observer; P. 20 Durham Morning Herald; P. 22 (L&R) Durham Morning Herald; P. 23 The News and Observer; P. 25 (top) The News and Observer, (bottom) Durham Morning Herald; P. 26 Durham Morning Herald; P. 29 Charles Cooper/Durham Morning Herald; P. 30 Burnie Batchelor; P. 31 The News and Observer; P. 33 South Carolina Sports Information; P. 34-35 (clockwise from top left) The News and Observer, Durham Morning Herald, Durham Morning Herald, William D. Cromer/Clemson Sports Information, The News and Observer; P. 36 Charles Cooper/Durham Morning Herald, N.C. State Sports Information (inset); P. 37 Charles Cooper/Durham Morning Herald; P. 39 The News and Observer; P. 41 The News and Observer; P. 42 N.C. State Sports Information; P. 44 (top) Basketball Hall of Fame, (bottom) UNC Sports Information; P. 45 Unknown; P. 47 UNC Sports Information; P. 48 Wake Forest Sports Information; P. 49 The News and Observer; P. 50-51 (clockwise from upper left) Durham Morning Herald, The News and Observer (remainder); P. 53 Durham Morning Herald; P. 54 Hugh Morton; P. 55 The News and Observer; P. 56 The News and Observer; P. 58 Duke Sports Information (3); P. 59 Clemson Sports Information; P. 61 The News and Observer (3); P. 62 Wake Forest Sports Information; P. 63 The News and Observer (3); P. 64 N.C. State Sports Information (4); P. 65 Charles Cooper/Durham Morning Herald; P. 68 N.C. State Sports Information; P. 71 Charles Cooper/Durham Morning Herald; P. 72 Burnie Batchelor.

The '60s

P. 75 Don M. Etheridge, (inset) N.C. State Sports Information; P. 79 N.C. State Sports Information (3); P. 81 The News and Observer; P. 83 Charles Cooper/Durham Morning Herald; P. 85 Sports Illustrated; P. 86 N.C. State Sports Information; P. 87 Harold Moore/Durham Morning Herald; P. 88 The News and Observer (2); P. 89 Maryland Sports Information; P. 91 Clemson Sports Information (3); P. 92 Charles Cooper/Durham Morning Herald; P. 93 Duke Sports Information; P. 95 Durham Morning Herald; P. 96 Charles Cooper/Durham Morning Herald; P. 97 Wake Forest Sports Information; P. 99 Columbia State; P. 100 Rich Clarkson; P. 101 (L) N.C. State Sports Information, (C) UNC Sports Information (2), (R) Wake Forest Sports Information; P. 102 Harold Moore/Durham Morning Herald; P. 103 Durham Morning Herald, (inset) UNC Sports Information; P. 105 Jim Sparks/Durham Morning Herald; 106-7 (L-R) Duke Sports Information, N.C. State Sports Information, Georgia Tech Sports Information, Columbia State, Duke Sports Information, Hugh Morton, Wake Forest Sports Information (2); P. 108 William D. Cromer/Clemson Sports Information; P. 111 N.C. State Sports Information; P. 112 Rich Clarkson; P. 113 Durham Morning Herald (2); P. 114 South Carolina Sports Information; P. 117 James Drake/Sports Illustrated; P. 118 UNC Sports Information, (inset) Harold Moore/Durham Morning Herald; P. 119 Charles Cooper/Durham Morning Herald; P. 120 (top) Charles Cooper/Durham Morning Herald; P. 121 Columbia State; P. 122 Charles Cooper/Durham Morning Herald; P. 124 James Drake/Sports Illustrated; P. 125 Rich Clarkson (2); P. 127 John Hanlon/Sports Illustrated; P. 128 (L) Charles Cooper/Durham Morning Herald, (R) Rich Clarkson; P. 129 Durham Morning Herald; P. 130 Duke Sports Information; P. 131 Harold Moore/Durham Morning Herald (2); P. 132 Jim Thornton/Durham Morning Herald, (inset) Duke Sports Information; P. 133 N.C. State Sports Information; P. 134-5 Charles Cooper/Durham Morning Herald; P. 137 The News and Observer; P. 138-9 Bob Donnan; P. 141 (L-R) UNC Sports Information, Durham Morning Herald, Harold Moore/Durham Morning Herald, Maryland Sports Information; P. 142 Larry Crouse/Maryland Sports Information.

The '70s

P. 147 Lane Stewart/Sports Illustrated; P. 151 Jim Stratford/Greensboro Daily News (2); P. 152 N.C. State Sports Information; P. 153 (top) Harold Moore/Durham Morning Herald, (bottom) Durham Morning Herald; P. 154 Harold Moore/Durham Morning Herald; P. 157 Wake Forest Sports Information; P. 158 The News and Observer; P. 159 Charles Cooper/Durham Morning Herald; P. 160 Columbia State (2); P. 163 Hugh Morton; P. 164 Hugh Morton; P. 166 The News and Observer; P. 167 (top) John Iacano/Sports Illustrated, (Bottom) The News and Observer (2); P. 168-9 (clockwise from bottom left) Harold Moore/Durham Morning Herald (2), Columbia State, UNC Sports Information, Columbia State; P. 171 Maryland Sports Information (2); P. 172 James Drake/Sports Illustrated; P. 173 Unknown; P. 174 Manny Millan/Sports Illustrated; P. 175 Hugh Morton; P. 176 Rich Clarkson/Sports Illustrated; P. 177 James Drake/Sports Illustrated, (inset) Rich Clarkson/Sports Illustrated; P. 178 Maryland Sports Information; P. 180 Manny Millan/Sports Illustrated; P. 181 Neil Liefer/Sports Illustrated; P. 183 Harold Moore/Durham Morning Herald; P. 184 Hugh Morton; P. 185 Manny Millan/Sports Illustrated; P. 186 (L) Jim Sparks/Durham Morning Herald, (R) Ned Hinshaw; P. 188-9 Jim Morton, (R) Hugh Morton; P. 190 Hugh Morton; P. 192 Kevin Keister/Durham Morning Herald; P. 193 Ned Hinshaw; P. 195 Manny Millan/Sports Illustrated; P. 197 Manny Millan/Sports Illustrated; P. 198 Manny Millan/Sports Illustrated, (inset) Duke Sports Information; P. 199 Hugh Morton (2); P. 200 Sally Sather/UNC Sports Information; P. 201 N.C. State Sports Information; P. 203 Sports Illustrated; P. 204 Hugh Morton; P. 206 Manny Millan/Sports Illustrated; P. 207 James Drake/Sports Illustrated (2); P. 208 Jim Thornton/Durham Morning Herald.

The '80s

P. 211 Hugh Morton (2); P. 212-3 Chuck Eaton/Winston-Salem Journal; P. 217 Harlem Globetrotters, (inset) Georgia Tech Sports Information; P. 218 (top) Hugh Morton (2), (bottom) Harold Moore/Durham Morning Herald (2); P. 219 Larry Crouse/Maryland Sports Information; P. 221 Al Steele; P. 222 Hugh Morton; P. 223 UNC Sports Information; P. 225 Hugh Morton; P. 227 Bob Jordan/Associated Press; P. 228 Hugh Morton (2); P. 229 Joe Rodriguez/Greensboro Daily News; P. 230 Hugh Morton (2); P. 231 Harold Moore/Durham Morning Herald (2); P. 232 Rich Clarkson/Sports Illustrated (2); P. 233 Andy Hyatt/Sports Illustrated; P. 234 Hugh Morton; P. 237 Bob Donnan; P. 238 N.C. State Sports Information, Duke Sports Information; P. 239 Sam Jones/Associated Press; P. 240 Bill Richards/The Chapel Hill Newspaper; P. 242 Harold Moore/Durham Morning Herald; P. 245 Bob Jordan/Associated Press; P. 246-7 (L-R) UNC Sports Information, Associated Press, Hugh Morton, Kevin Keister/Durham Morning Herald (2); P. 248 Hugh Morton; P. 249 (L) Bob Donnan, (R) Ned Hinshaw; P. 250 Bill Richards/The Chapel Hill Newspaper; P. 253 Associated Press; P. 254-5 (clockwise from near left) Hugh Morton, Clemson Sports Information, Hugh Morton, Clemson Sports Information, Harold Moore/Durham Morning Herald, Jim Sparks/Durham Morning Herald, Jamie Francis/Durham Morning Herald, Durham Morning Herald, Columbia State, Jim Thornton/Durham Morning Herald, Jim Sparks/Durham Morning Herald, Jim Thornton/Durham Morning Herald; P. 256 Bob Donnan; P. 257 Associated Press (2); P. 261 Kevin Keister/Durham Morning Herald; P. 262 (Top) Bob Donnan, (Bottom) Harold Moore/Durham Morning Herald; P. 263 (top) Kevin Keister/Durham Morning Herald, (bottom) ACC; P. 264 (L) Dan Charlson/Durham Morning Herald, (R) UNC Sports Information; P. 265 Sally Sather; P. 266-7 Bob Donnan; P. 270 (clockwise from top left) UNC Sports Information, Rich Clarkson, Hugh Morton (2); P. 271 Bob Donnan (2); P. 273 Hugh Morton; P. 274 (clockwise from top left) Columbia State, Kevin Keister/Durham Morning Herald (2), AP/Bob Jordan; P. 275 (top) unknown, (bottom) Bill Richards/Chapel Hill Newspaper.

Reference

ACC Player of the Year photos supplied by Sports Information Departments of ACC schools; P. 276 Hugh Morton; P. 313 Hugh Morton; P. 320 Jim Thornton/Durham Morning Herald; **Front and Back End Sheets** Charles Cooper/Durham Morning Herald.

ACKNOWLEDGEMENTS

Writing, editing and producing ACC Basketball: An Illustrated History turned out to be a monumental project that involved the hard work of several people and the enlisted help of many, many others.

Particularly helpful were those who located photographs. They included Hugh Morton; Harold Moore, chief photographer, and Barbara Semonche, head librarian of the *Durham Morning Herald*; Roger Jones of the North Carolina Department of Archives; Karen Carpenter of *Sports Illustrated*; and Bob Spear of the *Columbia Record*.

A special thanks also to Dave Birkhead and Kathy Stanford of Azalea Typography; Trish Bruce, Peter Krusa, Joanne Pegram, Terry Pegram and Lynn Roberts of PBM Graphics; Lynn Berry, Bernie Bohigas and Dan Kerns of Hi-Ke Color; Holly Kingdon of Liberated Types; Cricket Taylor and Susan Meyer, graphic artists; George Hollomon of TypEsthetics; Tim Farrell and Carol Sullivan of The Mailing Factor; Judy Wiles of The Mail Drop; Ashley Jackson, Mary Sakorski and Doris Shockley of the Duke University Library; and Bill King, Peggy Satterfield and Doris Parrish of the Duke University Archives.

The book could not have been completed without the endorsement of the Atlantic Coast Conference and the help of the entire ACC staff, particularly Commissioner Gene Corrigan, Service Bureau Director Skeeter Francis, and Assistant Service Bureau Director Brian Morrison.

The sports information office staff at each ACC school, plus South Carolina, contributed greatly. Those sports information directors include Bob Bradley, Clemson; John Roth, Duke; Mike Finn, Georgia Tech; Jack Zane and Herb Hartnett, Maryland; Rick Brewer, North Carolina; Ed Seaman and Mark Bockelman, N.C. State; Tom Price, South Carolina; Rich Murray, Virginia; and John Justus, Wake Forest.

In addition to the dozens of former ACC players, coaches and officials interviewed for the book, there were still others who in some way either contributed to the final product or gave valuable support. They included Lou Bello, Eddie Biedenbach, Wendell Carr, John Cole, Hugh Donohue, Lefty Driesell, Dan Engelhardt, Sam Esposito, Joel Fleishman, Don Gallagher, Ansley Giannini, Diane Gleason, John Godwin, Ann and Steve Hartman, Barbara MacDonald, Tom McMillen, Karen Olson-Miller, Jim Mills, Bill Millsaps, Peggy Nelson, Nick Pond, Dave Pritchett, Don Shea, Melissa Starr, Richard Walker, Bucky Waters, Frank Weedon, Rick Willenzik, Bruce Winkworth, Bill and Judy Woodward, Doug Verb and Carol Ann Zinn.

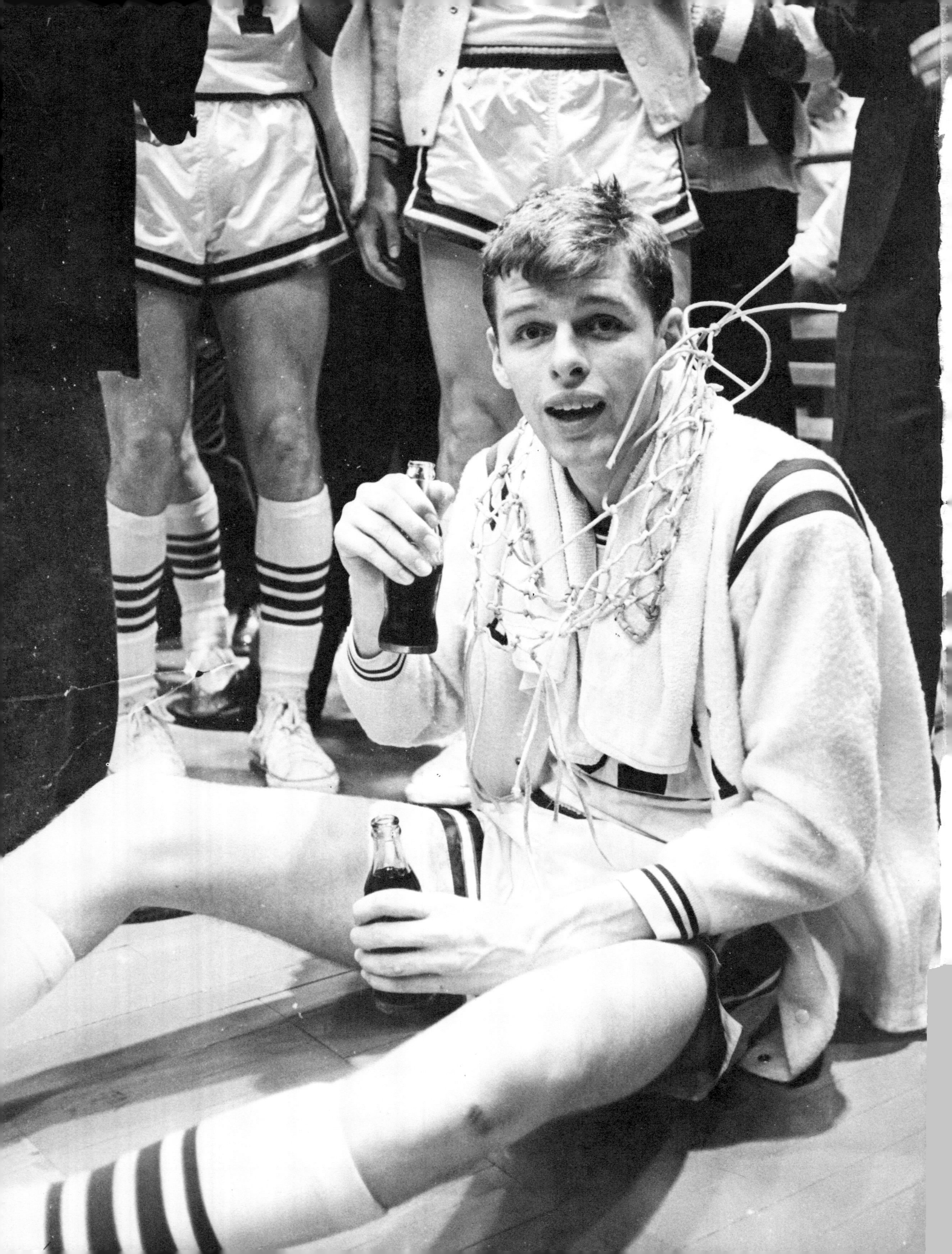